36: *British Novelists, 1890-1929: Modernists,* edited by Thomas F. Staley (1985)

37: *American Writers of the Early Republic,* edited by Emory Elliott (1985)

38: *Afro-American Writers After 1955: Dramatists and Prose Writers,* edited by Thadious M. Davis and Trudier Harris (1985)

39: *British Novelists, 1660-1800,* 2 parts, edited by Martin C. Battestin (1985)

40: *Poets of Great Britain and Ireland Since 1960,* 2 parts, edited by Vincent B. Sherry, Jr. (1985)

41: *Afro-American Poets Since 1955,* edited by Trudier Harris and Thadious M. Davis (1985)

42: *American Writers for Children Before 1900,* edited by Glenn E. Estes (1985)

43: *American Newspaper Journalists, 1690-1872,* edited by Perry J. Ashley (1986)

44: *American Screenwriters,* Second Series, edited by Randall Clark, Robert E. Morsberger, and Stephen O. Lesser (1986)

45: *American Poets, 1880-1945,* First Series, edited by Peter Quartermain (1986)

46: *American Literary Publishing Houses, 1900-1980: Trade and Paperback,* edited by Peter Dzwonkoski (1986)

47: *American Historians, 1866-1912,* edited by Clyde N. Wilson (1986)

48: *American Poets, 1880-1945,* Second Series, edited by Peter Quartermain (1986)

49: *American Literary Publishing Houses, 1638-1899,* 2 parts, edited by Peter Dzwonkoski (1986)

50: *Afro-American Writers Before the Harlem Renaissance,* edited by Trudier Harris (1986)

51: *Afro-American Writers from the Harlem Renaissance to 1940,* edited by Trudier Harris (1987)

52: *American Writers for Children Since 1960: Fiction,* edited by Glenn E. Estes (1986)

53: *Canadian Writers Since 1960,* First Series, edited by W. H. New (1986)

54: *American Poets, 1880-1945,* Third Series, 2 parts, edited by Peter Quartermain (1987)

55: *Victorian Prose Writers Before 1867,* edited by William B. Thesing (1987)

56: *German Fiction Writers, 1914-1945,* edited by James Hardin (1987)

57: *Victorian Prose Writers After 1867,* edited by William B. Thesing (1987)

58: *Jacobean and Caroline Dramatists,* edited by Fredson Bowers (1987)

59: *American Literary Critics and Scholars, 1800-1850,* edited by John W. Rathbun and Monica M. Grecu (1987)

60: *Canadian Writers Since 1960,* Second Series, edited by W. H. New (1987)

61: *American Writers for Children Since 1960: Poets, Illustrators, and Nonfiction Authors,* edited by Glenn E. Estes (1987)

62: *Elizabethan Dramatists,* edited by Fredson Bowers (1987)

63: *Modern American Critics, 1920-1955,* edited by Gregory S. Jay (1988)

64: *American Literary Critics and Scholars, 1850-1880,* edited by John W. Rathbun and Monica M. Grecu (1988)

65: *French Novelists, 1900-1930,* edited by Catharine Savage Brosman (1988)

66: *German Fiction Writers, 1885-1913,* 2 parts, edited by James Hardin (1988)

67: *Modern American Critics Since 1955,* edited by Gregory S. Jay (1988)

68: *Canadian Writers, 1920-1959,* First Series, edited by W. H. New (1988)

69: *Contemporary German Fiction Writers,* First Series, edited by Wolfgang D. Elfe and James Hardin (1988)

70: *British Mystery Writers, 1860-1919,* edited by Bernard Benstock and Thomas F. Staley (1988)

(Continued on back endsheets)

Dictionary of Literary Biography • Volume Ninety-three

British Romantic Poets, 1789-1832
First Series

Dictionary of Literary Biography • Volume Ninety-three

British Romantic Poets, 1789-1832 First Series

8238

Edited by
John R. Greenfield
McKendree College

A Bruccoli Clark Layman Book
Gale Research Inc.
Detroit, New York, London

Manufactured by Edwards Brothers, Inc.
Ann Arbor, Michigan
Printed in the United States of America

835 Penobscot Bldg.
Detroit, MI 48226-4094

Library of Congress Cataloging-in-Publication Data

British romantic poets, 1789-1832. First series/edited by John Greenfield.
p. cm.–(Dictionary of literary biography; v. 93)
"A Bruccoli Clark Layman book."
ISBN 0-8103-4573-0
1. English poetry–19th century–Dictionaries. 2. English poetry–19th century–Bio-bibliography. 3. Romanticism–Great Britain–Biography–Dictionaries. 4. Poets, English–19th century–Biography–Dictionaries. 5. Poets, English–18th century–Biography–Dictionaries. 6. English poetry–18th century–Bio-bibliography. 7. English poetry–18th century–Dictionaries. I. Greenfield, John. II. Series.
PR590.B86 1990
821'.709'03–dc20
[B]

90-2888
CIP

*For Judy
and for students and teachers
of Romantic studies*

Contents

Plan of the Series

. . . Almost the most prodigious asset of a country, and perhaps its most precious possession, is its native literary product—when that product is fine and noble and enduring.

Mark Twain*

The advisory board, the editors, and the publisher of the *Dictionary of Literary Biography* are joined in endorsing Mark Twain's declaration. The literature of a nation provides an inexhaustible resource of permanent worth. We intend to make literature and its creators better understood and more accessible to students and the reading public, while satisfying the standards of teachers and scholars.

To meet these requirements, *literary biography* has been construed in terms of the author's achievement. The most important thing about a writer is his writing. Accordingly, the entries in *DLB* are career biographies, tracing the development of the author's canon and the evolution of his reputation.

The purpose of *DLB* is not only to provide reliable information in a convenient format but also to place the figures in the larger perspective of literary history and to offer appraisals of their accomplishments by qualified scholars.

The publication plan for *DLB* resulted from two years of preparation. The project was proposed to Bruccoli Clark by Frederick G. Ruffner, president of the Gale Research Company, in November 1975. After specimen entries were prepared and typeset, an advisory board was formed to refine the entry format and develop the series rationale. In meetings held during 1976, the publisher, series editors, and advisory board approved the scheme for a comprehensive biographical dictionary of persons who contributed to North American literature. Editorial work on the first volume began in January 1977, and it was published in 1978. In order to make *DLB* more than a reference tool and to compile volumes that individually have claim to status as literary history, it was decided to organize volumes by topic, period, or genre. Each of these freestanding volumes provides a biographical-bibliographical guide and overview for a particular area of literature. We are convinced that this organization—as opposed to a single alphabet method—constitutes a valuable innovation in the presentation of reference material. The volume plan necessarily requires many decisions for the placement and treatment of authors who might properly be included in two or three volumes. In some instances a major figure will be included in separate volumes, but with different entries emphasizing the aspect of his career appropriate to each volume. Ernest Hemingway, for example, is represented in *American Writers in Paris, 1920-1939* by an entry focusing on his expatriate apprenticeship; he is also in *American Novelists, 1910-1945* with an entry surveying his entire career. Each volume includes a cumulative index of subject authors and articles. Comprehensive indexes to the entire series are planned.

With volume ten in 1982 it was decided to enlarge the scope of *DLB*. By the end of 1986 twenty-one volumes treating British literature had been published, and volumes for Commonwealth and Modern European literature were in progress. The series has been further augmented by the *DLB Yearbooks* (since 1981) which update published entries and add new entries to keep the *DLB* current with contemporary activity. There have also been *DLB Documentary Series* volumes which provide biographical and critical source materials for figures whose work is judged to have particular interest for students. One of these companion volumes is entirely devoted to Tennessee Williams.

We define literature as the *intellectual commerce of a nation:* not merely as belles lettres but as that ample and complex process by which ideas are generated, shaped, and transmitted. *DLB* entries are not limited to "creative writers" but extend to other figures who in their time and in their way influenced the mind of a people. Thus the series encompasses historians, journalists, publishers, and screenwriters. By this means readers of *DLB* may be aided to perceive litera-

---

*From an unpublished section of Mark Twain's autobiography, copyright © by the Mark Twain Company.

ture not as cult scripture in the keeping of intellectual high priests but firmly positioned at the center of a nation's life.

DLB includes the major writers appropriate to each volume and those standing in the ranks immediately behind them. Scholarly and critical counsel has been sought in deciding which minor figures to include and how full their entries should be. Wherever possible, useful references are made to figures who do not warrant separate entries.

Each *DLB* volume has a volume editor responsible for planning the volume, selecting the figures for inclusion, and assigning the entries. Volume editors are also responsible for preparing, where appropriate, appendices surveying the major periodicals and literary and intellectual movements for their volumes, as well as lists of further readings. Work on the series as a whole is coordinated at the Bruccoli Clark Layman editorial center in Columbia, South Carolina, where the editorial staff is responsible for accuracy of the published volumes.

One feature that distinguishes *DLB* is the illustration policy–its concern with the iconography of literature. Just as an author is influenced by his surroundings, so is the reader's understanding of the author enhanced by a knowledge of his environment. Therefore *DLB* volumes include not only drawings, paintings, and photographs of authors, often depicting them at various stages in their careers, but also illustrations of their families and places where they lived. Title pages are regularly reproduced in facsimile along with dust jackets for modern authors. The dust jackets are a special feature of *DLB* because they often document better than anything else the way in which an author's work was perceived in its own time. Specimens of the writers' manuscripts are included when feasible.

Samuel Johnson rightly decreed that "The chief glory of every people arises from its authors." The purpose of the *Dictionary of Literary Biography* is to compile literary history in the surest way available to us–by accurate and comprehensive treatment of the lives and work of those who contributed to it.

The *DLB* Advisory Board

Foreword

Dictionary of Literary Biography, volume 93: *British Romantic Poets, 1789-1832: First Series* takes as its beginning date not the more conventional date of the publication of the *Lyrical Ballads* (1798), important though that event certainly is, but the year in which the French Revolution began and in which William Blake's *Songs of Innocence*, William Bowles's *Sonnets*, and Erasmus Darwin's *The Loves of the Plants* were published. Although some of the older writers included herein—such as George Crabbe, and William Hayley—wrote some works before 1789, their important contributions to the Romantic movement came later. The poets treated in this volume, the "first wave" of British Romantic writers, were born prior to 1779 and wrote most of their important poems between 1789 and 1815, years of revolution, war, and great political and social change. A second volume will deal with British Romantic poets who were born in 1779 or later.

A movement as pervasive and complex as British Romanticism can be traced to many sources and influences, historical, philosophical, and literary. The ideas and ideals, the promises and disappointments associated with the events and personalities of the French Revolution and the Napoleonic period are so much a part of the Romantic movement in England that most of the writers recognized their importance either for themselves or for society. Blake, William Wordsworth, Samuel Taylor Coleridge, Robert Southey, and others wrote poems that comment directly and indirectly on the French Revolution and its aftermath.

The philosophical origins of British Romanticism may be found in the empiricism of John Locke, the skepticism of David Hume, the associational psychology of David Hartley, and the political radicalism of William Godwin and Mary Wollstonecraft, among others. These various writers helped to create an atmosphere in which received beliefs about human nature (especially the model of the mind), the natural world, the structure of society, and the place of tradition could be called into question.

In addition to addressing the uncertainties of political change, even upheaval, and the challenges of these new philosophies, often in a very personal way, the first generation of British Romantic writers was also conscious of developing a new aesthetic of poetry, emphasizing the imagination, the feelings, and the particular observation of nature. Drawing on the philosophers' emphasis on experience as the basis and organizing principle for thought and meaning, they formulated the concept of the organic imagination, suggesting that artistic productions reflect the shape of experience or the mind at work. M. H. Abrams in his seminal study of Romanticism, *The Mirror and the Lamp: Romantic Theory and the Critical Tradition* (1953), examines this aesthetic revolution as a reaction to the eighteenth-century mimetic model of art that developed into an expressive theory and practice of art.

But if the British Romantic movement may in one way be viewed as a reaction against the Augustan Age's neoclassical aesthetic premises of imitation, balance, and order, it must also be viewed as a continuation and outgrowth of literary developments that were already under way in the eighteenth century. The literary origins of the Romantic movement may be found in Jean Jacques Rousseau, especially in *Julie; ou La Nouvelle Heloise* (1761) and *The Confessions* (written 1765-1770); in the young Johann Wolfgang von Goethe, as the author of *The Sorrows of Young Werther* (1774); in so-called pre-Romantic English poets such as James Thomson and William Collins, who began to cultivate an interest in nature and in the feelings; in the cult of sensibility, of which Henry Mackenzie's *Man of Feeling* (1771) is the prime example; in the ballad revival, which was accompanied by an interest in things medieval and primitive in general; and in the popularity of Gothic literature, exemplified by Horace Walpole's *The Castle of Otranto* (1765) and M. G. Lewis's *The Monk* (1795), both of which fostered an interest in the supernatural.

The dominant topic or theme that emerges out of these various influences is the importance of the individual—his or her imagination, creativity, and feelings. Wordsworth captures this emphasis in the Prospectus to *The Recluse* (1814) when he proposes to lead the way in exploration of humanity's last frontier: "Into our Minds, into the Mind of Man– / My haunt, and the main region of my song." The emphasis on the primacy of the individual's mind is reflected in the predominance of lyric poetry, poems of feeling, reflection, and introspection. In the Preface to the 1800 edition of *Lyrical Ballads*, Wordsworth set down criteria for the new poetry: the democratizing idea of using the "real language of men"; the choice of humble, simple, or rustic subjects; the imagination's coloring of familiar objects; and the rendering of "emotion recollected in tranquility." Wordsworth's close observation and reading of nature stresses the mind and nature in a harmonious, reciprocal relationship:

> How exquisitely the individual Mind
>
> . . . to the external World
> Is fitted—and how exquisitely, too—
> Theme this but little heard of among men—
> The external World is fitted to the Mind.
>   (Prospectus to *The Recluse*)

Blake and other "visionary" poets place less stress on nature per se and more emphasis on the creative genius's capacity to re-create the universe as a "human form divine." With Blake and other writers, such as Percy Bysshe Shelley, the power of the visionary imagination has the potential to transform not only the individual mind but ultimately the collective mind of society. Wordsworth does, of course, depict visionary experiences (as in Book XIV of *The Prelude*, 1850), and, conversely, Blake does render meaning in nature (as in the *Songs of Innocence and of Experience*, 1794). Within the broad definition of Romanticism, there are many emphases.

The Romantic poets' contemporary critics saw these writers not as a monolithic movement all agreeing upon the basic premises of Romanticism, but as comprising various schools with different orientations concerning taste, religion, and politics. The literary milieu of the time was generally conservative and highly conscious politically, often condemning writers ostensibly for matters of taste but really for matters of politics. The reviewers created various schools of poetry such as: Joseph Johnson's radical circle of the 1790s, which included Blake, Godwin, and Wollstonecraft; the Lake Poets, which included Wordsworth, Coleridge, and Southey and which derived its name from the beautiful Lake District in northwest England; the "Cockney School," which

included John Keats and Leigh Hunt and referred to certain colloquialisms of style that may be found in their poetry; and the "Satanic School" of Shelley and George Gordon, Lord Byron, so called for Byron's reputation for immorality and Shelley's reputation for atheism and radicalism.

Of the twenty writers covered in *British Romantic Poets, 1789-1832: First Series*, three poets—Blake, Wordsworth, and Coleridge—receive extended treatment and four others—Crabbe, Walter Savage Landor, Sir Walter Scott, and Southey—receive more attention than minor writers. Yet the essays on the minor poets suggest a rich interplay of personalities, influences, and relationships. The lives and contributions of the minor poets, their voices seldom heard today over the dominant tones of the major writers, were part of an active literary milieu within a dynamic social context.

Included at the end of this volume is a selected bibliography that focuses on the most important studies of the historical, social, cultural, aesthetic, linguistic, and literary dimensions of British Romantic poetry.

The contributors to this volume, some of whom are friends or acquaintances of mine and many others whom I have never met, deserve special gratitude for their promptness in meeting deadlines, their conscientiousness in compiling bibliographies and in checking facts, their efficiency in making revisions, their helpfulness in making suggestions for illustrations, and perhaps most of all, for their cooperation and patience. I would also like to thank two former students of mine, Melissa Kaegel and Dawn Elmore-McCrary, for their editorial assistance performed under the auspices of the internship program at McKendree College. Three secretaries at McKendree, Nancy Ferguson, Annette Hug, and Naomia Severs, deserve thanks for the help they gave me in handling the correspondence associated with this volume. I would especially like to thank Karen Rood and the staff at Bruccoli Clark Layman for their tireless attention to accuracy and detail and their insistence upon high standards. Finally, I would like to thank Judy Durick Greenfield for her patience and understanding during all the time that I spent in editing this book.

—John R. Greenfield

Acknowledgments

This book was produced by Bruccoli Clark Layman, Inc. Karen L. Rood, senior editor for the *Dictionary of Literary Biography* series, was the in-house editor.

Production coordinator is James W. Hipp. Systems manager is Charles D. Brower. Photography editor is Susan Todd. Permissions editor is Jean W. Ross. Layout and graphics supervisor is Penney L. Haughton. Copyediting supervisor is Bill Adams. Typesetting supervisor is Kathleen M. Flanagan. Typography coordinator is Sheri Beckett Neal. Information systems analyst is George F. Dodge. Charles Lee Egleston and Laura Ingram are editorial associates. The production staff includes Rowena Betts, Anne L. M. Bowman, Teresa Chaney, Patricia Coate, Sarah A. Estes, Mary L. Goodwin, Willie M. Gore, Cynthia Hallman, Susan C. Heath, David Marshall James, Kathy S. Merlette, Laura Garren Moore, John Myrick, Cathy J. Reese, Laurrè Sinckler, Maxine K. Smalls, John C. Stone III, Jennifer Toth, and Betsy L. Weinberg.

Walter W. Ross and Parris Boyd did the library research with the assistance of the reference staff at the Thomas Cooper Library of the University of South Carolina: Gwen Baxter, Daniel Boice, Faye Chadwell, Cathy Eckman, Gary Geer, Cathie Gottlieb, David L. Haggard, Jens Holley, Jackie Kinder, Marcia Martin, Laurie Preston, Jean Rhyne, Carol Tobin, and Virginia Weathers.

Sara Hodson and Kay Peterson at the Henry E. Huntington Library provided valuable assistance in illustrating this volume.

British Romantic Poets, 1789-1832
First Series

Dictionary of Literary Biography

Joanna Baillie

(11 September 1762 - 23 February 1851)

Marlon B. Ross
University of Michigan

BOOKS: *A Series of Plays: in which it is attempted to delineate the stronger passions of the mind—each passion being the subject of a tragedy and a comedy* [commonly called *Plays on the Passions*], 3 volumes (volumes 1 and 2, London: Printed for T. Cadell, Jun. & W. Davies, 1798, 1802; volume 3, London: Printed for Longman, Hurst, Rees, Orme & Brown, 1812);

Miscellaneous Plays (London: Longman, Hurst, Rees & Orme, 1804);

De Monfort: a tragedy (London: Longman, Hurst, Rees, Orme & Brown, 1808; New York: D. Longworth, 1809);

The Family Legend: a tragedy (Edinburgh: J. Ballantyne & Co., 1810; New York: David Longworth, 1810);

Basil: a tragedy (Philadelphia: M. Carey, 1811);

The Election: a comedy, in five acts (Philadelphia: M. Carey, 1811);

The Tryal: a comedy (Philadelphia: M. Carey, 1811);

The Beacon: a serious musical drama, in two acts (New York: D. Longworth, 1812);

The Dream: a tragedy, in prose, in three acts (New York: D. Longworth, 1812);

Orra: a tragedy, in five acts (New York: D. Longworth, 1812);

The Siege: a comedy, in five acts (New York: D. Longworth, 1812);

Metrical Legends of Exalted Characters (London: Longman, Hurst, Rees, Orme & Brown, 1821);

The Martyr: a drama, in three acts (London: Longman, Rees, Orme, Brown & Green, 1826);

The Bride: a drama, in three acts (London: Henry Colburn, 1828; Philadelphia: C. Neal, 1828);

A View of the General Tenour of the New Testament regarding the nature and dignity of Jesus Christ; including a collection of the various passages in the Gospels, Acts of the Apostles, and the Epistles which relate to that subject (London: Longman, Rees, Orme, Brown & Green, 1831);

The Complete Poetical Works of Joanna Baillie (Philadelphia: Carey & Lea, 1832);

Dramas, 3 volumes (London: Longman, Rees, Orme, Brown, Green & Longman, 1836);

Fugitive Verses (London: Edward Moxon, 1840);

Ahalya Baee: a poem (London: Printed for private circulation by Spottiswoode & Shaw, 1849);

The Dramatic and Poetical Works of Joanna Baillie, complete in one volume (London: Longman, Brown, Green & Longmans, 1851).

PLAY PRODUCTIONS: *De Monfort,* London, Theatre Royal, Drury Lane, 29 April 1800;

Constantine Paleologus, Liverpool, Theatre Royal, 7 November 1808; produced again as *Constantine and Valeria,* London, Surrey Theatre, 1808;

The Family Legend, Edinburgh, Theatre Royal, 29 January 1810; London, Theatre Royal, Drury Lane, 29 May 1815;

The Separation, London, Theatre Royal, Covent Garden, 25 February 1836;

Henriquez, London, Theatre Royal, Drury Lane, 19 March 1836.

OTHER: *A Collection of Poems, chiefly manuscript, and from living authors,* edited by Baillie (London: Longman, Hurst, Rees, Orme & Brown, 1823);
"Epistles to the Literati: On the Character of Romiero," *Fraser's Magazine,* 14 (December 1836): 748-749.

In 1798, the same year that *Lyrical Ballads* was published anonymously, another anonymous publication appeared under the cumbersome title *A Series of Plays: in which it is attempted to delineate the stronger passions of the mind—each passion being the subject of a tragedy and a comedy.* Whereas Wordsworth and Coleridge's literary offering received little and ambivalent notice, this volume of plays created a sensation within the literary circles in London and Edinburgh. *Plays on the Passions,* for such the volume was rechristened, was immediately reviewed in all the major periodicals, and a frenzied debate ensued about the authorship of the plays. At first it was readily assumed that the plays had been written by some well-known man of letters who, for some mysterious reason, chose to remain incognito, but because none of the established poets seemed to possess the unique sensibility suffused throughout the plays, all of the possible suppositions—ranging from the lowly William Cowper to the lurid Matthew Gregory ("Monk") Lewis—were exhausted without a satisfactory suggestion. After Hester Piozzi and Mary Berry noted the dramatist's unprecedented focus on older heroines and an unusual predilection for intelligent women characters, speculation turned toward established women writers, with a general consensus divided erroneously between Ann Radcliffe and Anne Hunter.

It was not until 1800, with the publication of the third edition of *Plays on the Passions,* volume 1, that the true author identified herself, causing another sensation in the literary world. No one had suspected that this newly discovered genius was an unassuming, unimpressive Scottish spinster, fast approaching the age of forty, who occasionally frequented literary gatherings around London. Even Samuel Rogers, who had written a glowing first review of the plays, was astounded, for he had known Joanna Baillie for several years, but she had never crossed his mind as a candidate for such genius. Perhaps he had even praised the plays and speculated on their authorship right in her presence, as many others certainly had, and yet she had never said a word or blushed to reveal herself. As they embraced this newcomer on the literary scene, her contemporaries began to ask pertinent questions about the woman they ranked just beneath Shakespeare: Who was this new woman author? How did she come to compose such marvelous plays and to invent a complex dramatic theory? How would her accomplishment change expressed assumptions about what women writers could and could not do? What was the relation of her poetry to the literary tradition and to the poetry of her contemporaries, male and female? Finally, would she be as immortal as Shakespeare; for how long would she hold sway over all other women writers and over all male dramatists of her own time?

Baillie's beginnings are usually deemed inauspicious by her biographers. Her unnamed twin sister died several hours after their premature delivery on 11 September 1762. Dorothea Hunter Baillie and the Reverend James Baillie, who already had two children, Agnes (born in 1760) and Matthew (born in 1761), had just recently moved to the manse of Bothwell in Lanarkshire, Scotland, where the father had taken a position more desirable than his previous one in the parish of Shotts. When Baillie was six years old, her father was promoted to minister of the second charge at the collegiate church at Hamilton. Joanna, considered something of a tomboy by friends and relatives, enjoyed outdoor sports, especially horseback riding, in the countryside of Hamilton. While Matthew attended school in

Hamilton, James took charge of his daughters' education, heavily stressing moral over intellectual development, as was typical for girls at the time. According to Baillie, because she was not fond of her studies, she used to cry over her lessons and learned to read later than usual (perhaps as late as eleven).

It was not until she and Agnes were sent away to boarding school in Glasgow, around 1772, that she developed an interest in books. The elder sister, who was to be her lifetime companion in spinsterhood, "as partners link'd," initiated Baillie's literary interest and lent a sympathetic ear to the end. In "Lines to Agnes Baillie on her Birthday," Joanna wrote: " 'Twas thou who woo'dst me first to look / Upon the page of printed book, / That thing by me abhorr'd." Although Agnes may have redirected her sister's energy away from "fitful sports" and toward the "love of tale and story," Joanna retained a reputation among their schoolmates for boisterous adventure, such as scaling the roof of the school, and for gregarious leadership. She used to compose little dramas that she produced with the help of her friends, and she would often entertain them with hours of fascinating stories that she culled from others or that she invented herself. Alongside her nascent curiosity in the concrete drama of storytelling was a passion for the abstract science of mathematics. Mastering Euclid on her own, Joanna demonstrated an intellectual quality that would play a more subtle role in her literary career, an intense interest in abstract theorizing, problem solving, and philosophizing. Her plays were conceived as experiments, and one of her final compositions was a theological treatise on the hairsplitting question of Jesus' human-divine nature. Nonetheless, just as her physical energy had to be redirected from athletics and adventure to more appropriately feminine pastimes, so it seems that her intellectual energy had to be channeled from philosophy and mathematics to the less problematic occupation of writing poetry.

In 1778, only two years after the family moved to Glasgow due to the Reverend Baillie's having been appointed professor of divinity at the university there, Joanna experienced the first major disruption in her life, the death of her father. Not long after this, Matthew received a fellowship in Balliol College at Oxford. Having been left with a small inheritance, the family was dependent on the generosity of Dorothea's brother, William Hunter, a well-known London

Bothwell Manse in Lanarkshire, Scotland, the birthplace of Joanna Baillie

anatomist, who took Matthew under his wing as an apprentice in his School of Anatomy, and who provided his sister both a lifetime allowance and a home at the Hunter family estate in Long Calderwood, which he had inherited. During the next decade there was further uprooting of the three dependent women. Upon Dr. Hunter's death in 1783, Matthew inherited his uncle's medical school and London home, so the Baillie women moved to London to manage his new household. Upon Matthew's marriage in 1791, the women moved to Hampstead, where they remained for the rest of their lives. While these years of change must have been somewhat stressful to them, such instability was expected for a household of women without a significant inheritance.

Although the Baillie women could rely on their male relatives, it is difficult to know the true extent of the psychological strain that results from such dependence. One of the major themes

of Baillie's works involves the moral and psychological problems associated with feminine dependence, a theme also taken up by other women writers of the time, such as Ann Radcliffe, Jane Austen, Dorothy Wordsworth, Mary Shelley, Letitia E. Landon, and Felicia Hemans. In Baillie's dramas and poems we repeatedly encounter women who must make difficult decisions when their own domestic interest or security is in conflict with the demands of the state or the demands of men's desires. For instance, in her first play, *Basil* (*Plays on the Passions,* volume 1), Victoria playfully and unwisely seduces Count Basil, who, blinded by his love for her, makes fateful misjudgments in military strategy, causing the soldiers under him to mutiny. After forsaking his responsibility to the emperor and disgracing himself, Basil, who has been the kingdom's preeminent general, commits suicide. It is only then that Victoria fully realizes the relation between her playful love and serious loyalty, between her domestic responsibil-

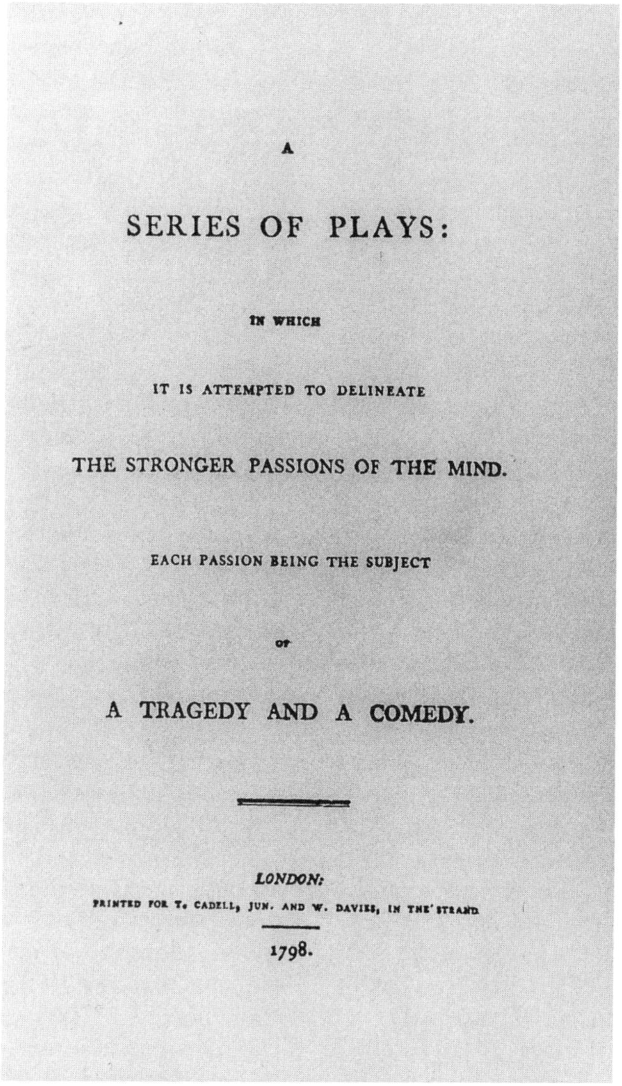

A

SERIES OF PLAYS:

IN WHICH

IT IS ATTEMPTED TO DELINEATE

THE STRONGER PASSIONS OF THE MIND.

EACH PASSION BEING THE SUBJECT

OF

A TRAGEDY AND A COMEDY.

LONDON:

PRINTED FOR T. CADELL, JUN. AND W. DAVIES, IN THE STRAND.

1798.

Title page for the first volume of Baillie's Plays on the Passions, *in which she attempted to depict human emotions "not only with their bold and prominent features, but also with those minute and delicate traits which distinguish them in an infant, growing, and repressed state"*

ity and the political world. Feeling remorse, she heroically sentences herself to live out the remainder of her life in a nunnery.

In *Ethwald, part 1* (*Plays on the Passions*, volume 2, 1802), Baillie portrays the opposite side of this picture, exploring the danger in placing political ambition above loyalty to family and loved ones. She charts the tragic demise of two contrasted women. Bertha attempts to regain Ethwald's affection and to restrict his ambition when she recognizes his obsessive drive for power. When she fails, she is left to wander hopelessly, like Ophelia, an innocent maiden doomed by her own loyalty and driven to madness by a state flooded with endless bloodshed. On the other hand, Elburga shifts her loyalty from the innocent and effeminate Edward, rightful heir to the throne and her fiancé, to the fiercely ambitious Ethwald. Even though her political instincts are validated when Ethwald takes the crown, murdering her father, the king, and imprisoning Edward in the process, Elburga soon discovers that she is as doomed as Bertha. After she marries Ethwald and becomes queen, she realizes that her only power lies in her wifely influence over her lord and husband, an influence that proves as vulnerable to the ruthless realpolitik of the state as Bertha's innocent love. In a later play, *The Family Legend* (1810), Helen heroically agrees to wed the defeated chieftain of a rival clan, only to discover that she and her baby are at the mercy of the malicious machinations of the vassals who manipulate her weak husband. Because these vassals see Helen, like her Greek namesake, as the source of the potential demise of their clan, they are willing to sacrifice her, along with the sanctity of marriage and their own honor. Only by luck (or providence) is Helen saved from the deserted island rock where she is left to die by the men who have sworn to protect her.

With these and many other examples we can see how Baillie's household predicament during these unstable years is reflected thematically in her poetry. We can also see it, as Piozzi and Berry first noted, in the sympathetic characterization of her heroines, even the misguided ones, who remain assiduous in the midst of tremendous political and domestic upheaval.

In Hampstead the Baillie women were finally able to establish a stable household and, just as important for Joanna, to participate in a busy social and literary scene, especially in the home of her aunt Anne Hunter, herself a "poetess." Among the literary notables with whom Joanna mingled were Samuel Rogers (who after her literary coming out became a lifelong devotee and her friend), Henry MacKenzie, the Reverend Richmount Barbauld, Anna Laetitia Barbauld, Mary Berry, and William Sotheby. While living in the Windmill Street house that Matthew inherited from Dr. Hunter, Baillie had made her first serious literary attempts. In 1790 she published an anonymous collection of poems, many of which were later included in the 1840 volume, *Fugitive Verses*. Although the 1790 volume encountered almost absolute silence and quickly sunk into oblivion (to the extent that no copy is known to be extant), Baillie did not give up her literary aspirations. She spent several months working on a play entitled "Arnold," which she evidently deemed unworthy and destroyed. Finally, at the age of thirty-six, Baillie achieved literary success with the first volume of *Plays on the Passions*, dramatically changing her literary prospects. Not surprisingly–considering her persistence, her even-tempered nature, and her determined modesty–she refused, as her friends and acquaintances repeatedly remarked, to let success change her mode of life, which was intimately interconnected with the philosophical orientation of her plays and poems, stressing a life of passionate commitment modulated and moderated by self-scrutiny and self-restraint.

Even more than the plays themselves, the "Introductory Discourse" led many people to believe that *Plays on the Passions* was authored by a male. According to the memoir prefacing the second edition of *The Dramatic and Poetical Works* (1851), even after the true author was acknowledged, some people persisted in declaring that this ambitious theoretical introduction had to be written by a man and attributed it, without any evidence, to Matthew Baillie. Joanna Baillie's "Introductory Discourse" is to her plays what Wordsworth's preface is to *Lyrical Ballads*, for both writers viewed their works as unprecedented experiments, needing theoretical explanation, to be tested on the reading public. In their projects Baillie and Wordsworth address these common concerns. Both want to rescue their national literature from what they perceive as a decadent trend toward unrealistic and unnatural impulses, identifiable as the fascination with the Gothic; yet both poets owe much in their theory and art to this genre. Both poets exploit the upsurge in nostalgia for the British literary past, Wordsworth turning to the "primitive" ballad and Baillie to Renaissance drama, while claiming to parent new literary forms. Both are concerned with the "natural" purity of linguistic representation and repeatedly appeal to a standard of ordinary "realness" even as they reaffirm that poetry must somehow purify the reality that is supposed to be the standard for poetic purity. Both poets stress the contemplation of readers' emotional response to universal and primordial human situations portrayed within the poetry, de-emphasizing the function of plot and action, the very elements that are normally stressed both in ballad and tragedy. Finally, both poets create a didactic literary theory that relates psychological behavior to moral decision making, a theory which advocates exploiting poetry as a way of regulating the passions in order to foster moral habits.

Baillie begins with the premise that there is an innate and universal "propensity," which she calls "sympathetic curiosity." There is, she writes, "no employment which the human mind will with so much avidity pursue, as the discovery of concealed passion, as the tracing the [sic] varieties and progress of a perturbed soul." This sympathetic curiosity "is our best and most powerful instructor. From it we are taught the proprieties and decencies of ordinary life, and are prepared for distressing and difficult situations. In examining others we know ourselves." Because the "dark and malevolent passions are not the predominant inmates of the human breast," even they ultimately contribute to our understanding of moral excellence. These ideas can, of course, be traced,

Joanna Baillie (portrait by John James Masquerier; by permission of the Hunterian Art Gallery, University of Glasgow)

along with Wordsworth's, to the sentimental writers of the latter part of the eighteenth century. However, Baillie and Wordsworth go beyond the eighteenth-century cult of feeling when they suggest that there is a kind of passion hidden beneath social feeling, subterranean, dark, and similar to the unconscious. Baillie states that however universal this propensity for sympathetic curiosity is, "with the generality of mankind it occupies itself in a passing and superficial way. . . . they look upon it singly and unconnected." On the other hand, for "those who reflect and reason upon what human nature holds out to their observation. . . . No stroke of nature which engages their attention stands insulated and alone. Each presents itself to them with many varied connections; and they comprehend not merely the immediate feeling which gave rise to it, but the relation of that feeling to others which are concealed." Baillie's objective, therefore, is to dig beneath the superficial social feeling–usually repre-

sented in novels, romances, plays, and lyrics–to the profound origin and natural consequence of passion, and to encourage the reader to reflect upon and make connections between "superficial" social behavior and "concealed" passion, between profound passion and a deepened sense of morality. Like Wordsworth, Baillie encourages the reader simultaneously to experience emotion vicariously as a primordial and spontaneous event in itself and to contemplate it as an idea that can be habituated as a calculated mental response.

In her series of plays, then, Baillie planned to represent the natural progress of passion from inception to realization by delving into the minds of "real and natural characters" and "unveiling the human mind under the dominion of those strong and fixed passions, which, seemingly unprovoked by outward circumstances, will from small beginnings brood within the breast." After classifying the various kinds of plays normally writ-

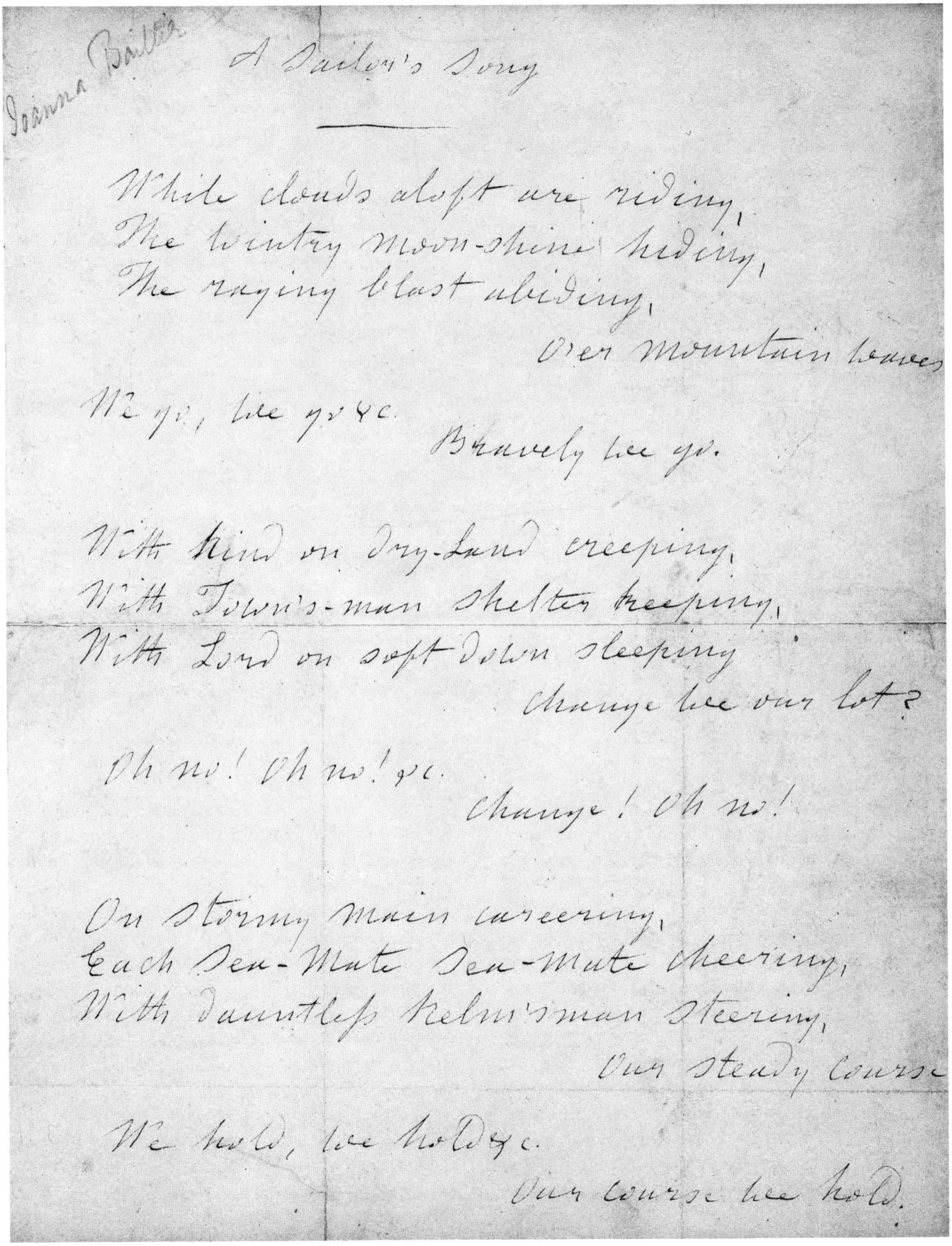

A Sailor's Song

———

While clouds aloft are riding,
The wintry moon-shine hiding,
The raging blast abiding,

   Over mountain leaves

We go, we go &c.

  Bravely we go.

With hind on dry-land creeping,
With Town's-man shelter keeping,
With Lord on soft down sleeping

   Change we our lot?

Oh no! Oh no! &c.

  Change! Oh no!

On stormy main careering,
Each Sea-Mate Sea-Mate cheering,
With dauntless Kelm's man steering,

   Our steady course

We hold, we hold &c.

  Our course we hold.

Manuscript for a poem Baillie contributed to Galt's Musical Selections *(HM 41083; by permission of the Henry E. Huntington Library and Art Gallery)*

Their sails with sunbeams whiten'd,
Themselves with glory brighten'd
From care their bosoms lighten'd

                                      Who shall return

The bold, the bold, &c.

                             Only the bold.

ten in the literary past, and explaining how they are inadequate in regard to developing intellectually sound moral sentiment, Baillie defines her project thus: "From this general view . . . , I have been led to believe, that an attempt to write a series of tragedies, of simpler construction, less embellished with poetical decorations, less constrained by that lofty seriousness which has so generally been considered as necessary for the support of tragic dignity, and in which the chief object should be to delineate the progress of the higher passions in the human breast, each play exhibiting a particular passion, might not be unacceptable to the public." In her first volume, she included a tragedy (*Basil*) and a comedy on love (*The Tryal*) and a tragedy on hatred (*De Monfort*). Baillie continued the series, publishing the second volume, comprising plays on hatred and ambition, in 1802, and the third volume, comprising three plays on fear and a musical drama on hope, in 1812. A fourth volume (the first volume of *Dramas*), comprising plays on jealousy and remorse, appeared in 1836. The plays sold well. New editions of *Plays on the Passions* were published almost yearly between 1798 and 1806, and editions of single plays were printed in Britain and America regularly throughout her life.

Baillie recognized that it was unusual to print plays before they had been staged, and she assured her readers that she did not intend them to be closet dramas. When the plays caught the eye of John Philip Kemble, Britain's best-known actor, he was determined to have one of them staged. On 29 April 1800 at the Drury Lane theater Kemble produced *De Monfort*, which quickly became Baillie's most popular and most frequently staged play. Kemble slightly altered the script to make it more stageable and took the part of the hero himself, a role which became one of his most celebrated, and one that the other great actor of the time, Edmund Kean, also relished. Kemble's sister, Sarah Siddons, took the part of Jane De Monfort, a role she so cherished that she asked Baillie to create more such heroines to test her skill.

It is not clear why *De Monfort* experienced more success than any of the other plays, since technically it is neither as ambitious nor as accomplished as some of her later tragedies, such as *Ethwald, parts 1 and 2* (*Plays on the Passions*, volume 2), *Orra* (*Plays on the Passions*, volume 3), or *Romiero* (*Dramas*, volume 1). Perhaps the success of *De Monfort* is related to the sensationalism of the play, which was occasionally criticized, and to

its Gothic undertones. The drama focuses on the consequences of its hero's intense hatred of Rezenvelt, a generous, honorable gentleman, whom De Monfort once challenged to a duel only to disgrace himself when Rezenvelt spared his life. De Monfort has felt overshadowed by Rezenvelt since childhood, and, despite Rezenfelt's exemplary character or rather because of it, De Monfort's envy and dislike increase with time. When his noble and loyal sister, Jane, attempts to intercede and to reconcile the two men, a tragedy of errors results. Having been led to believe that Jane and Rezenvelt have become romantically involved, De Monfort murders Rezenvelt. In a scene that proved controversial, De Monfort, who has been captured, is confined in a room with the corpse of his victim to await the arresting officers. Tormented to the point of a lucid insanity, he eventually dies in the wretchedness of his despair.

Except for the lugubriousness of the corpse incidents, *De Monfort* typifies Baillie's dramatic tendencies. The plots are usually well constructed and plausible, but unlike Shakespeare, whose influence is everywhere palpable, she restrains the action to classical simplicity and single-mindedness. As she explains in an article in *Fraser's Magazine* (December 1836), her interest is in the motive and motivation of behavior. She points out that in *Romiero*, her tragedy on jealousy that was often compared to *Othello*, she wanted to internalize the psychology of jealousy, rather than granting so much influence to a seemingly unmotivated villain like Iago. Baillie's defense of the plotting and characterization of *Romiero* and her theoretical excursions in various prefaces to the plays and poems reveal an astutely critical mind addressing a wide range of questions from poetics and diction to stage design and acting.

Despite her interest in near-Gothic emotional stimulation, Baillie's project is ironically classical and rationalist, stressing the fatefulness of passion and emphasizing how reason and self-knowledge can help us to control our deepest desires. At the same time, her project is romantic in that it internalizes characterization and explores the mental states of extreme agitation, madness, and criminality. In *Orra* once again the influence of the Gothic is felt. Because Orra wisely refuses to marry his son, Count Hughobert betrays his trust as her guardian by placing the heroine in the hands of the villainous Rudigere, who has convinced Hughobert that he can get Orra to change her mind. Rudigere in turn betrays Hughobert in an attempt to gain Orra's affection for himself. Knowing that she is inordinately superstitious and hoping that she will turn to him in her moment of weakness, Rudigere proceeds to inflict mental torture on Orra by confining her to a supposedly haunted castle, where she has only him to turn to. Despite her intense fear, Orra refuses to rely on Rudigere, just as she had refused her guardian, because not even fear can shake the foundation of her integrity. Baillie concentrates on the fluctuations in Orra's emotional states, demonstrating how courage of conviction can ironically be allied to superstition and fear. And even as Orra is reduced to insanity by her fear, she still retains her dignity as a heroine. Baillie repeatedly based her tragedies and narrative poems on such thin story lines, tinged with the Gothic but ultimately appealing to contemplation and restraint. And though the plays, like Shakespeare's, often mix humor with tragedy, they rarely deviate from unfolding singularly the main action or depict those violent catastrophes that consummate that action, preferring to have such incidents take place offstage in the classical manner.

Baillie's interest in superstition and in narrative poetry was probably intensified by her most important and intimate literary friendship, with Walter Scott, who admired Baillie's work greatly. Sotheby had introduced the two writers in London in 1806, the same year of Dorothea Baillie's death. Baillie and her sister seem to have been sedentary during the prolonged illness of their mother, who was both blind and paralyzed. After her death, they embarked on various travels over the next fifteen years, several times visiting with Scott in Scotland, and spending the summer and fall of 1816 in Switzerland. Perhaps it was this growing intimacy with Scott and these renewed links with Scotland that led Baillie to write *The Family Legend,* a play on a Scottish theme. Scott, who was a trustee of the Edinburgh theater, was instrumental in getting the play produced in early 1810, along with Henry Siddons, who took one of the leading roles. Scott kept Baillie informed of the tremendous success of the play. Baillie had requested that the drama be a charitable benefit for a financially distressed family she had taken an interest in—not an unusual endeavor for Baillie, who had long ago made a commitment of donating half of her income to charity. In 1806 she had interceded for the shoemaker-poet John Struthers through Scott, who encouraged Consta-

ble to publish *The Poor Man's Sabbath* (1805?, first Constable edition, 1808), and in 1823 she was to edit *A Collection of Poems* for the benefit of another friend. In the same year that she was collecting these poems from some of the best-known writers of her day, she was also nursing Matthew, who died in September of 1823. The quality of self-sacrifice that she repeatedly portrayed in her heroines she also endeavored to imitate in her own life.

The Family Legend proved once again that Baillie did not intend to be forgotten in the literary world. Even when she was not publishing new material, as in the hiatus between 1804 and 1810, she was busy thinking, writing, and revising. And although she remained disappointed, along with many critics, in the scarcity of productions of her plays, she persisted primarily because she was considering the verdict of posterity. As she notes several times in her prefaces, she felt that the theater of her time was not conducive to the kind of serious drama she was interested in writing. Byron seems to have agreed, for during 1815, when he was helping to manage the Drury Lane theater, he attempted without success to get Baillie's plays staged. It is not clear to what extent this failure led to her renewed interest in narrative poetry. With the publication of *The Lay of the Last Minstrel* in 1805, Scott had created a thirst for metrical romance, and Byron had, as Scott said, stolen his thunder with his world-weary, experimental, exotic romances. It is not surprising that when Baillie published her collection *Metrical Legends of Exalted Characters* in 1821, her romances returned to the more "naive" and nostalgic mode of Scott, rather than pursuing the racier route that Byron had taken. Baillie's romances, however, differ dramatically from Scott's in that they, like her dramas, stress characterization over plot. Like Scott's, however, her romances view the past with an almost sociological lens, and the narratives are supplemented with weighty footnotes to bolster the historicist claims, despite the obvious fictionalization that they are engaged in. Choosing to portray the "exalted characters" of William Wallace and Lady Griseld Baillie, both ancestors of hers, and Christopher Columbus, Baillie is again interested in the psycho-moral constitution of remarkable personalities thrown into the spotlight of demanding and distressing historical moments. The volume is filled out with ballads and ghost stories. That Baillie's name was still valuable on the literary market is demonstrated by the fact that her publisher

Joanna Baillie (engraving based on a portrait in Hampstead Parish Church)

was willing to pay her a thousand pounds for the volume.

With the publication of the three-volume collection *Dramas* in 1836, Baillie's career as a playwright came to a close, completing her series on the passions and giving to the public her last "miscellaneous" plays. Even her illness during 1831-1832 had not been able totally to diminish her persistence. In addition to a theological tract, *A View of the General Tenour of the New Testament* (1831; second edition, 1838), Baillie was able to present two new works to the public, *Fugitive Verses* in 1840 and *Ahalya Baee,* a narrative poem, in 1849. Predictably these poems demonstrate the same qualities as her plays. *Fugitive Verses* includes Scottish folk songs, for which she is sometimes ranked just beneath Robert Burns and James Hogg, as well as occasional poems, sacred hymns, loco-descriptive pieces, elegies for Scott and Sotheby, and love poems. Just before Baillie's death, a London bookseller requested a complete edition of her works. As usual, she was anxious to make whatever improvements she

could for the sake of posterity. Her career ended with what she called her "great monster book," published in 1851, the year of her death.

Like many of the early-nineteenth-century women writers who were well known during their own lifetimes but neglected soon afterward, Joanna Baillie's decline in fame was precipitous. Lauded by some of the most influential writers, such as Scott, Sotheby, Rogers, Thomas Campbell, Byron, and Wordsworth, Baillie was well known and respected among the literati, but she was never as popular among the massive reading public as Scott and Byron. Among the critics of her time, Francis Jeffrey, whom she eventually considered a close friend despite his consistently negative criticism of her work, and William Hazlitt stand out as dissenting voices. Jeffrey objected to the premises of her dramatic theory and thus to her plays, to the extent that those premises were fulfilled in them, but he occasionally praised isolated incidents, passages, and characters for their dignity of conception. Although Hazlitt praised *De Monfort,* he was not impressed with Baillie on the whole. Commenting on her theory in *Lectures on the English Poets,* he stated: "She is a Unitarian in poetry. With her passions are, like the French Republic, one and indivisible: they are not so in nature, or in Shakespeare." Hazlitt's objection to Baillie's plays, which he called "baby-house theatricals," is partly the result of their decidedly feminine aura. "She treats her grown men and women," he said, "as little girls treat their dolls." As the statements of other critics of the Romantic era indicate, the reception of female poets such as Baillie is intimately linked to complex matters of the relation between gender and literary taste. Literary historians and critics are only now beginning to explore these complex relations and to reexamine the influence within the Romantic period of women writers such as Baillie. It is clear, however, that Baillie's critical success helped to pave the way for the next generation of British women poets, headed by Felicia Hemans, who in turn made possible the success and more lasting renown of Elizabeth Barrett Browning and Christina Rossetti.

References:
Margaret S. Carhart, *The Life and Work of Joanna Baillie,* Yale Studies in English, 64 (New Haven: Yale University Press, 1923);

Donald Carswell, *Sir Walter: A Four-Part Study in Biography (Scott, Hogg, Lockhart, Joanna Baillie)* (London: John Murray, 1930);

Stuart Curran, "Romantic Poetry: The I Altered," in *Romanticism and Feminism,* edited by Anne K. Mellor (Bloomington: Indiana University Press, 1988), pp. 185-207;

Bertrand Evans, *Gothic Drama from Walpole to Shelley,* University of California Publications in English, 18 (Berkeley: University of California Press, 1947);

Catherine Jane Hamilton, *Women Writers: Their Works and Ways,* first series (London: Ward, Lock, 1892);

William Hazlitt, *Lectures on the English Poets* (London: Taylor & Hessey, 1818);

"A Life of Joanna Baillie," in *The Dramatic and Poetical Works of Joanna Baillie, complete in one volume,* second edition (London: Longman, Brown, Green & Longmans, 1853);

Alice C. Meynell, *The Second Person Singular and Other Essays* (London & New York: Oxford University Press, 1922);

M. Norton, "The Plays of Joanna Baillie," *Review of English Studies,* 23 (April 1947): 131-143.

William Blake

(28 November 1757 - 12 August 1827)

Charles Reinhart
Vincennes University

BOOKS: *Poetical Sketches* (London: Privately printed, 1783; facsimile, London: William Griggs, 1890);

There is No Natural Religion, series a and b (London: Printed by William Blake, 1788?; facsimile, 2 volumes, London: William Blake Trust, 1971);

All Religions are One (London: Printed by William Blake, 1788?; facsimile, London: William Blake Trust, 1970);

Songs of Innocence (London: Printed by William Blake, 1789); revised and enlarged as *Songs of Innocence and of Experience* (London: Printed by William Blake, 1794; facsimile, London: William Blake Trust, 1955);

The Book of Thel (London: Printed by William Blake, 1789; facsimile, London: William Blake Trust, 1965);

The Marriage of Heaven and Hell (London: Printed by William Blake, 1793?; facsimile, London: William Blake Trust, 1960);

Visions of the Daughters of Albion (London: Printed by William Blake, 1793; facsimile, London: William Blake Trust, 1959);

For Children: The Gates of Paradise (London: Printed by William Blake, 1793); revised and enlarged as *For the Sexes: The Gates of Paradise* (London: Printed by William Blake, 1818?; facsimile, London: William Blake Trust, 1968);

America. A Prophecy (Lambeth: Printed by William Blake, 1793; facsimile, London: William Blake Trust, 1963);

Europe (Lambeth: Printed by William Blake, 1794; facsimile, London: William Blake Trust, 1969);

The First Book of Urizen (Lambeth: Printed by William Blake, 1794; facsimile, London: William Blake Trust, 1975);

The Song of Los (Lambeth: Printed by William Blake, 1795; facsimile, London: William Blake Trust, 1975);

The Book of Los (Lambeth: Printed by William Blake, 1795; facsimile, London: William Blake Trust, 1975);

The Book of Ahania (Lambeth: Printed by William Blake, 1795; facsimile, London: William Blake Trust, 1973);

Milton (London: Printed by William Blake, 1804 [i.e., 1808?]; facsimile, London: William Blake Trust, 1967);

Jerusalem (London: Printed by William Blake, 1804 [i.e., 1820?]; facsimile, London: William Blake Trust, 1951);

A Descriptive Catalogue of Pictures, Poetical and Historical Inventions, Painted by William Blake in Water Colours, being the Ancient Method of Fresco Painting Restored: and Drawings . . . (London: Printed by D. N. Shury, 1809);

Illustrations of the Book of Job, in Twenty-One Plates, Invented and Engraved by William Blake (London: Printed by William Blake, 1826); facsimiles: *The Illustrations of the Book of Job,* edited by Lawrance Binyon and Geoffrey Keynes (New York: Pierpont Morgan Library, 1935) and in S. Foster Damon, *Blake's Job: William Blake's Illustrations to the Book of Job* (Providence: Brown University Press, 1966);

Blake's Illustrations of Dante. Seven Plates, designed and engraved by W. Blake (London, 1838).

Facsimiles of manuscripts for works not published during Blake's lifetime: *An Island in the Moon* [written 1784?] (Cambridge: Cambridge University Press, 1987);

Tiriel [written 1789?] (London: Oxford University Press, 1967);

The Notebooks of William Blake [written circa 1793-1818], edited by David Erdman and Donald Moore (London: Oxford University Press, 1973);

Vala, or The Four Zoas [written circa 1796-1807] (London: Oxford University Press, 1963);

Pickering Manuscript [written after 1807] (New York: Peirpont Morgan Library, 1972).

Collections: *The Writings of William Blake,* 3 volumes, edited by Geoffrey Keynes (London:

William Blake (portrait by Thomas Phillips; by permission of the National Portrait Gallery, London)

Oxford University Press, 1925); revised as *The Complete Writings of William Blake* (London: Oxford University Press, 1957; second revision, 1966);

The Complete Poetry and Prose of William Blake, edited by David Erdman (Berkeley: University of California Press, 1965; revised, 1982);

The Illuminated Blake, Annotated by David Erdman (Garden City, N.Y.: Anchor Press, 1974);

William Blake's Writings, 2 vols., ed. G. E. Bentley, Jr. (Oxford: Clarendon Press, 1978).

Reproductions of Pictorial Works: Geoffrey Keynes, ed. *Illustrations to Young's Night Thoughts Done in Water-Colour by William Blake* (Cambridge, Mass.: Harvard University Press, 1927);

Albert S. Roe, *Blake's Illustrations to the Divine Comedy* (Princeton: Princeton University Press, 1953);

Keynes, *Engravings by William Blake* (Dublin: E. Walker, 1956);

Keynes, ed., *William Blake's Illustrations of the Bible* (London: William Blake Trust, 1957);

William Wells and Elizabeth Johnston, *William Blake's "Heads of the Poets"* (Manchester: City of Manchester Art Gallery, 1969);

Irene Taylor, *Blake's Illustrations to the Poems of Gray* (Princeton: Princeton University Press, 1971);

William Blake's Water Colour Designs for the Poems of Thomas Gray (London: William Blake Trust, 1972);

Iain Bain, David Chambers, and Andrew Wilton, *The Wood Engravings of William Blake for Thornton's Virgil* (London: British Museum Publications, 1977);

Pamela Dunbar, *William Blake's Illustrations to the Poetry of Milton* (Oxford: Clarendon Press, 1980);

John Grant, Edward Rose, Michael Tolley, and David Erdman, eds., *William Blake's Designs for Edward Young's Night Thoughts* (Oxford: Clarendon Press, 1980);

Milton Klonsky, *Blake's Dante* (New York: Harmony Books, 1980);

Blake in his late twenties, drawn by his wife, Catherine Blake, probably from memory after his death (by permission of the Syndics of the Fitzwilliam Museum, Cambridge)

Martin Butlin, *The Paintings and Drawings of William Blake* (New Haven: Yale University Press, 1981).

OTHER: Edward Young, *The Complaint, and The Consolation; or Night Thoughts,* illustrated by Blake (London: R. Edwards, 1797);

William Hayley, *The Life and Posthumous Writings of William Cowper, Esqr.,* 3 volumes, includes plates engraved by Blake (Chichester: Printed by J. Seagrave for J. Johnson, 1803 [i.e., 1804]);

The Grave, A Poem. Illustrated by twelve Etchings Executed by Louis Schiavonetti, From the Original Inventions of William Blake (London: Cromek, 1808); facsimile, in *Robert Blair's The Grave Illustrated by William Blake. A Study with a Facsimile,* edited by Robert N. Essick and

Milton D. Paley (London: Scolar Press, 1982).

In his *Life of William Blake* (1863) Alexander Gilchrist warned his readers that Blake "neither wrote nor drew for the many, hardly for work'y-day men at all, rather for children and angels; himself 'a divine child,' whose playthings were sun, moon, and stars, the heavens and the earth." Yet Blake himself believed that his writings were of national importance and that they could be understood by a majority of men. Far from being an isolated mystic, Blake lived and worked in the teeming metropolis of London at a time of great social and political change that profoundly influenced his writing. After the peace established in 1762, the British Empire seemed secure, but the storm wave begun with the American Revolution

in 1775 and the French Revolution in 1789 changed forever the way men looked at their relationship to the state and to the established church. Poet, painter, and engraver, Blake worked to bring about a change both in the social order and in the minds of men.

One may wonder how a child born in moderate surroundings would become such an original artist and powerful writer. Unlike many well-known writers of his day, Blake was born into a family of moderate means. His father, James, was a hosier, one who sells stockings, gloves, and haberdashery, and the family lived at 28 Broad Street in London in an unpretentious but "respectable" neighborhood. Blake was born on 28 November 1757. In all, seven children were born to James and Catherine Harmitage Blake, but only five survived infancy. Blake seems to have been closest to his youngest brother, Robert, who died while yet young.

By all accounts Blake had a pleasant and peaceful childhood, made even more pleasant by his skipping any formal schooling. As a young boy he wandered the streets of London and could easily escape to the surrounding countryside. Even at an early age, however, his unique mental powers would prove disquieting. According to Gilchrist, on one ramble he was startled to "see a tree filled with angels, bright angelic wings bespangling every bough like stars." His parents were not amused at such a story, and only his mother's pleadings prevented him from receiving a beating.

His parents did, however, encourage his artistic talents, and the young Blake was enrolled at the age of ten in Pars' drawing school. The expense of continued formal training in art, however, was a prohibitive one, and the family decided that at the age of fourteen William would be apprenticed to a master engraver. At first his father took him to William Ryland, a highly respected engraver. William, however, resisted the arrangement telling his father, "I do not like the man's face: it looks as if he will live to be hanged!" The grim prophecy was to come true twelve years later. Instead of Ryland the family settled on a lesser-known engraver but a man of considerable talents, James Basire. Basire seems to have been a good master, and Blake was a good student of the craft. Blake was later to be especially grateful to Basire for sending the young student to Westminster Abbey to make drawings of monuments Basire was commissioned to engrave. The vast Gothic dimensions of Westminster and

the haunting presence of the tombs of kings affected Blake's romantic sensibilities and were to provide fertile ground for his active imagination.

At the age of twenty-one Blake left Basire's apprenticeship and enrolled for a time in the newly formed Royal Academy. It was as a journeyman engraver, however, that Blake earned his living. Booksellers employed him to engrave illustrations for publications ranging from novels such as *Don Quixote* to serials such as *Ladies' Magazine*.

One incident at this time affected Blake deeply. In June of 1780 riots broke out in London incited by the anti-Catholic preaching of Lord George Gordon but also by resistance to continued war against the American colonists. Houses, churches, and prisons were burned by uncontrollable mobs bent on destruction. On one evening, whether by design or by accident, Blake found himself at the front of the mob that burned Newgate prison. These images of violent destruction and unbridled revolution gave Blake powerful material for works such as *Europe* (1794) and *America* (1793).

Not all of the young man's interests were confined to art and politics. After one ill-fated romance, Blake met Catherine Boucher, an attractive and compassionate woman who took pity on Blake's tales of being spurned. After a year's courtship the couple were married on 18 August 1782. The parish registry shows that Catherine, like many women of her class, could not sign her own name. Blake soon taught her to read and write, and under Blake's tutoring she became an accomplished draftsman, helping in the execution of his designs.

By all accounts the marriage was a happy one, but no children were born to the couple. Catherine also managed the household and was undoubtedly of great help in making ends meet on Blake's always meager income.

Blake's friend John Flaxman introduced Blake to the bluestocking literary circle of the Rev. Henry Mathew and his wife, a leader of fashion whose drawing room was a gathering place for artists and musicians. Blake gained favor and read some of his early poems and sang his own songs. Mr. and Mrs. Mathew encouraged Blake and published his *Poetical Sketches*. Many modern critics have seen in these early poems evidence of Blake's great genius. Even here one can see his protest against

Catherine Blake, circa 1785 (portrait attributed to George Cumberland; The Complete Portraiture of William and Catherine Blake, *edited by Geoffrey Keynes, 1977)*

Erdman argues that the ballad "Gwin, King of Norway" is a protest against King George's treatment of the American colonies, a subject Blake treated more extensively in *America* (1793). Only about fifty copies of *Poetical Sketches* are known to have been printed, and the verses never reached a wide audience.

Blake's financial enterprises also did not fair well. In 1784, after his father's death, Blake used of the money he inherited to set up shop as a seller with his friend James Parker. The moved to 27 Broad Street, next door to the family home and close to Blake's brothers. The business did not do well, however, and the men moved out.

More concern to Blake was the deterioration of his favorite brother, Robert. Blake nursed his brother in his illness and according watched the spirit of his brother es-

cape his body in his death: "At the last solemn moment, the visionary eyes beheld the released spirit ascend heaven ward through the matter-of-fact ceiling, 'clapping its hands for joy.'"

Blake always felt the spirit of Robert lived with him. He even announced that it was Robert who informed him how to illustrate his poems in "illuminated writing." Blake's technique was to produce his text and design on a copper plate with an impervious liquid. The plate was then dipped in acid so that the text and design remained in relief. That plate could be used to print on paper, and the final copy would be then hand colored.

After experimenting with this method in a series of aphorisms entitled *There is No Natural Religion* and *All Religions are One* (1788?), Blake designed the series of plates for the poems entitled *Songs of Innocence* and dated the title page 1789.

Title page and interior page from Blake's book of "happy songs" that "Every child may joy to hear" (Copy N, Doheny Collection, auctioned by Christie, Manson and Woods International Inc., 21-22 February 1989)

Blake continued to experiment with the process of illuminated writing and in 1794 combined the early poems with companion poems entitled *Songs of Experience*. The title page of the combined set announces that the poems show "the two Contrary States of the Human Soul." Clearly Blake meant for the two series of poems to be read together, and Robert Gleckner has pointed out in reading the poems one should always consider the point of view of the speaker of the poem and the context of the situation.

The introductory poems to each series display Blake's dual image of the poet as both a "piper" and a "Bard." As man goes through various stages of innocence and experience in the poems, the poet also is in different stages of innocence and experience. The pleasant lyrical aspect of poetry is shown in the role of the "piper"

while the more somber prophetic nature of poetry is displayed by the stern Bard.

In the "Introduction" to *Songs of Innocence*, Blake presents the poet in the form of a simple shepherd: "Piping down the valleys wild / Piping songs of pleasant glee." The frontispiece displays a young shepherd simply dressed and holding a pipe, and it is clear Blake is establishing a pastoral world. The "piping songs" are poems of pure pleasure.

The songs of pleasure are interrupted by the visionary appearance of an angel who asks for songs of more seriousness:

> "Pipe a song about a Lamb!"
> So I piped with merry chear.
> "Piper, pipe that song again."
> So I piped: he wept to hear.

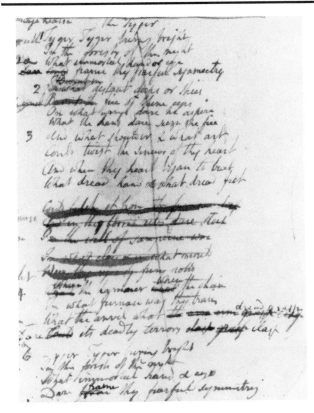

Draft for "The Tyger" and sketches from Blake's Notebook, *also known as the* Rossetti Manuscript *because it was once the property of Dante Gabriel Rosetti (Add. MS 49460, ff. 56 and 3v [details]; by permission of the British Library) and the poem as it appears in* Songs of Innocence and of Experience *(Copy Z, Rosenwald Collection, Library of Congress)*

The piper is no longer playing his songs for his own enjoyment. Now the piper is in the position of a poet playing at the request of an appreciative audience. The "song about a Lamb" suggests a poem about the "Lamb of God," Christ.

The child commands that the poet not keep the songs for himself but share them with his audience:

> "Piper sit thee down and write
> In a book that all may read."
> So he vanish'd from my sight
> And I pluck'd a hollow reed.

The "book" is *Songs of Innocence*, which is designed in a form that "all may read." The simple piper is now a true poet. He no longer writes only for his own enjoyment but for the delight of his audience. The piper is inspired by the directions of the child, and the poet is inspired by his vision of his audience. The child vanishes as the author interiorizes his vision of his audience and makes it a central part of his work. Immediately after the child's disappearance, the author begins the actual physical composition of the poem by plucking the hollow reed for his poem. At the end of the poem the poet is no longer the simple shepherd of Arcadia playing for his own amusement. Now he writes his poems for "Every child" of England.

The "Introduction" to *Songs of Experience* is a companion to the earlier poem, and, as a poem written in the state of experience, it presents a different view of the nature of the poet and his relation to his audience.

The strident tone of the first stanza provides a marked contrast to the gentle piping of the first poem and reminds us that we are now in the state of experience:

> Hear the voice of the Bard!
> Who Present, Past and Future sees:
> Whose ears have heard
> The Holy Word
> That walk'd among the ancient trees.

This is not an invocation, but a direct command to the reader to sit up and pay attention. Instead of playing at the request of his audience, the poet now demands that his reader listen to him. The speaker now has authority because of what he has heard. The voice of the poet is that of the ancient Bard and that also of the biblical prophet who has heard the "Holy Word," the word of God. Assuming the role of the prophet and the

Bard gives the modern poet a sense of biblical authority to speak on matters sacred and profane.

With his authority, the Bard is more willing to instruct his audience than is the piper. The Bard repeats the call of the Holy Word to fallen man. The message repeated by the Bard is that man still "might control" the world of nature and bring back the "fallen light" of vision.

Blake presents two sides of his view of the poet in these introductory poems. Neither one should be dismissed in favor of the other. The poet is both a pleasant piper playing at the request of his audience and a stern Bard lecturing an entire nation. In part this is Blake's interpretation of the ancient dictum that poetry should both delight and instruct. More important, for Blake the poet is a man who speaks both from the personal experience of his own vision and from the "inherited" tradition of ancient Bards and prophets who carried the Holy Word to the nations.

In reading any of the poems, one has to be aware of the mental "state" of the speaker of the poems. In some cases the speakers address the same issue, but from entirely different perspectives. The child of "The Chimney Sweeper" in *Songs of Innocence* lives in deplorable conditions and is clearly exploited by those around him: "So your chimneys I sweep & in soot I sleep." Yet in his childish state he explains away his misery with a dream of a promised afterlife where God will be his father and he will "never want joy." The same issue of child exploitation is addressed in "The Chimney Sweeper" of *Songs of Experience*. The speaker is also a child, but one who understands the social forces that have reduced him to misery:

> "And because I am happy, & dance & sing
> "They think they have done me no injury.
> "And are gone to praise God & his Priest & King.
> "Who make up a heaven of our misery."

In each poem the reader can see what the speaker can not always see because of his unique perspective: religion and government share a responsibility in the persecution of children.

The famous companion poems "The Lamb" and "The Tyger" are also written on the same subject: man's conception of God. Yet, how man understands God depends on man's view of God's divinity. In "The Lamb" the speaker makes the traditional association between a lamb and the "Lamb of God," Christ:

Title page and interior pages from the two series of poems in which Blake depicts contrasting aspects of the poet's vision (Copy Z, Rosenwald Collection, Library of Congress)

For he calls himself a Lamb:
He is meek & he is mild;
He became a little child:
I a child & thou a lamb.

The speaker sees God in terms he can understand. God is gentle and kind and very much like us. The close association between the "I," "child," and "lamb" suggests that all men share in the same spiritual brotherhood.

The speaker in "The Tyger" also sees God in terms he can understand, but he sees him from a different perspective. The raging violence of the animal forces him to ask what kind of God could create such terror:

When the stars threw down their spears,
And water'd heaven with their tears,
Did he smile his work to see?
Did he who made the Lamb make thee?

The answer, of course, is never given, but again the reader should be able to perceive more than the speaker of the poem. God did make both the lamb and the tyger, and his nature contains both the gentleness of the lamb and the violence of the tyger. Neither perspective is true by itself; both have to be understood.

The two states of innocence and experience are not always clearly separate in the poems, and one can see signs of both states in many poems. The companion poems titled "Holy Thursday" are on the same subject, the forced marching of poor children to St. Paul's Cathedral in London. The speaker in the state of innocence approves warmly of the progression of children:

'Twas on a Holy Thursday their innocent faces
     clean
The children walking two & two in red & blue &
     green
Grey headed beadles walkd before with wands as
     white as snow
Till into the high dome of Pauls they like Thames
     waters flow[.]

The brutal irony is that in this world of truly "innocent" children there are evil men who repress the children, round them up like so many herd of cattle, and force them to show their piety. In this state of innocence, experience is very much present.

The speaker of the companion "Holy Thursday" presents an entirely different perspective:

Is this a holy thing to see,
In a rich and fruitful land,

Babes reduc'd to misery,
Fed with cold and usurous hand?

The speaker of experience understands that the children have been brutalized and places the blame for this condition not just on the "Grey headed beadles" who have direct responsibility for the children but on the country at large. In a "rich and fruitful land" like England, it is appalling that children are allowed to suffer:

For where-e'er the sun does shine,
And where-e'er the rain does fall:
Babe can never hunger there,
Nor poverty the mind appall[.]

If experience has a way of creeping into the world of innocence, innocence also has a way of creeping into experience. The golden land where the "sun does shine" and the "rain does fall" is a land of bountiful goodness and innocence. But even here in this blessed land, there are children starving. The sharp contrast between the two conditions makes the social commentary all the more striking and supplies the energy of the poem.

The contrast between innocence and experience is also apparent in another illuminated book produced in 1789, *The Book of Thel*. Thel is a maiden who laments the passing of youth and of innocence: "O life of this our spring! why fades the lotus of the water, / "Why fade these children of the spring, born but to smile & fall?" Thel questions elements of nature, like the Lilly of the Valley and the Cloud, that are beautiful but transitory. Yet each understands that the transitory nature of beauty is necessary. The Cloud answers Thel's complaint by saying that "Every thing that lives / Lives not alone nor for itself." Thel is innocent but when one is stuck in a state of innocence there can be no growth.

Thel is allowed to enter into the world of experience, and she is startled by a voice from her own grave:

"Why a tender curb upon the youthful burning
     boy?
"Why a little curtain of flesh on the bed of our
     desire?"

The Virgin is shocked by this peek into her own sexuality and mortality and runs back to the quiet vales of Har "with a shriek." Blake satirizes those who are unable to see the necessary connection between innocence and experience, the spiri-

And Aged Tiriel. stood before the Gates of his beautiful palace

~~[deleted line]~~

With Myratana. once the Queen of all the western plains
But now his eyes were darkned. & his wife fading in death
They stood before their once delightful palace. & thus the Voice
Of aged Tiriel. arose. that his sons might hear in their gates

Accursed race of Tiriel. behold your father
Come forth & look on her that bore you. come you accursed sons.
In my weak arms. I here have borne your dying mother
Come forth sons of the Curse come forth. see the death of Myratana

His sons ran from their gates. & saw their aged parents stand
And thus the eldest son of Tiriel raisd his mighty voice

Old man unworthy to be called. the father of Tiriels race
For every one of those thy wrinkles. each of those grey hairs
Are cruel as death. & as obdurate as the devouring pit
Why should thy sons care for thy curses thou accursed man
Were we not slaves till we rebeld. Who cares for Tiriels curse
His blessing was a cruel curse. His curse may be a blessing

He ceast the aged man & raisd up his right hand to the heavens
His left supported Myratana shrinking in pangs of death
The orbs of his large eyes he opend. & thus his voice went forth

Serpents not sons. wreathing around the bones of Tiriel
Ye worms of death feasting upon your aged parents flesh
Listen & hear your mothers groans. No more accursed Sons
She bears. she groans not at the birth of Heuxos or Yuva
These are the groans of death ye serpents These are the groans of death
Nourishd with milk ye serpents. nourishd with mothers tears & cares
Look at my eyes blind as the orbless skull among the stones
Look at my bald head. Hark listen ye serpents listen
What Myratana. What my wife O Soul O Spirit O fire.
What Myratana. art thou dead. Look here ye serpents look
The serpents sprung from her own bowels have drawn her dry as this

First page of text from the manuscript for Tiriel *(EG 2876; by permission of the British Library, Department of Manuscripts)*

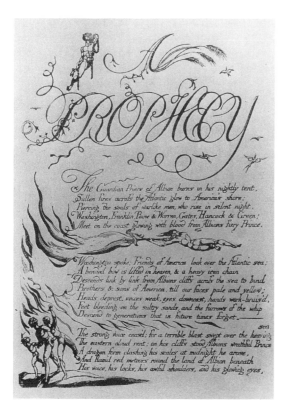

Frontispiece, title page, and interior pages from Blake's poetic commentary on the universal principles that underlie revolution
(Copy E, Rosenwald Collection, Library of Congress)

tual world and the physical world. Thel's world of soft watercolors is not enough. She cannot understand that even the lowly worm is loved by God and serves his part in creating life.

The storming of the Bastille in Paris in 1789 and the agonies of the French Revolution sent shock waves through England. Some hoped for a corresponding outbreak of liberty in England while others feared a breakdown of the social order. In much of his writing Blake argues against the monarchy. In his early *Tiriel* (written circa 1789) Blake traces the fall of a tyrannical king.

Politics was surely often the topic of conversation at the publisher Joseph Johnson's house, where Blake was often invited. There Blake met important literary and political figures such as William Godwin, Joseph Priestly, Mary Wollstonecraft, and Thomas Paine. According to one legend Blake is even said to have saved Paine's life by warning him of his impending arrest. Whether or not that is true, it is clear that Blake was familiar with some of the leading radical thinkers of his day.

In *The French Revolution* Blake celebrates the rise of democracy in France and the fall of the monarchy. King Louis represents a monarchy that is old and dying. The sick king is lethargic and unable to act: "From my window I see the old mountains of France, like aged men, fading away." The "old mountains" of monarchy are doomed to collapse under the pressure of the people and their representatives in the assembly. The "voice of the people" demand the removal of the king's troops from Paris, and their departure at the end of the first book signals the triumph of democracy.

On the title page for book one of *The French Revolution* Blake announces that it is "A Poem in Seven Books," but none of the other books has been found. The "Advertisement" to the poem promises "The remaining Books of the Poem are finished, and will be published in their Order." The first book was set in type in 1791, but exists only in proof copies. Johnson never published the poem, perhaps because of fear of prosecution, or perhaps because Blake himself withdrew it from publication. Johnson did have cause to be nervous. Erdman points out that in the same year booksellers were thrown in jail for selling the works of Thomas Paine.

In *America* (1793) Blake also addresses the idea of revolution, but the poem is less a commentary on the actual revolution in America as it is a

commentary on universal principles that are at work in any revolution. The fiery figure of Orc represents all revolutions:

> The fiery joy, that Urizen perverted to ten commands,
> What night he led the starry hosts thro' the wide wilderness,
> That stony law I stamp to dust; and scatter religion abroad
> To the four winds as a torn book, & none shall gather the leaves.

The same force that causes the colonists to rebel against King George is the force that overthrows the perverted rules and restrictions of established religions.

The revolution in America suggests to Blake a similar revolution in England. In the poem the king, like the ancient pharaohs of Egypt, sends pestilence to America to punish the rebels, but the colonists are able to redirect the forces of destruction to England. Erdman suggests that Blake is thinking of the riots in England during the war and the chaotic condition of the English troops, many of whom deserted. Writing this poem in the 1790s, Blake also surely imagined the possible effect of the French Revolution on England.

Another product of the radical 1790s is *The Marriage of Heaven and Hell*. Written and etched between 1790 and 1793, Blake's poem brutally satirizes oppressive authority in church and state. The poem also satirizes the works of Emanuel Swedenborg, the Swedish philosopher whose ideas once attracted Blake's interests.

The powerful opening of the poem suggests a world of violence: "Rintrah roars & shakes his fires in the burden'd air / Hungry clouds swag on the deep." The fire and smoke suggest a battlefield and the chaos of revolution. The cause of that chaos is analyzed at the beginning of the poem. The world has been turned upside down. The "just man" has been turned away from the institutions of church and state, and in his place are fools and hypocrites who preach law and order but create chaos. Those who proclaim restrictive moral rules and oppressive laws as "goodness" are in themselves evil. Hence to counteract this repression, Blake announces that he is of the "Devil's Party" that will advocate freedom and energy and gratified desire.

The "Proverbs of Hell" are clearly designed to shock the reader out of his commonplace notion of what is good and what is evil:

Prisons are built with stones of Law, Brothels with
  bricks of Religion.
The pride of the peacock is the glory of God.
The lust of the goat is the bounty of God.
The wrath of the lion is the wisdom of God.
The nakedness of woman is the work of God.

It is the oppressive nature of church and state
that has created the repulsive prisons and brothels. Sexual energy is not an inherent "evil," but
the repression of that energy is. The preachers
of morality fail to understand that God is in all
things, including the sexual nature of men and
women.

Blake is, of course, not advocating moral
and political anarchy, but a proper balance of energy and its opposing force, reason. Reason is defined as "the bound or outward circumference of
Energy." Reason is a vital and necessary force to
define Energy, and "Without Contraries is no progression." The problem now is that the forces of
reason have predominated, and the forces of energy must be let loose.

The Marriage of Heaven and Hell contains
many of the basic religious ideas developed in
the major prophecies. Blake analyzes the development of organized religion as a perversion of ancient visions: "The ancient Poets animated all sensible objects with Gods or Genuises, calling them
by the names and adorning them with the properties of woods, rivers, mountains, lakes, cities, nations, and whatever their enlarged & Numerous
senses could perceive." Ancient man created
those gods to express his vision of the spiritual
properties that he perceived in the physical
world. So far, so good, but the gods began to
take on a life of their own separate from man:
"Till a system was formed, which some took advantage of, & enslav'd the vulgar by attempting to realize or abstract the mental deities from their objects: thus began Priesthood." The "system" or
organized religion keeps man from perceiving
the spiritual in the physical. The gods are seen as
separate from man, and an elite race of priests is
developed to approach the gods: "Thus men forgot that All deities reside in the human breast." Instead of looking for god on remote altars, Blake
warns, man should look within.

In August of 1790 Blake moved from his
house on Poland Street across the Thames to the
area known as Lambeth. The Blakes lived in the
house for ten years, and the surrounding neighborhood often becomes mythologized in his poetry. Felpham was a "lovely vale," a place of trees
and open meadows, but it also contained signs of

human cruelty, such as the house for orphans.
At his home Blake kept busy not only with his illuminated poetry but also with the daily chore of
making money. During the 1790s Blake earned
fame as an engraver and was glad to receive numerous commissions.

One story told by Blake's friend Thomas
Butts shows how much the Blakes enjoyed the pastoral surroundings of Lambeth. At the end of
Blake's garden was a small summer house, and
coming to call on the Blakes one day Butts was
shocked to find the couple stark naked: "Come
in!" cried Blake; "it's only Adam and Eve you
know!" The Blakes were reciting passages from
Paradise Lost, apparently "in character."

Sexual freedom is addressed in *Visions of the
Daughters of Albion* (1793), also written during the
Lambeth period. Oothoon, the "soft soul of
America," expresses her unrestricted love for
Theotormon who cannot accept such love because he is limited by jealousy and possessiveness.
In the poem Oothoon is raped by Bromion, and
the enraged Theotormon binds the two together.
The frontispiece to the book shows Bromion and
Oothoon with their arms bound together back to
back while Theotormon hunched over stares at
the ground. The relationship between Bromion
and Oothoon is like that of marriage that is held together only by laws and not by love. In her lament to Theotormon, Oothoon denounces the destruction of a woman's sexual desire:

Till she who burns with youth, and knows no fixed
  lot, is bound
In spells of law to one she loathes? and must she
  drag the chain
Of life in weary lust?

The marriage "spells of law" bind a woman to
man much like a slave is bound to a master, and
marriage can become, in Mary Wollstonecraft's
phrase, a form of "legalized prostitution."

Oothoon calls for the freedom of desire:
"Open to joy and to delight where ever beauty ap-
pears" and even promises to provide women for
Theotormon to enjoy "in lovely copulation," but
Theotormon, bound by law and custom, cannot ac-
cept such love.

In 1793-1795 Blake produced a remarkable
collection of illuminated works that have come to
be known as the "Minor Prophecies." In *Europe*
(1794), *The First Book of Urizen* (1794), *The Book of
Los* (1795), *The Song of Los* (1795), and *The Book
of Ahania* (1795) Blake develops the major outlines of his universal mythology. In these poems

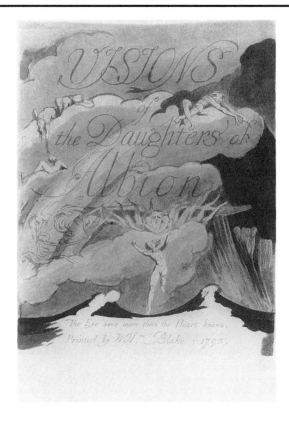

Frontispiece, title page, and interior pages for the poem in which Blake calls for love unbound by law and custom
(Copy A, British Museum Print Room)

Blake examines the fall of man. In Blake's mythology man and God were once united, but man separated himself from God and became weaker and weaker as he became further divided. Throughout the poems Blake writes of the destructive aspects of this separation into warring identities.

The narrative of the universal mythology is interwoven with the historical events of Blake's own time. The execution of King Louis XVI in 1793 led to an inevitable reaction, and England soon declared war on France. England's participation in the war against France and its attempt to quell the revolutionary spirit is addressed in *Europe*. In Blake's poem liberty is repressed in England after it declares war on France:

> Over the windows Thou shalt not; & over the chimneys Fear is written
> With bands of iron round their necks fasten'd into the walls of citizens

The very force of that repression, however, will cause its opposite to appear in the revolutionary figure of Orc: "And in the vineyards of reds France appear'd the light of his fury." Orc promises fire and destruction, but he also wars against the forces of repression.

Blake's minor prophecies are, of course, much more than political commentaries. In these poems Blake analyzes the universal forces at work when repression and revolution clash. Erdman has pointed out the historical parallel in *Europe* between Rintrah and William Pitt, the English Prime Minister who led his country into war against France. Yet in the same poem we see references to repression from the time of Christ to the Last Judgement. Blake saw English repression of the French Revolution as but one moment in the stream of history.

The causes of that repression are examined in *The First Book of Urizen*. The word *Urizen* suggests "your reason" and also "horizon." He represents that part of the mind that constantly defines and limits human thought and action. In the frontispiece to the poem he is pictured as an aged man hunched over a massive book writing with both hands in other books. Behind him stand the tablets of the ten commandments, and Urizen is surely writing other "thou shalt nots" for others to follow. His twisted anatomical position shows the perversity of what should be the "human form divine."

The poem traces the birth of Urizen as a separate part of the human mind. He broods upon himself and comes to insist on laws for all to follow:

> "One command, one joy, one desire
> "One curse, one weight, one measure,
> "One King, one God, one Law."

Urizen's repressive laws bring only further chaos and destruction. Like Milton's hell, Urizen's world is filled with the contradictions of darkness and fire: "no light from the fires." The lawgiver can only produce destruction, not understanding. Appalled by the chaos he himself created, Urizen fashions a world apart.

The process of separation continues as the character of Los is divided from Urizen. Los, the "Eternal Prophet," represents another power of the human mind. Los forges the creative aspects of the mind into works of art. Like Urizen he is a limiter, but the limitations he creates are productive and necessary. In the poem Los forms "nets and gins" to bring an end to Urizen's continual chaotic separation.

Los is horrified by the figure of the bound Urizen and is separated by his pity, "for Pity divides the Soul." Los undergoes a separation into a male and female form. His female form is called Enitharmon, and her creation is viewed with horror:

> Eternity shudder'd when they saw
> Man begetting his likeness
> On his own divided image.

This separation into separate sexual identities is yet another sign of man's fall. The "Eternals" contain both male and female forms within themselves, but man is divided and weak.

Enitharmon gives birth to the fiery Orc, whose violent birth gives some hope for radical change in a fallen world, but Orc is bound in chains by Los, now a victim of jealousy. Enitharmon bears an "enormous race," but it is a race of men and women who are weak and divided and who have lost sight of eternity.

Urizen explores the fallen world, spreading his "Net of Religion" over the cities of men:

> And their children wept, & built
> Tombs in the desolate places,
> And form'd laws of prudence, and call'd them
> The eternal laws of God.

In his fallen state man has limited senses and fails to perceive the infinite. Divided from God

Title page and interior pages from the seventh, and last, copy printed by Blake of the book he originally called The First Book of Urizen *(Copy G, Rosenwald Collection, Library of Congress). Before printing this copy, some time after 1815, Blake removed the word* First *from the plates for the pages on which the title appears.*

and caught by the narrow traps of religion, he sees God only as a crude lawgiver who must be obeyed.

The Book of Los also examines man's fall and the binding of Urizen, but from the perspective of Los whose task it is to place a limit on the chaotic separation begun by Urizen. The decayed world is again one of ignorance where there is "no light from the fires." From this chaos the bare outlines of the human form begin to appear:

> Many ages of groans, till there grew
> Branchy forms organizing the Human
> Into finite inflexible organs.

The human senses are pale imitations of the true senses that allow one to perceive eternity. Urizen's world where man now lives is spoken of as an "illusion" because it masks the spiritual world that is everywhere present.

In *The Song of Los,* Los sings of the decayed state of man, where the arbitrary laws of Urizen have become institutionalized:

> Thus the terrible race of Los & Enitharmon gave
> Laws & Religions to the sons of Har, binding them
>   more
> And more to Earth, closing and restraining,
> Till a Philosophy of five Senses was complete.
> Urizen wept & gave it into the hands of Newton &
>   Locke.

The "philosophy of the five senses" espoused by scientists and philosophers argues that the world and the mind are like industrial machines operating by fixed laws but devoid of imagination, creativity, or any spiritual life. Blake condemns this materialistic view of the world espoused in the writings of Newton and Locke.

Although man is in a fallen state, the end of the poem points to the regeneration that is to come:

> Orc, raging in European darkness,
> Arose like a pillar of fire above the Alps,
> Like a serpent of fiery flame!

The coming of Orc is likened not only to the fires of revolution sweeping Europe, but also to the final apocalypse when the "Grave shrieks with delight."

The separation of man is also examined in *The Book of Ahania,* which Blake later incorporated in *Vala, or The Four Zoas.* In *The Book of*

Ahania Urizen is further divided into male and female forms. Urizen is repulsed by his feminine shadow that is called Ahania:

> He groan'd anguish'd, & called her Sin,
> Kissing her and weeping over her;
> Then hid her in darkness, in silence,
> Jealous, tho' she was invisible.

Blake satirizes the biblical and Miltonic associations of sin and lust. "Ahania" in Blake's poem is only a "sin" in that she is given that name. Urizen, the lawgiver, can not accept the liberating aspects of sexual pleasure. At the end of the poem, Ahania laments the lost pleasures of eternity:

> "Where is my golden palace?
> "Where my ivory bed?
> "Where the joy of my morning hour?
> "Where the sons of eternity singing.

The physical pleasures of sexual union are celebrated as an entrance to a spiritual state. The physical union of man and woman is sign of the spiritual union that is to come.

At the same time as he was writing these individual poems that center on aspects of man's fall, Blake was also composing an epic poem on the fall of man into separate identities. Blake originally called the poem *Vala* and later changed the name to *The Four Zoas.* He worked on the poem for a number of years but never completed it. It survives in manuscript form with rough designs for illustrations, but it never became one of the "illuminated books."

The Four Zoas is subtitled "The Torments of Love and Jealousy in the Death and Judgement of Albion the Ancient Man," and the poem develops Blake's myth of Albion, who represents both the country of England and the unification of all men. Albion is composed of "Four Mighty Ones": Tharmas, Urthona, Urizen, and Luvah. Originally, in "Eden," these four exist in the unity of "The Universal Brotherhood." At this early time all parts of man lived in perfect harmony, but now they are fallen into warring camps. The poem traces the changes in Albion:

> His fall into Division & his Resurrection to Unity:
> His fall into the Generation of decay & death, & his
> Regeneration by the Resurrection from the dead.

The poem begins with Tharmas and examines the fall of each aspect of man's identity. The

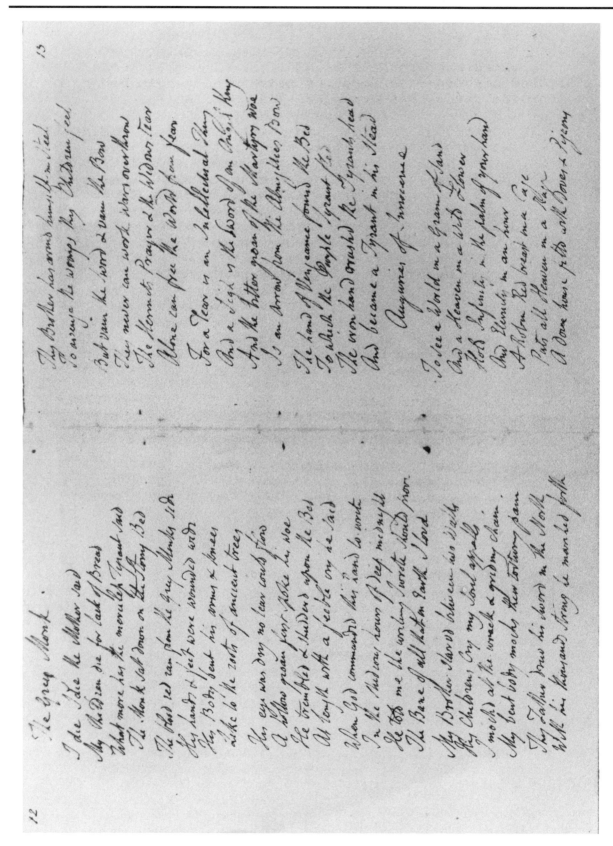

Pages from the Pickering Manuscript, *so-called because it was once the property of B. M. Pickering (MA 2879, gift of Mrs. Landon K. Thorne; by permission of the Pierpont Morgan Library). The manuscript, which dates from some time after 1807, comprises Blake's fair copies of ten poem written between 1800 and 1804.*

Page 29b from the manuscript for Vala, or The Four Zoas *(Add. MS 39764; by permission of the British Library, Department of Manuscripts)*

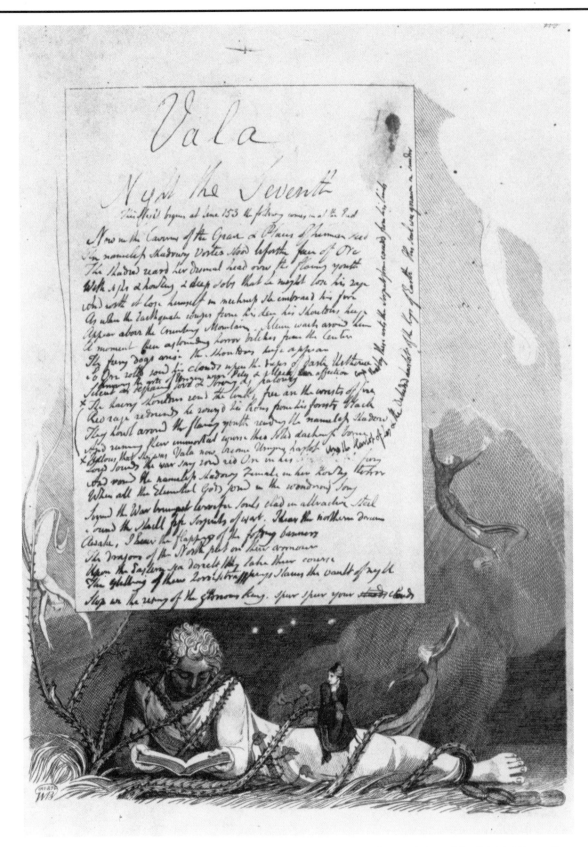

Page 45a from the manuscript for Vala, or The Four Zoas *(Add. MS 39764; by permission of the British Library, Department of Manuscripts). Forty-seven of the seventy leaves in this manuscript are proof sheets of Blake's illustrations for Edward Young's* Night Thoughts, *including this page, which is proof for plate 9, depicting the poet bound by chains and thorns.*

poem progresses from disunity toward unity as each Zoa moves toward final unification.

In the apocalyptic "Night the Ninth," the evils of oppression are overturned in the turmoil of the Last Judgment:

> The thrones of Kings are shaken, they have lost
>   their robes & crowns
> The poor smite their oppressors, they awake up to
>   the harvest.

The final overthrow of all kings and tyrants that earthly revolutions tried but failed to achieve will be accomplished on the last day. The "harvest" imagery is from the Book of Revelations and represents the process of gathering and discarding that marks the progress of man's soul on the last day.

As dead men are rejuvenated, Christ, the "Lamb of God," is brought back to life and sheds the evils of institutionalized religions:

> Thus shall the male & female live the life of Eter-
>   nity,
> Because the Lamb of God Creates himself a bride
>   & wife
> That we his Children evermore may live in Jerusa-
>   lem
> Which now descendeth out of heaven, a City, yet a
>   Woman
> Mother of myriads redeem'd & born in her spiritual
>   palaces,
> By a New Spiritual birth Regenerated from Death.

The heavenly City of Jerusalem is the true form of God's church. The earthly city of Jerusalem and the numerous forms of religions are but pale imitations of that true religion where God and the church are joined. In that City man's separate identities are reunited, and man is reunited with God.

Very little of Blake's poetry of the 1790s was known to the general public. His reputation as an artist was mixed. Response to his art ranged from praise to derision, but he did gain some fame as an engraver. He received several commissions, the most important probably being his illustrations to Edward Young's *Night Thoughts*. In 1795 the publisher and bookseller Richard Edwards commissioned Blake to illustrate the then-famous poems of Young. Blake produced 537 watercolor designs of which 43 were selected for engraving. The first volume of a projected four-volume series was published in 1797. However, the project did not prove finan-

cially successful, and no further volumes were published. After the disappointment of that project, Blake's friend and admirer Flaxman commissioned Blake to illustrate the poems of Thomas Gray. Blake painted 116 watercolors and completed the project in 1798. Blake was also aided by his friend Thomas Butts, who commissioned a series of biblical paintings. His commissions did not produce much in the way of income, but Blake never seems to have been discouraged. In 1799 Blake wrote to George Cumberland, "I laugh at Fortune & Go on & on."

Because of his monetary woes, Blake often had to depend on the benevolence of patrons of the arts. This sometimes led to heated exchanges between the independent artist and the wealthy patron. Dr. John Trusler was one such patron whom Blake failed to please. Dr. Trusler was something of a dabbler in a variety of fields. Aside from being a clergyman, he was a student of medicine, a bookseller, and the author of such works as *Hogarth Moralized* (1768), *The Way to be Rich and Respectable* (1750?), and *A Sure Way to Lengthen Life with Vigor* (circa 1819). Blake's friend Cumberland had recommended Blake to Trusler in hopes of providing some needed income for Blake. Blake, however, found himself unable to follow the clergyman's wishes: "I attempted every morning for a fortnight together to follow your Dictate, but when I found my attempts were in vain, resolv'd to shew an independence which I know will please an Author better than slavishly following the track of another, however admirable that track may be. At any rate, my Excuse must be: I could not do otherwise; it was out of my power!" Dr. Trusler was not convinced and replied that he found Blake's "Fancy" to be located in the "World of Spirits" and not in this world.

Blake's rebuttal is a classic defense of his own principles. To the charge that Blake needed someone to "elucidate" his idea, Blake replied with characteristic wrath: "That which can be made Explicit to the Idiot is not worth my care. The wisest of the Ancients consider'd what is not too Explicit as the fittest for Instruction, because it rouzes the faculties to act." Blake relies on a basic principle of rhetoric that is evident in his writing: it is often best to leave some things unsaid so that the reader must employ his imagination. To the charge that his visions were not of this world, Blake replied that he had seen his visions in this world, but not all men see alike: "As a man is, So he Sees. As the Eye is formed, such

Catherine Blake, circa 1802; pencil drawing by William Blake on the verso of a broadside printing of William Hayley's ballad "The Elephant" (by permission of the Tate Gallery, London)

are its Powers. You certainly Mistake, when you say that the Visions of Fancy are not to be found in This World. To Me This World is all One continued Vision of Fancy or Imagination." The problem then is not the location of Blake's subjects, but the relative ability of man to perceive. If Dr. Trusler could not understand Blake's drawings, the problem was his inability to see with the imagination.

Dr. Trusler was not the only patron that tried to make Blake conform to popular tastes. Blake's stormy relation to his erstwhile friend and patron William Hayley directly affected the writing of the epics *Milton* and *Jerusalem*. When Blake met him Hayley was a well-known man of letters who had produced several popular volumes of poetry. His *Triumphs of Temper* (1781), which admonishes women to control their tempers in order to be good wives, was very popular. In 1800 under Hayley's promptings Blake

moved from London to the village of Felpham, where Hayley lived. It was expected that Blake would receive numerous engraving commissions, and his financial problems would disappear.

Hayley did provide Blake with some small commissions. Blake began work on a series of eighteen "Heads of the Poets" for Hayley's library and worked on the engravings for Hayley's *Life of Cowper* (1802). Hayley also set Blake to work on a series of small portraits, but Blake soon bristled under the watchful eye of his patron. In January of 1803 Blake wrote to Butts that "I find on all hands great objections to my doing anything but the meer drudgery of business, & intimations that if I do not confine myself to this, I shall not live; this has always pursu'd me." In the same letter Blake argued that his duty to his art must take precedence to the necessity of making money: "But if we fear to do the dictates of our Angels, & tremble at the

The cottage at Felpham where the Blakes lived in 1800-1803 (engraving from a drawing by Herbert H. Gilchrist for Alexander Gilchrist's Life of Blake, *1880)*

Tasks set before us; if we refuse to do Spiritual Acts because of natural Fears of natural Desires! Who can describe the dismal torments of such a state!"

The "Spiritual Acts" Blake referred to include the writing of his epic poetry despite Hayley's objections. In the same month Blake wrote to his brother James that he is determined "To leave This Place" and that he can no longer accept Hayley's patronage: "The truth is, As a Poet he is frighten'd at me & as a Painter his view & mine are opposite; he thinks to turn me into a Portrait Painter as he did Poor Romney, but this he nor all the devils in hell will never do."

Blake left Felpham in 1803 and returned to London. In April of that year he wrote to Butts that he was overjoyed to return to the city: "That I can alone carry on my visionary studies in London unannoy'd, & that I may converse with my friends in Eternity, See Visions, Dream Dreams & Prophecy & Speak Parables unobserv'd & at lib-

erty from the Doubts of other Mortals." In the same letter Blake refers to his epic poem *Milton*, composed while at Felpham: "But none can know the Spiritual Acts of my three years' Slumber on the banks of the Ocean, unless he has seen them in the Spirit, or unless he should read My long Poem descriptive of those Acts."

In a later letter to Butts, Blake declares his resolution to have *Milton* printed:

This Poem shall, by Divine Assistance be progressively Printed & Ornamented with Prints & given to the Public. But of this work I take care to say little to Mr H., since he is as much averse to my poetry as he is to a Chapter in the Bible. He knows that I have writ it, for I have shewn it to him, & he has read Part by his own desire & has looked with sufficient contempt to inhance my opinion of it. But I do not wish to irritate by seeming too obstinate in Poetic pursuits. But if all the World should set their faces against This, I have Orders to set my face like flint (Ezekiel iiiC, 9v) against

William Blake, 1804 (drawing by John Flaxman; by permission of the Syndics of the Fitzwilliam Museum, Cambridge)

their faces, & my forehead against their foreheads.

Blake's letter reveals much of his attitude toward his patron and toward his readers. Blake believed that his poetry could be read and understood by the general public, but he was determined not to sacrifice his vision in order to become popular. Men of letters such as Hayley would not be allowed to dictate his art. Blake compares himself to the prophet Ezekiel, whom the Lord made strong to warn the Israelites of their wickedness. Blake's images of a stern prophet locked head to head with his adversary is a fitting picture of part of Blake's relation with his reader. Blake knew that his poetry would be derided by some readers. In *Milton* Blake tells us that "the idiot reasoner laughs at the Man of Imagination," and in the face of that laughter Blake remained resolute.

In his "slumber on the banks of the Ocean," Blake, surrounded by financial worries and hounded by a patron who could not appreciate his art, reflected on the value of visionary poetry. *Milton*, which Blake started to engrave in 1804 (probably finishing in 1808), is a poem that constantly draws attention to itself as a work of literature. Its ostensible subject is the poet John Milton, but the author, William Blake, also creates a character for himself in his own poem. Blake examines the entire range of mental activity involved in the art of poetry from the initial inspiration of the poet to the reception of his vision by the reader of the poem. *Milton* examines as part of its subject the very nature of poetry: what it means to be a poet, what a poem is, and what it means to be a reader of poetry.

In the preface to the poem, Blake issues a battle cry to his readers to reject what is merely fashionable in art:

Jacob's Dream, *circa 1805 (1949-11-12-2; by permission of the British Museum), one of the watercolors Blake exhibited in 1808*

Rouze up, O Young Men of the New Age! set your foreheads against the ignorant Hirelings! For we have Hirelings in the Camp, the Court & the University, who would, if they could, for ever depress Mental & prolong Corporeal War. Painters! on you I call. Sculptors! Architects! suffer not the fashionable Fools to depress your powers by the prices they pretend to give for contemptible works, or the expensive advertizing boasts that they make of such works; believe Christ & his Apostles that there is a Class of men whose whole delight is in Destroying. We do not want either Greek or Roman Models if we are but just & true to our own imaginations, those Worlds of Eternity in which we shall live for ever in Jesus our Lord.

In attacking the "ignorant Hirelings" in the "Camp, the Court & the University," Blake repeats a familiar dissenting cry against established figures in English society. Blake's insistence on being "just & true to our own Imaginations"

places a special burden on the reader of his poem. For as he makes clear, Blake demands the exercise of the creative imagination from his own readers.

In the well-known lyric that follows, Blake asks for a continuation of Christ's vision in modern-day England:

> I will not cease from Mental Fight,
> Nor shall my Sword sleep in my hand
> Till we have built Jerusalem
> In England's green & pleasant Land.

The poet-prophet must lead the reader away from man's fallen state and toward a revitalized state where man can perceive eternity.

"Book the First" contains a poem-within-a-poem, a "Bard's Prophetic Song." The Bard's Song describes man's fall from a state of vision. We see man's fall in the ruined form of Albion as a representative of all men and in the fall of Palamabron from his proper position as prophet to a nation. Interwoven into this narrative are the Bard's addresses to the reader, challenges to the reader's senses, descriptions of contemporary events and locations in England, and references to the life of William Blake. Blake is at pains to show us that his mythology is not something far removed from us but is part of our day to day life. Blake describes the reader's own fall from vision and the possibility of regaining those faculties necessary for vision.

The climax of the Bard's Song is the Bard's sudden vision of the "Holy Lamb of God": "Glory! Glory! to the Holy lamb of God: / I touch the heavens as an instrument to glorify the Lord." The vision of the "Lamb of God" is traditional in apocalyptic literature. In this case the Bard's final burst of vision is important not only for its content, but also for its placement in the poem. The Bard's sudden vision of the Lamb of God testifies that man need not remain "in chains of the mind Lock'd up." The Bard begins by describing the fall from vision, but he ends with a vision of his own that indicates that man still possesses the powers of vision.

At the end of the Bard's Song, the Bard's power of vision is questioned much as Blake's prophecies were criticized. The Bard's spirit is incorporated into that of the poet Milton. Blake portrays Milton as a great but flawed poet who must unify the separated elements of his own identity before he can reclaim his powers of vision and become a true poet. Upon hearing the Bard's Song, Milton is moved to descend to earth and begin the process of becoming an inspired poet. It is a journey of intense self-discovery and self-examination that requires Milton to cast off "all that is not inspiration."

As Milton is presented as a man in the process of becoming a poet, Blake presents himself as a character in the poem undergoing the transformation necessary to become a poet. As Milton is inspired by the "Bard's Song," Blake is inspired by the spirit of Milton:

> Then first I saw him in the Zenith as a falling star
> Descending perpendicular, swift as the swallow or swift:
> And on my left foot falling on the tarsus, enter'd there
> But from my left foot a black cloud redounding spread over Europe.

This sudden moment of inspiration extends to the very end of book one. Like Saul on the road to Damascus, the character Blake is not fully

aware of the importance of this moment of illumination. Like Milton, Blake is in the process of becoming a poet.

In a moment of sudden inspiration, Blake overcomes his "earthly lineaments" and binds "this Vegetable World" as a sandal under his foot so that he can "walk forward thro' Eternity." Blake's act of creativity enables him to merge with Los:

> And I became One Man with him arising in my strength
> 'Twas too late now to recede. Los had enter'd into my soul:
> His terrors now possess'd me whole! I arose in fury & strength!

Blake's act of faith in the world of the imagination enables him to increase his powers of perception and sets a pattern for the reader to follow. Blake's union with Los marks the end of one stage of the unification process that began at the completion of the Bard's Song. In each case faith in the power of the imagination precedes union.

Only Milton believes in the vision of the Bard's Song, and the Bard takes "refuge in Milton's bosom." As Blake realizes the insignificance of this "Vegetable World," Los merges with Blake, and he arises in "fury and strength." This ongoing belief in the hidden powers of the mind heals divisions and increases powers of perception. The Bard, Milton, Los, and Blake begin to merge into a powerful bardic union. Yet it is but one stage in a greater drive toward the unification of all men in a "Universal Brotherhood."

In the second book of *Milton* Blake initiates the reader into the order of poets and prophets. Blake continues the process begun in book one of taking the reader through different stages in the growth of a poet. Ololon, Milton's female form, descends to earth to unite with Milton. Her descent gives the reader a radically new view of this world. Ololon's unique perspective turns the reader's world of time and space upside down to make him see the decayed and limited nature of this world. If he can learn to see his familiar world from a new perspective, then the reader can develop his own powers of perception. Indeed "learning to see" is the first requirement of the poet.

The turning of the outside world upside down is a preliminary stage in an extensive examination of man's internal world. A searching inquiry into the self is a necessary stage in the development of the poet. Milton is told he must first

The creative act and the Eagle of Inspiration, *from Blake's* Milton *(Copy D, Rosenwald Collection, Library of Congress)*

look within: "Judge then of thy Own Self: thy Eternal Lineaments explore, / What is Eternal & what Changeable, & what Annihilable." Milton descends within himself and judges the separate parts of his own identity; he must distinguish between what is permanent and what transitory. Central to the process of judging the self is a confrontation with that destructive part of man's identity Blake calls the Selfhood. The Selfhood continually hinders man's spiritual development. Only by annihilating the Selfhood, Blake believes, can one hope to participate in the visionary experience of the poem. Unless the Selfhood is annihilated, one cannot become a true poet, for the Selfhood continually blocks "the human center of creativity."

The Selfhood places two powerful forces to block our path: the socially accepted values of "love" and "reason." In its purest state love is given freely with no restrictions and no thought of return. In its fallen state love is reduced to a form of trade: "Thy love depends on him thou lovest, & on his dear loves / Depend thy pleasures, which thou hast cut off by jealousy." "Female love" is given only in exchange for love received. It is bartering in human emotions and is not love at all. When Milton denounces his own Selfhood, he gives up "Female love" and loves freely and openly.

As Blake attacks accepted notions of love, he also forces the reader to question the value society places on reason. The Seven Angels of the Presence warn that the "memory is a state Always, & the Reason is a State / Created to be Annihilated & a new Ratio Created." Both Memory and Reason exercise the lesser powers of the mind. Nothing new can be created by the mental processes involved in memory and reason. In his struggle with Urizen, who represents man's limited power of reason, Milton seeks to cast off the deadening effect of the reasoning power and free the mind for the power of the imagination. Milton gains control of Urizen, and it is clear that in Milton's mind it is now the imagination that directs reason.

Destroying the Selfhood allows Milton to unite with others. He descends upon Blake's path and continues the process of uniting with Blake that had begun in book one. This union is also a reflection of Blake's encounter with Los that is described in book one and illustrated in book two. As was the case with seeing Los, Blake is startled by Milton's arrival. Los appears as a "terrible flaming Sun," and Milton's arrival turns Blake's path into a "solid fire, as bright as the Clear Sun." Both events describe the process of union and the assumption of the powers of the imagination necessary to become a true poet. All of this comes about through the individual annihilation of the Selfhood. To become a poet and prophet, the man of imagination must first look within and destroy the Selfhood.

Milton's final speech in praise of the virtue of self-annihilation is followed by Ololon's own annihilation of the Selfhood. She rejects her virgin Selfhood and joins with Milton:

> Then as a Moony Ark Ololon descended to
>   Felpham's Vale
> In clouds of blood, in streams of gore, with dread-
>   ful thunderings
> Into the fires of Intellect that rejoic'd in Felpham's
>   Vale
> Around the Starry Eight; with one accord the
>   Starry Eight became
> One Man, Jesus the Savior, wonderful!

As Noah's Ark saved lives upon earth, the "Moony Ark" of Ololon preserves man's individual nature. The Seven Eyes of God that had instructed Milton are now merged with Milton, Blake, and all men on earth. Jesus is "One Man," for he unites all men in a Universal Brotherhood. By destroying the Selfhood, we do not lose our identity but rather gain a new identity in the body of the universal brotherhood. Our entry into this union prepares us for the promise of vision.

The apex of Blake's vision in Felpham is the brief image of the Throne of God. In Revelation, John's vision of the Throne of God is a prelude to the apocalypse itself. Similarly Blake's vision of the throne is also a prelude to the coming apoca-

lypse. Blake's vision is abruptly cut off as the Four Zoas sound the Four Trumpets, signaling the call to judgment of the peoples of the earth. The trumpets bring to a halt Blake's vision, as he falls to the ground and returns to his mortal state. The apocalypse is still to come.

Blake's falling to the ground is not a mystic swoon, but part of his design to take himself out of the poem and leave it to the reader to continue the vision of the coming apocalypse. The author falls before the vision of the Throne of God and the awful sound of the coming apocalypse. However, the vision of the author does not fall with him to the ground. In the very next line after Blake describes his faint, we see his vision soar: "Immediately the lark mounted with a loud trill from Felpham's Vale." We have seen the lark as the messenger of Los and the carrier of inspiration. Its sudden flight here demonstrates that the vision of the poem does not end but continues. It is up to the reader to follow the flight of the lark to the Gate of Los and continue the vision of *Milton*.

Milton does not come to a firm conclusion, for it can only be concluded by the reader. The reader, armed with the creative power of poetry and the power of his own imagination, is asked to continue the work of the poet and prophet.

Before Blake could leave Felpham and return to London, an incident occurred that was very disturbing to him and possibly even dangerous. Without Blake's knowledge, his gardener had invited a soldier by the name of John Scofield into his garden to help with the work. Blake seeing the soldier and thinking he had no business being there promptly tossed him out. In a letter to Butts, Blake recalled the incident in detail:

> I desired him, as politely as possible, to go out of the Garden; he made me an impertinent answer. I insisted on his leaving the Garden; he refused. I still persisted in desiring his departure; he then threaten'd to knock out my Eyes, with many abominable imprecations & with some contempt for my Person; it affronted my foolish Pride. I therefore took him by the Elbows & pushed him before me till I had got him out; there I intended to leave him, but he, turning about, put himself into a Posture of Defiance, threatening & swearing at me. I, perhaps foolishly & perhaps not, stepped out at the Gate, &, putting aside his blows, took him again by the Elbows, &, keeping his back to me, pushed him forwards down the road about fifty yards—he all the while endeavouring

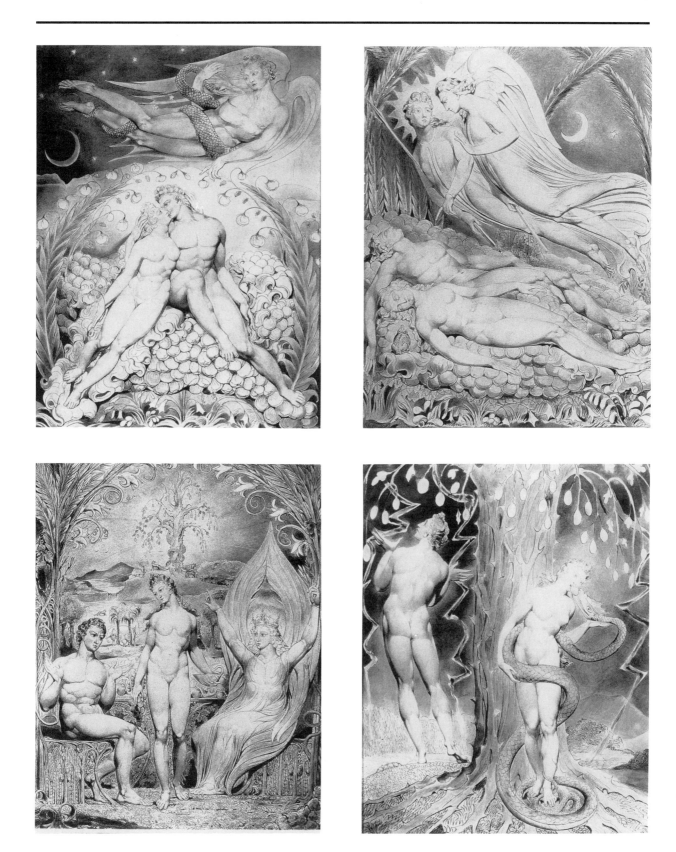

Pen and watercolor illustrations for John Milton's Paradise Lost, *signed "W Blake 1808" (by permission of the Museum of Fine Arts, Boston):* Satan Watching the Endearments of Adam and Eve *(90.96),* Adam and Eve Asleep *(90.102),* Raphael Warns Adam and Eve *(90.97), and* The Temptation and Fall of Eve *(90.97)*

Four of Blake's pen and watercolor illustrations for Milton's "L'Allegro" and "Il Penseroso," circa 1816-1820 (by permission of the Pierpont Morgan Library): Mirth *and* Night Startled by the Lark (*for "L'Allegro"*); The Youthful Poet's Dream *and* The Wandering Moon (*for "Il Penseroso"*)

to turn round & strike me, & raging & cursing, which drew out several neighbours. . . .

What made this almost comic incident so serious was that the soldier swore before a magistrate that Blake had said "Damn the King" and had uttered seditious words. Blake denied the charge, but he was forced to post bail and appear in court. Hayley came to Blake's aid by helping to post the bail money and arranging for counsel.

Blake left Felpham at the end of September 1803 and settled in a new residence on South Molton Street in London. His trial was set for the following January at Chichester. Hayley was almost forced to miss the trial because of a fall he suffered while riding his horse, but he was determined to help Blake and appeared in court to testify to the good character of the accused. The soldier's testimony was shown to be false, and the jury acquitted Blake. A local newspaper, the *Sussex Weekly Advertiser* (16 January 1804), reported on the acquittal: "After a very long and patient hearing, he was by the Jury acquitted, which so gratified the auditory, that the court was, in defiance of all decency, thrown into an uproar by their noisy exultations."

Blake's radical political views made him sometimes fear persecution, and he wondered if Scofield had been a government agent sent to entrap him. In any event Blake forever damned the soldier by attacking him in the epic poem *Jerusalem*. One positive result of the trial was that Blake was reconciled with Hayley, whose support during the trial was greatly appreciated.

Jerusalem is in many ways Blake's major achievement. It is an epic poem consisting of 100 illuminated plates. Blake dated the title page 1804, but he seems to have worked on the poem for a considerable length of time after that date.

In *Jerusalem* Blake develops his mythology to explore man's fall and redemption. As the narrative begins, man is apart from God and split into separate identities. As the poem progresses man's split identities are unified, and man is reunited with the divinity that is within him.

In chapter one Blake announces the purpose of his "great task":

To open the Eternal Worlds, to open the immortal Eyes
Of Man inwards into the Worlds of Thought, into Eternity
Ever expanding in the Bosom of God, the Human Imagination.

It is sometimes easy to get lost in the complex mythology of Blake's poetry and forget that he is describing not outside events but a "Mental Fight" that takes place in the mind. Much of *Jerusalem* is devoted to the idea of awakening the human senses, so that the reader can perceive the spiritual world that is everywhere present.

At the beginning of the poem, Jesus addresses the fallen Albion: " 'I am not a God afar off, I am a brother and friend; / 'Within your bosoms I reside, and you reside in me.' " In his fallen state Albion rejects this close union with God and dismisses Jesus as the "Phantom of the overheated brain!" Driven by jealousy Albion hides his emanation, Jerusalem. Separation from God leads to further separation into countless male and female forms creating endless division and dispute.

Blake describes the fallen state of man by describing the present day. Interwoven into the mythology are references to present-day London. There one finds: "Inspiration deny'd, Genius forbidden by laws of punishment." Instead of inspiration man is driven by the "Reasoning Power" which Blake calls "An Abstract objecting power that Negates everything." It is against this mental error that Los wars: " 'I must create a System or be enslav'd by another Man's. / 'I will not Reason & Compare : my business is to Create.' " Like the poet Blake, Los emphasizes the importance of the human imagination. Systems of thought, philosophies or religions, when separated from men, destroy what is human. To put an end to the destructive separation, Los struggles to build "The Great City of Golgonooza." Like a work of art, Golgonooza gives form to abstract ideas. It represents the human form and is composed of bodies of men and women.

In chapter two the "disease of Albion" leads to further separation and decay. As the human body is a limited form of its divine origin, the cities of England are limited representations of the Universal Brotherhood of Man. Fortunately for man, there is "a limit of contraction," and the fall must come to an end.

Caught by the errors of sin and vengeance, Albion gives up hope and dies. The flawed religions of moral law cannot save him: "The Visions of Eternity, by reason of narrowed perceptions, / Are become weak Visions of Time & Space, fix'd into furrows of death." Our limited senses make us think of our lives as bounded by time and space apart from eternity. In such a framework physical death marks the end of exis-

Page from Jerusalem, *with an illustration depicting the creation of Eve (Copy E, Collection of Paul Mellon)*

tence. But there is also a limit to death, and Albion's body is preserved by the Savior.

Before Albion can rise from the dead, the errors of religion must be corrected. Each of the last three chapters begins with addresses to what Blake saw as the three large bodies of religion: Jews, Deists, and Christians. Each is flawed, and each is founded on negation. Blake believed that the ancient religion of Judaism preached the union of all men, but that Jews practice the Old Testament idea of sin and vengeance and deny man's divinity. Deists similarly deny the religion of Jesus and follow the religion of this world, beliving in the material world and denying man's spiritual nature. Christians claim to follow Jesus but have so perverted his teachings that they turned Jesus into a moralizer and law giver. For Blake the essence of Christ's teachings was the "Continual Forgiveness of Sins." Without such forgiveness man can never realize his divine nature.

The cruelty of vengeance is displayed in chapter three in the bloody sacrifices of the Druids, whose rituals are performed at Stonehenge. Divisions of man's nature into separate sexual identities are further indications of his fallen nature as is the creation of a separate "Female Will." The multiple divisions of man's identities lead to chaos and war. Against this chaos Los struggles to create a "World of Generation" to place an end to the endless wars of separation and abstraction.

That *Jerusalem* is concerned with mental regeneration is made obvious in Blake's address "To the Christians" at the beginning of chapter four: "Let every Christian, as much as in him lies, engage himself openly & publicly before all the World in some Mental pursuit for the Building up of Jerusalem." "To build" Jerusalem is to reconstruct man's fallen nature, so that he can grow closer to the divinity that is within him. Primarily this is to come about through the libera-

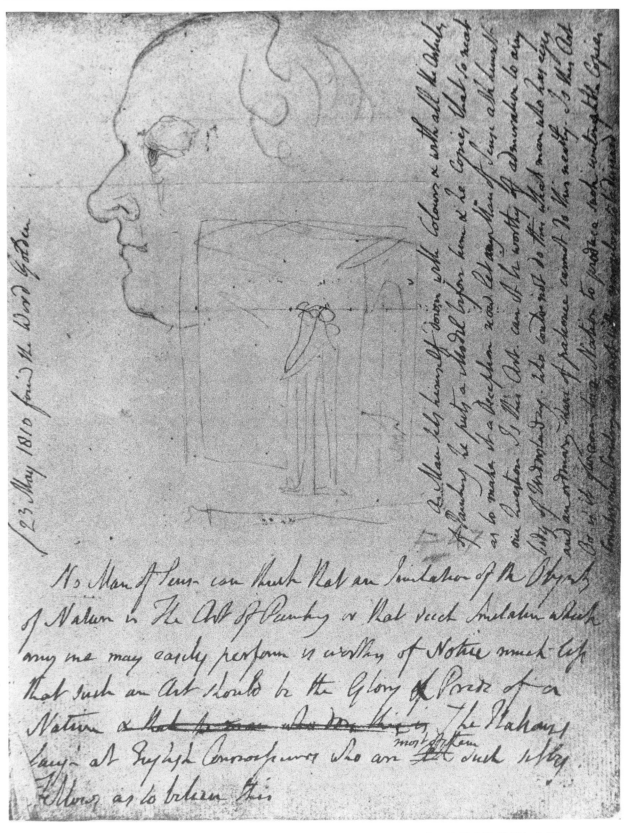

Self-portrait by Blake on a page from the Notebook, *or* Rossetti Manuscript *(Add. MS 49460; f. 33; by permission of the British Library)*

tion of the senses, so that man can perceive eternity. Much of *Jerusalem* is concerned with the expansion of the human senses.

The separation of man into male and female forms leads to the formation of a destructive "Female Will" that forever opposes unification and leads man away from eternity. As Enitharmon rejects Los, a terrible image is revealed: "Thus was the Covering Cherub reveal'd, majestic image / Of Selfhood, Body put off, the Antichrist accursed." The Covering Cherub demonstrates the destructive power of the Selfhood, that part of the mind that makes man think only of the self and not of eternity. But its revelation also shows its true nature, and the discovery of error leads to "that Signal of the Morning which was told us in the Beginning."

As in the Book of Revelations, the appearance of such horrors as "The God of This World, & the Goddess Nature, Mystery, Babylon the Great" mark the beginning of the apocalypse. "The Breath Divine" revives the figure of Albion, and Jesus appears to Albion. The separate parts of man's identity begin to reunite as One Man. In the final vision of the poem, "All Human Forms" are identified, and man is no longer separate from the spiritual world.

Today *Jerusalem* is recognized as one of the major works of the Romantic period, but in its own time it was not widely read. In 1827 Blake wrote to George Cumberland, who had inquired about his work: "The Last Work I produced is a Poem Entitled Jerusalem the Emanation of the Giant Albion, but find that to Print it will Cost my Time the amount of Twenty Guineas. One I have Finish'd. It contains 100 Plates but it is not likely that I shall get a Customer for it."

Blake experienced similar disappointments in his engraving work. The fame that he had hoped to acquire on returning to London never materialized. He did receive a commission from Cromeck to design engravings for Blair's poem *The Grave*, but he was disturbed that the actual engraving was left to the engraver Louis Schiavonetti.

Aside from commercial engraving, Blake produced watercolors. In 1808 he exhibited some of his watercolors, including "Christ in the Sepulcher guarded by Angels" and "Jacob's Dream," in the Royal Academy. He made two sets of watercolors for Milton's *Paradise Lost* and two sets of six watercolors for Milton's "On the Morning of Christ's Nativity."

Unhappy with the reception given his art by critics and publishers alike, Blake decided in May of 1809 to exhibit his works at his brother James's house on Broad Street. In his *Descriptive Catalogue* (1809) prepared for the exhibition, Blake blasts contemporary tastes of the time: "Mr. B. appeals to the Public, from the judgment of those narrow blinding eyes, that have too long governed art in a dark corner." In the catalogue Blake establishes his own views on the necessity of firm line: "The great and golden rule of art, as well as of his life, is this: That the more distinct, sharp, and wirey the bounding line, the more perfect the work of art; and the less keen and sharp, the greater is the evidence of weak imitation, plagiarism, and bungling."

The exhibition caused some interest among the London literati. Charles Lamb visited the exhibit and, in a letter to Bernard Barton, described his impressions: "He paints in water colours, marvelous strange pictures, visions of his brains which he asserts that he has seen. They have great merit." Robert Southey also visited the exhibit but was less enthusiastic: "Some of the designs were hideous, especially those which he considered as most supernatural in their conception and likenesses. In others you perceived that nothing but madness had prevented him from being the sublimest painter of this or any other country." Robert Hunt's review in the *Examiner* criticized the paintings as "fresh proof of the alarming increase of the effects of insanity." In the "Public Address" written in his notebook, Blake answered his critics: "I know my Execution is not like Any Body Else. I do not intend it should be so; none but Blockheads Copy one another."

Despite being panned by the critics, Blake maintained a belief in the public reception of his work: In his notebook Blake wrote, "It has been said of late years The English Public have no Taste for Painting. This is a Falsehood. The English are as Good Judges of Painting as of Poetry, & they prove it in their Contempt for Great Collection of all the Rubbish of the Continent brought here by Ignorant Picture dealers." Blake saw his own obscurity as the fault of booksellers, publishers, and critics, not the fault of common Englishmen.

Blake's fortunes fell after the exhibit, and his reputation dwindled although he seems to have been the object of interest among a few. Southey visited Blake at his home, and Crabb Robinson prepared an article on Blake for a German

Four of Blake's illustrations to Milton's Paradise Regained, *circa 1816-1820 (by permission of the Syndics of the Fitzwilliam Museum, Cambridge):* The Baptism of Christ *(PD 14),* The First Temptation *(PD 15),* Satan in Council *(PD 17), and* Christ Refusing the Banquet Offered by Satan *(PD 18)*

Blake and painter John Varley (1821); drawing by John Linnell, who studied art under both men (by permission of the Syndics of the Fitzwilliam Museum, Cambridge)

Job and his Family Restored to Prosperity, *a pen and watercolor painting from Linnell's set (1821) of Blake's illustrations for the Book of Job (Rosenwald Collection, B. 11083; National Gallery of Art, Washington, D.C.)*

magazine. Robinson seems to have been fascinated by Blake, and Robinson's diary records his conversations with men such as Joseph Mallord William Turner, William Hazlitt, Walter Savage Landor, and Wordsworth on the subject of Blake's art and poetry. Coleridge's letters also reveal his interest in Blake's poetry. Blake's poetry was not well known by the general public, but enough was thought of him to mention him in *A Biographical Dictionary of the Living Authors of Great Britain and Ireland,* published in 1816.

In his later years, Blake was fortunate enough to have become friends with a young artist, John Linnell, who studied under him and helped to support him. In 1820 Blake produced a remarkable series of watercolors illustrating the Book of Job for his patron Thomas Butts. Under Linnell's sponsorship the designs were engraved and published in 1826.

In 1821 the Blakes moved to 3 Fountain Court, Strand, in a house owned by Mrs. Blake's brother-in-law. Their first floor apartment was modest, and Blake seems constantly to have had financial problems. In 1822 Linnell was able to persuade the Royal Academy council to give Blake a grant of twenty-five pounds.

In his later years Blake had his own followers, a group of young artists who called themselves "the Ancients." Samuel Palmer, Edward Calvert, George Richmond, Francis Oliver Finch, Henry Walter, and Charles Heathcote Tatham would meet at Blake's house to discuss art. At times they would travel to the country to sketch, and Blake seems to have enjoyed these artistic expeditions.

In October of 1825 Linnell commissioned Blake to design a series of illustrations for Dante's *Divine Comedy,* and Blake continued to work on these designs until his death. Many of the water-color drawings were composed while Blake was forced to stay in bed. At the time of his death Blake had engraved seven of them, which were published in 1838.

Blake's letters at this time show his ill health. He complained to Linnell of "shivering fits" and of jaundice, and he suffered from gallstones. Blake died on 12 August 1827. George Richmond wrote to Samuel Palmer of Blake's death: "Just before he died His countenance became fair–His eyes Brighten'd and He burst out in Singing of the things he saw in Heaven."

In his lifetime the public knew of Blake primarily as an artist and engraver. Perhaps as a result of his unusual method of "publication,"

Blake's poetry never received the wide public recognition given to the works of Wordsworth and Coleridge, but it was read by Wordsworth and Coleridge and other prominent literary figures of the time. After Blake's death, John Thomas Smith devoted thirty-five pages of his book *Nollekens and his Times* (1828) to a biography of Blake. Blake was also thought to be of enough importance to receive mention in Allan Cunningham's 1830 edition of *Most Eminent British Painters, Sculptors, and Architects.* For a long time, however, Blake's reputation floundered. The publication in 1863 of Alexander Gilchrist's *Life of William Blake: Pictor Ignotus* helped to save Blake's works from obscurity and established Blake as a major literary figure. Gilchrist's biography motivated other studies of Blake, including Swinburne's 1868 study of Blake's prophecies. Blake influenced several later poets. Most important is his influence on William Butler Yeats. Yeats studied Blake's works and often speaks of him in his poetry. Ellis and Yeats's 1893 edition of Blake's works is unreliable, but it does show Blake's influence on Yeats.

In the early twentieth century John Sampson's 1905 edition of *The Poetical Works* provided a solid text for serious study of Blake as did A. G. B. Russell's 1912 catalogue *The Engravings of William Blake* which reproduced many engravings. Joseph Wicksteed's 1910 study, *Blake's Vision of the Book of Job* provided a close analysis of Blake's designs and helped to demonstrate that Blake's art should be interpreted in careful detail.

Modern scholarship is in large part based on the herculean efforts of Geoffrey Keynes, whose 1921 *A Bibliography of William Blake* (along with his 1953 *Census of William Blake Illuminated Books*) set a firm foundation for a critical examination of Blake's works. Keynes's 1925 edition of the *Writings of William Blake* (and subsequent revisions) became the standard text for decades. S. Foster Damon's pioneering *William Blake: His Philosophy and Symbols,* published in 1924, argued that Blake's major prophecies, sometimes thought to be incomprehensible or the product of an irrational mind, could be interpreted through a systematic appreciation of his use of symbol.

Renewed interest in Blake's life and his times is evident in Mona Wilson's 1927 *Life of William Blake.* Jacob Bronowski's *Life of William Blake: A Man Without a Mask* (1945) and Mark Schorer's *William Blake: The Politics of Vision* (1959) both examine the political and social forces that helped

Blake (top) on the hill near John Linnell's Hampstead cottage, circa 1825 (drawing by Linnell; by permission of the Syndics of the Fitzwilliam Museum, Cambridge); and "The Circle of the Corrupt Officials. The Devil tormenting Ciampolo" (below), plate 2 from the illustrations for Dante's Inferno, *commissioned by Linnell, that Blake was engraving at the time of his death (Doheny Collection, auctioned by Christie, Manson & Woods International Inc., 21-22 February 1989)*

My dearest Friend

This sudden Cold Weather has cut up all my hopes by the roots. Every one who knows of our intended flight into your delightful Country. concur in saying Do not Venture till Summer appears again. I also feel Myself weaker than I was aware. being not able as yet to Sit up longer than six hours at a time I also feel the Cold too much to dare venture beyond my present precincts — My heartiest Thanks for your care in my accomodation & the trouble you will yet have with me But I get better & stronger every day tho weaker in muscle & bone than I supposed. — As to pleasantness of Prospect it is All pleasant Prospect at North End. Mrs Hards I think like as well as any — But think of the Expense & how it may be spared & never mind appearances

I intend to bring with me besides our necessary change of apparel. Only My Book of Drawings from Dante & one Plate shut up in the Book. All will go very well in the Coach which at present would be a rumble I fear I am not go thro'. So that I conclude another Week must pass before I dare Venture upon what I ardently desire the Seeing you with your happy Family once again & that for a longer period than I had ever hoped in my health-full hours   I am dear Sir
Yours most gratefully
William Blake

Letter to John Linnell, postmarked 2 July 1826, in which Blake mentions his illustrations for Dante's Inferno *(Doheny Collection, auctioned by Christie, Manson & Woods International Inc., 21-22 February 1989)*

to shape Blake's art. A modern critical biography still remains to be written, but G. E. Bentley's *Blake Records* (1969) carefully records all known evidence about Blake's life, including contemporary accounts of him. Bentley's *Blake Books* (1977) provides a comprehensive catalogue of Blake's writings and of works about him.

In 1948 Northrop Frye's seminal work *Fearful Symmetry* opened the field of Blake scholarship by showing the mythic structure of the major works and making the claim for Blake as a major poet of English literature. David Erdman's *Blake: Prophet Against Empire* (first published in 1954, revised 1969) is important in showing Blake as a commentator and critic of the age in which he lived. Among the numerous explications of Blake's poetry that followed, Harold Bloom's *The Visionary Company* (first published in 1961, revised 1971) and *Blake's Apocalypse* (published in 1963), influenced many critics in the reading of individual poems.

Modern textual study of Blake has been aided by new editions of the poetry. David Erdman's *The Complete Poetry and Prose of William Blake* (first published in 1965) contains a commentary by Harold Bloom. G. E. Bentley's two-volume *William Blake's Writings* (1978) provides a scholarly text and contains numerous reproductions of the designs. Students interested in the relationship between text and design have been aided by the excellent facsimiles of the illuminated books produced by the Trianon Press for the William Blake Trust. Erdman's *The Illuminated Blake* (1974) provides inexpensive black-and-white reproductions of all of the illuminated books.

Today Blake scholarship continues at a rapid pace with many critics now concentrating on the relationship between text and design in Blake's major poetry. From the relative obscurity of his reputation in his own time, Blake is now recognized as one of the major poets of the Romantic period and one of the most original and challenging figures in the history of English literature.

Letters:
Letters from William Blake to Thomas Butts 1800-1803, facsimile, edited by Geoffrey Keynes (London: Oxford University Press, 1926);
The Letters of William Blake, third edition, revised and amplified, edited by Keynes (Oxford: Clarendon Press, 1980).

Bibliographies:
Geoffrey Keynes, *A Bibliography of William Blake* (New York: Grolier Club, 1921);
Keynes and Edwin Wolf, *William Blake's Illuminated Books: A Census* (New York: Grolier Club, 1953);
Keynes, *Engravings by William Blake: The Separate Plates* (Dublin: E. Walker, 1956);
G. E. Bentley, Jr., and Martin K. Nurmi, *A Blake Bibliography: Annotated Lists of Works, Studies, and Blakeana* (Minneapolis: University of Minnesota Press, 1964);
Bentley, *Blake Books* (Oxford: Clarendon Press, 1977).

Biographies:
Alexander Gilchrist, *Life of William Blake: Pictor Ignotus,* 2 volumes (London: Macmillan, 1863; enlarged, 1880);
Mona Wilson, *The Life of William Blake* (London: Nonesuch Press, 1927); third edition, edited by Geoffrey Keynes (London: Oxford University Press, 1965);
G. E. Bentley, Jr., *Blake Records* (Oxford: Clarendon Press, 1969);
Geoffrey Keynes, *Blake Studies: Essays on His Life and Work,* second edition, revised and enlarged (Oxford: Clarendon Press, 1971);
Michael Davis, *William Blake: A New Kind of Man* (Berkeley: University of California Press, 1977).

References:
Hazard Adams, *Blake and Yeats: The Contrary Vision* (Ithaca: Cornell University Press, 1955);
Adams, *William Blake: A Reading of the Shorter Poems* (Seattle: University of Washington Press, 1963);
Thomas Altizier, *The New Apocalypse: The Radical Christian Vision of William Blake* (East Lansing: Michigan State University Press, 1974);
John Beer, *Blake's Humanism* (Manchester: Manchester University Press, 1968);
G. E. Bentley, ed., *William Blake: The Critical Heritage* (Boston: Routledge & Kegan Paul, 1975);
Harold Bloom, *Blake's Apocalypse: A Study in Poetic Argument* (Garden City, N.Y.: Doubleday, 1963);
Bloom, *The Visionary Company,* revised edition (Ithaca: Cornell University Press, 1971);
Bloom, ed., *Modern Critical Views: William Blake* (New York: Chelsea House, 1985);

Anthony Blunt, *The Art of William Blake*, Hampton Lectures in America, no. 12 (New York: Columbia University Press, 1959);

Jacob Bronowski, *William Blake and the Age of Revolution* (London: Routledge & Kegan Paul, 1972);

Stuart Curran and Joseph Wittreich, Jr., eds., *Blake's Sublime Allegory: Essays on the Four Zoas, Milton, and Jerusalem* (Madison: University of Wisconsin Press, 1973);

Samuel Foster Damon, *A Blake Dictionary: The Ideas and Symbols of William Blake* (Providence: Brown University Press, 1965);

Damon, *William Blake: His Philosophy and Symbols* (Boston: Houghton Mifflin, 1924);

John Davies, *The Theology of William Blake* (Oxford: Clarendon Press, 1948);

George Digby, *Symbol and Image in William Blake* (New York: Oxford University Press, 1957);

Deborah Dorfman, *Blake in the Nineteenth Century: His Reputation as a Poet from Gilchrist to Yeats* (New Haven: Yale University Press, 1969);

David Erdman, *Blake: Prophet Against Empire*, revised edition (Princeton: Princeton University Press, 1969);

Erdman, ed., *A Concordance to the Writings of William Blake*, 2 volumes (Ithaca: Cornell University Press, 1967);

Erdman and John E. Grant, eds., *Blake's Visionary Forms Dramatic* (Princeton: Princeton University Press, 1970);

Robert Essick, *The Visionary Hand: Essays for the Study of William Blake's Art and Aesthetics* (Los Angeles: Hennesy & Ingalls, 1973);

Peter Fisher, *The Valley of Vision: Blake as Prophet and Revolutionary*, edited by Northrop Frye, University of Toronto Department of English Studies and Texts, no. 9 (Toronto: University of Toronto Press, 1961);

Thomas Forsch, *The Awakening of Albion: The Renovation of the Body in the Poetry of William Blake* (Ithaca: Cornell University Press, 1974);

Susan Fox, *Poetic Form in Blake's Milton* (Princeton: Princeton University Press, 1976);

Northrop Frye, *Fearful Symmetry: A Study of William Blake* (Princeton: Princeton University Press, 1947);

Frye, ed., *Blake: A Collection of Critical Essays* (Englewood Cliffs, N.J.: Prentice Hall, 1966);

Charles Gardner, *Vision and Vesture: A Study of William Blake in Modern Thought*, revised edition (New York: Dutton, 1929);

Stanley Gardner, *Infinity on the Anvil: A Critical Study of Blake's Poetry* (Oxford: Blackwell, 1954);

D. G. Gillam, *Blake's Contrary States: The "Songs of Innocence and Experience" as Dramatic Poems* (Cambridge: Cambridge University Press, 1966);

Gillam, *William Blake* (London: Cambridge University Press, 1973);

Robert Gleckner, *Blake and Spenser* (Baltimore: Johns Hopkins University Press, 1985);

Gleckner, *The Piper and the Bard: A Study of William Blake* (Detroit: Wayne State University Press, 1959);

Jean Hagstrum, *William Blake: Poet and Painter, An Introduction to the Illuminated Verse* (Chicago: University of Chicago Press, 1964);

George Harper, *The Neoplatonism of William Blake* (Chapel Hill: University of North Carolina Press, 1961);

Raymond Lister, *William Blake: An Introduction to the Man and His Work* (London: Bell, 1968);

Anne Katherine Mellor, *Blake's Human Form Divine* (Berkeley: University of California Press, 1974);

W. J. T. Mitchell, *Blake's Composite Art: A Study of the Illuminated Poetry* (Princeton: Princeton University Press, 1978);

Martin K. Nurmi, *Blake's Marriage of Heaven and Hell: A Critical Study* (Kent, Ohio: Kent State University Press, 1957);

Nurmi, *William Blake* (Kent, Ohio: Kent State University Press, 1976);

Alicia Ostriker, *Vision and Verse in William Blake* (Madison: University of Wisconsin Press, 1965);

Morton D. Paley, *Energy and Imagination: A Study of the Development of Blake's Thought* (Oxford: Clarendon Press, 1970);

Paley, ed., *Twentieth Century Interpretations on "Songs of Innocence and of Experience"* (Englewood Cliffs, N.J.: Prentice Hall, 1969);

Paley and Michael Phillips, eds., *William Blake Essays in Honour of Geoffrey Keynes* (Oxford: Clarendon Press, 1973);

Milton Percival, *William Blake's Circle of Destiny* (New York: Columbia University Press, 1938);

Vivian De Sola Pinta, ed., *The Divine Vision: Studies in the Poetry and Art of William Blake* (London: Gollancz, 1957);

Kathleen Raine, *Blake and Tradition*, 2 volumes, A. W. Mellon Lectures in the Fine Arts,

1962 (Princeton: Princeton University Press, 1968);

Alvin Rosenfeld, ed., *William Blake: Essays for S. Foster Damon* (Providence: Brown University Press, 1969);

A. G. B. Russell, *The Engravings of William Blake* (London: Richards, 1912);

Denis Saurat, *Blake and Milton* (Bordeaux: Y. Cadoret, 1920; New York: MacVeagh/Dial, 1924);

Mark Schorer, *William Blake: The Politics of Vision* (New York: Vintage Books, 1959);

Algernon Charles Swinburne, *William Blake* (London: J. C. Hotlen, 1868);

Leslie Tannenbaum, *Biblical Tradition in Blake's Early Prophecies: The Great Code of Art* (Princeton: Princeton University Press, 1982);

Ruthven Todd, "The Techniques of William Blake's Illuminated Printing," *Print*, 6, no. 1 (1948): 53-65;

Thomas Vogler, *Preludes to Vision: The Epic Venture in Blake, Wordsworth, Keats, and Hart Crane* (Berkeley: University of California Press, 1971);

David Wagenknecht, *Blake's Night: William Blake and the Idea of the Pastoral* (Cambridge, Mass.: Belknap Press, 1973);

Joseph Wicksteed, *Blake's Innocence and Experience* (New York: Dutton, 1928);

Wicksteed, *Blake's Vision of the Book of Job* (London: Dent, 1910);

Joseph Wittreich, *Angel of Apocalypse: Blake's Idea of Milton* (Madison: University of Wisconsin Press, 1975).

Papers:
The British Museum contains an important collection of Blake's illuminated works, including Blake's notebook and the manuscripts for *Tiriel* and *Vala, or The Four Zoas*. The Tate Gallery in London has one of the best collections of Blake's art. Another major collection of illuminated works, including the manuscript for *An Island in the Moon*, is located in the Fitzwilliam Museum in Cambridge, England. In the United States major collections of Blake's works can be found at Harvard, the Huntington Library in San Marino, California, the Library of Congress, and the J. Pierpont Morgan Library in New York, which has the *Pickering Manuscript*.

Robert Bloomfield

(3 December 1766 - 19 August 1823)

Jonathan N. Lawson
University of Hartford

BOOKS: *The Farmer's Boy; A Rural Poem* (London: Printed for Vernor & Hood by T. Bensley, 1800; New York: Printed & sold by George F. Hopkins, 1801; Philadelphia: Printed by J. Humphreys, 1801);

Rural Tales, Ballads, and Songs (London: Printed for Vernor & Hood and Longman & Rees by T. Bensley, 1802; Baltimore: S. Sower, 1802; Boston: Printed for J. Nancrede, 1802);

Extract from a Poem, entitled "Good Tidings, or News from the Farm," by Robert Bloomfield. Recited at the Anniversary Meeting of the Royal Jennerian Society, Thursday, 17th of May, 1804 (London: James Whiting, 1804);

Good Tidings; or, News from the Farm. A Poem (London: Printed for Vernor & Hood and Longman & Rees by James Swan, 1804; Philadelphia: Hugh Maxwell, 1805);

Wild Flowers; or Pastoral and Local Poetry (London: Printed for Vernor, Hood & Sharpe and Longman, Hurst, Rees & Orme, 1806; Philadelphia: Jacob Johnson, 1806);

The Banks of the Wye; A Poem (London: Printed for the author; Vernor, Hood & Sharp; and Longman, Hurst, Rees, Orme & Brown, 1811; New York: R. Scott, 1812; Philadelphia: Bradford & Inskeep, 1812);

The History of Little Davy's New Hat (London: Printed for Darton, Harvey & Darton, 1815);

May Day with the Muses (London: Printed for the author and for Baldwin, Cradock & Joy, 1822);

Hazelwood Hall: A Village Drama (London: Printed for Baldwin, Cradock & Joy, 1823);

The Remains of Robert Bloomfield, 2 volumes, edited by Joseph Weston (London: Printed by Thomas Davison, published by Baldwin, Cradock & Joy, 1824).

Collection: *Collected Poems, 1800-1822*, facsimile reproductions, with an introduction by Jonathan N. Lawson (Gainesville, Fla.: Scholars' Facsimiles & Reprints, 1971).

Robert Bloomfield is perhaps the best of England's rural or "uneducated" poets, as Robert Southey termed them. Certainly his first and best work, *The Farmer's Boy*, struck an amazingly resonant chord with English readers, who bought some twenty-six thousand copies of the poem—there were fourteen separate editions during Bloomfield's lifetime—for the most part during the three years following its publication in 1800. An unmatched chronicler of rural life, its people, traditions, and landscapes, Bloomfield described country life in Suffolk at the close of the eighteenth century, providing a sympathetic yet realistic view of a culture and its values. While his romantic themes and subjects are often set forth in conventional verse that is constantly in danger of succumbing to an excess of nostalgia, something of the authentic voice of the countryman, his humor, and the accurate details of his portraits allow his poetry to stand with a respectability that will surprise the modern reader.

Robert Bloomfield was born on 3 December 1766 in the tiny Suffolk village of Honington to George Bloomfield, the village tailor, and Elizabeth Manby Bloomfield, the schoolmistress. He was the youngest of their six children. The death of his father from smallpox before Bloomfield's first birthday left the family with only the small resources his mother could manage from spinning wool and conducting the village school in her home. Nevertheless, young Bloomfield's first years were fruitful, and the family enjoyed village life, most especially activities on Honington's large commons.

Bloomfield learned to read—if we can trust the fond memories of his brother George—almost before he could walk. Available to him, in addition to school readings and the family copies of the Bible and John Bunyan's *Pilgrim's Progress* (1678), were Thomas Gray's *Elegy Written in a Country Churchyard* (1751), Oliver Goldsmith's *Deserted Village* (1770), and Isaac Watts's *Hymns*. Some of the deficiencies of his home schooling were addressed with the financial help of friends

Robert Bloomfield

when–before he was seven–he was sent to a Mr. Rodwell of Ixworth for several months' tutoring. Soon after he returned home, his mother remarried, adding more children to an already crowded household. When he was eleven, Bloomfield was sent to the farm of his mother's brother-in-law, William Austin of Sapiston, where he spent four years as "the farmer's boy." Bloomfield was not well suited for heavy farm labor. Barely five feet as an adult, he was never robust. His time on the Sapiston farm, however, was happy and ultimately the source of images and experiences on which he would draw for his best poetry.

By the time Bloomfield was fifteen, Mr. Austin had advised the boy's mother that a more suitable employment should be found for him. His oldest brother, George, then a shoemaker in London, agreed to take him in and teach him the trade, and Nathaniel, the next oldest brother and a tailor, offered to clothe him. So on 29 June 1781, after selling his youthful clothes for a shilling and washing his best hat in a horse pond, Bloomfield, accompanied for the trip by his mother, rode the London stage to join his brother in rented quarters in Pitcher's Court, Bell Alley, Coleman Street. Five shoemakers worked in the garret where the brothers lived. Because Robert's time was judged the least valuable, he was soon assigned the task of reading aloud to the other cobblers from newspapers and six-penny weekly numbers of a *History of England*, the *British Traveler,* and a geography. Encouraged by the gift of a dictionary and the discovery of the poetry and reviews in the *London Magazine*, Bloomfield soon had more than country walks on Sundays to break the drudgery of learning his trade and waiting on his companions. He read, attended the occasional public lecture, and by the mid 1780s was attempting to place some of his own verse in the "Poets Corner" of the *London Magazine.*

Illustration from the third 1800 edition of The Farmer's Boy

Apparently, Bloomfield composed in his mind while he cobbled, and there is a strong likelihood that he turned over in his thought those images from his rural childhood, ultimately setting them in verse, as a reaction to his growing dislike of the city and his dreary confinement. A real paradox of his life and art is that the city he would later condemn as the destroyer of the best of rural culture taught him the language of the conservative writers of the eighteenth century which would become the vehicle for his poetry. Further, had he been physically capable of making his way at farming, what he felt for his rural heritage might never have been written. A ditty of small merit, "A Village Girl," soon appeared in Say's *Gazetteer* (24 May 1786). With "The Sailor's Return" and several other brief pieces, it shows a sentimental cast of mind that would be far less evident in his better works. Clearly, however, an idealized vision of what rural life had been or might have been was there when in his eighteenth year Bloomfield was plowing through works by John Milton and James Thomson, and what novels he could lay his hands on.

In 1784 Bloomfield left London for a brief return to Mr. Austin's farm occasioned by a labor dispute regarding his apprenticeship. After his return to London he learned to play the violin and handcrafted aeolian harps (one of which he later sold to Scottish poet James Montgomery). He married Mary-Anne Church on 12 December 1790, and their first daughter was born the following October. Bloomfield set up his family in a rented second-story room in Bell Alley and supported them by shoemaking. By May 1796, when he began to compose his best and most famous work, *The Farmer's Boy,* they had two daughters. In a letter to his brother George, he wrote of *The Farmer's Boy:*

> When I first began it, I thought to myself that I could compleat it in a twelvemonth, allowing myself three months for each quarter; but I soon found that I could not, and indeed made it longer than I first intended. Nine tenths of it was put together as I sat at work, where there are usually six of us; no one in the house has any knowledge of what I have employed my thoughts about when I did not talk.

I chose to do it in rhime for this reason; because I always found that when I put two or three lines together in blank verse, or something that sounded like it, it was a great chance if it stood right when it came to be wrote down, for blank verse has ten-syllables in a line, and this particular I could not adjust, or bear in mind as I could rhimes. Winter, and half of Autumn were done long before I could find the leisure to write them. (British Library, Additional Manuscript 28,266, 85r–85v)

From April of 1798 to the time of its appearance in the shops in March of 1800, the unsolicited manuscript from a journeyman shoemaker passed through many hands, finally finding a sponsor and champion in Capel Lofft, a nephew of Edward Capel, writer, Shakespearean commentator, and deputy inspector of plays. Lofft, a barrister and lord of the manor at Troston, was himself a fair writer on legal and political affairs and had earned a local reputation as a patron of the arts that Byron would later lampoon in *English Bards and Scotch Reviewers* (1809). Lofft found Bloomfield a publisher, meddled a bit with the regionalisms in the manuscript, and later assisted in introducing the poet into London social and literary circles.

The Farmer's Boy; A Rural Poem follows the course of life on a small Suffolk farm through the four seasons—four books, each following the simple, seasonal activities of Giles, the farmer's boy. While Bloomfield clearly knew the works of Thomson, Goldsmith, and others, his poem seems to come directly from nature, and he wisely and deliberately distanced himself from those literary progenitors. In fact, Bloomfield was conscious of differences between the more literary pastoral tradition and rural or peasant poetry. Although he would at times ape the stylistic elements of the former, he strove for the voice of the latter.

The very length of the poem and the temperate climate of Suffolk, together with the single locale and single central character, make almost inevitable Bloomfield's concentration on local detail, small incident, and accurate description. Whether it is marking the order of precedence that cows led home from pasture establish or the characteristics of a chalky manure bed, Bloomfield's sense of realism keeps the reader focused on a single place (his uncle's farm) at a single point in time (that of his own boyhood) as Giles does his own chores and observes the activities of the farm in each of the seasons. While this nar-

row focus might have doomed the work to flatness interspersed with maudlin sentiment, Bloomfield's skill at contrasts, reversals, balance, and sense-imparting transitions allowed him to create a rural poem of the first order despite his limitations as a versifier.

Bloomfield's themes in *The Farmer's Boy* are drawn in part from the values he sensed in rural life and custom and in part from the threat to those values he saw in such forces as enclosure of pasture lands, urbanization of the country, and city values. What Bloomfield prized and celebrated in Suffolk rural life was a connectedness of life and labor to nature with its generally predictable cycles—a knowable life where predictability encouraged trust as a basis for social contracts. The nobility of labor, a sense of classlessness in a society dependent on the land, benevolence to people and creatures alike, good and careful husbandry that balanced human need with respect for nature, and joy in simple living are all expounded in narrative and description. By setting the poem in the past and presenting a generally positive picture of rural life, Bloomfield could argue against unwanted change—be it London market demands causing a deterioration in the quality of cheese making or a shift away from egalitarian social attitudes—as persuasively as the contrast with earlier times would allow. He was no fool about the darker realities of the rural life of his childhood, and he took care to present it selectively and balance it with the good that he celebrated.

The success of the book soon had Bloomfield fighting to balance his shoemaking, which remained necessary to the support of his family, with the social demands of friends, supporters, and the curious. In addition to Capel Lofft; Augustus Henry Fitzroy, Duke of Grafton (his first great patron); and Dr. Nathan Drake, he became acquainted to varying degrees with Charles Lamb, Dr. Edward Jenner, George Dyer (who introduced him to Lamb and others), Robert Southey, Samuel Rogers, George Crabbe, William Holloway, James Montgomery, Bernard Barton, and later John Clare. Southey wrote a supportive review in the *Critical Review* (May 1800); dozens of small literary publications such as the *Lady's Monthly* began to follow his career, testifying to his popularity and specific appeal to women readers; and Wordsworth wrote to Coleridge of having seen Bloomfield in London and found him far more interesting than expected. Years later when Bloomfield's financial affairs had soured,

PREFACE.

THE Poems here offered to the Public were chiefly written during the interval between the concluding and the publishing of THE FARMER's BOY, an interval of nearly two years. The pieces of a later date are, *the Widow to her Hour-Glass, the Fakenham Ghost, Walter and Jane,* &c. At the time of publishing the Farmer's Boy, circumstances occurred which rendered it necessary to submit these Poems to the perusal of my Friends: under whose approbation I now give them, with some confidence as to their moral merit, to the judgment of the Public. And as they treat of village manners, and rural scenes, it appears to me not ill-tim'd to avow, that I have hopes of

vi   PREFACE.

meeting in some degree the approbation of my Country. I was not prepar'd for the decided, and I may surely say extraordinary attention which the Public has shewn towards the Farmer's Boy: the consequence has been such as my true friends will rejoice to hear; it has produc'd me many essential blessings. And I feel peculiarly gratified in finding that a poor man in England may assert the dignity of Virtue, and speak of the imperishable beauties of Nature, and be heard, and heard, perhaps, with greater attention for his being poor.

Whoever thinks of me or my concerns, must necessarily indulge the pleasing idea of gratitude, and join a thought of my first great friend Mr. LOFFT. And on this head, I believe every reader, who has himself any feeling, will judge rightly of mine: if otherwise, I would much rather he would lay down this volume, and grasp hold of

PREFACE.   vii

such fleeting pleasures as the world's business may afford him. I speak not of that gentleman as a public character, or as a scholar. Of the former I know but little, and of the latter nothing. But I know from experience, and I glory in this fair opportunity of saying it, that his private life is a lesson of morality; his manners gentle, his heart sincere: and I regard it as one of the most fortunate circumstances of my life, that my introduction to public notice fell to so zealous and unwearied a friend.*

I have received many honourable testimonies of esteem from strangers; letters without a name, but fill'd with the most cordial advice, and almost

* I dare not take to myself a praise like this; and yet I was, perhaps, hardly at liberty to disclaim what should be mine and the endeavour of every one to deserve. This I can say, that I have reason to rejoice that Mr. *George Bloomfield* introduced *the Farmer's Boy* to me. C. L.

viii   PREFACE.

a parental anxiety, for my safety under so great a share of public applause. I beg to refer such friends to the great teacher Time: and hope that he will hereafter give me my deserts, and no more.

One piece in this collection will inform the reader of my most pleasing visit to *Wakefield Lodge:* books, solitude, and objects entirely new, brought pleasures which memory will always cherish. That noble and worthy Family, and all my immediate and unknown Friends, will, I hope, believe the sincerity of my thanks for all their numerous favours, and candidly judge the Poems before them.

R. BLOOMFIELD.

SEPT. 29, 1801.

Preface to Rural Tales, Ballads, and Songs *(1802). C. L., who signed the footnote on page vii, is Capel Lofft, who had found a publisher for Bloomfield's first book,* The Farmer's Boy.

Southey sought a subscription plan that might have aided the poet, and, after Bloomfield's death, Southey wished a place in literary history for him.

While not as popular as *The Farmer's Boy*, a second book of verse, *Rural Tales, Ballads, and Songs,* appeared in January of 1802 to some critical acclaim. Most of the pieces had been composed in odd seasonal bouts (spring to fall) in 1798 and 1799 while Bloomfield awaited the publication of his first book, and all were complete by the fall of 1801. The book, which John Clare later thought contained the poet's best verse, is a distinct change from the conservative meter and sometimes elevated style of *The Farmer's Boy*. A wide variety of rural characters–often presented in the social context of a village–are portrayed in eighteen "ballads," "tales," and "songs." Love among old couples and young, the solitude of age, country traditions, and superstitions are some of the subjects; the verse forms are varied and often sprightly. Bloomfield even attempted a "shaped" poem with surprising success in "The Widow to Her Hour-Glass."

Bloomfield's loss of his father and several other family members to smallpox led him to become an early and public supporter of the then controversial work of Dr. Edward Jenner. Having had his children vaccinated as early as 1800, Bloomfield turned his support for the cause into verse with the composition of *Good Tidings; or, News from the Farm.* Happily discarding such titles as "Vaccine Rose" and "Vaccine Inoculation," Bloomfield brought to print in 1804 an epideictic poem extolling the value of the vaccine. While the sentimental lapses of the piece and its voice, which loses rural authenticity, do not recommend it, *Good Tidings* may be notable for its comment on Bloomfield's intellect and enthusiasm. He researched the writings of Jenner's coworker, William Woodville, and became a friendly acquaintance of Jenner. The poem was "improved" and included in Bloomfield's next collection in 1806.

While waiting for the publication of *Rural Tales,* Bloomfield wrote a children's tale extolling rural virtues. *The History of Little Davy's New Hat* was not published until 1815. He was also at work on the pieces which would be included in *Wild Flowers; or Pastoral and Local Poetry,* which appeared to somewhat diminished critical acclaim in 1806. With more distance from *The Farmer's Boy* and without the influence of Capel Lofft, Bloomfield, however, introduced there additional variety of character and incident and verse. Sev-

eral of the poems in *Wild Flowers*–the humorous courtship of "Abner and the Widow Jones," the meditative "To My Old Oak Table," and "The Horkey," celebrating the harvest festival–catch themes from the earlier two books and stand up well to modern reading. Although the volume was not without merits, the *Critical Review* (June 1806) damned it with faint praise as below the expected standard of so well known a poet as Bloomfield.

Still, his popularity continued, and the struggle to handle his public affairs, manage the financial end of his literary affairs, and produce necessary income from making shoes and harps led him to escape the city yet again, this time to tour the Wye River valley with friends. The store of images he brought back in a journal along with the novelty of trying his own hand at sketching from memory carried him through the next winter and beyond as he transformed the journal into verse. The result, published in 1811, was *The Banks of the Wye; A Poem.* The travel poem in four books records scenery and some local history. While its images are often appealing, it is the voice of the visitor, the tourist, not the countryman that speaks throughout. The result is undistinguished verse which drops the themes Bloomfield could follow with intensity and skill.

The lack of warm public response to the work, however, paled in comparison to the troubling effect on the poet brought on by the deaths that year of his patron, the duke of Grafton, and of Thomas Hood, the more active partner at the firm of his publishers. Those events precipitated the long decline of Bloomfield's financial fortunes, and, although some early biographers (with the intent of having a good literary story) blamed what followed on a Burnsian carelessness with money and drink, there is not much truth in that and less in the notion that his decline brought nothing but hopelessness and bitterness. On the contrary, Bloomfield's relative innocence in business matters led him through much of the rest of his life always to be hopeful for a reverse of fortune and often disappointed. His character was such that he often shared what wealth he had with needy relatives, always fretted over the fortunes of his children, and, for the most part, moved through his later years facing each disappointment with determination to struggle on and perhaps to find his muse.

When in 1816 illness and more financial trouble led friends to issue a modestly successful subscription in his behalf in an effort to purchase

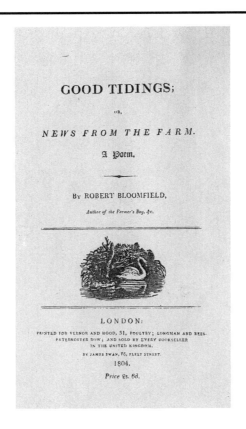

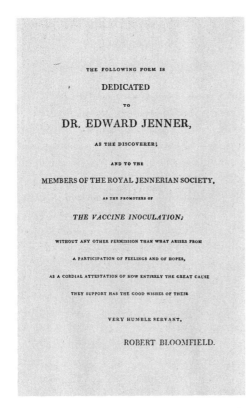

Decorated title page, dedication, and advertisement from the first complete edition of the poem in which Bloomfield celebrated the invention of a vaccine for smallpox

Frontispiece to The Poems of Robert Bloomfield *(1827), published four years after the poet's death*

for him an annuity, he was grateful and with characteristic humor noted the limited success: "The Subscription—Aye, the Subscription goes on very much like a donkey in a dirt lane with its legs tied" (British Library, Additional Manuscript 28,268 366v). By the winter of 1817, with many of his children placed in acceptable employment, with some money in hand from the subscription and the publication of his children's book, Bloomfield had begun to write again, picking up the text for *May Day with the Muses*, which he had begun years earlier.

By fall 1819 Bloomfield had apparently finished the pieces that would appear in *May Day*, his last, slim volume of verse. For two vexing years he pursued a publisher for the work. His first try was John Murray, who, he thought, was about to pay "Parson Crabbe" three thousand pounds for his *Tales*. Learning that his own publishers, Baldwin, Cradock and Joy, were to publish Crabbe immediately and being rejected by Murray were difficult. Being simultaneously at

the center of rumors questioning his loyalty to church and state did little to improve his state of mind. Nor were his spirits improved when he found it necessary to sell his late mother's cottage in Honington. When *May Day with the Muses* finally appeared in 1822, his preface referred to his tribulations, and he signed himself "with remembrance of what is past." The book, however, was a modest success, and a second edition was called for in the same year.

Bloomfield's long frustration with lack of patronage and his financial plight is reflected in more than the preface to *May Day*. The entire poem may be an elaborate exercise in wish fulfillment, for its subject is rewards for rural poets. In this case, an aging baronet who loves rural song and poetry accepts verse for rent money from all his tenants who will write. The poetic frame tale has all the folk of Oakly Manor gathering to read their verses, and after the disappointments the reader may have had with *The Banks of the Wye*, the quality of the poetry Bloomfield created for these rustic bards is surprisingly high. Back on his native ground, Bloomfield again spices the tales and ballads with romance, singular characters, and country virtue. While there was scant critical notice of *May Day*, Bloomfield himself was pleased and sent a copy to John Clare, with whose works he was newly acquainted. The two corresponded warmly in Bloomfield's last years. Clare was an admirer.

Bloomfield's bouts of melancholy, years of precarious health and failing eyesight, lapses of memory, and always bothersome finances might have silenced a less determined writer. Bloomfield wrote on. In his fifty-sixth year he was working with his son, Charles, on a natural history for children entitled "The Bird and Insect Post Office" (published in *The Remains of Robert Bloomfield*, 1824), and he finished a dramatic sketch contemplated as early as 1805—*Hazelwood Hall: A Village Drama*—in his final year. While all that plagued him was never far away, his final letters in the British Library collection reveal a spirit troubled but not defeated. His daughter Hannah found a scrap of verse in his pocket toward the very end of his life (British Library Additional MS 30,809, fol. 32). The lines were occasioned by May Day night of 1822 and the recent publication of his *May Day with the Muses*. The verse says more of his character and determination during his hardest years than any biographer could, and it reveals his awareness of his place in the tradition of rural poetry:

> It is the voice thou gavest me, God of Love
> And all I see & feel still bears thy sway
> And when the Spring breaks forth in mead & grove
> Thou art my God, thou art the God of May.

Editions of Bloomfield's collected works and inclusions of his poems in anthologies continued through the late nineteenth century. His influence and reputation, however, faded far earlier. The month after his death on 19 August 1823, the *Monthly Magazine* attacked his poetry viciously, and there were few supporters to reply. Within the tradition of the peasant poets, however, he was remembered in the verse of John Clare and others. And there is a strong possibility that the popularity of Wordsworth and the other Romantics, who on a far different literary plane used rural tales and images drawn from the English countryside, was in part the result of a vast audience whose appetite for such subjects was whetted by the writings of the farmer's boy.

Letters:

Selections from the Correspondence of Robert Bloomfield, The Suffolk Poet, edited by W. H. Hart, F.S.A. (London: Spottiswoode, 1870); facsimile edition, edited by Robert Ashby (Redhill, Surrey: Commercial Lithographic Company, 1969).

Bibliography:

The Earl of Cranbrook and John Hadfield, "Some Uncollected Authors XX: Robert Bloomfield, 1766-1823," *Book Collector*, 8 (Summer 1959): 170-179.

Biographies:

James Storer and John Greig, eds., *Views of Suffolk, Norfolk, and Northhamptonshire; Illustrative of the Works of Robert Bloomfield; Accompanied with Descriptions: To which is Annexed, A Memoir of the Poet's Life*, by Edward Wedlake Brayley (London: Vernor, Hood & Sharpe, 1806);

A Biographical Sketch of Robert Bloomfield, with a Portrait (London, 1825);

William Wicket and Nicholas Duval, *The Farmer's Boy: The Story of a Suffolk Poet, Robert Bloomfield* (Levenham, Suffolk: Terence Dalton, 1971).

References:

Edmund Blunden, *Nature in English Literature* (London: Leonard & Virginia Woolf, 1929);

Jonathan Lawson, *Robert Bloomfield* (Boston: Twayne, 1980);

Robert Southey, *The Lives and Works of the Uneducated Poets*, edited by J. S. Childers (London: Humphrey Milford, 1925);

Rayner Unwin, *The Rural Muse: Studies in the Peasant Poetry of England* (London: Allen & Unwin, 1954).

Papers:

The manuscript for *The Farmer's Boy* is now in the Houghton Library of Harvard University. The majority of the extant manuscripts for Bloomfield's verse and original letters can be found in the British Library (Additional Manuscripts, 26,265, 28,266, 28,268, 30,809). A letter to John Clare is in that library's Egerton collection (MS 2245, fol. 186).

William Lisle Bowles

(24 September 1762 - 7 April 1850)

Thomas L. Blanton

Central Washington University

BOOKS: *Fourteen Sonnets, Elegiac and Descriptive, Written During a Tour* (Bath: Printed by R. Cruttwell & sold by C. Dilly, London, 1789); enlarged as *Sonnets, Written Chiefly on Picturesque Spots, During a Tour* (Bath: Printed & sold by R. Cruttwell & sold also by C. Dilly, London & J. Rann, Oxford, 1789); enlarged again as *Sonnets, (3d Ed.), With Other Poems* (Bath: Printed by R. Cruttwell & sold by C. Dilly, London, 1794); corrected as *Sonnets, and Other Poems* (Bath: Printed by R. Cruttwell & sold by C. Dilly, London, 1796; enlarged again, 1796); enlarged again as *Sonnets, and Other Poems, by the Reverend W. L. Bowles . . . 6th Edition. To Which is Added Hope, An Allegorical Sketch on Recovering Slowly from Sickness* (Bath: Printed by R. Cruttwell for C. Dilly, London, 1798; reprinted, 1800); republished as volume one of *Poems*, 2 volumes (London: T. Cadell, 1800, 1801);

Verses to John Howard, F.R.S. On His State of Prisons and Lazarettos (Bath: Printed by R. Cruttwell & sold by C. Dilly, London & C. Rann, Oxford, 1789);

The Grave of Howard, A Poem (Salisbury: Printed by E. Easton & sold by C. Dilly, T. Hookham & J. Dodsley, London, 1790);

Verses on the Benevolent Institution of the Philanthropic Society, for Protecting and Educating the Children of Vagrants and Criminals (Bath: Printed by R. Cruttwell & sold by C. Dilly, T. Becket, T. Hookham & J. Johnson, London, 1790);

A Poetical Address to the Right Honourable Edmund Burke (London: Printed for C. Dilly, 1791);

Elegy Written at the Hot-Wells Bristol, Addressed to the Rev'd William Howley (Bath: Printed by R. Cruttwell & sold by C. Dilly, T. Becket, T. Hookham & J. Johnson, London, 1791);

Monody, Written at Matlock, October, 1791 (Salisbury: Printed by E. & J. Easton & sold by C. Dilly, London & R. Cruttwell, Bath, 1791);

A Sermon Preached in the Cathedral Church of Sarum at the Triennial Visitation of John Lord Bishop of the Diocese, on Friday, August 7, 1795 (Salisbury: Printed by & for J. Easton; C. Dilly, London; J. Fletcher & Co., Oxford; J. Burden & Son, Winchester; R. Cruttwell, Bath; W. Sollers, Blandford; T. Adams, Shaston, 1795);

Elegiac Stanzas, Written During Sickness at Bath, December, 1795 (Bath: Printed by R. Cruttwell & sold by C. Dilly, London, 1796);

Hope, An Allegorical Sketch, on Recovering Slowly from Sickness (London: Printed for C. Dilly, Cadell & Davies, and Cruttwell, Bath, 1796);

St. Michael's Mount, A Poem (Salisbury: Printed by B. C. Collins for T. Adams, Shaftesbury & sold by C. Dilly, London, 1798);

Coombe Ellen: A Poem, Written in Radnorshire, September, 1798 (Bath: Printed by R. Cruttwell & sold by C. Dilly and Cadell & Davies, London, 1798);

A Discourse, Delivered to the Military Associations for the Town and District of Shaftesbury, On Monday, December 3, 1798 (Salisbury: Printed by J. Easton for F. & C. Rivington, London; T. Adams, Shaston; W. Sollers, Blandford; T. Baker, Southampton; R. Cruttwell, Bath; & J. Easton, Salisbury, 1799);

Song of the Battle of the Nile (London: Printed for T. Cadell, Jun. & W. Davies, and C. Dilly, 1799);

A Sermon Preached at the Anniversary Meeting of the Sons of the Clergy, in the Cathedral Church of St. Paul, on Thursday, May 7, 1801 (London: Printed by Ann Rivington, and sold by F. & C. Rivington, and Cadell & Davies, 1801);

Poems, Vol. II (London: Printed for T. Cadell, Jun. & W. Davies and C. Dilly, 1801);

The Sorrows of Switzerland: A Poem (London: Printed for T. Cadell, Jun. & W. Davies, J. Mawman; and R. Cruttwell, Bath, 1801);

The Picture, Verses Written in London, May 28, 1803, Suggested By a Magnificent Landscape of Ru-

bens (London: Printed by W. Bulmer for Cadell & Davies, and James Carpenter, 1803);

The Spirit of Discovery, or, The Conquest of Ocean. A Poem, in Five Books: With Notes, Historical and Illustrative (Bath: Printed by R. Cruttwell & sold by Cadell & Davies, and Mawman, London, 1804);

Bowden Hill, The Banks of the Wye, Cadland, Southampton River (Southampton: Printed by Baker & Fletcher, 1806);

Poems (Never Before Published), Written Chiefly at Bremhill, in Wiltshire, Vol. IV (London: Printed for Cadell & Davies; and Cruttwell, Bath, 1809);

The Missionary, A Poem (London: Printed by J. Innes & sold by J. Murray, 1813; Philadelphia: M. Carey, 1815; corrected and enlarged edition, London: J. Murray, 1815); re-

published as *The Missionary of the Andes* (N.p., 1822); republished as *The Ancient Missionary of Chili* (London: James Bulcock, 1835);

A Few Plain Words for the Bible, and a Word on the Prayer-Book, and the Spirit (Calne: Printed & sold by W. Baily, also sold by Brodie & Dowding, Salisbury, circa 1815);

Sermons on Some Important Points Respecting the Faith, the Feelings, the Spirit, and The Dispositions of Christians, Preached Before a Country Congregation, To Which Are Added Small Hymns for Charity Schools (Bath: Printed by R. Cruttwell & sold by Murray, London, 1815);

Thoughts on the Increase of Crimes, the Education of the Poor, and the National Schools; in A Letter to Sir James Mackintosh (Salisbury: Printed & sold by Brodie & Dowding, sold also by Longman, Hurst, Rees, Orme & Brown, London, 1818);

Vindiciæ Wykehamicæ; or, A Vindication of Winchester College: In a Letter to Henry Brougham, Esq.; Occasioned by His Letter to Sir Samuel Romilly, on Charitable Abuses (Bath: Printed by R. Cruttwell & sold by Longman, Hurst, Rees, Orme & Brown, London, 1818);

The Triumphant Tailor; Or, A True Account of the Especial Visitation of the Spirit; in These Days, on William Cowhorne, P.E. & T.S.C. of Trowbridge, in the County of Wilts, One of the Despised and Persecuted People Called Tailors (N.p., 1818);

The Plain Bible, and the Protestant Church in England: With Reflections on Some Important Subjects of Existing Religious Controversy (Bath: Printed by R. Cruttwell & sold by Longman, Hurst, Rees, Orme & Brown, 1818);

The Invariable Principles of Poetry, In a Letter Addressed to Thomas Campbell, Esq.; Occasioned by Some Critical Observations in His Specimens of the British Poets. Particularly Relating to the Poetical Character of Pope (Bath: Printed by R. Cruttwell & sold by Longman, Hurst, Rees, Orme & Brown, London, 1819);

A Reply to an "Unsentimental Sort of Critic," the Reviewer of "Spence's Anecdotes" in the Quarterly Review for October 1820; Otherwise to a Certain Critic and Grocer, The Longinus of "In-Door" Nature (Bath: Printed by R. Cruttwell & sold by Longman, Hurst, Rees, Orme & Brown and Baldwin, Cradock & Joy, 1820);

A Vindication of the Late Editor of Pope's Work, from Some Charges Brought Against Him, by a Writer in the Quarterly Review, for October, 1820: With Further Observations on "The Invariable Principles of Poetry;" and A Full Exposure of the Mode of Criticising Adopted by Octavius Gilchrist, second edition corrected [first separate edition] (London: Printed by A. J. Valpy & sold by Cadell, Colburn & Warren, 1821);

*Two Letters to the Right Honorable Lord Byron, in Answer to His Lordship's Letter to **** ****** on the Rev. Wm. L. Bowles's Strictures on the Life and Writings of Pope* (London: John Murray, 1821);

The Grave of The Last Saxon, Or, The Legend of The Curfew, A Poem (London: Printed for Hurst, Robinson & Co., and Archibald Constable, Edinburgh, 1822);

Ellen Gray, Or, The Dead Maiden's Curse, A Poem, By the Late Dr. Archibald Macleod [pseud.] (Edinburgh: Printed for Archibald Consta-

ble, and Hurst, Robinson & Co., London, 1823);

A Voice from St. Peter's and St. Paul's; Being a Few Plain Words Addressed Most Respectfully to the Members of Both Houses of Parliament, on Some Late Accusations against the Church Establishment (London: Published by Hurst, Robinson & Co., and sold by J. Parker and Munday & Slater, Oxford; Deighton & Sons, Cambridge, 1823);

The Church and Parochial School. A Sermon, Preached at Bremhill, For the Benefit of the National Schools; August 31st, 1823 (Calne: Printed by Baily, 1823);

The Ark: A Dramatic Oratorio. Written Expressly for Musical Effect (Bath: Printed by R. Cruttwell, 1824?);

A Final Appeal to the Literary Public, Relative to Pope, in Reply to Certain Observations of Mr. Roscoe, in His Edition of that Poet's Works. To Which Are Added, Some Remarks on Lord Byron's Conversations, As Far as They Relate to the Same Subject and the Author (London: Hurst, Robinson & Co., 1825);

The Little Villager's Verse Book: Consisting of Short Verses, for Children to Learn by Heart, in Which the Most Familiar Images of Country Life are Applied to Excite the First Feelings of Humanity and Piety, 3rd edition (London: Printed for Mary R. Stockdale, 1826);

Paulus Parochialis, or a Plain and Practical View of the Object, Arguments, and Connection, of St. Paul's Epistle to the Romans, in a Series of Sermons Adapted to Country Congregations (Bath: Printed by R. Cruttwell, 1826);

Lessons in Criticism to William Roscoe, Esq.; F.R.S. Member of the Della Crusca Society of Florence, F.R.S.L. In Answer to his Letter to the Reverend W. L. Bowles on the Character and Poetry of Pope. With Further Lessons in Criticism to a Quarterly Reviewer (London: Hurst, Robinson & Co., 1826);

Hermes Britannicus, A Dissertation on the Celtic Deity, Teutates, the Mercurius of Caesar, in Further Proof and Corroboration of the Origin and Designation of the Great Temple of Abury, in Wiltshire (London: Printed by & for J. B. Nichols & Son, 1828);

The Parochial History of Brenhill (London: J. Murray, 1828);

Days Departed, Or, Banwell Hill: A Lay of the Severn Sea (London: Murray / Bath: R. Cruttwell, 1828); republished, with a revision of *Ellen Gray,* as *Days Departed, or Banwell Hill, a Lay of the Severn Sea, including the Tale of the Maid of Cornwall; or, Spectre and Prayer-Book* (London: Murray, 1829);

The Poetical Works of Milman, Bowles, Wilson, and Barry Cornwall (Paris: A. & W. Galignani, 1829);

The Life of Thomas Ken, D.D., 2 volumes (London: J. Murray, 1830-1831);

A Word on Cathedral-Oratorios, and Clergy-Magistrates, Addressed to Lord Mountcashel (London: J. Murray, 1830);

A Few Words, Most Respectfully Addressed to the Lord Chancellor Brougham, on the Misrepresentations, Exaggerations, and Falsehoods Respecting the Property and Character of the Cathedral Clergy of the Church of England (Salisbury: W. B. Brodie & Co., sold also by Rivington, London, 1831);

St. John in Patmos: a Poem, By One of the Old Living Poets of Great-Britain (London: J. Murray, 1832); enlarged as *St. John in Patmos; Or, the Last Apostle: A Sacred Poem, from the Revelations, by the Rev. W. L. Bowles, To Which are Added Some Minor Poems of Early Youth* (London: J. Murray, 1835);

The Grave of Anna, In the Island of Madeira (From the "Spirit of Discovery") Now First Corrected (Bath: Printed by H. E. Carrington, 1833);

A Last and Summary Answer to the Question "Of What Use Have Been, and Are, the English Cathedral Establishments?" With a Vindication of Anthems & Cathedral Services; in a Letter to Lord Henley (London: Rivington & Turril, printed by H. E. Carrington, Bath, 1833);

Annals and Antiquities of Lacock Abbey in the County of Wilts, by Bowles and John Gough Nichols (London: J. B. Nichols & Son, 1835);

Scenes and Shadows of Days Departed, With Selections from Poems, Illustrative of a Long Journey Through Life, From the Earliest Recollections to Age (London: J. Murray / Bath: Meyler Ford & Binns, Printed by H. E. Carrington, 1835); enlarged as *Scenes and Shadows of Days Departed, A Narrative Accompanied With Poems of Youth and Some Other Poems of Melancholy and Fancy in the Journey of Life from Youth to Age* (London: William Pickering, 1837);

Further Observations on the Last Report of the Church Commissioners, Particularly as Respects the Patronage of Deans and Chapters, and Cathedral Music (Devizes: Printed by Simpson, 1836);

A Discourse, Preached in Salisbury Cathedral, on King Charles's Martyrdom (Salisbury: W. B. Brodie

& Co., sold also by Rivingtons, London, 1836);

Some Account of the Last Days of William Chillingworth, Author of "The Religion of Protestants a Safe Way to Salvation;" With Remarks on the Character of Cromwell, and the Late Report of the Church Commissioners (Salisbury: W. B. Brodie & Co., sold also by Rivingtons, London, 1836);

The Patronage of the English Bishops. Two Addresses to the Houses of Lords and Commons (Bristol: Gutch & Martin, 1837);

The English Village Church, A Sermon, Preached at Bremhill, Wilts, for the Benefit of the Society for Building and Repairing Churches; To Which Are Added A Series of Discourses, Preached in Bowood, on Six Subjects, from the Cartoons of Raphael (London: J. Murray, 1837);

The Cartoons of Raphael. A Series of Discourses, Preached in Bowood Chapel (London: John Murray, 1838);

A Final Defence of the Rights of Patronage in Deans and Chapters: Being a Few Plain Words in Answer to One Material Part of the Bishop of Bristol and Gloucester's Charge, Delivered at Chippenham, August 30TH, 1838 (London: J. Murray, Printed by Meyler & Son, Bath, 1838);

Pudens and Claudia of St. Paul. On the Earliest Introduction of the Christian Faith, to These Islands (Calne: Printed at the Office of E. Baily, 1838?).

Collections: *The Poetical Works of William Lisle Bowles,* 2 volumes, edited by George Gilfillan (Edinburgh: J. Nichol, 1855; New York: D. Appleton, 1855);

The Poetical Works of Bowles, Lamb, and Hartley Coleridge, edited by William Tirebuck (London: W. Scott, 1887);

Fourteen Sonnets . . . Monody Written at Matlock . . . Coombe Ellen, edited by Donald H. Reiman (New York: Garland, 1978);

Hope, an Allegorical Sketch, St. Michael's Mount . . . Ellen Gray, edited by Reiman (New York: Garland, 1978);

Poems and The Missionary, edited by Reiman (New York: Garland, 1978);

Sonnets and Other Poems, and The Spirit of Discovery, edited by Reiman (New York: Garland, 1978).

OTHER: *The Works of Alexander Pope, Esq. in Verse and Prose,* 10 volumes, edited, with a mem-

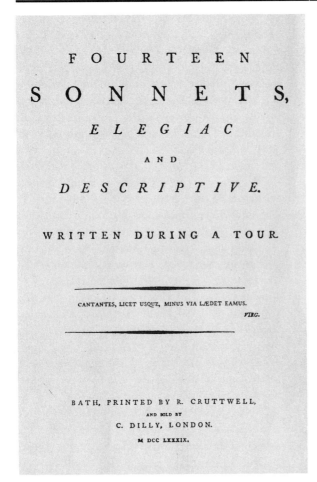
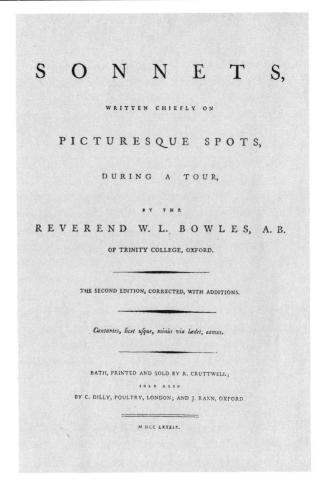

Title pages for the first edition and the second, revised and enlarged, edition of Bowles's first book. Coleridge wrote in his Biographia Literaria *of discovering Bowles's* Sonnets *at seventeen and falling under "the genial influence of a style of poetry, so tender, and yet so manly, so natural and real, and yet so dignified, and harmonious. . . ."*

oir by Bowles (London: Printed for J. Johnson, 1806).

Thomas Moore–William Lisle Bowles's friend, fellow minor poet, and longtime Wiltshire neighbor–recorded in a journal for 20 March 1819 that he found the middle-aged vicar "in the bar of the White Hart, dictating to a waiter (who acted as an amanuensis for him) his ideas of the true Sublime in Poetry." He concluded by recalling the innocent, absentminded, and benevolent country parson in Henry Fielding's *Joseph Andrews* (1742): "Never was there such a Parson Adams, since the real one. . . ." Here, Moore seems to express the view of those contemporaries who found in this clergyman-poet-antiquarian-controversialist-musician a human being of warmth and good nature in spite of his vanities, naïveté, and uncritical self-esteem. His discerning friends, as well as critical readers of the day,

knew Bowles was not a major poet–or, often enough, not even a passable one. What reputation he had rested not on widespread acclaim but on a seventeen-year-old's enthusiasm for a slender volume of twenty-one sonnets Bowles published in 1789.

That teenager was Samuel Taylor Coleridge, who could still, on mature reflection, acknowledge in *Biographia Literaria* (1817), "My obligations to Mr. Bowles were indeed important, and for radical good. At a very premature age, . . . I had bewildered myself in metaphysicks, and in theological controversy. Nothing else pleased me. Poetry . . . became insipid to me. . . . This preposterous pursuit was, beyond doubt, injurious both to my natural powers, and to the progress of my education. . . . But from this I was auspiciously withdrawn, . . . chiefly . . . by the genial influence of a style of poetry, so tender and yet so manly, so natural and real, and yet so dignified and harmoni-

ous, as the sonnets &c. of Mr. Bowles!" Wordsworth found that he, too, could not put down
that volume of Bowles's sonnets until he had
read them all. Robert Southey and Charles Lamb
also admitted to being admirers of Bowles's early
poetry. Yet this enthusiasm on the part of his
youthful admirers did not extend much beyond
the 1790s. Wordsworth, for example, never acknowledged Bowles as an influence or as a writer
of any significance. Hazlitt did not include
Bowles in his *Lectures on the English Poets* (1818),
and in *The Spirit of the Age* (1825) merely portrayed him as an early interest of Coleridge's and
as the cause in the 1820s of the Alexander Pope
controversy into which George Gordon, Lord
Byron was drawn. Indeed, one may ask why
Bowles should receive even a footnote in literary
history when it is difficult to find among his
poems even a handful with intrinsic merit, and
when the vast bulk of his prodigious output in
verse and prose is not only considered unreadable today but was scarcely better judged in his
own day.

George Gilfillan, writing in 1855, five years
after Bowles's death, offered perhaps the most favorable possible estimate of his work: "In his
larger poems, he is often diffuse and verbose,
and you see more effort than energy. But in his
smaller, and especially in his sonnets, and his
pieces descriptive of nature, Bowles is always true
to his own heart, and therefore always successful." Few today would accept the final statement,
but the case for Bowles rests on his having managed at one brief time, almost in spite of himself,
to have found a way to bring a sympathetic response to nature and the private emotion of a moment of introspection together, in verse, in a way
that seemed fresh and vital. Limited as his poetic
achievement is, it nonetheless exists as the first expression of a sensibility and a style which would
soon be fully realized in the work of Coleridge
and especially Wordsworth. Thus, Bowles's importance as a poet is historical and rests on those
few poems Gilfillan mentioned. His work as editor of Pope, antiquarian, historian, controversial-
ist, and writer of sermons belongs as a minor
entry in the history of taste and British culture.
Yet the fact remains that Bowles's was a household name, at least among the readers of poetry
and the literary journals of the period, largely because of the force of his own belief in himself
and in the causes he fought for. In his journal
Thomas Moore wrote that Bowles was "an excellent fellow notwithstanding, and if the waters of

his inspiration be not those of Helicon, they are
at least very-sweet waters, and to my taste pleas-
anter than some that are more strongly impreg-
nated." His friend was a Parson Adams who
could cheerfully find compliments in a less than
laudatory article about him in an influential literary quarterly, thereby prompting Moore to conclude, "How lucky it is that self love has always
something comfortable to retire upon."

Born to the Reverend William Thomas
Bowles and Bridget (Biddy) Grey Bowles at
King's Sutton near Banbury in Northamptonshire, Bowles was the son and grandson of clergy-
men and a descendant of a notable Wiltshire family. In 1769 his father received the living of
Uphill and Brean in Somerset, a rural area over-
looking the great estuary of the Severn, not quite
fifteen miles to the northeast of Nether Stowey,
where Coleridge settled in 1797 and where he
and Wordsworth collaborated on *Lyrical Ballads*
(1798). A sensitive child, rather like the young
Wordsworth in his physical enjoyment of sea-
shore and hillside, he inherited, as he recalled in
Scenes and Shadows of Days Departed (1835), his father's love for landscape and his mother's love of
music, particularly sacred music.

He showed early promise as a student, and although there was little money to spare, his father
resolved to provide his son, the eldest of seven children, with a good education. Consequently, in
1781 Bowles went to Winchester, where he attracted the attention and tutelage of the headmaster, Joseph Warton. From Warton the critic he
learned of Pope's lesser status in the poetic hierar-
chy. Warton the poet, as "Monody on the Death
of Dr. Warton" reveals, awakened him to nature:

> I gazed
> Delighted 'round; awaked, inspired, amazed,
> I marked another world, and in my choice
> Lovelier, and decked with light! On fairy ground
> Methought I buoyant trod, and heard the sound
> As of enchanting melodies, that stole,
> Stole gently, and entranced my captive soul.
> Then all was life and hope! 'Twas thy first ray,
> Sweet Fancy, on the heart. . . [.]

Warton reinforced and refined Bowles's youthful
enthusiasm for nature, emphasizing not only the
pleasures of the wild and the picturesque, but
also those beauties of nature which could be rendered particularly in the verse he encouraged his
young pupil to write. With Warton, he discovered Homer and Sophocles, "the lonely heights

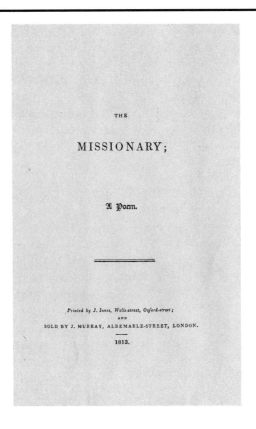

THE

MISSIONARY;

A Poem.

Printed by J. Innes, Wells-street, Oxford-street;
AND
SOLD BY J. MURRAY, ALBEMARLE-STREET, LONDON.

1813.

Preface.

SOUTH AMERICA has, of late, received additional importance, from the eventful circumstances of the present times.

Of all the countries in South America, the least known, but the most beautiful, picturesque, and interesting, is Chili:—beautiful, from the amenity of its climate, and the objects of its natural history—the humming-bird, the Llama, the Alpaca, &c.; picturesque, from its lakes, cataracts, and most magnificent elevation of the Andes; and interesting, from the bravery and character of its natives, whom the Spaniards, in their day of dominion, were never able to subdue,—and who remain free, to the present hour.

The following poem is founded upon a fact,

iv

recorded in all the historical accounts of that country, viz.—That at the battle of Arauco in Chili, the Spaniards, under Valdivia, were destroyed by the Indians, and the victory gained in consequence of the treachery of Valdivia's page, a native of Chili, who, in the most critical moment of the engagement, turned against his master, animated his countrymen, and became afterwards the most renowned leader of the Indians against the invaders of their country.—The same histories relate, that at this battle, Valdivia and an old priest, his confessor, who was present, were the only persons taken alive.

Garcilasso, from whom all other accounts are taken, briefly says — "The governor Pedro de "Valdivia, and *a priest that was with him*, they took "alive, and tied them to trees until they had "dispatched all the rest, that they might, in cool "blood, consider with what death they should "punish them."

Upon these incidents the following poem is founded.

Title page and preface for Bowles's most popular long poem

v

It may be unnecessary to add, that Ercilla, the Spanish poet, who was present at the scene he describes, has made the wars of Arauco the subject of a long and celebrated poem. The poem I have never seen; the analysis, since these lines were written, has been shown me in Hayley's Essay on History. It may be observed, that Ercilla has not confined himself to one action; that he has made no poetical use of the priest on whom this poem depends; and, above all, has imagined no incident to reconcile us to the apparent treachery of Lautaro, without which it appears to me impossible to sympathise with his character.

Ercilla has given him a mistress, and I have taken the liberty of giving him a father, a sister, a Spanish wife, and child; and I must, on this account, request the reader's indulgence for supposing him to be somewhat older than he is said to have been in all the historical accounts.

If we may imagine him to have been twenty, instead of sixteen years old, at the battle of Arauco, and to have been taken a prisoner when he was a

vi

boy of thirteen, all the rest is, I trust, reconcileable to the *vra-semblable* that is allowed to the province of poetry: the same apology must be used for abridging the time, and deviating in trifling instances from the exact line of history, for the sake of coherence and unity of disposition in the plan.

The whole action may be supposed to be comprised in two months, the time of Valdivia's march from Baldivia to the city of Conception, from which he proceeded immediately to the field of battle, in the vale of Arauco.

It may appear unnatural that Lautaro should have been in his native country without deserting from Valdivia,—and, above all, that he should have been present at the battle against his own countrymen: I have endeavoured to reconcile the mind to the last circumstances, by an imaginary incident, which at the same time tends to give an union to the story; for the other, I need only give the following passage from Garcilasso:—

" The Indians of Peru held this maxim or

vii

" principle, that if any yielded himself, or having " been taken by a Spaniard in war, he was thereby " become his absolute slave, and esteemed him by " whom he was taken, to be *his idol and his God;* " and that he ought to honour and revere him " as such; and to obey, serve, and be faithful to " him, unto the death; and not to deny him, " either for the sake of his country, parents, wife, " or children. Upon this preamble they preferred " the welfare of a Spaniard who was their master, " before all other considerations whatever."——— Book i. p. 487.

I have also had recourse to imagination to account for the priest being in battle, and for all the incidents of his history and character, on which the poem is founded.—For an illustration of the local imagery, and other characteristic circumstances of the country, I must refer generally to Molina, and all accounts of Chili. One word more—For fear I might be thought guilty of something like an anachronism, in making the Missionary, in the first book, speak of Tibet, the chief knowledge of which country may be considered as

viii

comparatively recent; I must request the reader to bear in mind that it was to the eastern parts of the globe the first missionaries were sent. So early as the thirteenth century Carpini was sent there, by the pope; and Rubruquis, by the king of France. Tibet was first mentioned by Rubruquis; and afterwards, more particularly by Marco Paulo, who visited it in 1272. The first edition of M. Paulo's Travels was published at Lisbon, and translated into Portuguese in 1502.

The Reader is requested to pay attention to the following Errata of the Press.

PAGE 5, LINE 4.
For Huge Andes' snows, all desolate, were spread,
Read Andes, thy wintry solitudes were spread.

PAGE 25, LINE 25.
For linger
Read lingers

PAGE 28, LINE 14.
For turns
Read turns

PAGE 33, LINE 8.
For clos'd again the emboss'd book.
Read clos'd again th' embossed book.

PAGE 46, LINE 5.
For " I came, with moving lips intent to pray; —
Read " I came — with moving lips intent to pray,

where Shakespeare sat sublime," Ossian's "wild song," and "Great Milton's solemn harmonies."

From Winchester, Bowles matriculated to Trinity College, Oxford, where he studied with Joseph Warton's brother, Thomas, professor of poetry and senior fellow, who later became poet laureate. Miltonist, historian of English poetry, and writer of sonnets and odes, Thomas Warton, like his brother, was influential in Bowles's development as a writer. Clearly the brothers shaped the receptive youth into an early romantic who was to become the direct link between them and the greater Romantic writers to follow.

At Oxford, Bowles won a prize for Latin verse. After receiving his A.B. in 1786, he attended the university intermittently for the next three years, eventually obtaining his A.M. in 1792. He did not, however, receive a hoped-for fellowship. Having taken orders, he was appointed to a curacy in southwest Wiltshire, the county in which he was to spend the rest of his life. Other ecclesiastical appointments followed, most notably in 1804 to the living in Bremhill, a Wiltshire hamlet between Chippenham and Calne. In 1804 he also became a prebendary of Salisbury cathedral and in 1828, canon residentiary. In the latter capacity one of his duties for the three months he spent in Salisbury each year allowed him to indulge his lifelong interest in church music. In 1845 ill health forced him to resign as vicar of Bremhill. He retired to Salisbury, where he died in 1850, shortly after the death of William Wordsworth, briefly outliving the last of his youthful admirers of sixty years before.

Some time between 1785 and 1788 Bowles became engaged to a young woman, only to have the relationship terminated by parents who were less than sanguine about the young man's prospects. To heal his broken heart Bowles set out on a tour which took him from the north of England and Scotland to Belgium, the Rhine, and eventually to Switzerland. His was the itinerary of the romantic wanderer who sought the picturesque in nature. Landscape provided occasions for "poetical meditations" which he did not write down at the time. After his return home, however, they found form, in 1789, as sonnets. As he explained, he took the fourteen he had recollected, perhaps in tranquillity but definitely in a state of financial need, to a printer in Bath who agreed, somewhat reluctantly, to print an anonymous edition of one hundred copies in quarto. A second, expanded edition of five hundred copies, the edition Coleridge read, was published in the

same year. By 1805 nine editions had been published. In addition to some short poems, which were topographical, descriptive, or elegiac in nature, they included as well those sonnets he had composed as consolation after experiencing the sudden death of his fiancée, Harriet Wake, in 1793. (In 1797 he married her older sister Magdalen.) In the preface to the ninth edition (1805) Bowles wrote that the sonnets, in describing the poet's "personal feelings . . . can be considered as exhibiting occasional reflections which naturally arose in his mind . . ." as he encountered scenes in nature, "and wherever such scenes appeared to harmonize with his disposition at the moment, the sentiments were involuntarily prompted." Years later, in an introduction to some of these poems in the 1837 edition of *Scenes and Shadows of Days Departed*, he explained his use of the sonnet form: "I confined myself to fourteen lines, because fourteen lines seemed best adapted to unity of sentiment. I thought nothing about the strict Italian model; the verses naturally flowed in unpremeditated harmony, as my ear directed. . . . The subjects were chiefly from river scenery. . . ." Perhaps to emphasize the importance of place and time, the second, expanded edition was retitled *Sonnets, Written Chiefly on Picturesque Spots*, with the individual titles indicating these "spots of time": "To the River Tweed," "On Dover Cliffs. July 20, 1787." Thus, Bowles's general remarks on composition, content, and form suggest the descriptive / meditative pattern which is evident in the sonnets. "The typical single poem," writes M. H. Abrams, "Begins with a rapid sketch of the external scene . . . then moves on to reminiscence and moral reflection."

It was the association, however incomplete and formulaic it now seems, of natural objects and the emotions inspired by them that made Bowles's sonnets exciting reading for Coleridge. Bowles's "To the River Itchin" expressed a poetic sensibility Coleridge recognized as his own in the way a lyric speaker could link feelings of loss with a place associated with the speaker's past. In his own "To the River Otter" (1796), a superior sonnet frankly written in imitation of Bowles's "To the River Itchin," Coleridge too could associate details of place and private feeling. Yet Coleridge and the other major Romantic poets went beyond Bowles's limited use of landscape or scene and his meditative tone of bittersweet melancholia. For all of their superficial similarity with great meditative lyrics such as Wordsworth's "Tintern Abbey" and Coleridge's "Frost at Midnight," Bowles's poems of place have more in common with the landscape poetry of the eighteenth century, especially in their imagery, diction, and syntax. Yet, for a brief time in the 1790s, Bowles seemed the first poet of a new age. Sixty years later the ever sympathetic George Gilfillan could make that very claim. In retrospect we see that Bowles was able only to suggest a new poetic idiom which he himself was incapable of fully achieving.

Between 1789 and 1809 Bowles published scores of shorter poems in addition to sonnets. In poems such as *Monody, Written at Matlock* (1791), *Coombe Ellen* (1798), and *St. Michael's Mount* (1798) natural scenes and places are invoked, but in these poems verbal scene painting and evocation of the picturesque have given way to didacticism. Forced sublimity in the form of Miltonisms and other eighteenth-century stylistic excesses has replaced the simpler, more natural style of the early sonnets. Effective passages, reminiscent of the descriptive / meditative style of the best of the sonnets, are lost in a torrent of wordiness.

More than half of the two-volume Gilfillan edition of Bowles's poetry (1855) is devoted to five long poems: *The Spirit of Discovery* (1804), *The Missionary* (1813), *The Grave of The Last Saxon* (1822), *Days Departed, Or, Banwell Hill* (1828), and *St. John in Patmos* (1832).

In *The Spirit of Discovery* Bowles expanded his earlier "The Spirit of Navigation" into a poem of epic pretensions. Its Miltonic beginning, with its personal invocation and self-consciously elevated style–"Awake a louder and a loftier strain!"–announces the poet's desire for "loftier utterance" from his "beloved harp." Until now "I only asked / Some stealing melodies the heart might love, / And a brief sonnet to beguile my tears!"

For his pains, and for his unself-conscious parody of Milton, Bowles set himself up for Byron's ridicule in *English Bards and Scotch Reviewers* (1809):

Now to soft themes thou scornest to confine
The lofty numbers of a harp like thine:
'Awake a louder and a loftier strain,'
Such as none heard before, or will again;
Where all discoveries jumbled from the flood,
Since first the leaky ark repos'd in mud,
By more or less, are sung in every book,
from Captain NOAH down to Captain COOK.

Indeed, in five books and more than two thousand lines of blank verse *The Spirit of Discovery* sings and moralizes the history of great discoverers from Noah to Captain Cook.

The Missionary, first published anonymously, narrates in eight cantos and two thousand lines of heroic couplets the story of Lautaro, a Chilean Indian who was taken from his family in childhood to become the page of Valdivia, commander of the Spanish armies. Lautaro is forced to accompany the Spaniards in a military campaign against his own people, but at a critical point he turns against the Spaniards and brings about their defeat. The story also includes a humane missionary, Anselmo, and some Chilean Indians. With its exotic characters and Andean setting, as well as its sentimental heroics and moralizing, *The Missionary* was the most popular of Bowles's longer works.

In *The Grave of the Last Saxon*, a poem of two thousand lines of blank verse, the scene is England at the time of the Norman Conquest. In this poem Bowles combines his historical and antiquarian interests with his usual didacticism and heroic melodrama to produce yet another pastiche. Bowles surely had in mind Sir Walter Scott's success with verse romance when he wrote this poem. *Days Departed, Or, Banwell Hill*, on the other hand, in two thousand blank-verse lines and five parts, is a "local poem." But its evocation of place, Banwell Cave and its antediluvian remains, while it reveals once again the author's antiquarian interests, occupies only a portion of the poem. Reflections on the ruins of time blend with childhood reminiscences of rural Somerset and thoughts about those who die at sea. The rest of the poem contains "reflections on the moral and religious state of parishes, past and present"; a canto of narrative about unrequited love, previously published as *Ellen Gray* (1823); a *Prelude*-like section with passages about his youth near Bristol and the Severn Sea; and finally, visions of the deluge followed by a poetic farewell to "Banwell Cave, and Banwell Hill, / And Banwell Church . . . ," all concluding on a note of prayer and thanksgiving.

In the preface to his last long poem, *St. John in Patmos*, first published anonymously as the work of "One of the Old Living Poets of Great Britain," Bowles declares that "It is a consolation that, from youth to age, I have found no line I wished to blot, or departed a moment from the severer taste which I imbibed from the simplest and purest models of classical composition."

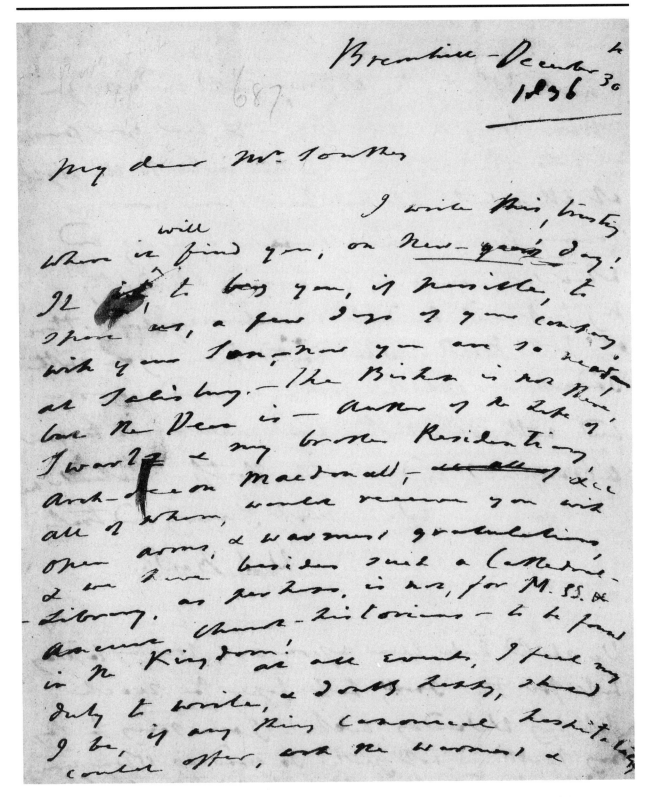

Letter from Bowles to Robert Southey, who had recently visited Bowles at Bremhill (HM 11484; by permission of the Henry E. Huntington Library and Art Gallery)

most expect. —

most affectionate esteem, could induce you —
now *longa e est via* — to bend your course
— into the North — a few miles to the right!
at all events let me hear from you
(Conway House) and wherever you go, and
wherever you are, be assured, that both
my best and kindest remembrances with those
of Mrs. Bowles who parted from you with
sorrow, — will be with you and yours —
and with affectionate kind remembrance to your
accomplished and amiable North — believe me,
ever — most sincerely and truly
W L Bowles

We should have been upon our journey to day
but for the rain, but hope to reach
Salisbury Wednesday next. — I am sorry to say
my health is not quite so good as when you
were here — but this at my time of life I

Once again the indefatigable man of letters undertook a major project in blank verse extending to more than twenty-one hundred lines. In this work about the revelations of Saint John the Divine, the picturesque landscape of rural England of the previous long poem "is replaced," as George S. Fayen, Jr., has noted, "by the apostle's lonely cave and his vision: the seven candlesticks and the churches of Asia. Contrasting stanza forms, presumably used for variety, dramatize and distinguish the appeal of angelic harmonies and the enticements of earthly love."

All of Bowles's long poems, Gilfillan conceded, are "more distinguished by the ambition of their themes than by the success of their treatment." Coleridge, in a letter of 1802, commented on the growing didacticism in Bowles's verse even before the publication of the first of the five long poems and observed that "There reigns through all the blank verse poems such a trick of moralizing everything, which is very well, occasionally, but never to see or describe any interesting appearance in nature without connecting it, by dim analogies, with the moral world proves faintness of impression." In 1814 Bowles's publisher, John Murray, tactfully suggested that if the poet could condense the "beauties" of *The Missionary* "into two thirds its present size, I do think I could sell thousands, and it is a great pleasure to be universally read." Bowles seems not to have gotten the message.

Bowles published his ten-volume edition of Pope's works in 1806. His criticism of Pope's moral and poetical character revived the reaction against Pope which had begun in the previous century, most notably through Bowles's Winchester master, Joseph Warton. Bowles was a mediocre editor. Thomas Moore noted in his journal in 1819: "Was struck by the characteristic weakness and maudlin wordiness of his notes, contrasted as they are with the original remarks and rich erudition of [Joseph] Warton's, that accompany them. . . ." Byron first attacked Bowles for his devaluing of Pope in *English Bards and Scotch Reviewers*. Thomas Campbell defended Pope's character in *Specimens of the British Poets* (1819), to which Bowles replied with his *Invariable Principles of Poetry* (1819). When a long article in the *Quarterly Review* (July 1820) ridiculed Bowles's principles, he promptly answered his critics in two pamphlets. Byron reentered the fray in 1821 with two letters which were immediately followed by two more from Bowles. More articles and pamphlets appeared, and whatever the issues might have been

at the beginning, they were lost in the sound and fury. In the pamphlet war, as in his long poems, Bowles was verbose and pretentious, ever confident in his purpose and culpable for never blotting a line.

In a preface to *The Little Villager's Verse Book* (third edition, 1826) Bowles wrote, "The following compositions were written originally to be learned by heart by the poor children of my own parish, who had been instructed every Sunday through the summer, on the garden lawn before the parsonage house, by Mrs. Bowles." The marchioness of Lansdowne, wife of Bowles's local patron and friend, wrote to Mrs. Bowles, "We are quite delighted with the *Little Hymn Book*. The simplicity and beauty of the compositions quite charm us, and I am sure they will be very popular amongst our children. It is quite admirable of Mr. Bowles to lower his Muse in so kind a manner to adapt it to such early readers." Indeed, in composing such simple, unpretentious verses as "The Withered Leaf " Bowles may well have used his "harp" more memorably than at any other time in his long poetic career:

Oh! mark the withered leaves that fall
  In silence to the ground;
Upon the human heart they call,
  And preach without a sound.

They say, So passes man's brief year!
  To-day, his green leaves wave;
To-morrow, changed by time and sere,
  He drops into the grave.

Let Wisdom be our sole concern,
  Since life's green days are brief !
And faith and heavenly hope shall learn
  A lesson from the LEAF.

Letters:

A Wiltshire Parson and His Friends: The Correspondence of William Lisle Bowles, edited by Garland Greever (London: Constable, 1926; Boston: Houghton Mifflin, 1926).

Bibliography:

Cecil Woolf, "Some Uncollected Authors XVII: William Lisle Bowles," *Book Collector*, 7 (Autumn 1958): 286-294; (Winter 1958): 407-416;

Geoffrey Little and Elizabeth Hall, "Cecil Woolf 'William Lisle Bowles': Additions to Check-List," *Book Collector*, 26 (Summer 1977): 262-263.

Portrait by Daniel Maclise in the Fraser's Magazine *"Gallery of Illustrious Literary Characters" (1830-1838)*

Biography:

"Memoir of the Rev. Wm. Lisle Bowles," *New Monthly Magazine,* 82 (November 1820): 480-484.

References:

M. H. Abrams, "Structure and Style in the Greater Romantic Lyric," in *From Sensibility to Romanticism: Essays Presented to Frederick A. Pottle,* edited by Frederick W. Hilles and Harold Bloom (New York: Oxford University Press, 1965), pp. 527-557;

"Anecdotes, Observations, and Character of Books and Men," *Quarterly Review,* 23 (July 1820): 400-434;

T. E. Casson, "William Lisle Bowles," in *Eighteenth Century Literature: An Oxford Miscellany* (Oxford: Clarendon Press, 1909), pp. 151-183;

Oswald Doughty, "Coleridge and a Poets' Poet: William Lisle Bowles," *English Miscellany,* 14 (1963): 95-114;

A. Harris Fairbanks, " 'Dear Native Brook': Coleridge, Bowles, and Thomas Warton, the Younger," *Wordsworth Circle,* 6 (Autumn 1975): 313-315;

George S. Fayen, Jr., "The Pencil and the Harp of William Lisle Bowles," *Modern Language Quarterly,* 21 (December 1960): 301-314;

Rudolf Kaiser, "Vier Sonette (Thomas Warton 'To the River Lodon'; W. L. Bowles 'To the River Itchin'; S. T. Coleridge 'To the River Otter'; W. Wordsworth 'To the River Dudden')," *Die Neueren Sprachen,* new series 6 (1963): 252-262;

Alfred L. Kellogg, "William Lisle Bowles: The 'Sonnets' and Criticism of Pope," Ph.D. dissertation, Yale University, 1941;

J. J. van Rennes, *Bowles, Byron and the Pope-Controversy* (Amsterdam: H. J. Paris, 1927);

A. J. A. Waldock, "William Lisle Bowles," in his *James, Joyce, And Others* (London: Williams & Norgate, 1937), pp. 79-103;

Lucyle Werkmeister, "Coleridge, Bowles, and 'Feelings of the Heart,'" *Anglia,* 78 (1960): 55-73;

W. K. Wimsatt, Jr., "The Structure of Romantic Nature Imagery," in his *The Verbal Icon* (Lexington: University of Kentucky Press, 1954): pp. 103-116.

Papers:

In Great Britain letters are to be found in the Bodleian Library at Oxford, the British Library, and the library of the University of Edinburgh. The University of Michigan Library has a collection of letters from the marquis of Lansdowne and Lady Lansdowne to Bowles and his wife, Magdalen. Rutgers University Library has letters Bowles wrote to Harriet Wake and to Magdalen Wake Bowles. Letters are also held by the libraries of Harvard and Yale and by the Huntington Library.

Thomas Campbell

(27 July 1777 - 15 June 1844)

Mary Ruth Miller
North Georgia College

BOOKS: *The Wounded Hussar* (Glasgow, 1799);

The Pleasures of Hope; with other Poems (Edinburgh: Printed for Mundell & Son and for Longman & Rees and J. Wright, London, 1799; New York: Printed by John Furman for Jones Bull, 1800);

Poems (Edinburgh: Printed by James Ballantyne, 1803);

Annals of Great Britain from the Ascension of George III to the Peace of Amiens, 3 volumes (Edinburgh: Printed for Mundell, Doig & Stevenson, Constable, and J. Fairbairn, Edinburgh; J. & A. Duncan, Glasgow; and T. Ostell, London, 1807);

Gertrude of Wyoming, a Pennsylvanian Tale; and other Poems (London: Printed by T. Bensley & published for the author by Longman, Hurst, Rees & Orme, 1809; New York: Printed & published by D. Longworth, 1809);

Specimens of the British Poets; with Biographical and Critical Notices, and an Essay on English Poetry, 7 volumes (London: John Murray, 1819);

Miscellaneous Poems (London: W. Dugdale, 1824);

Theodric, a Domestic Tale; and other Poems (London: Longman, Hurst, Rees, Orme, Brown & Green, 1824; Philadelphia: H. C. Carey & I. Lea, 1825);

Inaugural Discourse of Thomas Campbell, Esq. on Being Installed Lord Rector of the University of Glasgow, Thursday April 12th, 1827 (Glasgow: John Smith & Son; Bell and Bradfute, Edinburgh; and Henry Colburn, London, 1827);

Letters on the History of Literature, Addressed to the Students at the University of Glasgow (Glasgow: Distributed by J. Smith, 1829);

Address of the Literary Polish Association to the People of Great Britain to which is added a Letter from Samuel T. Howe, Esq. of the United States, to Thomas Campbell, Esq. (London: George Eccles, 1832);

Life of Mrs. Siddons (2 volumes, London: Wilson, 1834; 1 volume, New York: Harper, 1834);

Letters from the South, 2 volumes (London: Colburn, 1837); republished as *The Journal of a Residence in Algiers*, 2 volumes (London: Colburn, 1842);

Life of Petrarch (2 volumes, London: Colburn, 1841; 1 volume, Philadelphia: Carey & Hart, 1841);

The Pilgrim of Glencoe, and other Poems (London: Moxon, 1842).

Collections: *The Poetical Works of Thomas Campbell. Including several pieces from the original manuscript, never before published in this country. To which is prefixed a biographical sketch of the author, by a gentleman of New-York* [Washington Irving] (Baltimore: Printed by Fry & Kammerer for Philip H. Nicklin & Co., also for D. W. Farrand & Green, Albany; D. Mallory & Co., Boston; Lyman & Hall, Portland; and E. Earle, Philadelphia, 1810);

The Poetical Works of Thomas Campbell, edited by W. Alfred Hill (London: Edward Moxon, 1851; Boston: Little, Brown, 1854); republished, with a biographical sketch, by William Allingham, Aldine Edition (London: G. Bell & Sons, 1875);

The Complete Poetical Works of Thomas Campbell, Oxford Edition, edited by J. Logie Robertson (London & New York: Henry Frowde for Oxford University Press, 1907).

OTHER: *New Monthly Magazine and Literary Journal*, edited by Campbell, 1821-1830;

Metropolitan: A Monthly Journal of Literature, Science, and the Fine Arts, edited by Campbell, 1831-1832;

The Scenic Annual, for 1838, edited by Campbell (London: Virtue, 1838);

The Dramatic Works of William Shakspeare, with remarks on his life and writings, edited, with remarks, by Campbell (London: Routledge, 1838);

Frederick the Great, His Court and Times, 2 volumes, edited, with an introduction, by Campbell (London: Colburn, 1842-1843);

History of Our Own Times, 2 volumes, edited by Campbell (London: Colburn, 1843, 1845).

PERIODICAL PUBLICATIONS–UNCOLLECTED:
"Lectures on Poetry, the Substance of Which Was Delivered at the Royal Institution," *New Monthly Magazine,* new series 1-17 (January 1821-November 1826);

"Proposal on a Metropolitan University in a Letter to Henry Brougham, Esq.," *Times* (London), 9 February 1825;

"Suggestions Respecting the Plan of an University in London," *New Monthly Magazine,* new series 13, no. 52 (1825): 404-419; part 2, "Suggestions Respecting Plan of a College in London," 14, no. 55 (1825): 1-11.

Thomas Campbell was an important transitional figure. Although he lived and wrote during the height of the Romantic period, he preferred the classical poetry of the eighteenth century. Yet like many other writers and thinkers of his day, he was caught up in the enthusiasm for expanded freedom generated by the American Revolution and the early days of the French Revolution. His major work, "The Pleasures of Hope," embodies the humanitarian idealism he shared with the great Romantics. Today he is remembered as a poet of freedom, patriotism, and social concern, and for his influence on many contemporaries and successors.

The youngest of the eleven children of Alexander and Margaret Campbell, Thomas Campbell was a native of Glasgow, Scotland. He received a traditional literary education at Glasgow University, where he enrolled in autumn 1791 at the age of fourteen. He attended five six-month sessions, leaving in May 1796. The next year he

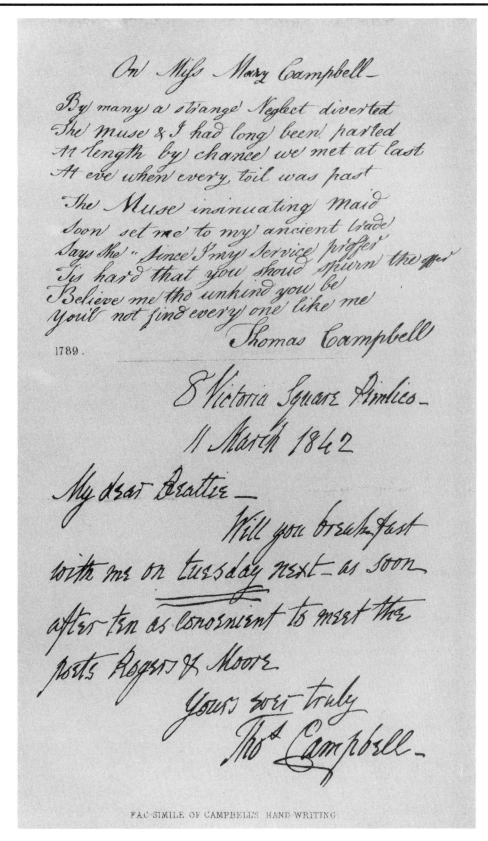

On Miss Mary Campbell—

By many a strange Neglect diverted
The Muse & I had long been parted
At length by chance we met at last
At eve when every toil was past

The Muse insinuating Maid
Soon set me to my ancient trade
Says she "Since I my Service proffer
Tis hard that you should spurn the offer
Believe me tho unkind you be
You'll not find every one like me

Thomas Campbell

1789.

8 Victoria Square Pimlico—
11 March 1842

My dear Beattie—
                 Will you breakfast
with me on tuesday next—as soon
after ten as convenient to meet the
poets Rogers & Moore

                 Yours very truly
                 Thos Campbell—

FAC-SIMILE OF CAMPBELL'S HAND-WRITING

Lines from a poem the twelve-year-old Campbell addressed to his sister and a letter the adult poet wrote to his biographer William Beattie (frontispiece to volume 2 of Beattie's Life and Letters of Thomas Campbell, *1849)* moved to Edinburgh to find work as a tutor and compiler of books for the booksellers. There he wrote most of "The Pleasures of Hope." When *The Pleasures of Hope; with other Poems* appeared in April 1799, three years after the death of Robert Burns, Campbell was hailed by the Scots as the "bard of hope, liberty, independence, patriotism!," according to his biographer William Beattie.

"The Pleasures of Hope," 1,078 lines of heroic couplets, presents a series of didactic vignettes and abstractions on the theme of hope: part 1 on the temporal or human level and part 2 on the eternal or divine. Both parts stress the importance of anticipation as they discourse on love, imagination, and amelioration: " 'Tis distance lends enchantment to the view." Hope, personified as a female guardian deity, aids, inspires, and consoles: "The light of Hope" must abide, despite the realization that one's "winged hours of bliss have been, / Like angel-visits, few and far between."

In part 1 people benefiting from Hope include a ship's pilot, a military man, a youth seeking fame, poverty-stricken parents and children, a prisoner, a maniac, and a wanderer. Social issues of the day are addressed, including the civilization of the American Indians and the tribes of Africa, freedom for Poland, an end to the slave trade, and cessation of the British exploitation of India: "Come, bright Improvement! on the car of Time, / And rule the spacious world from clime to clime."

Part 2 is concerned with the alliance of Hope and Imagination, expressing a belief in the eternity of Hope beyond "Nature's funeral pile." It contains an episode in which a convicted criminal, Conrad, about to be transported to Australia, bids farewell to his daughter Ellenore, promising her that they will be reunited "beyond the realms of Nature and Time."

That Campbell caught the sentiments of liberal thinkers of his day is reflected in the early reviews of "The Pleasures of Hope." The *Analytical Review* (June 1799) praised it with reservations, judging that only "a small portion of it can be allowed to be descriptive of the *pleasures of hope*. The second part, which we think inferior to the first, describes rather the pleasures of *sympathy*." The July 1799 issue of the *British Critic*, a Tory and High Church journal unsympathetic to Campbell's Whiggism, criticized his libertarian principles as ones to be corrected by maturity while at the same time praising his genius. This re-

viewer also disliked part 2, terming it "an afterthought" and urging the poet to practice self-criticism. He pointed out faults which subsequent critics have also noticed: lack of clarity, obscure allusions, inadequate transitions, weak expressions, and verses which do not clearly relate to the subject. In August the *Monthly Review* criticized Campbell's arrangement of episodes without clear transitions and the poem's lack of a story. The reviewer, Alexander Hamilton, a conservative professor and scholar of Sanskrit, termed its "characteristic style" to be "*the pathetic*" and lamented that Campbell had not included the excesses of the French Revolution among the social ills of the day. Unlike other reviewers he praised the "sublimity" of part 2 and judged the poem "entitled to rank among the productions of our superior Bards of the present day."

Other writers also differed in their assessments of "The Pleasures of Hope." Samuel Rogers, whose *The Pleasures of Memory* (1792) had helped inspire Campbell, said it was "no great favorite" of his. He reported William Wordsworth's feeling that it was "strangely overrated." Samuel Taylor Coleridge criticized it for its lack of a "fixed design." William Hazlitt termed it "too artificial and antithetical," and Leigh Hunt found faults with the prosody. Walter Scott preferred the shorter poems, but George Gordon, Lord Byron, in his *English Bards and Scotch Reviewers* (1809), termed "The Pleasures of Hope" one of "the most beautiful didactic poems in our language."

The popularity of "The Pleasures of Hope" is evident in the fact that a ninth edition appeared in 1806. Its early success enabled Campbell in 1800 to go to Germany, an important cultural center. His travel plans were altered by the Napoleonic Wars, but the excitement of military events, together with a battle he actually witnessed at Ratisbon, inspired several of his best-known poems, including "Ye Mariners of England," "The Battle of the Baltic," and "Hohenlinden."

These war songs epitomize the spirit of Campbell's age, expressing nationalism, patriotism, love for the sea, and belief in the importance of British sea power. "Ye Mariners of England: a Naval Ode" is a rhetorical salute in four stanzas to the British navy and its proud tradition. Thomas Carlyle, Walter Scott, and Washington Irving were among its admirers. An alteration of the old ballad "Ye Gentlemen of

England," it was first published in the *Morning Chronicle* of London in 1801.

"The Battle of the Baltic" is an ode in eight stanzas celebrating Admiral Horatio Nelson's victory on 2 April 1801 at the Battle of Copenhagen, which Campbell almost witnessed. (He saw the preparations from shipboard as he fled the hostilities.) The original version, written in winter 1804-1805 and entitled "The Battle of Copenhagen," was twenty-seven stanzas but was shortened at the suggestion of Scott and other friends. After newspaper publication, it was included in *Gertrude of Wyoming, a Pennsylvanian Tale; and other Poems* (1809). "The Battle of the Baltic" recounts the preparations, the battle itself, and the victory celebration, ending with a memorial to dead heroes. Its appropriate sound effects and oratorical lyricism contributed to its success. Like "Ye Mariners of England," it has been set to music; one version is by Gerard Manley Hopkins, who liked Campbell's handling of rhythm. The poem also influenced the work of Alfred Tennyson and Robert Browning.

"Hohenlinden" gives a generalized picture of a land battle between the French and the Austrians at Hohenlinden in Bavaria on 3 December 1800. The visual and auditory imagery in its eight stanzas captures the excitement of warfare but also emphasizes its human cost—an ambivalence which creates a powerful tension. "Hohenlinden," published anonymously with "Lochiel's Warning" in *Poems* (1803) and later in *Gertrude of Wyoming . . . and other Poems*, was well liked and widely praised. Scott claimed credit for encouraging Campbell to publish it.

Two years after his return from Germany, Campbell married Matilda Sinclair, his second cousin, on 10 October 1803. They settled permanently in London, where he made a living writing, lecturing, editing, and publishing editions of his poems. They had two sons: Thomas Telford (born in 1804) and Alison (born in 1805). In 1805 Campbell was awarded a lifetime royal pension of two hundred pounds a year, and later he received several legacies.

Campbell's own favorite of his long poems, "Gertrude of Wyoming, or, The Pennsylvanian Cottage," appeared in 1809. A tragic love story, it is set in an idealized version of the Wyoming valley of the Susquehanna River in eastern Pennsylvania before and at the time of the American Revolution, with which the poem expresses sympathy. Its theme is freedom violated by evil. The eighty-seven Spenserian stanzas tell Gertrude's life

story, including her marriage to the poem's romantic hero, their friendship with a noble savage, and Gertrude's death in the hero's arms when the forces of a villainous Indian attack the white settlers. Sentiment, pathos, and hope for immortality are the prevailing emotions.

Contemporary reviewers included Scott, writing for the Tory *Quarterly Review* (May 1809). He called the poem less than "honourable to our national character" for dealing with atrocities committed by Britain's Indian allies during the Revolution. The story line he thought difficult to follow, with improbabilities and unexplained motivations. Yet despite these and other faults, he was complimentary to his friend Campbell. Francis Jeffrey in the *Edinburgh Review* (April 1809) liked the story's exquisite pathos but criticized missing links, faults in diction, and overrefinement. The *Scots Magazine*, the *Monthly Review*, the *London Review*, the *Antijacobin Review*, and the *British Critic* were likewise mixed in their reactions. William Hazlitt and Leigh Hunt liked the poem even with its faults, such as excessive antithesis and possible borrowing from Wordsworth's "Ruth." Hazlitt stated in *The Spirit of the Age* (1825) that Campbell had "succeeded in engrafting the wild and more expansive interest of the romantic school of poetry on classic elegance and precision."

The public enjoyed the first well-known English poem set in North America with Indians as characters. Three British editions and an American one sold out in two years. In the United States "Gertrude of Wyoming" was also popular; Washington Irving and Oliver Wendell Holmes both expressed their appreciation for it; school children memorized it. Today, however, "Gertrude of Wyoming" is out of print and no longer anthologized.

One of Campbell's short poems, "The Last Man," is popular today because of its eschatological theme. That last surviving human heroically defies the "darkening universe." One of several literary works on a subject current in 1823, when Campbell published it in the *New Monthly Magazine,* which he edited from 1820 until 1830, "The Last Man" follows logically the conclusion of "The Pleasures of Hope," where Hope survives "Nature's funeral pile." Campbell had discussed the subject with Lord Byron many years earlier, and when he saw Byron's "Darkness" (1816) he realized that their conversation might have helped to inspire Byron's poem.

Fifteen years after "Gertrude," in 1824, Campbell's next long poem, "Theodric," ap-

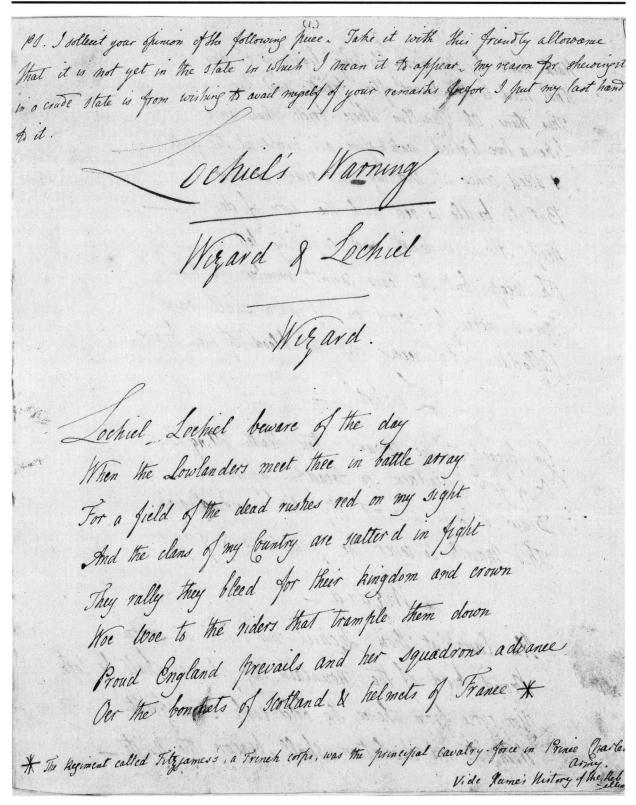

Pages from a draft for "Lochiel's Warning" sent to Dr. James Currie (HM 31476; by permission of the Henry E. Huntington Library and Art Gallery). On 4 September 1802 Campbell thanked Currie for having pointed out errors in the poem and added, "Pray do not let 'Lochiel' be seen in his present state. . . ."

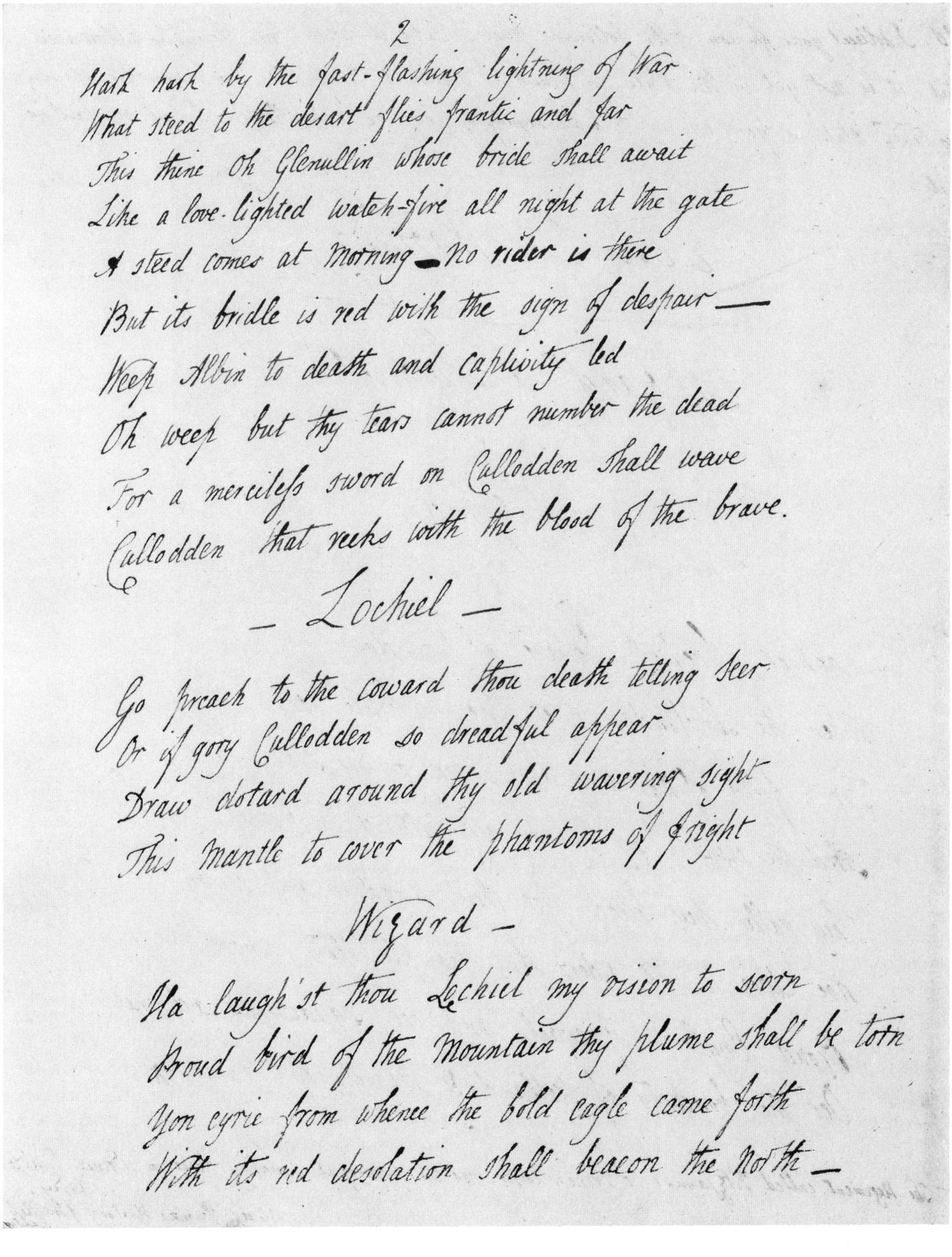

2

Hark hark by the fast-flashing lightning of War
What steed to the desart flies frantic and far
Tis thine Oh Glenullin whose bride shall await
Like a love-lighted watch-fire all night at the gate
A steed comes at morning—No rider is there
But its bridle is red with the sign of despair—
Weep Albin to death and captivity led
Oh weep but thy tears cannot number the dead
For a merciless sword on Cullodden shall wave
Cullodden that reeks with the blood of the brave.

— Lochiel —

Go preach to the coward thou death telling seer
Or if gory Cullodden so dreadful appear
Draw dotard around thy old wavering sight
This mantle to cover the phantoms of fright

Wizard —

Ha laugh'st thou Lochiel my vision to scorn
Proud bird of the mountain thy plume shall be torn
Yon eyrie from whence the bold eagle came forth
With its red desolation shall beacon the North—

Thomas Campbell (engraving by H. Robinson, based on a portrait by Sir Thomas Lawrence)

peared. Another domestic love tragedy, the poem comprises 577 lines in heroic couplets (and one triplet); it is set in Switzerland and England. Theodric is an Austrian colonel beloved by two ladies, one Swiss and one English, epitomes of the angelic woman much admired at the time. Both die in the poem, their deaths inadvertently caused by the triangle with Theodric. Young love, idealism, honor, loyalty, chance, self-blame, premonitions, and broken hearts combine with a healthy dose of sentiment to make up the story. The obscurity of Campbell's narration may be due in part to hidden allusions to personal sorrows—the death of one son, Alison, from scarlet fever in 1810; the mental illness of the other, Thomas, which had become apparent by 1821;

and the failing health of his wife, who died on 9 May 1828.

Campbell's friend Jeffrey reviewed "Theodric" in the *Edinburgh Review* for January 1825. Hard put to compliment his friend and fellow Whig's work, Jeffrey admired its "chastened elegance of words and images," but criticized its "poverty of invention," its abruptness, and its lack of clarity and motivation—Campbell's old problems. *Blackwood's Edinburgh Magazine* (April 1825), Tory rival of the *Edinburgh Review*, chided Jeffrey for his efforts to praise "a weak, silly, puerile, ineffective, unimaginative, unreadable screed of trash." Other reviewers, less virulent, were generally disappointed with what they considered a failure, a work unworthy of Campbell.

Yours truly,

T. Campbell

THE EDITOR OF THE NEW MONTHLY

Portrait by Daniel Maclise in the Fraser's Magazine *"Gallery of Illustrious Literary Characters" (1830-1838)*

"The Pilgrim of Glencoe," the last of his long poems, was published in 1842, two years before Campbell's death. Set in the Western Highlands of Scotland, the poem tells of the reconciliation of a Campbell and a Macdonald, archenemies after the massacre of the Macdonalds by the Campbells, who were allied with the English troops at Glencoe in February 1692. During the time span of the poem the battle of Culloden (16 April 1746) takes place, but the poem does not describe it. In the sentimental story, in which Campbell partly expiates the crimes of his anti-Jacobite forefathers, he reuses earlier themes and subjects—Scottish history, heroic warriors, a visitor, exemplary womanhood, death, and a democratic philosophy. Campbell could undoubtedly identify with

the two old men he created for the poem.

Most of the critics of the day ignored the poem. The *Spectator* (5 March 1842) admitted "The Pilgrim of Glencoe" contained some of "the higher qualities of art," but found it deficient "in subject and matter." Scenes and characters are well sketched, however, especially old Norman, the Highlander. The *Literary Gazette* (5 March 1842) observed "some sparkles of Campbell" but was "forcibly impressed with the image of the flickering of expiring flame." The *Eclectic Review* (June 1842) pointed out that Campbell is "preeminently a lyrical poet" rather than a narrative one, but "The Pilgrim of Glencoe" is a story "worthy of poetry, as being connected with traits of national manners which are fading away into tradition."

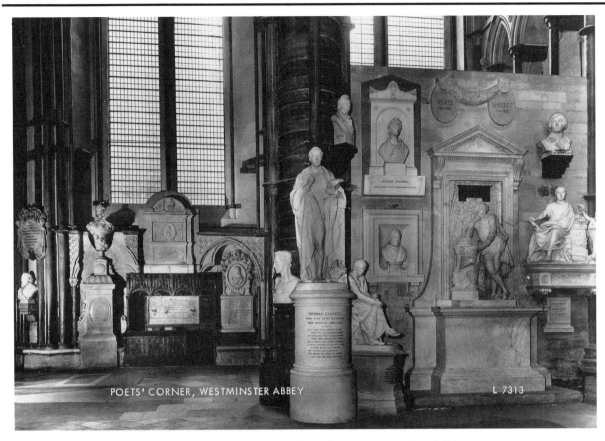

Postcard of Poets' Corner, Westminster Abbey. The monument to Campbell is at center.

Besides battle songs, Campbell also wrote many other short poems, including historical and legendary poems, most of them set in Scotland. Depending upon one's taste, many of them are appealing and strike chords of empathy.

As long as he lived Campbell managed his finances badly and had to write for booksellers and periodicals to meet his needs, but his prose writing gave him little pleasure. To him it was drudgery, much of it anonymous hackwork. His prose works include the *Annals of Great Britain* (1807), a historical work; *Specimens of the British Poets* (1819), short biographies and selections from poets' works, with an opening "Essay on English Poetry"; *Life of Mrs. Siddons* (1834), a biography of the great actress Sarah Siddons; *Letters from the South* (1837), a travelogue of his visit to Algeria in the winter of 1834-1835; and *Life of Petrarch* (1841), which grew out of his attempt to edit an earlier biography by Archdeacon Coxe. In addition he edited the *Scenic Annual, for 1838,* an edition of *The Dramatic Works of William Shakspeare* (1838), *Frederick the Great, His Court and Times* (1842, 1843), and *History of Our Own Times*

(1843, 1845). His lectures on poetry appeared in the *New Monthly Magazine* (January 1821-November 1826), and the same magazine published his "Letters to the Students of Glasgow" (July 1827-August 1828), written while he served as Lord Rector of Glasgow University (November 1826-1829).

In 1843, beset by financial and other worries and the debilities of his old age, Campbell moved from London to Boulogne, France, taking his niece Mary Campbell with him as housekeeper. He continued trying to write, working on a volume of ancient geography, but his health gradually weakened. His medical adviser, executor, and later biographer, Dr. William Beattie, with others, crossed the Channel to be with him at the time of his death, 15 June 1844. At a large funeral on 3 July he was interred in the Poets' Corner of Westminster Abbey.

In his work habits Campbell was dilatory, and in his standards he was a perfectionist—a combination which limited his output and took away much of the spontaneity from his poems. Part of the controversy about his work during his own day stemmed from politics. He made no effort to hide his strong Whig partisanship, which provoked responses from the opposition. His health problems, which included venereal disease, depression, and alcoholism, combined with his limitations in time and talent to disappoint his readers' expectations of him. Still, other better-known poets have felt his influence: Crabbe, Byron, Shelley, Tennyson, Robert Browning, Elizabeth Barrett Browning, Peacock, Hopkins, Swinburne, Carlyle, Emerson, and Whittier.

In addition to his writing, Campbell is remembered for his philanthropy, notably for his role, beginning in 1825, as one of the leading instigators and founders of London University as an institution for higher education with religious toleration. In 1834 the Polish people honored him as the "Poet of Freedom" for his efforts in their behalf. Numerous other causes also made claims on his purse, pen, and tongue.

Today Thomas Campbell is regarded as a minor poet and humanitarian, popular in his own day but largely unread now. True to his classical heritage, he spoke as a social voice. Much of his poetry is didactic, rhetorical, or sentimental—qualities no longer admired. Yet his poems about individual yearning and striving, rebellion against tyranny, the past, the common man, children, exiles, and the wild in nature characterize him as a Romantic. The Romantic quest and the heroic ideal are themes he used many times. Even though his flaws are numerous, he is remembered for his poetry of human dignity and hope.

Letters:

Life and Letters of Thomas Campbell, edited by William Beattie, 3 volumes (London: Moxon, 1849; New York: Harper, 1850).

Biographies:

Cyrus Redding, *Fifty Years' Recollections, Literary and Personal, with Observations on Men and Things,* 3 volumes (London: Skeet, 1858);

Redding, *Literary Reminiscences and Memoirs of Thomas Campbell,* 2 volumes (London: Skeet, 1860);

J. Cuthbert Hadden, *Thomas Campbell,* Famous Scots Series (Edinburgh: Oliphant Anderson, 1899).

References:

H. Hale Bellot, *University College London, 1826-1926* (London: University of London Press, 1929);

Edmund Blunden, "Campbell's Political Poetry," *English Review,* 46 (June 1928): 703-706;

George M. C. Brandes, "The British Spirit of Freedom," in his *Main Currents in Nineteenth Century Literature,* 6 volumes (London: Heinemann / New York: Macmillan, 1906), IV: 189-194;

Kenneth Walter Cameron, "Emerson, Thomas Campbell, and Bacon's Definition of Poetry," *Emerson Society Quarterly,* no. 14 (First Quarter 1959): 48-56;

Lewis Campbell, "Thomas Campbell, the Poet," *Monthly Review,* 10 (February 1903): 110-122;

Edgar Castle, "Kangaroo with Flowers," *Southern Review: An Australian Journal of Literary Studies,* 1, no. 2 (1964): 24-29;

James Coutts, *A History of the University of Glasgow* (Glasgow: Maclehose, 1909);

W. Macneile Dixon, *An Apology for the Arts* (New York: Longmans, 1944), pp. 165-178;

Charles Duffy, "Thomas Campbell: A Critical Biography," Ph.D. dissertation, Cornell University, 1939;

Duffy, "Thomas Campbell and America," *American Literature,* 13 (January 1942): 346-355;

Stanton Garner, "Melville and Thomas Campbell: the 'Deadly Space Between,'" *English Language Notes,* 14 (June 1977): 289-290;

Frank G. Garvin, Jr., "Thomas Campbell and the Reviewers: A Study of Evolving Literary Criteria in the Periodical Reviews, 1798-1824," Ph.D. dissertation, University of Illinois, Urbana-Champaign, 1973;

Lafcadio Hearn, "Note on Thomas Campbell," in his *On Poets,* edited by R. Tanabe, T. Ochiai, and I. Nishizaki (Tokyo: Hokeuseido, 1938), pp. 640-653;

Stanley Jones, "Three Notes on Howe's Edition of Hazlitt: Paine, Porson, and Campbell," *Notes & Queries,* 30 (June 1983): [228], 230-232;

Peter S. Macaulay, "Thomas Campbell: A Revaluation," *English Studies,* 50 (February 1969): 39-46;

George McKnight, "The Poetic Development of Thomas Campbell," Ph.D. dissertation, University of Toronto, 1979;

Mary Ruth Miller, "Five Recently Found Letters by Thomas Campbell," *Modern Language Review,* 83 (April 1988): 287-296;

Miller, *Thomas Campbell* (Boston: Twayne, 1978);

Kenneth H. Ober and Warren U. Ober, "Zukovskij's Translation of Campbell's 'Lord

Ullin's Daughter,' " *Germano-Slavica: A Canadian Journal of Germanic and Slavic Comparative Studies,* 51 (Fall 1977): 295-305;

Frederick E. Pierce, *Currents and Eddies in the English Romantic Generation* (New Haven: Yale University Press, 1918);

George Richards, "Thomas Campbell and Shelley's *Queen Mab,*" *American Notes & Queries,* 10 (September 1971): 5-6;

Daniel B. Shumway, "Thomas Campbell and Germany," in *F. E. Schelling Anniversary Papers by His Former Students* (New York: Russell, 1923), pp. 233-261;

Jack Stillinger, "Whittier's Early Imitation of Thomas Campbell," *Philological Quarterly,* 38 (October 1959): 502-504;

Francis J. Sypher, "Swinburne's Debt to Campbell in 'A Forsaken Garden,' " *Victorian Poetry,* 12 (Spring 1974): 74-78;

Albert M. [Turner] Bierstadt, "Gertrude of Wyoming," *JEGP,* 20 (October 1921): 491-501;

Albert M. Turner, "Wordsworth's Influence on Thomas Campbell," *PMLA,* 38 (June 1923): 253-266.

Papers:

Major collections of Campbell's manuscript poems and letters are located in the National Library of Scotland, the British Museum, the Bodleian Library, London University and University College, London, the University of Glasgow, and the Henry E. Huntington Library.

Samuel Taylor Coleridge

(21 October 1772 - 25 July 1834)

A. C. Goodson
Michigan State University

BOOKS: *The Fall of Robespierre. An Historic Drama*, act 1 by Coleridge, acts 2 and 3 by Robert Southey (Cambridge: Printed by Benjamin Flower for W. H. Lunn and J. & J. Merrill, sold by J. March, Norwich, 1794);

A Moral and Political Lecture, delivered at Bristol (Bristol: Printed by George Routh, 1795);

Conciones ad Populum, or Addresses to the People (Bristol, 1795);

The Plot Discovered; or an Address to the People, against Ministerial Treason (Bristol, 1795);

The Watchman: A Periodical Publication, in Prose and Verse, nos. 1-10 (Bristol: Published by the author and by Parsons, London, 1 March - 13 May 1796);

Poems on Various Subjects, by Coleridge, with four sonnets by Charles Lamb and part of another by Southey (London: C. G. & J. Robinsons/Bristol: J. Cottle, 1796); revised and enlarged as *Poems*, with poems by Lamb and Charles Lloyd (Bristol: Printed by N. Biggs for J. Cottle and Robinsons, London, 1797; third edition with deletions, London: Printed by N. Biggs for T. N. Longman & O. Rees, 1803);

Fears in Solitude, Written in 1798 during the alarm of an invasion. To which are added, FRANCE, AN ODE; and FROST AT MIDNIGHT (London: Printed for J. Johnson, 1798);

Lyrical Ballads, with a few Other Poems, by Coleridge and William Wordsworth (Bristol: Printed by Biggs & Cottle for T. N. Longman, London, 1798; London: Printed for J. & A. Arch, 1798; enlarged edition, 2 volumes, London: Printed for T. N. Longman & O. Rees, by Biggs & Co., Bristol, 1800; Philadelphia: Printed & sold by James Humphreys, 1802);

The Friend: A Literary, Moral, and Political Weekly Paper, 27 parts, plus one supernumerary (Penrith: Printed & published by J. Brown and sold by Longman & Co., and Clement, London, 1 June 1809 - 15 March 1810); republished as *The Friend; A Series of Essays* (London: Printed for Gale & Curtis, 1812); new edition, with added material (3 volumes, London: Rest Fenner, 1818: 1 volume, Burlington, Vt.: Chauncey Goodrich, 1831);

Remorse, A Tragedy, in Five Acts (London: Printed for W. Pople, 1813; New York: D. Longworth, 1813);

Christabel: Kubla Khan, a Vision; The Pains of Sleep (London: Printed for John Murray, 1816; Boston: Published by Wells & Lilly, sold by Van Winkle & Wiley, New York, and M. Carey, Philadelphia, 1816);

The Statesman's Manual; or the Bible the Best Guide to Political Skill and Foresight: A Lay Sermon (London: Printed for Gale & Fenner, 1816; Burlington, Vt.: Chauncey Goodrich, 1832);

Sibylline Leaves: A Collection of Poems (London: Rest Fenner, 1817); republished in part as *Selections from the Sybilline Leaves of S. T. Coleridge* (Boston: True & Greene, 1827);

Biographia Literaria; or, Biographical Sketches of my Literary Life and Opinions, 2 volumes (London: Rest Fenner, 1817; New York: Published by Kirk & Mercein, 1817);

Zapolya: A Christmas Tale (London: Rest Fenner, 1817);

Aids to Reflection in the Formation of a Manly Character on the Several Grounds of Prudence, Morality, and Religion: Illustrated by Select Passages from our Elder Divines, especially Archbishop Leighton (London: Printed for Taylor & Hessey, 1825; Burlington, Vt.: Chauncey Goodrich, 1829);

The Poetical Works of S. T. Coleridge, 3 volumes (London: Pickering, 1828);

The Devil's Walk; A Poem. By Professor Parson [pseud.]. *Edited with a biographical memoir and notes by H. W. Montagu* [pseud.], by Coleridge and Southey (London: Marsh & Miller/ Edinburgh: Constable, 1830);

On the Constitution of Church and State (London: Hurst, Chance, 1830);

Samuel Taylor Coleridge, 1795 (portrait by Pieter van Dyke; by permission of the National Portrait Gallery, London)

Specimens of the Table Talk of the late Samuel Taylor Coleridge, 2 volumes, edited by Henry Nelson Coleridge (London: John Murray, 1835; New York: Harper & Brothers, 1835);

The Literary Remains in Prose and Verse of Samuel Taylor Coleridge, 4 volumes, edited by Henry Nelson Coleridge (London: Pickering, 1836-1839);

Confessions of an Inquiring Spirit, edited by Henry Nelson Coleridge (London: Pickering, 1840; Boston: Munroe, 1841);

Hints towards the Formation of a more Comprehensive Theory of Life, edited by Seth B. Watson (London: Churchill, 1848; Philadelphia: Lea & Blanchard, 1848);

Essays on His Own Times; forming a second series of

"The Friend," 3 volumes, edited by Sara Coleridge (London: Pickering, 1850);

Seven Lectures upon Shakespeare and Milton, by the late S. T. Coleridge [corrupt text], edited by J. Payne Collier (London: Chapman & Hall, 1856).

Edition and Collections: *Biographia Literaria,* 2 volumes, edited by J. Shawcross (Oxford: Clarendon Press, 1907);

The Complete Poetical Works of Samuel Taylor Coleridge, 2 volumes, edited by Ernest Hartley Coleridge (Oxford: Clarendon Press, 1912);

The Philosophical Lectures of Samuel Taylor Coleridge, edited by Kathleen Coburn (London & New York: Pilot Press, 1949; New York: Philosophical Library, 1949);

The Notebooks of Samuel Taylor Coleridge, edited by Coburn, 3 volumes to date (New York: Pantheon, 1957-);

The Collected Works of Samuel Taylor Coleridge, general editor Coburn, 13 volumes to date (Princeton: Princeton University Press, 1969- ; London: Routledge & Kegan Paul, 1969-);

Samuel Taylor Coleridge, The Oxford Authors, edited by H. J. Jackson (Oxford & New York: Oxford University Press, 1985).

OTHER: [Sonnets from various authors], edited, with contributions, by Coleridge (N.p., 1796).

Coleridge is the premier poet-critic of modern English tradition, distinguished for the scope and influence of his thinking about literature as much as for his innovative verse. Active in the wake of the French Revolution as a dissenting pamphleteer and lay preacher, he inspired a brilliant generation of writers and attracted the patronage of progressive men of the rising middle class in the west country around Bristol. As William Wordsworth's collaborator and constant companion in the formative period of their careers as poets, Coleridge participated in the sea change in English verse associated with *Lyrical Ballads* (1798). His poems of this period, speculative, meditative, and strangely oracular, put off early readers but survived the doubts of Wordsworth and Robert Southey, future poets laureate, to become recognized classics of the romantic idiom.

Coleridge renounced poetic vocation in his thirtieth year and set out to define and defend the art as a practicing critic. His promotion of Wordsworth's verse, a landmark of English literary response, proceeded in tandem with a general investigation of epistemology and metaphysics. Coleridge was preeminently responsible for importing the new German critical philosophy of Immanuel Kant and Friedrich von Schelling; his associated discussion of imagination remains a fixture of institutional criticism while his occasional notations on language proved seminal for the foundation and development of Cambridge English in the 1920s. In his distinction between culture and civilization Coleridge supplied means for a critique of the utilitarian state which has been continued in our own time. And in his late theological writing he provided principles for reform in the Church of England. Coleridge's various and imposing achievement, a cornerstone of

modern English culture, remains an incomparable source of informed reflection on the brave new world whose birth pangs he attended.

Coleridge's example is a living one, but it has always been controversial. A notorious opium addict, prevaricator, and plagiarist, he was more appreciated among his contemporaries for his talk than for his prose style, for his vivid imagination than for the quality of his response to society in transition. George Gordon, Lord Byron, who successfully urged publication of "Kubla Khan," characterized Coleridge's voice for the age in *Don Juan* (1819-1824):

> And Coleridge, too, has lately taken wing,
> But, like a hawk encumber'd with his hood,
> Explaining metaphysics to the nation,
> I wish he would explain his Explanation.

Both the aspiration and the celebrity of the career show through the satire. William Hazlitt, whose enthusiasm for the dissenting Coleridge would turn to recrimination at his later conformity, exemplifies an ambivalence evident elsewhere in Wordsworth and Thomas De Quincey, among Coleridge's distinguished associates. Writing in "My First Acquaintance with Poets" (1823), Hazlitt recalled his youthful pilgrimage to hear "this celebrated person preach" at Bridgwater in January 1798; he was reminded of John the Baptist crying in the wilderness, of "an eagle dallying with the wind." Hazlitt's vision of poetry and philosophy uniting in this vatic voice is important for grasping what Coleridge was about, and not only in his verse. As Hazlitt put it in a beautiful homage, "that my understanding also did not remain dumb and brutish, or at length found a language to express itself, I owe to Coleridge." Yet the acolyte's homage was qualified elsewhere by a dismissive account of the poetry and the judgment that Coleridge's prose "is utterly abortive." In *The Spirit of the Age* (1825) Hazlitt contrasted his old friend with William Godwin, the radical author of *Political Justice* (1793), whose single-minded concentration showed up Coleridge's abstraction, diffuseness, and inconsequence. The admitted genius appeared to his contemporaries as a human failure.

Such judgments should be weighed against the testimony in the next generation of John Stuart Mill, for whom the significant contrast was between Coleridge and Jeremy Bentham, dominating spirits of their generation, "to whom their country is indebted not only for the greater part

The vicarage (left) and church at Ottery St. Mary. The man who is about to mount his horse is the Reverend John Coleridge (engraving based on an eighteenth-century aquatint).

of the important ideas which have been thrown into circulation among its thinking men in their time, but for a revolution in its general modes of thought and investigation" ("Bentham," 1838). Coleridge, as the exponent of speculative philosophy, teacher of the teachers, paragon of the conservative cast of mind in a changing society, had led his contemporaries to ask the question, "What is the meaning of it?" On the basis of a "philosophy of mind" he had demonstrated the urgency of first questions and first principles in the practical functioning of society. As a poet he was counted by Mill "among the greatest names in our literature"; as a critic he was praised for "the healthier taste, and more intelligent canons of poetic criticism, which he was himself mainly instrumental in diffusing." And memorably, "as a philosopher, the class of thinkers has scarcely yet arisen by whom he is to be judged" ("Coleridge," 1840). It was not only as a speculative but as a reflective intelligence responding to the life of his time that Coleridge counted in this capacity for Mill. At the moment of his death in 1834 his name was already associated in England and America— by Ralph Waldo Emerson as by Thomas Carlyle and Mill—with the penetrating critique of modern culture which had been largely ignored.

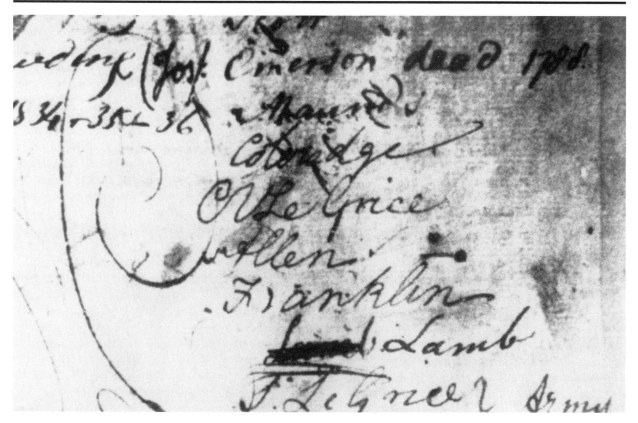

Signatures in a copy of Homer's Iliad *shared by Coleridge, Charles Valentine Le Grice, Robert Allen, and Charles Lamb at Christ's Hospital (Richard Holmes,* Coleridge: Early Visions, *1989)*

Samuel Taylor Coleridge was born on 21 October 1772 in the remote Devon village of Ottery St. Mary, the tenth and youngest child of Ann Bowdon Coleridge and John Coleridge, a schoolmaster and vicar whom he was said to resemble physically as well as mentally. In vivid letters recounting his early years he describes himself as "a genuine Sans culotte, my veins uncontaminated with one drop of Gentility." Laying stress on his father's foundling origins and gnawing poverty, he paints a picture of himself at one remove: the man of learning as outcast and social misfit. Yet Coleridge's older brothers were successful enough in conventional careers, three of them after training at Pembroke College, Oxford, where Samuel Johnson had endured two lean years. The childhood of isolation and self-absorption which Coleridge describes in these letters has more to do, on his own telling, with his position in the family. Feelings of anomie, unworthiness, and incapacity persisted throughout a life of often compulsive dependency on others.

A reader seemingly by instinct, Coleridge grew up surrounded by books at school, at home, and in his aunt's shop. "At six years old I remember to have read Belisarius, Robinson Crusoe, & Philip Quarle–and then I found the Arabian Nights' entertainments–one tale of which made so deep an impression on me that I was haunted by spectres, whenever I was in the dark." The dreamy child's imagination was nourished by his father's tales of the planets and stars and enlarged by constant reading. Through this, "my mind had been habituated *to the Vast*–& I never regarded *my senses* in any way as the criteria of my belief. I regulated all my creeds by my conceptions not by my *sight* –even at that age." Romances and fairy tales instilled in him a feeling of "the Great" and "the Whole." It was a lesson he never forgot. Experience he always regarded as a matter of whole and integrated response, not of particular sensations. Resolving conflicted feelings into whole response occupies much of his best verse, and his developed philosophical synthesis represents a comparable effort of resolution.

A year after the death of his father in 1781 Coleridge was sent to Christ's Hospital, the London grammar school where he would pass his adolescence training in Hebrew, Latin, and Greek, at which he excelled, and in English composition. His basic literary values were formed here under the tutelage of the Reverend James Bowyer, a larger-than-life figure who balanced classical models with native English examples drawn from Shakespeare and Milton. While Wordsworth was imitating Thomas Gray at Hawkshead Grammar School, Coleridge was steeping in this long tradition of distinguished writing, learning to compose on Bowyer's principles. These included an insistence on sound sense and clear reference in phrase, metaphor, and image: literary embroidery was discouraged. So were conventional similes and stale poetic diction. Coleridge's later development as a poet may be characterized as an effort to arrive at a natural voice which eschewed such devices. Critical of the rhetorical excesses of the poetry of sensibility which prevailed at the time, he would join forces with Wordsworth in promoting "natural thoughts with natural diction" (*Biographia Literaria,* chapter 1).

Charles Lamb's evocative portrait of "Christ's Hospital Five and Thirty Years Ago" (1820) suggests what a hothouse environment the school was at the time. The student population included boys who went on to important careers in letters, church, and state. Even in such company Coleridge stood out unmistakably: "Come back into memory, like as thou wert in the day-spring of thy fancies, with hope like a fiery column before thee–the dark pillar not yet turned–Samuel Taylor Coleridge–Logician, Metaphysician, Bard!– How have I seen the casual passer through the Cloisters stand still, intranced with admiration (while he weighed the disproportion between the *speech* and the *garb* of the young Mirandula), to hear thee unfold, in thy deep and sweet intonations, the mysteries of Jamblichus, or Plotinus (for even in those years thou waxedst not pale at such philosophic draughts), or reciting Homer in his Greek, or Pindar–while the walls of the old Grey Friars re-echoed to the accents of the *inspired charity-boy!*" The opening notes of awe and eventual disappointment are characteristic, but the portrait of the artist as a young prodigy is more disturbing than Lamb admits. The vatic voice was already alive to its social possibilities, the sole resource of an isolated personality.

At Christ's Hospital, Coleridge acquired an exalted idea of poetry to match this waxing voice. From Bowyer he would learn that "Poetry, even that of the loftiest and, seemingly, that of

the wildest odes, had a logic of its own, as severe as that of science." The comparison of poetry and science was an important one, leading to his mature definition of the art as a form of composition whose immediate aim was pleasure while science was concerned first of all with truth. Yet poetry arrived at truth in its own way, and that way was "more difficult, because more subtle, more complex, and dependent on more, and more fugitive causes." The logic of science was derived from pure reason; the logic of poetry depended on human understanding, which was anything but pure. Understanding belonged to the world of sensation, generalization, and language, and through it poetry was committed to ordinary human experience. Hence its tangled condition. The words of the common tongue kept the poet in touch with this common world.

Poetry as distinguished from science in this way might include not only verse but what we now call prose, including all sorts of fictive discourse as well as the essay. Pleasure is the point; good writing pleases first, making its claim on truth through its management of the language. "In the truly great poets," Coleridge quotes Bowyer as saying, "there is a reason assignable, not only for every word, but for the position of every word." On this basis in part Coleridge would go on to distinguish between verse and prose composition. Verse "demands a severer keeping," exciting "equal and continuous attention" where prose is less particular, and less exacting. Stressing some syllables while counting out the unstressed ones, regular meter compels constant attention. Poetic diction makes additional demands, and it was on this difference that Coleridge would rely in defending the art against Wordsworth's radical claim that there was "no essential difference" between the language of verse and prose composition. Coleridge's defense of poetry remains an important one, and it reverts directly to his training at Christ's Hospital.

Poetry as living speech, poetry as act of attention: the commitments of Christ's Hospital encouraged fresh judgment on the state of the art, and on what rang true now. Pope's couplets had begun to sound contrived while the more masculine energies of Shakespeare and Milton were welling up in the imagination of a generation of young writers. In the sonnets of the Reverend William Lisle Bowles, the schoolboy Coleridge found a contemporary model whose voice struck him as "tender" yet "manly," at once "natural and real." These words are Coleridge's own, and they de-

To late each Flower that sweetest blows
  I pluck'd, the Garden's pride;
Within the petals of a Rose
  A sleeping Love I spy'd.

Around his brows a lucid wreath
  Of many a mingled hue;
And purple glow'd his cheek beneath
  Inebriate with Dew.

I softly seiz'd th'unguarded Power,
  Nor scar'd his balmy rest;
And plac'd him cag'd within the Flower
  On Angelina's Breast.

But when all reckless of the Guile
  Awoke the Slumberer sweet,
He struggled to escape awhile,
  And stamp'd his angry feet.

Ah! soon the soul-entrancing Sight
  Subdued th'impatient Boy:
He gaz'd, he thrill'd with deep delight,
  Then clapt his Wings for Joy.
And—oh! he cried what charms refin'd This magic Throne endear.
Another Love may Venus find—Ill fix my empire here!

Page from Coleridge's 28 June 1793 letter to his brother George, including a poem published in Poems on Various Subjects
(1796) as "Effusion xxvii" (auctioned by Sotheby's, 27 September 1988)

scribe his aspirations at least as much as they do Bowles's fulsome versifications. Long after the model had lost its grip on him, he would credit Bowles with drawing him out of a metaphysical daze, restoring him to "the love of nature, and the sense of beauty in forms and sounds." To the poet in his first flush, Bowles represented the modern possibilities of "the more sustained and elevated style" in English verse.

The sonnets which Coleridge composed under Bowles's influence are of little lasting interest, though "To the River Otter" has been admired for its natural detail and pensiveness. As an improvement on Bowles's rather aimless voice, it does show Coleridge adapting current conventions to his own temperamental requirements. First published in 1796 in a volume of sonnets from various authors assembled around specimens of Bowles's poetastery, the poem speaks for the early impact of his example. In his prefatory remarks to this volume Coleridge locates the sonnet form halfway between epigram and elegy. And he characterizes not only Bowles's practice but his own assumptions when he considers that "in a Sonnet then we require a development of some lonely feeling . . . in which moral Sentiments, Affections, or Feelings, are deduced from, and associated with, the scenery of Nature."

As a statement of working premises this obscure definition shows how Coleridge thought about poetry at the beginning of his practice of the art. The sonnet was a conventional starting point. Its long lineage and compact scale suited his sense of purpose. Bowles's approach to the form sorted well with his own idea of poetry's vocation. Bowles was continuing the plaintive tone and elegiac manner of the poetry of sensibility descending from Thomas Gray and William Collins, among others. This rambling, melancholic, pictorial idiom came to dominate English verse in the half century following the death of Pope in 1744.

William Blake has been accounted the culminating figure in the development of the poetry of sensibility, but Coleridge is surely more representative of its destination. With William Cowper, he stands at the end of a line of disturbed and disturbing voices which exercise the suppressed fears of a complacent time. Coleridge has much to say of this line of English verse in the opening chapter of his *Biographia Literaria* (1817) and elsewhere. Isolated in a literary lull between the age of Pope and that of Wordsworth, the poetry of sensibility does not appeal to modern taste. Yet it

was from this uncertain source that both Coleridge and Wordsworth took their bearings.

At Jesus College, Cambridge, where Coleridge matriculated in October 1791, he composed a mass of occasional poetry. Full of the rhetorical machinery of the middling verse of the period, and often cloying in sentiment, these early poems have little in common with the work of 1795 and after, on which his reputation would be founded. They do not even show him developing in the direction of his mature voice. Some of the phrasing of this college phase bears witness to the force of Milton's example on the student's impressionable ear. It is worth noticing since it looks forward to Coleridge's later struggle with Milton's haunting melody. There are fashionable Anacreontica, satirical couplets, lines imitated from Ossian, quatrains, and irregular odes. Some were included in letters, others apparently read aloud to college friends. Some were published in the *Morning Chronicle*, gaining a foothold which Coleridge would make use of later. A number of these early efforts are included in his *Poems on Various Subjects* (1796).

The backward ambience of Cambridge in the 1790s seems to have retarded Coleridge's muse, setting him to composing an arid (and ungrammatical) prize poem in Greek (in summer 1792), while driving him to escape from "bog and desolation." Reports of his college life suggest that he was absorbing not only Greek texts but English political pamphlets at this interesting moment. Edmund Burke's *Reflections on the Revolution in France* (1790) had met the rising sympathy for events in France with questions about the legitimacy and future of the state. Coleridge is said by a Cambridge contemporary to have consumed Burke's various productions on first publication, reciting them from memory to company at supper. His sympathies were broadly liberal–critical of William Pitt's government and the slave trade, yet wary of the situation in France. He was active in defense of William Frend, a Unitarian and Fellow of Jesus College who was expelled for publishing a pamphlet advocating *Peace and Union* (1793). This episode marks the beginning of a convergence between politics and poetry in Coleridge's career which is characteristic and important. For he was never a disinterested observer. His poetry participated in ongoing reactions to events at home and abroad, and he recognized its vocation in this public setting.

Some idea of Coleridge's attitude toward the troubling situation in France can be gathered

Than the love-wilder'd Maniac's Brain hath seen
Shaping celestial forms in vacant air;
If these demand th'empassion'd Poet' care —
If Mirth, and soften'd Sense, and Wit refin'd,
The blameless features of a lovely mind;
Then haply shall my trembling hand assign
No fading wreath to Beauty's saintly throne.
Nor, Sara! thou these early flowers refuse:
No serpent lurks beneath their simple hues.
From Flatt'ry's Night-shade brings
A Child of Nature as I feels, I sings.

Nor, Sara! thou these early flowers refuse
Ne'er lurk'd the Snake beneath their simple hues.
Nature's pure Child from Flatt'ry's night-shade brings
No blooms rich-purpling: as he feels, he sings.

✻. Put as a note the fourteenth line of this Poem these
lines.

When eager patriots fly the news & spread
Of glorious conquest and of thousands dead;
'all feel the mighty glow of victory joy:

But if extended on the gory plain
And snatch'd in conquest some lov'd friend be slain.
Affection's tears will dim the sorrowing eye,
And suffering Nature grieve that one should die.
From the Retrospect by Robert Southey
published by Dilly.

Page from the manuscript for "To a Young Lady" in The Watchman, *no. 1 (1 March 1796), with Coleridge's instructions to the printer about the placement of a footnote (MA 1916 f19; by permission of the Pierpont Morgan Library)*

from the sonnets and effusions, as he would call them, written in the course of events. "To a Young Lady" (written in 1792) includes lines which show him taking the cause of freedom to heart while regretting the hard fate of the "oppressor." The ambivalence is characteristic; it appears in another form in a sonnet to Burke, where an allegorical Freedom honors the man despite his siding with the monarchists. Freedom figures again in a sonnet to Thomas Erskine as a defiled shrine honored by his eloquence. Both sonnets are oratorical in inspiration and manner. In *The Fall of Robespierre* (1794), whose brief opening act is Coleridge's work, the morality of the reign of terror is dramatized through the growing conviction among the protagonist's advisers that he had sacrificed everything to an inhuman principle. On Christmas Eve of the same year, in "Religious Musings," Coleridge would image human nature as

> A sea of blood bestrewed with wrecks, where mad
> Embattling interests on each other rush
> With unhelmed rage!

History was no longer heroic. Its horror made sense only in the scheme of Christian redemption.

On the basis of seemingly contradictory responses, Coleridge has sometimes been depicted as a turncoat who betrayed his original revolutionary sympathies. His poems suggest, and his lay sermons of the period confirm, that his allegiance was always to an ideal of freedom, not to democratic insurgency. Danton's doubts were more honorable than Robespierre's murderous crusade, as *The Fall of Robespierre* intimates. Comparison with Georg Buchner's *Dantons Tod* (1835) shows Coleridge's scruples to have been consistent with the best revisionist thinking about the revolution. The quality of his ambivalence did not prevent his speaking out in situations which damaged his reputation among Burke's party, his natural constituency. Pitt's reactionary government actually sent a spy to find out what he was doing in the course of the decade; he was regarded as potentially dangerous, a natural ally of the French. The Jacobin label stuck in a suspicious time and among the patriotic west-country populace, but Coleridge remained substantially true to his convictions despite the liabilities.

What sort of revolutionary would enlist in the king's army in this perilous moment? Coleridge did so on 2 December 1793 under an as-

sumed name, fleeing debts and discouragement at college. He was rescued by family and friends after serving locally for some five months. In the end the interlude was a comic one, but it shows what instability underlay the oratorical certitudes of the sonnets. Escape, servitude, and retreat would become a familiar pattern in Coleridge's life.

The Fall of Robespierre was a collaboration undertaken with Southey, whom he met at Oxford in June 1794, while on a walking tour from Cambridge. With Southey he hatched another escape route, a utopian scheme for immigration to America, where a small group was to found a commune on the banks of the Susquehanna in Pennsylvania. The ideals of Pantisocracy, as they called their project, involved shared labor and shared rewards. Servitude in this setting was exalted as "aspheterism," a Christian selflessness. "Religious Musings" envisions the dismal historical world which they hoped to escape, as well as their aspiration:

>   'Tis the sublime of man,
> Our noontide majesty, to know ourselves
> Parts and proportions of one wondrous whole!
> This fraternises man, this constitutes
> Our charities and bearings!

Pantisocracy occupied Coleridge's energies and continued to influence his sense of vocation for some time after the scheme's collapse in 1795. A communitarian ideal remained essential to his writing, as to the life he now proposed to live.

For he left Cambridge, without taking a degree, in December 1794, in the midst of this communitarian enthusiasm and was soon thrown back on his own resources. In the course of the next year Coleridge delivered a series of lectures on politics and religion in Bristol, where Southey had connections. He considered various journalistic enterprises and made influential friends, including Joseph Cottle, a local publisher, who was interested enough in his poetry to advance him living expenses against copyright. The volume of *Poems on Various Subjects* (including four sonnets by Lamb and part of another by Southey) which Cottle would publish in 1796 represents a rite of passage. Behind him, the young author's school verse, sonnets, and rambling effusions trace a course of aimless poetasting. Before him, in "The Eolian Harp" (included in the 1796 volume as "Effusion xxxv") and in "Religious Musings" (which concluded the volume), something is stirring. The former, addressed to Sara Fricker, whom he

Coleridge in 1796 (portrait by Robert Hancock; by permission of the National Portrait Gallery, London)

married in Bristol on 4 October 1795, looks forward to the conversational line which he would develop and share with Wordsworth. The latter, on which he claimed in a letter to "build all my poetic pretensions," is an affirmation of Christian principle in troubled times. Both poems are broadly communitarian in aspiration.

Dating from just after Coleridge's departure from Cambridge, "Religious Musings" is earlier in point of composition. With the old world seemingly behind him and the new world clearly in view, he contrasted the "meek Galilean" figure of Christ with the civilization which had come of his sacrifice. The humble biblical shepherd had been succeeded by greedy individualists, "Each for himself"; his flock and unbounded horizons had given way to Property. Imagination fed the ram-

pant desires of modern man, spurring him on to material prosperity and its associated social ills. Science had arisen in reaction; freedom was its child. Joseph Priestley, chemist and political radical recently exiled in America, was the muse of the poem's conclusion. He pointed the way to a better world.

Coleridge expanded on "Religious Musings" over the next two years. A section of it was published as "The Present State of Society" in *The Watchman,* a periodical which Coleridge conducted through ten issues (1 March - 13 May 1796). Its contents were various, including reports from Parliament, foreign intelligence, and responses to current issues. The loaf was leavened with bits of poetry, some of it the editor's own. *The Watchman* failed despite Coleridge's

Sara Fricker Coleridge, 1809 (engraving based on a miniature by Matilda Betham)

strenuous efforts to enlist subscribers, but it bears witness to his seriousness of purpose. As a commentary on English society in transition, it remains a valuable source despite some incongruities. Foremost among these is the literary tone of the production, including the occasional verse offerings. "Religious Musings" illustrates the problem. Its social vision is compromised by congested thinking and histrionic expression. The poetry does not do justice to the politics.

This conjunction was where Coleridge had staked his claim. Poetry as a vatic art in the service of a general social revival: the restless England of George III, reeling from the shock of American and French revolutions, was surely prepared to listen. The scientific and political culture which had emerged in the 1770s was gaining force among the dissenters, Unitarians in

particular, whom Coleridge cultivated in and around Bristol. They were his constituency and his means of support. He spoke to them in sermons and lectures, through *The Watchman* and also, as he hoped, through his verse.

His move with Sara to Clevedon, Somersetshire, along the Bristol Channel, in October 1795 was a change of air though not of social context. From here he continued his attack on the king and his ministers, returning occasionally to Bristol to lecture or walking to Bridgwater to speak at the Unitarian chapel. At his cottage he wrote "The Eolian Harp," a meditative poem different in every way from "Religious Musings" and the real inauguration of his mature voice. In its primitive form, as the effusion of 1796, it reflects the conflict between natural response–"the sense of beauty in forms and sounds," as he put it in the

Biographia Literaria —and higher responsibility. Nature as an animated, omnipresent life force, a benevolent companion, is memorably characterized through the image of the wind harp, which is identified with the poet's "indolent and passive brain." Poetic imagination is simply an instrument of this Nature, one "organic harp" among others in its universal symphony.

As an expression of the pantheist vision of God-in-nature descending from Benedict de Spinoza, "The Eolian Harp" has made a strong appeal to readers, though early reviewers made little of it. It has a special place in Coleridge's intellectual development as a statement of pantheist sympathy. The God-in-nature idea exerted a magnetic attraction, which he resisted through his Christian conviction of the personeity of God. This is brought to bear in the poem's final stanza, where his admonishing wife stands against "vain Philosophy's aye-babbling spring." It is neither a graceful nor a convincing conclusion, but it is true to a conflict which Coleridge felt intensely. In the exemplary setting of the new life he was undertaking, the claims of enlightenment thinking succumbed to faith.

"The Eolian Harp" establishes the terms of this important conflict, which was not simply intellectual but broadly social in implication. For pantheism was associated with the progressive scientific culture for which the empirical world of nature was simply reality itself. A personal God had no empirical reality. Unitarians and various sorts of deists adhered to a divinity which was known through sensation: a Nature god of sorts. This was Coleridge's intellectual milieu, and he tried out its ideas in his Bristol period. Yet his enduring commitments showed through. The community espoused in the conclusion of "The Eolian Harp" is not the egalitarian utopia of scientific aspiration, but "the family of Christ." The ideals of Pantisocracy triumph over the temptations of the new science. In his extensive correspondence of the period Coleridge proclaimed himself a Necessitarian for whom everything had a place in the divine scheme. "The Eolian Harp" shows how the lure of an alternative vision of human experience dominated by sensation could provoke an equal and opposite reaffirmation of first principles to the contrary. A traditional faith was confirmed through temptation.

The other significant poem of Coleridge's cottage residence at Clevedon explains his early departure. "Reflections on Having Left a Place of Retirement" takes the ambling voice of "The

Eolian Harp" to overtly social conclusions. The cottage is now a bower of bliss, edenic in a fallen world, an alluring but necessarily short-lived haven of peace and tranquillity. The view from a nearby promontory provides an icon of man's settlement in an accommodating nature. This view and the idea which informs it make a strong appeal, yet they are the occasion of the poet's reaction against his own rustication. In the end it is the thought of human suffering that drives him back to the world of society and history "to fight the bloodless fight / Of science, freedom, and the truth in Christ."

Community after the collapse of Pantisocracy meant a wife and family, impassioned friendships based on shared concerns, and the company of kindred spirits. Thomas Poole, a prosperous tanner of good family in the tiny Somerset village of Nether Stowey, became Coleridge's closest associate in the uncertain period following his return to Bristol in 1796. The arduous and ultimately futile enterprise of *The Watchman* led him to seek a steady haven where he might work and write in sympathetic surroundings. Supporting Sara and their newborn son, Hartley (born September 1796), was a priority: "Literature will always be a secondary Object with me." There was something desperate in such a resolution, and it proved hard to keep after their move to a small thatched cottage in Nether Stowey at the end of 1796.

"This Lime-Tree Bower My Prison," composed from Poole's cottage garden the next year, relates to the community which he made there. Poole had proved a loyal friend and steady companion; his patronage was crucial to the success of the resettlement. Wordsworth, whom Coleridge had met in Bristol some time before, came to visit with his sister, Dorothy, and they soon occupied a substantial house at Alfoxden, walking distance from Nether Stowey. Charles Lloyd lived at Coleridge's cottage for a time, providing steady income in exchange for tuition. Lamb, the old friend from Christ's Hospital, and the youthful Hazlitt joined Cottle and other Bristol connections to make up a real if transient community of socially interested parties. All were writers at least by aspiration; all were involved in the reformation of English values for which "romanticism" has since come to stand. The lives they were leading on the fringes of conventional society would become the subject of their work.

So it was in "This Lime-Tree Bower My Prison," which describes a walk some of them

The Coleridges' cottage in Nether Stowey (illustration by Edmund H. New for William Knight's Coleridge and Wordsworth in the West Country, *1913)*

took one day in Coleridge's absence. The jealous Sara had spilled a pan of boiling milk on his foot, excluding him from the company of Dorothy and William Wordsworth, as well as Charles Lamb, on a jaunt in the surrounding spur of low hills–*combes*, in local parlance–the Quantocks. From his confinement in the garden, he celebrates the pleasures of the natural world as seen from within this harmonious community of like-minded individuals. The detailed evocation of their itinerary marks the apogee of his response to landscape. In the end, the poet's imagination triumphs over his separation: his bower reveals pleasures of its own; Nature is hospitable to human response. Sensation proves adequate to human need; Nature is a providential resource against isolation. The poem's conclusion dwells on the joy of companionship in such a world.

Coleridge's new community was instrumental in bringing him to such feeling, and to such expression. This proved to be the most satisfying arrangement he would ever enjoy. It was the setting of his verse breakthrough, of the annus mirabilis in which most of his enduring poems were written. Here he built on the achievement of Clevedon, writing reflectively about his inner life in a social environment which excited and encouraged the questions he was asking. Was the human place in nature a merely passive one, comparable to the wind harp's? Was natural beauty sufficient to our moral needs? And more speculatively, what was the meaning of nature conceived as an organ of divine will? How did this bear on our idea of society?

These questions haunt the reflective idiom which he developed in the course of this resi-

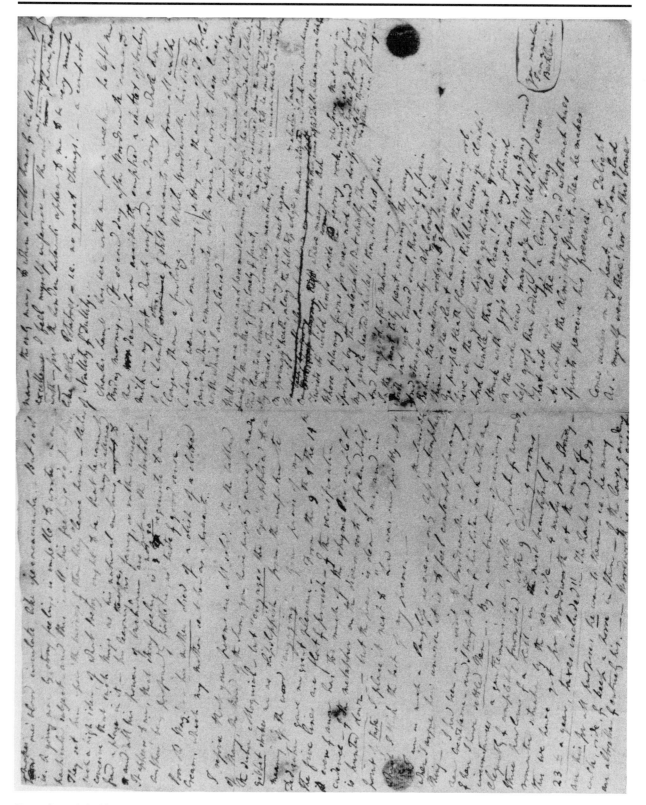

Pages from Coleridge's circa 17 July 1797 letter to Robert Southey, including an early draft of "This Lime-Tree Bower My Prison" and a description of the events that led to its composition (MA 1848; by permission of the Pierpont Morgan Library)

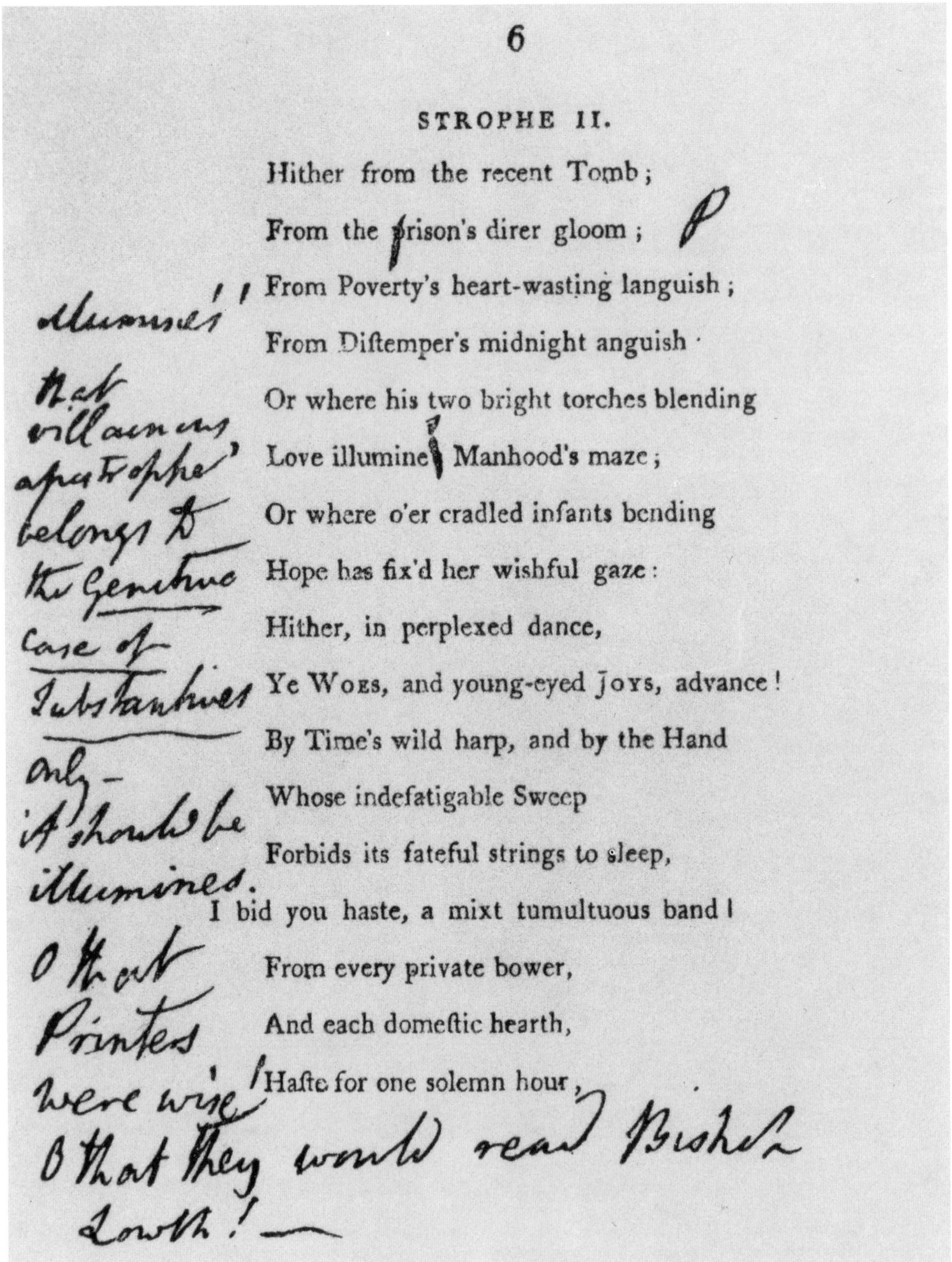

6

STROPHE II.

Hither from the recent Tomb;

From the prison's direr gloom;

From Poverty's heart-wasting languish;

From Diftemper's midnight anguish ·

Or where his two bright torches blending

Love illumines Manhood's maze;

Or where o'er cradled infants bending

Hope has fix'd her wishful gaze:

Hither, in perplexed dance,

Ye Woes, and young-eyed Joys, advance!

By Time's wild harp, and by the Hand

Whose indefatigable Sweep

Forbids its fateful strings to sleep,

I bid you haste, a mixt tumultuous band!

From every private bower,

And each domeftic hearth,

Hafte for one solemn hour,

illumines'

that villainous apostrophe' belongs to the Genitive Case of Substantives only,—

it should be illumines.

O that Printers were wise,

O that they would read Bishop Lowth!—

Pages from Coleridge's proofs for "Ode on the Departing Year" in his 1797 Poems *(from Thomas J. Wise,* A Bibliography of the Writings in Prose and Verse of Samuel Taylor Coleridge, *1913)*

15

By livid fount, or roar of blazing stream,

~~Or if, distemper'd by the corse of god~~ *of*

If ever to her idless dragon eyes,

O ALBION ! thy predestin'd ruins rise,

The Fiend-hag on her perilous couch doth leap,

Mutt'ring distemper'd triumph in her charmed sleep.

Away, my soul, away !

In vain, in vain, the birds of warning sing—

And hark ! I hear the famin'd brood of prey

Flap their ~~dark~~ *lank* pennons on the groaning wind !   *lank*

Away, my soul, away !

I unpartaking of the evil thing,

With daily prayer/ and daily toil/   *·/, ·/,*

Soliciting for food my scanty soil,

Have wail'd my country with a loud lament.

Now I recenter my immortal mind

I suspect, almost suspect, that the word "dark" was intentionally substituted for "lank" — if so, 'twas the most tasteless thing thou ever didst, dear Joseph!—

dence of a year and a half at Nether Stowey, with storm clouds brewing on the horizon. The topographic realism of "This Lime-Tree Bower My Prison" reverts via Wordsworth's *An Evening Walk* (1793) to James Thomson and *The Seasons* (1730), but the voice at work here is that of "a man speaking to men," in the parlance of the "Preface" to the 1800 edition of *Lyrical Ballads.* Speech replaces stale poetic convention from the start. The character of the poet lies at the center of the exercise. The self-consciousness of Wordsworth's poetically premature ramble is turned to good effect in Coleridge's effort at something true to the occasion. The sense of occasion is conveyed in fresh blank verse, not the rattling heroic couplets of Wordsworth's first extended production. The prickly personifications and moralizing eye of "An Evening Walk" are vestigially present in "This Lime-Tree Bower My Prison," but the effect is not of conventional chatter. Coleridge's diction is clear and direct for the most part, his apostrophes natural to the drama of the situation which he develops.

Walking was more than recreation for the writers' colony in the Quantocks. It provided the fresh air which their assumptions required. If Nature were to be their muse, and the source of their living values, it would have to be observed in all its sorts and conditions. Coleridge's plan for an expansive treatment in verse of the course of a brook from source to river shows how his walks in the nearby combes contributed to his reflection on the human condition. "The Brook" as he conceived it would mix "description and incident" with "impassioned reflection on men, nature, society." He traced a local stream to its wellsprings, recording occasional images in his notebook, but these are all that survive of an ambitious and characteristic project of the period.

Wordsworth's move to Alfoxden in the summer of 1797 stimulated further projects. Cottle had Coleridge busy preparing for a second edition of his poems, this time with more material by Lamb and poems by Lloyd–a reminder of the sense of collective enterprise involved in the Nether Stowey encampment. A commission for a tragedy for Drury Lane was on his mind as well; he would soon be drafting *Osorio*, an unsatisfactory treatment which was rejected and later revised and produced at Drury Lane on 23 January 1813 under the title of *Remorse*. And he was writing book reviews, including four for the *Critical Review* on the new Gothic fictions, trying to keep body and soul together. At loose ends Cole-

ridge found in Wordsworth a catalyst for his thinking about poetry. The year following his friend's move to the area would prove to be his most productive, and the beginning of a collaboration which culminated in the *Lyrical Ballads* volume.

On his own telling, his conversations with Wordsworth during this year "turned frequently on the two cardinal points of poetry, the power of exciting the sympathy of the reader by a faithful adherence to the truth of nature, and the power of giving the interest of novelty by the modifying colors of imagination." The first point may be described as Wordsworthian, the second as basically Coleridgean. Imagination was already one of his preoccupations; he was interested in Erasmus Darwin's idea that "the excess of fancy is delirium, of imagination mania." Extraordinary states of mind, or casts of spirit, color his major poems of this period of innovation, and the effects which he achieved through them have earned enduring recognition.

Most extraordinary of all, in the eyes of later readers, is "Kubla Khan," an opium-induced, orientalizing fantasia of the unconscious. It is important to recognize that Coleridge himself claimed nothing for this production's "supposed *poetic* merits." He did not publish it until 1816, under financial pressure as usual and at the urging of Lord Byron, and only as an appendage to the more substantial *Christabel*, which Wordsworth had excluded from the second edition of *Lyrical Ballads* (1800). The poem was not liked even then. As a "psychological curiosity" it was interesting to its author mainly as evidence of a state of extreme imaginative excitement. "Kubla Khan" had nothing to do with the reflective idiom to which Coleridge was committed. It might be verse, but it was not good poetry.

The story of its genesis is one of the prodigies of English literature. In the course of a solitary walk in the combes near the Bristol Channel in the fall of 1797, Coleridge took two grains of opium for the dysentery which had been bothering him for some time. He retired to an old stone farmhouse some distance from Porlock, where he fell asleep while reading an old travel book, *Purchase His Pilgrimage* (1613), by Samuel Purchase. He awoke hours later to record the extraordinary train of images which arose during his opiated stupor. The act of composition was interrupted by a "person from Porlock"–often conjured by later poets as a figure of life intruding on art–and it proved impossible to continue afterward. Much ink has been spilled over these circumstances, but their oddity makes them generally plausible, even considering Coleridge's habits of prevarication.

If they are significant at all it is because they epitomize his reputation as the truant phantast of romantic legend. He did much to encourage it, certainly, but he lived to regret what his friends made of him and to defend himself against charges of idleness and premature decay. The Coleridge phenomenon, as it might be called, has been recounted in every literary generation, usually with the emphasis on wonder rather than disappointment, though sometimes–among moralizing critics, never among poets–with a venom which recalls the disillusionment of his associates. Henry James's story, "The Coxon Fund" (1895), based on table talk of the genius who became a nuisance, is indicative of both attitudes. The Coleridge phenomenon has distorted Coleridge's real achievement, which was unique in scope and aspiration if all too human in its fits and starts.

The case for "Kubla Khan" has been made in various ways. The marvelous imagery surrounding a river rising from underground to drop into the sea has been adduced as a prototype of the distinctive imagism of modern verse: it points the way to "thinking in images." This affiliation would not have pleased its author, whose promotion of reflective poetry made him uneasy with such stunning images. For these distracted from real thinking. His apprehensions have been confirmed by the poem's success. The sources and associations of its imagery have been traced at exhaustive length. Coleridge's evocative images have consumed critical response, leading to a conventional view of "Kubla Khan" as an allegory of imagination. The poem has become an oracle of sorts, Xanadu the sacred ground of this arch-romantic power.

Recent studies lay stress on the poem's dialectical structure and observe its heteroglossia. It develops through a series of opposing images which are resolved into "mingled measures" and committed to an ideal harmony. The animating spirit remains mysterious to the poet. Imagination appears here as an esemplastic or unifying power, a source of vision which Coleridge would explore in his reflections on the critical philosophy of Kant and Schelling. In a quite different vein of response, "Kubla Khan" can be read as exemplifying Coleridge's search for a voice. Antecedents from Milton, Collins, and Gray to Wordsworth and Cowper are incorporated here into a per-

sonal poetic idiom. The poem orchestrates the haunting voices of English poetry, enacting a struggle for expression within poetic language, not through a transcendental power of imagination.

The compelling imagery of "Kubla Khan" might be regarded as preparation for "The Rime of the Ancient Mariner," conceived soon after on a walk to the port of Watchet on the Bristol Channel in the company of Wordsworth and his sister. Some time before, John Cruikshank, a local acquaintance of Coleridge's, had related a dream about a skeleton ship manned by spectral sailors. This became the germ of a momentous project in which Wordsworth acted as collaborator. The plot was hatched on the walk, according to Wordsworth's own later recollections, and it was he who conceived of the tale of crime and punishment which Coleridge would treat, in Christian terms, as a story of transgression, penitence, and atonement. Wordsworth also claimed to have suggested that the Old Navigator, as Coleridge initially called him, kill an albatross and be set upon by the "tutelary spirits" of Cape Horn, where the deed is done. He contributed some few lines of verse to the poem in addition.

The collaboration on "The Rime of the Ancient Mariner" is interesting on several counts. It underlines the collective enterprise involved in the inauguration of the new poetic idiom which would eventually be called Romantic. Creation of this kind is more than a matter of oracular power. It has much to do with rational inquiry and exchange. Further, the episode gives some idea of the working relations between Coleridge and Wordsworth at the moment when the scheme for *Lyrical Ballads* (1798) was being hatched. Their constant companionship on walks, at Alfoxden and elsewhere, gave rise to extended discussion of poetry present and past. Both proved open to suggestion; both grew as poets through their conversations. Most of what is known of this process is known through the *Lyrical Ballads* volume and its later "Preface." The conclusions which it expresses, in Wordsworth's voice more than Coleridge's, have long been seen as foundations of modern poetry.

The genesis of the "Ancient Mariner" is more than the story of one poem. It is the story of a project. In Coleridge's own account of events, they decided on two sorts of poems for *Lyrical Ballads*: "In the one, the incidents and agents were to be, in part at least, supernatural; and the excellence aimed at was to consist in the interest-

In Xannadù did Cubla Khan
A stately Pleasure-Dome decree;
Where Alph, the sacred River, ran
Thro' Caverns measureless to Man
Down to a sunless Sea.
So twice six miles of fertile ground
With Walls and Towers were compass'd round:
And here were Gardens bright with sinuous Rills
Where blossom'd many an incense-bearing Tree,
And here were Forests ancient as the Hills
Enfolding sunny spots of Greenery.
But o! that deep romantic Chasm, that slanted
Down a green Hill athwart a cedarn Cover,
A savage Place, as holy and inchanted
As e'er beneath a waning Moon was haunted
By Woman wailing for her Daemon Lover:
From forth
And from this Chasm with hideous Turmoil seething,
As if this Earth in fast thick Pants were breathing,
A mighty Fountain momently was forc'd,
Amid whose swift half-intermitted Burst
Huge Fragments vaulted like rebounding Hail,
Or chaffy Grain beneath the Thresher's Flail:
And mid these dancing Rocks at once & ever
It flung up momently the sacred River.
Five miles meandring with a mazy Motion
Thro' Wood and Dale the sacred River ran,
Then reach'd the Caverns measureless to Man
And sank in Tumult to a lifeless Ocean;
And mid this Tumult Cubla heard from far
Ancestral Voices prophesying War.
   The Shadow of the Dome of Pleasure
   Floated midway on the Wave
   Where was heard the mingled Measure
   From the Fountain and the Cave.
   It was a miracle of rare Device,
   A sunny Pleasure-Dome with Caves of Ice!

    A Damsel with a Dulcimer

The earliest known manuscript for "Kubla Khan" (Crewe MS; by permission of the British Library)

In a vision once I saw:
It was an Abyssinian Maid,
And on her Dulcimer she play'd
Singing of Mount Amara.
Could I revive within me
Her Symphony & Song,
To such a deep Delight 'twould win me,
That with Music loud and long,
I would build that Dome in Air,
That sunny Dome! those Caves of Ice!
And all, who heard, should see them there,
And all should cry, Beware! Beware!
His flashing Eyes! his floating Hair!
Weave a circle round him thrice,
And close your Eyes in holy Dread,
For He on Honey-dew hath fed
And drank the Milk of Paradise.————

This fragment with a good deal more, not
recoverable, composed, in a sort of Reverie brought
on by two grains of Opium, taken to check a
dysentery, at a Farm House between Porlock &
Linton, a quarter of a mile from Culbone Church,
in the fall of the year, 1797.————

                                        S. T. Coleridge

ing of the affections by the dramatic truth of such emotions, as would naturally accompany such situations, supposing them real. And real in this sense they have been to every human being who, from whatever source of delusion, has at any time believed himself under supernatural agency."

It was this line that Coleridge was set to pursue. The "Ancient Mariner," the opening poem of the volume as it appeared in 1798 and after, represents a kind of case study in derangement and perception if we take his account of things at face value. De Quincey corroborates this assumption with his story that "Coleridge, shortly before writing his 'Ancient Mariner,' had been thinking of writing a poem on delirium, confounding its own dream-scenery with external things, and connected with the imagery of high latitudes."

Lyrical Ballads was deliberately experimental, as the authors insisted from the start. The "Ancient Mariner" pointed the way. The fact that it was a collaboration meant that both authors took responsibility for the design of the experiment. This was more than a volume of poems from various hands. The largely negative reviews which it excited on publication concentrated on the "Ancient Mariner," in part because it was the most substantial poem in the collection, but also because of its self-consciously archaic diction and incredible plot. Southey described it in a dismissive (and anonymous) review as "a Dutch attempt at German sublimity." Elsewhere it was reckoned "the strangest story of a cock and a bull that we ever saw on paper." The character of the Mariner also caused confusion.

It is evident that the collaboration had something to do with these difficulties. The ballad form adopted for the purpose typically included a strong central figure. Coleridge's Old Navigator became an Ancient Mariner without acquiring personality or the strong appeal characteristic of the type. Coleridge later said that he had the Wandering Jew in mind; one of the ballads from Thomas Percy's *Reliques of Ancient English Poetry* (1765) took him as its subject. The sacrificial victim sorts well enough with Coleridge's scheme of sin and penance, rather less well with Wordsworth's original notion of crime and punishment. The unresolved sense of direction produced an aimless protagonist whose sufferings appeared excessive if not actually pointless.

Despite the problems, the poem flourished on the basis of strong local effects–of its pictures of the "land of ice and snow" and of the ghastly ship in the doldrums, in association with a drumming ballad meter. Wordsworth frankly disliked it after the reviews came in, but Lamb led the way in appreciating its odd mix of romance and realism. Satires were published in leading periodicals; Coleridge fiddled with the diction, toning down his original "Ancyent Marinere" for the second edition of *Lyrical Ballads*. He added glosses in the margins when it was included in *Sibylline Leaves* (1817), trying to straighten things out. Nothing he attempted really answered the confusion about the character of the protagonist, nor about supernatural agents which seemed more than figments of the Mariner's delirious fancy.

It is perhaps as a poem of pure imagination, in the words of Robert Penn Warren's landmark reading, that the "Ancient Mariner" has appealed. In this respect among others it bears comparison with "Kubla Khan"; they are usually classified, with *Christabel*, as poems of the supernatural. All answer to the formula proposed for Coleridge's contributions to *Lyrical Ballads:* supernatural, or at least preternatural, phenomena dignified by association with a human voice. For most readers this is the line of Coleridge's verse that has mattered. Whatever their liabilities of dramatic construction, the highly charged imagery of these poems has made a strong impression. Its influence rings clear in Shelley and Keats in the next generation, and in Tennyson, Browning, Rossetti, and Swinburne among their Victorian inheritors. In the title of W. H. Auden's *Look, Stranger!* (1936) the echo of the Mariner's exhortation, "Listen, Stranger!," from the text of 1798, shows how far Coleridge's oracular voice would carry.

Christabel, whose first part dates from the winter of 1797 and spring 1798, the most productive period of Coleridge's brief residence at Nether Stowey, proved the most influential of his poems of the supernatural. The imagery of this opening part reflects the winter landscape of the surrounding area. But the air of romance is pronounced from the beginning, and the details of Sir Leoline's castle and wood are charged with otherworldly significance. The tension between sensible particulars and informing values runs very high throughout. Here Coleridge came as near as he ever would to sustaining the distinctive blend of image and idea at work in his best verse. Even in its unfinished state the poem compels attention, and not only for local effects of imagery. Coleridge tried out a new metric scheme in *Christabel*, counting four accents per line instead of eight syllables as in ordinary iambic te-

Cartoon by James Gillray, published in the 1 August 1798 issue of the Anti-Jacobin Review and Magazine. *Among the worshipers at the altar of the French Revolutionary "trinity" are Coleridge (standing ass), Robert Southey (kneeling ass), Charles Lamb and Charles Lloyd (frog and toad), John Thelwall (on the shoulders of the Leviathan), and Charles James Fox (behind Thelwall), leader of the opposition party in Parliament. The Leviathan is Francis Russell, Fifth Duke of Bedford, one of Fox's supporters.*

trameter. Most of the verse actually conforms to the normal pattern, but the syllables number from seven to twelve per line "in correspondence with some transition, in the nature of the imagery or passion."

The dramatic action is accentuated in this way through the poet's inflections. The effect, as in the "Ancient Mariner," is of a voice speaking, not of disembodied spectacle. But the character of the narrator is not in question here; the conventions of romance operate without interference from an unsympathetic or intrusive observer. Christabel, daughter of Sir Leoline, is an attractive if vulnerable protagonist whose midnight walk in the nearby wood introduces a parable of innocence undone by evil. Her encounter with the mysterious Geraldine is carefully staged for disarming effect; she accepts without question Geraldine's woolly story of abduction and abandonment. Carrying her frail foundling over the threshold into the castle grounds, Christabel takes an incubus into her heart and into her bed. The lyrical "Conclusion to Part I" recapitulates the imagery and significance of the opening movement of the story, drawing preliminary conclusions. Though extraneous to the dramatic action, it underlines the authority of the narrating voice.

Christabel was meant for the *Lyrical Ballads* volume in progress at the time of its first composition, but its completion was deferred: first until 1800, when the second edition was in sight, then

until "my poetic powers" recovered from "a state of suspended animation," as Coleridge put it in his preface to the first edition of 1816. At that late date he still expected to add three parts "in the course of the present year" to what he had on hand. This included "Part II" and its attached lyric conclusion, composed at Keswick in 1800. The imagery of the second part belongs not to the Quantock combes but to the ghylls and pikes of the north English lake district. Sir Leoline dominates the dramatic action, which turns on his infatuation with Geraldine, and with her transformation in Christabel's eyes. Wordsworth's decision not to include the poem in the second edition of *Lyrical Ballads* after the strenuous effort which Coleridge had made toward completing this part was a turning point. For he found himself unable to go on with *Christabel*, unable even to continue to think of himself as a poet. Wordsworth confirmed, if he did not actually cause, the state of suspended animation referred to in the 1816 preface to the still-unfinished text.

Coleridge's contributions to the *Lyrical Ballads* volume included a short piece from *Osorio* called "The Foster-Mother's Tale," and a meditative poem in blank verse, "The Nightingale," as well as "The Ancient Mariner." The collaboration with Wordsworth is perhaps most striking in their development of the conversational idiom for which the subtitle of "The Nightingale, A Conversation Poem, Written in April, 1798" provided a name. It was not the first of the conversation poems; these are considered to begin from "The Eolian Harp" and to include "Reflections on Having Left a Place of Retirement" and "This Lime-Tree Bower My Prison" among his earlier meditative verses. Coleridge himself never distinguished them in this way, nor has Wordsworth's poetry of the kind ever been described as conversational. Yet the term has come to stand for Coleridge's decisive innovation as a poet and for his contribution to the formation of Wordsworth's voice.

"The Nightingale" exemplifies the type. Coleridge had been to tea at Alfoxden with William and Dorothy Wordsworth, and on his walk back to Nether Stowey the train of thoughts and images arising as he went provided material for a meditative poem written with his hosts in mind. What he produced was not a conversation, as Cowper had done in his "Table Talk" for instance. It was "conversational," a sort of soliloquy among friends. The poem begins from the spectacle of twilight, fixes on a line of Milton which Wordsworth had employed in his *An Evening Walk*, accounts for the nightingale's supposed melancholy, and culminates in a tale of a maid in a wood brought to joy by the birds' "choral minstrelsy." All of this is clearly designed to please his friends, in its casual manner of association and delivery as much as in its conviction of a benevolent Nature. The poem concludes with a reflection on the education of his infant son, Berkeley (born 14 May 1798), to natural feeling. This should be read in the setting of Wordsworth's reflections on childhood elsewhere in *Lyrical Ballads*. Comparison shows how dialogic the poem's soliloquy actually is.

It was at this moment of intense exchange that Coleridge wrote his most imposing conversational verse, and that Wordsworth wrote "Lines Written A Few Miles Above Tintern Abbey," his startling initiation in the conversational idiom. Wordsworth's poem stands at the end of *Lyrical Ballads* rather as the "Ancient Mariner" stands at the beginning. It stands out, a monument to the realized achievement of the experiment. From the title, with its particularity about time and place, and the graceful discursive manner, through the association of ideas and the praise of Nature to the address in the concluding stanza to his sister, this poem is virtually a homage to Coleridge's conversational manner. What Wordsworth would make of the conversation poem is the story of the most distinguished poetic career of the period.

Silhouette of Sara Hutchinson in early middle age (by permission of the Wordsworth Trust)

Their achievement in the developing conversational line has seemed more momentous in retrospect than it did at the time. "Tintern Abbey" was noticed only fitfully in early reviews, while "The Nightingale" was associated with Cowper's meditative verse, which enjoyed greater currency throughout Coleridge's lifetime. Yet the example of the conversation poems took where it mattered most, among the poets of the next generation and every generation since. Shelley's "Julian and Maddalo" (1818) represents an early effort to expand on the possibilities of conversational verse. Matthew Arnold and T. S. Eliot in England and Robert Frost in America elaborated variously on the conversational convention. The recent testimony of Charles Tomlinson, an English poet, shows how the influence of Coleridge's innovation has been transmitted by modern writers: "The distinguishable American presences in my own work, so far as I can tell, were, up to then, Pound, Stevens, and Marianne Moore, and yet, if through them the tonality sounded American, the tradition of the work went back to Coleridge's conversation poems." The meditative verse of Geoffrey Hill in the same postwar generation rings changes on the Coleridgean originals of this line of modern verse.

Wordsworth made the conversation poem the vehicle of his celebration of enlightenment values: of nature as spiritual home, of man as the measure of things. Coleridge's conversational verse points in the same direction under the influence of his great friend, yet it is deeply conflicted under the surface. The conviction of a benevolent nature is compromised by mounting fears. In the earlier poems of the kind these are indicated only indirectly. In "Frost at Midnight," composed from the front room of the Lime Street cottage in the winter of 1798, the poet's isolation drives him to test the resources of nature conceived as a mediating agent. The opening image, and the concluding stanza which recalls it, represent an affirmation of this idea of nature, which is fundamentally Wordsworthian.

But there is more to "Frost at Midnight" than affirmation. The poem dramatizes Coleridge's sense of vulnerability in the face of a threatening outside world. Part of this feeling must have come from the growing hostility of the community in which he was living. Fear of a French invasion was widespread, and the outsiders were suspected of democratic sympathies, even of collusion with the national enemy. Walking home from Bristol, Coleridge heard himself described as a "vile Jacobin villain." The spy sent by the government found nothing much to report against him, but there was open mistrust of his motives and way of life. A local parson, William Holland, writing in 1799 in a diary first published in 1986, recounted seeing "that Democratic hoyden Mrs. Coleridge who looked so like a friskey girl or something worse that I was not surprised that a Democratic Libertine should choose her for a wife." Such testimony provides incidental evidence of social pressures which Coleridge expressed in "Frost at Midnight" in an intensely personal way.

The poem begins from a winter night's view out the poet's cottage window. With nothing stirring, he is driven back to the fire in the grate, where a fluttering film reminds him of his own "idling Spirit." *Strangers*, as such films are known—and as his footnote calls to attention—identifies not only the grate film but also the soliloquist's alien condition. The central movement of the poem characterizes him in his schoolboy isolation and homesickness, anticipating the arrival of friends or relations when the fluttering *stranger* appeared on the fire grate. This word fires his imagination, providing the impetus which the world outside his window had not. Yet it is "the secret ministry of frost" which is credited in the concluding stanza, in the final version of the poem, with intervening in his dark night of the spirit.

"Frost at Midnight" is the most psychodramatic of Coleridge's conversation poems even if the conclusion is not really consistent with the imaginative process which gives rise to it. For it exposes the deep fears behind the passion for Nature conceived in this way, as an intentional agent and life companion. "Religious meanings in the forms of nature" practically defines the idea as Coleridge understood it. In "Fears in Solitude," written soon after, and the source of this fine characterization, the sense of danger and vulnerability is directly related to political apprehensions. Less a conversation poem than a monody or extended peroration like "Religious Musings," "Fears in Solitude" shows Coleridge trying to associate the scenery around Nether Stowey with feelings for his country without giving way to the government which he despised. It is an uncertain performance, rambling and disjointed, yet interesting as a portrait of political conviction under pressure.

Despite the difficulties, this was a time of rare promise for the young writer. Wordsworth's presence was catalytic. It was through the *Lyrical Ballads* volume that Coleridge's voices, conversational and "romantic," were developed and rationalized. Dorothy Wordsworth's journal of 1798 shows how collaborative were all of their undertakings of this formative moment. Yet their auspicious beginning was to prove the beginning of the end of Coleridge's poetic powers. While Wordsworth would carry on with the experiment for some ten years after that spring in the Quantocks, his companion in the art was all but finished with it. Reasons for the divergence are bound to be conjectures after the fact, but two at least remain worth considering. The collaboration turned out to be a struggle for poetic primacy, and Wordsworth's personal domination eventually meant loss of conviction—and loss of face—for his troubled colleague. There was room for only one strong voice of this kind. Coleridge was drawn to other roles in any case, and to other causes. Poetry was his means, not his vocation.

What was his vocation then? He is usually described as a man of letters–as the prototype of the modern writer who lives from his earnings as journalist, book reviewer, and jack of all literary trades. The man of letters is typically considered as free of the constraints imposed by patronage on his convictions. In certain respects Coleridge fits this mold. He was repelled on principle by the Anglican ministry for which he was being trained at Christ's Hospital and Jesus College. This was the conventional career for a boy of his modest means and scholarly temperament. Dissenting theology made a strong appeal to his convictions and temperament; he considered accepting the post of minister offered him at the Unitarian chapel at Shrewsbury early in 1798. He was suited to the work, which provided both a pulpit and free time for his own writing.

He turned down the prospect of settled work and community only because he was provided, quite unexpectedly, a life annuity of 150 pounds sterling by Josiah and Thomas Wedgwood, heirs to the pottery and friends of reliable standing. There were no strings attached. The point was to free him of the routine material difficulties which were already closing in on him from all sides. This was a godsend, but it also put Coleridge on his mettle. For he was now faced with the imperative to choose and define a vocation for himself. Freedom imposes its own obligations, and patronage remains patronage even without the strings. The imminent departure of the Wordsworths, whose one-year lease at Alfoxden was not renewed in June 1798 due to local doubts about their character, precipitated a personal crisis of sorts. The upshot was an extended residence in Germany, separation from family and friends in Nether Stowey, and a change of direction.

Coleridge was drawn to Germany for its literary ferment and new learning. He proposed to stay "3 or 4 months, in which time I shall at least have learnt the language," but his real motive was larger: "I think the realization of the scheme of high importance to my intellectual utility; and of course to my moral happiness." He sailed with the Wordsworths in tow in September, returning only in June 1799, with more than the language to show for his wanderings. His residence of some months at the university in Göttingen ex-

posed him to the earlier Germanic languages and literatures and also to the new scriptural criticism which would change the face of modern theology. He read Friedrich Gottlieb Klopstock and Gotthold Ephraim Lessing rather than Johann Wolfgang von Goethe; he met the first, by then an elderly gentleman, in Hamburg, and projected a life of the second, among many other things, in the course of his studies. Enlightenment thinking–not *Sturm und Drang*–was the object lesson.

Germany opened doors whose existence he had hardly imagined. It was here that he learned the language sufficiently to approach the critical philosophy of Immanuel Kant, which consumed his thinking from about 1800. Göttingen supplied a working idea of language which he would turn to his own uses on his return. And it involved him in historical inquiries–on the origin of the free farming class, for example–which he communicated to his correspondents at home. The impression left by his notebooks and letters of this period of residence abroad is of unusual intellectual attentiveness.

The intellectual turn is what distinguishes Coleridge from others, including his friends Hazlitt and Lamb, whose activity as writers in the period was more clearly in the native grain. His example was followed by De Quincey and Carlyle with differing emphases; "men of letters" would appear less apt to their cases than "literary intellectuals," with the stress on fresh thinking. Literature, or "polite literature" as Coleridge sometimes called it, included the prose essay for all of them. Verse and prose did not live separate lives; they were distinctive in means but not different in ends as Coleridge explained them. Both gave scope to the same human understanding.

Coleridge rejoined his family in Nether Stowey in midsummer 1799, some time after having returned from Germany. It was an uncomfortable homecoming on several counts. Wordsworth was soon on his way to Dove Cottage at Grasmere in the remote north country, and Coleridge was not far behind. There was trouble with Southey and a difficult leavetaking from Thomas Poole. "The Devil's Thoughts" (later published as *The Devil's Walk*, 1830), a finely honed satirical collaboration undertaken with Southey at this time, is an odd memorial to the rural society he was leaving. The devil as country gentleman finds himself in good company on "his snug little farm the Earth," in his element among lawyers, booksellers, turnkeys, clerks (in the old sense of scholars), and Methodists. With such feelings about the populace of the west country, it is no wonder that Coleridge was ready to go north. His home thoughts from abroad had been warm, but Nether Stowey now seemed hopelessly parochial.

On his way north he tarried in London as political correspondent for the *Morning Post*, writing a brilliant piece on Pitt, the prime minister, showing what his own convictions counted for. For readers interested only in the poetry, such topical work is bound to seem tedious; yet it represents the heart of Coleridge's commitment in the period when he was writing his best verse. His *Essays on His Own Times* (1850), collected long after in three volumes, show how serious and capable a critic of society he was. The promotion of his most personal and individualistic work by later readers has obscured his constant attention to social arrangements and social ideals. Far from the lunatic visionary evoked by "Kubla Khan," Coleridge was always concerned for the whole, the public arena of human experience; not merely for the parts–the private mind, the estate, the poem as text.

His move to Keswick in summer 1800 (not long before the birth of his third son, Derwent, on 14 September) did represent a kind of retreat from the discouraging world of city politics and city life. The Wedgwood annuity made it feasible, Wordsworth's presence nearby practically inevitable. *Lyrical Ballads* was to be republished in a new edition; *Christabel* was still unfinished, and here he added the second part, with its altered landscape reflecting the scenery of Langdale Pike and "Borodale." It was a critical time in his professional transition. Wordsworth's rejection of the still unfinished poem contributed to Coleridge's sense of personal incapacity. He came to feel that he was not a poet; not a great poet, at least–not like Wordsworth. Yet his valedictory ode, "Dejection," first composed as a letter in 1802, shows him at the peak of his powers. Writing in the shadow of Wordsworth's "Intimations" ode, Coleridge here cultivated a more colloquial delivery while remaining true to his own muse. This is his magisterial conversation poem, the most compelling (though not the most celebrated) achievement of his foreshortened poetic career.

"Dejection" began as a verse epistle to Sara Hutchinson, sister of Wordsworth's soon-to-be wife, and the object of a desperate passion which afflicted Coleridge's life at home and within. In its original form it is rambling and effusive, yet exceptionally energetic, and this at a time when Cole-

ridge had seemingly gone to ground. The original should be compared with the finished piece, which is trimmed and shaped, orchestrated for dramatic effect with rare attention to detail. It should also be considered in the complex and interesting intertextual setting of Wordsworth's "Intimations" ode, and also of his exasperated "Leech-Gatherer" (later "Resolution and Independence"), which responds with determination to the despair of "Dejection." The mingled measures of their voices are nowhere more evident, nor more effective. Wordsworth galvanized Coleridge's natural powers but feared the echo of his own voice and the intimacy which it involved. In his "Leech-Gatherer" he put Coleridge and all his problems behind him, choosing to continue in a poetic isolation which would eventually deplete his powers.

Coleridge's testament, as "Dejection" might be considered, begins from a verse of "Sir Patrick Spence," relying on language for inspiration. It follows "The Nightingale" and "The Eolian Harp" in turning from natural impressions to human voices for dialogic context. The opening stanza dramatizes the insufficiency of sensation for the inner life, already evident in those poems. Wordsworth's companionable nature has failed; in Coleridge's valedictory it appears as a dark and stormy setting of personal psychodrama. Observed more than felt, its beauty is alien to the estrangement and terror of the human condition. Wordsworth would go on to solve this problem by invoking the compensating power of memory, which bound the grown man to the child's spontaneous feeling for the world around him. There is no such compensation in "Dejection."

Coleridge was now on his own as never before, unsettled, constantly ill, searching for a way through his difficulties. He decided at this time on a career as a critic, at first proposing "an Essay on the Elements of Poetry / it would in reality be a *disguised* System of Morals & Politics–." The real orientation of his poetics is indicated here. It was refined but not fundamentally altered by subsequent reflection and formulation. By 1804 he was calling the same project *"On the Sources of Poetic Pleasure*–in which without using the words bad or good, I simply endeavor to detect the causes & sources of the Pleasures, which different styles &c have given in different ages, & then determining their comparative Worth, Permanency, & Compatibility with the noble parts of our nature to establish in the utmost depths, to

Pages from the first version of "Dejection," written as a verse epistle to Sara Hutchinson (by permission of the Wordsworth Trust).
This version, written in an accounts ledger, is more than twice as long as the final version.

Coleridge in 1804, just before he left England for Malta (portrait by James Northcote by permission of the Wordsworth Trust)

which I can delve, the characteristics of Good & Bad Poetry– & the intimate connection of Taste & Morals.–" The lectures delivered at the Royal Institution in 1808 on "The Principles of Poetry" apparently fleshed out this program, beginning from Shakespeare and concluding "On Modern Poetry." They were the first of several lecture series conducted by Coleridge in the years 1808-1814. Their contents are known mainly from unreliable reports when they are known at all.

The lectures of 1811-1812 on Shakespeare were influential in the general revival of interest in the Elizabethan drama. Dr. Johnson's 1765 preface to his edition of Shakespeare's works had de-

fended him as the poet of nature who held up a mirror to life and manners. Against this mimetic emphasis Coleridge lay stress on Shakespeare's expressive language and the psychological acumen associated with it: "In the plays of Shakespeare, every man sees himself, without knowing that he does so." In his notes on *Hamlet* and *Macbeth*, Coleridge can be seen teasing out elements of his own personality while exploring two models of poetic identity: poet as idealist, poet as obsessive imagist. Both revert to a meditation on the "poetical character" in his early letters and notebooks. Character analysis would become the stock-in-trade of a tribe of Victorian commentators working in Coleridge's wake, though not always in accord with his commitment to the integrity of Shakespeare's dramatic construction. Maurice Morgann and A. C. Bradley, to name two celebrated practitioners, concentrated on the characters at the expense of the plays, something which Coleridge did only where, as in *Hamlet*, the character consumes the fabric of the text.

A more important legacy of the lectures on Shakespeare is the idea of organicism, which has deep roots in his earlier critical reflection. In lecture notes on Shakespeare, Coleridge evokes organic form in terms which mimic the contemporary German critic August Wilhelm Schlegel: "The form is mechanic when on any given material we impress a pre-ordained form, not necessarily arising out of the properties of the material, as when to a mass of wet clay we give whatever shape we wish it to retain when hardened. The organic form, on the other hand, is innate; it shapes as it develops itself from within, and the fullness of its development is one and the same with the perfection of its outward form." The form of Shakespeare's dramas grew out of his characters and ideas, on Coleridge's telling; the old dramatic conventions did not impede the conception. The structural variety of his plays–the seeming irregularities of *The Tempest*, in particular–arose from expressive requirements. Organic form redeemed Shakespeare's unconventional dramatic constructions.

The importance of the organic metaphor and idea for later thinking about poetry can hardly be exaggerated. The sense of the work of art as an organism, self-germinating and self-enclosed, pervades modern writing and modern criticism. Coleridge's elaboration on the idea of imagination in this period owes something to the distinction of mechanic and organic form as well. His definitions of primary and secondary imagination and of fancy have become canonical; they served I. A. Richards, notably, as a theoretical basis of the "semasiology" which he proposed in 1935. This putative science of meaning was meant to shore up the foundations of English as an academic discipline and proved influential not only at Cambridge but throughout the English-speaking world, including the United States, where it provided impetus for the development of the New Criticism, as it was called. Coleridge on imagination practically underwrote this enterprise. In chapter 13 of his *Biographia Literaria* Coleridge defines the key terms as follows:

The IMAGINATION then, I consider either as primary, or secondary. The primary IMAGINATION I hold to be the living Power and prime Agent of all human Perception, and as a repetition in the finite mind of the eternal act of creation in the infinite I AM. The secondary Imagination I consider as an echo of the former, co-existing with the conscious will, yet still as identical with the primary in the *kind* of its agency, and differing only in *degree*, and in the *mode* of its operation. It dissolves, diffuses, dissipates, in order to recreate; or where this process is rendered impossible, yet still at all events it struggles to idealize and to unify. It is essentially *vital*, even as all objects (*as* objects) are essentially fixed and dead.

FANCY, on the contrary, has no other counters to play with, but fixities and definites. The Fancy is indeed no other than a mode of Memory emancipated from the order of time and space; while it is blended with, and modified by that empirical phenomenon of the will, which we express by the word CHOICE. But equally with the ordinary memory the Fancy must receive all its materials ready made from the law of association.

These compact definitions, grounded in a long philosophical investigation, remain problematic. The theological conception of primary imagination does not sort with the aesthetic orientation of the secondary, which is derived directly from the German philosopher Friedrich Wilhelm Joseph von Schelling. Coleridge soon abandoned it along with the aesthetic ideal which it expresses. Yet it is this aesthetic ideal which Richards and modern criticism in general have drawn from a very partial reading of Coleridge's criticism. Treating him as a provincial outpost of the new German critical philosophy of Immanuel Kant, English and American readers have usually abandoned the complex record of his reading and response in favor of one or two manageable ideas. The result has been general misapprehension about his orientation and commitments. Coleridge does not make sense as a model of aesthetic reading despite the efforts of Richards and others to bend him to this purpose.

What sort of reader was he, then? Moral and political, certainly, but something more. On his return from Germany in 1799, Coleridge had undertaken "a metaphysical Investigation" of "the affinities of the Feelings with Words & Ideas," to be composed "under the title of 'Concerning Poetry & the nature of the Pleasures derived from it.'" The connection of his philosophi-

Unfinished portrait of Coleridge painted by Washington Allston in early 1806 while Coleridge was in Rome
(by permission of the Harvard University Art Museums [Fogg Art Museum], Washington Allston Trust)

cal studies with his critical ambition is important for understanding how Coleridge imagined the critical function. He was not interested in judging writing by current standards. Conventional judgments of good or bad relied on unspoken assumptions which he was concerned to test and modify, where appropriate, by the light of reason. Adjudicating taste is the usual purview of the "man of letters." Coleridge was trying for something more philosophical, of larger scope and bearing: "acting the arbitrator between the old School & the New School to lay down some plain, & perspicuous, tho' not superficial Canons of Criticism respecting poetry."

In the wake of the republication of *Lyrical Ballads* in early 1801 (with '1800' on the title page), Coleridge's critical project became a protracted effort to come to terms with Wordsworth's radical claims in the "Preface" for a poetry composed "in the real language of men." This was the "New School" of "natural thoughts in natural diction": Coleridge's own school despite his differences with Wordsworth. His effort to make the case for the new verse in the teeth of pitched hostility on the part of reviewers culminated in his *Biographia Literaria* (1817), where the "Old School" is treated anecdotally in the opening chapters on the way to the triumph of Wordsworth's voice. The fifteen years between the "Preface" and *Biographia Literaria* were consumed with working through the critical agenda which Coleridge set himself at the turn of the century.

Coleridge in 1814 (portrait by Washington Allston; by permission of the National Portrait Gallery, London)

The process was a fitful, often tortuous one. The metaphysical investigation assumed a life of its own, waylaid by deep plunges into Kant and Schelling, among others. It culminates in the first volume of the *Biographia Literaria* with an effort to provide rational ground for the critical exercise which follows in the second. The definition of imagination in chapter 13 is usually accounted the most important of Coleridge's critical propositions though its bearing remains uncertain. The long native tradition of thinking about imagination was supplemented here by an aesthetic idea borrowed from Schelling. The judgment that Coleridge was badly off his philosophic form in the first volume of the *Biographia Literaria* is now widely accepted. His definition of imagination remains an important part of his poetic legacy, nevertheless, since it underwrites the development of a symbolist aesthetic still associated with

his name though at odds with his enduring commitments.

The thoughtful approach to Wordsworth in the second volume represents Coleridge's understanding of poetry at its best. His account of the *Lyrical Ballads* project challenges some of Wordsworth's claims in the "Preface" to the second edition in a way which distinguishes the effective from the peculiar in his verse. He begins by developing a definition of poetry based on something more than its metric properties. It is not so much meter as the calculus of the parts in the whole that makes poetry different from novels and romances, which share its primary aim of communicating pleasure. "Equal and continuous attention" characterizes the reader's response to poetry. Such concerted effect is the product of the faculty of imagination: "The poet, described in *ideal* perfection, brings the whole soul of man

269

And to repay the other !   Why rejoices
   Thy heart with hollow joy for hollow good,
   Why cowl thy face beneath the Mourner's hood,
Why waste thy sighs, and thy lamenting voices,
   Image of Image, Ghost of Ghostly Elf,
That such a thing, as thou, feel'st warm or cold!
Yet what and whence thy gain, if thou withhold
   These costless shadows of thy shadowy self?
Be sad ! be glad! be neither ! seek, or shun !
Thou hast no reason why !   Thou can'st have none !
Thy being's being is contradiction.

Coleridge's notes on "Human Life" in a set of sheets for Sibylline Leaves *(1817) bound in 1897 and believed to have been his author's proofs (auctioned by Christie, Manson & Woods Ltd, 13-14 June 1979)*

Portrait by Daniel Maclise in the Fraser's Magazine *"Gallery of Illustrious Literary Characters" (1830-1838)*

into activity, with the subordination of its faculties to each other, according to their relative worth and dignity. He diffuses a tone and spirit of unity, that blends, and (as it were) *fuses,* each into each, by that synthetic and magical power, to which we have exclusively appropriated the name of imagination."

This esemplastic or unifying faculty thus becomes definitive of poetry. Wordsworth is extolled for his "gift of IMAGINATION in the highest and strictest sense of the word." But not only for this, nor only in terms which recur to the definition of imagination. Coleridge does not actually describe the operation of the faculty of imagination in particular passages, though he points to several which appear to illustrate his idea. Readers have often taken his theoretic pronouncements about imagination as constituting his poetics, while the account of Wordsworth's verse shows

him applying more conventional standards in new and thoughtful ways. This discussion of the new school in English poetry includes a detailed treatment of the question of poetic language as raised by Wordsworth, and it is Coleridge's response to his positions in the *Lyrical Ballads* "Preface" that makes up the real centerpiece of the argument. The defense of poetic diction in particular is important for understanding his idea of poetry. Its roots lie in a long meditation on language, not in a philosophically derived faculty of imagination.

This meditation on language occupied Coleridge occasionally during the years between his return from Germany in 1799 and the composition of the *Biographia Literaria*. Among projects which he undertook during these long years of opium addiction, physical disability, and aimless wandering, *The Friend* (1809) stands out for its originality and influence. After two years away, in Malta, Sicily, and Rome, he returned to Keswick in 1806, separated from his wife (who had given birth to their daughter, Sara, on 23 December 1802), lectured and dilated, and finally settled on publishing "a weekly essay" which ran from 1 June 1809 to 15 March 1810. Unlike his earlier periodical enterprise, *The Watchman* (1796), which was resolutely political, *The Friend* was dedicated "to found true PRINCIPLES, to oppose false PRINCIPLES, in Criticism, Legislation, Philosophy, Morals, and International Law." The cultural setting of this project was the general malaise of the English intelligentsia during the French wars. The publication rose and fell by subscriptions, relying on Coleridge's name and reputation, and finally collapsed under the weight of his private difficulties. Eclectic in approach, broadly literary in style, its various essays remain worth considering for what they indicate of the evolution of letters in the period. *The Friend* established a high discursive tone which was influential among Coleridge's inheritors, including Carlyle and Emerson, for whom it was counted among his most valuable works.

In 1812 the Wedgwood annuity was reduced by half due to financial difficulties related to the war. Coleridge continued to wander, staying with friends all over the kingdom and occasionally with his family in Keswick. In 1816 he published *Christabel* with "Kubla Khan" and "The Pains of Sleep" in a single volume; the next year his collected verse, *Sibylline Leaves*, appeared. He moved into the house of Dr. James Gillman, a physician in Highgate, now a north London village, trying to cure or at least to treat his opium problem. Here he would pass the remainder of his life, writing only occasional verse while preparing philosophical lectures (delivered in 1818), revising the text of *The Friend* for publication as a book, and collating the moral and theological aphorisms which appeared as *Aids to Reflection* (1825). These were popular and influential in America as well as in England. Coleridge published a meditation on political inspiration in *The Stateman's Manual* (1816) among other tracts on subjects theological and political. *On the Constitution of Church and State* appeared in 1830; *Confessions of an Inquiring Spirit* posthumously in 1840. He planned a comprehensive philosophical synthesis which he was unable to realize, conjuring with a system which lived only in his constantly working mind. The most finished text from among his philosophical papers was published in

1848 as *Hints towards the Formation of a more Comprehensive Theory of Life*. The reconstruction of his abortive synthesis is in progress.

Coleridge died in 1834 after years of personal discomfort and disappointment. A legend in his time, he came to be seen by friends and contemporaries as the genius who failed. The failure was largely relative to early expectations, however, and to hopes defeated by disease and drugs. Despite everything, Coleridge can still be regarded as a groundbreaking and, at his best, a powerful poet of lasting influence. His idea of poetry remains the standard by which others in the English sphere are tried. If the philosophical investigation appears less convincing than it once did, it still represents the trajectory of idealist thinking in the most searching English mind of the nineteenth century. As a political thinker, and as a Christian apologist, Coleridge proved an inspiration to the important generation after his own. The achievement is more considerable than his detractors have admitted, of greater moment than he dared to hope in despair of his broken life. Recent publication of his private notebooks has provided further evidence of the constant ferment and vitality of his inquiring spirit.

Letters:

The Letters of Samuel Taylor Coleridge, 2 volumes, edited by Ernest Hartley Coleridge (London: Heinemann, 1895; Boston & New York: Houghton, Mifflin, l895);

Unpublished Letters of Samuel Taylor Coleridge, 2 volumes, edited by Earl Leslie Griggs (London: Constable, 1932; New Haven: Yale University Press, 1933);

Collected Letters of Samuel Taylor Coleridge, 6 volumes, edited by Griggs (Oxford: Clarendon Press, 1956-1973);

Samuel Taylor Coleridge: Selected Letters, edited by H. J. Jackson (Oxford: Clarendon Press, 1987).

Bibliographies:

Thomas J. Wise, *A Bibliography of the Writings in Prose and Verse of Samuel Taylor Coleridge*, 2 volumes (London: Bibliographical Society, 1913);

Wise, *Coleridgeiana, Being a Supplement to the Bibliography of Coleridge* (London: Bibliographical Society, 1919);

Richard & Josephine Haven and Maurianne Adams, *Samuel Taylor Coleridge: An Annotated Bibliography of Criticism and Scholarship*, vol-

Coleridge in 1832 (portrait by Moses Haughton; by permission of Christ's Hospital)

ume 1: 1793-1899 (Boston: G. K. Hall, 1976);

Jefferson D. Caskey and Melinda M. Stapper, *Samuel Taylor Coleridge: A Selective Bibliography of Criticism, 1935-1977* (Westport, Conn.: Greenwood, 1978);

Mary Lee Taylor Milton, *The Poetry of Samuel Taylor Coleridge: An Annotated Bibliography of Criticism, 1935-1970* (New York: Garland, 1981).

Biographies:

Thomas Allsop, *Letters, Conversations, and Recollections of Samuel Taylor Coleridge*, 2 volumes (London: Moxon, 1836; New York: Harper, 1836);

Joseph Cottle, *Early Recollections, chiefly relating to the late Samuel Taylor Coleridge, during his long residence at Bristol*, 2 volumes (London: Longman, Rees/Hamilton, Adams, 1837); revised, with additional materials, as *Reminiscences of Samuel Taylor Coleridge and Robert Southey* (London: Houlston & Stoneman, 1847; New York: Wiley & Putnam, 1848);

James Gillman, *The Life of Samuel Taylor Coleridge*, volume one [no more published] (London: Pickering, 1838);

Henry Nelson Coleridge and Sara Coleridge, "Biographical Supplement" to *Biographia Literaria*, second edition (London: Pickering, 1847; New York: Putnam, 1848);

H. D. Traill, *Coleridge*, English Men of Letters (London: Macmillan, 1884; New York: Harper, 1884);

James Dykes Campbell, *Samuel Taylor Coleridge: a Narrative of the Events of his Life* (London & New York: Macmillan, 1894);

E. K. Chambers, *Samuel Taylor Coleridge: A Biographical Study* (Oxford: Clarendon Press, 1938);

Lawrence Hanson, *The Life of Samuel Taylor Coleridge: The Early Years* (London: Allen & Unwin, 1938; New York: Oxford University Press, 1939);

Walter Jackson Bate, *Coleridge*, Masters of World Literature (New York: Macmillan, 1968; London: Weidenfeld & Nicolson, 1969);

Berta Lawrence, *Coleridge and Wordsworth in Somerset* (Newton Abbot: David & Charles, 1970);

John Cornwell, *Coleridge: Poet and Revolutionary, 1772-1804* (London: Allen Lane, 1973);

Oswald Doughty, *Perturbed Spirit: The Life & Personality of Samuel Taylor Coleridge* (Rutherford, Madison & Teaneck, N. J.: Farleigh Dickinson University Press, 1981);

Richard Holmes, *Coleridge: Early Visions* (London: Hodder & Stoughton, 1989).

References:

M. H. Abrams, *Natural Supernaturalism: Tradition and Revolution in Romantic Literature* (New York: Norton, 1971);

Richard W. Armour and Raymond F. Howes, eds., *Coleridge the Talker: A Series of Contemporary Descriptions and Comments* (Ithaca: Cornell University Press/London: Humphrey Milford, Oxford University Press, 1940);

Owen Barfield, *What Coleridge Thought* (Middletown, Conn.: Wesleyan University Press, 1971);

J. Robert Barth, S.J., *The Symbolic Imagination: Coleridge and the Romantic Tradition* (Princeton: Princeton University Press, 1977);

J. B. Beer, *Coleridge's Poetic Intelligence* (London & Basingstoke: Macmillan, 1977);

Beer, "The Languages of *Kubla Khan*," in *Coleridge's Imagination*, edited by Richard Gravil, Lucy Newlyn, and Nicholas Roe (Cambridge: Cambridge University Press, 1985), pp. 218-262;

Beer, ed., *Coleridge's Variety: Bicentenary Studies* (London & Basingstoke: Macmillan, 1974);

Jerome Christensen, *Coleridge's Blessed Machine of Language* (Ithaca: Cornell University Press, 1981);

John Colmer, *Coleridge: Critic of Society* (Oxford: Clarendon Press, 1959);

Thomas De Quincey, "Samuel Taylor Coleridge, by the English Opium-Eater," *Tait's Edinburgh Magazine*, new series 1 (September 1834): 509-520; (October 1834): 588-596;

(November 1834): 685-690; new series 2 (January 1835): 2-10; republished in *Recollections of the Lakes and the Lake Poets*, edited by David Wright (Harmondsworth: Penguin, 1970), pp. 33-111;

James Engell, *The Creative Imagination, Enlightenment to Romanticism* (Cambridge, Mass.: Harvard University Press, 1981);

Norman Fruman, *Coleridge, the Damaged Archangel* (New York: Braziller, 1971);

A. C. Goodson, "Kubla's Construct," *Studies in Romanticism*, 18 (Fall 1979): 405-425;

Goodson, *Verbal Imagination: Coleridge and the Language of Modern Criticism* (New York & Oxford: Oxford University Press, 1988);

Anthony John Harding, *Coleridge and the Inspired Word* (Kingston & Montreal: McGill-Queen's University Press, 1985);

Richard Haven, "The Ancient Mariner in the Nineteenth Century," *Studies in Romanticism*, 11 (Fall 1972): 360-374;

William Hazlitt, "Mr. Coleridge," in *The Spirit of the Age: or Contemporary Portraits* (London: Colburn, 1825);

Hazlitt, "My First Acquaintance with Poets," *Liberal*, 3 (April 1823): 23-46;

Humphry House, *Coleridge: The Clark Lectures* (London: Hart-Davis, 1953);

Charles Lamb (Elia), "Christ's Hospital Five-and-thirty Years Ago," *London Magazine* [Baldwin's], 2 (November 1820): 483-490;

John Livingston Lowes, *The Road to Xanadu: A Study in the Ways of the Imagination* (Boston & New York: Houghton Mifflin, 1927);

Paul Magnuson, *Coleridge and Wordsworth: A Lyrical Dialogue* (Princeton: Princeton University Press, 1988);

Emerson Marks, *Coleridge on the Language of Verse* (Princeton: Princeton University Press, 1981);

Thomas McFarland, *Coleridge and the Pantheist Tradition* (Oxford: Clarendon Press, 1969);

McFarland, *Originality and Imagination* (Baltimore & London: Johns Hopkins University Press, 1985);

McFarland, *Romanticism and the Forms of Ruin: Wordsworth, Coleridge, and the Modalities of Fragmentation* (Princeton: Princeton University Press, 1981);

John Stuart Mill, "Coleridge," *London and Westminster Review*, 33 (1840): 257-302;

John T. Miller, Jr., *Ideology and Enlightenment: The Political and Social Thought of Samuel Tay-

lor Coleridge (New York & London: Garland, 1987);

Reeve Parker, *Coleridge's Meditative Art* (Ithaca: Cornell University Press, 1975);

Walter Pater, "Coleridge," in his *Appreciations* (London & New York: Macmillan, 1889);

I. A. Richards, *Coleridge on Imagination* (New York: Harcourt, Brace, 1935);

Nicolas Roe, *Wordsworth and Coleridge: The Radical Years* (Oxford & New York: Oxford University Press, 1987);

Eleanor Shafer, *"Kubla Khan" and the Fall of Jerusalem: the Mythological School in Biblical Criticism and Secular Literature 1770-1880* (Cambridge: Cambridge University Press, 1975);

Robert Penn Warren, "A Poem of Pure Imagination: An Experiment in Reading," in *The Rime of the Ancient Mariner* (New York: Reynal & Hitchcock, 1946), pp. 61-148;

Raymond Williams, *Culture and Society: 1780-1950* (London: Chatto & Windus, 1958), pp. 30-86;

Williams, "Notes on English Prose: 1780-1950," in his *Writing in Society* (London: Verso, 1984), pp. 67-118;

Carl Woodring, *Politics in the Poetry of Coleridge* (Madison: University of Wisconsin Press, 1961);

Ian Wylie, *Young Coleridge and the Philosophers of Nature* (Oxford: Oxford University Press, 1988).

Papers:

The British Library and Victoria University in the University of Toronto have important Coleridge collections.

George Crabbe

(24 December 1754 - 3 February 1832)

David R. Anderson
Texas A&M University

BOOKS: *Inebriety, A Poem, In Three Parts* (Ipswich: Printed & sold by C. Punchard, 1775);

The Candidate; A Poetical Epistle To The Authors Of The Monthly Review (London: Printed for H. Payne, 1780);

The Library. A Poem (London: Printed for J. Dodsley, 1781);

The Village: A Poem. In Two Books (London: Printed for J. Dodsley, 1783; New York: Printed for Berry & Rogers and sold by Thomas & Andrews, Boston, 1791);

The News-paper: A Poem (London: Printed for J. Dodsley, 1785);

A Discourse, Read in the Chapel at Belvoir Castle, After the Funeral of His Grace the Duke of Rutland, Late Lord Lieutenant of the Kingdom of Ireland, &c. &c. (London: Printed for J. Dodsley, 1788);

Poems (London: Printed for J. Hatchard, 1807; New York: Published by Inskeep & Bradford, printed by Robert Carr, 1808)–comprises *The Village, The Parish Register, The Library, The Newspaper, The Birth of Flattery, Reflections Upon The Subject–, Sir Eustace Grey, The Hall of Justice, Woman!*;

The Borough: A Poem, in Twenty-Four Letters (London: Printed for J. Hatchard, 1810; Philadelphia: Published by Bradford & Inskeep; Inskeep & Bradford, New York; Wm. M'Ilhenny, Boston, 1810);

Tales (1 volume, London: Printed for J. Hatchard, 1812; 2 volumes, New York: Published by James Eastburn, 1813);

A Variation of public Opinion and Feelings considered, as it respects Religion. A Sermon, Preached before the Right Reverend the Lord Bishop of Sarum, on his Visitation, Held at Devizes, On Friday the 5th of August 1817 (London: Printed for J. Hatchard, 1817);

Tales of the Hall, 2 volumes (London: John Murray, 1819; Boston: Wells & Lilly, 1819);

The Works of the Rev. George Crabbe, 5 volumes (London: John Murray, 1823).

Collections: *The Poetical Works of the Rev. George Crabbe: With His Letters And Journals, and His Life, By His Son*, 8 volumes (London: John Murray, 1834)–includes posthumous tales and *Farewell and Return*;

The Posthumous Sermons of George Crabbe, edited by J. D. Hastings (London: J. Hatchard, 1850);

Poems by George Crabbe, Cambridge English Classics, 3 volumes, edited by A. W. Ward (Cambridge: Cambridge University Press, 1905-1907);

New Poems by George Crabbe, edited by Arthur Pollard (Liverpool: Liverpool University Press, 1960);

George Crabbe: The Complete Poetical Works, 3 volumes, edited by Norma Dalrymple-Champneys and Arthur Pollard, general editor: Norma Dalrymple-Champneys (Oxford: Clarendon Press, 1988).

OTHER: "The Natural History of the Vale of Belvoir," in *The History and Antiquities of the County of Leicester* (London: Printed by & for John Nichols, 1795), I: cxci-ccii.

George Crabbe's literary career began with the assistance of Edmund Burke and the blessing of Samuel Johnson, spanned the lives of Burns, Blake, Byron, Keats, and Shelley, and ended just five years before Queen Victoria ascended the throne. He lived through the American and French revolutions and the fall of Napoleon. He witnessed the beginnings of the Industrial Revolution and its political consequences in the struggle over the first Reform Bill. During this time of extraordinary social, political, and literary change, Crabbe wrote prolifically, chiefly tales in heroic couplets, and, during the Regency period, he won critical acclaim, mingled in high society, and pleased the common reader. His poetry in general displays a keen awareness of the unhappiness into which humans lead themselves, tempered by sympathy for human suffering, impatience with self-deceit and illusion, a steady be-

George Crabbe (portrait by H. W. Pickersgill; by permission of the National Portrait Gallery, London)

lief in the providential governance of natural and human affairs, and an active sense of humor. Crabbe stands as a key link between the eighteenth and nineteenth centuries, as a barometer of the pressures exerted by social change upon his times, and—not least—as a poet to whom readers can still turn for profit and pleasure.

The son of George and Mary Lodwick Crabbe, George Crabbe was born on Christmas Eve in 1754 in Aldeburgh, a seaside village in Suffolk on the eastern coast of England. Crabbe's son describes it as "a poor and wretched place.... It consisted of two parallel and unpaved streets, running between mean and scrambling houses, the abodes of seafaring men, pilots, and fishers." Crabbe's father, a minor customs offi-

cial, occasionally read "Milton, Young, or some other of our graver classics" to his family. Crabbe was educated at the local dame school and then sent to school at Bungay and, later, Stowmarket, both in Norfolk. It had been decided that he would become a physician, but, after finishing school, he worked as a dock laborer briefly, before being apprenticed to an apothecary in 1768 at the age of fourteen. In 1771 he was released and apprenticed to a surgeon at Woodbridge, near Aldeburgh. While there he fell in love with Sarah Elmy and acquired a reputation in his circle as a poet, publishing some of his early verse in a ladies' magazine.

In 1775 Crabbe published anonymously an amusing pastiche called *Inebriety, A Poem.* It sati-

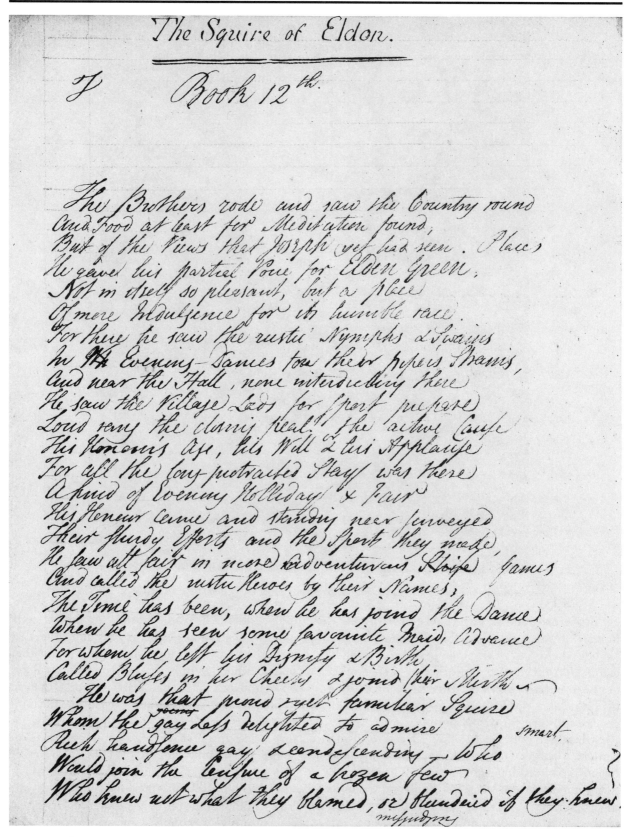

The Squire of Elden.

Book 12th.

The Brothers rode and saw the Country round
And Food at last for Meditation found;
But of the Views that JOSEPH yet had seen. Places
He gave his partial Voice for Elden Green,
Not in itself so pleasant, but a place
Of more Indulgence for its humble race.
For there he saw the rustic Nymphs & Swains
In the Evening-Games toss their pipers Swains,
And near the Hall, none interdicting there
He saw the Village Lads for Sport prepare
Loud rang the closing peal! the active Cause
His Honour's Axe, his Will & his Applause
For all the long-protracted Stay was there
A kind of Evening Holliday & Fair
His Honour came and standing near surveyed
Their sturdy Efforts and the Sport they made,
He saw all fair in more adventurous Strife Games
And called the rustic Heroes by their Names;
The Time has been, when he has joind the Dance
When he has seen some favourite Maid, advance
For whom he left his Dignity & Birth,
Called Blushes in her Cheeks & joind their Mirth
He was that proud yet familiar Squire
Whom the gay Lass delighted to admire
Rich handsome gay & condescending — who
Would join the Censure of a frozen few
Who knew not what they blamed, or blundered if they knew.

Pages from the manuscript for Tales of the Hall *(HM 27621; by permission of the Henry E. Huntington Library and Art Gallery)*

Say not it is beneath my Care
    I cannot Truth like this allow these cold
The Thought may not afflict me there
    But O! they pain and vex me now
Raise me no Turf, nor set a Stone
    That Man or Maiden's Grave may trace
But there my Lucy come alone
    And let Affection find the Place.
Long, long may the dear Girl survive
    And still her fair Example give.
She lives when all will wish to live   Living!
She dies when none will wish to live   When I am gone!

O take me from a World I hate
    Men Cruel, selfish, sensual Cold
And in that pure that blessed State
    Let me my Sister Minds behold! their
The Good & quiet & pure, the warm
From gross & impure refined!
    All Heavens of Love for Hearts to share
For generous gentle Souls designed
    And not a Man! to meet us there —

Come let us go & find the Hill
    Beneath those the Water flow base
There spreads a Brook. "so still o looks so still
    It moves. "You cannot And there a bird hungry, glew

Come go with me & find the Hill
    Beneath whose Height the waters grew
Where   the Hill
That bids on either side
   the Waters slide
And by that Brook so pure & still
    You see the sweetest Violet blow
There And there the Insect lies until
    the new born bird it cease to glow!

         Glenroom

rizes the effects of liquor on various kinds and classes of people, from laborers to parsons to fine ladies. Footnotes to the poem identify the particular passages from Alexander Pope's *Essay on Man* (1733-1734) and *The Dunciad* (1743 version) which Crabbe parodies, but the poem's most effective section is a mock-heroic account of the return of a drunken husband to his angry wife and the ensuing battle. Crabbe's preface declares that this poem was principally composed for "The Ladies," and its third part is devoted entirely to satirizing the effects of drink on women, ironically exhorting them to ape the failings of men.

His apprenticeship completed, Crabbe returned to Aldeburgh and, after working on the docks again, established himself as an apothecary, with the intention of going to London to finish his medical training. His mother was ill, and his father had become alcoholic, moody, and violent. Crabbe had become interested in botany, and he spent his spare time courting Sarah Elmy, writing poetry, and collecting specimens of the local flora.

In 1776-1777 Crabbe found the means to go to London to complete his medical education. However, he had only enough money to survive there and not enough to pay for proper instruction. When he returned to Aldeburgh he found much of his practice taken over by a rival. Furthermore, one of his obstetrics patients died prematurely, which shook both his confidence and reputation. He was very poor and very unhappy. In April 1780 Crabbe decided to abandon Aldeburgh and his profession and go to London to seek his fortune in literature. Sarah Elmy, to whom he had become engaged, supported him in this decision. He left with "a box of clothes, a small case of surgical instruments, and three pounds in money."

It appeared that Crabbe would fail miserably. As the "Journal to Mira" (Sarah Elmy) shows, he was desperately poor, and his writings were consistently rejected as not suiting the taste of the town. The exception was *The Candidate; A Poetical Epistle To The Authors Of The Monthly Review*, published anonymously in 1780. Crabbe published the poem "with a view of obtaining the opinion of the candid and judicious reader on the merits of the writer as a poet. . . ." The response of the reviewers was negative, however, and Crabbe was forced to appeal for patronage to powerful figures in government, all of whom rejected him.

In desperation, just as he was on the verge of being arrested for debt in February or March 1781, Crabbe wrote a letter to Edmund Burke which changed his life. "I am one of those outcasts on the World who are without a Friend without Employment & without Bread," he wrote. "I appeal to You Sir as a good & let me add a great Man; I have no other Pretensions to your Favor than that I am an unhappy One. It is not easy to support the Thoughts of Confinement; & I am Coward enough to dread such an End to my Suspense." In the concluding paragraph Crabbe turned from thoughts of prison to thoughts of death, hinting at suicide: "if I have not the Happiness to obtain Credit with You, I will submit to my Fate: My Existence is a Pain to me, & every one near & dear to me are distress'd in my Distresses; My Connections once the Source of Happiness now embitter the Reverse of my Fortune; & I have only to hope a speedy End to a Life so unpromisingly begun: In which (tho it ought not to be boasted of) I can reap some Consolation from looking to the End of it." With this letter Crabbe enclosed some of his manuscript poetry. Burke read the work, interviewed the man, and saved him.

Burke arranged for the publication of *The Library*, the work he selected as the most promising from among those submitted by Crabbe, in July 1781. *The Library* is Crabbe's poem of dedication, for in it he determines what kind of poetry he will write, grappling with and finally rejecting the lure of romance. He laments the contempt with which romance is treated and in a powerful passage pays tribute to the appeal of visionary poetry about "Ghosts, fairies, daemons. . . ." But he realizes that he has outgrown this visionary world:

> But lost, for ever lost, to me these joys,
> Which Reason scatters, and which Time destroys;
> Too dearly bought, maturer Judgment calls
> My busied mind from tales and madrigals;
> My doughty Giants all are slain or fled,
> And all my Knights, blue, green, and yellow, dead;
> ....
> Enchantment bows to Wisdom's serious plan,
> And pain and prudence make and mar the man.

The poem concludes by arguing that in a world of inevitable pain, consolation should be sought in the mind, not in "vision," and by arguing for the value of poetry that does not seek escape in the visions of romance but rather seeks a "cautious freedom" of numbers and opposes vice. This rejection of "vision" for "reality" was the central choice of Crabbe's poetic career and became

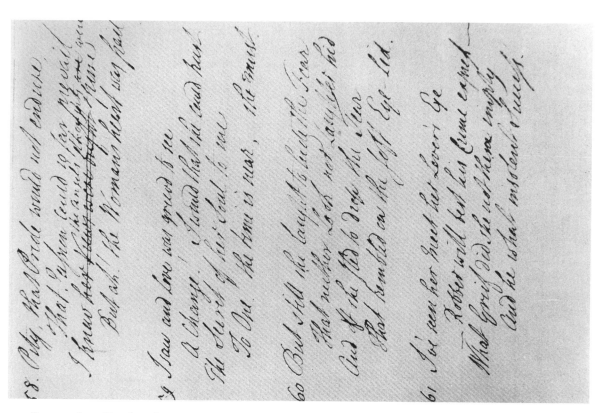

Passages from "Joseph and Jesse," an incomplete poem in a notebook Crabbe kept circa 1822 (Notebook O, No. 4,
by permission of John Murray Ltd)

the central issue on which his poetry would be judged.

Burke's efforts on Crabbe's behalf continued. He arranged for Crabbe to enter the church, and in 1781 the poet was appointed curate to the rector of his native Aldeburgh. Soon after that, in August 1782, Crabbe was ordained and became chaplain to Charles Manners, Fourth Duke of Rutland, at Belvoir Castle in Leicestershire, a post he held for eight years.

On 23 May 1783 Crabbe published the work that would establish his reputation as a poet and remains today his best-known poem, *The Village*. Burke had read the poem in manuscript as had Samuel Johnson, who thought it "original, vigorous, and elegant.... I do not doubt of Mr. Crabbe's success." Johnson proposed several emendations to the poem, including four lines (I.15-18) which Crabbe substituted for his own.

The Village seems to reflect Crabbe's dedication, in *The Library*, to sober realities rather than to "visionary" poetry:

> cast by Fortune on a frowning coast,
> Which neither groves nor happy vallies boast;
> Where other cares than those the Muse relates,
> And other shepherds dwell with other mates;
> By such examples taught, I paint the cot,
> As truth will paint it, and as bards will not.

The village dwellers, "a wild amphibious race," fish the sea by day and smuggle by night. The inhabitants of the plain have a somewhat kinder natural setting, but their lives, darkened by excessive labor and poverty, are no happier, and old age finds pain, disease, and contempt. Crabbe is particularly hard on the institutions and professions meant to alleviate the sufferings of the poor. His well-known lines on the poorhouse are matched by angry portraits of the doctor and the parish priest.

The Village puts some of the blame for the evils in the lives of the poor on the victims themselves. The "village vices" play a part as well. Here the poor and the great meet, for they each display characteristic vices:

> And each in all the kindred vices trace
> Of a poor, blind, bewilder'd erring race;
> Who, a short time in varied fortune past,
> Die, and are equal in the dust at last.

The poem's ending is controversial. Crabbe argues that the poor, despite the evils that con-

front them, should not envy the great, who face evils of their own, such as sloth, fear, and guilt. If there were a noble person who faced pains and dangers greater than theirs, the poor should "Think, think of him, and take your lot in peace." Such a person was Lord Robert Manners, younger brother of Crabbe's employer, the duke of Rutland. The poem concludes with a lengthy portrait of Manners's virtues and a consolation on his recent death.

Criticism of *The Village* has focused on Crabbe's supposed attack on the pastoral and upon his attempt to balance the sufferings of the poor and the rich. It has been tempting to read the poem as a revolutionary attack on the pastoral mode. As many critics have pointed out, however, there is a long tradition of realistic pastoral poetry in English which includes works by Jonathan Swift, John Gay, Allan Ramsay, Charles Churchill, and others, and Crabbe writes in this tradition. *The Village* certainly questions the vision of rural happiness which is one version of pastoral, but it ultimately responds with another version of pastoral–the possibility of human greatness exemplified by the life and conduct of the great man, Robert Manners.

Some readers have criticized the poem's conclusion as a betrayal of Crabbe's theme and purpose in a venal quest for patronage or preferment. Whatever his motives may have been, it certainly is true that Crabbe's diagnosis of social evils presented in *The Village* did not lead him to call for social change to correct them. It is possible, however, to see the conclusion as Crabbe's attempt to show how individuals can rise above the limitations of their environment through qualities of mind and soul. Manners had the benefits of wealth and privilege, which laid him open to the vices of the wealthy. In overcoming what could have been the determining factors of his environment, he proves that environment can be transcended.

On 15 December 1783 Crabbe married Sarah Elmy after an eleven-year engagement. At about this time the duke of Rutland was sent as lord-lieutenant to Ireland. Crabbe remained in England, becoming curate at Stathern in Leicestershire. For the rest of his life he would hold a succession of country livings, sometimes engaging in the common eighteenth-century practice of holding multiple livings and hiring others to serve the parishes where he was not in residence.

In March 1785 Crabbe published a satire, *The News-paper*, dedicated to Edward Thurlow,

George Crabbe (engraving by W. Holl, based on a portrait by Thomas Phillips)

First Baron Thurlow, the lord high chancellor of England. The poem attacked newspapers chiefly as enemies to literature, charging that their "party-rage" drowns out all peaceful and general subjects. He advises poets to band together, like Greeks attacking the Trojans, and scorn and deride newspapers and the taste that makes them so popular. Crabbe attacks the rage for news created by newspapers, the puffery of advertising, the ephemeral verse newspapers publish, and other topics. It is a political poem, in the sense that it seems to have been prompted in part by newspaper attacks on Crabbe's friends and patrons, but it does not take sides on any political issue. Like Pope, whom he attempts to imitate closely in the poem, Crabbe portrays the poet as above the rage and temporality of politics and periodical literature. The poem was well received

by contemporary critics, who found it energetic and "manly."

At this point an extraordinary thing happened in Crabbe's career: he ceased to publish poetry for twenty-two years. Despite the encouragement he had received from both patrons and critics, Crabbe simply dropped out of the public's sight, devoting himself to his parish duties, to botany, and to writing at home. He published a natural history of the Vale of Belvoir in 1795, but the rest of his writing during this period, including an essay on botany and three novels, he burned. His son describes these "grand incremations": "I can well remember more than one grand incremation not in the chimney, for the bulk of paper to be consumed would have endangered the house—but in the open air—and with what glee his children vied in assisting him, stirring up the fire, and bringing him fresh loads of the fuel as fast as their little legs would enable them."

In February 1789 Crabbe left Stathern to become rector of Muston in Leicestershire and West Allington in Lincolnshire. In November 1792 he moved again, to Parham in Suffolk, his wife's native village, placing a curate in his church at Muston. He replaced a popular priest at Parham, and it appears that the parishoners were not entirely pleased with the successor. In March 1796 Crabbe's son Edmund died, and the grief of losing this child precipitated a nervous disorder–alternating fits of depression and mania– in Sarah Crabbe which lasted the rest of her life. Of the seven children she had borne, only two, George and John, had survived early childhood. Crabbe himself had been taking opium–in constant and slightly increasing doses–since about 1790 for what his doctor diagnosed as gastric distress.

In July 1800 Crabbe's bishop required him to return to Muston within four years. He returned in October 1805 and was apparently not welcomed by many of his former parishioners. A Methodist preacher had attracted much of Crabbe's congregation, and Crabbe's sermons attacking dissent won him few friends.

In October 1807, motivated in part by the expenses of his sons' education, Crabbe reappeared in print with *Poems. By The Rev. George Crabbe, LL.B.* This volume contains both some previously published work and some new work. The most significant poem is *The Parish Register,* in which Crabbe takes up the voice and themes which characterize his greatest poetry.

In his preface to the *Poems,* Crabbe describes *The Parish Register* as "an endeavour once more to describe Village-Manners, not by adopting the notion of pastoral simplicity or assuming ideas of rustic barbarity, but by more natural views of the peasantry, considered as a mixed body of persons sober or profligate, and from hence, in a great measure, contented or miserable." The poem has three parts–"Baptisms," "Marriages," "Burials"–each recording scenes of life in the parish connected with these central human events. Unlike Crabbe's later poetry, which consists of extended and developed narratives, *The Parish Register* contains vignettes from the lives of the parishioners.

The poem's opening lines declare that we inhabit a fallen world–"*Auburn* and *Eden* can no more be found"–but that we need not be unhappy:

Hence good and evil mix'd, but Man has skill
And power to part them, when he feels the will;
Toil, care, and patience bless th' abstemious few,
Fear, shame, and want the thoughtless herd pursue.

The opening paints contrasting pictures of a happy, clean, and reverent country cottage and a filthy, rude, and unhappy one, concluding that the cause of woe in the second picture is "want of virtuous will, / Of honest shame, of time-improving skill. . . ." In reading the poem, however, our attention falls mainly on the compelling vignettes rather than on the moral. Whether he tells the story of a miller's daughter and her illegitimate child, chastises Gaffer Kirk for a May-and-December wedding, or relates the unlamented death of the grasping Widow Goe, Crabbe's parish priest largely refrains from explicit moralizing on the fates of his parishioners. Within the cycles of the seasons and of birth, marriage, and death, with which the poem opens and closes, the poet treats a broad range of human emotion anchored in a particularity which *The Village* had not sought. As Crabbe developed and expanded his narrative style and sharpened his handling of poetic voices, this particularity was to increase and become one of the hallmarks of his verse.

Sir Eustace Grey, another of the new poems in the 1807 volume, shows Crabbe's handling of poetic voices at this point in his career as well as an interest in the visions of insanity. Set in a madhouse, the poem approaches the dramatic monologue in its focus upon the voice of the insane Sir Eustace Grey, "The Sport of Madness, Misery's Prey." Upon discovering the adulterous affair between his best friend and his wife, Sir Eustace murdered the friend and watched his wife and children die shortly after. Sir Eustace describes the visitations of the demons that haunt him and the religious visions with which he opposes them. Written in eight-line stanzas of alternately rhyming tetrameters, the poem exhibits both new form and new subject matter for the Anglican clergyman who had been silent for twenty-two years.

The Hall of Justice, another new poem, focuses sharply again on a single voice, in this case that of a female vagrant who has been brought before a magistrate for theft. The magistrate allows her to tell the moving story of her life, after which he counsels her to seek God's mercy by repenting her sins. The poem clearly implies that offenders like the vagrant cannot be held totally responsible for their crimes–she had stolen bread to feed her starving grandchild–and though the magistrate does not explicitly remit her punishment, the boldness and pathos with which the woman speaks reveal the poet's sympathy with her.

Contemporary critical response to the 1807 *Poems* was enthusiastic. Crabbe was praised as a poet of nature and as a moral poet. The reviewers found not only that he portrayed the truth about village life and the states of mind of his speakers but also that the portrayal tended to promote the public good and private virtue. Among his most vocal champions was Francis Jeffrey in the *Edinburgh Review* (April 1808), who used the occasion of his review to attack Wordsworth, Coleridge, and Southey as poets who could benefit from reading the works of Crabbe.

In the spring of 1810 Crabbe published *The Borough,* a series of twenty-four loosely connected verse letters which describe the lives and minds of the inhabitants of an imaginary Borough. Many of the letters treat general topics through portraits of individuals–the professions, amusements, prisons, the poor, and so on. The most memorable are those which focus entirely on specific persons, such as the three letters devoted to inhabitants of the almshouse and those devoted to the parish clerk, Ellen Orford, Abel Keene, and Peter Grimes. Crabbe describes the poem's subject and theme in his preface: "the sea, and the country in the immediate vicinity; the dwellings, and the inhabitants; some incidents and characters, with an exhibition of morals and manners, offensive perhaps to those of extremely delicate feelings, but sometimes, I hope, neither unamiable nor unaffecting."

The fiction governing the poem's structure is that the narrator is describing the Borough in a series of letters to a friend. Crabbe writes at one remove from the subjects of the poem, and this distance gives him an objectivity which saves the poem from didacticism or sentimentality. This distance was necessitated in part by the fact that some portraits in the poem were based on originals whom Crabbe knew. In a 1 December 1816 letter to Mary Leadbetter, Crabbe discussed the relationship between his art and reality: "There is not one [of his characters] of whom I had not in my Mind the Original, but I was obliged in most Cases to take them from their real Situations & in one or two Instances, even to change the Sex and in many the Circumstances. The nearest to real Life, was the proud ostentatious Man in the Borough [Sir Denys Brand],

who disguised a little Mind by doing great things. . . ."

The Borough shows the complexity of human motives, the intricacy of causation in human affairs, and the influence of social environment on behavior. It teaches, finally, a sad–perhaps tragic–acceptance of the inevitability of human suffering tempered by Crabbe's continuing belief in the power of human will to combat much of the evil we suffer through faith, action, and endurance.

The critical reception of *The Borough* was mixed. Critics continued to comment upon Crabbe's originality in his choice of subject matter, his descriptive accuracy, the fluency of his verse, and in general upon his power to please. However, an increasing number of critics complained of a lack of taste–of excessive description, excessive realism in the descriptive passages, too restricted a subject, and formlessness. Additionally, Crabbe was criticized for presenting too gloomy and pessimistic a view of life.

Crabbe responded to these criticisms in the preface to his next work, *Tales. By the Rev. George Crabbe, LL.B.,* published in 1812, arguing that the relative formlessness of his poems allowed for "greater variety of incident and more minute display of character, by accuracy of description, and diversity of scene. . . ." Crabbe also rejected the charge that he was prosaic: "nor was I aware that by describing, as faithfully as I could, men, manners, and things, I was forfeiting a just title to a name which has been freely granted to many whom to equal, and even to excel, is but very stinted commendation." In a passage that recalls *The Library*, Crabbe argues that visionary poetry is not the only kind, and that those who address "plain sense and sober judgment" rather than "fancy and imagination" (including Chaucer, Dryden, and Pope) have an equal claim to the title of poet. Finally, Crabbe argues that realistic poetry can give literary pleasure, so long as the painful realities it portrays are not the present concern of the reader. This defense of his art contains Crabbe's most important critical writing, for here he defends his right to be called a poet.

The *Tales* offers no framing device–simply twenty-one verse narratives on such subjects as "The Patron," "The Frank Courtship," "The Struggles of Conscience," and "The Wager." It is difficult to generalize about the *Tales,* which blend humor and tragedy in portraying individuals often at moments of profound ethical choice. Like Jane Austen, Crabbe realized that one's

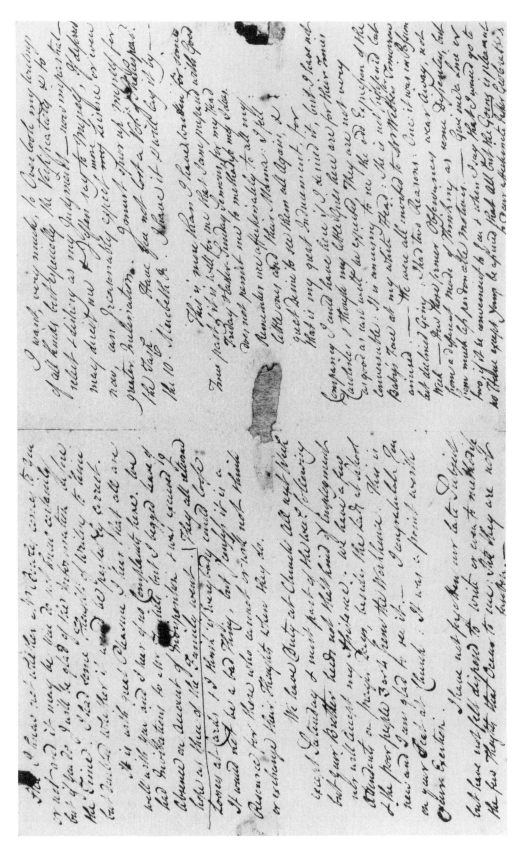

Pages from Crabbe's 1 March 1828 letter to his son George (MA 2927; by permission of the Pierpont Morgan Library)

choice of a spouse is often a choice of a way of life, and many of the tales treat the trials of love, courtship, and marriage as keys to character. He continues to be interested in the ways in which powerful emotion can form and deform character, and he maintains his view that–whatever the pressures individuals feel from social forces or emotional states–faith, reason, and will can still permit them to endure.

Crabbe's wife died on 21 September 1813. In a letter written a month later Crabbe observed, "I cannot weigh Sorrows in a Ballance or make Comparisons between different Kinds of Affliction, nor do I judge whether I should have suffered most to have parted with my poor Sally, as I did . . . or to have seen her pass away with all her Faculties, feelings, senses acute & awake as my own. . . . For with Respect to Intellect & the more enquiring & reasoning of the Faculties, she, dear Creature had lost those even years since. . . ." Crabbe himself was acutely ill after his wife's death, but he gradually recovered and resumed his parish duties.

In 1814 Crabbe moved to the living he would occupy for the rest of his life, at Trowbridge in Wiltshire. There he was briefly engaged to a young woman named Charlotte Ridout, but her family opposed the match, and the engagement ceased. In 1816 Crabbe's son John became his curate at Trowbridge; the following year his son George became curate at nearby Pucklechurch.

Crabbe's years at Trowbridge were happy ones, punctuated by visits to Bath, London, and elsewhere. When Burke had rescued Crabbe from oblivion early in his life, Crabbe had enjoyed the company of Burke, Sir Joshua Reynolds, and members of their circle. Since then, however, he had lived mainly in the country. Now, near the end of his life, he returned to London society as a distinguished literary figure. Crabbe kept a journal of his activities and thoughts during a London visit in 1817 which reveals his acquaintance at this time with leading literary figures and members of London's fashionable society. In 1822 Crabbe journeyed to Scotland to visit Sir Walter Scott, with whom he had corresponded for years.

Crabbe published one major work during the Trowbridge years, *Tales of the Hall,* which appeared in two volumes on 3 July 1819. The publisher John Murray offered Crabbe three thousand pounds for the copyright to this volume and all his previous works. Crabbe carried the ac-

tual currency home to Trowbridge to show his sons, who might hardly believe the sum he had gotten if they did not see the bills. *Tales of the Hall,* regarded by many as Crabbe's greatest work, begins with the meeting of two brothers, George and Richard, who have been separated for years. George, the elder, lives a wealthy but lonely life at the hall in their native village. Richard, married and a father, has led a more active and wide-ranging but less successful life. The two brothers have never understood one another, and each approaches the reunion with ambivalent feelings. Richard makes an extended visit, during which the brothers exchange life stories, visit some of George's neighbors, hear stories about others, and gradually come to know and understand one another and to appreciate what they have in common.

In the preface to *Tales of the Hall* Crabbe disclaims any attempt at novelty: "I have no peculiar notion to defend, no poetical heterodoxy to support, nor theory of any kind to vindicate or oppose. . . ." His key pronouncement, however, concerns the relationship of pleasure to instruction in literature: "The first intention of the poet must be to please; for, if he means to instruct, he must render the instruction which he hopes to convey palatable and pleasant." At the same time, Crabbe assures his reader that he has not deliberately written anything that could excuse or excite vice.

Tales of the Hall is Crabbe's most unified work. The poet continues to be distanced from his characters by one or more narrative frames, but the overarching relationship of the brothers– in particular its development from awkwardness to affection and the focus on particular subjects of interest to the two narrators–gives the collection of tales considerable unity. A major preoccupation continues to be love and marriage and the importance of an individual's choices in love as keys to character and moral stature. Some readers have found Crabbe a stern, overly pessimistic observer of human life. *Tales of the Hall* offers a mellowing of Crabbe's vision, particularly because of the reunion and reconciliation of the brothers. The narrator still maintains a detachment from the fate of the characters, but the sympathy that underlies all of Crabbe's tales is most apparent in this work.

Crabbe's collected works were published by Murray in 1823. He continued to write until his death, and in 1834 his posthumous verse appeared in an edition of his works, letters, and journals prepared by his son George, his first biographer. Crabbe died in his Trowbridge rectory on 3 February 1832.

On the whole, Crabbe was regarded favorably as a poet by his contemporaries, though he was seen as in many ways outside the mainstream of English poetry because of his persistent use of the heroic couplet, his reliance on descriptive detail, and his reticence as a commentator. Byron, in *English Bards and Scotch Reviewers* (1809), called him "Though Nature's sternest painter, yet the best"; Wordsworth, however, though he occasionally spoke approvingly of Crabbe, doubted that he was a poet: "nineteen out of twenty of Crabbe's Pictures are mere matters of fact; with which the Muses have just about as much to do as they have with a Collection of medical reports or of Law Cases" (letter to Samuel Rogers, 29 September 1805). The great Romantic attack upon Crabbe, however, came from Hazlitt, who declared in "Living Authors–No. V, Crabbe" (*London Magazine,* May 1821) that he was not a poet. "His song is one sad reality, one unraised, unvaried note of unavailing woe. Literal fidelity serves him in the place of invention. . . ."

Hazlitt did not succeed in ruining Crabbe's reputation during the rest of the nineteenth century, but neither did Crabbe's supporters succeed in raising it. The same charges made by Romantic readers reappear in Victorian criticism. Crabbe's supporters were not silent, however. In the 1837 edition of his *The Idea of a University* John Henry, Cardinal Newman, called *Tales of the Hall* "A work which can please in youth and age . . . a Classic," but Crabbe's great defender was Edward Fitzgerald, who labored to have a selection of Crabbe's *Tales of the Hall* published.

Crabbe's modern admirers include E. M. Forster, Ezra Pound, T. S. Eliot, F. R. Leavis, and the composer Benjamin Britten, who based his opera *Peter Grimes* in large part on "Tale XXII" from *The Borough.* Crabbe's selected letters and journals have recently been published in a new edition, and biographical and critical studies of him continue to appear regularly. A new edition of his complete poetical works was published in 1988. There is much yet to say about Crabbe. In particular, his attitudes toward and treatment of women and the social and economic politics implicit in his work require further study. More work on Crabbe will certainly be forthcoming, for his understanding of the complexities of moral choice, his studies of the importance of environment to behavior, and his genuine sympathy for the human failings he so clearly portrayed give his verse–despite its bulk–lasting significance and value.

Letters:

Selected Letters and Journals of George Crabbe, edited by Thomas C. Faulkner (Oxford: Clarendon Press, 1985).

Bibliography:

T. Bareham and S. Gatrell, *A Bibliography of George Crabbe* (Folkestone, U.K.: Wm Dawson /Hamden, Conn.: Archon Books, 1978).

Biographies:

[George Crabbe, Jr.], "Memoirs of Eminent Persons: Biographical Account of the Rev. G. Crabbe," *New Monthly Magazine* (January 1816);

George Crabbe [Jr.], *The Life of the Rev. George Crabbe, LL.B.,* volume 1 of *The Poetical Works of the Rev. George Crabbe,* 8 volumes (London: John Murray, 1834);

A. C. Ainger, *Crabbe,* English Men of Letters Series (New York & London: Macmillan, 1903);

René Huchon, *Un Poète Réaliste Anglais. George Crabbe 1754-1832* (Paris, 1906); translated by Frederick Clarke as *George Crabbe and His Times, 1754-1832* (London: John Murray, 1907);

Neville Blackburne, *The Restless Ocean: The Story of George Crabbe The Aldeburgh Poet 1754-1832* (Lavenham, U.K.: Terence Dalton, 1972).

References:

Terence Bareham, *George Crabbe* (London: Vision Press, 1977);

John Barrell, *The Dark Side of the Landscape: The Rural Poor in English Painting, 1730-1840* (Cambridge: Cambridge University Press, 1980);

Robert L. Chamberlain, *George Crabbe* (New York: Twayne, 1965);

Rodney Stenning Edgecombe, *Theme, Embodiment and Structure in the Poetry of George Crabbe,* Salzburg Studies in English Literature (Salzburg: Institut für Anglistik und Amerikanistik, Universität Salzburg, 1983);

Lillian Haddakin, *The Poetry of Crabbe* (London: Chatto & Windus, 1955);

Ronald B. Hatch, *Crabbe's Arabesque: Social Drama in The Poetry of George Crabbe* (Montreal &

London: McGill-Queen's University Press, 1976);

F. R. Leavis, *Revaluation* (London: Chatto & Windus, 1936);

Beth Nelson, *George Crabbe and the Progress of Eighteenth-Century Narrative Verse* (Lewisburg, Pa.: Bucknell University Press, 1976);

Peter New, *George Crabbe's Poetry* (London: Macmillan Press Ltd., 1977);

Arthur Pollard, ed., *Crabbe: The Critical Heritage* (London & Boston: Routledge & Kegan Paul, 1972);

Roger Sales, *English Literature in History 1780-1830: Pastoral and Politics* (New York: St. Martin's Press, 1983);

Oliver Sigworth, *Nature's Sternest Painter: Five Essays on The Poetry of George Crabbe* (Tucson: University of Arizona Press, 1965);

Raymond Williams, *The Country and the City* (Oxford: Oxford University Press, 1973).

Papers:

Crabbe did much of his composing and revising in notebooks and pocket diaries. The most significant collection of these is in the archives of the British publisher John Murray, with other important holdings at the Cambridge University Library, the Henry E. Huntington Library, Wellesley College, and the Brotherton Collection at the University of Leeds. The University of Chicago holds an important collection of manuscripts for Crabbe's sermons. Full details about Crabbe's papers may be found in the *Index of English Literary Manuscripts*, volume 3, part 1, compiled by Margaret M. Smith with contributions by Penny Boumella (London: Mansell, 1986), pp. 293-330.

Erasmus Darwin

(12 December 1731 - 18 April 1802)

Desmond King-Hele
The Royal Society of London

BOOKS: *The Botanic Garden.* part 2, *The Loves of the Plants* (Lichfield: Printed by John Jackson & sold by J. Johnson, London, 1789); part 1, *The Economy of Vegetation* (London: Printed for Johnson, 1791); parts 1 and 2, 1 volume (New York: Printed by T. & J. Swords, 1798);

Zoonomia; or, the Laws of Organic Life. part 1 (London: Printed for J. Johnson, 1794; New York: Printed by T. & J. Swords, 1796); part 1 (revised) and parts 2 and 3, 2 volumes (London: Printed for Johnson, 1796); parts 2 and 3 (Philadelphia: Printed by T. Dobson, 1797);

A Plan for the Conduct of Female Education, in Boarding Schools (Derby: Printed by J. Drewry for J. Johnson, London, 1797; Philadelphia: Printed by John Ormrod, 1798);

Phytologia; or, the Philosophy of Agriculture and Gardening (London: Printed for J. Johnson by T. Bensley, 1800);

The Temple of Nature; or, the Origin of Society (London: J. Johnson, 1803; New York: Printed & sold by T. & J. Swords, 1804).

OTHER: Poem on the death of Prince Frederick, in *Academiae Cantabrigiensis Luctus in obitum Frederici celsissimi Walliae Principis* (Cambridge: Printed by Joseph Bentham, 1751);

A System of Vegetables. . . . Translated from the thirteenth edition (as published by Dr. Murray) of the Systema Vegetabilium of the Late Professor Linneus; and from the Supplementum Plantarum of the present Professor Linneus . . . By a Botanical Society, at Lichfield, translated by Darwin, published in parts (1782-1785); 2 volumes (Lichfield: Printed by John Jackson for Leigh & Sotheby, London, 1783 [i.e. 1785]);

The Families of Plants. . . . Translated from the last edition (as published by Dr. Reichard) of the Genera Plantarum of the Elder Linneus; and From the Supplementum Plantarum of the Younger Linneus. . . . By a Botanical Society at Lichfield, 2 volumes, translated by Darwin (Lichfield:

Printed by John Jackson & sold by J. Johnson, London; T. Byrne, Dublin; and J. Balfour, Edinburgh, 1787).

SELECTED PERIODICAL PUBLICATIONS:
"Remarks on the Opinion of Henry Eeles, Esq., concerning the Ascent of Vapour," *Philosophical Transactions of the Royal Society of London,* 50 (1757): 240-254;

"An Account of an Artificial Spring of Water," *Philosophical Transactions of the Royal Society of London,* 75 (1785): 1-7;

"Frigorific Experiments on the Mechanical Expansion of Air," *Philosophical Transactions of the Royal Society of London,* 78 (1788): 43-52.

For the first fifty-seven years of his life Erasmus Darwin worked hard as a physician in the Midland counties of England and earned the highest reputation as a doctor. He was also an ingenious experimenter in physical science, a compulsive inventor of mechanical gadgets, and a leader in the technological innovations associated with the Lunar Society of Birmingham. Another of his interests was botany, and in the 1780s he spent several years translating the botanical works of Linnaeus. In 1789 he began a new career as a poet with the publication of *The Loves of the Plants.* This long poem in rhyming couplets was the second part of a longer poem, *The Botanic Garden.* (Part 1 was published in 1792 with "1791" on its title page and is usually bound with the third, 1791 edition of part 2.) The verse was augmented by more than a hundred pages of "Notes" providing an up-to-date, select encyclopedia of science. The poem was highly praised, and for a few years Darwin was regarded as the leading English poet of the day. But he had turned away from verse to complete a massive treatise on animal life, *Zoonomia* (1794-1796), where he expounded his system of medicine and also his concept of biological evolution (as we now call it), later redeveloped much more fully by his grand-

Erasmus Darwin, 1770 (portrait by Joseph Wright of Derby; by permission of the Master and Fellows of Darwin College, Cambridge)

son Charles. Next came a lengthy volume on plant life, *Phytologia* (1800), and his second (and better) long poem, *The Temple of Nature* (1803), where he traced the evolution of life from microscopic specks to the human animal. The Romantic poets liked Darwin's integrated view of nature and humankind, respected his scientific authority, and were impressed by the popular success of *The Botanic Garden.* He had much influence, both verbally and intellectually, on William Blake, William Wordsworth, Samuel Taylor Coleridge, Percy Bysshe Shelley, and (to a lesser extent) John Keats.

The son of Robert and Elizabeth Hill Darwin, Erasmus Darwin was born in 1731 in central England, at the village of Elston, near Newark in Nottinghamshire. His father was a lawyer who had retired early, and Erasmus was the youngest

of his seven children. After attending Chesterfield School from 1741 to 1750, Erasmus studied for four years at Cambridge University, where in 1751 he wrote a smooth poem on the death of Prince Frederick, the Prince of Wales, and another on shorthand, an art at which he was adept. After leaving Cambridge and studying for a further two years at the Edinburgh Medical School in 1754-1756, Darwin started his career as a doctor at Lichfield, then a more important town than its growing neighbor Birmingham. His success as a doctor was rapid and continued throughout his twenty-five years at Lichfield. On 30 December 1757 he married Mary Howard, and they had five children, of whom three sons survived past infancy. The eldest, Charles, was a brilliant medical student, but died tragically at the age of nineteen, from an infection sustained

Elston Hall, Nottinghamshire, the birthplace of Erasmus Darwin

Robert and Elizabeth Darwin, the parents of Erasmus Darwin (by permission of the Master and Fellows of Darwin College, Cambridge)

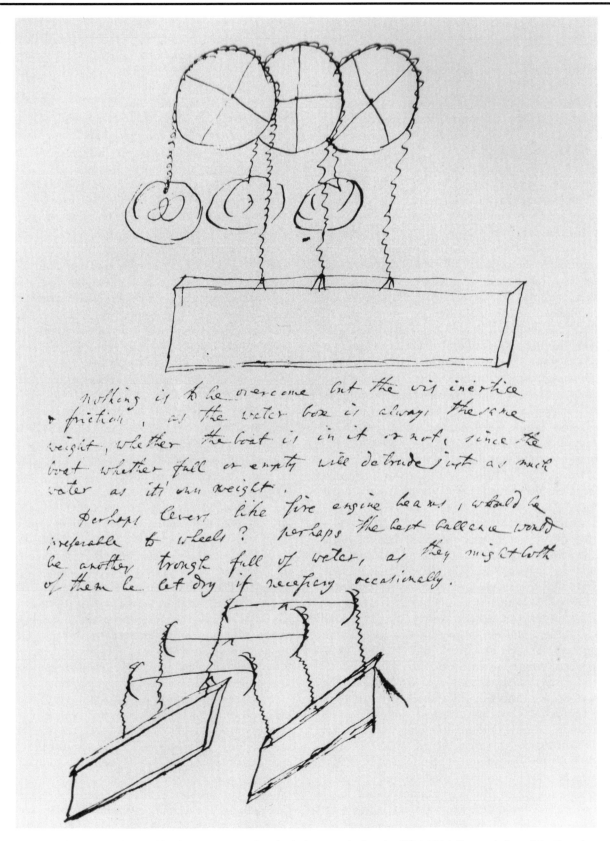

Sketches for a canal lift (1777) from a commonplace book that Darwin kept in 1776-1786 (by permission of the Darwin Museum, Down House, Downe, Kent, and the Royal College of Surgeons of England)

after cutting his hand while dissecting. The second son, Erasmus, became a lawyer. The third, Robert, was a successful doctor at Shrewsbury and the father of the naturalist Charles Robert Darwin.

In these early years Darwin's main intellectual interests were in physical science and mechanical invention, and his scientific paper about "the Ascent of Vapour" in 1757 earned him election as a fellow of the Royal Society of London four years later.

In person Darwin was a tall and powerful-looking man, very energetic and with a great talent for friendship. Among his earliest friends were Matthew Boulton, later England's leading manufacturer, and Benjamin Franklin, already famous for his electrical discoveries, who introduced Boulton and Darwin to Dr. William Small, the honored teacher of Thomas Jefferson. In 1765 Small settled at Birmingham, and the meetings of Boulton, Darwin, and Small to discuss science developed into the informal "Lunar Society of Birmingham," as it is usually known. Other friends of Darwin joined the group, including Josiah Wedgwood, the potter, James Watt, the engineer, and James Keir, pioneer of the chemical industry. The Lunar group was perhaps the strongest intellectual driving force of the Industrial Revolution in Britain, and Darwin did much to keep up their enthusiasm for improving technology.

During the 1760s Darwin's reputation as a doctor grew, but he had no cure for his wife, Mary, who died in 1770, aged thirty. Darwin continued to live at Lichfield, unmarried, in the 1770s, and his sister Susannah acted as foster mother to his youngest son, Robert. He was not without other female company: her name was Mary Parker, and she bore him two illegitimate daughters, known as Susan and Mary Parker, who were brought up in his home.

In the 1770s Darwin participated in the Lunar Society and also in the literary circle of the Cathedral Close at Lichfield, presided over by Canon Seward and his daughter Anna, soon to be known as "the Swan of Lichfield." Brooke Boothby, the confidant of Jean-Jacques Rousseau, was another member, and Samuel Johnson an occasional visitor. But at this time Darwin's literary work was limited to short poems, and much of his abundant energy went into mechanical inventions. These included a speaking machine that astonished everyone, a "horizontal windmill" that worked for many years at Wedgwood's pot-

tery, a superb copying machine, new methods of steering and springing for carriages, and dozens of sketches for designs that only became practicable later, such as canal lifts, an "artificial bird," and multimirror telescopes.

In the mid 1770s Darwin fell in love with Mrs. Elizabeth Pole, the young wife of Col. Sacheverel Pole, a military hero who owned Radburn Hall near Derby. In 1780 Colonel Pole died, and to everyone's surprise his widow accepted the aging Darwin in preference to younger and wealthier suitors. They were married on 6 March 1781 and moved to Derby, where they lived for twenty-one years. It was a happy marriage, to judge from the comments of their seven children. Darwin continued in medical practice at Derby, and in his later years his fame as a doctor became excessive, provoking many semilegendary anecdotes, such as King George III saying (over and over again) "why does not Dr Darwin come to London?"

About 1777 Darwin had begun creating a botanical garden at Lichfield. This project led to ten years of enthusiasm for botany. He formed the Lichfield Botanical Society, with the ambitious aim of translating the botanical works of Linnaeus into English. The society had only two other members, both rather inactive, and was little more than a useful pseudonym for Darwin, who spent much of the 1780s working on the translations. They were published first in parts and then as 1,000-page books, each in two volumes, *A System of Vegetables* (1785) and *The Families of Plants* (1787). In this painstaking work, essentially lists of plants and their characters, it was necessary almost to invent a new language, as Darwin remarked, and more than fifty of the new words he devised have entered the English language: they range from *bract* to *vernation*. The books won a warm welcome from botanists at the time, but they have now passed into virtual oblivion, apart from the verbal progeny.

As a compensation for the tedium of translating the Linnaean listings, Darwin began a playful retranslation into rhyming couplets, transforming the stamens and pistils of the plants into humanized lovers. The completed poem was published anonymously in April 1789 as *The Loves of the Plants*. First on the list in Linnaeus, and therefore also in the poem, is *Canna* (Indian reed): "First the tall CANNA lifts his curled brow / Erect to heaven, and plights his nuptial vow." The touch of the risqué here is one of Darwin's many tricks for enlivening the catalogue of flow-

Elizabeth Pole, who became Darwin's second wife in 1781 (by permission of the Darwin Museum, Down House, Downe, Kent, and the Royal College of Surgeons of England)

ers and their fertilization processes. Another of his techniques is to slide from the plant to the human activities linked with it: thus *papyrus* leads to printing and its role in human culture; while *papaver* provokes a chilling cameo of opium addicts. His rhyming couplets are smooth and skillful, "with a boldness of projection," said William Cowper in his review, "unattainable by any hand but that of a master" (*Analytical Review*, May 1789). Darwin overdressed his verse in glittering ornamentation, and his readers liked it. The spirit of the poem is sportive and mildly subversive, as in this line about "promiscuous marriage" in Tahiti: "And the Loves laugh at all but Nature's laws." The poem was an attractive novelty and became "all the rage" among the reading pub-

lic: "I send you the most delicious poem upon earth," wrote Horace Walpole to Mary and Agnes Berry (28 April 1789), and he was speaking for the majority of its readers.

The Loves of the Plants was published as part 2 of a longer poem, *The Botanic Garden*, and, encouraged by his success, Darwin extended and completed part 1. He kept the original title, *The Economy of Vegetation*, though the final version ranged over all science (and much else), and not just plant life. *The Economy of Vegetation* runs to 2,440 lines, rather longer than *The Loves of the Plants* (1,936 lines in the third edition), and there are about 100,000 words of "Notes," chiefly essays on selected topics in science that appealed to Darwin: particularly in geology, astronomy, mete-

so well, (which I mind much more.)

Why will not you live at Derby? I want learning from you of various kinds, & would give you in exchange _cheerfulness_ which by some parts of your letter, you seem to want. — & of which I have generally a pretty steady supply.

Why the D—l do you talk of your mental faculties decaying, have not you more mechanical invention, *accuracy*, ~~accuracy~~, & execution then any other person alive? — besides an inexhaustible fund of wit, when you please to call for it? (so misers talk of their poverty ~~that~~ that their companions may contradict them.) your headachs & asthma would ~~relieve~~ regieve permanent relief from warm bathing I dare say. — but perhaps you are too indolent to try it' use? — or have some theory against it?

Page from Darwin's 19 January 1790 letter to James Watt, in which Darwin praises Watt's invention of the steam engine
(by permission of the Birmingham Public Libraries)

orology, and plant physiology. *The Economy of Vegetation* is divided into four cantos, ostensibly on the subjects of fire, earth, water, and air, though again Darwin selected whatever subjects he fancied. In the first canto he paints pictures of the earth's creation as a child of the fiery sun, the moon being torn out of the earth, volcanic lavas, Vulcan's forge, and the production of electrical sparks. Fire creates steam to power engines, and these "or some other explosive material" may in future "drive the rapid car" and "the flying-chariot." He celebrates the existing achievements of steam in providing power for mills and for Boulton's coining machine, and he looks forward to piped water supplies and the industrial use of electricity. And so the poem proceeds, jumping from one subject to another: it is a real ragbag of topics, all animated and validated by Darwin's burning prophetic zeal for the advance of science and technology.

Like its predecessor, *The Economy of Vegetation* seems an effortless exhibition of smooth and showy couplets, and Darwin avoids the danger of too much science and industry by digressing into classical legends. These are either pastoral, set against a comforting background of kindly nature, or rather spicy, as when Vulcan throws a wiry net over Mars and Venus to "lock the embracing lovers on their bed" for the "festive Gods" to chortle over. Another of his techniques was to bring in current events, with praise for the American and French revolutions and a tirade against slavery. Readers found the mixture attractive, and they never knew what was coming next; they also felt virtuous because they were painlessly educating themselves in science. Another pleasing feature of the poem was Darwin's verbal inventiveness, carried over from the Linnaean translations: more than a hundred words are recorded as (or are earlier than) the earliest examples in the *Oxford English Dictionary*, mostly adjectives such as *brineless, convoluted, frenzied,* and *iridescent.*

The Botanic Garden won over nearly all the critics. William Cowper wrote long and glowing reviews of both parts: "no poet since Pope," he said, had excelled Darwin "in delicacy and harmony of versification" (*Analytical Review,* March 1793). Horace Walpole wrote to Mrs. Hannah More, "You will agree with me that the author is a great poet" (22 April 1789). In a 6 February 1797 letter to John Thelwall, Coleridge called Darwin "the first *literary* character in Europe, and the most original-minded Man," and on 23 June

1801 he wrote to William Godwin, "I have myself met with persons who professed themselves idolatrous admirers of Milton, & yet declared it to be their opinion that Dr Darwin was as great a poet." Darwin's overinflated reputation as a poet could not last and was vulnerable to ridicule. The most wounding parody was "The Loves of the Triangles," published in the political magazine the *Anti-Jacobin* in 1798. In the same year Wordsworth complained in the preface to the first edition of *Lyrical Ballads* about the "gaudiness" of Darwin's verse, though later acknowledging he had been influenced by "the dazzling manner of Darwin." Relics of Darwin's high reputation endured until the 1860s, however, when the third edition of G. L. Craik's *History of English Literature* (1866) gave Byron three pages, Milton twelve, and Darwin eighteen.

Darwin's forty years of medical study and practice had led him to formulate a comprehensive theory of biology and medicine, which he expounded in the first volume of his *Zoonomia; or, the Laws of Organic Life,* published in 1794 as a weighty quarto book of 586 pages. As well as explaining the basis of his system of medicine, Darwin has chapters on general subjects, such as instinct, reverie, sleep, and vertigo, which appealed strongly to Wordsworth and Coleridge. In an arresting final chapter he tells why he believed that species have gradually changed in response to environmental forces and that all creatures now alive have derived from microscopic organisms. Volume 2 of *Zoonomia,* published in 1796 and even longer than volume 1, divides diseases into various classes and offers treatments for each. For a time *Zoonomia* raised Darwin's reputation still higher. Dr. Thomas Beddoes thought it would "place the Author among the greatest of mankind, the founders of sciences," and he was not alone in this opinion. Darwin's system of medicine was soon abandoned, but his insight into biological evolution stands as one of his major achievements in biology.

In 1794 Darwin's daughters Susan and Mary Parker set up a school for girls at Ashbourne, not far from Derby. To help them, Darwin wrote a little book published in 1797 as *A Plan for the Conduct of Female Education, in Boarding Schools.* He had no patience with the idea of the featherbrained feeble female, and he proposed a curriculum that would nourish the brains and bodies of the pupils and equip them for life ahead. The school was a great success, though it seems unlikely that his radical program

THE

BOTANIC GARDEN;

A Poem, in Two Parts.

PART I.

CONTAINING

THE ECONOMY OF VEGETATION.

....

PART II.

THE LOVES OF THE PLANTS.

WITH

Philofophical Notes.

LONDON,
PRINTED FOR J. JOHNSON, ST. PAUL's CHURCH-YARD.
....
MDCCXCI.
𝔈ntered at 𝔖tationers 𝔥all.

Title page for the first complete edition of the long poem inspired by Darwin's desire "to inlist Imagination under the banner of Science" and to convince his readers "to cultivate the knowledge of Botany"

was fully adopted. Still, his book has a distinctive place in the history of girls' education in England and is a significant step toward sexual equality.

Meanwhile, Darwin had been writing a massive treatise about plant life, *Phytologia* (1800). It is a much better book than *Zoonomia*, because many of Darwin's insights into plant physiology and nutrition have proved to be valid, and pregnant with future realities. There are two major achievements. The first is a nearly complete description of photosynthesis, the basis of all plant life: Darwin stated that, in plants exposed to light, carbon dioxide and water are converted into oxygen and sugar. His second achievement was to seize on the essential plant nutrients, nitrogen, carbon, and phosphorus. With both these insights Darwin was well ahead of contemporary opinion and has turned out to be right. He made

many other suggestions for improvements in agriculture, including a detailed design for an improved drill plough. By 1800 Darwin's reputation had declined, and *Phytologia*, despite its many merits, did not receive the recognition it deserved: it was the only book of his not to be published in the United States, and there was only one translation (into German).

Darwin died of a heart attack in 1802 at the age of seventy, leaving a second long poem ready for publication. This poem is generally seen as his finest literary achievement, and he gave it the title *The Origin of Society*. The poem first explains how he believes animals originated and developed under environmental pressures (a thesis argued more fully by his grandson in *The Origin of Species,* 1859); Erasmus sees the human animal as the culmination of the process and tells how hu-

Erasmus Darwin (bust by William Coffee; by permission of the Darwin Museum, Down House, Downe, Kent, and the Royal College of Surgeons of England)

Darwin (right) playing chess with his son Erasmus (by permission of Dr. John L. Moilliet)

mans, when they refrain from violence, can create society. Darwin's title was changed to the neutral *The Temple of Nature* by his publisher Joseph Johnson, who had been imprisoned for selling an irreligious pamphlet and was understandably nervous about a poem in which natural forces deprived God of his usual role.

The Temple of Nature is in four cantos, backed up with long essay-notes. Canto 1, "Production of life," begins in the lifeless ocean: "Nurs'd by warm sun-beams in primeval caves, / Organic Life began beneath the waves." Darwin then neatly summarizes the subsequent course of evolution:

> First forms minute, unseen by spheric glass,
> Move on the mud, or pierce the watery mass;
> These, as successive generations bloom,
> New powers acquire, and larger limbs assume;
> Whence countless groups of vegetation spring,
> And breathing realms of fin, and feet, and wing.

"After islands or continents were raised above the primeval ocean, great numbers of the most simple animals would attempt to seek food" along the shores, and "might thence gradually become amphibious." So he sees the progression to amphibia, reptiles, and eventually the "human animal," to use his customary phrase. Canto 2, "The reproduction of life," expresses his strong approval of sex, which enhances organic happiness and leads (via variety and competition) to improvement of the species. Canto 3, "Progress of the mind," balances this physicality with praise of art, science, and sympathy, and the ideal of universal love. Canto 4, "Of good and evil," reverts to the war in nature, with the wolf savaging "the guiltless lamb," and the lamb feeding on the plants, which are themselves in continuous "vegetable war" with each other. Human ills are plentiful too, but they can be outweighed by the delights of nature, the satisfactions of art, science, and scholarship, and "the raptures of delirious love."

This farseeing poem did not enjoy the fame of its predecessor. The climate had changed during the 1790s: with England on the brink of invasion by Napoleon, a poem so deeply subversive of the established order was not welcome. The reviewer in the *British Critic* (February 1804) gave up in disgust: "we are full of horror, and will write no more." Despite the reviews, the poem went through three editions and did influence Shelley and Keats, who were impressed by the calm certainty of Darwin's picture of nature and humanity developing under the action of natural forces.

Darwin is admired today for his breadth of talent: it can be argued that he achieved more in a wider range of intellectual disciplines than anyone since his day. Like Johann Wolfgang von Goethe, who acknowledged a debt to him, he has his place in both scientific and literary history, and if today there were any real wish to reunite these two cultures, Darwin would be an essential name on the curriculum. In his own day *The Botanic Garden* was seen as justifying the ways of science to man. He celebrated the idea of progress via the march of science and technology. He was the laureate of the Industrial Revolution, glorifying the entrepreneurs and engineers such as Boulton, Wedgwood, Watt, and Brindley, and ignoring the grief and grime of the factories. Instead, almost everything in *The Botanic Garden* is lovely: the episodes are played out against a background of gentle and luxuriant nature, with death usually either sublimated into classical legend or overthrown by rebirth, as in real gardens. There is no crime or squalor in Darwin's science park. Science expounded in glittering couplets seems an unlikely recipe for popular success; yet the world applauded, and Darwin was acclaimed as the leading English poet of the day for a few years (about 1792-1795). No subsequent poet has won similar success. His years of fame were brief, but they left a lasting legacy because Darwin touched the nerves of the Romantic poets, who were nearly all indebted to him, both verbally and via his "Orphic" idea of the integration of nature and humankind into an organic whole. This integrated view is best expressed in Darwin's second poem, *The Temple of Nature*, which describes biological evolution under the action of natural forces; but it was *The Botanic Garden* that chiefly influenced Blake, Wordsworth, and Coleridge.

Letters:
The Letters of Erasmus Darwin, edited by Desmond King-Hele (Cambridge & New York: Cambridge University Press, 1981).

Biographies:
Anna Seward, *Memoirs of the Life of Dr Darwin* (London: Johnson, 1804; Philadelphia: Poyntell, 1804);
Charles Darwin, *The Life of Erasmus Darwin*, in *Erasmus Darwin*, by Ernst Krause, translated by W. S. Dallas (London: Murray, 1879; New York: Appleton, 1880);

Hesketh Pearson, *Doctor Darwin* (London & Toronto: Dent, 1930);

Desmond King-Hele, *Doctor of Revolution: the Life and Genius of Erasmus Darwin* (London: Faber & Faber, 1977).

win (Princeton, N.J.: Princeton University Press, 1936);

Maureen McNeil, *Under the Banner of Science: Erasmus Darwin and his Age* (Manchester, U.K. & Wolfeboro, N.H.: Manchester University Press, 1987).

References:

Donald M. Hassler, *The Comedian as the letter D: Erasmus Darwin's Comic Materialism* (The Hague: Nijhoff, 1973);

Hassler, *Erasmus Darwin* (New York: Twayne, 1973);

Desmond King-Hele, *Erasmus Darwin and the Romantic Poets* (London: Macmillan, 1986; New York: St. Martin's Press, 1986);

J. V. Logan, *The Poetry and Aesthetics of Erasmus Dar-*

Papers:

Erasmus Darwin's commonplace book is at the Darwin Museum, Down House, in Downe, Kent. The most extensive collections of letters and other papers are also in England, at Birmingham Reference Library and the libraries of Keele University, University College London, and Cambridge University, with some in private hands. A fuller list is given in *The Letters of Erasmus Darwin,* pp. xv-xvi.

George Dyer

(15 March 1755 - 2 March 1841)

Nicholas Roe
University of St. Andrews

BOOKS: *An Inquiry into the Nature of Subscription to the Thirty-Nine Articles* (Cambridge, 1789; revised and enlarged edition, London: Printed for J. Johnson, 1792);

Poems (London: Printed for J. Johnson, 1792);

The Complaints of the Poor People of England (London, 1793; revised and enlarged edition, London: Printed for J. Ridgway & H. D. Symonds, 1793);

A Dissertation on the Theory and Practice of Benevolence (London: Printed for Kearsley, 1795);

Memoirs of the Life and Writings of Robert Robinson (London: Printed for G. G. & J. Robinson, 1796);

The Poet's Fate. A Poetical Dialogue (London: Printed for G. G. & J. Robinson, J. Johnson, & J. Debrett, 1797);

An Address to the People of Great Britain on the Doctrine of Libels (London: Sold by Hurst, 1799; London: Printed for the author & sold by H. D. Symonds, 1799);

Poems (London: Printed for the author & sold by Longman & Rees, 1801);

Poems and Critical Essays, 2 volumes (London: Printed for T. N. Longman & O. Rees, 1802);

Poetics, or a Series of Poems and Disquisitions on Poetry, 2 volumes (London: Printed for J. Johnson, 1812);

Four Letters on the English Constitution (London: J. Johnson, 1812);

History of the University and Colleges of Cambridge, 2 volumes (London: Printed for Longman, Hurst, Rees, Orme & Brown, 1814);

Academic Unity (London: Longman, Rees, Orme, Brown & Green, 1827).

OTHER: Robert Robinson, *The History of Baptism,* edited by Dyer (London: Printed by Couchman & Fry for Thomas Knott, 1790);

George Thompson, *Slavery and Famine, Punishments for Sedition; or, an Account of the Miseries and Starvation at Botany Bay,* includes preliminary remarks by Dyer (London: Printed for J. Ridgway, 1794);

An English Prologue and Epilogue to the Latin Comedy of Ignoramus; Written by George Ruggle, preface and notes by Dyer (London: Printed for G. G. & J. Robinson, J. Johnson & J. Debrett, 1797);

The Privileges of the University of Cambridge, 2 volumes, compiled by Dyer (London: Printed for Longman, 1824).

George Dyer's reputation has largely derived from anecdotes about his eccentric character and behavior. Leigh Hunt told a story about Dyer's leaving a dinner wearing only one shoe and not discovering his loss until halfway home. Charles Lamb affectionately portrayed his friend Dyer in "Oxford in the Vacation" (1820) and "Amicus Redivivus" (1823). The former essay gently teases Dyer's pedantic scholarship; in the latter essay Elia whimsically comments, "I do not know when I have experienced a stranger sensation, than on seeing my old friend G. D. . . . at noon day, deliberately march right forwards into the midst" of the New River at Islington. But Dyer also needs to be taken seriously, first as an active republican and dissenter in the revolutionary 1790s; second as a man of letters who over a long life maintained an astonishingly diverse output as poet, pamphleteer, biographer, historian, and editor.

Dyer was born in London on 15 March 1755, the son of John Dyer, a shipwright. When seven years old he was admitted to Christ's Hospital, 1 July 1762, and he remained there until 1774. In the meantime he had been admitted as a sizar at Emmanuel College, Cambridge, but he did not take up residence until 25 October 1774–possibly due to financial problems. He gained his B.A. in 1778. While at Emmanuel he met a number of men who would be influential in later life. Among them was William Taylor, who occupied adjacent rooms in college and who was subsequently William Wordsworth's headmas-

George Dyer, 1795 (aquatint by E. Cristall, based on a portrait by J. Cristall)

ter at Hawkshead Grammar School and his first poetic mentor. Dyer was also acquainted with Gilbert Wakefield of Jesus College, a man who became one of the most outspoken radical dissenters of the 1790s; it was through Dyer that Wakefield was introduced to Samuel Taylor Coleridge, most probably in 1794.

Looking back in old age, Dyer said that Cambridge had been a "ruling star" in his career after leaving the university. Having graduated in 1778, he worked for a short time as usher (assistant master) at Dedham Grammar School and at Northampton Grammar School before returning to Cambridge once again as tutor to the family of Robert Robinson, Baptist minister and founder of the reformist Cambridge Constitutional Society. Dyer's presence in Robinson's house placed him at the center of dissenting and radical activity in Cambridge during the 1780s, and this in-

fluenced the way in which his own political and religious opinions developed. In 1781 Dyer preached "with no very happy results" to the Oxford Baptist Congregation, but during the next few years both Robinson and Dyer moved toward Unitarianism. This shift is evident in Dyer's *An Inquiry into the Nature of Subscription to the Thirty-Nine Articles,* published at Cambridge in 1789. Dyer's religious dissent ensured his approval of the French Revolution and encouraged his support for a democratic parliamentary reform in Britain. In this way his Cambridge background exercised a ruling influence on his intellectual life and his publications during the 1790s.

In 1792 Dyer moved from Cambridge to London and settled at Clifford's Inn, where he was to live for the rest of his life. Later that year the second edition of Dyer's *Inquiry* was published by the liberal and dissenting bookseller Joseph Johnson. The revised pamphlet is republican and sympathetic to the French Revolution, and it reveals the influence of Thomas Paine's *Rights of Man* (1791-1792). But while he responded to Paine's political theory, Dyer's strength as a pamphleteer in the 1790s also lay in advocating practical, compassionate change in an unjust society: "I am not pleading the cause of the dissenter merely," Dyer wrote, "but of the citizen and the man." *The Complaints of the Poor People of England* (1793), Dyer's preliminary remarks to George Thompson's *Slavery and Famine* (1794), and *A Dissertation on the Theory and Practice of Benevolence* (1795) each addresses the contemporary crisis of social upheaval caused by the French war and the government's repressive policies in Britain. Besides calling for a reform in parliamentary representation, Dyer also looked for freedom of conscience and far-reaching changes in taxation, the legal system, prisons, poor rates, workhouses, schools, and the army and navy. His pamphlets from this period place him at the forefront of contemporary opposition alongside other friends of liberty such as John Thelwall, William Frend, Thomas Holcroft, and William Godwin—all of whom he knew personally. It was for this reason that Dyer was an important London contact for Coleridge and Robert Southey between 1794 and 1797. In 1794, for example, he distributed twenty-five copies of Coleridge and Southey's *Fall of Robespierre;* two years later, in May 1796, he came to Coleridge's rescue with a gift of money to offset losses on his failed periodical *The Watchman.*

Like Coleridge, Wordsworth, Southey, and other liberals and reformists, Dyer moved away from active politics after 1795 to a life of literature and the imagination. In 1796 he published his *Memoirs of the Life and Writings of Robert Robinson,* a book which again looks back to his Cambridge years in the 1770s and 1780s and which Wordsworth admired as one of the best biographies in the language. As a poet, however, Dyer's achievement is rather less distinguished, despite a prolific output of verse. In his lifetime he published five substantial collections of poetry: *Poems* (1792), *The Poet's Fate* (1797), and *Poems* (1801) were followed by two collections of verse with supporting essays, *Poems and Critical Essays* (1802) and *Poetics* (1812). Dyer's poetry is most generously described as "occasional" verse. Charles Lamb emphasized its motley, derivative qualities in a letter to Thomas Manning (9 August 1800) when he described Dyer's poetry as "Ode, pastoral, sonnet, Elegy, Spenserian, Horation, aken-

sidish, & Masonic, verse." But Dyer also tackled larger, public themes in his poems. He welcomed the French Revolution in "Ode on Liberty" and similarly in "Ode on Peace, Written, in Part, in Jesus College Garden"—characteristically including in both a celebration of the "patriot zeal" of his Cambridge friends Wakefield, Frend, and Robert Tyrwhitt.

Dyer's early friendship with Coleridge is evidence of his generosity to other writers; but his own ambitions as a literary critic and theorist met with early disappointment. Having prepared during 1800 a volume of critical essays as a companion to his forthcoming *Poems,* Dyer discovered, as Charles Lamb recalled, "that in the very first page of said preface he had set out with a principle of criticism fundamentally wrong" (letter to Manning, 27 December 1800). As a result he delayed publication of the volume of essays until 1802. A single copy of his canceled preface survives in the British Library, bound with Dyer's *Poems* (1801) and containing manuscript notes by Lamb and Coleridge (British Library catalogue reference C.45 f. 18. 1). In this 1800 preface Dyer makes a sustained "vindication" of lyrical poetry and describes his own intention as a poet in giving "free rein to [his] imagination . . . to impose no restraint on [his] feelings; to let [his] thoughts run loose to what extent they please; to seize the rudest ideas, while yet lively and warm." Dyer's casual attitude toward his own verse caused Lamb much amusement, particularly in the case of one of the copious footnotes to his 1801 *Poems:* "Discrimination is not the *aim* of the present volume. It will be more strictly attended to in the next" (quoted with delight by Lamb in a letter to Manning, 15 February 1801). Despite the setback of his canceled preface Dyer persevered with writing verse, and in 1812 he published *Poetics,* in two volumes, as "a systematic edition of [his] poetical writings . . . a life . . . composed out of his poems" supported by critical "disquisitions" on "Arts and Sciences," "Poetical Genius," "The Number of Excellent Poets," and "The Use of Topography in Poetry."

While cheerfully continuing to write his poetry, Dyer also devoted his later years to scholarly and editorial work. Once again, much of this takes its bearings from his earlier Cambridge links. In 1814 he published a two-volume *History of the University and Colleges of Cambridge,* which remains valuable as a historical survey and also as a source of information about Dyer's own contemporaries at the university—especially the dissent-

Dyer with his dog, Tobit (portrait by Henry Meyer; by permission of the Syndics of the Fitzwilliam Museum, Cambridge)

ing community. Ten years afterward Dyer's *The Privileges of the University of Cambridge* appeared as a supplement to his history. It included the charters of the university along with various endowments, graces, statutes, and manuscripts in college libraries. Dyer also included in the second volume his own 145-page "Dissertatio Generalis," which–somewhat fancifully–he thought, "in conformity with the greater part of the Privileges, would appear better in the Latin language than in the English." (An English translation, *Academic Unity*, appeared in 1827.) But this instance of Dyer's mild eccentricity also serves as a reminder that he was an accomplished classicist; between 1819 and 1830 he worked as an editor on Valpy's

141-volume edition of the classical authors. The labor involved in this task almost certainly contributed to the failure of his eyesight. This, coupled with his consistent unworldliness, made him all the more dependent upon his friends' care and especially upon that of an elderly widow, Mrs. Mather, who lived in neighboring rooms at Clifford's Inn and whom Dyer married when he was fifty-nine. The marriage turned out happily, and Dyer's last years were spent in a contented retirement. He died at Clifford's Inn on 2 March 1841. An autobiography which existed in manuscript at the time of his death has since vanished.

Dyer's literary achievement is a mixture of oddity and genuine seriousness. His pamphlets of the 1790s are indispensable to an understanding of the democratic reform movement in London at that time and to the important connections between Cambridge dissenters and London radicalism. He maintained his political interests as late as 1812, when he published *Four Letters on the English Constitution* in Leigh Hunt's *Reflector* and later as a separate book. As a poet Dyer's reputation is slight, but his verse retains the interest of its reference to contemporary characters and affairs. Lamb's account of Dyer's researches in "Oxford in the Vacation" casts a humorous light upon the man who compiled the *History* and *Privileges* of Cambridge University; but in other respects these two works retain a genuine scholarly value. Dyer is an engaging and wayward figure, and his writings are most helpful to an understanding of the literary, political, and religious contexts of his times.

References:

Martin Ray Adams, "George Dyer and English Radicalism," in his *Studies in the Literary Backgrounds of English Radicalism*, Franklin and Marshall College Studies, no. 5 (Lancaster, Pa., 1947), pp. 227-266;

British Public Characters of 1798 (London: Printed for R. Phillips, 1798), pp. 454-462;

S. Butterworth, "Charles Lamb: some new Biographical and other Details," *Bookman*, 60 (July 1921): 165-170;

Winifred Courtney, *Young Charles Lamb* (London: Macmillan, 1982), pp. 201-209;

"George Dyer," *Emmanuel College Magazine*, 15 (1905): 194-213;

Harriet Jump, " 'Snatch'd out of the Fire': Lamb, Coleridge, and George Dyer's cancelled Preface," *Charles Lamb Bulletin*, new series 58 (April 1987): 54-67;

Ernest A. Payne, "The Baptist Connections of George Dyer," *Baptist Quarterly*, new series 10 (1940-1941): 260-267;

J. J. Raven, "George Dyer of Emmanuel," *Emmanuel College Magazine*, 7 (1895): 39-42;

Nicholas Roe, "Radical George. Dyer in the 1790s," *Charles Lamb Bulletin*, new series 49 (January 1985): 17-26.

Papers:

Collections of Dyer's correspondence and papers are in the archives of Emmanuel College, Cambridge, and at the Guildhall Library in London.

William Hayley

(29 October 1745 - 12 November 1820)

John R. Holmes
Franciscan University of Steubenville

BOOKS: *A Poetical Epistle to an Eminent Painter* (London: Printed for T. Payne and Son, J. Dodsley, and Robson and Co., 1778); republished as *An Essay on Painting: In Two Epistles to Mr. Romney* (London: Printed for J. Dodsley, 1781);

An Elegy, on the Ancient Greek Model (Cambridge: Printed by Francis Hodson; sold by T. Payne, London, and T. & J. Merrill, Cambridge, 1779);

Epistle to Admiral Keppel (London: Printed for Fielding & Walker, 1779);

Epistle to a friend, on the death of John Thornton, esq. (London: Printed for J. Dodsley, 1780);

An Essay on History; in Three Epistles to Edward Gibbon, Esq., with Notes (London: Printed for J. Dodsley, 1780);

Ode Inscribed to John Howard (London: Printed for J. Dodsley, 1780; Philadelphia: Printed & sold by Enoch Story, 1780);

Poems and Plays, 2 volumes (London: J. Dodsley, 1780, 1784);

The Triumphs of Temper; a Poem. In six cantos (London: Printed for J. Dodsley, 1781; Newburyport: Printed by John Mycall for Joseph H. Seymour, Boston, 1781);

An Essay on Epic Poetry; in Five Epistles to the Rev. Mr. Mason. With Notes (London: Printed for J. Dodsley, 1782);

Ode to Mr. Wright of Derby (Chichester: Printed by Dennet Jacques, 1783);

Plays of three acts, written for a private theatre (London: Printed for T. Cadell, 1784)—comprises *The Happy Prescription, Marcella, The Two Connoisseurs, Lord Russel*, and *The Mausoleum*;

A Philosophical, Historical, and Moral Essay on Old Maids. By a Friend to the Sisterhood, 3 volumes (London: Printed for T. Cadell, 1785);

Two Dialogues; Containing a Comparative View of the Lives, Characters, and Writings of Philip, the Late Earl of Chesterfield, and Dr. Samuel Johnson (London: Printed for T. Cadell, 1787);

Occasional Stanzas, Written at the Request of the Revolution Society, and Recited on their Anniversary, November 4, 1788. To Which is Added, Queen Mary to King William, During his Campaign in Ireland, 1690, a Poetical Epistle (London: Printed for T. Cadell, 1788);

The Young Widow; or, the History of Cornelia Sedley, in a Series of Letters, 3 volumes (London: Printed for G. G. J. & J. Robinson, 1789);

The Eulogies of Howard, a Vision (London: G. G. J. & J. Robinson, 1791);

The National Advocates; a Poem, Affectionately Inscribed to the Honourable Thomas Erskine, and Vicary Gibbs, Esquire (London: Printed for J. Debrett, 1795);

An Elegy on the Death of the Honourable Sir William Jones, a Judge of the Supreme Court of Judicature in Bengal, and President of the Asiatic Society (London: Printed for T. Cadell, Jun. & W. Davies, 1795);

The Life of John Milton, in Three Parts. To Which are Added, Conjectures on the Origin of Paradise Lost: with an Appendix (London: Printed for T. Cadell, Junior & W. Davies, 1796);

An Essay on Sculpture, in a Series of Epistles to John Flaxman, with Notes (London: Printed by A. Strahan for T. Cadell jun. & W. Davies, 1800);

Little Tom the Sailor. Printed for & Sold by the Widow Spicer of Folkstone for the Benefit of her Orphan, October 5, 1800 [broadside], by Hayley, with engravings by William Blake (Felpham: Printed by William Blake, 1800);

A Series of Ballads, nos. 1-4, by Hayley, with engravings by Blake (Chichester: Printed by J. Seagrave, 1802);

The Life and Posthumous Writings of William Cowper, esq. (3 volumes, Chichester: Printed by J. Seagrave for J. Johnson, London, 1803; 2 volumes, Boston: Published by W. Pelham, Manning & Loring, and E. Lincoln, 1803);

Desultory Remarks on the Letters of Eminent Persons, Particularly Those of Pope and Cowper (London, 1804);

William Hayley, circa 1779 (mezzotint by J. Jacobe, based on a portrait by George Romney)

The Triumphs of Music; a Poem: in Six Cantos (Chichester: Printed by & for J. Seagrave and sold by T. Payne, London, 1804);

Ballads, By William Hayley, Esq. Founded On Anecdotes Relating To Animals, With Prints, Designed and Engraved by William Blake (London: Printed by J. Seagrave for Richard Phillips, 1805);

Supplementary Pages to the Life of Cowper, Containing the Additions Made to that Work, on Reprinting it in Octavo (Chichester: Printed by J. Seagrave for J. Johnson, London, 1806);

The Stanzas of an English Friend to the Patriots of Spain (London: Printed for Westley & Parish, 1808);

The Life of George Romney (Chichester: Printed by W. Mason for T. Payne, London, 1809);

Eudora. A Tragedy (London: Printed by William Mason for T. Cadell & W. Davies, 1811);

Three Plays (Chichester: Printed by W. Mason for T. Cadell & W. Davies, London, 1811)–comprises *Eudora, The Viceroy,* and *The Heroine of Cambria;*

Poems on serious and sacred subjects, printed only as private tokens of regard, for the particular friends of the author (Chichester: Printed at the private press of W. Mason, 1818);

Memoirs of the life and writings of William Hayley, Esq. The Friend and Biographer of Cowper, written by himself, edited by John Johnson, 2 volumes (London: H. Colburn, 1823).

PLAY PRODUCTIONS: *Lord Russel,* London, Theatre Royal, Haymarket, 18 August 1784;

Portrait (1800) by William Blake of Thomas Alphonso Hayley, the recently deceased son of William Hayley, based on the subject's self-portrait (by permission of the City of Manchester Art Galleries). The portrait by Blake is one of eighteen "Heads of the Poets" that Blake painted to be hung as a frieze in Hayley's library at Felpham.

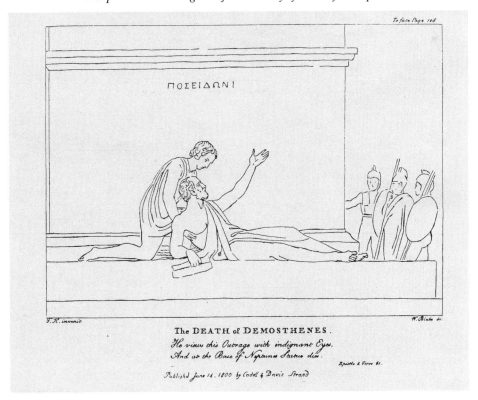

Illustration for Hayley's long poem An Essay on Sculpture *(1800), engraved by Blake after a drawing by Hayley's son, Thomas*

Broadside by Hayley, illustrated by William Blake. This copy, in the George C. Smith Collection at the Princeton University Library, has been cut in half to form two leaves.

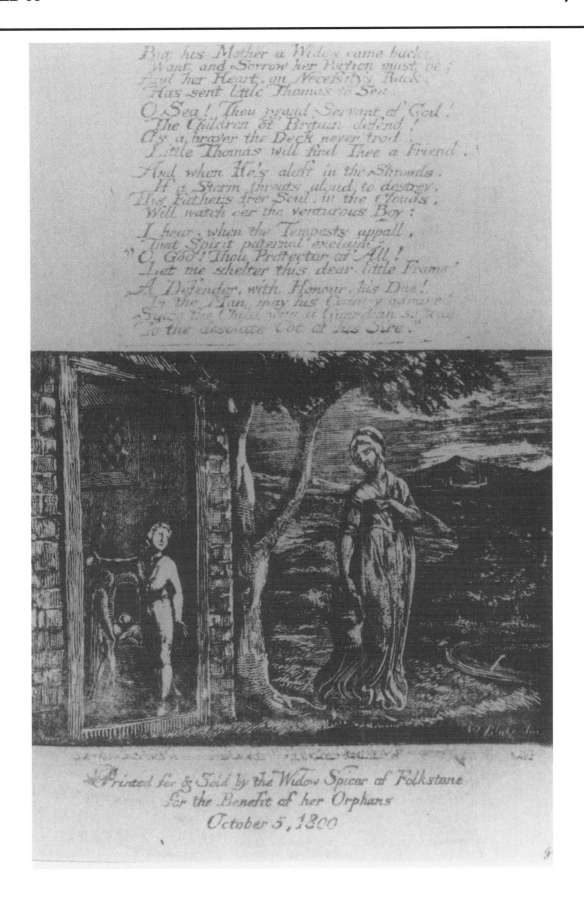

The Two Connoisseurs, London, Theatre Royal, Haymarket, 2 September 1784;

Marcella, London, Theatre Royal, Drury Lane, 7 November 1789;

Eudora, London, Theatre Royal, Covent Garden, 29 February 1790.

OTHER: "The Life of John Milton," in *The Poetical Works of John Milton,* 3 volumes, edited by Hayley (London: John & Josiah Boydell, 1794-1797), I:i-cxxxiii;

Select Poems, &c., by the Late John Dawes Worgan, of Bristol, who died on the Twenty-fifth of July 1809, aged Nineteen Years. To Which are Added, Some Particulars of his Life and Character, by an Early Friend and Associate. With a Preface, by William Hayley, Esq. (Philadelphia: Published by Kimber & Richardson, printed by Merritt, 1813).

William Hayley is perhaps destined to remain known more as the object of the satirical scorn of his betters than for his own voluminous and popular poetic output. Blake in *Milton* (1808?) and *Jerusalem* (1820?)–and more scurrilously in his notebook epigrams–Byron in lines 309-318 of his *English Bards and Scotch Reviewers* (1809), and Southey in a *Quarterly Review* essay (March 1825), all satirize Hayley's verse. Yet Hayley never pretended to genius. When he was asked to be poet laureate after the death of Thomas Wharton in 1790, he declined the honor.

William Hayley was born in Chichester, the second son of Thomas and Mary Yates Hayley. Thomas Hayley died when William was three, and two years later William's older brother died from an inoculation intended to protect him. In the same year, 1750, his mother moved to London, and sent William to Kingston Grammar School, where a young Edward Gibbon had studied just three years before under the same master, Richard Wooddeson. There Hayley was struck by an illness which left him lamed for life. His mother nursed him back to health, and on 31 August 1757 the boy was enrolled at Eton. In the summer of 1763, before entering Trinity College, Cambridge, he met and fell in love with Frances Page, for whom he wrote his earliest verse. His self-designed curriculum at Cambridge was erratic, and he left after three years without taking a degree.

In the spring of 1767, Hayley toured Scotland. When he returned to claim Frances Page's

hand, her father rebuffed him. A year later, she had married another, and Hayley proposed to Eliza Ball, a younger girl who had been the courier between him and Frances. On 23 October 1769, William and Eliza were married in Chichester Cathedral and settled with his mother on Queen Street in London, where Hayley prepared to become a playwright. His first attempt, "The Afflicted Father," was politely rejected by David Garrick in 1770. Next he translated Corneille's *Rodogune* (1644) as "The Syrian Queen," which George Colman the Elder turned down just as politely in 1771.

Failing at the drama, Hayley turned his hand to the epic, beginning a massive work on the Magna Carta. But this project was interrupted by an eye infection, which forced him to give up writing for a while, and from which his eyes never fully recovered. In 1774 Hayley returned to a villa his father had built at Eartham, where he continued to write poetry and developed a friendship with the painter George Romney.

The friendship with Romney resulted in Hayley's first successful poem, *An Essay on Painting* (1781), and in Romney's portrait of Hayley. The poetical epistle on painting was soon followed by other compositions in the same vein, mostly unsuccessful, with the notable exception of his *Essay on History* (1780), which sold well and won him the company of its dedicatee, the celebrated historian Edward Gibbon.

On 5 October 1780, Hayley's illegitimate son, Thomas Alphonso, was born to his housemaid. Shortly after, Hayley's wife, Eliza, left him to live in Bath, though Hayley's *Memoirs* (1823) suggest that the breach, which he attributed to her frigidity, was felt much earlier. Nevertheless, Eliza enjoyed being known in Bath as Mrs. Hayley, particularly since her husband's most successful work, *The Triumphs of Temper,* appeared just as she arrived there in the spring of 1781.

In 1783 Hayley met the sculptor John Flaxman, who remained a lifelong friend and would introduce him to William Blake. The following year Flaxman created a chimneypiece at the Eartham villa, establishing Hayley as a patron of the arts. After years of neglect, Hayley's tragedy *Lord Russel* and his comedy *The Two Connoisseurs* were produced at the Haymarket theater in August and September of 1784, without much notice. Hayley's last attempts to conquer the theater were his 1788 revision of a German opera (also a failure); a tragedy, *Marcella,* which created the flat-

"Adam Naming the Beasts," frontispiece by William Blake for Hayley's A Series of Ballads *(1802)*

tering circumstance of having the Drury Lane and Covent Garden theaters fight over it in 1789; and *Eudora*, which was given a wretched production on 29 February 1790 and closed after one performance. His only literary triumph of this period was the anonymous prose book *A Philosophical, Historical, and Moral Essay on Old Maids* (1785): by being almost universally condemned as a scandalous attack on spinsterhood, it became a best-seller.

For the next decade, most of Hayley's energy was taken up by entertaining prominent writers (Edward Gibbon, William Cowper) and artists (George Romney, John Flaxman) at Eartham each summer and plotting various schemes to improve the fortunes of England's neglected ge-

niuses. The one exception was the summer of 1790, which Hayley spent in France, where he hired a governess for his son Tom. The only other notable outcome of the trip was his composition of a verse comedy in French, "Les préjugés aboli, ou l'Anglois juste envers les François," though it was never produced and never published. Hayley's most ambitious scheme of literary benevolence, securing a pension for Cowper, was successful, but only after Cowper had grown too ill, both mentally and physically, to benefit by it.

Nevertheless, Hayley's acquaintance with the great minds of his day led to the next stage of his writing career, as a literary biographer. When Gibbon died in 1794, his executor, John Baker Holroyd, Earl of Sheffield, turned to Hayley for

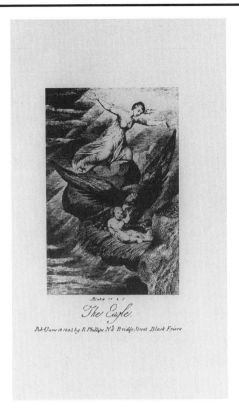

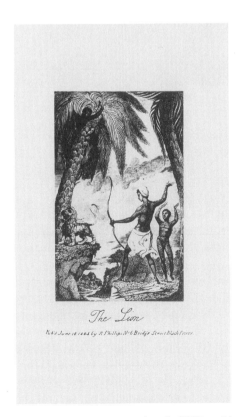

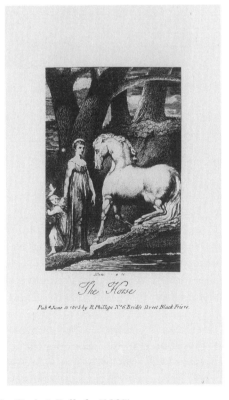

Engravings by William Blake for Hayley's Ballads *(1805)*

William Hayley (portrait by Henry Howard; by permission of the National Portrait Gallery, London)

help in editing Gibbon's papers. Hayley had already been working on a life of Milton to preface Cowper's translations of Milton's Latin poems and would in turn chronicle the lives of his friends Cowper (1803) and Romney (1809)–as well as his own (1823). Though they would never achieve the popularity of *The Triumphs of Temper*, these biographies, particularly Cowper's, were the most-read works of Hayley's last period.

One of the artists Hayley helped was his own son, Tom. Convinced of his boy's genius (of which there was indeed evidence), he apprenticed Tom to John Flaxman. In the summer of 1796 Tom returned to his father, who rented out the Eartham villa and took a more modest cottage at Felpham, anxious to conserve his dwindling income and convinced that the sea air was

necessary to the invalid boy's recovery. A series of deaths in the next few years–that of his estranged wife on 8 November 1797, of Cowper on 25 April 1800, and of his son, Tom, exactly a week later, changed Hayley's mood. He threw himself into the work of editing Cowper's letters and writing his life. While pursuing this work in London, he convinced William Blake to accompany him to Felpham, where Hayley promised to find the engraver some commissions.

Hayley's patronage of Blake from 1800 to 1803 is an important chapter in Blake's life, but a relatively minor episode in Hayley's. In addition to turning over his works in progress, both poetical and biographical, for Blake to illustrate, Hayley took time away from more important projects to dash off a series of juvenile ballads for the sole purpose of giving Blake more to engrave. There is no evidence that Hayley even knew of Blake's own poetry. In a copy of *The Triumphs of Temper* which he presented to Blake, Hayley wrote:

> Accept, my gentle visionary, Blake,
> Whose thoughts are fanciful and kindly mild;
> Accept and fondly keep for friendship's sake,
> This favour'd vision, my poetic child!

Though a rift grew between Blake and Hayley from the summer of 1802, their last meeting was Hayley's enthusiastic support for the defendant as a character witness at Blake's sedition trial. Blake's last letter to Hayley, 11 December 1805, shows no sign of their quarrel.

In the last decade of his life, Hayley's literary output continued, though his popularity was behind him. He was married for a second time on 28 March 1809 to twenty-eight-year-old Mary Welford. This marriage was no more successful than the first. By the summer of 1812 Mary had left Hayley. After another eight years of entertaining artists and literati and hatching benevolent schemes, Hayley died on 12 November 1820.

Hayley's verse is typical of late-eighteenth-century sentimental poetry, mostly in absolutely regular heroic couplets. While most such verse is unreadable by a modern audience, the minute analysis of human feelings it affords is sometimes of interest for its psychological insight. Unfortunately, however, Hayley's observations tend to be either bland or pedestrian or both, and always presented authoritatively, as immutable truth. Nevertheless, it was exactly these qualities which made *The Triumphs of Temper* a best-seller. Its heroine, Serena, represents the ideal balanced temper, which is triumphant over a series of emotional upsets in the poem, including a fair imitation of Pope's "Cave of Spleen" passage in *The Rape of the Lock* (1712, 1714). She avoids the extremes of wantonness, represented by nymphs, and prudishness, represented by her maiden aunt Penelope:

> Mild *Serena* scorn'd the prudish play,
> To wound warm love with frivolous delay;
> Nature's chaste child, not Affectation's slave,
> The heart she meant to give, she frankly gave.

Hayley's dramas are full of the sentimental, although his comic "Receipt for a Tragedy" in *The Triumph of Temper* suggests that he was merely following his own advice on how to write for an audience which demanded (and got) spectacle and melodrama on the stage:

> Now stir all together these separate parts
> And season them well with Ohs! fainting, and
>   starts:
> Squeeze in, while they're stirring, a potent infusion
> Of rage and of horror, of love and illusion:
> With madness and murder complete the conclusion.

Public taste turned away from Hayley's style of verse in his own lifetime, and he had little or no influence on subsequent English poetry. He was, however, one of the first to observe the extent to which Milton had revolutionized the epic, and to call for experimentation in the traditional form. Joseph Anthony Wittreich, Jr., has convincingly argued that Hayley's epic theory in *An Essay on Epic Poetry* (1782) and parts of his *Life of Milton* (1796) parallels Blake's practice in *Milton*, and may even have influenced it. Though his own poems tended to follow neoclassic rules, Hayley echoed his Romantic contemporaries in insisting that the poet is a visionary ruled "by Fancy's boundless power alone." Hayley is more important as a friend of poets than as a poet himself. Robert Southey's conclusion in a review of Hayley's *Memoirs* (*Quarterly Review*, March 1825), echoed by modern critics, is perhaps the best summary of Hayley's place in Romantic literature: "everything about that man is good except his poetry."

Biography:
Morchard Bishop, *Blake's Hayley* (London: Golancz, 1951).

References:
G. E. Bentley, Jr., "Blake, Hayley, and Lady Hesketh," *Review of English Studies,* 7 (July 1956): 264-286;

Joseph A. Wittreich, Jr., "Domes of Mental Pleasure: Blake's Epics and Hayley's Epic Theory," *Studies in Philology,* 69 (January 1972): 101-129.

Papers:
Hayley's manuscripts and unpublished letters are in the British Library.

James Hogg

(November ? 1770 - 21 November 1835)

N. C. Smith
University of Victoria

BOOKS: *Scottish Pastorals, Poems, Songs, Etc.* (Edinburgh: Printed by John Taylor, 1801);

The Mountain Bard (Edinburgh: Printed by J. Ballantyne for A. Constable, and J. Murray, London, 1807; enlarged edition, Edinburgh: Oliver & Boyd, 1821);

The Shepherd's Guide (Edinburgh: Printed by J. Ballantyne for A. Constable, and J. Murray, London, 1807);

The Forest Minstrel, by Hogg and others (Edinburgh: Printed for the editor & sold by A. Constable, and by Constable, Hunter, Park & Hunter, London, 1810; Philadelphia: M. Carey, 1816);

The Spy (nos. 1-52, Edinburgh, 1 September 1810 - 24 August 1811; 1 volume, Edinburgh: Sold by Constable, 1811);

The Queen's Wake (Edinburgh: Printed by A. Balfour for G. Goldie, and for Longman, Hurst, Rees, Orme & Brown, London, 1813; Baltimore: Coale & Maxwell, 1815);

The Hunting of Badlewe, A Dramatic Tale, as J. H. Craig of Douglas (London: Printed for Henry Colburn & George Goldie, Edinburgh, 1814);

The Pilgrims of the Sun (Edinburgh: Printed for W. Blackwood, and sold by J. Murray, London, 1815; Philadelphia: Published by Moses Thomas, printed by J. Maxwell, 1815);

The Ettricke Garland; being Two Excellent New Songs on The Lifting of the Banner of the House of Buccleuch, at the great foot-ball match on Carterhaugh, Dec. 4, 1815, by Hogg and Walter Scott (Edinburgh: Printed by James Ballantyne, 1815);

A Selection of German Hebrew Melodies, lyrics by Hogg (London: Printed & sold by C. Christmas, 1815);

Mador of the Moor (Edinburgh: Printed for W. Blackwood, and J. Murray, London, 1816; Philadelphia: Published by Moses Thomas, printed by J. Maxwell, 1816);

The Poetic Mirror (London: Printed for Longman, Hurst, Rees, Orme & Brown and John Ballantyne, Edinburgh, 1816; Philadelphia: Published by M. Carey, 1817);

Dramatic Tales, 2 volumes (Edinburgh: Printed by J. Ballantyne for Longman, Hurst, Rees, Orme & Brown, London & John Ballantyne, Edinburgh, 1817);

The Long Pack (Newcastle: Printed for John Bell, 1817);

A Border Garland. Containing Nine New Songs, lyrics by Hogg, music by Hogg and others (Edinburgh: Engraved for the editor by Walker & Anderson and sold by Nathaniel Gow & Son, 1819); enlarged as *A Border Garland, containing Twelve New Songs* (Edinburgh: Printed & sold by R. Purdie, n.d.);

The Brownie of Bodsbeck, and Other Tales (2 volumes, Edinburgh: Printed for W. Blackwood, and J. Murray, London, 1818; 1 volume, Philadelphia: Robert Dunlap, 1833);

Winter Evening Tales, 2 volumes (Edinburgh: Printed for Oliver & Boyd and for G. & W. B. Whitaker, London, 1820; New York: Published by Kirk & Mercein, Wiley & Halsted, W. B. Gilley, and Haley & Thomas, printed by C. S. Van Winkle, 1820);

The Poetical Works of James Hogg (4 volumes, Edinburgh: Printed for A. Constable, and Hurst, Robinson & Co., London, 1822; 2 volumes, New York: D. Mallory, 1825);

The Royal Jubilee. A Scottish Mask (Edinburgh: W. Blackwood / London: T. Cadell, 1822);

The Three Perils Of Man, 3 volumes (London: Longman, Hurst, Rees, Orme & Brown, 1822);

The Three Perils Of Woman (3 volumes, London: Printed for Longman, Hurst, Rees, Orme, Brown & Green, 1823; 2 volumes, New York: E. Duyckinck, 1823);

The Private Memoirs and Confessions of a Justified Sinner (London: Printed for Longman, Hurst, Rees, Orme, Brown & Green, 1824);

Queen Hynde (London: Printed for Longman, Hurst, Rees, Orme, Brown & Green, and W. Blackwood, Edinburgh, 1825);

Select and Rare Scotish [sic] *Melodies*, lyrics by Hogg, music by Henry R. Bishop (London: Published by Goulding & D'Almaine, 1829);

The Shepherd's Calendar, 2 volumes (Edinburgh: W. Blackwood / London: T. Cadell, 1829; New York: Goodrich, 1829);

Songs (Edinburgh: W. Blackwood / London: T. Cadell, 1831; New York: W. Stodart, 1832);

Altrive Tales (London: Cochrane, 1832);

A Queer Book (Edinburgh: W. Blackwood / London: T. Cadell, 1832);

Familiar Anecdotes of Sir Walter Scott (New York: Harper & Brothers, 1834); republished as *The Domestic Manners and Private Life of Sir Walter Scott* (Glasgow: John Reid & Co. / Edinburgh: Oliver & Boyd / London: Black,

Young & Young, 1834);

A Series of Lay Sermons on Good Principles and Good Breeding (London: J. Fraser, 1834);

Tales of the Wars of Montrose (3 volumes, London: Cochrane, 1835; 2 volumes, Philadelphia: E. L. Carey & Hart, 1836);

Tales and Sketches, 6 volumes (Glasgow, Edinburgh & London: Blackie & Son, 1837).

Collections: *The Works of the Ettrick Shepherd*, 2 volumes, edited by Rev. Thomas Thomson (London, Glasgow & Edinburgh: Blackie & Son, 1865; facsimile, New York: AMS Press, 1973);

Selected Poems, edited by Douglas S. Mack (Oxford: Clarendon Press, 1970);

A Shepherd's Delight: A James Hogg Anthology, edited by Judy Steel (Edinburgh: Canongate, 1985);

Hogg's birthplace, near Ettrick Kirk in Selkirkshire (engraving by Daniel Wilson, based on a drawing by D. O. Hill)

Walter Scott (seated at center) talking to Hogg and his mother while collecting ballads and stories for his Minstrelsy of the Scottish Border *(1802, 1803). Seated at left is Scott's friend William Laidlaw, Hogg's distant cousin.*

James Hogg: Selected Poems and Songs, edited by David Groves (Edinburgh: Canongate, 1986).

OTHER: *The Jacobite Relics of Scotland*, edited by Hogg (Edinburgh: Printed for W. Blackwood and for T. Cadell & W. Davies, London, 1819);

The Jacobite Relics of Scotland . . . Second Series, edited by Hogg (Edinburgh: Printed for W. Blackwood and for T. Cadell & W. Davies, London, 1821).

For the last twenty years of his life, James Hogg, "The Ettrick Shepherd," was perhaps as well known in his native Scotland as any of his contemporaries, save only Sir Walter Scott. This reputation derived not only from his numerous poems, stories, sketches, and novels that appeared in the leading literary magazines and in book form, but also from his having become a "character" (in both senses of the word) in the long-running satirical series, *Noctes Ambrosianae* (*Blackwood's Magazine*, 1822-1835) by critic John Wilson ("Christopher North"). Hogg's public image as a rural shepherd with no formal education was both a true picture and an attempt to capitalize on similarities with his famous predecessor Robert Burns. Throughout the nineteenth century Hogg was known as an untutored, bluff, rustic farmer, a maker of graceful songs and lyrics primarily, who had also written long poems imitative of Scott. Queen Victoria noted in her diary that she spent time in her Holyrood Palace garden reading Hogg's poems. By the beginning of the twentieth century, Hogg's works were largely unknown, but the beginnings of a modest revival came about largely through the republication of his best novel, *The Private Memoirs and Confessions of a Justified Sinner*, in 1947 with an introduction by André Gide. Since that time several editions of his works and several critical studies and articles have appeared.

Although both Hogg and his friends exaggerated the "Shepherd" of *Noctes Ambrosianae*, this persona did have its basis in fact, and, given his beginnings, Hogg's final achievement was considerable. Hogg was the second son of Robert Hogg, a tenant farmer in Selkirkshire, about forty miles south of Edinburgh, and Margaret Laidlaw Hogg, known for her knowledge of folk songs and stories. He was probably born in late November of 1770. (The Ettrick parish register gives the date of his baptism as 9 December 1770; however, Hogg himself usually provided a birth date of 25 January 1772, possibly as an attempt to appear younger, perhaps as the result of genuine carelessness about keeping records, but certainly as an endeavor to promote further parallels between himself and Burns, who had been born on 25 January 1759.) He attended school for only a few months before his father's farm failed, and for the next twenty-five years worked as a laborer and shepherd. He had to reteach himself to read and write in his late teens, when he began composing verse on a slate while tending flocks. In 1802 Walter Scott, collecting material for his *Minstrelsy of the Scottish Border* (1802, 1803), met Hogg, whose mother sang for Scott some songs that she remembered. Between 1794 and 1810 Hogg wrote songs which appeared in magazines and in two small collections–the patriotic "Donald M'Donald" became a popular success throughout the country–but his main job continued to be that of shepherd. Finally, at the age of forty, unable to maintain a farm or find other work, Hogg determined to move to Edinburgh and attempt to earn a living by writing–a most unlikely career at such an age and with such a background.

Improbable as the move was, even stranger was his initial literary endeavor: a weekly paper, modeled on *The Spectator* (1711-1712, 1714) that would satirize the foibles of the town–written by someone who knew very little about either town life or literary work. Yet Hogg managed to keep *The Spy* going for nearly a year, by filling it primarily with his own poems and tales. Nearly all his main motifs (the supernatural, manners and morals, good and evil) and techniques (anecdotes, frame stories, doubles, lyrics, hoaxes) appeared in *The Spy*, and Hogg would rework these devices over and over again for the rest of his career. In some ways Hogg can be considered a hack writer who knew the formulas for poetry and prose that would sell; he often said in later life that he wrote to earn money to support his family or his farm in specific instances, such as having to buy a new cow. Yet, at the same time, his naïveté–which shows itself in the constant tension between fantasy and realism in his works–his good humor, and his joy in earthy pleasures often inject a liveliness into even the most mundane of his pieces.

Hogg nearly starved for the next two years, but in 1813, encouraged by the popularity of the narrative poems of Scott and Byron, he returned to poetry. He collected some earlier verse, wrote new pieces, and added a framing narrative to pro-

James Hogg (portrait by William Nicholson; by permission of the Scottish National Portrait Gallery)

duce *The Queen's Wake*, which became an enormous success. The book's frame story involves a poetry contest held to celebrate the return of Queen Mary to Scotland in 1561. Minstrels come from every region of the country to display their distinct local talents in seventeen poems that educate the young queen–and Hogg's contemporary audience–about the variety and vitality of Scottish poesy. Two prize harps, one won by a Highland poet, the other by a bard of Ettrick, are borne away to their respective lands, where they disappear, until, the poem concludes, the magic harp won by the Ettrick poet is rediscovered by Walter Scott, who brings the magic of poetry back into the land. The nationalistic themes and the variety of poetic forms deservedly made Hogg's reputation, as the book went through six editions in the next six years, and two more after his death.

Two of Hogg's most-praised short pieces appear in *The Queen's Wake* (though neither won a prize in the poem's contest). "Kilmeny" depicts a journey to a peaceful, heavenly world of thought; written mainly in rhymed couplets and

sung by a religious mystic, the poem contrasts the fairy world with the harsh realities of earth. The sensuous descriptions of the heavenly world show the strength of Hogg's portrayals of the unearthly. Hogg's friend John Wilson, who often disparaged the Shepherd's works, called this poem "the finest Pastoral Lyric in our tongue," while one of Hogg's modern editors, Douglas S. Mack, who sees "Kilmeny" in a Christian context, calls the first section "one of the most beautiful passages in Scottish literature" and regards the whole poem as "the achievement of a poet of considerable importance."

In a quite different vein is "The Witch of Fife," a comic ballad which traces the adventures of a bawdy, pleasure-loving old man who follows his wife, a witch, on a wild flight with her coven. Getting drunk on the Bishop of Carlisle's wine, the old man is captured and nearly burned at the stake before his wife forgives his disbelief in her and rescues him. In the tradition of Burns's "Tam O' Shanter" (1791), a poem which Hogg loved, "The Witch of Fife," with its earthy hero, exotic adventures, comic dialogue, and witty exuber-

Facsimile of the Ettrick Shepherd's handwriting.

The Blackbird
By the Ettrick Shepherd

Sing on thou bonny bird of Spring
Thy little heart with love is heaving
Far hast thou wandered on the wing
But not thy love behind thee leaving
But I have left my native glade
The plant bower and printed blossom
And I have left the sweetest maid
That ever heaved a snowy bosom

Alas I fear the sylvan bower
Has lost its sweets of morn and even
Since I have flung the sweetest flower
That ever breathed the breeze of heaven
How often from the evening fall
I've wooed her fondly till the morrow
She gave her heart it was her all
And yet I left that heart to sorrow

Sing on thou bonny bird of morn
Above the broomwood waving yellow
Thy love sits listening in the thorn
Delighted with thy music mellow
Lang may thy melody renew
The fondest hope of faithful lover
And morning weave her mantle blue
Thy chanting in the greenwood over

THESE VERSES ARE FROM THE POEM ENTITLED "REGRET," PAGE 396.

Facsimile, included in the so-called Centenary Edition (1874) of The Works of the Ettrick Shepherd, *of a manuscript for a version of a poem first published in* The Spy, *no. 43 (1811), and collected in* The Poetical Works of James Hogg *(1822)*

ance, displays Hogg's variety and originality. Written in what Mack calls "a kind of pseudo-antique Scots, clearly an imitation of the Middle Scots of the old Makars," the poem testifies to Hogg's genius for exaggeration and extravagance. Walter Scott told Hogg, "There never was such a thing written for genuine and ludicrous humour," and even today, the poem delights for its genuine joy in life.

Hogg's next two books tried to capitalize on these strains in his work, with varying degrees of success. *The Pilgrims of the Sun* (1815) attempts to expand the lyric fragility of "Kilmeny" into an extended discussion of the nature of man and religion. An over-ambitious four-part epic, which ranges from a tour of the solar system and the planets to a Scottish Gothic tale, and which provides thematic variations of metrical form, *The Pilgrims of the Sun* was not as successful as Hogg had hoped, probably because the Shepherd was perhaps the least philosophical and intellectual of men. Although he was deeply religious, moral, and humanitarian, Hogg's artistic genius tends toward the comic, the lively, the horrific, and the surface rather than toward the meditative. As in "Kilmeny," the pure heroine of *The Pilgrims of the Sun* leaves Scotland, this time to tour a somewhat Miltonic universe, where she sees evidence of humanity's growing perfection as all people gradually move toward the godhead. Although competent in execution, the poem is often inconsistent in conception, and though fascinating for students of Hogg's beliefs, *The Pilgrims of the Sun* offers little for the modern reader.

Far more successful, and unduly neglected, is Hogg's collection of parodies of his Romantic contemporaries, *The Poetic Mirror* (1816). Hogg had originally asked each of his fellow poets to contribute an original piece for an anthology which he would edit; only Wordsworth, among the major poets, sent a poem, so Hogg determined that he would retain the original format but would write all the works himself. Using his gifts for mimicry and gentle comedy, his facility for various poetic techniques, and his literary knowledge, Hogg published anonymously a book of poems purportedly by Wordsworth, Byron, Coleridge, Scott, Southey, Wilson, and Hogg. George Kitchin, in *A Survey of Burlesque and Parody in English* (1931), called the book "one of the more considerable books of parodies in our language," and whether Hogg deals with Byronic excess, Scott's romantic descriptions, or Wordsworthian vapidity, his parodies are gentle, humorous,

and quite accurate. His self-parody, "The Gude Greye Cat," includes most of the elements of his other poems, couched in an almost unreadable exaggeration of the pseudo-Scots language. While poking fun at the originals, Hogg's parodies also stand alone as interesting and readable works—the mark of the best parody.

The rest of Hogg's poetry is of considerably less interest. He continued to contribute songs and lyrics to magazines, but the only sustained efforts were two long narrative poems in imitation of Scott and Byron. Both *Mador of the Moor* (1816) and *Queen Hynde* (1825), however, contain only occasional flashes of Hogg's best writing. Essentially a writer of anecdotes and sketches, he always had difficulty with extended narratives. *Mador of the Moor*, written in uncharacteristic Spenserian stanzas, seems especially derivative of such poems as Scott's *Lady of the Lake* (1810), with its disguised king and its relative lack of action. *Queen Hynde*, begun at about the same time, then abandoned, and finally completed some years later, has two of Hogg's typical delightful heroines, enough story to more than make up for the lack of incident in *Mador of the Moor*, and much of Hogg's most inept verse. Also in imitation of Scott, Hogg published two collections of Highland songs and music, *The Jacobite Relics*, but the Shepherd's editorial abilities were limited, and the collections have proven unreliable.

In 1817 *Blackwood's Magazine* appeared in answer to the more liberal *Edinburgh Magazine*; Hogg became one of the major contributors, and a kind of dubious fame was also realized when *Noctes Ambrosianae*, comic sketches and dialogues which featured a buffoon character called the Ettrick Shepherd, began appearing in *Blackwood's* in 1822. By this time, however, Hogg had been gone from Edinburgh for five years, having returned to the Ettrick farmlands, where he married Margaret Phillips in April 1820, and raised five children: James, Jessie, Maggy, Harriet, and Mary. Maintaining two farms for a time and supporting his wife's parents as well, he continued to produce stories, poems, and novels, more often to support his farming ventures than from any great commitment to art. Since Scott's Waverley novels had become immensely popular, Hogg also turned to fiction, in imitation of his acknowledged master. In 1818 appeared Hogg's short novel, *The Brownie of Bodsbeck*, like Scott's *Old Mortality* (1816) an historical account set in 1685, the days of the Covenanters and the persecutions by John Graham of Claverhouse. Hogg's tale, told

Hogg in 1824 (pastel portrait by William Bewick; by permission of the Scottish National Portrait Gallery)

from the point of view of the common people–always his most comfortable approach–mixes history, effective characterization, and interesting supernatural elements to create one of his best works. Other novels, novelettes, and stories appeared regularly over the next six years, including *Winter Evening Tales* (1820), *The Three Perils of Man* (1822), and *The Three Perils of Woman* (1823), mainly historical tales of uneven quality and consistency which nonetheless display the range of his traditional fiction.

Hogg's final extended prose narrative, however, *The Private Memoirs and Confessions of a Justified Sinner* (1824), serves as the basis of his modern reputation. In this remarkable novel Hogg uses a sophisticated narrative structure to explore religious fanaticism and to provide a marvelously ambiguous supernatural tale and an early example of the doppelgänger motif in literature. An introductory "Editor's Narrative" provides a

straightforward historical account of the century-old activities of Robert Wringhim, including the murder of his half-brother and his own eventual disappearance; the body of the book reproduces Wringhim's diary, found in his recently discovered grave in Scotland; a third part recounts the editor's trip to Scotland, a meeting with an uncouth shepherd, James Hogg, and the editor's thoughts about the diary and the events. Wringhim's diary tells of his strict religious upbringing at the hands of his mother and his eventual meeting with a fascinating young man, Gil-Martin, who convinces Wringhim that because they are "saved," any earthly acts will have no effect on their afterlife. For the glory of God, then, the pair commit murder, fratricide, matricide, and seduction in the name of religious rectitude. Trying finally to escape from Gil-Martin, who has the power to change his appearance, Wringhim is pursued by demons, until he commits suicide.

A.Croquis

James Hogg

THE AUTHOR OF "THE CHALDEE MANUSCRIPT."

Portrait in the Fraser's Magazine *"Gallery of Illustrious Literary Characters" (1830-1838)*

The novel shows Hogg's usual skills of dealing with the supernatural, providing a range of excellent comic characters, and pointing a moral against the evils of excess. It is unusual, though, in the psychological insights into the mind of a religious fanatic who nevertheless manages to elicit sympathy; in its uses of doubles, which recur in many forms throughout the novel; and in the creation of the Devil figure, Gil-Martin, of whom Walter Allen has said, "it is doubtful whether a more convincing representation of the power of evil exists in our literature" (*The English Novel*, 1954). The book did not enhance Hogg's reputation, however, until Gide's praise, when it began to attract significant attention. Gide wondered why the novel had failed to become famous, since it is "so singular and so enlightening, so especially fitted to arouse passionate interest both in those who are attracted by religious and moral ques-

tions, and, for quite other reasons, in psychologists and artists, and above all in surrealists who are so particularly drawn by the demoniac in every shape."

At the end of his life Hogg suffered from financial problems. At age sixty-two he made his first visit to London, where he was honored by literary society, especially at a Burns birthday dinner devoted to Hogg. His last major work was the memoir *Familiar Anecdotes of Sir Walter Scott* (1834), which recounted highlights of their relationship. The book, in fact, tells us much more about Hogg than Scott, but it angered Scott's biographer John Gibson Lockhart, who attacked Hogg and probably damaged his subsequent reputation. Wordsworth wrote the "Extempore Effusion Upon the Death of James Hogg" (1835), lamenting the deaths of Scott, Coleridge, Crabbe, as well as Hogg, but the Shepherd's fame slipped quickly, and only a few collections of poems and "collected" works appeared for nearly a century.

In recent years, however, the rediscovery of *The Private Memoirs and Confessions of a Justified Sinner* and renewed interest in Scottish literature have brought new attention to Hogg. Most of his important fiction has been republished, and two recent editions of selected poems provide a useful introduction to the important poetry. Clearly, Hogg will never be considered a major writer (though in *The Private Memoirs and Confessions of a Justified Sinner* he undoubtedly produced a major work): he was not a profound thinker, nor was he deeply committed to art. He wrote too much, both in poetry and prose, and much of what he wrote was derivative, designed for popular consumption in the magazines. His writing did not seem to develop significantly in either content, thought, or technique. Yet he was a gifted entertainer. He could tell a story in prose or poetry–especially a comic one or a supernatural one–with a skill that remains evident today. His simple beliefs–in God, in a moderate Calvinist religion, in the interaction of the real and the supernatural worlds, in simple retribution, in the power of good and the reality of evil–all come from his rural, uneducated background; likewise, his narrative skills derive from the ballads, hymns, folk tunes, seduction stories, and comic anecdotes of his youth. His poems lack a deep insight into humanity, but he can effectively convey moral, supernatural, and comic narratives with grace and skill, and he had a musical, lyrical gift; above all, he can communicate a joy in the pleasures of life.

Bibliographies:

Edith C. Batho, "Bibliography," *The Ettrick Shepherd* (Cambridge: Cambridge University Press, 1927), pp. 183-221;

Batho, "Notes on the Bibliography of James Hogg," *Library: Transactions of the Bibliographical Society*, fourth series 16 (December 1935): 309-326.

Biographies:

Edith C. Batho, *The Ettrick Shepherd* (Cambridge: Cambridge University Press, 1927);

Alan Lang Strout, *The Life and Letters of James Hogg: Volume I (1770-1825)* [no more published] (Lubbock: Texas Tech Press, 1946).

References:

Douglas Gifford, *James Hogg* (Edinburgh: Ramsay Head Press, 1976);

Louis Simpson, *James Hogg: A Critical Study* (Edinburgh: Oliver & Boyd, 1962);

Nelson C. Smith, *James Hogg* (Boston: Twayne, 1980).

Papers:

Hogg letters and some manuscripts are in the National Library of Scotland, the Bodleian Library, the British Library, the Yale University Library, the Alexander Turbull Library (Wellington, New Zealand), and the Stirling University Library.

Charles Lamb

(10 February 1775 - 27 December 1834)

Winifred F. Courtney

BOOKS: *Blank Verse,* by Lamb and Charles Lloyd (London: Printed by T. Bensley for J. & A. Arch, 1798);

A Tale of Rosamund Gray and Old Blind Margaret (Birmingham: Printed by Thomas Pearson, 1798; London: Printed for Lee & Hurst, 1798);

John Woodvil: A Tragedy (London: Printed by T. Plummer for G. & J. Robinson, 1802);

The King and Queen of Hearts (London: Printed for Thos Hodgkins, 1805);

Tales from Shakespear. Designed for the Use of Young Persons, 2 volumes, by Charles Lamb and Mary Lamb, attributed to Charles Lamb (London: Printed for Thomas Hodgkins at the Juvenile Library, 1807; Philadelphia: Published by Bradford & Inskeep, and by Inskeep & Bradford, New York, printed by J. Maxwell, 1813);

The Adventures of Ulysses (London: Printed by T. Davison for the Juvenile Library, 1808; New York: Harper, 1879);

Mrs. Leicester's School, by Charles Lamb and Mary Lamb (London: Printed for M. J. Godwin at the Juvenile Library, 1809; George Town: J. Milligan, 1811);

Poetry for Children, Entirely Original, 2 volumes, by Charles Lamb and Mary Lamb (London: Printed for M. J. Godwin at the Juvenile Library, 1809; Boston: West & Richardson, and E. Cotton, 1812);

Prince Dorus: Or, Flattery Put Out of Countenance. A Poetical Version of an Ancient Tale (London: Printed for M. J. Godwin at the Juvenile Library, 1811);

Mr. H., or Beware a Bad Name. A Farce in Two Acts [pirated edition] (Philadelphia: Published by M. Carey, printed by A. Fagan, 1813);

The Works of Charles Lamb, 2 volumes (London: Ollier, 1818);

Elia: Essays which have appeared under that signature in the London Magazine (London: Printed for Taylor & Hessey, 1823; [pirated edition] Phil-

adelphia: Carey, Lea & Carey, printed by Mifflin & Parry, 1828);

Elia: Essays which have appeared under that name in the London Magazine Second Series [pirated edition] (Philadelphia: Carey, Lea & Carey, printed by J. R. A. Skerret, 1828)–includes three essays not written by Lamb;

Album Verses, with a Few Others (London: Moxon, 1830);

Satan in Search of a Wife (London: Moxon, 1831);

The Last Essays of Elia (London: Moxon, 1833; Philadelphia: T. K. Greenbank, 1833).

Collections: *The Works of Charles and Mary Lamb,* 7 volumes, edited by E. V. Lucas (London: Methuen, 1903-1905; New York: Putnam's, 1903-1905);

Charles Lamb on Shakespeare, edited by Joan Coldwell (Gerrards Cross: Colin Smythe, 1978);

Lamb as Critic, edited by Roy Clark (London & Henley: Routledge & Kegan Paul, 1980).

PLAY PRODUCTION: *Mr. H----,* London, Theatre Royal, Drury Lane, 10 December 1806.

OTHER: Samuel Taylor Coleridge, *Poems on Various Subjects,* includes four poems by Lamb (London: C. G. & J. Robinson/Bristol: J. Cottle, 1796); enlarged as *Poems, Second Edition, to which are now added Poems by Charles Lamb, and Charles Lloyd,* includes ten poems by Lamb (Bristol: Printed by N. Biggs for J. Cottle and Robinsons, London, 1797);

Charles Lloyd, *Poems on the Death of Priscilla Farmer,* includes one poem by Lamb (Bristol: Printed by N. Biggs & sold by James Phillips, London, 1796);

Specimens of English Dramatic Poets, Who Lived About the time of Shakspeare, edited, with commentary, by Lamb (London: Printed for Longman, Hurst, Rees & Orme, 1808; New York: Wiley & Putnam, 1845).

Charles Lamb
1819.

Charles Lamb achieved lasting fame as a writer during the years 1820-1825, when he captivated the discerning English reading public with his personal essays in the *London Magazine,* collected as *Essays of Elia* (1823) and *The Last Essays of Elia* (1833). Known for their charm, humor, and perception, and laced with idiosyncrasies, these essays appear to be modest in scope, but their soundings are deep, and their ripples extend to embrace much of human life–particularly the life of the imagination. Lamb is increasingly becoming known, too, for his critical writings. *Lamb as Critic* (1980) gathers his criticism from all sources, including letters. A new edition of his entertaining letters is also underway. While Lamb was an occasional journalist, a playwright (of small success), a writer for children, and a poet, it is his prose which has endured. He early realized that poetry was not his vocation; his best poetry was written in youth.

The son of John and Elizabeth Field Lamb, Charles Lamb, a Londoner who loved and celebrated that city, was born in the Temple, the abode of London lawyers, where his father was factotum for one of these, Samuel Salt. The family was ambitious for its two sons, John and Charles, and successful in entering Charles at Christ's Hospital, a London charity school of merit, on 9 October 1782. Here he met Samuel Taylor Coleridge, a fellow pupil who was Lamb's close friend for the rest of their lives and who helped stir his growing interest in poetry. Lamb left school early, on 23 November 1789. (Because he had a severe stammer, he did not seek a university career, then intended to prepare young men for orders in the Church of England.) In September 1791 he found work as a clerk at the South Sea House, but he left the following February, and in April he became a clerk at the East India Company, where he remained for thirty-three years, never feeling fitted for the work nor much interested in "business," but managing to survive, though without promotion.

Soon after leaving school, he was sent to Hertfordshire to his ill grandmother, housekeeper in a mansion seldom visited by its owners. Here he fell in love with Ann Simmons, subject of his earliest sonnets (though his first to be published, in the 29 December 1794 issue of the *Morning Chronicle,* was a joint effort with Coleridge to the actress Sarah Siddons–evidence of his lifelong devotion to the London theater). His "Anna" sonnets, which appeared in the 1796 and 1797 editions of Coleridge's *Poems,* have a sentimental, nostalgic quality: "Was it some sweet device of Faery / That mocked my steps with many a lonely glade, / And fancied wanderings with a fair-hair'd maid?"; "Methinks how dainty sweet it were, reclin'd"; "When last I roved these winding wood-walks green"; "A timid grace sits trembling in her eye." All were written after the love affair had ended, to Lamb's regret. His early novel, *A Tale of Rosamund Gray* (1798), is also rooted in the Ann episode.

After the death of Samuel Salt in 1792 the Lambs were in straitened circumstances, mother and father both ill. The elder brother, John, was living independently and was not generous to his family. On Charles (after an unpaid apprenticeship) and his elder sister, Mary, a dressmaker who had already shown signs of mental instability, fell the burden of providing for the family, and Mary took on the nursing as well. Two of Lamb's early sonnets are addressed to her: Mary, who was ten years older than Charles, had mothered him as a child, and their relationship was always a close one. Charles continued to write–a ballad on a Scottish theme, poems to friends and to William Cowper on that poet's recovery from a fit of madness. "A Vision of Repentance" ("I saw a famous fountain, in my dream") treats a truly Romantic theme–the hope of God's forgiveness for the sin of a repentant Psyche. It has a Keatsian charm but little lasting distinction.

The tragedy of 22 September 1796–when Mary, exhausted and deranged from overwork, killed their mother with a carving knife–changed both their lives forever. She was judged temporarily insane, and Lamb at twenty-one took full legal responsibility for her for life, to avoid her permanent confinement in a madhouse. Thereafter she was most often lucid, warm, understanding, and

much admired by such friends as the essayist William Hazlitt. She also developed skills as a writer. But she was almost annually visited by the depressive "illness" which led to her confinement for weeks at a time in a private hospital in Hoxton. (Lamb too had been confined briefly at Hoxton for his mental state in 1795, but there was no later recurrence.) Both were known for their capacity for friendship and for their mid-life weekly gatherings of writers, lawyers, actors, and the odd but interesting "characters" for whom Lamb had a weakness.

For the moment Lamb "renounced" poetry altogether, but he soon took it up again and began work on a tragedy in Shakespearean blank verse, *John Woodvil* (1802), which has autobiographical elements. While there are a few fine lines and the writing in general is competent but unoriginal, plotting and character are weak: it was never produced. "The Wife's Trial," a late play in blank verse, is of minor interest. It was published in the December 1828 issue of *Blackwood's Magazine.* His only play to reach the stage, *Mr. H----* (in prose), was roundly hissed in London when it opened on 10 December 1806, but it was successfully produced in the United States thereafter.

Though soon after his mother's death he announced his intention to leave poetry "to my betters," Lamb continued to write verse of various kinds throughout his life: sonnets, lyrics, blank verse, light verse, prologues and epilogues to the plays of friends, satirical verse, verse translations, verse for children, and finally *Album Verses* (1830), written to please young ladies who kept books of such tributes. By 1820 he had developed what was to be his "Elia" prose style. He was the first intensely personal, truly Romantic essayist, never rivaled in popularity by his friends Leigh Hunt and William Hazlitt. Many of Lamb's essays before those he signed Elia came out in Hunt's publications.

For students of Lamb and for his recent biographers, Lamb's poetry is mainly of interest as autobiography and as light on the essays, often treating the same subjects. The great French critic Charles-Augustin Sainte-Beuve admired Lamb's early sonnet "Innocence" so much that he translated it, but most critics then and now agree with Leigh Hunt that Lamb "wanted sufficient heat and music to render his poetry as good as his prose." Alaric A. Watts, another of Lamb's contemporaries, wrote a jingle on Lamb that includes these lines: "For what if thy Muse will be sometimes perverse, / And present us with prose

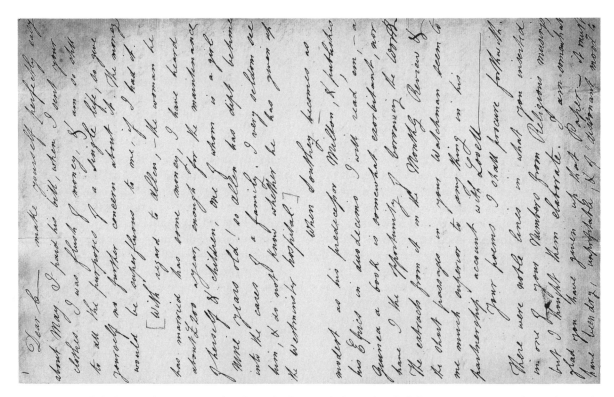

Letter, postmarked 27 May 1796, to Samuel Taylor Coleridge, in which Lamb included "To My Sister" (HM 7482; by permission of the Henry E. Huntington Library and Art Gallery). Lamb's sonnet was first published in Coleridge's Poems *(1797). May, mentioned in the first paragraph, is a London landlord to whom Coleridge owed money. The letter also mentions Robert Allen and Charles Valentine Le Grice, friends from Lamb and Coleridge's school days at Christ's Hospital, and it refers to Coleridge's recently failed "Paper,"* The Watchman, *as well as Lamb's 1795 confinement in a mental asylum.*

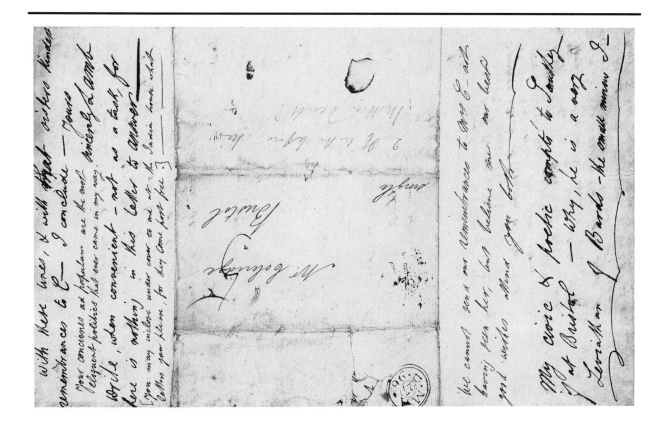

Lamb dressed as a Venetian senator, 1804 (portrait by William Hazlitt; by permission of the National Portrait Gallery, London)

when she means to give verse?" He noted that Lamb's *prose* is often admirably poetic, so that "we miss not the rhyme." In the twentieth century A. C. Ward has effectively demonstrated that Lamb's poetry lacks both the inspiration and discipline of his prose, concluding that in his poetry "his intensity of emotion is never once matched with an intensely personal manner of expression: he does not find the one perfect mould, and hardly ever lights upon the miraculous right word...." (For "never once" one should substitute "rarely.") E. V. Lucas, Edmund Blunden, George L. Barnett, and William Kean Seymour, however, find in much of it charm, honesty, strength of feeling, and originality. "His poetry," Seymour concludes, "makes a pendant to his Essays, and it is a lustrous and significant pendant." The roles of artist and critic, of course, demand very different abilities: Lamb was, in correspondence, an able critic of the poetry of Coleridge and Wordsworth, who sometimes took his advice. (He met Wordsworth, who became a lifelong friend, through Coleridge in 1797.)

Of considerable interest are Lamb's blank-verse poems, which reveal–with passion that comes through–his spiritual struggles after the tragedy, as he sought consolation in religion. In one, he doubts whether atheists or deists (such as his friend William Godwin, novelist, philosopher, and publisher of children's books) have adequate answers for the larger questions of life; other poems dwell on the death of the old aunt whose favorite he was (she also appears in his essay "Witches and Other Night-Fears"), on his dead mother with regrets for days gone, on his father's senility, on Mary's fate, and on his growing doubts about institutional religion. Yet these poems are among his most "prosy," with only an

Jowis ratherish unwell
Chs Lamb.

THE AUTHOR OF 'ELIA'.

Portrait by Daniel Maclise in the Fraser's Magazine *"Gallery of Illustrious Literary Characters" (1830-1838)*

occasional impressive passage; their grammatical complexities are hard to follow. Several were published with poems by his Quaker friend Charles Lloyd in their *Blank Verse* (1798).

Soon after composing this group he contributed a piece on his grandmother (later developed in "Dream-Children") to Lloyd's *Poems on the Death of Priscilla Farmer* (1796). The culmination of this period was "The Old Familiar Faces" (written in 1798 and published in *Blank Verse*), which ends:

some they have died.and some they have left me,
And some are taken from me; all are departed;
All, all are gone, the old familiar faces.

This poem is still anthologized; it tells with grace the story of his own youth, touching a universal human chord. Written in 1803 and published in Lamb's 1818 *Works*, "Hester" takes as its subject a young Quaker whom he had often seen but to whom he had never spoken, though he said he was "in love" with her. She married early and soon died; his poem, a delicate tribute to a charming girl who enhances even Death, ends with lines addressed to her:

My sprightly neighbour, gone before
To that unknown and silent shore,
Shall we not meet, as heretofore,
    Some summer morning,

When from thy cheerful eyes a ray
Hath struck a bliss upon the day,
A bliss that would not go away,
    A sweet fore-warning?

These are his poetic triumphs. After them came more poems to friends, and also political verses, which are often sharp and clever, even venomous. "The Triumph of the Whale," on the prince regent, whom he sincerely hated, was published in Hunt's *Examiner* (15 March 1812) and may have had a part in Hunt's two-year incarceration for libel, though the official charge was based on Hunt's editorial a week later. "The Gipsy's Malison," another harsh poem of Lamb's later years–on the ill-born child who is destined to hang–is sometimes anthologized. Like "The Triumph of the Whale," it reveals a bitter aspect of Lamb's complex nature, which shows rarely but persistently in his work. Among Lamb's humorous light-verse pieces, "A Farewell to Tobacco" is one of the best. (He never gave up smoking or lost his taste for drink, though he tried often.)

In 1808 he published his *Specimens of English Dramatic Poets, Who Lived About the time of Shakspeare,* with commentary that was later admired by the younger generation of Romantics, particularly Keats, and established Lamb as a critic. For needed cash, he and Mary, at Godwin's request, wrote *Poetry for Children* (1809), in which their fondness for children shines through the moral verses. It did not reach a second edition, but the Lambs were much more successful with *Mrs. Leicester's School* (1809) and *Tales from Shakespear* (1807), which has never since been out of print.

In 1818 Lamb published his early *Works,* and in 1819 he proposed to Fanny Kelly, a popular comic actress who was later a friend of Dickens and founder of the first dramatic school for girls. She refused him, confiding to a friend that she could not carry Mary's problems too. Charles and Mary did know a sort of parenthood in their 1823 "adoption" of a teenage orphan, Emma Isola, who regarded their home as hers until she married Lamb's new young publisher, Edward Moxon, in 1833.

In the years 1820-1825 Lamb made his reputation as Elia in the *London Magazine.* By 1825, though he was still a clerk, Lamb's salary had risen after long service, and he was able to retire at fifty with a good pension and provision for Mary. He occupied his new leisure for several years at the British Museum, compiling more dramatic excerpts, which appeared in William Hone's *Table Book* throughout 1827, and contributing other writings to periodicals. When *Album Verses* appeared in 1830, followed by the humorous ballad *Satan in Search of a Wife* (1831), critics found them disappointing fluff. His *Last Essays of Elia* (1833), from the *London Magazine,* reminded readers of his true stature.

Brother and sister had had to move many times as the reason for Mary's increasing absences from home became known. Their last move was to a sort of sanitarium at Edmonton, near London, in 1833. Here, while out walking one day in 1834, Lamb fell. He died of erysipelas a few days later. Mary lived on, with a paid companion, till 1847.

Lamb's essays were taught in schools until World War II, when reaction set in–from critics such as F. R. Leavis and others–dulling the sentimental admiration Lamb had till then enjoyed. Yet in the 1970s serious scholars increasingly discovered new virtues in his fine letters and criticism, and new subtleties in the old essays: too long had it been said that the affection he inspired precluded criticism. New biographies and studies have recently appeared, and in the 1980s there began a renewed appreciation for Lamb's prose–though not for his poetry. The Charles Lamb Society of London flourishes, and publishes a bulletin which has become impressively scholarly since its new series began in the 1970s.

Letters:

The Letters of Charles Lamb, to Which Are Added Those of His Sister Mary Lamb, 3 volumes, edited by E. V. Lucas (London: Dent / Methuen, 1935; New Haven: Yale University Press, 1935);

The Letters of Charles and Mary Anne Lamb, 3 volumes to date, edited by Edwin W. Marrs, Jr. (Ithaca & London: Cornell University Press, 1975-   ).

Bibliographies:

Luther S. Livingston, *A Bibliography of the First Editions in Book Form of the Writings of Charles and Mary Lamb Published Prior to Charles Lamb's Death in 1834* (New York: Printed for J. A. Spoor, 1903);

Thomas Hutchinson, "Bibliographical List (1794-1834) of the Published Writings of Charles and Mary Lamb," in *The Works of Charles Lamb,* edited by Hutchinson (London & New York: Oxford University Press, 1908), pp. xvii-xlvii;

Joseph C. Thomson, *Bibliography of the Writings of Charles and Mary Lamb* (Hull: Tutin, 1908);

George L. Barnett and Stuart M. Tave, "Charles Lamb," in *The English Romantic Poets & Essayists: A Review of Research and Criticism,* revised edition, edited by Carolyn Washburn Houtchens and Lawrence Huston

Mary and Charles Lamb, 1834 (portrait by F. S. Cary; by permission of the National Portrait Gallery, London)

Houtchens (New York: Published for the Modern Language Association of America by New York University Press, 1966).

Biographies:

Barry Cornwall (Bryan Waller Procter), *Charles Lamb: A Memoir* (London: Moxon, 1866; Boston: Roberts, 1866);

Alfred Ainger, *Charles Lamb*, English Men of Letters Series (London: Macmillan, 1882; New York: Harper, 1882);

Jules Derocquigny, *Charles Lamb: sa vie et ses oeuvres* (Lille: Le Bigot, 1904);

E. V. Lucas, *The Life of Charles Lamb*, 2 volumes (London: Methuen, 1905); revised edition, 1 volume (London: Methuen, 1921);

Edmund Blunden, comp., *Charles Lamb: His Life Recorded by His Contemporaries* (London: Leonard & Virginia Woolf at the Hogarth Press, 1934);

Henry Crabb Robinson, *Henry Crabb Robinson on Books and Their Writers,* 3 volumes, edited by Edith J. Morley (London: Dent, 1938);

Ernest C. Ross, *The Ordeal of Bridget Elia: A Chronicle of the Lambs* (Norman: University of Oklahoma Press, 1940);

Will D. Howe, *Charles Lamb and His Friends* (New York & Indianapolis: Bobbs-Merrill, 1944);

Winifred F. Courtney, *Young Charles Lamb, 1775-1802* (London: Macmillan, 1982; New York: New York University Press, 1982);

David Cecil, *A Portrait of Charles Lamb* (London: Constable, 1983).

References:

George L. Barnett, *Charles Lamb* (Boston: Twayne, 1976);

Barnett, *The Evolution of Elia*, Indiana University Humanities Series, no. 53 (Bloomington, 1964);

Edmund Blunden, *Charles Lamb and His Contemporaries* (Cambridge: Cambridge University Press, 1933);

Charles Lamb Bulletin (1935-1972; new series 1973-);

Reginald L. Hine, *Charles Lamb and His Hertfordshire* (London: Dent, 1949);

Edith C. Johnson, *Lamb Always Elia* (London: Methuen, 1935);

E. V. Lucas, *Charles Lamb and the Lloyds* (London: Smith, Elder, 1898);

Wallace Nethery, *Charles Lamb in America to 1848* (Worcester, Mass.: St. Onge, 1963);

Nethery, *Eliana Americana: Charles Lamb in the United States 1849-1866* (Los Angeles: Plantin Press, 1971);

Roy Park, Introduction to *Lamb as Critic,* edited by Park (London & Henley: Routledge & Kegan Paul, 1980);

Claude A. Prance, *Companion to Charles Lamb: A Guide to People and Places, 1760-1847* (London: Mansell, 1983);

S. M. Rich, comp., *The Elian Miscellany: A Charles Lamb Anthology* (London: Joseph, 1931);

Frank P. Riga and Claude E. Prance, *Index to The London Magazine* (New York & London: Garland, 1978);

William Kean Seymour, "Charles Lamb as a Poet," *Essays by Divers Hands,* new series 26 (March 1954): 103-126;

A. C. Ward, *The Frolic and the Gentle: A Centenary Study of Charles Lamb* (London: Methuen, 1934);

George Whalley, "Coleridge's Debt to Charles Lamb," *Essays and Studies by Members of the English Association,* new series 11 (1958): 68-85.

Papers:

There are significant collections in the Henry E. Huntington Library, the New York Public Library, the Pierpont Morgan Library, the British Library, and libraries at Harvard University, Yale University, Princeton University, the University of Texas, and the University of Kentucky. The Charles Lamb Society Library, which holds some autograph items, is now housed in the Guildhall Library, London.

Walter Savage Landor

(30 January 1775 - 17 September 1864)

Keith Hanley
University of Lancaster

BOOKS: *The Poems of Walter Savage Landor* (London: Printed for T. Cadell & W. Davies, 1795);

Moral Epistle, Respectfully dedicated to Earl Stanhope (London: Printed for Cadell & W. Davies, 1795);

To the Burgesses of Warwick (Warwick, 1797); edited by R. H. Super (Oxford: Printed for the Luttrell Society by B. Blackwell, 1949);

Gebir; A Poem in Seven Books (London: Sold by Rivingtons, 1798; enlarged and corrected edition, Oxford: Printed by & for Slatter & Munday & sold by R. S. Kirby, London, 1803); translated by Landor as *Gebirus, Poema* (Oxford: Printed & sold by Slatter & Munday & sold by R. S. Kirby, London, 1803);

Poems from the Arabic and Persian (Warwick: Printed by H. Sharpe & sold by Rivingtons, London, 1800);

Iambi (Oxford: Privately printed, circa 1802);

Poetry by the Author of Gebir (London: Sold by F. & C. Rivington, 1802);

Simonidea (Bath: Printed by W. Meyler & sold by G. Robinson, London, 1806);

Three Letters, Written in Spain, to D. Francisco Riguelme Commanding the Third Division of the Gallician Army (Bath: Printed by W. Meyler & sold by J. Robinson and J. Harding, London, 1809);

Ode ad Gustavum Regem. Ode ad Gustavum Exulem (London: Printed by A. J. Valpy, 1810);

Count Julian: A Tragedy (London: Printed for John Murray by James Moyes, 1812);

Commentary on Memoirs of Mr. Fox [printed but suppressed] (London: Printed for the author by T. Davison & sold by J. Murray, 1812); edited by Stephen Wheeler as *Charles James Fox, A Commentary on his Life and Character* (New York: Putnam's, 1907; London: J. Murray, 1907);

Letter from Mr. Landor to Mr. Jervis (Bath, 1814);

Letters addressed to Lord Liverpool, and The Parliament, on the Preliminaries of Peace, by Calvus (London: Printed for Henry Colburn & sold by George Goldie, Edinburgh, 1814);

Idyllia Nova Quinque Heroum atque Heroidum (Oxford: Sold by Slatter & Munday & by Longman, Hurst, Rees, Orme & Brown, London, 1815);

Sponsalia Polyxenae (Pistoia, 1819);

Idyllia Heroica Decem (Pisa: S. Nistri, 1820);

Poche Osservazioni (Naples, 1821);

Imaginary Conversations of Literary Men and Statesmen, volumes 1 and 2 (London: Printed for Taylor & Hessey, 1824; corrected and enlarged edition, London: H. Colburn, 1826);

Imaginary Conversations of Literary Men and Statesmen, volume 3 (London: Henry Colburn, 1828);

Imaginary Conversations of Literary Men and Statesmen . . . Second Series, 2 volumes (London: James Duncan, 1829);

Gebir, Count Julian, and Other Poems (London: E. Moxon, 1831);

Citation and Examination of William Shakspeare (London: Saunders & Otley, 1834; Boston: Roberts Brothers, 1888);

Pericles and Aspasia (2 volumes, London: Saunders & Otley, 1836; abridged, unauthorized edition, Philadelphia: Carey & Hart, 1839; complete edition, 1 volume, Boston: Roberts Brothers, 1871);

The Letters of a Conservative (London: Saunders & Otley, 1836);

A Satire on Satirists, and Admonition to Detractors (London: Saunders & Otley, 1836);

Terry Hogan: An Eclogue (London: Printed by J. Wertheimer, 1836);

The Pentameron and Pentalogia (London: Saunders & Otley, 1837); republished in *The Pentameron etc.* (Boston: Roberts Brothers, 1888);

Andrea of Hungary, and Giovanna of Naples (London: R. Bentley, 1839);

Fra Rupert, The last part of a Trilogy (London: Saunders & Otley, 1840);

The Works of Walter Savage Landor, 2 volumes (London: E. Moxon, 1846);

The Hellenics of Walter Savage Landor. Enlarged and Completed (London: E. Moxon, 1847); enlarged as *The Hellenics of Walter Savage Landor; comprising Heroic Idyls, &c.* (Edinburgh: J. Nichol/London: R. Griffin, 1859);

Poemata et Inscriptiones (London: E. Moxon, 1847);

The Italics of Walter Savage Landor (London: Reynell & Weight, 1848);

Imaginary Conversation of King Carlo-Alberto and the Duchess Belgioioso, on the Affairs and Prospects of Italy (London: Longman, Brown, Green & Longmans, 1848);

Statement of Occurrences at Llanbedr (Bath: Printed by Meyler & Son, 1849);

Popery: British and Foreign (London: Chapman & Hall, 1851);

Tyrannicide (N.p., 1851);

Imaginary Conversations of Greeks and Romans (London: E. Moxon, 1853);

The Last Fruit off an Old Tree (London: E. Moxon, 1853);

Letters of an American, mainly on Russia and Revolution (London: Chapman & Hall, 1854);

Antony and Octavius. Scenes for the Study (London: Bradbury & Evans, 1856);

Letter from W. S. Landor to R. W. Emerson (Bath: E. Williams, 1856);

Selections from the Writings of Walter Savage Landor, edited by George Stillman Hillard (Boston: Ticknor & Fields, 1856);

Walter Savage Landor and the Honourable Mrs. Yescombe (Bath, 1857);

Landor's birthplace, Warwick

Mr. Landor Threatened (Bath, 1857);

Dry Sticks, Fagoted by Walter Savage Landor (Edinburgh: J. Nichol/London: J. Nisbet, 1858);

Mr. Landor's Remarks On a Suit Preferred against him, at the Summer Assizes at Taunton, 1858 (London: Holyoake, 1859);

Savonarola e il Priore di San Marco (Florence, 1860);

Heroic Idyls, with additional poems (London: T. C. Newby, 1863);

Imaginary Conversations, 5 volumes (Boston: Roberts, 1876-1877).

Editions and Collections: *Imaginary Conversations,* 6 volumes; *Poems Dialogues in Verse and Epigrams,* 2 volumes; and *The Longer Prose Works,* 2 volumes, edited by Charles G. Crump (London: Dent, 1891-1893);

The Complete Works of Walter Savage Landor, 16 volumes: volumes 1-12 [prose] edited by T. Earle Welby, volumes 13-16 edited by Stephen Wheeler (London: Chapman & Hall, 1927-1936); volumes 13-16 republished as

The Poetical Works of Walter Savage Landor, 3 volumes (Oxford: Clarendon Press, 1937);

Landor as Critic, edited by Charles L. Proudfit (London: Routledge & Kegan Paul, 1979);

Walter Savage Landor. Selected Poetry and Prose, edited by Keith Hanley (Manchester: Carcanet Press, 1981).

As a poet, Walter Savage Landor has enjoyed a permanent minority reputation for the classicism of his epigrams and idyls. He was a seriously emulative classicist and wrote a significant proportion of his poetry in Latin, which was also the original language of some of the long and short poems that he published in English. Indeed, he was deterred from making it his chief medium only by the example of John Milton and the advice of Robert Southey and William Wordsworth, and as an old man he remarked, "I am sometimes at a loss for an English word, for a Latin never." Though the "Latin savour" (Arthur Symons's phrase) and the formal skills of his works have always attracted the particular atten-

Landor in 1804 (engraving by J. Brown, based on a portrait by George Dance)

tion of fellow poets, so that Wordsworth, for instance, wrote to Landor that he would rather have been the author of his verses "than of any produced in our time," T. S. Eliot summed up Landor's achievement as that of "only a magnificent by-product," limited by a single-minded adherence to the classical humanist tradition that was under siege in the age of industrialization. William Butler Yeats in *A Vision* (1925), on the other hand, admired the completeness of Landor's cultural mask and saw it as one peculiarly appropriate for a notorious firebrand: "The most violent of men, he uses his intellect to disengage a visionary image of perfect sanity . . . seen always in the most serene and classic art imaginable."

A recognition of the art and the mask, however, including Landor's patrician contempt for popularity, should not prevent acknowledgment of the political vision of liberal republicanism, critically opposed to the dominant forces of Romantic reaction, that varies from the esoteric to the propagandist in Landor's poetry. That vision is related to the resilient structure of feeling even in the miniaturism of his epigrams, idyls, and dramatic scenes, with their emphasis on physical pleasure and noble attitudes. In this respect he is best viewed in the light of a live classical tradition he shared with contemporaries such as George Gordon, Lord Byron, Percy Bysshe Shelley, and Thomas Love Peacock.

It was through his prose writings that Landor became well known, especially with the series of *Imaginary Conversations* (1824-1829) between literary and political personalities from all periods of European history. But the prose is linked to the verse by the control or "mastership" that

Jane Sophia Swift, the "Ianthe" of Landor's poems. This portrait, attributed to Horace Hone, once belonged to Landor (Malcolm Elwin, Landor, A Replevin, *1958)*

Friedrich Nietzsche described as "its polite warfare with poetry." They are common representations of what Ezra Pound called "a whole culture," extending from Greece and Rome to the Enlightenment, and through Landor to the English modernists and beyond. His long life span enabled him personally to influence Robert Browning and Algernon Charles Swinburne in the formation of a countertradition in nineteenth-century English poetry concerned with the difficult and adverse relaying of past culture–a tradition especially influential on Pound, Landor's greatest advocate, for whom Landor was the most important English writer between Pope and Browning.

    Walter Savage Landor was born at Warwick, the eldest son of Walter Landor, a physician who inherited a large estate in Staffordshire, and his second wife, Elizabeth Savage, heiress to a more modest Warwickshire fortune. In 1783 he became a boarder at Rugby School, where he displayed remarkable tendencies for excelling in the daily exercises in Latin translation and composition and for rebelliousness. Proud and unruly from early boyhood, he fixed on the role of precocious classicist as a mark of superiority to his contemporaries and of equality to his elders. His unofficial mentor was Samuel Parr, the celebrated Latin scholar, political controversialist, and zealous supporter of Charles James Fox. Parr, who had taken up a curacy near Warwick, respectfully fostered Landor's classicism throughout his youth and also his political enthusiasm in the broad Whig tradition of his father. Parr's protégé's schooldays culminated in insubordination, for which he was removed from school at the age of fifteen. He became a pupil of a private tutor near Ashbourne, Derbyshire, the following year, translating Cowley into Latin verse, "correcting his extravagance," before matriculating at Trinity College, Oxford, in 1792.

Southey, who avoided him at Oxford, remembered him there as "a mad Jacobin," wearing his hair conscientiously unpowdered. In his second year Landor was rusticated for prevarication over a shooting incident in which he fired against the shutters of a neighboring student's windows during college prayers. He did not return to Oxford, so that he quarreled with his father and went to live in London, where he devoted himself to the private study of French, Italian, and Greek. His first publication, *The Poems of Walter Savage Landor,* which came out in 1795, includes university satires, an imaginary verse epistle, "Abelard to Eloise," in the vogue of Pope's poem on the same subject, and other fashionable imitations. It established the pattern of commercial failure that all his poetic volumes were to undergo and did not nearly cover its expenses. But, despite its private jokes and derivativeness, it was not without the spice of topical urgency: one piece, "Apology for Poetry," celebrated the French victories over the allies and charged the British government with repression at home and abroad. He had embarked on a lifelong engagement in political literature. In the same year he produced the *Moral Epistle,* an attack on the Tory government dedicated to Charles, Earl Stanhope, who had denounced British intervention in French domestic affairs in the House of Lords, and in 1797 he took part in the hot political debatings of his hometown, producing a pamphlet, *To the Burgesses of Warwick,* scorning William Pitt's current policies, including the continuation of the war against France.

Having made a financial arrangement with his father, he went to Swansea, where he lived with Nancy Jones (the "Iöne" of early poems), a local girl with whom he had started an affair in 1793 on an undergraduate holiday in South Wales. They had a child who died, as did Nancy herself (probably from tuberculosis) at some time in or before 1806. At Swansea in 1796 he met Rose Aylmer, whose tragic early death was to occasion one of his best-known epigrams. He wrote that they were "not indifferent" to one another before she accompanied her aunt in 1799 to Calcutta, where her uncle was judge in the Supreme

Court of Bengal and where in 1800 she died of cholera at age twenty.

At Swansea he continued the program of leisured learning and unprofitable publication that extended throughout his life, enabled by an allowance and later a private income. In autumn 1796 he began his first considerable work, the heroic poem *Gebir* (1798), in seven books, parts of which were originally written in Latin, and of which he produced a Latin version in 1803. It is an epic with an Oriental setting (though most evocative of Greek pastoral) that describes the invasion of Egypt by Gebir, a Spanish king, according to a childhood oath, and his assassination by the nurse of the Egyptian queen, Charoba, tragically unaware that her mistress had fallen in love with him.

Landor had now renounced the heroic couplet that had presided in the longer pieces of his first publication. His reading of Milton had convinced him that blank verse was a heroic medium superior to the classical hexameter in conveying in English an impression of weight and dignity, and "repeated perusals of Pindar" conditioned the severity of his own style. After his previous disappointment, he had it printed in Warwick in 1798 in an inconspicuous paper-covered pamphlet, with the imprint of the London publisher Rivingtons. It went largely unnoticed. Southey, however, gave it prominent and enthusiastic attention in his piece for the *Critical Review* (September 1799) and in writing to his friends, later acknowledging its influence on *Thalaba* (1801, 1809). The ardor expressed in the *Critical Review* caused other journals to review *Gebir* far less admiringly. It suffers from a lack of narrative movement characteristic of Landor, and most contemporary responses refer to its unevenness and patchy beauties. But both Thomas De Quincey as an Oxford undergraduate in 1803 and later Shelley as a student were fascinated by the poem. Other notable admirers were Henry Cary, Landor's school and university friend who was to translate Dante, and Wordsworth.

A supplementary essay in Oriental poetry was the hoax pamphlet of nine short poems, *Poems from the Arabic and Persian,* published in 1800, purporting to be based on French translations but actually originals by Landor. It was produced in a similar manner to *Gebir* and went largely unnoticed apart from a bait-swallowing piece in the *Monthly Review* (July 1804).

Landor was conscious of a political subtext in *Gebir,* which he summarizes in the extended

Julia Thuillier Landor with her children Julia and Arnold, circa 1825 (portrait by Trajan Wallis; Malcolm Elwin, Landor, A Replevin, *1958)*

preface to the second edition of 1803, where it takes on an anti-Napoleonic resonance as "the folly, the injustice, and the punishment of Invasion." He projected another long heroic poem about the disruption and restoration of civilization to be entitled "The Phoceans," two fragments of which (possibly written before *Gebir*) were published in 1802, in a book actually printed in 1800: *Poetry by the Author of Gebir.* The project revolves around the Persian invasion of Ionia and the consequent flight of one of its nations to Spain. Another heroic poem belonging to this project is "Crysaor." The title character is the last survivor of "a race of earth-born giants," associated with the Titans, the old order of the gods being routed by Zeus, as he takes over the rule from Chronos. To Landor, the giant embodies the forces of reactionary tyranny, attempting to defy the inevitability of moral progress. Lan-

dor was aiming in this heroic sequence to supply a missing link in ancient literature by evoking the "classic land" of ancient Spain which Greek and Latin authors had strangely neglected. He characteristically moved to the arcane and remote margins of ancient history to occupy territory where he is unchallenged and unpreceded, but the political subtext is lost in esotericism. As Southey commented in the *Annual Review* (1802), "While the poet involves his meaning in such allegory and such language, he may continue to publish without danger of comments by the Attorney General." The volume met with mostly abusive rejection from the reviewers, and Landor did not pursue this heroic vision of a postrevolutionary society. Besides, his political sympathies were clouding.

After the Peace of Amiens in 1802 he visited Paris and lost his revolutionary ardor when

Landor in Florence, 12 September 1826 (drawing by William Bewick; by permission of the British Museum)

he actually witnessed Napoleon's assumption of the title First Consul for life and the French submission to a new despotism. In his notes to the second edition of *Gebir* in 1803 he recanted the praise for Napoleon in the original poem and registered his disillusionment with the French Revolution. Without representation for his republican idealism in any British faction he allowed his political opinions to run along the grooves of his master principles—in Sidney Colvin's phrase, "the elementary principles of love of freedom and hatred of tyranny"—as they began to find expression in the rise of liberal nationalism throughout Europe.

A major event in his personal life occurred at Bath in the spring of 1802 when he met and fell in love with Jane Sophia Swift, the "Ianthe" of his poems. She married a cousin, in the tradition of her family, in 1803; but a liaison with Landor extending into this marriage is probable.

The invention of the pseudonym owes something to discretion as well as to euphony. She was widowed in 1814 and married Comte Pelletier de Molandé. She became a widow once more about 1827, and by then in possession of a large fortune, she was wooed by the duke of Luxembourg. She remained Landor's grand passion, and her path recrossed his at Florence in 1829 and at Bath in 1839 and 1849-1850, before she died at Versailles in 1851.

From 1803 until his marriage in 1811 Landor moved about in fashionable circles, mostly at Bath. The chief fruit of the period was the exquisite collection of epigrams (including some in Latin), *Simonidea* (1806), named after the Greek elegist Simonides. These lyrics, mostly devoted to Nancy Jones and Ianthe, hark back ultimately in simplicity of theme and form to the *Greek Anthology*. They define the characteristic tension of his lyrical pieces, in which the classical commonplace

Bust of Landor by John Gibson, completed in July 1828 (by permission of the National Portrait Gallery, London). Landor called Gibson "the only man who has not either flattered or abused me."

of the brevity of love is invested with a personal coloring, while the pressure of private feeling is soothed by its conventionality. Though it was noted in the reviews, it did not sell well.

In 1805 his father died, and Landor succeeded to the estates at Rugeley, Staffordshire, assured of still greater wealth at the death of his mother–an event that occurred in 1829. In the same year he sold his inherited and some prospective property to buy Llanthony Abbey, Monmouthshire, a half-ruined thirteenth-century Austin priory and the valley it occupied, though he continued to move restlessly round the West Country and it was some years before he tried to settle there. It was while he was at Bristol in 1808 that he finally met Southey, who was to become a lifelong friend and literary ally, a kind of association Landor generally avoided. When he heard that

Southey had stopped producing poetry because he could not afford to write it, Landor promised to have printed anything Southey wrote, and though the offer was declined Southey acknowledged its effect in encouraging him to go on writing verse. Then, later that year, Landor left impulsively for Corunna to aid the Spanish revolt against Napoleon. He gave £100 for the relief of Venturada, almost destroyed by the French, and paid the expenses of a force of volunteers he collected to join Gen. Joachim Blake's army, though he never got the chance of active service. After his return he published *Three Letters, Written in Spain* (1809), addressed to the Spanish general Francisco Riquelme, on military and political topics. He was now violently anti-Napoleonic, calling for "the termination both of the war and of the warrior."

Villa Gherardesca in Fiesole, where Landor lived from 1829 until 1835, when he left his family and returned to England

Landor's first poetic drama, *Count Julian: A Tragedy* (1812), influenced by his Spanish adventure, was written at Bath between November 1810 and January 1811 and was probably prompted by the arrival of the first manuscript installment of Southey's new "Tragic Poem," *Roderick, the Last of the Goths* (1814), in July 1810. *Count Julian* tells the story of a Christian general of the Goths, who in order to revenge the dishonoring of his daughter by his sovereign, Roderigo, in Edward Gibbon's words, "solicited the disgraceful honour of introducing [Moslem] arms into the heart of Spain." He had difficulty in getting it published: Longman, Southey's publisher, would not print it even at Landor's own expense, and Landor was so indignant that he burned another tragedy he had been working on. When *Count Julian* did appear, anonymously, in an edition of 250 copies, it was popularly mistaken for a work by Byron. Wordsworth thought it had "very fine touches," but as Landor acknowledged, it lacked action and development, as do

the subsequent dramatic efforts. In the 1846 edition of Landor's works it was included with other pieces under the heading "Acts and Scenes" with the note: "None of these poems of a dramatic form were offered to the stage, being no better than *Imaginary Conversations* in metre."

Back in Bath he met and within several months, on 24 May 1811, had married Julia Thuillier, about seventeen years old and, in Landor's words, "a girl without a sixpence, and with very few accomplishments." He had simply decided to settle down–immediately. The marriage eventually failed, but it produced four children and spells of calming and affectionate domesticity, though he never addressed any verses to his wife. The couple took up residence in the half-ruined abbey at Llanthony while a house was being built there. Landor's attempts to manage the estate proved disastrous. His literary and political interests were obviously more congenial, as he completed the first significant collection of his Latin verse, *Idyllia Nova Quinque*, eventually pub-

Walter Savage Landor, 1838 (portrait by William Fisher; by permission of the National Portrait Gallery, London)

lished in 1815. He also continued his contentious political interventions, producing *Commentary on Memoirs of Mr. Fox* (1812), which was printed but suppressed by its would-be publisher. After negotiations involving Southey, Murray declined to publish a book containing attacks on the Tory administration and dedicated to President James Madison, with whom England was on the brink of war. At this time Landor also composed the *Letters addressed to Lord Liverpool,* published in early 1814 under the pseudonym Calvus, concerning the peace settlement after the battle of Leipzig. Landor demanded Napoleon's total loss of power and the stripping of all France's territory acquired since the revolution. Harassed by lawsuits and debts, Landor was forced to leave England in May 1814 and determined to live in France. The Welsh estate was taken over and managed by his family, who resolved his debts and allotted him and his wife a moderate income (doubled after his mother's death). After an ominous quar-

rel, during which they separated, his wife rejoined him at Tours in February 1815. They remained in France until October 1815, but with the restoration of the monarchy after Waterloo they moved to Como, where they remained for the next three years and where Southey visited them in 1817.

Landor's Italian period extended some twenty years, from 1815 to 1835, years during which he opened himself to a more comprehensive encounter with the European past and achieved a degree of hard-won fame. The peace was not unruffled. He was compelled to leave Como in late September 1818 after forcefully objecting to the censorship of some Latin poems and threatening to cane the royal delegate, a series of disagreements that resulted in the family's move south to Albaro, near Genoa, and then to Pisa. He was beginning to attract a small reputation, especially in the English Lakes. Greatly impressed at this time by the "stupendous" poetry of Wordsworth that Southey sent him, he made a translation (nonextant) of Wordsworth's critical essays into Italian, and in 1820 he and Wordsworth began their congratulatory correspondence. De Quincey praised Landor in the *Westmorland Gazette* (early May 1819) as "the English poet who most resembles Goethe, but infinitely his superior." Landor refused to make Shelley's acquaintance at Pisa during the winter of 1820, when both poets were there, because of the rumors of Shelley's mistreatment of his first wife, though he later regretted deeply having missed the opportunity after meeting Shelley's friend Edward Trelawny and Mary Shelley, the poet's second wife.

His Latin poetry was published at Pisa in 1820 in *Idyllia Heroica Decem*, though his contemptuous remarks on Italian officials were cut by the Pisan censor. Landor's lifelong intervention in the revolutionary uprisings that were breaking out became more open, beginning at Naples in 1819. He sent off pamphlets, including the three "orations," *Poche Osservazioni* (1821), against the Holy Alliance. His political opinions now differed radically from those of Southey, though they managed to smooth over their differences. Landor supported Catholic emancipation and electoral reform and rejected the reaction inaugurated throughout the Continent by the victory at Waterloo.

Landor claimed to have left Pisa because he heard Byron was coming: "His character in Italy was infamous." The family moved to Florence in 1821, and in November they took a large apartment in a palace belonging to the marchese de' Medici-Tornaquinci, marking the start of an extended period of peace and consolidation for him. There he began the sustained writing of the "Imaginary Conversations" that were to attract the wider attention his verse never achieved. Though Landor claimed to have written "two or three" Conversations in 1797, the crucial impetus toward this form of composition was Southey's announcement in a letter of 14 August 1820 that he was commencing "a series of Dialogues." Landor probably started composition soon after in 1820, though the first Conversation to be published appeared in the *London Magazine* of July 1823, and the first two-volume collection, *Imaginary Conversations of Literary Men and Statesmen*, appeared in 1824.

The form had a lengthy pedigree, deriving from the dialogue tradition of Plato and Cicero that had been reintroduced in the eighteenth-

century "Dialogues of the Dead," practiced by Fontenelle, Fénelon, and especially Lord Lyttleton and Bishop Hurd, who introduced the term *conversation* for this kind of writing. Landor's originality rests on his combination of a succinct portrayal of character with a fastidious prose style. Some conversations are little more than extended essays, covering a pleasing variety of topics, often including pet hobbyhorses; others are dramatic scenes of a tragic or pathetic nature that parallel his heroic idyls and verse scenes. But his creative delight is most evident in the conception of ironically self-revealing villains of the sort Robert Browning was to develop in the dramatic monologue. Landor's Fra Filippo Lippi in his Conversation with Pope Eugenius the Fourth, for instance–his most charming extension of creative sympathy to moral imperfection–evidently fed into Browning's later treatment.

He experienced difficulties in finding a publisher for the first Conversations and had to undergo political and religious censorship to get them produced, but once published they attracted positive attention from the literary reviews. He had received his first payment for a manuscript, and the book even sold well. Wordsworth wrote, "I long for the third volume," and heavily corrected his own neoclassical poem, "Laodamia," in accordance with the strictures raised in the conversation between Southey and Porson. A new, enlarged edition appeared in 1826, and there followed the third volume in 1828, and a second series, comprising two more volumes, in 1829.

For two years, beginning in summer 1827, the family lived at the Villa Castiglione just outside Florence. Though Landor's explosiveness with servants, tradesmen, and government officials eventually led to his being banished from Florentine society and a month's retirement to Lucca in 1829, a renewed sense of poise was established that year when, with the financial assistance of a close friend, the family resettled at the Villa Gherardesca in Fiesole, above Florence. It was an epicurean phase of some six years in which he composed less than at any other period in his writing life and in which a chief enthusiasm was his collection of paintings showing a particular taste for the fourteenth- and fifteenth-century Italian primitives. A doting paterfamilias, he was submerged in the small dramas of domesticity and the study, tending the garden and orchard on the spot, as he told Southey, "where Boccaccio led his women to bathe when they had left

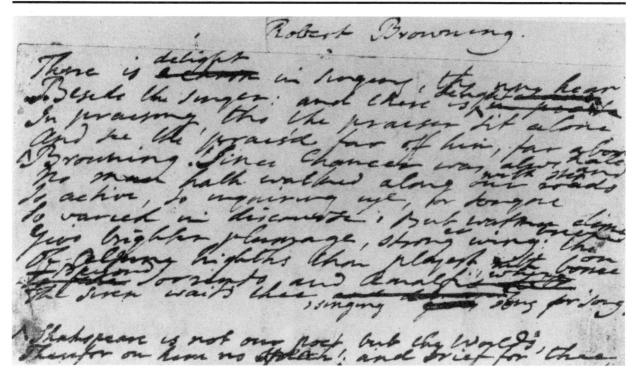

Draft for "To Robert Browning," first published in the 22 November 1845 issue of the Morning Chronicle *and collected in Landor's 1846* Works *(by permission of the British Library)*

the first scene of their story-telling."

Though poetry had given way to the successful production of prose, the vein never dried up. In addition to revising the title poems, he added some new lyrical pieces to the collection *Gebir, Count Julian, and Other Poems,* which was published on commission by Moxon in 1831. Though it brought back the poetry hauntingly to Lamb, it sold only forty copies in the first nine months, and it was above all as the author of the celebrated Conversations that he revisited England in 1832 and made the literary rounds, visiting the Lambs and Coleridge, and traveling to the Lakes to see Southey and for the first time Wordsworth. Back in Fiesole his reputation was attracting tribute. In 1833 he was visited by the young Ralph Waldo Emerson, who was struck by his formal courtesy and by what he conceived to be a typically English "love of freak" and "appetite for action and heroes." In 1834 Landor extended the conversational format in the *Citation and Examination of William Shakspeare,* which presents Shakespeare's supposed trial for his legendary deer stealing. It was brought out anonymously and greeted warmly in the *Examiner* (30 November 1834) by John Forster, the young critic who was to become Landor's most active literary aide,

his first editor and biographer. But the book has never attracted significant interest.

When his marriage broke down completely in 1835, Landor made over his income to his family, keeping for himself only a subsistence allowance, left wife and children in Fiesole, and returned to England. He settled in Bath, where he remained for more than twenty years, writing continuously. While still in Italy he had been preparing his epistolary novel set in ancient Athens, *Pericles and Aspasia* (1836), for which he had made a systematic study of Greek life and literature. The interspersed prose fragments and verses are ostensibly written by ancient writers, some invented. One of the best is "The Shades of Agamemnon and Iphigeneia," the dramatic scene in blank verse with choral odes attributed to Aspasia. For the volume, which was immediately greeted by the *Examiner* (27 March 1836) and several of his friends as his masterpiece, Landor was paid the single sum of £100. He was also paid the indirect compliment of a pirated American edition of selections made from it. The only unfortunate consequence was *A Satire on Satirists* (1836), his reply to a series of mocking dialogues in *Blackwood's Magazine.* Landor combined his attack on that magazine with one on Wordsworth, as a chivalric im-

69

Acon and Rhodope.
A Sequel to "The Hamadryad"
by Walter Savage Landor.

The year had roll'd its varying months away;
The snow had left the mountain-top; freshly flowers
Had wither'd in the valley; prune and fig
Were wrinkled; the last apple glow'd amidst
Its freckled leaves; and weary oxen paus'd
Between the trodden corn and twisted vine
Under whose bunches stood the empty crates,
To creak ere long beneath them carried home.
This was the season when, twelve months before,
O gentle Hamadryad true to love!
Thy mansion, thy dim mansion in the wood
Was blasted and laid desolate: but none
Dared violate its precincts, none dared pluck
The moss beneath it which alone remain'd
Of what was thine!
                    Old Thallinos sat mute
In solitary sadness. The strange tale
Not until Raicos died, but then the whole,
Echion had related, whom no force
Could ever make look back upon the oaks.
The father said,
            "Echion! thou must weigh,
Carefully, and with steddy hand, enough
(Altho no longer comes the store as once)
Of wax, to burn all day and night upon
That hollow stone where milk and honey lie.
So may the Gods, so may the dead be pleas'd!"
Thallinos bore it thither in the morn,
And lighted it, and left it.
                        First of those
Who visited upon this solemn day

On this and the next two pages: manuscript for a poem first published in Landor's 1847 volume of Hellenics *(HM 44721; by permission of the Henry E. Huntington Library and Art Gallery)*

The Hamadryad's oak, were Rhodopè
And Acon: of one age, one hope, one trust.
Graceful was she as was the Nymph whose fate
She sorrowed for; he, slender, pale and first
Lapt by the flame of love: his father's lands
Were fertile, herds lowed over them afar.
Now stood the two aside the hollow stone
And lookt with stedfast eyes toward the oak
Shiver'd and black and bare.
                                         'May never we
love as they loved!" said Acon. She at this
Smiled: for he said not what he meant to say,
And thought not of their bliss but of its end.
He caught the flying smile and blusht, and vow'd
Nor time nor that power whereto the might
Of love hath yielded and may yield again,
Should alter his. The father of the youth
Wanted not beauty for him, wanted not
Song, that could lift earth's weight from off his breast,
Discretion, that could guide him thro' the world,
Innocence, that could clear his way to heaven:
Silver and gold and land, not great before
The ancestral gate, but ample under skies
Bending far off, he wanted for his heir.
      Fathers had given life but virgin heart
They never gave; and dare they then controll
Or check it harshily? dare they break a bond
Girt round it by the holiest Power on high?
      Acon was griev'd, he said, griev'd bitterly;
But Acon had complied: 'twas dutiful!
      Crush thy own heart, Man! Man! but fear to wound
The gentler that relies on thee alone,
By thee created weak or strong by thee:
Touch it not but for worship; tile are closed
The temple doors, and the last lamp is spent.

Rhodopè in her soul's waste solitude,
Sate mournful by the dull-resounding sea,
Often not hearing it, and many years
Had the cold breezes hardend on her cheek.
Meanwhile he saunterd in the wood of oaks,
Nor shunned to look upon the hollow stone
That held the milk and honey, nor to lay
His plighted hand where recently 'twas laid
Opposite hers, when finger playfully
Advanced and push't back finger, on each side.
He did not think of this, as she would do
If she were there alone. The day was hot;
The moss invited him; it cool'd his cheek,
It cool'd his hands; he thrust them into it
And sank to slumber. Never was there dream
Divine as his. He saw the Hamadryad;
She took him by the arm and led him on
Along a valley, where profusely grew
The smaller lilies with their pendent bells,
And, hiding under mint, chill drosera,
The violet shy of butting cyclamen,
And the sweet rose above them all, intact
By mortal hand, and blossoming for gods.
The fragrance fill'd his breast with such delight
His senses were bewilderd, and he thought
He saw again the face he most had loved.
He stopd: the Hamadryad at his side
Now stood between; then drew him farther off.
He went, compliant as before; but soon
Verdure had ceast: altho' the ground was smooth,
Nothing was there delightful. At this change
He would have spoken, but his guide represt
All questioning, and said,
           Weak youth! what brought
Thy footstep to this wood, my native haunt,
My lifelong residence; this bath where first
I saw with him the faithful (now I know,
Too late!) the faithful Rhaïcos. Haste thee home,
Be happy, if thou canst, but come no more
Where those whom death alone could sever, died.
         He started up: the moss whereon he slept
Was dried and withered: deadlier paleness spred
Over his cheek: he sickened; and the sire
Had land enough; it held his only son.

Landor circa 1854 (portrait by Robert Faulkner; by permission of the National Portrait Gallery, London)

pulse to defend what he believed had been Wordsworth's slighting of Southey's poetry and his fancied coolness toward Landor.

He continued to publish his experiments with different genres. In August 1837-April 1838 Leigh Hunt printed Landor's dramatized commentary *High and Low Life in Italy* in the *Monthly Repository*. It had been written in 1831, but no publisher would bring it out at that time. Also in 1837 the fruit of his study of Italian literature was published as *The Pentameron*, a series of five day-long interviews between Boccaccio and Petrarch, dwelling largely on criticisms of Dante, the *Decameron*, and the poetry of Virgil and Horace. With it was published *The Pentalogia*, five scenes in blank verse of crucial moments from Greek myth and European history. Landor had little power of extended construction, but such scenes, summing up a whole narrative or historical development, were his dramatic forte. He then produced a historical trilogy—the first two

parts of which, *Andrea of Hungary, and Giovanna of Naples,* were published in 1839, and the last, *Fra Rupert,* in 1840—excelling in the (often unhistorical) depiction of female suffering. The profits from these plays Landor wished to be given to the Grace Darling Fund.

He allowed himself to be lionized, especially by Marguerite, Countess of Blessington, participating in her brilliant salons at Gore House, Kensington, and benefiting from her help as an unofficial literary agent. His longevity in effect enabled him to bestride distinct literary periods, so that he was able to make many admiring acquaintances in the new literary generation, including Robert Browning and Elizabeth Barrett, Crabb Robinson, and Thomas Carlyle. In 1840 he met Alfred Tennyson and became friendly with the twenty-eight-year-old Charles Dickens, who was to caricature him as Lawrence Boythorn in *Bleak House* (1852-1853), with his violent warmheartedness and tremendous superlatives. Most in-

Landor in Siena, July 1859 (drawing by William Wetmore Story; Malcolm Elwin, Landor, A Replevin, *1958)*

fluential was his relationship with Browning. Landor praised *Paracelsus* (1835), and the younger poet acknowledged his encouragement publicly in *Sordello* (1840), and dedicated to Landor in 1846 the final number of *Bells and Pomegranates,* comprising "Luria" and "A Soul's Tragedy."

Forster was now the most important presence behind Landor's literary activities. As editor of the *Foreign Quarterly,* Forster encouraged him to write two close textual analyses–of Catullus (July 1842) and Theocritus (October 1842)–and a biographical-critical account of Petrarch (July 1843). In 1846 he helped Landor to collect his English output in *The Works of Walter Savage Landor,* which was a considerable success. Selections were pirated in America, and the first edition was reprinted by his British publisher in 1853, 1868, and 1895. A complementary volume came out in 1847, *Poemata et Inscriptiones,* in which Landor gathered nearly all his previously published works in

Latin, adding about 170 shorter pieces. His publisher, Moxon, claimed to have sold only one copy–to the bishop of St. Andrews. Landor then translated his ten Latin *Idyllia* and collected them with the group of poems on Greek themes he had called the "Hellenics" in the *Works* of 1846. The volume so compiled was entitled *The Hellenics of Walter Savage Landor. Enlarged and Completed* (1847) and contained the verse most admired by both Swinburne and Richard Aldington. The Landorian idyl, which he defines as "a small image of something greater," was a distinctive invention in English narrative poetry. Like the dramatic scenes, it tends to the arrangement of posed tableaux, reminiscent of figures from sculpture and painting.

From 1847 to 1853 was a period of extraordinary activity for Landor as he contributed about one hundred prose pieces and more than seventy poems to the periodicals, especially the *Examiner.*

The outbreak of revolution all over Europe in 1848 ignited his political ardor. In that year he produced two pamphlets: *The Italics,* seven poems urging the Italians to strive for glorious freedom, and *Imaginary Conversation of King Carlo-Alberto and the Duchess Belgioioso, on the Affairs and Prospects of Italy,* devoting the profits from the latter to the relief of the sufferers in the Sicilian revolt at Messina. Then he had printed Latin odes to his contemporary heroes and heroines, leaflets supporting the Roman uprising in 1849, the Hungarian revolutionary movement, and the complete independence of Poland, corresponding with workers' leaders in Birmingham. His literary productivity became apparent in 1853 when he brought out a miscellaneous volume of selected pieces written since the *Works* of 1846, *The Last Fruit off an Old Tree,* including Conversations, letters, a pamphlet, dramatic scenes, and an assortment of poems. In the same year he published a collection of the Conversations between classical speakers, *Imaginary Conversations of Greeks and Romans,* dedicated to Dickens.

Landor was now an old man, disheveled and often abstracted, though until the end he did not lose his gift for firm and simple expression. In 1856 he became embroiled in a Bath scandal involving a sixteen-year-old girl to whom he had been fondly overgenerous and an older woman who defrauded him and who had exerted an unsavory influence over the girl. Landor's misconceived denunciations took the form of pamphlets and, after being forced into a legal retraction, abusive verses directed at the woman in his next volume, *Dry Sticks* (1858). The book contained all the poetry written since *The Last Fruit off an Old Tree* and also included recently discovered old verses as well as some amorously addressed to the girl. To avoid libel charges he abruptly left for a final exile in Italy.

Back in Fiesole, he inevitably quarreled with his family, left the villa, and was kindly helped by the Brownings, eventually renting a house in Florence. In 1859 he brought out a revised and extended edition of *The Hellenics,* illustrating his lifelong process of revision. For this book he retranslated the original Latin *Idyllia* into different English versions, attempting, as Forster noted, a more "severe and simple character," though they have been considered relatively lax and prosaic. His last book, *Heroic Idyls* (1863), which was published in his eighty-eighth year, includes a remarkable variety of verse. During his final year he was visited by the twenty-six-year-old Swinburne and

accepted the dedication of "Atalanta in Calydon" in a consciously symbolic act of continuity. He died in Florence at the age of eighty-nine and was buried there in the Protestant Cemetery.

Hugh Whitemeyer has described Landor's contribution to Pound's cultural ventriloquism and to his sympathetic conception of the artist figure in isolation, a persona of dedicated unpopularity and expatriation. Pound's particular interest in Landor's poetic style, seeing him as a master of the "hardness" effected by minute control of emotion and technical detail, has stimulated the attention of several poet-critics to Landor's play with conventional language, most notably Donald Davie and Robert Pinsky. Pinsky has characterized Landor's poetry as distinguished above all by an urbane awareness of rhetorical and stylistic convention—"a voice more resonant than any particular moment of history." Landor now stands to gain fresh attention because of the current examination of canonicity in Romanticism.

Letters:

The Literary Life and Correspondence of the Countess of Blessington, 3 volumes, edited by R. R. Madden (London: T. C. Newby, 1855), II: 361-395;

The Blessington Papers, in *The Collection of Autograph Letters and Historical Documents Formed by Alfred Morrison,* second series, 1882-1893 (London: Printed for private circulation, 1895);

Letters and Other Unpublished Writings of Walter Savage Landor, edited by Stephen Wheeler (London: Bentley, 1897);

Letters of Walter Savage Landor, Private and Public, edited by Wheeler (London: Duckworth, 1899);

George Somes Layard, *Mrs. Lynn Linton, Her Life, Letters, and Opinions* (London: Methuen, 1901);

Edward H. R. Tatham, "Some Unpublished Letters of W. S. Landor," *Fortnightly Review,* 93 (February 1910): 361-373;

Baylor University Browning Interests, fifth series, edited by A. Joseph Armstrong (Waco, Tex.: Baylor University, 1932);

H. C. Minchin, *Walter Savage Landor: Last Days, Letters and Conversations* (London: Methuen, 1934);

R. H. Super, "Landor's 'Dear Daughter,' Eliza Lynn Linton," *PMLA,* 59 (December 1944): 1059-1085;

Super, "Landor's Letters to Wordsworth and Cole-ridge," *Modern Philology*, 55 (November 1957): 73-83;

A. Lavonne Ruoff and Edwin Burton Levine, "Landor's Letters to the Reverend Walter Birch," *Bulletin of John Rylands Library*, 51 (1968): 200-261;

Ruoff, "Landor's Letters to his Family: 1802-25," *Bulletin of John Rylands Library*, 53 (1971): 465-500;

Ruoff, "Landor's Letters to his Family: 1826-29," *Bulletin of John Rylands Library*, 54 (1972): 398-433;

John F. Mariani, "The Letters of Walter Savage Landor to Marguerite Countess of Blessington," Ph.D. dissertation, Columbia University, 1973;

Ruoff, "Walter Savage Landor's Letters to His Family, 1830-1832," *Bulletin of John Rylands Library*, 58 (1976): 467-507.

Bibliographies:

Thomas James Wise and Stephen Wheeler, *A Bibliography of the Writings in Prose and Verse of Walter Savage Landor* (London: Printed for the Bibliographical Society by Blades, East & Blades, 1919);

Wise, *A Landor Library. A Catalogue of Printed Books, Manuscripts and Autograph Letters* (London: Printed for private circulation, 1928);

R. H. Super, *The Publication of Landor's Works* (London: Bibliographical Society, 1954);

Super, "Walter Savage Landor," in *The English Romantic Poets & Essayists: A Review of Research and Criticism*, revised edition, edited by Carolyn Washburn Houtchens and Lawrence Huston Houtchens (New York: Published for the Modern Language Association of America by New York University Press/London: University of London Press, 1966), pp. 221-253.

Biographies:

John Forster, *Walter Savage Landor. A Biography* (2 volumes, London: Chapman & Hall, 1869; 1 volume, Boston: Fields, Osgood, 1869);

Sidney Colvin, *Landor*, English Men of Letters Series (London: Macmillan, 1881; New York: Harper, 1881);

Malcolm Elwin, *Savage Landor* (London: Macdonald, 1941); revised and enlarged as *Landor. A Replevin* (London: Macdonald, 1958);

R. H. Super, *Walter Savage Landor: A Biography* (New York: New York University Press, 1954).

References:

Richard Aldington, "Landor's 'Hellenics,'" in his *Literary Studies and Reviews* (London: Allen & Unwin, 1924), pp. 141-154;

William Bradley, *The Early Poems of Walter Savage Landor* (London: Printed by Bradbury, Agnew & Co., 1913);

John Buxton, "Walter Savage Landor," in his *The Grecian Taste. Literature in the Age of Neo-Classicism 1740-1820* (London: Macmillan, 1978), pp. 105-127;

Donald A. Davie, "Attending to Landor," *Ironwood*, 12 (Fall 1984): 103-111;

Davie, "The Shorter Poems of Landor," in *Essays in Criticism*, 1 (1951): 345-355; republished in his *Purity of Diction in English Verse* (London: Chatto & Windus, 1952; New York: Oxford University Press, 1953), pp. 183-196;

Ernest Dilworth, *Walter Savage Landor* (New York: Twayne, 1971);

Felice Elkin, *Walter Savage Landor's Studies of Italian Life and Literature* (Philadelphia: University of Pennsylvania, 1934);

R. W. Emerson, *English Traits* (Boston: Phillips, Sampson, 1856; London: Routledge, 1856);

Edward Waterman Evans, Jr., *Walter Savage Landor. A Critical Study* (New York: Putnam's/London: Knickerbocker, 1892);

Hermann M. Flasdieck, "Walter Savage Landor und seine 'Imaginary Conversations,'" *Englische Studien*, 58 (1924): 390-431;

Guido Fornelli, *W. S. Landor e l'Italia* (Forli: La Poligrafia Romagnola, 1930);

G. Rostrevor Hamilton, *Walter Savage Landor*, Writers and Their Work, no. 126 (London: Published for the British Council & the National Book League by Longmans, Green, 1960);

W. Brooks Drayton Henderson, *Swinburne and Landor* (London: Macmillan, 1918);

Andrea Kelly, "The Latin Poetry of Walter Savage Landor," in *The Latin Poetry of the English Poets*, edited by J. W. Binns (London & Boston: Routledge Chapman & Hall, 1974);

F. R. Leavis, "Landor and the Seasoned Epicure," *Scrutiny*, 11 (December 1942): 148-150;

Vernon Lee, "The Rhetoric of Landor," in her *The Handling of Words and Other Studies in Liter-*

ary Psychology (London: John Lane/New York: Dodd, Mead, 1923), pp. 157-174;

A. H. Mason, "Walter Savage Landor, Poète Lyrique," Paris, university thesis, 1924;

Bruce McKinnon, "Three Latin Poems by W. S. Landor," *Durham University Journal*, 72, part 1 (December 1979): 55-59;

Vivian Mercer, "The Future of Landor Criticism," in *Some British Romantics: A Collection of Essays*, edited by J. V. Logan, J. E. Jordan, and Northrop Frye (Columbus: Ohio State University Press, 1966), pp. 43-85;

Richard Monckton Milnes, Lord Houghton, *Monographs Personal and Social* (London: J. Murray, 1873; New York: Holt & Williams, 1873);

Elizabeth Nitchie, "The Classicism of Walter Savage Landor," *Classical Journal*, 14 (December 1918): 147-166;

Robert Pinsky, *Landor's Poetry* (Chicago & London: University of Chicago Press, 1968);

Ezra Pound, *ABC of Reading* (London: Routledge, 1934; New Haven: Yale University Press, 1934);

Pound, "The Case of Landor," *Observer* (London), 14 January 1934, p. 9;

Pound, *Guide to Kulchur* (London: Faber & Faber, 1938); republished as *Culture* (Norfolk, Conn.: New Directions, 1938);

Pound, *How to Read* (London: Harmsworth, 1931);

Ernest de Selincourt, "Classicism and Romanticism in the Poetry of Landor," in *England und die Antike*, edited by F. Saxl (Berlin, 1932);

Leslie Stephen, "Landor's Imaginary Conversations," in his *Hours in a Library*, third series (London: Smith, Elder, 1879);

A. C. Swinburne, *Miscellanies* (London: Chatto & Windus, 1886; New York: Worthington, 1886);

Arthur Symons, "Walter Savage Landor," in his *The Romantic Movement in English Poetry* (London: Constable, 1909; New York: Dutton, 1909);

Francis Thompson, "Landor," *Academy* (27 February 1897): 258-259;

Pierre Vitoux, *L'Oeuvre de Walter Savage Landor* (Paris: Presses Universitaires de France, 1964);

Hugh Whitemeyer, "Walter Savage Landor and Ezra Pound," in *Romantic and Modern: Revalu-*

ations of Literary Tradition, edited by George Bornstein (Pittsburgh: University of Pittsburgh Press, 1977);

Stanley T. Williams, "Walter Savage Landor as a Critic of Literature," *PMLA*, 38 (December 1923): 906-928;

Wordsworth Circle, special Landor issue, edited by Charles L. Proudfit, 7 (Winter 1976).

Papers:
Various British and American libraries hold important Landor materials. The only major poetic manuscript to survive–that of "Count Julian"–is in the Forster Collection at the Library of the Victoria and Albert Museum, together with letters from Landor to Forster (mostly published in Forster's *Walter Savage Landor. A Biography*). The British Library has various manuscripts for prose and verse compositions, including the sonnet "To Robert Browning," and letters to a variety of correspondents, including Charles Lamb, Swinburne, and the countess of Blessington. The Bodleian Library, Oxford; Edinburgh University Library; and John Rylands University Library of Manchester also have significant manuscript collections of correspondence. The Henry E. Huntington Library holds many items, including literary manuscripts, correspondence, and private papers. The Baylor University Browning Collection has many letters from Landor to Browning (unreliable texts of these letters are published in Minchin's *Walter Savage Landor: Last Days, Letters and Conversations*). Arkansas University Library has correspondence with Elizabeth Barrett Browning; the Beinecke Rare Book and Manuscript Library at Yale holds a collection of mostly unpublished letters to Kenneth Robert Henderson Mackenzie; the Chicago University Library holds letters, including some to John Forster on literary topics; the Harry Ransom Humanities Research Center at the University of Texas at Austin has correspondence with Dickens. Other items are in the Henry W. and Albert A. Berg Collection, New York Public Library; the Houghton Library, Harvard University; Iowa University Library; Knox College Archives; the Carl H. Pforzheimer Library, New York; the Pierpont Morgan Library, New York; and the University of Virginia Library.

James Montgomery

(4 November 1771 - 30 April 1854)

Mark Minor
Westmar College

BOOKS: *Prison Amusements, and Other Trifles: Principally written during Nine Months of Confinement in the Castle of York*, as Paul Positive (London: Printed for Joseph Johnson, 1797);

The Whisperer; or, Tales and Speculations, as Gabriel Silvertongue (London: Printed & sold by J. Johnson, 1798);

The Wanderer of Switzerland, and Other Poems (London: Published by Vernor & Hood, and by Longman, Hurst, Rees & Orme, printed by J. Montgomery, Sheffield, 1806; New York: Printed for S. Stansbury, 1807);

Poems on the Abolition of the Slave Trade, by Montgomery, James Graham, and E. Benger (London: R. Bowyer, 1809);

The West Indies, and Other Poems (London: Printed for Longman, Hurst, Rees & Orme, 1810; Boston: Printed by Munroe & Francis, 1810);

The World Before The Flood, A Poem, in Ten Cantos; with Other Occasional Pieces (London: Printed for Longman, Hurst, Rees, Orme & Brown, 1813; New York: Published by Eastburne & Kirk, printed by Pray & Bowen, Brooklyn, 1814);

Verses to the Memory of the Late Richard Reynolds, of Bristol (London: Printed for Longman, Hurst, Rees, Orme & Brown, 1816);

Greenland and Other Poems (London: Longman, Hurst, Rees, Orme & Brown, 1819; New York: Printed for Kirk & Mercein, C. Wiley & Co., W. B. Gilley, and Wells & Lilly, Boston, 1819);

Songs of Zion (London: Longman, Hurst, Rees, Orme & Brown, 1822; Boston: Wells & Lilly, 1823);

Prose by a Poet, 2 volumes (London: Longman, Hurst, Rees, Orme, Brown & Green, 1824; Philadelphia: A. Small, 1824);

The Poetical Works, 4 volumes (London: Longman, Rees, Orme, Brown & Green, 1826-1827);

The Pelican Island (London: Longman, Rees, Orme, Brown & Green, 1827; Philadelphia: Littell & Grigg, 1827);

Lectures on Poetry and General Literature (London: Printed for Longman, Rees, Orme, Brown, Green & Longman, 1833); republished as *Lectures on General Literature, Poetry, &c.* (New York: Harper, 1838);

Original Hymns For Public, Private, and Social Devotion (London: Longman, Brown, Green & Longmans, 1853).

OTHER: *The Chimney-Sweeper's Friend and Climbing-Boy's Album*, edited by Montgomery (London: Longman, Hurst, Rees, Orme, Brown & Green, 1824);

The Christian Psalmist; or, Hymns, Selected and Original (Glasgow: Printed for Chalmers & Collins, 1825).

James Montgomery may be the most representative poet of the British Romantic period. In form, style, and subject matter his poetry reflects the concerns of the age more completely than does that of any of his contemporaries. By an interesting paradox he is today one of the least-read poets of the time and yet one of the most familiar. His long epic and narrative poems, once very popular, are read today almost solely by scholars interested in his possible influence on his greater contemporaries Byron, Shelley, and Keats. Yet anyone who attends a Christian church encounters Montgomery's poetry regularly, for several dozen of his hymn texts are in common use in both Protestant and Catholic worship.

Whatever his readership, there is no doubt of the admirable qualities of Montgomery's character. He was born in Ayrshire, Scotland, of Irish parents, John and Mary Blackley Montgomery, who were members of the Moravians, an evangelical Protestant group. Montgomery's parents took the family to live in Ireland in 1775, and in 1777 they sent him, at age six, to a Moravian settlement and school near Leeds, Yorkshire. His must have been a lonely childhood, for his parents remained in Ireland, and then in 1783, when their son was twelve, they sailed as missionaries to the

West Indies. They never returned to Britain. His mother died in October of 1790 at Tobago and his father the following June at Barbados. In 1787 James Montgomery had run away from the Moravians and found work in Wath as a grocer's assistant. Ambitious to be a poet, he went to London to find a publisher, but after a year without success, he returned to his old employment at Wath. In April 1792, when he was twenty, he was hired as assistant to the editor of the *Sheffield Register*. When the editor was imprisoned in 1794 during the height of the repression directed against sympathizers with the French Revolution, Montgomery took over the paper, renamed it the *Iris*, and outlined a middle-of-the-road editorial position: opposing the war with France and sympathizing with reform, but upholding the British Constitution. Even this mildly reformist stance could not keep him out of trouble, however. Accused

of printing seditious libel, Montgomery was fined and imprisoned twice–for three months in 1795 and for six months in 1796. Upon release from his second term, dogged by depression, religious doubts, and fear of further imprisonment, Montgomery prudently decided against further involvement with controversy. Nevertheless, by nature a strong supporter of moral causes, he began to look for ways of channeling his interests into more politically acceptable forms. Writing poetry was to become the solution.

Perhaps in part because of the intimidation involved, the first volume of poetry he published, *Prison Amusements* (1797), does not in fact deal with his experiences in or opinions about prison. It simply shows how he passed his time there. The poems are filled with conventional imagery and are often tame allegories about free-spirited robins and captive nightingales. The vol-

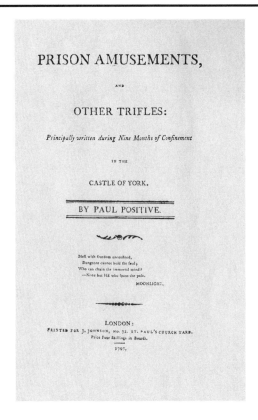

PRISON AMUSEMENTS,

AND

OTHER TRIFLES:

Principally written during Nine Months of Confinement

IN THE

CASTLE OF YORK.

BY PAUL POSITIVE.

Blest with freedom unconfined,
Dungeons cannot hold the foul;
Who can chain the immortal mind?
—None but HE who spans the pole.
MOONLIGHT.

LONDON:
PRINTED FOR J. JOHNSON, No. 72. ST. PAUL'S CHURCH YARD.
Price Four Shillings in Boards.
1797.

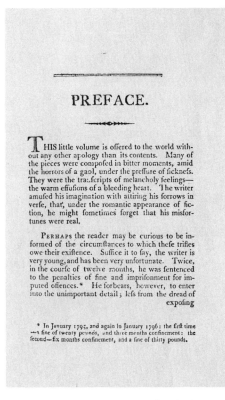

PREFACE.

THIS little volume is offered to the world without any other apology than its contents. Many of
the pieces were composed in bitter moments, amid
the horrors of a gaol, under the pressure of sickness.
They were the transcripts of melancholy feelings—
the warm effusions of a bleeding heart. The writer
amused his imagination with attiring his sorrows in
verse, that, under the romantic appearance of fiction, he might sometimes forget that his misfor-
tunes were real.

PERHAPS the reader may be curious to be informed of the circumstances to which these trifles
owe their existence. Suffice it to say, the writer is
very young, and has been very unfortunate. Twice,
in the course of twelve months, he was sentenced
to the penalties of fine and imprisonment for im-
puted offences.* He forbears, however, to enter
into the unimportant detail; less from the dread of
exposing

* In January 1795, and again in January 1796: the first time
—a fine of twenty pounds, and three months confinement: the
second—six months confinement, and a fine of thirty pounds.

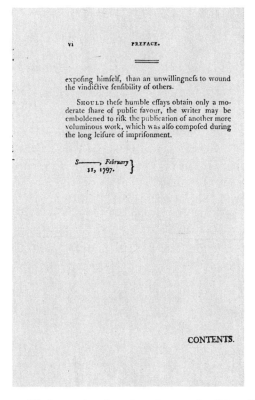

vi PREFACE.

exposing himself, than an unwillingness to wound
the vindictive sensibility of others.

SHOULD these humble essays obtain only a moderate share of public favour, the writer may be
emboldened to risk the publication of another more
voluminous work, which was also composed during
the long leisure of imprisonment.

S———, *February*
11, 1797.

CONTENTS.

*Title page and preface for Montgomery's first book, poems written while he was imprisoned on charges of seditious libel after
having published editorials opposing war with France and advocating reform at home*

ume is thus a disappointment, but it does carry promise of Montgomery's later mastery of certain lyric forms and reveals his gift for rhyme. A few years later, like many of his contemporaries, he had come to sympathize with France's enemies in the wake of the transformation of that nation into an aggressor.

His contribution to the public debate over Napoleon was to write his first long narrative poem, "The Wanderer of Switzerland," concerning an elderly citizen of that nation who is forced to emigrate when the French invade and destroy his country. This poem was published at the beginning of 1806 in a volume with some shorter lyrics. The book proved instantly popular; the first edition sold out in three weeks, and two more editions were printed that same year. Most of the reviews were favorable, though not the one in the *Edinburgh Review* (January 1807), which pointed out many of the same faults in Montgomery's verse that later generations of readers and critics have come to notice. Montgomery's preface to the volume shows something of what went wrong. In the title poem, he says, "An heroic subject is celebrated in a lyric measure, on a dramatic plan." Further, Montgomery claims, he wanted "To unite with the majesty of epic song, the fire, rapidity and compression of the ode. . . ." The poet himself recognizes his confusion about genre as well as his almost impossible ambitions–problems that were to plague him throughout his poetic career. Nevertheless, the success of the volume led to Montgomery's being hired to review for the new *Eclectic Review*. Byron liked the poems and defended the author in his *English Bards and Scotch Reviewers* (1809), and Robert Southey complimented Montgomery, thus initiating a regular correspondence that was to last until Southey's death forty years later.

Certainly the poems of this volume show improvement over his earlier work. The ballad meter is more suitable to the intention, and the subject of the title poem, together with Montgomery's obvious sincerity, helped make the work popular. Although "Alpine" poems had been written before this–including Coleridge's "Hymn Before Sunrise in the Vale of Chamouni" (1802)–Montgomery's "Wanderer of Switzerland" was the first one to be widely read and admired, thus preparing the way for the more impressive efforts of Byron in *Manfred* (1817) and Shelley in "Mont Blanc" (1817). The shorter poems in the volume may have been even more responsible for its popularity, however. In "The Grave," for example, the personification of the grave as it speaks to man is grimly effective, something in the manner of a "Christian" Thomas Hardy. Charles Lamb declared that "The Common Lot" was one of four or five poems in English that he would have been proud to have written, and there is evidence that "The Vigil of St. Mark" was the inspiration for Keats's "Eve of St. Mark" (written in 1819).

Montgomery had now begun to establish the characteristic pattern of his long poetic career: that of writing poetry with the intention of moral reform, never just entertainment. He was likewise using the editorial pages of the *Iris*, of which he had now been editor for a decade, to inveigh against abuses such as the slave trade and the misery of child chimney sweepers. As a result of the popularity of *The Wanderer of Switzerland, and Other Poems*, a London publisher asked him to contribute to a volume of poetry and prose supporting abolition of slavery. The result was a poem called "The West Indies," in which Montgomery traces the history of the slave trade from Columbus forward to the present, showing the moral degeneration that profiteering in human lives brought on master and slave alike. The poem is well conceived, skillfully constructed, and reflects perhaps as well as anything else he wrote the poet's eloquence and sincerity when he hits on a subject consonant (as the subject of his earlier "Wanderer of Switzerland" was not) with his essentially religious sensibility. The faults of the poem are related to those of Montgomery's other long poems: after so long the heroic-couplet rhyme scheme becomes tiresome, as does the temptation to be "epical" about everything. The author finally claims too much for abolition, as the concluding lines make clear:

> –All hail!–the age of crime and suffering ends;
> The reign of righteousness from heaven descends;
> Vengeance for ever sheathes the afflicting sword;
> Death is destroy'd, and Paradise restored;
> Man, rising from the ruins of his fall,
> Is one with God, and God is All in All.

The volume did not sell well, but when Montgomery published his poem in a book of his own the next year (1810), it was widely praised by critics and public alike.

Montgomery was always an ambitious poet, and his next major effort, a biblical epic, was already well under way by 1811. The poetry of John Milton constituted an imposing influence on all the Romantics in one way or another. Tak-

GEORGE BENNET.   ROWLAND HODGSON.   JAMES MONTGOMERY.   SAMUEL ROBERTS.

The Four Friends.

Montgomery with three close friends who shared his religious and social views (frontispiece to volume 2 of John Holland and James Everett's Memoirs of the Life and Writings of James Montgomery, *1855)*

ing off from book 11 of *Paradise Lost* and from the biblical book of Genesis, Montgomery conceived a story about the antediluvian patriarchs, the invasion of Eden by the progeny of Cain, the love of Javan (a poet) and Zillah, and the final deliverance of the patriarchal families from a race of giants. The publication of the poem was delayed for more than a year while the author spent time in London, attending lectures by Coleridge and meetings of religious societies to which he belonged. Undoubtedly also contributing to the delay was another bout of his periodic depression, and his condition was not helped by the fact that he found the noise of the city unbearable. Finally in the spring of 1813, *The World Before The Flood* was published and proved as popular as his two immediately preceding volumes. In the title poem Javan, tempted by fame and glory, leaves the paradisal homeland of the patriarchs only to return, prodigallike, when he realizes that his earlier way of life was closer to his needs. Again, the poem shows significant development over

Montgomery's previous efforts: a greater variety of interesting and dramatic incident, more compelling characterization, and greater sureness in handling of the usual verse form he employed in his longer works, the heroic couplet. It is true that the poem shows Montgomery too much under the spell of Milton and his eighteenth-century imitators. He did not seem to recognize the inappropriateness of the form for what he was attempting, nor its irrelevance for the revolutionary age of literature in which Montgomery found himself. One may notice, however, that "The World Before The Flood" is the only religious epic of the Romantic period which dares to invent new incidents to fill in the gaps in the scriptural story. Unlike Milton, but like his early-nineteenth-century contemporaries, Montgomery's approach to the epic was to transform such materials into romance form. Undoubtedly, part of the popularity of this work was due to its combining sacred history and an exotic setting to appeal to the rage for escapist narrative (though Montgomery him-

220

self would have resisted such a verdict, given his predominantly religious interests).

It may not be coincidence that the plot of "The World Before The Flood" concerns a prodigal poet's return to a godly society, since a few months after publishing the poem, Montgomery himself returned to the Moravians, having been estranged from them for some twenty-five years. This was not the conversion of an unbeliever, however, for during those years he had not only attended the services of other denominations but had been active in promoting various Christian causes; most recently, he had been one of the founders of the Methodist Missionary Society. And since boyhood, at least according to Montgomery himself, he had been writing hymn texts; he had probably composed more than a hundred by this time.

A hymn may achieve wide appeal for a variety of reasons—one obvious one being the nature of the music to which the words are set—but Montgomery's philosophy of hymn writing shows how thoroughly he grasped what was needed: "A hymn ought to be as regular in its structure as any other poem; it should have a distinct subject, and that subject should be simple, not complicated, so that . . . there should be little or no [skill] required on the part of the reader to understand it. . . . There should be a manifest gradation in the thoughts; and their mutual dependence should be so perceptible that they could not be transposed without injuring the unity of the piece; every line carrying forward the connection, and every verse adding a well-proportioned limb to a symmetrical body." Montgomery helped ensure his success in this endeavor by making many of his hymns paraphrases of Old Testament psalms or of various New Testament passages such as incidents from the life of Jesus and exhortations from Paul's letters. One cause of the continuing popularity of Montgomery's hymns, then, is that their theology tends to retain its basic appeal over a wide span of denominations and time. Writing verse paraphrases of biblical passages, especially of psalms, was a fairly common practice among Romantic poets; the list of those who did so successfully includes Cowper, Blake, Coleridge, Clare, and Byron. Although Montgomery was engaging in a common poetic practice of his day, only he (and Cowper to a much lesser extent) attempted to take verse paraphrase of scripture a step further into the popular form of the hymn.

Montgomery wrote more than four hundred hymns, of which at least thirty are now or were until recently in use in Catholicism and in many different Protestant denominations. His most popular hymn is the Christmas song "Angels From The Realms Of Glory," followed closely by "In The Hour Of Trial," "Hail To The Lord's Anointed," and "Go To Dark Gethsemane." Montgomery's sense of drama, his ability to capture the essence of an important incident or idea, and his gift for description are perhaps nowhere better illustrated than in the texts of his best hymns.

The experiences of missionaries had long been of interest to Montgomery, not least because of the fate of his own parents in the West Indies. After his return to the Moravians he wrote a series of editorials in the *Iris* about the poverty and sufferings of Moravian missionaries in Greenland. This research soon became the basis for his next long poem, "Greenland," published in 1819. More than any other major poem he had written to date, "Greenland" demonstrates that Montgomery's forte is not narration but description. The awe-inspiring landscape of Greenland allowed the poet full opportunity to display his ability to render the sublime according to the taste of the times. These descriptions wear at least as well as those of Mary Shelley, who described the same Arctic region in her novel *Frankenstein,* written the same year as "Greenland." However, given the lack of a central character, the author's rather tame piety, and his familiar inability to make the heroic couplet sustain long passages of narrative, "Greenland" must, like his other epics, be judged ultimately a failure. In fact the poem as he published it is unfinished; the best guess is that Montgomery probably printed it anyway in order to help save the missions in that far off country.

As Montgomery approached his fiftieth birthday, his income from his poetry had become such that he could begin to think of retiring from newspaper work. He had always hated the controversy that such employment involved, and his increasingly active role in religious organizations also sapped the energy needed to run the paper. After editing a volume of poems designed to arouse public concern about abuse of chimney sweeps (1824), Montgomery sold the *Iris* and was honored at a retirement dinner in 1825 by some of the leading literary, political, and religious figures of his day. While the verdict on his poetic abilities was decidedly mixed, he was univer-

James Montgomery (engraving by Joseph Brown)

sally admired, even loved as one of the kindest, gentlest persons in England. His final attempt at a long poem, *The Pelican Island*, was published in 1827. For the first (and last) time, Montgomery broke away from the heroic couplet in a narrative poem, writing instead in blank verse. Set in Australia and based on travelers' journals, *The Pelican Island* has even less human interest than "Greenland." The poet's struggle with the unfamiliar blank-verse medium makes the poem so convoluted that it becomes difficult to follow. It delighted some reviewers with its descriptive passages, but merely puzzled and irritated others, as it has most modern readers.

The thirty years of life remaining to Montgomery were devoted to editing volumes of religious writing, lecturing on English poetry, collecting his work for uniform publication, and to his usual variety of tasks within the several religious and humanitarian organizations and causes to

which he belonged or subscribed. In 1835 he was granted a pension from the Literary Fund of £150 per annum. In 1841 he took a long-postponed tour of Moravian sites in Scotland and began editing work on a new Moravian hymnbook as well as other collections of hymns in the Protestant tradition. Two years later, at the death of Southey, the poet laureate, Montgomery's name was prominently mentioned as a worthy successor, but Wordsworth's greatness was too obvious for Montgomery to have had a realistic chance at the post. He died in 1854, in his eighty-third year, honored as a poet and as an editor, but above all as a human being.

The accepted verdict on Montgomery's poetry may never change substantially. Yet literary historians sometimes succeed (albeit unwittingly) in burying a poet's work completely when that is not what it deserves. Montgomery was not an original thinker in verse–he did not comprehend, for example, that a revolutionary age demands profound changes in artistic form–but his long poems contain passages of real power, and some of his short lyrics can stand comparison with lyrics of the major Romantics. Thus he deserves to be thought of (and read) as something more than a contemporary who had some influence on Byron, Shelley, and Keats.

Biographies:

John Holland and James Everett, *Memoirs of the Life and Writings of James Montgomery*, 7 volumes (London: Longman, Brown, Green & Longmans, 1854-1857);

Mrs. Helen C. Knight, *Life of James Montgomery* (Boston: Gould & Lincoln, 1857).

References:

Stuart Curran, *Poetic Form & British Romanticism* (Oxford: Oxford University Press, 1986);

A. D. Harvey, *English Poetry in a Changing Society, 1780-1825* (London: Allison & Busby, 1980);

A. S. Holbrook, "The Life & Work of James Montgomery," *London Quarterly*, 179 (1954): 134-137;

Judy Page, "The Garland Facsimiles of the Poetry of James Montgomery," *Blake: An Illustrated Quarterly*, 15 (Summer 1981): 38-45;

Donald H. Reiman, Introduction in *Prison Amusements and The Wanderer of Switzerland*, facsimile (New York & London: Garland, 1978); also published in *Verses to the Memory of the Late Richard Reynolds* [and] *The World before the Flood*, facsimile (New York & London: Garland, 1978); *Greenland and Abdallah*, facsimile (New York & London: Garland, 1978); and *The West Indies*, facsimile (New York & London: Garland, 1979).

Samuel Rogers

(30 July 1763 - 18 December 1855)

Patricia L. Skarda
Smith College

BOOKS: *An Ode to Superstition, with some other Poems* (London: Printed for T. Cadell, 1786);

The Pleasures of Memory (London: Printed by J. Davis & sold by T. Cadell, 1792; Boston: Printed by Manning & Loring for David West, 1795);

An Epistle to a Friend, with Other Poems (London: Printed by R. Noble for T. Cadell Jr. & W. Davies, 1798);

The Voyage of Columbus (London: T. Cadell & W. Davies, 1810);

Poems (London: Printed by T. Bensley for T. Cadell & W. Davies, 1812; Philadelphia: Published by Bradford & Inskeep and Inskeep & Bradford, New York, 1813);

Lara, A Tale [by George Gordon, Lord Byron]; *Jacqueline, A Tale* [by Rogers] (London: Printed for J. Murray by T. Davison, 1814; Boston: Wells & Lilly, 1814; New York: Eastburn & Kirk, 1814)–*Jacqueline* also published separately (1814);

Human Life, a Poem (London: John Murray, 1819; Philadelphia: Published by M. Thomas, printed by J. Maxwell, 1819);

Italy a Poem, part 1 (London: Printed for Longman, Hurst, Rees, Orme & Brown, 1822; revised and enlarged edition, London: John Murray, 1823; Philadelphia: E. Littell / New York: N. Henry, 1823); part 2 (London: John Murray, 1828);

Poems (London: Printed for T. Cadell & E. Moxon, 1834; Philadelphia: Lea & Blanchard, 1843);

Recollections of the Table-Talk of Samuel Rogers, edited by Alexander Dyce (London: Moxon, 1856; New York: Appleton, 1856);

Poetical Works (London: Moxon, 1856; Philadelphia: E. H. Butler, 1857);

Recollections, edited by William Sharpe (London: Longman, Brown, Green, Longmans & Roberts, 1859; Boston: Bartlett & Miles, 1859);

The Italian Journal of Samuel Rogers. Edited, with an Account of Rogers' Life and of Travel in Italy, by J. R. Hale (London: Faber & Faber, 1956).

Samuel Rogers had considerably more taste than poetic talent, more friends than favorable reviews. His seven rooms at 22 St. James's Place, London, were, according to Donald Weeks, "the first small home to become a great museum," and there Rogers reigned supreme as an arbiter of taste, noted as much for the sharpness of his tongue as the kindness of his heart, the openness of his purse, and the power of his influence. He built his reputation on the success of *The Pleasures of Memory* (1792), which went through fifteen editions by 1806 and which was quoted by William Wordsworth in *Descriptive Sketches* (1793) and admired by him throughout the writing of *Lyrical Ballads* (1798). As if in return, Rogers arranged, by a timely comment to Sir William Lowther, Lord Lonsdale, for Wordsworth to be appointed Distributor of Stamps for Westmorland in 1813, and in 1843, when Wordsworth was appointed poet laureate, Rogers dressed him in his own court suit, as he was, in 1850, to dress Alfred, Lord Tennyson.

In addition to aiding these two figures, larger both in size and in literary history, Rogers had sent £150 to keep the dying Richard Brinsley Sheridan from being evicted in 1816 and £500 to Thomas Campbell in 1831 so that Campbell could purchase a share in the *Metropolitan* magazine. Throughout his life he befriended Thomas Moore, assisting him financially in his Bermuda difficulties. He set up Henry Moxon in the publishing business in 1830 and contributed to the popularity of the illustrated gift book by advancing enormous sums to the publication of his poetry with illustrations by J. M. W. Turner and Thomas Stothard. Moore, who was to dedicate *Lalla Rookh* (1817) to Rogers, introduced him to George Gordon, Lord Byron, in 1811. Byron dedicated *The Giaour* (1813) to Rogers and published his *Lara* with Rogers's *Jacqueline* in 1814 but later asked if Rogers were "Vampire, ghost, or ghoul,"

Samuel Rogers (portrait by Thomas Phillips; by permission of the National Portrait Gallery, London)

a comment on both his cadaverous appearance and his verbal bloodletting. Charles Dickens dedicated *Master Humphrey's Clock* (1840, 1841), which includes *The Old Curiosity Shop* and *Barnaby Rudge*, to Rogers but lampooned him in *Bleak House* (1852) as the small-minded, deaf, and surly Grandfather Smallweed, slipping down in his chair and down in regard.

Rogers counted among his friends almost everyone of significance in the age, including such Americans as William Cullen Bryant, Ralph Waldo Emerson, Henry Wadsworth Longfellow, and Herman Melville. In fact, most members of the social, political, and literary elite of the day were invited to Rogers's handsome home to breakfast or dinner and conversation, occasions worthy of record in a host of journals and letters. They enjoyed Rogers's caustic wit, admired his reputation, and read his poetry with varying degrees of enthusiasm. The decline in Rogers's poetic reputation comes not merely because he was a relic of Augustan England (his models were Thomas Gray,

Oliver Goldsmith, and Samuel Johnson), but because his smooth, competent verse was overshadowed by the rougher but more powerful measures of the major Romantic poets, whom he readily recognized as his superiors.

Rogers's long life spanned nearly a century, from Strawberry Hill to the Great Exhibition, from Sir Joshua Reynolds to the Pre-Raphaelites, from John Wesley to John Henry, Cardinal Newman, from Gray to Tennyson. His talent was moderate, but he crafted all his works fastidiously and polished each to the dull sheen of his capability.

Rogers was born into advantageous circumstances at The Hill, Newington Green, the home of his maternal grandfather, a linen draper and strong English Presbyterian, to Mary Radford Rogers and Thomas Rogers, a successful glass manufacturer who had liberal and nonconformist principles. Samuel was the third son of eight children, five of whom lived long lives, though none longer than Samuel. He began his education in

Illustration by Thomas Stothard for "A Wish"

Hackney, where he met his lifelong friend William Maltby, later librarian of the London Institute, and he continued his studies in Stoke Newington and Islington under the masterful hand of James Burgh, a Scotsman whose belief in liberty of the press and reform in Parliamentary representation led the young Samuel Rogers to embrace such unpopular causes as the right of the American colonists to revolt. When Samuel was thirteen his mother died. His father, then a banker in Cornhill, lived a dozen years after Samuel had reluctantly joined him at the bank. Rogers's own choice of vocation was to enter the Presbyterian ministry, for in his boyhood he "thought there was nothing on earth so *grand*" as to figure in a pulpit and to have the polished manners of Dr. Richard Price, a well-known preacher at Newington Green and a close friend of the family. By conscientiously launching a literary career while fulfilling his responsibilities to the bank, Rogers managed to strike something of the pose he sought in his youth, considerably assisted by the comfortable annuity of £5,000, received after

his father's death. On long holidays at either Margate or Brighton, where sea bathing bolstered his indifferent health, Samuel Rogers read voraciously in English, Latin, and French, as well as Greek in translation. With Maltby, he went to see Dr. Samuel Johnson, but with his "hand on the knocker," courage failed him and he retreated, missing his only opportunity to meet the great man of letters of the eighteenth century.

Rogers's literary career began, as Johnson's had, in prose. In 1781-1782, when he was still in his teens, Rogers contributed to the *Gentleman's Magazine* eight short essays modeled on Johnson's *Rambler* (1750-1752) in subject though not in style. With that success he turned his attention to opera in 1782 (only fragments remain of his "Vintage of Burgundy") and then finally to poetry, which attracted him for the immortality he assumed it offered. In 1786 he published anonymously *An Ode to Superstition, with some other Poems,* imitating Gray in diction, rhythm, and the use of personification. In *Table-Talk* (1856), Rogers admitted to reading a pocket edition of

Gray's poems every morning during his walks to his father's banking house in town, but his subsequent comments indicate that his admiration of Gray was qualified. Throughout his career, Rogers relied on models but conscientiously avoided plagiarism or direct echoes by working hard and long on each poem. "An Ode to Superstition," consisting of only 156 lines, was revised for two years before it was published. Rogers recognized its lack of originality and freshness in all but the characterization of superstition as a demon of darkness opposing truth and inhibiting the human mind. "A Wish," first published with the ode, anticipates Wordsworth and Coleridge in its expression of desire for simple domesticity in a "cot" with "Lucy" spinning amid nature's pleasant sounds, but the scene Rogers created, and that Stothard illustrated, remains but a picture, free of the mystery and suggestiveness that distinguish *Lyrical Ballads*.

In 1788 the death of Rogers's older brother Thomas imposed heavier family and banking responsibilities on Samuel. Realizing that he had not yet reached the literary standard he set for himself, he decided to enlarge his experience and his circle of friends. He solicited the friendship of Mrs. Anna Laetitia Barbauld by sending her a copy of *An Ode to Superstition,* and in 1789 he visited Scotland, meeting historian William Robertson, economist Adam Smith, novelist Henry Mackenzie, and Walter Scott. In fact he made the acquaintance of nearly every Scottish man of letters save Robert Burns. Associating with the literati rekindled his hope for personal excellence, and he systematically continued to accumulate friends, among them Lafayette, whom he met on a brief journey to Paris in 1791. There he saw for the first time the magnificent collection of pictures in the Palais Royal and was inspired to become a liberal patron of the fine arts.

In 1792 Rogers produced *The Pleasures of Memory*, not fashioned after Gray but resembling Goldsmith's *Deserted Village* (1770). Rogers's poem is inferior in power to *The Pleasures of Imagination* (1744) by Mark Akenside and *The Pleasures of Melancholy* (1747) by Thomas Warton–which preceded it–and in episodic competence to *The Pleasures of Hope* (1799) by Thomas Campbell–which it suggested–but it satisfied the taste of the day. The *Monthly Review* (June 1792) applauded the "correctness of thought, delicacy of sentiment, variety of imagery, and harmony of versification" in the poem, and J. R. Watson finds amid its "stylistic conservatism" an anticipation of Coleridge's as-

sociation of memory with the workings of fancy and "the domestic-rural scene beloved of Victorian painters." Some years later Coleridge accused Rogers of stealing the tale of "Florio," the memorable narrative in the second half of Rogers's poem, from the *Lochleven* of Michael Bruce (completed in 1766), but Charles Lamb exonerated Rogers, and Coleridge retracted his charge publicly in the second edition (1797) of his first volume of verse. The tale of Florio's love for Julia, who drowns before love can be consummated, gave Rogers an opportunity to end his poem with his personal testimony to the healing powers of memory in a moving invocation to his deceased brother, Thomas:

> Still o'er my life preserve thy mild control,
> Correct my views, and elevate my soul;
> Grant me thy peace and purity of mind,
> Devout yet cheerful, active yet resigned;
> Grant me, like thee, whose heart knew no disguise,
> Whose blameless wishes never aimed to rise,
> To meet the changes Time and Chance present,
> With modest dignity and calm content.

The Pleasures of Memory adheres to what M. H. Abrams calls the "loco-descriptive" form, a meditation on a rural scene, here, specifically, that of Rogers's home village of Newington Green. The strict iambic-pentameter couplets, with balanced phrasing, are replete with classical allusions and needless personification, but the form aptly idealizes both the place and the power of memory that were to mean much more to the later, greater Romantics.

After the death of his father in 1793 Rogers took chambers in the Temple, where he could entertain his friends, many of them politically and artistically influential. Eventually giving up the family home at Newington Green, he took an active interest in Parliamentary reforms advocated by Horne Tooke and others, and he decorated his rooms with antique casts and engravings after Raphael. His next poem demonstrates the growth of his artistic interests, at least in its allusions. *An Epistle to a Friend* (1798)–a directed response to a verse epistle by a friend, the sage literary judge Richard Sharp–somewhat disingenuously sets forth the advantages of simple tastes and country life over the pleasures of town. Rogers argues for elegant sufficiency, for good taste, making his point that the genius of "a Michael's grandeur, and a Raphael's grace" flows from any "modest ornament" that "attracts the eye to exercise the mind," an argument that

Illustrations by J. M. W. Turner for The Pleasures of Memory

Rogers with the Hon. Mrs. Norton and Mrs. Phipps (painting by F. Stone; by permission of the National Portrait Gallery, London)

seems false to his own situation. He combines in this poem a Romantic sentimentality with an Augustan rationalism revealed in the predictability of his reaction to the pleasures of pastoral harmonies. Rarely does Rogers surprise the reader with unexpected or profound insights into human behavior; his poetry states the obvious rather than suggesting the subtle connections made by the greater Romantic poets.

Politically and socially, Rogers was something of a contradiction, alternately acting on personal ethics or the unstated rules of prevailing fashion. He could as easily be selfless, compassionate, and generous as self-aggrandizing, cruel, and niggardly. Rogers attended Horne Tooke's trial for treason in 1794 and visited him and others in prison, but Rogers's liberal principles did not keep him from cultivating the attention of the aristocrats of the day. Sarah Sophia Villiers, Lady Jersey, and Frances, Lady Crewe–as well as that consummate host and hostess Henry Richard Vassall Fox, Lord Holland, and Elizabeth Vassall Fox,

Lady Holland–entertained him, but no salon claimed his full allegiance until he created his own. He became a fellow of the Royal Society in 1796, but he was blackballed, probably for his political and religious opinions, by the Literary Club, established by Samuel Johnson and Sir Joshua Reynolds. Another trip to Paris, in 1802, took him to the Louvre, where Napoleon's trophies were attracting a crowd of viewers, including artists. There he met Henry Fuseli and John Flaxman, Benjamin West and John Opie, and he took up art collecting, an avocation he shared with his brother-in-law Sutton Sharpe and his dear friend Charles James Fox.

In 1803 Rogers moved to 22 St. James's Place, where he could display his growing collection, which included works by his artistic friends. Flaxman designed the ceiling, cornice, and mantelpiece of the drawing room; Stothard, a cabinet; round the staircase ran a frieze copied from that of the Parthenon; and in the dining room stood a sideboard carved by Francis Chantry from one

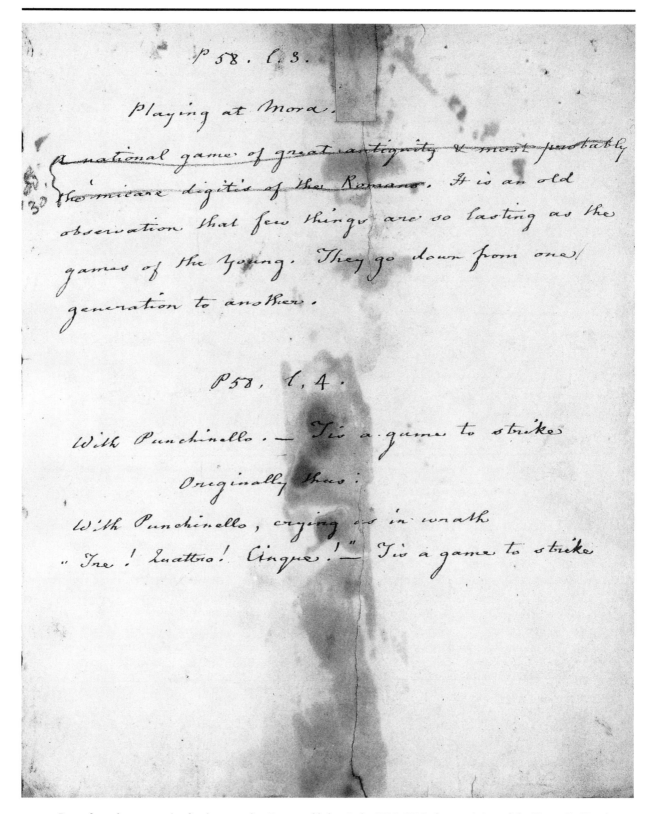

P 58. l. 3.

Playing at Mora.

A national game of great antiquity & most probably the 'micare digitis' of the Romans. It is an old observation that few things are so lasting as the games of the Young. They go down from one generation to another.

P 58. l. 4.

With Punchinello. — 'Tis a game to strike

Originally thus:

With Punchinello, crying as in wrath
"Tre! Quattro! Cinque!" — 'Tis a game to strike

Pages from the manuscript for the notes that Rogers added to Italy *(HM 6028; by permission of the Henry E. Huntington Library and Art Gallery)*

South of the Church, east of the belfry-tower:

This Quarter of the City was in the fourteenth Century
the scene of a romantic incident that befell a ~~young~~ Lady
of the Amieri family, ~~a Lady, no less distinguished for~~
~~her worth than her beauty;~~ who, being crossed in love
& sacrificed by her Father, to his avarice or his
ambition, was in the fourth year of an unhappy
marriage, consigned to the grave.

With the usual solemnities she was conveyed to
the Cemetery of the Cathedral & deposited in a tomb
of the family that ~~in still~~ was long pointed out; but she was
~~long~~ not to remain there. For she had been buried in
a trance; &, awaking ~~soon~~ at midnight ~~afterwards~~ among them
that slept, she disengaged in the darkness her hands
& her feet, & climbing up the narrow stair-case to
a gate that had been left unlocked, she came
abroad into the moon-shine, wondering where she
was & what had befallen her.

When at length she had in some degree recovered herself,

of Hope's designs. Over time Rogers's home became a private gallery, eventually including 2,466 books, 744 drawings, engravings, and manuscripts, 224 paintings, 210 Greek vases, 161 articles of furniture, 82 Egyptian antiquities, and more than a hundred bronzes, marbles, modern statues, and casts. So extensive a collection would result in clutter in the rooms and halls of lesser men, but in Rogers's home all was harmony, order, and elegance. He became one of the first connoisseurs of both people and objets d'art, and when his brother relieved him almost entirely of business cares, he lived wholly for letters, art, and society. He willed three paintings to the National Gallery: Guido Reni's *Ecce Homo*, Titian's *Noli Me Tangere*, and Giorgione's *Man in Armour*. The rest of his art collection and his library, sold at auction in May 1856, produced fifty thousand pounds in a sale lasting twenty-two days. Charles Robert Leslie, in his *Autobiographical Recollections* (1860), summarizes the many tributes to Rogers as collector by writing: "Whatever place may be assigned to Samuel Rogers among poets, he deserves to hold the highest place among men of taste; not merely of taste for this and that, but of general good taste in all things."

It was for his poetry that he wished to be remembered, but that was not to be. He set himself almost impossible tasks in his eagerness to improve upon the popular success of *The Pleasures of Memory*. In 1810 Rogers had printed for private circulation *The Voyage of Columbus*, a cumbersome poetic rendering, presented as a translation, of an epic theme. Rogers attempts to honor Columbus for bringing the light of Christianity to the dark region of the world, a subject worthy of Milton but seriously marred by obvious Miltonic resonances and contrived fragmentation. By departing from the moralizing tone of his earlier work, Rogers hoped to match the inventiveness of Burns, Scott, Moore, Byron, and Wordsworth, but Rogers's imagination failed him in execution though it led him often to a theatrical style Byron rather liked and improved upon in his *Giaour*.

Rogers had played the peacemaker in a dispute between Byron and Thomas Moore in 1811, and Rogers and Byron's friendship prospered for seven years until reports of Rogers's sharp tongue knocked him from second place on Byron's "Gradus ad Parnassum" (second only to Scott); from being acclaimed by Byron as "the Nestor of our inferior race of living poets" Rogers sunk to being called "the cancer of the species

. . . Plague personified and famine / Devil, whose sole delight is damning!" In 1822, when Rogers visited Byron and Shelley at Pisa, Byron entertained himself by managing to get Rogers to sit upon a cushion under which the cruel lampoon "On Sam Rogers: Question and Answer" had been thrust, but Rogers was unaware of Byron's malignant lines until long after Byron's death, a loss Rogers felt keenly and ably recorded in *Italy* (1822, 1828). Byron admired Rogers's verse, though not his tongue, to the end. In tribute to "melodious Rogers" (Byron's epithet in *English Bards and Scotch Reviewers*, 1809) Byron had published his *Lara* with Rogers's *Jacqueline* in 1814. Byron, however, was almost alone among careful readers in finding music in Rogers's singsong meter and sympathy in the melodrama of Jacqueline, who left her father for her lover and then thought better of it. Reviewers contrasted the two brutally, calling Rogers's verse "a pretty trifle" (*Monthly Review*, September 1814), gleaming "palely like the moon-beams in the presence of the sun" of Byron's tragedy.

Although the joint publication was a popular success, Rogers left the limelight dimmed by the reviewers to visit Italy with his sister Sarah to take notes for a poem, *Italy*, planned to rival and complete Byron's *Childe Harold's Pilgrimage* (1812-1818). His Italian journal was edited and published on its own merits in 1956. But before embarking on *Italy*, his last and most successful work, Rogers completed *Human Life* (1819), begun as soon as *Columbus* was in the publisher's hands. Of all his works Rogers preferred *Human Life* not only for its freer versification but also for its maturity of thought. The poem presents various scenes from the cradle to the grave in the career of an Englishman of gentle birth and liberal training. The life Rogers depicts is not his own, for his nameless subject marries for love, fathers a son, and watches carefully as the lad becomes a man and has a family of his own. The poignance of the poem comes not only from the life Rogers imagines for himself if he had married, but from the sensitive account of the son's gradual maturation into fatherhood and the father's grief at the death of the child. Rogers intrudes into the poem twice, with addresses first to his sister Maria and then to his friend Charles James Fox, both of whom died in 1806. Rogers knew suffering firsthand, and it is characteristic of him to console himself by direct poetic address to the deceased. He had great sympathy for the suffering and the dying, and in his long life he bade al-

THE AUTHOR OF "THE PLEASURES OF MEMORY"

Portrait by Daniel Maclise in the Fraser's Magazine *"Gallery of Illustrious Literary Characters" (1830-1838)*

most all his friends good-bye. He had kind words for Byron, whose marital dispute resulted in his self-exile, and he consoled both Wordsworth and Moore on the deaths of their children. Rogers recognized adversity and alleviated it for his friends when he could, practicing what he preached in *Human Life:* "Through the wide world he only is alone / Who lives not for another." In most of his poetry Rogers observed misfortune as if from a height above it, but in *Human Life* his tone is more personal.

When the first part of *Italy* appeared anonymously in 1822, Rogers was out of the country, hoping to have his work evaluated separately from his personality. He was markedly disappointed in its reception but not daunted; the sec-

ond part appeared under his name in 1828. The second part sold no better than the first, but Rogers did not give up hope for this, his longest work. He commissioned Turner and Stothard to illustrate a second edition, which appeared in 1830. Success elevated Rogers to something of a potentate in the world of letters and made possible astonishing sales of his *Poems,* also illustrated, in 1834. Byron's friend Marguerite, Lady Blessington, commented that *Italy* "would have been dished were it not for the plates." The poem is rarely read today, but it has value for more than the tourist, for whom it was designed. Its blank verse marks Rogers's awareness of his Romantic contemporaries, and its narratives, usually suggested by place, often have an affective dimen-

Rogers in 1848 (drawing by George Richmond; by permission of the National Portrait Gallery, London)

sion. His prose notes, richly allusive and anecdotal, were widely admired for their clarity and grace. The character of the poet, however, has no depth; he observes as he goes, and he recounts what he sees in the present by what he knows of the past. Interestingly, John Ruskin so admired Rogers's *Italy* that he credited it with having "determined the main tenor of my life." Ruskin placed higher value on Turner's vignettes than on Rogers's poetry or prose or suggestions for the drawings, but echoes of Rogers can be found throughout Ruskin's work, and Ruskin thanked Rogers sincerely for his words and feeling, especially on Venice.

Rogers had learned to enhance the commercial appeal of his work by illustrations much earlier, when he added thirty-four vignettes by Stothard to the 1810 edition of *The Pleasures of Memory,* and he continued to do so by adding seven illustrations by Turner to the 1834 edition of *The Voyage of Columbus.* Since the sumptuous editions of his work were financed by Rogers per-

sonally, he retained control over the subject and manner of each illustration. His exacting requirements testify to his taste for a composite art form that remains popular even now.

After *Italy,* Rogers wrote but a few brief lyrics and occasional poems. In 1844 his bank was robbed, occasioning Edward Everett to write, "It is the only part of your fortune which has gone for any other objects than those of benevolence, hospitality, and taste." Most of the money was recovered, and Rogers used it as wisely as before. Although his taste, benevolence, and wit could sometimes be controlling and although he never could suppress a bon mot, even when uncharitable, Rogers recognized excellence in others and refused the laureateship following Wordsworth's death in 1850, out of deference to Tennyson and because of his own advanced age. Shortly thereafter, in June 1850, he was struck by a carriage, and his thigh was shattered in the socket. From then until his tranquil death in 1855 he was an invalid, attended by a devoted niece. Dickens's friend

Daniel Maclise had captured in caricature the antiquated Rogers, "lean as if he had been fed on bank-notes, and drunk ink: sallow as if he had breathed no air that was not imbued with the taint of gold," but Dickens himself had seen Rogers more generously and, perhaps, much more fairly when he defended Rogers from an attack by John Overs, telling him: "I do not know and have never known a man on whom riches and honors have had less corrupting influence than the venerable old gentleman who is the subject of our discussion. I do not know and have never known a more amiable, charitable, or just man in all he says and does. A kinder-hearted or more gentle creature I have never seen. And that he does, every day, a thousand worthy and generous acts, *I know*." Although the quality of Rogers's life cannot compensate for the mediocrity of his poetry or even for the occasional sharpness of his tongue, his hospitality and refined taste made him a legend in his own time and earn him a place among his more powerful contemporaries.

Letters:

Samuel Rogers and William Gilpin: Their Friendship and Correspondence, edited by Carl Paul Barbier (London: Published for Glasgow University by Oxford University Press, 1959).

Biographies:

Edward Bell, Memoir of Rogers, in *The Poetical Works of Samuel Rogers* (London: G. Bell & Sons, 1875);

P. W. Clayden, *The Early Life of Samuel Rogers* (London: Smith, Elder, 1887; Boston: Roberts, 1888);

Clayden, *Rogers and His Contemporaries,* 2 volumes (London: Smith, Elder, 1889);

Richard Ellis Roberts, *Samuel Rogers and His Circle* (London: Methuen, 1910).

References:

Doris Alexander, "The Poet in Grandfather Smallweed," *Dickensian,* 80, part 2 (Summer 1984): 66-73;

William Bates, *The Maclise Portrait Gallery of Illustrious Literary Characters with Memoirs* (London: Chatto & Windus, 1898), pp. 12-22;

Shelley M. Bennett, "Thomas Stothard's Adaptation to the Semi-Industrial Arts," *Eighteenth Century Life,* 7 (January 1982): 19-30;

Joseph Firebaugh, "Samuel Rogers and American Men of Letters," *American Literature,* 13 (January 1942): 331-334;

Avery F. Gaskins, "Samuel Rogers: A Revaluation," *Wordsworth Circle,* 16 (Summer 1985): 146-149;

Ernest Giddey, "Byron and Samuel Rogers," *Byron Journal,* 7 (1979): 4-19;

J. R. Hale, "Samuel Rogers the Perfectionist," *Huntington Library Quarterly,* 25 (November 1961): 61-67;

Adele M. Holcomb, "A Neglected Classical Phase of Turner's Art: His Vignettes to Rogers's *Italy,*" *Journal of the Warburg and Courtauld Institutes,* 32 (1969): 405-410;

Bernard Knieger, "Samuel Rogers: Forgotten Maecenas," *College Language Association Journal,* 3 (March 1960): 187-192;

David E. Latané, Jr., "Samuel Rogers' *The Voyage of Columbus* and Turner's Illustrations to the Edition of 1834," *Wordsworth Circle,* 14 (Spring 1983): 108-112;

Ben Harris McClary, "Alaric Watts on Samuel Rogers: An Unpublished Personal Remembrance," *Bulletin of Research in the Humanities,* 84 (Spring 1981): 121-125;

McClary, "An Exchange of Verse Epistles: Richard Sharp and Samuel Rogers," *Notes and Queries,* new series 30 (June 1983): 212-213;

Jeffrey L. Spear, "Ruskin's Italy," *Browning Institute Studies: An Annual of Victorian Literary and Cultural History,* 12 (1984): 73-92;

J. R. Watson, "Samuel Rogers: The Last Augustan," in *Augustan Worlds: New Essays in Eighteenth Century Literature,* edited by J. C. Hilson, M. M. B. Jones, and J. R. Watson (New York: Harper & Row, 1978), pp. 281-297;

Donald Weeks, "Samuel Rogers: Man of Taste," *PMLA,* 62 (1947): 472-486.

Sir Walter Scott

(15 August 1771 - 21 September 1832)

Alan Richardson
Boston College

BOOKS: *The Chase, and William and Helen: Two Ballads from the German of Gottfried Augustus Bürger* (Edinburgh: Printed by Mundell & Son for Manners & Miller and sold by T. Cadell, Jun. & W. Davies, 1796);

The Eve of Saint John. A Border Ballad (Kelso: Printed by James Ballantyne, 1800);

The Lay of the Last Minstrel (London: Printed for Longman, Hurst, Rees & Orme, and A. Constable, Edinburgh, by James Ballantyne, Edinburgh, 1805; Philadelphia: Printed for I. Riley, New York, 1806);

Ballads and Lyrical Pieces (Edinburgh: Printed by James Ballantyne for Longman, Rees & Orme, London, and Archibald Constable, Edinburgh, 1806; Boston: Published & sold by Etheridge & Bliss and by B. & B. Hopkins, Philadelphia, 1807);

Marmion: A Tale of Flodden Field (Edinburgh: Printed by J. Ballantyne for Archibald Constable, Edinburgh, and William Miller & John Murray, London, 1808; Philadelphia: Hopkins & Earle, 1808);

The Lady of the Lake; A Poem (Edinburgh: Printed for John Ballantyne, Edinburgh, and Longman, Hurst, Rees & Orme and William Miller, London, by James Ballantyne, 1810; Boston: Published by W. Wells & T. B. Wait, printed by T. B. Wait, 1810; New York: E. Sargeant, 1810; Philadelphia: E. Earle, 1810);

The Vision of Don Roderick: A Poem (Edinburgh: Printed by James Ballantyne for John Ballantyne, Edinburgh, and Longman, Hurst, Rees, Orme & Brown, London, 1811; Boston: Published by T. B. Wait, 1811);

Rokeby; A Poem (Edinburgh: Printed for John Ballantyne, Edinburgh, and Longman, Hurst, Rees, Orme & Brown, London, by James Ballantyne, Edinburgh, 1813; Baltimore: J. Cushing, 1813);

The Bridal of Triermain, or The Vale of St John. In Three Cantos (Edinburgh: Printed by James Ballantyne for John Ballantyne and for Longman, Hurst, Rees, Orme & Brown and Gale, Curtis & Fenner, London, 1813; Philadelphia: Published by M. Thomas, printed by W. Fry, 1813);

Waverley; or, 'Tis Sixty Years Since (3 volumes, Edinburgh: Printed by James Ballantyne for Archibald Constable, Edinburgh, and Longman, Hurst, Rees, Orme & Brown, London, 1814; 1 volume, Boston: Published by Wells & Lilly and Bradford & Read, 1815; 2 volumes, New York: Van Winkle & Wiley, 1815);

Guy Mannering; or, The Astrologer. By the Author of "Waverley" (3 volumes, Edinburgh: Printed by James Ballantyne for Longman, Hurst, Rees, Orme & Brown, London, and Archibald Constable, Edinburgh, 1815; 2 volumes, Boston: Published by West & Richardson and Eastburn, Kirk, New York, printed by T. W. White, 1815);

The Lord of the Isles, A Poem (Edinburgh: Printed for Archibald Constable, Edinburgh, and Longman, Hurst, Rees, Orme & Brown, London, by James Ballantyne, 1815; New York: R. Scott, 1815; Philadelphia: Published by Moses Thomas, 1815);

The Field of Waterloo; A Poem (Edinburgh: Printed by James Ballantyne for Archibald Constable, Edinburgh, and Longman, Hurst, Rees, Orme & Brown, and John Murray, London, 1815; Boston: T. B. Wait, 1815; New York: Van Winkle & Wiley, 1815; Philadelphia: Published by Moses Thomas, printed by Van Winkle & Wiley, 1815);

The Ettricke Garland; Being Two Excellent New Songs on The Lifting of the Banner of the House of Buccleuch, At the Great Foot-Ball Match on Carterhaugh, Dec. 4, 1815, by Scott and James Hogg (Edinburgh: Printed by James Ballantyne, 1815);

The Antiquary. By the Author of "Waverley" and "Guy Mannering" (3 volumes, Edinburgh: Printed by James Ballantyne for Archibald Constable, Edinburgh, and Longman, Hurst, Rees,

Walter Scott (portrait by William Nicholson; by permission of the Scottish National Portrait Gallery)

Orme & Brown, London, 1816; 2 volumes, New York: Van Winkle & Wiley, 1816);

Paul's Letters To His Kinfolk (Edinburgh: Printed by James Ballantyne for Archibald Constable, Edinburgh, and Longman, Hurst, Rees, Orme & Brown, and John Murray, London, 1816; Philadelphia: Republished by M. Thomas, 1816);

Tales of My Landlord, Collected and Arranged by Jebediah Cleishbotham, Schoolmaster and Parish-Clerk of Gandercleugh [The Black Dwarf and *Old Mortality]* (4 volumes, Edinburgh: Printed for William Blackwood and John Murray, London, 1816; 1 volume, Philadelphia: Published by M. Thomas, 1817);

Harold the Dauntless; A Poem (Edinburgh: Printed by James Ballantyne for Longman, Hurst, Rees, Orme & Brown, London, and Arch-

ibald Constable, Edinburgh, 1817; New York: Published by James Eastburn, printed by Van Winkle, Wiley, 1817);

Rob Roy, by the Author of "Waverley," "Guy Mannering," and "The Antiquary" (3 volumes, Edinburgh: Printed by James Ballantyne for Archibald Constable, Edinburgh, and Longman, Hurst, Rees, Orme & Brown, London, 1818; 2 volumes, New York: J. Eastburn, 1818; New York: Published by Kirk & Mercein, printed by E. & E. Hosford, Albany, 1818; Philadelphia: Published by M. Thomas, printed by J. Maxwell, 1818);

Tales of My Landlord, Second Series, Collected and Arranged by Jedediah Cleishbotham, Schoolmaster and Parish-Clerk of Gandercleugh [The Heart of Mid-Lothian], 4 volumes (Edinburgh: Printed for Archibald Constable, 1818; Philadelphia: M. Carey & Son, 1818);

Walter and Anne Rutherford Scott, the poet's parents, at the time of their marriage in 1758 (portraits attributed to Robert Harvie; with kind permission of Mrs. Maxwell-Scott of Abbotsford)

Tales of My Landlord, Third Series, Collected and Arranged by Jedediah Cleishbotham, Schoolmaster and Parish-Clerk of Gandercleugh [The Bride of Lammermoor and A Legend of Montrose], 4 volumes (Edinburgh: Printed for Archibald Constable, Edinburgh, and Longman, Hurst, Rees, Orme & Brown and Hurst, Robinson, London, 1819; New York: Published by Charles Wiley, W. B. Gilley and A. T. Goodrich, printed by Clayton & Kingsland, 1819; Philadelphia: M. Thomas, 1819);

Ivanhoe; A Romance, by "the Author of Waverley" &c. (3 volumes, Edinburgh: Printed for Archibald Constable, Edinburgh, and Hurst, Robinson, London, 1819; 2 volumes, Philadelphia: M. Carey & Son, 1820);

The Monastery. A Romance. By the Author of "Waverley" (3 volumes, Edinburgh: Printed for Longman, Hurst, Rees, Orme & Brown, London, and for Archibald Constable and John Ballantyne, Edinburgh, 1820; 1 volume, Philadelphia: Published by M. Carey & Son, 1820);

The Abbot. by the Author of "Waverley" (3 volumes, Edinburgh: Printed for Longman, Hurst, Rees, Orme & Brown, London, and for Archibald Constable and John Ballantyne,

Edinburgh, 1820; 2 volumes, New York: J. & J. Harper, 1820; 1 volume, Philadelphia: M. Carey & Son, 1820);

Kenilworth; A Romance. By the Author of "Waverley," "Ivanhoe," &c. (3 volumes, Edinburgh: Printed for Archibald Constable and John Ballantyne, Edinburgh, and Hurst, Robinson, London, 1821; Hartford: S. G. Goodrich, 1821; Philadelphia: M. Carey & Son, 1821);

The Pirate. By the Author of "Waverley," "Kenilworth," &c. (3 volumes, Edinburgh: Printed for Archibald Constable, and Hurst, Robinson, London, 1821; 2 volumes, Boston: Wells & Lilly, 1822; 1 volume, Hartford: S. G. Goodrich and Huntington & Hopkins, 1822; 2 volumes, New York: E. Duyckinck, 1822; 1 volume, Philadelphia: H. C. Carey & I. Lea, 1822);

The Fortunes of Nigel. By the Author of "Waverley," "Kenilworth," &c. (3 volumes, Edinburgh: Printed for Archibald Constable, Edinburgh, and Hurst, Robinson, London, 1822; 2 volumes, New York: T. Longworth, 1822; Philadelphia: Carey & Lea, 1822;

Halidon Hill: A Dramatic Sketch (Edinburgh: Printed for Archibald Constable, and Hurst,

Robinson, London, 1822; New York: S. Campbell, printed by E. B. Clayton, 1822; Philadelphia: H. C. Carey & I. Lea, 1822);

Peveril of the Peak. By the Author of "Waverley, Kenilworth," &c. (4 volumes, Edinburgh: Printed for Archibald Constable, Edinburgh, and Hurst, Robinson, London, 1823; 3 volumes, Philadelphia: H. C. Carey & I. Lea, 1823);

Quentin Durward. By the Author of "Waverley, Peveril of the Peak," &c. (3 volumes, Edinburgh: Printed for Archibald Constable, Edinburgh, and Hurst, Robinson, London, 1823; 1 volume, Philadelphia: H. C. Carey & I. Lea, 1823);

St Ronan's Well. By the Author of "Waverley, Quentin Durward," &c. (3 volumes, Edinburgh: Printed for Archibald Constable, Edinburgh, and Hurst, Robinson, London, 1823; Philadelphia: H. C. Carey & I. Lea, 1824);

Redgauntlet. A Tale of the Eighteenth Century. By the Author of "Waverley" (3 volumes, Edinburgh: Printed for Archibald Constable, Edinburgh, and Hurst, Robinson, London, 1824; 2 volumes, Philadelphia: H. C. Carey & I. Lea, 1824);

Tales of the Crusaders, by the Author of Waverley [The Betrothed and *The Talisman]* (4 volumes, Edinburgh: Printed for Archibald Constable, Edinburgh, and Hurst, Robinson, London, 1825; New York: Published by E. Duyckinck, Collins & Hannay, Collins, E. Bliss & E. White, and W. B. Gilley, printed by J. & J. Harper, 1825; 2 volumes, Philadelphia: H. C. Carey & I. Lea, 1825);

Woodstock; or, the Cavalier. A Tale of the Year Sixteen Hundred and Fifty-One. By the Author of "Waverley, Tales of the Crusaders," &c. (3 volumes, Edinburgh: Printed for Archibald Constable, Edinburgh, and Longman, Rees, Orme, Brown & Green, London, 1826; 2 volumes, Philadelphia: H. C. Carey & I. Lea, 1826);

Chronicles of the Canongate; By the Author of "Waverley," &c. *[The Highland Widow; The Two Drovers; The Surgeon's Daughter]* (2 volumes, Edinburgh: Printed for Cadell, Edinburgh, and Simpkin & Marshall, London, 1827; 1 volume, Philadelphia: Carey, Lea & Carey, 1827);

The Life of Napoleon Bonaparte, 9 volumes (Edinburgh: Printed by Ballantyne, for Longman, Rees, Orme, Brown & Green, London, 1827; Philadelphia: Carey, Lea & Carey, 1827);

Chronicles of the Canongate. Second Series. By the Author of "Waverley" &c. *[The Fair Maid of Perth]* (3 volumes, Edinburgh: Printed by Cadell, Edinburgh, and Simpkin & Marshall, London, 1828; 1 volume, Philadelphia: Carey, Lea & Carey, 1828);

Anne of Geierstein; or The Maiden in the Mist. By the Author of "Waverley," &c. (3 volumes, Edinburgh: Printed for Cadell, Edinburgh, and Simpkin & Marshall, London, 1829; 2 volumes, Philadelphia: Carey, Lea & Carey, 1829);

The Doom of Devorgoil, A Melo-drama. Auchindrane; or, the Ayrshire Tragedy (Edinburgh: Printed for Cadell, Edinburgh, and Simpkin & Marshall, London, 1830; New York: Printed by J. & J. Harper, 1830;

Letters on Demonology and Witchcraft (London: J. Murray, 1830; New York: J. & J. Harper, 1830);

Tales of My Landlord, Fourth and Last Series Collected and Arranged by Jedediah Cleishbotham, Schoolmaster and Parish-Clerk of Gandercleugh [Count Robert of Paris and *Castle Dangerous]* (4 volumes, Edinburgh: Printed for Robert Cadell, Edinburgh, and Whitaker, London, 1832; 3 volumes, Philadelphia: Carey & Lea, 1832);

The Journal of Sir Walter Scott, edited by W. E. K. Anderson (Oxford: Clarendon Press, 1972).

Collections: *Waverley Novels,* 48 volumes, with Scott's prefaces and final revisions (Edinburgh: Cadell, 1829-1833);

Miscellaneous Prose Works, 30 volumes, edited by John Gibson Lockhart (Edinburgh: R. Cadell, 1834-1846);

The Poetical Works of Sir Walter Scott, With the Author's Introductions and Notes, edited by J. Logie Robertson (London: H. Frowde, 1894);

Scott on Himself: A Collection of the Autobiographical Writings of Sir Walter Scott, edited by David Hewitt (Edinburgh: Scottish Academic Press, 1981).

OTHER: *Goetz of Berlichingen, With the Iron Hand: A Tragedy. Translated from the German of Goethe,* translated by Scott (London: Printed for J. Bell, 1799);

"The Fire King," "Glenfinlas," "The Eve of Saint John," "Frederick and Alice," and "The Wild Huntsmen," in *Tales of Wonder; Written and Collected by M. G. Lewis, Esq. M.P.,* 2 volumes (London: Printed by W. Bulmer for

Scott at age six (by permission of the Scottish National Portrait Gallery)

the author & sold by J. Bell, 1801), I: 62-69, 122-136, 137-147, 148-152, 153-163;

Minstrelsy of the Scottish Border, 2 volumes, edited by Scott (Kelso: Printed by James Ballantyne for T. Cadell, Jun. & W. Davies, London, and sold by Manners & Miller and A. Constable, Edinburgh, 1802); enlarged edition, 3 volumes (Edinburgh: Printed by James Ballantyne for Longman & Rees, London, and sold by Manners & Miller and A. Constable, Edinburgh, 1803; Philadelphia: Carey, 1813;

Sir Tristrem; A Metrical Romance of the Thirteenth Century; by Thomas of Ercildoune, edited and completed by Scott (Edinburgh: Printed by James Ballantyne for Archibald Constable, Edinburgh, and Longman & Rees, London, 1804);

The Works of John Dryden, 18 volumes, edited, with a biography, by Scott (London: Miller, 1808);

The Works of Jonathan Swift, 19 volumes, edited by Scott (Edinburgh: Constable, 1814).

Writing toward the close of 1818 on the state of contemporary literature, John Keats remarked: "We have seen three literary kings in our Time–Scott–Byron–and then the scotch novels." The same year, William Hazlitt had stated in the last of the *Lectures on the English Poets* that "Walter Scott is the most popular of all the poets of the present day, and deservedly so." Today, Scott's poetry has been all but forgotten, although the "scotch novels" continue to be read and occasionally taught. Scott's poetic career and reputation present an especially intriguing problem for literary biography: Why one of the most popular British poets of all time should at present find only a small place, if that, in anthologies and histories of British Romantic poetry. The answer probably has as much to do with the history of literature and literary criticism since the Roman-

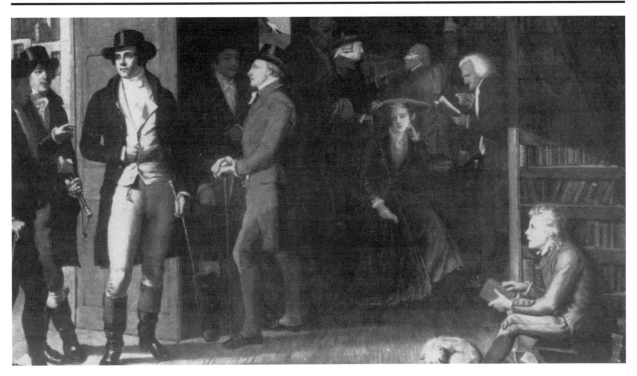

James Sibbald's Bookshop, 1786 (painting by William Borthwick Johnston; by permission of the Edinburgh Booksellers' Society). The people portrayed are Hugh Blair; Henry Mackenzie; Robert Burns; Alexander Nasmyth; David Allan; James Bruce; James Burnett, Lord Monboddo; Elizabeth Burnett; James Sibbald; Adam Ferguson; and Scott.

Young Scott meeting Robert Burns, at Sciennes Hill House, the home of Professor Adam Ferguson, winter 1786-1787

tic period as it does with the nature and quality of Scott's poetic works.

The son of Walter and Anne Rutherford Scott, Walter Scott was born in Edinburgh, 15 August 1771 (or possibly 1770). His father was a lawyer and strict Presbyterian; Scott singled out among his ancestors some of the romantic Border figures he commemorated in his poetry, such as "Auld Watt of Harden and his fair dame, the Flower of Yarrow," and his paternal great-grandfather Walter Scott ("Beardie"), a near-martyr to the Jacobite cause. In Scott's genealogy one can see already the tension between realism and romanticism that would mark his life and literary career, and which he would embody in the hero of his first novel, *Waverley* (1814). When a fever (probably a symptom of infantile paralysis) left his right leg lame, Scott, then eighteen months old, was sent to live at Sandyknowe, his grandfather Robert Scott's farm, where it was hoped that fresh air and "natural exertion" would cure him. Here Scott spent a pastoral childhood, hearing tales of Border outlaws (including his ancestor Watt) and Jacobite martyrs, and learning to recite ballads before he could read.

Scott returned to live with his parents in 1775 and, beginning in October 1779, attended the High School and University at Edinburgh, which then boasted one of the finest educational systems in Europe. Scott began reading law under his father in March 1786 and took more university courses in 1789-1792, but he described himself as a dilatory student and as largely self-educated. Scott was an omnivorous reader, especially (like Edward Waverley) of "all that was adventurous and romantic"; he wrote in retrospect that he had "read as much nonsense of this class as any man now living." His youthful reading of Edmund Spenser, Torquato Tasso, and of Thomas Percy's *Reliques of Ancient English Poetry* (1765) did much to shape his later poetic career, as did his many expeditions to the countryside collecting ballads, local legends, and folklore. A half-year spent (in 1788) in the country at Kelso, "the most beautiful, if not the most romantic village in Scotland," again for reasons of health, left him with an "insatiable passion" for natural beauty. While Scott apprenticed in his father's profession, passing the examination in Scots Law in July 1792, he continued his voracious reading and joined several literary and debating societies, which exposed him to Edinburgh's vital intellectual world. Encouraged by his Edinburgh friends, Scott translated (or, as he put it, "bal-

ladized") Gottfried Augustus Bürger's *Lenore* and *Der Wilde Jäger*, which led to his first publication, a small quarto volume entitled *The Chase, and William and Helen: Two Ballads from the German of Gottfried Augustus Bürger* (1796). Although not much noticed in London, the volume was praised by Scott's friends, and he followed up with a prose translation of Johann Wolfgang von Goethe's *Goetz von Berlichingen* in 1799. Meanwhile, Scott began his association with Matthew Gregory Lewis, whose novel *The Monk* had made a sensation in 1796, and (influenced by Lewis's own poetry) Scott contributed several ballads to Lewis's *Tales of Wonder* (1801). On 24 December 1797, only about a year after losing a woman he had loved passionately for three years, Scott married Charlotte Carpenter, the daughter of a Frenchwoman living in England.

Scott's first important publication was the *Minstrelsy of the Scottish Border,* which appeared in two volumes in 1802 and in an enlarged, three-volume edition in 1803. In these volumes Scott's interests as a poet, an antiquarian, and a Scottish cultural nationalist came together for the first time. In the first two volumes Scott gathered together a large number of Scottish ballads and, in the copious introductions, appendices, and notes, a great deal of Scottish folklore, legends, and historical curiosities. The third volume was devoted to "Imitations of the Ancient Ballad" by Scott and his collaborators; already Scott had begun the patronage of lesser Scottish writers which he would continue throughout his career. Scott's contributions included "Glenfinlas," a powerful ballad somewhat in Lewis's style with thematic affinities to Samuel Taylor Coleridge's *Christabel* (1816) and John Keats's *Lamia* (1820), and "The Gray Brother," an early example of the Romantic fragment poem. "Thomas the Rhymer" shows the continuity between Scott's antiquarianism and his poetry: "Part First" is a transcription of a fifteenth-century ballad attributed to Thomas; "Part Second" a "cento" of prophecies traditionally attributed to Thomas; "Part Third" Scott's own continuation of the ballad based on popular legends regarding Thomas's return to fairyland. *Sir Tristrem,* originally intended for *Minstrelsy of the Scottish Border* but published separately in 1804, similarly moves from Scott's redaction of a late medieval poem attributed to Thomas of Erceldoune (the same "Thomas the Rhymer") to a continuation in Scott's own style.

The publication of *The Lay of the Last Minstrel* in 1805 marked the real beginning of Scott's

Scott at twenty-six or twenty-seven, wearing the uniform of the Royal Edinburgh Light Dragoons (portrait by an unknown artist; with kind permission of Mrs. Maxwell-Scott of Abbotsford)

prolific literary career. Up to this point Scott's work as antiquary, translator, editor, and poet had remained secondary to his career as a barrister (which he followed with indifferent success) and his sinecure as sheriff of Selkirkshire, which began in 1800 and led to his taking Ashestiel, "situated in a wild pastoral country" on the banks of the Tweed, as his country house in 1804. Scott had begun writing *The Lay of the Last Minstrel* as a Border ballad for the third volume of *Minstrelsy of the Scottish Border;* its subject was suggested by Scott's "lovely chieftainess," Harriet, Countess of Dalkeith (later Duchess of Buccleuch), who requested a ballad on Gilpin Horner, a goblinlike figure from Border lore. Scott took the meter from Coleridge's as yet unpublished *Christabel,* which he had heard recited the year before and had characteristically retained in his prodigious memory.

The work grew under Scott's hands and resulted in a romance of six cantos, which he completed "at about the rate of a canto per week." It was an immediate success with the public and went through fourteen editions; Scott's biographer (and son-in-law) John Gibson Lockhart states that "in the history of British Poetry nothing had ever equalled the demand for *The Lay of the Last Minstrel.*" Its success allowed Scott to "resign the active pursuit of an honorable profession for the more precarious resources of literature." At this time also Scott began his partnership with the printer, and later publisher, James Ballantyne, which initially helped Scott realize still greater profits from his works but eventually proved his financial undoing.

The frame of the poem, in which the last of the Border minstrels sings his "unpremeditated

Scott's wife, Charlotte (portrait by James Saxon; with kind permission of Mrs. Maxwell-Scott of Abbotsford)

Ashetiel, Scott's country house from 1804 until 1812 (engraving based on a watercolor by J. M. W. Turner)

Harriet, Countess of Dalkeith, the friend who inspired Scott to write The Lay of the Last Minstrel *(in the collection of the Duke of Buccleuch and Queensberry KT)*

Illustration by Scott's friend Sir William Allan for The Lay of the Last Minstrel *(pen and wash drawing; by permission of the National Gallery of Scotland)*

lay" to the then countess of Dalkeith, is set in the late seventeenth century; the minstrel's narrative itself concerns the feudal exploits of the Scott clan in the mid sixteenth century. *The Lay of the Last Minstrel* is in a variable ballad stanza (still less regular than that of its model, *Christabel)* and employs a loose narrative structure that allows for digressions, lays within the lay, and periodic returns to the frame. It is filled with references to Border superstitions, historical and quasi-historical events, and chivalric doings. As with *Minstrelsy of the Scottish Border,* and indeed many of Scott's works, the notes add much to the poem's interest. The story itself, which concerns the Ladye of Branksome Hall, a sorceress and widow to Sir Walter Scott of Buccleuch (an ancestor of both the duke of Buccleuch and Walter Scott himself), her feuds with the Cranstoun clan and with the English across the border, and the Romeo and Juliet romance between her daughter Margaret and the heir of the Cranstouns, often seems a mere vehicle for the poem's antiquarian, folkloric, and historical references and its descriptive passages. In the sixth canto the narrative is suspended altogether and the work becomes a kind of ballad anthology as a group of bards takes turns at the harp; one of the songs, that of the bard Fitzraver beginning " 'Twas All-soul's eve," is in Spenserian stanzas and anticipates Keats's *Eve of St. Agnes* (1820).

Scott, however, was not particularly interested in attaining unity in his poems; as long as the narrative held interest (and it did for generations of readers) he was content. Indeed, Scott valued the romance form precisely for its openness: "the author is absolute master of his country and its inhabitants, and everything is permitted to him, excepting to be heavy or prosaic, for which, free and unembarrassed as he is, he has no manner of apology." *The Lay of the Last Minstrel* succeeds more in parts than as a whole: the introduction, which describes the ancient and dejected bard, and constitutes an implicit commentary on the debased status of poetry in nineteenth-century society; the famous description of the half-ruinous Melrose Abbey, which Fanny Price cites approvingly in Jane Austen's *Mansfield Park* (1814); the Gothicism surrounding the tomb of the wizard, Michael Scott; the ritualistic single combat between the English and Scots champions. A more serious charge against the poem, made by its first reviewers and ever since, concerns the author's frequent carelessness in matters of composition. As a poet if not as a man,

Scott conforms too well to the popular image of the Romantic poet: he wrote hastily and hated to revise. Despite the advantages of an irregular stanza and measure, Scott botches an occasional rhyme, relies on awkward ellipses, too often fills out lines with repetitions, and, in Francis Jeffrey's phrase, "presented us with such combinations of meter, as must put the teeth of his readers, we think, into some jeopardy" *(Edinburgh Review,* April 1805). Nevertheless, Scott succeeded in his object, the "attempt to return to a more simple and natural style of poetry" through reviving the open form of the romance and the earthy vocabulary of the ballad; if overrated by Scott's generation, *The Lay of the Last Minstrel* is underrated by ours.

From this period on, Scott led the life of a Scottish man of letters so engagingly evoked by Lockhart in his well-known biography. Scott was too practical to depend entirely on literature: in addition to his sheriffship, he was appointed Clerk of Sessions in 1806, although he did not begin receiving his sinecure until 1812. He wrote essays for the *Edinburgh Review,* edited by his friend Francis Jeffrey, and in 1808 brought out a critical edition in eighteen volumes of Dryden's works with a biography. He continued as silent partner to Ballantyne, who expanded his printing business to a publishing house after Scott quarreled with his Edinburgh publishers over delays with his edition of Swift's works (eventually published, in nineteen volumes, in 1814). During the same period Scott worked sporadically on his next poetic romance, *Marmion: A Tale of Flodden Field,* also published in 1808.

Like *The Lay of the Last Minstrel, Marmion* is in six cantos and employs a variable stanza composed mostly of tetrameter lines, irregularly varied with trimeter lines. Again Scott uses a framing technique to great effect: here the "Border Minstrel" is Scott himself, who in introductory epistles to each canto addresses his friends, describes his life and surroundings, and defends his use of popular superstitions, his "wild measure rude and bold," and his revival of "legendary lay" and "old romance." Although the narrative is more unified than that of *The Lay of the Last Minstrel,* it still allows for digressive descriptive passages and interpolated tales, ballads, and lyrics, including "Lochinvar." The story mingles historical facts, legends, and conventional chivalric motifs– "Fiction's fair romantic range" and "tradition's dubious light"–with Scott's masterly natural and architectural descriptions and his adaptations of

Scott in the ruins of Hermitage Castle with the mountains of Liddesdale in the background, 1808 (portrait by Henry Raeburn; in the collection of the Duke of Buccleuch and Queensberry KT)

contemporary literary modes as well. Scott borrows most effectively from the Gothic novel, another form based in part on reviving the romance, and the influence especially of Lewis's *The Monk* and Ann Radcliffe's *The Italian* (1797) is seen in the poem's obsessive Abbess, Constance's live burial in a convent vault, and the ambivalent character of the hero-villain, Marmion. Even Marmion's most abject deed–the forgery which Scott's contemporaries found so unchivalric as to spoil the poem's full effect–works quite well within the world of Gothic conventions, with the fragmentary, lost, or illegible texts and general semiotic confusion that mark so many Gothic novels of the time. The poem's conclusion, in which Marmion's apparently supernatural encounter with the "Elfin Knight" is ex-

posed as a meeting between Marmion and his disguised archrival, de Wilton, is also typical of Radcliffe's novels.

Marmion was another huge success with the reading public: it went through thirteen editions and sold more than thirty thousand copies between 1808 and 1825. Its critical reception was less spectacular. Jeffrey, who had reviewed *The Lay of the Last Minstrel* quite favorably, attacked *Marmion* in the *Edinburgh Review* (April 1808), faulting Scott for "tedious, hasty, and injudicious composition" and characterizing his poetry as "a broken narrative–a redundancy of minute description–bursts of unequal and energetic poetry–a general tone of spirit and animation, unchecked by timidity or affectation, and unchastised by any great delicacy of taste, or elegance

Where hedge-rows spread a verdant screen
And spires and forests intervene
And the neat cottage peeps between?
No, no! for there will he exchange
His dark Lochaber's boundless range
Nor for gay Devon's meads forsake
Benevis grey and Garry's lake.

Thus, while I ape the measure wild
Of tales that charmed me yet a child
Rude though they be still with the chime
Returns the thoughts of early time
And feelings waked in life's first day †
Glow in the line and prompt the lay.
Then rise that hill, that mountain tower
That fixed Attention's dawning hour
Where no broad river swept along †
To wake perchance heroic song
Where sighed no groves in summer gale
To prompt of love a softer tale
Where scarce a puny streamlet's speed †
Claimed homage from a shepherd's reed
                lonely
It was a ~~naked~~ scene and wild
Where ~~between scene as lonely~~ naked rocks were
                                rudely piled
But ever and anon between
Lay velvet tufts of loveliest green
And well the lonely infant knew
Recesses where the woodbine grew ✗

Page from the manuscript for Marmion *(Adv. Ms. 19.1.16; by permission of the Trustees of the National Library of Scotland, Edinburgh)*

of fancy." Soon after, Scott ceased reviewing for the *Edinburgh Review* and helped found its rival, the *Quarterly Review,* although the move probably had more to do with politics (Scott was a conservative Tory, Jeffrey a liberal Whig) than with personal resentment. Hearing that Scott had been paid an unprecedented thousand pounds for *Marmion* sight unseen, Byron included a scathing passage in *English Bards and Scotch Reviewers* (1809) on Scott's "prostituted Muse," dismissing Marmion as "Not quite a Felon, yet but half a Knight, / . . . / A mighty mixture of the great and base." Ironically, *Marmion* is now remembered chiefly as a source for Byron's verse tales, and particularly as the medium between such Gothic villains as Lewis's Ambrosio and Radcliffe's Schedoni and the morally ambivalent "Byronic hero." Scott and Byron eventually became friends, and Byron staunchly supported Scott's poetry over that of Wordsworth and Coleridge.

In the third and last of his truly successful romances, *The Lady of the Lake* (1810), Scott shifted his ground from the Border to the Highlands. Again in six cantos, and composed mostly of rather facile tetrameter couplets, *The Lady of the Lake* is the most unified of the three poems and the only one which is well plotted. It is also the poem of Scott's which is most "Romantic" as the term has been conventionally understood. Much of the natural description is quite compelling, particularly the opening portrayal of Loch Katrine, with the Highland peaks depicted as fantastic architecture and the rocky outcroppings nearer the loch as "fragments of an earlier world." Scott's use of popular superstitions in this work for once evokes less Gothicism or local-color writing such as Maria Edgeworth's than the "supernaturalism" associated with Coleridge and Shelley; the description of the half-pagan Brian the Hermit especially anticipates such Shelleyan figures as the Alastor poet and Prince Athanase. Ellen Douglas, the only engaging heroine in Scott's poetry, initially seems with her "light skiff " another figure out of Shelley. Other elements are developed from Scott's earlier romances: the chivalric middle-aged hero, James Fitz-James (James V); the hero-villain, Roderick Dhu, who inherits traits from Deloraine (in *The Lay of the Last Minstrel)* and Marmion; the prophetic minstrel, Allan-bane; and the general emphasis on feudal manners and furniture.

The popular reception of *The Lady of the Lake* was, again, everything Scott could wish: five editions were exhausted within a year, bringing the early sales to some twenty thousand copies. The poem even helped boost the Scottish tourist industry. According to Lockhart, "the whole country rang with the praises of the poet–crowds set off to view the scenery of Loch Katrine, till then comparatively unknown; and as the book came out just before the season for excursions, every house and inn in that neighborhood was crammed with a constant succession of visitors." (Scott's novel *Waverley* would later inspire a fashion for wearing plaids which is still with us.) The critical reception was on the whole the warmest accorded to any of Scott's poems. Jeffrey rehabilitated Scott as a kind of literary paradox: the great original poet of the commonplace and derivative. Although objecting to the usual flaws, he named *The Lady of the Lake* "one of the most attractive poems in the language" *(Edinburgh Review,* August 1810). Coleridge, on the other hand, demolished the poem in a letter to Wordsworth (early October 1810), going through stanzas line by line for faults in diction, usage, and grammar, detecting borrowings from his own and Wordsworth's poetry, and summarizing: "In short, what I felt in *Marmion,* I feel still more in the Lady of the Lake–viz. that a man accustomed to cast words in metre and familiar with descriptive Poets & Tourists, himself a Picturesque Tourist, must be troubled with a mental Stangury, if he could not lift up his leg six times at six different Corners, and each time p– a canto." Scott himself, who though proud of his popular success remained rather suspicious toward it, seems to have agreed more with Coleridge than with the reviewers: when Ballantyne asked Scott's daughter what she thought of the poem, she answered, "Oh, I have not read it: papa says there's nothing so bad for young people as reading bad poetry."

In 1811 Scott brought out *The Vision of Don Roderick,* a relatively short work in Spenserian stanzas, which he wrote to benefit the relief fund for Portuguese victims of the Peninsular conflict. Although the "vision" is set up promisingly, in a medieval Spain "Where wonders wild of Arabesque combine / With Gothic imagery of darker shade," the pageant of Spanish history from the Moorish conquest to the British involvement in the campaign against Bonaparte is dull and frequently obscure; Scott's portrayal of Napoleon is no more than a chauvinistic caricature; and even the concluding list of British heroes was attacked in the reviews for Scott's partisan bias (a noted Whig hero, though a fellow Scot, was conspicuously left out). During this year Scott let the lease

1)

The Lady of the Lake
Canto Third

Time rolls his ceaseless course. ǁ The race of yore
    Who danced our infancy upon their knee,
And told our marvelling boy-hood legends store,
    Of their strange ventures hap'd by land or sea,
How are they blotted from the things that be!
    How few, all weak and ~~wrinkled~~ withovd of their force,
Wait on the verge of dark eternity,
    Like stranded wrecks, the tide returning hoarse
To sweep them from our sight! ǁ Time rolls his ceaseless
                                            course. ⸿

Yet live there still who can remember well
    How, when a mountain Chief his bugle blew,
Both field and forest, dingle, cliff, and dell
    And solitary heath the signal knew;
And fast the faithful clan around him drew,
    What time the warning note was keenly wound,
What time aloft the kindred banner flew,
    While clamorous war-pipes yell'd the gathering
                                            sound, ⸿
And while the Fiery Cross glanced, like a meteor, round.

Abbotsford in 1812 (engraving from a 1901 edition of John Gibson Lockhart's Memoirs of the Life of Sir Walter Scott) *and in 1837, after Scott's extensive renovations and additions (engraving by Thomas Prior, based on a drawing by Thomas Allom)*

of Ashestiel expire and bought the estate he called Abbotsford. Scott obsessively enlarged and improved the property over the next dozen years, transforming the main house into a neo-Gothic manor and becoming known as the "Laird of Abbotsford." His hunger for adjoining estates helped keep his finances on the stretch and contributed to his later crash.

Scott's obsession with Abbotsford affected his literary output as well; toward the end of 1811 he wrote his friend John Bacon Sawney Morritt, who held the estate of Rokeby: "I want to build my cottage a little better than my limited finances will permit out of my ordinary income; and although it is very true that an author should not hazard his reputation, yet, as Bob Acres says, I really think Reputation should take some care of the gentleman in return." The result was *Rokeby* (1813), another romance in six cantos, again in the easy octosyllabic couplets Scott had used for *The Lady of the Lake*. The poem is set in Yorkshire immediately after Marston Moor (3 July 1644), one of the decisive battles of the English Revolution, but the Cavalier-Puritan conflict is only incidental to the complicated plot. Far too much of the poem is devoted to describing the Rokeby estate and surrounding countryside, which Scott visited for the purpose. The poem's sales were more than respectable, and the reviews somewhat less than respectful. Although Scott's descriptive and narrative powers were again attested to, Scott was seen as beginning to repeat himself, in the verse form, in the plot's by-now formulaic heroics, in particular images (one reviewer complained of too many "bowers and towers": "wherever we see the one, we may be sure the other is not far behind"). Lockhart detected Scott's self-portrait in Wilfrid, the "sickly boy" grown "visionary" poet, who, like Scott, loses his first love. As a poet, however, Scott is much more successful at describing the middle-aged and old than the young; the sections of *Rokeby* dealing with the young people, especially canto 5, are stilted and melodramatic even for Scott. And without the feudal Scottish setting, much of the poetry's incidental charm is lost. *Rokeby* most comes alive when featuring Bertram, a grizzled, amoral buccaneer who, like Scott's earlier heroic villains, is "irregularly great"; surprisingly, even his sixth-canto change of heart is convincing.

In the *Edinburgh Annual Register* for 1809 Scott had anonymously published three imitations of popular living poets–George Crabbe,

Thomas Moore, and himself. Scott was sufficiently pleased with the success of this hoax that he developed the self-imitation into a poem in three cantos, *The Bridal of Triermain* (1813), which appeared anonymously shortly after *Rokeby*. Scott's friend William Erskine supplied a preface, written from Scott's notes, which gives an important early definition of "romantic poetry" (basically opposing the open romance form to the more structured epic). The poem is a romance based on a variant of "Sleeping Beauty": Sir Roland of Triermain wakes the sleeping Gyneth, who 501 years earlier (as we learn in an interpolated tale) was fathered by King Arthur on the half-mortal, half-genie Guendolen. The romance is enclosed by a syrupy modern frame tale in which Arthur, a middle-class poet, tells the aristocratic Lucy the story of Triermain in the process of luring her into an elopement and marriage. The reviewers were taken in and accepted the poem as a clever imitation of Scott. This same year Scott was offered the laureateship, which he turned down in favor of Robert Southey, less from his modesty regarding his own poetry (he did not think much more highly of Southey's) than because he held two lucrative government sinecures already.

In retrospect, one can see in the elaborately plotted *Rokeby* Scott moving toward the novel form, as the next year saw the anonymous publication of *Waverley* (1814). Perhaps Scott's greatest work, *Waverley* was an immediate popular and critical success, and in the novel Scott found a form still more congenial than the romance: as Lockhart wrote, "he had seized on an instrument of wider compass, and which, handled with whatever rapidity, seemed to reveal at every touch treasures that had hitherto slept unconsciously within him." With the success of his next novel, *Guy Mannering*, and the relative failure of another verse romance, *The Lord of the Isles*, occurring in the same year (1815), Scott turned his energies almost exclusively to what became known as the "Waverley novels" (Scott did not publicly acknowledge his authorship until 1827). Despite its Scottish setting and the presence of Robert the Bruce, the Scottish national hero, at its center, *The Lord of the Isles* did not sell terribly well and the reviews were quite hard on it. Francis Hodgson wrote in the *Monthly Review* (March 1815): "We really believe that he *cannot* write correct English; and we therefore dismiss him as an *incurable*. . . ." At the same time, Scott's popular reputation was being eclipsed by that of Byron,

Sir Walter Scott, 1822 (portrait by Sir Henry Raeburn; by permission of the Scottish National Portrait Gallery)

whose verse tales owed more than a little to Scott's romances. Scott, "the Monarch of Parnassus" (according to Byron in 1813), now effectively abdicated in favor of the younger poet, although he was to publish two more poetic volumes. *The Field of Waterloo*, published in 1815, was, like *The Vision of Don Roderick*, a benefit performance, and, also like it, it featured a chauvinistic attack on Napoleon which offended the reviewers. Due to its topicality (it appeared only a few months after the battle of Waterloo, much of it being written on a visit to the battlefield), the work was more successful than either *Rokeby* or *The Lord of the Isles* had been. Scott continued putting most of his creative spirit into the "Scotch novels" (the novels with Scottish settings written before *Ivanhoe); The Antiquary, The Black Dwarf*, and *Old Mortality* all appeared in 1816. In 1817 Scott brought out his

last six-canto romance, *Harold the Dauntless*, published anonymously as by "the author of *The Bridal of Triermain*": like this earlier poem, it was begun as an imitation. The cartoonlike narrative, featuring a boisterous, club-wielding Viking, does nothing to redeem the hasty writing; if Scott was imitating himself in *The Bridal of Triermain* and *The Lord of the Isles*, he seems to be parodying himself (and Byron) in *Harold the Dauntless*. The poem was treated dismissively in the reviews.

Scott's poetic career did not end entirely with his last book-length romance, however, as he brilliantly worked a number of ballads, songs, and other lyrics into his novels. Gothic writers such as Radcliffe (in *The Romance of the Forest*, 1791) and Lewis (in *The Monk*) had revived the convention of interspersing lyric poems in prose narratives, characteristic of earlier English romances

Scott with family and friends, 1825: Archibald Constable, James Hogg, John Gibson Lockhart, Scott, Anne Scott, Lady Scott, Sophia Scott Lockhart, Maria Edgeworth, Walter Scott (son), Anne Scott (niece), Harriet Edgeworth, Charles Scott, and R. Shortreed (painting by William Stewart Watson; from a 1901 edition of Lockhart's Memoirs of the Life of Sir Walter Scott, Bart.*)*

such as Sir Philip Sidney's *Arcadia* (1590, 1593) and Thomas Lodge's *Rosalynde* (1590). But Scott used this device to much greater effect than did his Gothic predecessors. Scott's early mastery of song and ballad forms enabled him to use such pieces quite deftly to establish atmosphere and character, and his use of interpolated lyrics to comment on or foreshadow the action of the novels is often quite subtle and effective. In *Waverley*, for example, Flora's oral translation of the bardic "Battle Song" is dramatically interrupted by Fergus just at the point where it would reveal to Waverley his own growing implication in the Jacobite uprising; earlier in the novel Waverley's poem "Mirkwood Mere" not only does much toward revealing his romantic character but foreshadows (in a manner the poet himself cannot yet appreciate) the eventual destruction of his "fond ideal world" as well.

Scott continued to write novels at the rate of more than one a year until the end of his life, including *Rob Roy* (1818), *The Heart of Mid Lothian*

(1818), *The Bride of Lammermoor* (1819), *Ivanhoe* (1819), *Quentin Durward* (1823), and *Redgauntlet* (1824); while he tried his hand at drama and continued to produce antiquarian and historical works, his later career belongs mainly to the history of the novel. The growing popularity and fame of the "Waverley novels" made Scott one of the foremost writers in Europe as well as in Great Britain. In 1820 he was created baronet, and in 1822 he stage-managed George IV's visit to Scotland. In 1826 the printing firm of James Ballantyne was implicated in the bankruptcy of publishing houses in London and Edinburgh; Scott, as Ballantyne's partner, assumed the firm's considerable debts (about fourteen thousand pounds). He worked out a compromise with the creditors through which he would hold on to Abbotsford but lose all profits from his literary work until the debts were paid; always prolific, Scott forced himself to become even more so in order to clear his name. On 21 September 1832 Scott died at Abbotsford.

Portrait by Daniel Maclise in the Fraser's Magazine *"Gallery of Illustrious Literary Characters" (1830-1838)*

If Scott's reputation as a novelist has had its fluctuations, his reputation as a poet, once so high, has steadily decreased until, at present, his poems are virtually unknown beyond their titles even to many scholars of the Romantic period. Part of the blame at least must be laid to Scott's haste and his carelessness as a stylist: he wrote too quickly, and too much. Jeffrey's harsh review of *Marmion* asked Scott to think on his posthumous reputation, but Scott seemed almost congenitally unable to hold back his poems long enough to revise them; as he wrote his friend Anne, Lady Abercorn, regarding *The Lady of the Lake:* "I have always been, God help me, too poor and too impatient to let my poems lie by me for years, or for months either; on the contrary, they have hitherto been always sent to the press before they were a third part finished. This is, to be sure, a very reprehensible practice in many re-

spects, and I hope I shall get the better of it next time." He never did. Perhaps more important, Scott's poetry seemed lacking in depth and complexity at a time when these qualities were becoming more and more looked for in "modern poetry." Jeffrey's characterization of Scott as the poet of the commonplace stuck; William Hazlitt located the secret of Scott's success in the obviousness of his poetry: "It has neither depth, height, nor breadth in it; neither uncommon strength, nor uncommon refinement of thought, sentiment, or language. It has no originality." The flatness of Scott's poetry became seen increasingly as an almost total lack of interiority. Thomas Carlyle wrote in reviewing Lockhart's biography that "there is nothing spiritual in him; all is economical, material, of the earth earthly" (*London and Westminster Review,* January 1838). William Wordsworth similarly remarked in 1844, "as a poet

Scott *cannot* live, for he has never in verse written anything addressed to the immortal part of man." Hazlitt's later comment on Scott's poetry in *The Spirit of the Age* (1825) sums it up: "it wanted *character*."

Unlike most twentieth-century readers, however, Scott's contemporaries located strengths in Scott's poetry as well. For Hazlitt as for Jeffrey, Scott excelled at description: "He describes that which is most easily and generally understood with more vivacity and effect than any body else." Wordsworth followed Jeffrey in acknowledging Scott's almost unparalleled excellence as a "master of bodily movement"; Ruskin praised Scott for his masterly use of color in physical description. What Hazlitt called Scott's "picturesque power," however, is a quality not much looked for any longer in poetry, and yet it was the one Scott himself most admired in the "ancient ballad": "Above all, to attain the highest point of his profession, the poet must have that original power of embodying and detailing circumstances, which can place before the eyes of others a scene which only exists in his own imagination." As is clear from Scott's now anachronistic uses of "original" and "imagination," his aesthetics differed significantly from that of such contemporaries as Wordsworth, Coleridge, and Shelley, and it is their terms which have shaped our own critical practice.

Another reason for the eclipse of Scott's poetic reputation can be located in the modern poet's and critic's emphasis on the short, intense lyric, a tendency that goes back at least to Edgar Allan Poe's contention that "the phrase, 'a long poem,' is simply a flat contradiction in terms." Indeed, throughout the first half of the twentieth century, Scott's slender claim to poetic fame rested almost entirely on the ballads and songs interpolated throughout the longer poems and the novels. And for a still later critical generation that saw the "greater Romantic lyric" as the English Romantic genre par excellence, Scott barely existed. When his narrative romances, however, are placed alongside those of his contemporaries–Byron's Eastern tales, Moore's *Lalla Rookh* (1817), Wordsworth's *White Doe of Rylstone* (1815), Keats's *Isabella* (1820)–*The Lay of the Last Minstrel*, *Marmion*, and *The Lady of the Lake* can more than stand up to the comparison. At one time, Scott's narrative "force" was universally acknowledged, as by Hazlitt: "He selects a story such as is sure to please, full of incidents, characters, peculiar manners, costume, and scenery; and he tells it in

a way that can offend no one. He never wearies or disappoints you." It is quite possible that in the present critical climate, marked by a much greater interest in narrative poetry, a predilection for historically engaged writing, and a more receptive attitude toward "popular" literature, Scott's poetry will come in for a minor revival, guided by an appreciation of Scott's historicism such as that of Karl Kroeber in *Romantic Narrative Art* (1960).

At the very least, Scott's role in shaping the poetic practice of his time needs to be more widely recognized in histories and general studies of British Romantic poetry. Scott enriched the poetry of his time not only in bringing the "Byronic" hero, energetic and amoral, into narrative verse, but also through incorporating elements of the traditional ballad into modern poetry, helping to define a "more simple and natural" poetic style, adding dialect and archaic terms to the poetic lexicon, reviving (with Southey) a more open narrative romance form inspired by Spenser, and helping to establish a climate for mixed genres, complex framing effects, the use of poetic fragments, and the vogue for literary "medievalism." Although we may well hesitate to bring Scott back into the Romantic canon, we cannot understand the "spirit of the age" without giving his poetry more serious attention than the past century has done.

Letters:

The Letters of Sir Walter Scott, 12 volumes, edited by H. J. C. Grierson (London: Constable, 1932-1937);

James C. Corson, *Notes and Index to Sir Herbert Grierson's Edition of the Letters of Sir Walter Scott* (Oxford: Clarendon Press, 1979).

Bibliographies:

William Ruff, *A Bibliography of the Poetical Works of Sir Walter Scott, 1796-1832* (Edinburgh: Edinburgh Bibliographical Society, 1938);

James C. Corson, *A Bibliography of Sir Walter Scott: A Classified and Annotated List of Books and Articles Relating to His Life and Works, 1797-1940* (Edinburgh: Oliver & Boyd, 1943);

James T. Hillhouse and Alexander Welsh, "Sir Walter Scott," in *The English Romantic Poets & Essayists: A Review of Research and Criticism,* revised edition, edited by Carolyn Washburn Houtchens and Lawrence Huston Houtchens (New York: Published for the

Scott in 1832 reading the proclamation issued by Mary Queen of Scots prior to her marriage to Henry Stuart, Lord Darnley (portrait by Sir William Allan; by permission of the National Portrait Gallery, London)

Modern Language Association by New York University Press, 1966), pp. 115-154;

Jill Rubenstein, *Sir Walter Scott: A Reference Guide* (Boston: G. K. Hall, 1978).

Biographies:

John Gibson Lockhart, *Memoirs of the Life of Sir Walter Scott, bart.*, 7 volumes (Edinburgh: Cadell, 1837-1838); revised edition, 10 volumes (Edinburgh: Cadell, 1839);

Edgar Johnson, *Sir Walter Scott: The Great Unknown*, 2 volumes (London: Hamilton, 1970; New York: Macmillan, 1970).

References:

J. L. Adolphus, *Letters to Richard Heber, Esq.* (London: Rodwell & Martin, 1821);

J. H. Alexander, *The Lay of the Last Minstrel: Three Essays* (Salzburg: Institut für Englische

Sprache und Literatur, 1978);

Alexander, *Marmion: Studies in Interpretation and Composition* (Salzburg: Institut für Englische Sprache und Literatur, 1981);

Alexander, *The Reception of Scott's Poetry by his Correspondents: 1796-1817*, 2 volumes (Salzburg: Institut für Englische Sprache und Literatur, 1979);

Alexander, *Two Studies in Romantic Reviewing: The Reviewing of Walter Scott's Poetry, 1805-1817* (Salzburg: Institut für Englische Sprache und Literatur, 1976);

Alexander and David Hewitt, eds., *Scott and His Influence: The Papers of the Aberdeen Scott Conference, 1982* (Aberdeen: Association for Scottish Literary Studies, 1983);

Sir R. H. Anstice, *The Poetical Heroes of Sir Walter Scott* (Aberdeen: Cornwall, 1917):

Sir Walter Scott (portrait by Edwin Landseer; in the collection of the Duke of Buccleuch and Queensberry KT)

Alan Bold, ed., *Sir Walter Scott: The Long-Forgotten Memory* (London: Vision Press, 1983);

Allston Burr, *Sir Walter Scott: An Index Placing the Short Poems in His Novels and in His Long Poems and Dramas* (Cambridge, Mass.: Harvard University Press, 1936);

Thomas Crawford, *Scott* (Edinburgh: Scottish Academy Press, 1982), pp. 1-50;

Crawford, "Scott as a Poet," *Etudes Anglaises*, 24 (October-December 1971): 478-491;

Donald Davie, "The Poetry of Sir Walter Scott," *Proceedings of the British Academy*, 47 (1961): 61-75;

Ruth Eller, "Themes of Time and Art in *The Lay of the Last Minstrel*," *Studies in Scottish Literature*, 13 (1978): 43-56;

Nancy Moore Goslee, "*Marmion* and the Meta-phor of Forgery," *Scottish Literary Journal*, 7 (May 1980): 85-96;

Goslee, "Romance as Theme and Structure in Scott's *The Lady of the Lake*," *Texas Studies in Literature and Language*, 27 (Winter 1976): 737-757;

Goslee, *Scott the Rhymer* (Lexington: University Press of Kentucky, 1988);

Goslee, "Witch or Pawn: Women in Scott's Narrative Poetry," in *Romanticism and Feminism*, edited by Anne K. Mellor (Bloomington: Indiana University Press, 1988), pp. 115-136;

Sir Herbert Grierson, "The Problem of the Scottish Poet," *Essays and Studies*, 21 (1936): 105-123;

Grierson, "Scott: The Man and the Poet," in *Sir Walter Scott Lectures 1940-1948*, edited by

Grierson (Edinburgh: Edinburgh University Press, 1950), pp. 3-30;

Ann M. Guest, "Imagery of Color and Light in Scott's Narrative Poems," *Studies in English Literature*, 12 (Autumn 1972): 705-720;

A. D. Harvey, *English Poetry in a Changing Society 1780-1825* (New York: St. Martin's Press, 1980), pp. 98-106;

John O. Hayden, *The Romantic Reviewers 1802-1824* (London: Routledge & Kegan Paul, 1969), pp. 125-134;

Hayden, *Scott: The Critical Heritage* (New York: Barnes & Noble, 1970);

William Hazlitt, *Lectures on the English Poets* (London: Printed for Taylor & Hessey, 1818);

Hazlitt, *The Spirit of the Age: or, Contemporary Portraits* (London: H. Colburn, 1825);

Francis Jeffrey, *Contributions to the Edinburgh Review* (London: Longman, Brown, Green & Longmans, 1853), pp. 455-482;

Karl Kroeber, *Romantic Narrative Art* (Madison: University of Wisconsin Press, 1960), pp. 168-187;

Claire Lamont, "The Poetry of the Early Waverley Novels," *Proceedings of the British Academy*, 61 (1975): 315-336;

Andrew Lang, *Sir Walter Scott and the Border Minstrelsy* (London & New York: Longmans, Green, 1910);

Jane Millgate, *Walter Scott: The Making of the Novelist* (Toronto: University of Toronto Press, 1984), pp. 3-34;

Jerome Mitchell, *Scott, Chaucer, and Metrical Romance* (Lexington: University Press of Kentucky, 1987), pp. 40-86;

G. H. Needler, *Goethe and Scott* (Toronto: Oxford University Press, 1950);

Alfred Noyes, "The Poetry of Sir Walter Scott: A Revaluation," *Quarterly Review*, 290 (April 1952): 211-225;

John Pikoulis, "Scott and 'Marmion': The Discovery of Identity," *Modern Language Review*, 66 (October 1971): 738-750;

James Reed, *Sir Walter Scott: Landscape and Locality* (London: Athlone Press, 1980), pp. 23-50;

Marlon B. Ross, "Scott's Chivalric Pose: The Function of Metrical Romance in the Romantic Period," *Genre*, 19 (Fall 1986): 267-297;

Jill Rubenstein, "The Dilemma of History: A Reading of Scott's *Bridal of Triermain*," *Studies in English Literature*, 12 (Autumn 1972): 721-734;

Rubenstein, "Symbolic Characterization in *The Lady of the Lake*," *Dalhousie Review*, 51 (Autumn 1971): 366-373;

D. Nichol Smith, "The Poetry of Sir Walter Scott," *University of Edinburgh Journal*, 15 (1951): 63-80;

Arthur Symons, *The Romantic Movement in English Poetry* (London: Constable, 1909), pp. 108-119;

Graham Tulloch, *The Language of Sir Walter Scott: A Study in Scottish and Period Language* (London: Deutsch, 1980).

Papers:

The Pierpont Morgan Library, New York, has the largest single collection of manuscripts of Scott's works. The National Library of Scotland, Edinburgh, holds additional Scott manuscripts as well as the largest collection of manuscripts relating to Scott, including the Abbotsford Collection and the Walpole Collection of about six thousand letters to Scott. Much of the Scott collection at the National Library is becoming available on microform: see *The Sir Walter Scott Manuscripts* (Brighton: Harvester Press Microform, 1986-   ).

William Sotheby

(9 November 1757 - 30 December 1833)

Thomas L. Cooksey
Armstrong State College

BOOKS: *Poems: Consisting of a Tour through parts of North and South Wales, Sonnets, Odes, and an Epistle to a Friend of Physiognomy* (Bath: Printed by R. Cruttwell, 1790); republished as *A Tour Through Parts of Wales, Sonnets, Odes and other Poems* (London: Printed by J. Smeeton for R. Blamir, 1794);

The Battle of the Nile: A Poem (London: Hatchard, 1799);

The Cambrian Hero; or, Llewelyn the Great, and Historical Tragedy, tentatively attributed to Sotheby (Egham: Printed by Wettons, 1800?);

The Siege of Cuzco: A Tragedy in Five Acts (London: Printed for J. Wright by W. Bulmer & Co., 1800);

Julian and Agnes: or, The Monks of the Great St. Bernard: A Tragedy in Five Acts: As it was performed at the Theatre Royal, Drury Lane (London: J. Wright, 1801); revised as *Ellen; or, The Confession: A Tragedy in Five Acts* (London: John Murray, 1816);

A Poetical epistle to Sir George Beaumont, bart., on the Encouragement of the British School of Painting (London: Printed for J. Wright, 1801);

Oberon: or, Huon de Bordeaux: a Mask. and Orestes: a Tragedy (London: Sold by T. Cadell & W. Davies, printed by J. Mills, Bristol, 1802; facsimile, New York: Garland, 1978);

Saul: A Poem in two parts (London: Printed for T. Cadell & W. Davies by W. Bulmer, 1807; Boston: Printed by D. Carlisle for John West, 1808);

Constance de Castile: a Poem in Ten Cantos (London: Printed for T. Cadell & W. Davies, 1810; Boston: West & Blake, printed by Greenough & Stebins, 1812);

A Song of Triumph (London: Printed for John Murray by W. Bulmer & Co., 1814);

Tragedies (London: Printed for John Murray by W. Bulmer & Co., 1814);

Ivan: a Tragedy in Five Acts (London: Printed for John Murray, 1816);

Farewell to Italy, and Occasional Poems (London: Printed by W. Bulmer, 1818); revised and enlarged as *Poems* (London: Printed by W. Nichol, 1825); enlarged again as *Italy and Other Poems* (London: John Murray, 1828);

Lines Suggested by the Third Meeting of the British Association for the Advancement of Science, held at Cambridge, in June, 1833. By the Late William Sotheby . . . with a Short Memoir of his Life (London: G. & W. Nicol and John Murray, 1834).

PLAY PRODUCTION: *Julian and Agnes; or The Monks of the Great St. Bernard: a Tragedy*, London, Theatre Royal, Drury Lane, 25 April 1801.

OTHER: Christoph Martin Wieland, *Oberon, a Poem from the German of Wieland*, translated by Sotheby (1 volume, London: Printed for Cadell & Davies, 1798; 2 volumes, Newport, R.I.: L. Rousmaniere / Boston: J. Belcher, 1810);

Publius, Vergilius Maro, *The Georgics of Virgil*, translated, with notes, by Sotheby (London: Printed for J. Wright, 1800; Middletown, Conn.: Printed by Richard Alsop for I. Riley, New York, 1808; revised edition, London: Printed for John Murray by W. Bulmer, 1815); enlarged as *Georgica Publii Virgilii Maronis hexaglotta*, edited by Sotheby with the Latin of C. G. Heyne and with translations in Italian by G. F. Soave, Spanish by J. de Guzmán, German by J. H. Voss, French by Delille, and English by Sotheby (London: Printed by W. Nicol, 1827);

Homer, *The First Books of the Iliad; the Parting of Hector and Andromache; and the Shield of Achilles: Specimens of a New Version of Homer*, translated by Sotheby (London: John Murray, 1830); enlarged to *The Iliad of Homer* (London: John Murray, 1831);

Homer, *The Odyssey of Homer, illustrated by the designs of Flaxman*, translated by Sotheby (London: G. & W. Nicol and John Murray, 1834).

William Sotheby (portrait by Sir Thomas Lawrence; by permission of the National Portrait Gallery, London)

William Sotheby was the consummate gentleman of letters in the Romantic era, a role that both tied him to the past as well as pointed to the future. While George Gordon, Lord Byron, found him a patronizing bore and satirized him in *Beppo* (1818) as Mr. Botherby, an "antique gentleman of rhyme," most literary men and women, from Samuel Taylor Coleridge to Sir Walter Scott, found him a loyal friend and a generous patron. Sotheby was a prodigious poet, playwright, and translator, though aside from his translation of Christoph Martin Wieland's verse fantasy *Oberon* few of his works transcended the conventions of the day or exercised an enduring influence. Despite its conventionality, his artistic output does serve to provide a literary and aesthetic context that sets the work of William Wordsworth and others into full relief, showing both their relationship with their aesthetic environment and their originality. Sotheby's most important role, however, was personal. The friend of Scott, Wordsworth, Coleridge, and even Byron, as well as Thomas Moore, Robert Southey, Joanna Baillie, Maria Edgeworth, Samuel Rogers, Henry Hallam, and many others, Sotheby represented a focal point that joined various literary and intellectual circles together, giving coherence to British Romanticism. It was as a unifier, more than as a poet, that Sotheby provided an enduring influence.

O B E R O N,

A POEM,

FROM THE GERMAN OF WIELAND.

By WILLIAM SOTHEBY, Esq.

IN TWO VOLUMES.

VOL. I.

L O N D O N:

PRINTED FOR CADELL AND DAVIES, STRAND; EDWARDS,
PALL MALL; FAULDER, BOND STREET;
AND HATCHARD, PICCADILLY.

1798.

TO

Sir H. C. ENGLEFIELD, Bart.

Dear Sir Harry,

If the following version of a Poem, deservedly held in the highest estimation in its native country, can give any delight to your cultivated mind, it will add to that which I feel in dedicating it to you, as a trifling testimony of my esteem and friendship.

Yours, affectionately,

WILLIAM SOTHEBY.

Seymour Place, May Fair,
May 12th, 1798.

Title page and dedication for Sotheby's best-known work. Although Coleridge expressed the reservation that it "had not at all caught the manner of the original," Sotheby's translation remained the standard English version of Wieland's poem for at least a quarter of a century.

William Sotheby was born in London 9 November 1757, the oldest son of William Sotheby, a colonel in the Coldstream Guards, and his wife, Elizabeth Sloane. When Sotheby was eight years old, his father died, bringing him under the joint guardianship of Charles Philip York, Fourth Earl of Hardwicke (later Lord Chancellor) and his maternal uncle, Hans Sloane. This death also led to Sotheby's succession to the hereditary estate of Sewardstone, near Epping Forest. Following the pattern of many affluent gentlemen, Sotheby received his first formal education at Harrow. When he was seventeen, he bought a commission in the Tenth Dragoons. Almost at once, he received leave to further his military studies at the military academy at Angers in the Loire Valley. This was followed in the winter and spring by visits to Vienna and Berlin. He rejoined his regiment at the close of 1777, quartered at Knaresborough, near Edinburgh. At this time, Britain was in the midst of the American Revolution, and the mission of Sotheby's regiment was to guard the Scottish coast against threatened raids by John Paul Jones. Walter Scott recalled that as a schoolboy, he had seen Sotheby lead a troop of the Tenth Dragoons against a mutinous Highland regiment. To this he added, "had the Highlanders fired down the street, we poets might both have been swept away." Sotheby was not entirely consumed by his regimental duties. He also began to occupy himself with the close study of William Shakespeare and the other classics of British literature, especially his perennial favorite, Alexander Pope. He also began writing poetry.

In 1779 the regiment was transferred to Northamptonshire. During this time he made the acquaintance of Mary Isted (28 December 1759 - 14 October 1834), daughter of his old friend Ambrose Isted of Ecton and Anne Isted, heiress of Sir Charles Buck, baronet. On 17 July 1780, Sotheby and Mary Isted married, forming a union that added considerably to his already sizable resources. At this point Sotheby retired from the Dragoons, buying Bevis Mount near Southampton, once the residence of the earl of Peterborough and frequented by Pope. Independently wealthy, Sotheby settled down to the life of a gentlemen of letters, devoting himself to poetry and the careful study of the Greek and Latin classics.

In 1788 Sotheby and his younger brother, Thomas (1759-1831)–later an admiral in the British navy–followed the fashion of the day with a walking tour through Wales. The experience gave rise to a series of poetic descriptions. These were much in the landscape-tourist poetic tradition of John Denham and John Dyer that was later satirized in Thomas Rowlandson and William Combe's *The Tour of Dr. Syntax in Search of the Picaresque* (1812). Taking his landscape poems as the core, Sotheby collected them with some of the sonnets and odes that he had composed while living at Bevis Mount as *Poems, Consisting of a Tour through parts of North and South Wales* (1790). In 1794 he republished this book as *A Tour Through Parts of Wales,* which included aquatint engravings based on drawings by T. Smith.

Composed in blank verse, the poems in Sotheby's first book are conventional in their imagery and sentiments. His vision of Mount Snowdon is representative, reflecting the typical diction of an Augustan poet in search of the sublime: "–thus ardent I behold, / Raised o'er the rocky scenery sublime, / Thee Snowdon! king of Cambrian mountains hail!" Perhaps more important, however, is the sharp contrast between Sotheby's response to Mount Snowdon and Wordsworth's profounder experience of the same scene some nine years later. Where Sotheby, scanning the panorama, observes:

Amid the vast horizon's stretch,
In restless gaze the eye of wonder darts
O'er the expanse; mountains on mountains piled,
Are winding bays, and promontories huge,
Lakes and meandering rivers, from their source,
Traced to the distant ocean.

Wordsworth, witnessing a similar prospect, writes in the *Prelude,*

As I looked up,
The moon hung naked in a firmament
Of azure without cloud, and at my feet
Rested a silent sea of hoary mist.
A hundred hills their dusky backs upheaved
All over this still ocean; and beyond,
Far, far beyond, the solid vapours stretched,
In headlands, tongues, and promontory shapes,
Into the main Atlantic. . . .

Distanced from the experience by the formality of his language, Sotheby's version of Snowdon represents an accurate if ponderous description. By contrast, Wordsworth's presents a more direct and immediate apprehension of the scene. The reader experiences through the poem, not a sublime sight, but the unmediated experience of the poet's mind.

While the vision of Mount Snowdon is typical of Sotheby's poetry, he did occasionally achieve some memorable lines, as in his ode "Netly Abbey," a work that Coleridge claimed to have memorized. Included in *Poems,* the ode describes the wanderings of the poet's imagination at night among the ruins of the abbey:

Bright on the silvered tower the moon-beam shines,
And the grey cloister's roofless length illumes;
Upon the mossy stone I lie reclined,
And to a visionary world resigned
Call the pale spectres forth from the forgotten tombs.

In a bow to tradition, however, the ode ends with the triumph of reason and enlightenment over the free play of imagination: "wisdom shall curb wild fancy's magic power, / And as with life's gay dawn, the illusion cease. . . ."

At Bevis Mount Sotheby also composed the first of a series of five-act verse tragedies based on historical subjects. *Bertram and Matilda* was never published, though it was performed privately at Wincester by Sotheby and some friends. Another play, *The Cambrian Hero; or, Llewelyn the Great* (1800?), has been attributed to Sotheby and may have been written during this period, though the authorship is not entirely certain.

After the death of Sotheby's mother in 1791, he moved his family to London in order to have "a more extensive literary society." Thereafter he divided his time between his residence in London and his hereditary property at

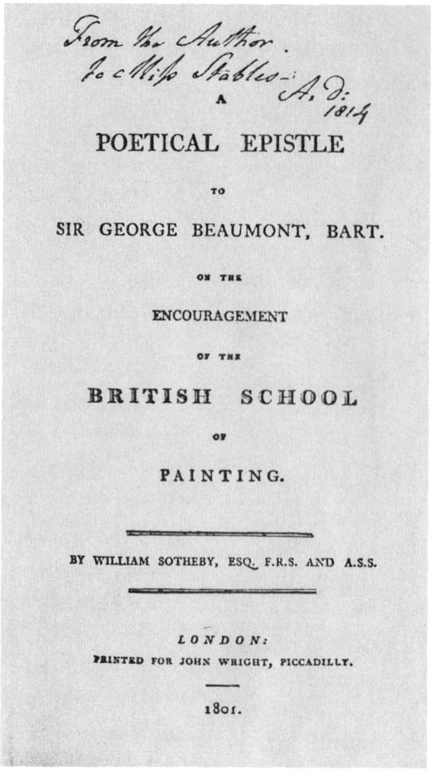

From the Author.
To Miss Stables— *A. D:*
1814

A

POETICAL EPISTLE

TO

SIR GEORGE BEAUMONT, BART.

ON THE

ENCOURAGEMENT

OF THE

BRITISH SCHOOL

OF

PAINTING.

BY WILLIAM SOTHEBY, ESQ. F.R.S. AND A.S.S.

LONDON:
PRINTED FOR JOHN WRIGHT, PICCADILLY.

1801.

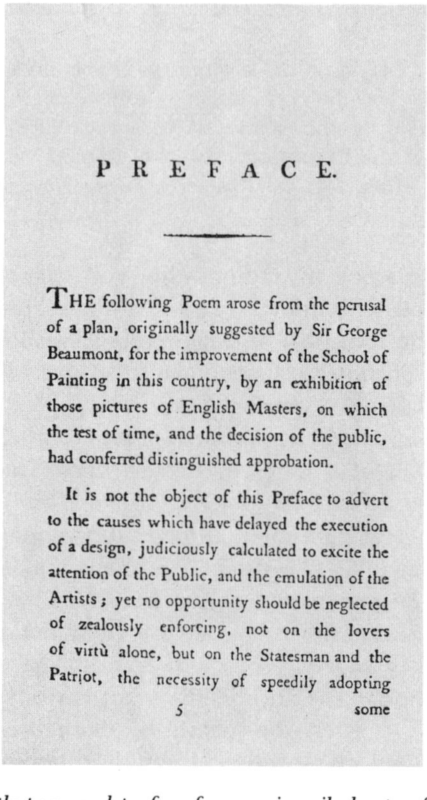

PREFACE.

THE following Poem arose from the perusal of a plan, originally suggested by Sir George Beaumont, for the improvement of the School of Painting in this country, by an exhibition of those pictures of English Masters, on which the test of time, and the decision of the public, had conferred distinguished approbation.

It is not the object of this Preface to advert to the causes which have delayed the execution of a design, judiciously calculated to excite the attention of the Public, and the emulation of the Artists; yet no opportunity should be neglected of zealously enforcing, not on the lovers of virtù alone, but on the Statesman and the Patriot, the necessity of speedily adopting

5   some

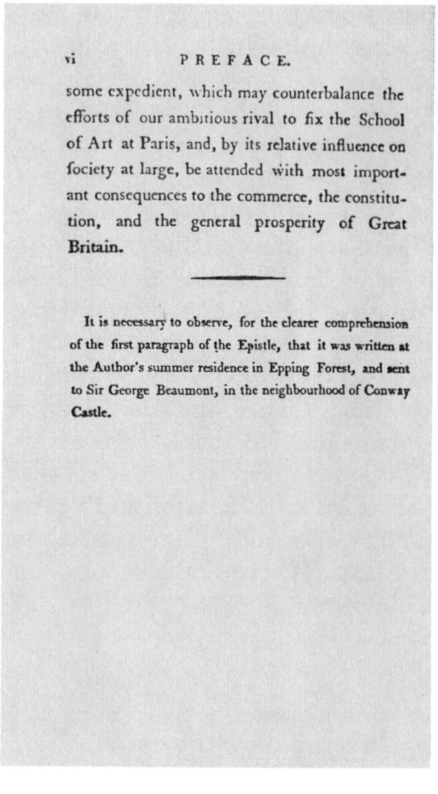

vi   PREFACE.

some expedient, which may counterbalance the efforts of our ambitious rival to fix the School of Art at Paris, and, by its relative influence on society at large, be attended with most important consequences to the commerce, the constitution, and the general prosperity of Great Britain.

It is necessary to observe, for the clearer comprehension of the first paragraph of the Epistle, that it was written at the Author's summer residence in Epping Forest, and sent to Sir George Beaumont, in the neighbourhood of Conway Castle.

Title page and preface from an inscribed copy of a poem Sotheby addressed to one of the friends he later enlisted as a patron for Coleridge (Yale University Library, In. So 77.801p)

Sewardstone, where he also served as master keeper of the Epping Forest. Once in London, Sotheby soon found the literary society that he desired, being elected in 1792 to the Dilettante Society, where he soon became a leading voice. In 1794 came his election as a Fellow to the Society of Antiquaries and as a member of the Royal Society. In the latter case, although Sotheby's knowledge of science was limited, he had a sustained interest in it. Toward the end of his life, he even composed a poem on the occasion of the meeting of the British Association for the Advancement of Science (1834).

Early in his stay in London, Sotheby made the acquaintance of William Taylor (1765-1836), among the first men to introduce and translate German literature into British culture. By the time of Sotheby's move to London, Taylor had already published a translation of G. E. Lessing's *Nathan the Wise* (1791), followed shortly thereafter by Johann Wolfgang von Goethe's *Iphigenia in Tauris* (1793). He was to become best known, however, for his rendition of the macabre ballad *Lenore* (1797), composed by the Sturm und Drang poet Gottfried August Bürger. Perhaps recalling his earlier visits to Vienna and Berlin, Sotheby turned to the mastery of German. In December 1795, Taylor began the first of a series of five reviews discussing the works of the Weimar poet Christoph Martin Wieland. These reviews seem to have intrigued Sotheby, leading him to the production of his most important work, a translation of Wieland's 1780 rococo fantasy, *Oberon*, which he published in 1798.

Wieland's *Oberon*, based on the thirteenth-century French chanson *Huon de Bordeaux*, Geoffrey Chaucer's "Merchant's Tale," and Shakespeare's *A Midsummer Night's Dream*, traces the fantastic and suicidal quest of the young knight Huon de Bordeaux, who–to atone for killing Charlemagne's son–is sent to the court of Caliph of Baghdad, where he is to behead the person seated at the caliph's left, claim the heiress to the throne as a bride, and take four of the caliph's teeth and a handful of his beard. After many adventures, Huon is successful in his quest and reconciled with Charlemagne. The key to his success, however, rested with the magic intervention of Oberon, "King of the daemons and the elements," a figure that Werner W. Beyer compares to Shakespeare's Prospero and Ovid's Medea.

Sotheby's literary fame rests on his *Oberon*, which became the "classic" version in English. There had been an earlier translation by James

Six, and Coleridge claimed to have abandoned a similar project when he saw Sotheby's work. The same was true of a translation completed by John Quincy Adams when he was the United States minister in Berlin. (Adams's version was first published in 1940.) William Taylor praised Sotheby's efforts in the *Monthly Review* (August 1798), but expressed a telling reservation that the poem affected him more powerfully in German than in English. Coleridge drew a similar conclusion when he remarked that "Sotheby's translation had not at all caught the manner of the original." Both Coleridge and Taylor observed that Sotheby had chosen to turn Wieland's ottava-rima stanzas into nine-line Spenserian stanzas, which meant that he had to embellish the original in order to fill out the stanzas. The effect was to diffuse the spontaneity of the original, a defect that was exacerbated by casting Wieland in Augustan diction and syntax. His adherence to the poetic conventions, which had limited much of his original poetry, also hindered the spontaneity of his translation. To further complicate matters Sotheby often exercised a moral restraint over his text that led him to expurgate some stanzas. Yet, in a review of the fourth edition (1806), Taylor observed, "if Sotheby loses something of the easy familiarity and picturesque precision of the original *Oberon*, he makes ample amends by smoothness of versification, elegance of phrase and majesty of diction." Thus, despite its shortcomings, Sotheby's *Oberon* represented what was considered the best translation of the day. Wieland himself praised Sotheby's efforts, and John Keats, who fell under the spell of *Oberon*, was deeply influenced. Indeed, praise for Sotheby's translation was sustained as late as 1825, when Thomas Carlyle declared that it, along with Coleridge's translation of Friedrich von Schiller's *Wallenstein* (1800), was "the best, indeed the only sufferable translation from the German with which our literature has yet been enriched."

Oberon was not the only work to come from Sotheby's pen at this time. In 1799 he published his poem *The Battle of the Nile*, an occasional piece celebrating Nelson's victory over the Napoleonic fleet. This work was a personal celebration as well, for Sotheby's second son, Charles, an officer in the British navy, was present for the battle. More important to his literary fame, however, was the publication of his translation of the *Georgics of Virgil*. In this project he found a subject harmonious with his talents. Francis Jeffrey praised Sotheby as a refined and elegant scholar in the

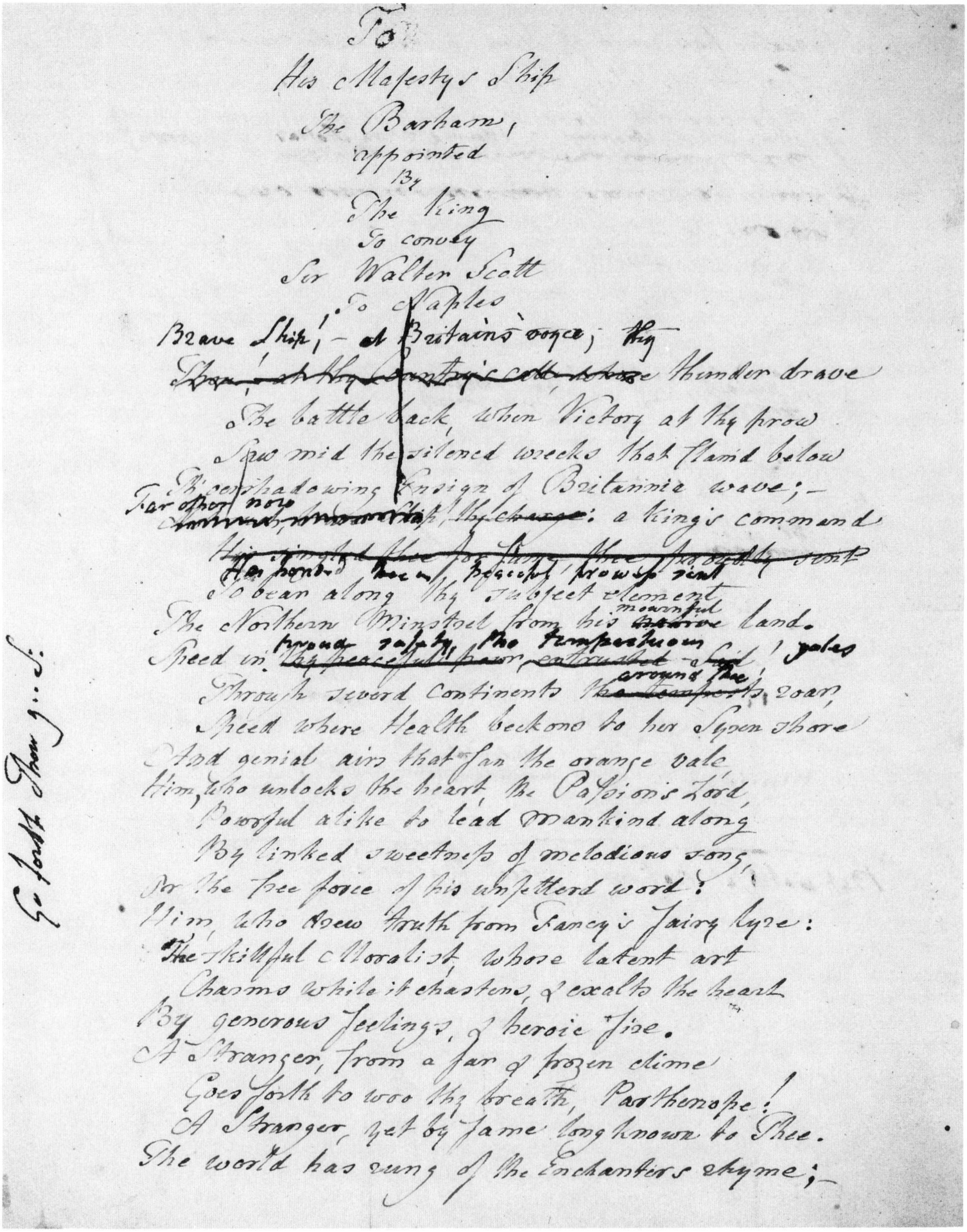

To
His Majesty's Ship
The Barham,
appointed
By
The King
To convey
Sir Walter Scott
To Naples

Brave Ship! — at Britain's once; thy
~~Thou, at thy country cost, whose~~ thunder drave
The battle back, when Victory at thy prow
Saw mid the silenced wrecks that flam'd below
Thy overshadowing Ensign of Britannia wave; —
Far ~~often~~ now ~~o'er main, thyself~~: a king's command
~~Thy inmost~~ ~~Respond~~ ~~peaceful prow~~ ~~sent~~
To bear along thy subject element
The Northern Minstrel from his ~~native~~ mournful land.
Speed in ~~proud~~ ~~safety~~ ~~the tempestuous~~ ~~The peaceful pair entrusted~~ gales
Through sever'd Continents the ~~crown's the~~ roar,
Speed where Health beckons to her Syren shore
And genial airs that fan the orange vale
Him, who unlocks the heart, the Passion's Lord,
Powerful alike to lead mankind along
By linked sweetness of melodious song,
Or the free force of his unfetterd word!
Him, who drew Truth from Fancy's fairy lyre:
The skillful Moralist whose latent art
Charms while it chastens, & exalts the heart
By generous feelings, & heroic fire.
A Stranger, from afar & frozen clime
Goes forth to woo thy breath, Parthenope!
A Stranger, yet by fame long known to Thee.
The world has rung of the Enchanter's rhyme;

Go forth thou ....

Draft for a poem Sotheby wrote on the occasion of Scott's October 1831 voyage to Italy (SY 148; by permission of the Henry E. Huntington Library and Art Gallery)

266

Thy realm has rung of Him whose wide renown
Gathers its glory as the years roll on.
Who has not heard of dauntless Marmion?
Of ~~her whose charms~~ ~~burned than~~ Scotia's ~~crown~~?
~~[struck through line]~~
Of ~~[struck]~~ the wild Witches dark sublimity?
Of ~~Her~~ one who swerved not from her hard career
To save a Sister, and the burning tear
That gush'd through flame from Douglas' iron eye?
Who has not thrill'd o'er the unbroken flow
              purest   that sweetly
Of ~~sweetest~~ Poesy, ~~[struck]~~ ~~one~~ wound
The Hunter's horn ~~and~~ Katrine's lake around;
When through the Trossachs burst the Artherd brow?
Bright Sun of Italy! soft Southern clime,
~~the gales~~ that breathe of Health refresh his frame!
Not yet consummated his glorious aim.
Forms yet unseen, the beauteous the sublime,
From his creative spirit life ~~[struck]~~ implore.
                                exultant
Then — gallant Ship! — erelong — ~~[struck]~~ bear
From soft Parthenope's reviving air
                  Caledonian   joyful shore.
The ~~Northern~~ Bard to ~~[struck]~~ ~~[struck]~~.
Not Britain thy return alone shall hail — —
~~For the [struck] Nations wait & watch for thy sail~~
But watchful Nations greet the Ausonian Sail — — — —

267

Edinburgh Review (July 1804). Comparing his *Georgics* with the efforts of John Dryden, Jeffrey declared that Sotheby had "run the same race with some of the first and most celebrated worthies of English poetry, and has manifestly distanced his competitors." This success led Sotheby to republish his version of the *Georgics* several times, eventually putting out at his own expense *The Hexaglott* (1827), a limited folio edition with Virgil's poem translated into five languages. This volume was presented to the various sovereigns of Europe, garnering for Sotheby gold medals from the king of Prussia and the emperor of Austria as well as a silver medal from Pope Pius VIII. But not all of Sotheby's literary ventures were so successful.

On 25 April 1801, Sotheby's verse tragedy *Julian and Agnes; or The Monks of the Great St. Bernard* was staged at the Drury Lane theater. The production featured Mrs. Sarah Siddons and John Kemble in the title roles. The production proved to be a disaster, closing after one night. In part this failure was due to Sotheby's limits as a dramatist, but the bungling of the cast also contributed. While Kemble was reviewed as "particularly fine," Mrs. Siddons inadvertently hit the head of a dummy baby she was carrying against a doorpost with a resounding noise that shattered the solemnity of a scene, leaving her and the audience laughing. Sotheby renamed the play *The Confession,* and later republished it as *Ellen; or, The Confession* (1816). None of the other six tragedies he wrote ever made it to the stage, though *Ivan* was nearly produced. When Byron was casting about for plays to produce at the Drury Lane theater around 1816, Sotheby offered him all of his plays—including the infamous *Julian and Agnes, The Siege of Cuzco* (1800), and *Orestes* (1802), as well as *Ivan, The Death of Darnley,* and *Zamorin and Zama*—all published with *Julian and Agnes* and *Orestes* in *Tragedies* (1814). As Byron recollected, "Mr. Sotheby obligingly offered *all* his tragedies, and I pledged myself, and, notwithstanding many squabbles with my committed brethren, did get *Ivan* accepted, read, and parts distributed." After several rehearsals, however, Edmund Kean, who was to play Ivan, objected that he was unable to develop his part. This complaint led to a heated exchange followed by Sotheby's withdrawal of the play, ending his last attempt at the theater.

While on a tour near Grasmere with his family in the summer of 1802, Sotheby made the acquaintance of Coleridge. Sharing a common interest in German literature, they discussed Salomon Gessner's poem "Der erste Schiffer." This conversation began Sotheby's sustained, if trying, patronage of Coleridge. At an early state they exchanged compliments on one another's works. Soon, however, Sotheby was encouraging Coleridge to finish *Christabel,* promising to form a committee to publish it. By 1804 it was necessary to lend Coleridge one hundred pounds to get his debts in order and to facilitate his trip to Malta. By 1812 Sotheby had formed a committee of patronage with Sir T. Bernard, Sir G. Beaumont, and Sir H. Davy to support Coleridge's *Lectures on the Drama,* a project whose start was delayed by the assassination of the prime minister, Spencer Perceval, on 11 May 1812. As late as 1816, he was petitioning the Committee of the Literary Fund and others on Coleridge's behalf. Yet throughout his dealings with Coleridge, he remained a loyal friend and supporter, a role that was indicative of most of his dealings with the poets and artists around him.

In 1807, Sotheby published *Saul: A Poem in two parts.* Despite the title, the subject is the life of David from his appearance as a harpist through the death of Saul, and the poem often closely paraphrases the biblical account. While Coleridge praised it in a letter to Sotheby as "the best epic poem in our language," others were less sanguine. Jeffrey expressed his disappointment in a review in the *Edinburgh Review* (April 1807), complaining that it lacked animation or character development. In remarks that are telling, he added, "Mr. Sotheby's blank verse is as remarkable for harshness, constraint, and abruptness, as his stanzas are for ease and melody; and his muse, we are afraid, is like one of those old beauties, who, having been long accustomed to move gracefully in tight stays, high shoes, and hooped petticoats, feels her supports withdrawn when disencumbered of her shackles and totters and stumbles when there are no longer any restraints on her movement." Sotheby's poetic language belonged to an earlier era.

The allied triumph over Napoleon in 1814 was marked by Sotheby with his *A Song of Triumph,* one of many similar works that emerged from that historic occasion. On a sadder note, Sotheby's eldest son, William, a colonel in the Guards, died on 1 August 1815 as a result of illness following the Spanish and Walcheren campaigns. Sotheby seems to have been seriously depressed by this event, and, after the debacle over *Ivan* the following year, he left with his family for a tour through Europe, returning to England

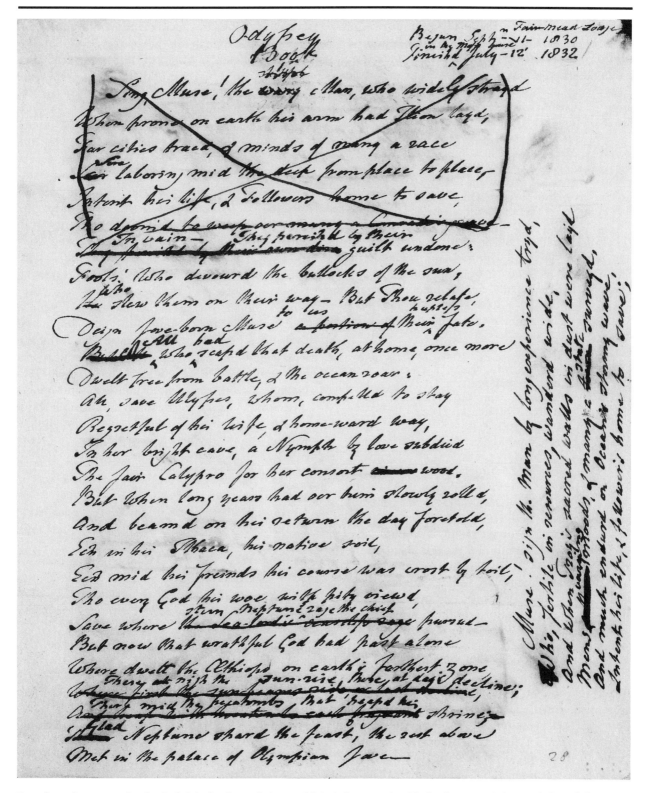

Page from the manuscript for Sotheby's final translation, published the year after his death (SY 146; by permission of the Henry E. Huntington Library and Art Gallery)

through Germany in 1817. The artistic product of this journey was *Farewell to Italy*, published with other poems in 1818. *Farewell to Italy* is another descriptive poem in the spirit of the earlier *Tour through parts of North and South Wales*. Describing the various sights and cities, he takes his leave of Italy in characteristic form:

> Realm of the Sun! bright Italy! farewell!
> My parting lay receive!
> Now, as beneath this waving canopy,
> The green leaf purpled by the beam of eve,
> On the fern's fragrant bed I lonely lie, . . .

The work received little attention, aside from a bitter satire by Byron, who—perhaps remembering the difficulties over *Ivan* and convinced that Sotheby had sent him an anonymous negative review—vented his wrath against him in a letter to publisher John Murray (8 January 1818). Byron wrote,

> Then you've Sotheby's tour,
> No great thing, to be sure,–
>   You could hardly begin with a less work;
> For the pompous rascallion,
> Who didn't speak Italian
>   Nor French, must have scribbled by guesswork.

After the publication of *Farewell to Italy*, Sotheby's poetic production began to taper off. He wrote only a few additional poems that were published with *Farewell to Italy* in *Poems* (1825) and *Italy and Other Poems* (1828). Although sixty-one years old, he continued his rounds of literary circles in London. In 1828 he hosted a major literary dinner honoring his old friend Sir Walter Scott. The courtesy was returned by Scott the following year at Abbotsford. Sotheby also began to devote himself to the massive task of translating Homer.

In 1830 Sotheby published the first volume of his *New Version of Homer*. It was followed in 1831 by a complete *Iliad*. He completed his translation of the *Odyssey* in July 1832, though it did not come off the press until 1834, the year after his death. Reviews of Sotheby's Homer praised its fidelity to the original. A reviewer for the *London Monthly Review* (May 1831), proclaimed that "we know of no book in any tongue but this single one of Sotheby's in which any thing like a just conception of Homer can be conveyed to an unlearned reader." While his efforts were compared to those of Pope and William Cowper, he was praised by this reviewer as much for the immensity of his undertaking as for the results. Others found his verse stiff, lacking vigor and directness, and owing too much to Pope. By the Victorian era his efforts were largely dismissed.

Sotheby died at his residence on Lower Grosvenor Street on 30 December 1833 at the age of seventy-six. In command of his faculties to the end, he was attended by his friend Henry Hallam. While Sotheby's poetry often looked back toward an outmoded poetic tradition, he was capable of writing some fine lyrics. While his translations often suffered from his adherence to the Augustan model, his *Oberon* nevertheless captured the Romantic imagination. But more important than his poetry or translations, was his influence as a friend and patron, encouraging young poets and artists. While he might rankle the sensibilities of a Byron, most found him loyal and generous. Sotheby clung to the aesthetic sensibilities of an earlier generation in his own poetry, but he willingly aided in the birth of the poetry of the next.

References:

Werner W. Beyer, *Keats and the Daemon King* (New York: Oxford University Press, 1947), pp. 19-23;

Beyer, "Two Translators, John Richardson of York and William Sotheby and Wieland's Prestige in England," in *Christoph Martin Wieland: Nordamerikanische Forschungsbeiträge zur 250. Wiederkehr seines Geburtstages 1983*, edited by Hansjörg Schelle (Tubingen: Max Niemeyer, 1984), pp. 209-223;

Ralph Cohen, "S. T. Coleridge and William Sotheby," *Modern Language Review*, 52 (January 1957): 19-27;

Albert Bernhardt Faust, Introduction to *Oberon: A Poetical Romance in Twelve Books Translated from the German of Wieland (1799-1801) by John Quincy Adams* (New York: F. S. Crofts, 1940), pp. xvii-xxix.

Robert Southey

(12 August 1774 - 21 March 1843)

Ernest Bernhardt-Kabisch
Indiana University

BOOKS: *The Fall of Robespierre. An Historic Drama,* act 1 by Samuel Taylor Coleridge, acts 2 and 3 by Southey (Cambridge: Printed by Benjamin Flower for W. H. Lunn and J. & J. Merrill, sold by J. March, Norwich, 1794);

Poems: Containing The Retrospect, Odes, Elegies, Sonnets, etc., by Southey and Robert Lovell (Bath: Printed by R. Cruttwell, 1795);

Joan of Arc, an Epic Poem (1 volume, Bristol: Printed by Bulgin & Rosser for Joseph Cottle, Bristol, and Cadell & Davies and G. G. & J. Robinson, London, 1796; revised edition, 2 volumes, Bristol: Printed by N. Biggs for T. N. Longman and J. Cottle, 1798; Boston: Printed by Manning & Loring for J. Nancrede, 1798);

Letters Written During a Short Residence in Spain and Portugal. With some Account of Spanish and Portugueze Poetry (Bristol: Printed by Bulgin & Rosser for J. Cottle, 1797); third edition revised as *Letters Written during a Journey in Spain, and a Short Residence in Portugal,* 2 volumes (London: Printed for Longman, Hurst, Rees & Orme, 1808);

Poems, 2 volumes (Bristol: Printed by N. Biggs for Joseph Cottle and G. G. & J. Robinson, London, 1797, 1799; volume 1, Boston: Printed by Manning & Loring for Joseph Nancrede, 1799);

The Annual Anthology, 2 volumes, by Southey and others (Bristol: Printed for T. N. Longman & O. Rees, London, 1799, 1800);

Thalaba the Destroyer, 2 volumes (London: Printed for T. N. Longman & O. Rees by Biggs & Cottle, Bristol, 1801; Boston: Published by T. B. Wait & Charles Williams, 1812);

Madoc, 2 volumes (London: Longman, Hurst, Rees & Orme, 1805; Boston: Printed by Munroe & Francis, 1806);

Metrical Tales, and Other Poems (London: Longman, Hurst, Rees & Orme, 1805; Boston: C. Williams, 1811);

Letters from England: By Don Manuel Alvarez Espriella. Translated from the Spanish (3 volumes, London: Printed for Longman, Hurst, Rees & Orme, 1807; 1 volume, Boston: Printed by Munroe, Francis & Parker, 1808; New York: Ezra Sargent, 1808);

The Curse of Kehama (London: Printed for Longman, Hurst, Rees, Orme & Brown by J. Ballantyne, 1810; New York: Published by David Longworth, 1811);

History of Brazil, 3 volumes (London: Longman, Hurst, Rees, Orme & Brown, 1810, 1817, 1819; volume 1 revised, 1822);

Omniana, or Horae Otiosiores, 2 volumes (London: Longman, Hurst, Rees, Orme & Brown, 1812)—also includes contributions by Coleridge;

The Origin, Nature, and Object of the New System of Education (London: Printed for J. Murray, 1812);

The Life of Nelson, 2 volumes (London: Printed for John Murray, 1813; New York: Eastburn, Kirk / Boston: W. Wells, 1813);

Roderick, the Last of the Goths (London: Printed for Longman, Hurst, Rees, Orme & Brown by James Ballantyne, Edinburgh, 1814; Philadelphia: E. Earle / New York: Eastburn, Kirk, printed by W. Fry, 1815);

Odes to His Royal Highness The Prince Regent, His Imperial Majesty The Emperor of Russia, and His Majesty the King of Prussia (London: Longman, Hurst, Rees, Orme & Brown, 1814); republished as *Carmen Triumphale, for the Commencement of the Year 1814. Carmina Aulica. Written in 1814 on the Arrival of the Allied Sovereigns in England* (London: Printed for Longman, Hurst, Rees & Orme, 1821);

The Minor Poems of Robert Southey, 3 volumes (London: Printed for Longman, Hurst, Rees, Orme & Brown, 1815);

The Poet's Pilgrimage to Waterloo (London: Longman, Hurst, Rees, Orme & Brown, 1816; New York: W. B. Gilley and Van Winkle &

Robert Southey (portrait attributed to Edward Nash; from Jack Simmons, Southey, *1945)*

Wiley, printed by T. & W. Mercein, 1816; Boston: Published by Wells & Lilly, 1816);

The Lay of the Laureate. Carmen Nuptiale (London: Printed for Longman, Hurst, Rees, Orme & Brown, 1816);

Wat Tyler. A Dramatic Poem (London: Printed for Sherwood, Neely & Jones, 1817; Boston: J. P. Mendum, 1850);

A Letter to William Smith, Esq., M.P. (London: J. Murray, 1817);

The Life of Wesley; and the Rise and Progress of Methodism, 2 volumes (London: Printed for Longman, Hurst, Rees, Orme & Brown, 1820; New York: Published by Evert Duyckinck & George Long, printed by Clayton & Kingsland, 1820; New York: Wm. B. Gilley, 1820);

A Vision of Judgement (London: Longman, Hurst, Rees, Orme & Brown, 1821); republished in *The Two Visions; or, Byron v. Southey* (Lon-

don: W. Dugdale, 1822; New York: W. Borradaile, 1823);

The Expedition of Orsua; and the Crimes of Aguirre (London: Longman, Hurst, Rees, Orme & Brown, 1821; Philadelphia: Hickman & Hazard, 1821);

History of the Peninsular War, 3 volumes (London: J. Murray, 1823, 1827, 1832);

The Book of the Church, 2 volumes (London: J. Murray, 1824; Boston: Wells & Lilly, 1825);

A Tale of Paraguay (London: Longman, Hurst, Rees, Orme, Brown & Green, 1825; Boston: S. G. Goodrich, 1827);

Vindiciæ Ecclesiæ Anglicanæ (London: J. Murray, 1826);

All for Love; and the Pilgrim to Compostella (London: J. Murray, 1829);

Sir Thomas More: or, Colloquies on the Progress and Prospects of Society, 2 volumes (London: J. Murray, 1829);

Southey in 1796 (portrait by Robert Hancock; by permission of the National Portrait Gallery, London)

The Devil's Walk; A Poem. By Professor Porson [pseud.]. *Edited with a biographical memoir and notes by H. W. Montagu* [pseud.], by Southey and Coleridge (London: Marsh & Miller / Edinburgh: Constable, 1830);

Essays, Moral and Political, 2 volumes (London: J. Murray, 1832);

Lives of the British Admirals, with an Introductory View of the Naval History of England, 5 volumes, volume 5 by Robert Bell (London: Longman, Rees, Orme, Brown, Green & Longmans, 1833, 1834, 1837, 1840);

The Doctor, &c., 7 volumes, volumes 6 and 7 edited by J. W. Warter (London: Longman, Rees, Orme, Brown, Green & Longmans, 1834-1847; volumes 1-3 republished in 1 volume, New York: Harper, 1836);

The Poetical Works (10 volumes, London: Printed for Longman, Orme, Brown, Green & Longmans, 1837, 1838; 1 volume, New York: D. Appleton, 1839);

The Life of the Rev. Andrew Bell. . . . Comprising the History of the Rise and Progress of the System of Mutual Tuition, volume 1 (London: Murray / Edinburgh: Blackwood, 1844 [volumes 2 and 3 by Charles Cuthbert Southey]);

Oliver Newman: A New-England Tale (Unfinished): With Other Poetical Remains, edited by Herbert Hill (London: Longman, Brown, Green & Longmans, 1845);

Robin Hood: A Fragment. By the Late Robert Southey and Caroline Southey. With Other Fragments and Poems by R. S. & C. S. (Edinburgh & London: Blackwood, 1847);

Southey's Common-Place Book, edited by John Wood Warter, 4 series (London: Longman, Brown, Green & Longmans, 1849-1851);

Journal of a Tour in the Netherlands in the Autumn of 1815, edited by W. Robertson Nicoll (Boston & New York: Houghton, Mifflin, 1902; London: Heinemann, 1903);

Journal of a Tour in Scotland in 1819, edited by C. H. Herford (London: Murray, 1929);

Journal of a Residence in Portugal 1800-1801 and a Visit to France in 1838, edited by Adolfo Cabral (Oxford: Clarendon Press, 1960);

First page of a translation written in June 1797 at Christ Church in one of Southey's commonplace books (auctioned by Christie, Manson & Woods Ltd, 11-12 June 1980). This poem appears in Southey's Common-Place Book. Fourth Series, *edited by John Wood Warter (1851).*

The Contributions of Robert Southey to the Morning Post, edited by Kenneth Curry (University: University of Alabama Press, 1984).

OTHER: *On the French Revolution, by Mr. Necker*, 2 volumes, volume 2 translated by Southey (London: Printed for T. Cadell & T. Davies, Jun., 1797);

The Works of Thomas Chatterton, 3 volumes, edited by Southey and Joseph Cottle (London: T. N. Longman & O. Rees, 1803);

Vasco Lobeira, *Amadis of Gaul*, 4 volumes, translated by Southey (London: Printed by N. Biggs for T. N. Longman & O. Rees, 1803);

Francisco de Moraes, *Palmerin of England*, 4 volumes, translated by Southey (London: Printed for Longman, Hurst, Rees & Orme, 1807);

Specimens of the Later English Poets, 3 volumes, edited, with notes, by Southey and Grosvenor Bedford (London: Longman, Hurst, Rees & Orme, 1807);

The Remains of Henry Kirke White, of Nottingham, late of St. John's College, Cambridge; With an Account of His Life, 3 volumes, edited, with a biography, by Southey (volumes 1 and 2: London: Printed by W. Wilson for Vernor, Hood & Sharp; Longman, Hurst, Rees & Orme; J. Dighton, T. Barret & J. Nicholson, Cambridge; W. Dunn & S. Tupman, Nottingham, 1807; Philadelphia: Printed & sold by J. & A. Y. Humphreys, 1811; volume 3: London: Printed for Longman, Hurst, Rees, Orme & Brown, 1822; Boston: Wells & Lilly, 1822);

Chronicle of the Cid, translated by Southey (London: Longman, Hurst, Rees & Orme, 1808; Lowell, Mass.: Bixby, 1846);

The Byrth, Lyf, and Actes of King Arthur, 2 volumes, edited by Southey (London: Printed for Longman, Hurst, Rees, Orme & Brown by T. Davison, 1817);

John Bunyan, *The Pilgrim's Progress. With a Life of John Bunyan*, edited, with a biography, by Southey (London: John Murray and John Major, 1830; Boston: Crocker & Brewster / New York: Jonathan Leavitt, 1832);

Select Works of the British Poets, from Chaucer to Jonson, edited, with biographical sketches, by Southey (London: Longman, Rees, Orme, Brown & Green, 1831);

Attempts in Verse, by John Jones, an Old Servant; with Some Account of the Writer, Written by Himself: and an Introductory Essay on the Lives and Works of the Uneducated Poets, introduction by Southey (London: J. Murray, 1831); republished as *Lives of the Uneducated Poets, to Which Are Added Attempts in Verse by John Jones, an Old Servant* (London: H. G. Bohn, 1836);

Isaac Watts, *Horae Lyricae. Poems, Chiefly of the Lyric Kind, in Three Books*, edited, with a memoir, by Southey (London: J. Hatchard & Son, 1834);

The Works of William Cowper, Esq., Comprising His Poems, Correspondence, and Translations. With a Life of the Author, 15 volumes, edited, with a biography, by Southey (London: Baldwin & Craddock, 1835-1837).

SELECTED PERIODICAL PUBLICATIONS
UNCOLLECTED: Review of *Lyrical Ballads, Critical Review*, second series 24 (October 1798): 197-204;

Review of *Gebir*, by Walter Savage Landor, *Critical Review*, second series 27 (September 1799): 29-39;

"Malthus's Essay on the Principles of Population," *Annual Review*, 2 (1804): 292-301;

"Ritsons Ancient English Romances," *Annual Review*, 2 (1804): 515-533;

"Thomas Clarkson's History of the Abolition of the African Slave Trade," *Annual Review*, 7 (1809): 127-148;

"The State of Public Affairs," by Southey and R. Grant, *Quarterly Review*, 22 (January 1820): 492-560;

"The Life of Cromwell," *Quarterly Review*, 25 (July 1821): 279-347;

"Superstition and Knowledge," by Southey and F. Cohen, *Quarterly Review*, 29 (July 1823): 440-475;

"Dr. [Frank] Sayers's Work," *Quarterly Review*, 35 (January 1827): 175-220;

"History of the Dominion of the Arabs and Moors in Spain," *Foreign Quarterly Review*, 1 (July 1827): 1-60;

"On the Corn-Laws," *Quarterly Review*, 51 (March 1834): 228-283.

Robert Southey (Byron correctly, if scathingly, rhymed the name with "mouthey") presents a paradox. Arguably the most prolific, inventive, and diversified of the English Romantics, he was early regarded as the leader of the "Lake School" of radical poets (whose other "members" were William Wordsworth, Samuel Taylor Coleridge, and Charles Lamb), and then for thirty

Edith Fricker Southey at thirty-five (portrait by Matilda Betham; by permission of the Fitz Park Museum, Keswick)

years held the office of poet laureate of England—the first laureate of stature since Ben Jonson and the first to restore the office from the aura of sinecure and sycophancy that had come to surround it. The prime epic poet of that Romantic Indian summer of the epopee, an indefatigable chronicler of both English and Portuguese history, and—as leading essayist for the *Quarterly Review* and other publications—a prominent voice in the political and socioeconomic controversies of that turbulent time, Southey was one of the foremost men of letters of his age. Yet his multitudinous writings are mostly forgotten today. With all his talent, ambition, and tenacity, Southey lacked the concentration and incandescence of genius. His early renown was based on controversy—both literary and political—more than on aesthetic worth, and it faded when those controversies lost their virulence. After almost a half-century of tireless writing, Southey is today remembered for only a few lyrics and ballads, his masterful, much-admired *Life of Nelson* (1813) and his immortal "Tale of the Three Bears." Though there have been some recent efforts to readmit him to the canon, Sou-

they will for the most part remain in the precincts of literary history and biography. Since he was himself an insatiable, even obsessive, antiquarian, book collector, and encyclopedist, it is perhaps an inevitable irony that he should have survived more as a grand museum piece than as a living voice.

Southey's significance is nevertheless considerable, both literarily and with regard to the ideological climate of the day. As a poet, Southey was boldly experimental. In his long poems he revitalized the epic by opening new territories for it and by implementing Richard Hurd's concept of the romance as "romantic epic." As a lyricist he cultivated such innovative forms as the eclogue and the monodrama and played a major role in the Romantic revival of the ballad and the sonnet. As a prose writer he pioneered a more sympathetic, descriptive, and objective mode of reviewing and developed a prose style that is precise, perspicuous, and economical. Above all, as a religious and political thinker and a social and economic analyst, he exemplified both the millennial republican fervor generated among the young intellectuals of

Greta Hall, Keswick (top), where the Southeys settled in September 1803 and continued to live, with Coleridge's wife and children, for the rest of Southey's life; and (bottom) Crosthwaite Church and Bassenthwaite Lake from the garden at Greta Hall (engraving by William Westall, published in volume 6 of Charles Cuthbert Southey's The Life and Correspondence of Robert Southey, *1850)*

his day by the French Revolution in its early stages and the disillusioned about-face performed by many of these enthusiasts in reaction to the Reign of Terror and the subsequent Napoleonic threat. In Southey's case the disenchantment grew at length into a militant Tory conservatism and paternalism and even a bigoted adulation of Church-and-King and the status quo ante. His authoritarianism was all the more fanatical because it compensated for a persistent skepticism regarding the ultimate grounds of belief and authority. Both revolt and reaction, both fame and failure, have their roots in Southey's formative years.

Southey was born on 12 August 1774, the oldest surviving child of Robert Southey, a rather unsuccessful Bristol draper, and his wife, Margaret Hill Southey. One of nine siblings of whom five died in childhood, Southey at two was farmed out to his mother's older half sister, Elizabeth Tyler of Bath, an eccentric and domineering spinster, whose neurotic and compulsive behavior left little Robert at once overprotected and emotionally deprived, imprisoned and in exile, a condition reinforced by the various schools to which he was sent and where he suffered from petty tyranny and lack of nurture. The child early sought compensation in literature and the theater, which was his aunt's passion: he saw his first play at four and was reading William Shakespeare and Francis Beaumont and John Fletcher before he was eight. Not long thereafter he discovered Torquato Tasso's *Jerusalem Delivered,* Ludovico Ariosto's *Orlando Furioso,* and Edmund Spenser's *Faerie Queen,* John Milton's *Paradise Lost,* and Luis de Camoëns's *Lusiad,* among other works, and thence derived his lifelong passion for epic and romance and, in particular, an idolatrous love for Spenser, whose great poem he read some thirty times and once dreamed of completing. He also found relief in the company of his aunt's "half-saved" brother William Tyler, the prototype of the kindly, half-witted William Dove who is the narrator of "The Tale of the Three Bears" in Southey's late, quasi-Shandean work, *The Doctor* (1834-1847).

At thirteen Robert was placed by his uncle, the Reverend Herbert Hill, at Westminster public school, intended to be the eventual gateway to Christ Church College, Oxford. Robert suffered under the obsolete curriculum and fitful discipline as well as the bullying and fagging endemic at British public schools. But he also experienced the joys of close and lasting friendships and of liberating intellectual discoveries, including Voltaire,

Jean-Jacques Rousseau, Edward Gibbon, and Bernard Picart's *Religious Ceremonies,* first English translation, 1731-1739). Fired by their example, Southey published a pseudonymous satire on corporal punishment in *The Flagellant,* a school periodical, of which he had become coeditor, and was promptly found out and expelled by the headmaster, who also effectively denounced him to the authorities at Christ Church. Deeply wounded, and further humiliated by his father's bankruptcy, he plunged into a suicidal mood, from which he rescued himself by reading the stoic Epictetus, ever after his favorite regimen for what he called his "mimosa sensibility."

Early in 1793 Southey entered Balliol College, Oxford, to study for holy orders in accordance with his uncle's wishes. But he soon grew restive again. By now a confirmed republican, as well as a stoic, an enthusiastic supporter of the French Revolution and admirer of the radicalism of Thomas Paine's *Rights of Man* (1791, 1792) and William Godwin's *Enquiry concerning Political Justice* (1793), Southey detested both the pedantry and soulless, quasimonastic regimentation of the masters and the licentiousness and snobbery of the scholars—and signaled his contumacy by refusing to powder his hair. Moreover, he was skeptical about Church dogma and opposed both the idea of priesthood and the Test Act. Essentially a sentimental deist, he prized Christianity for its spirit of charity and its promise of personal immortality and posthumous happiness rather than for its message of sin and salvation.

From this state of uncertainty and anxiety emerged three developments that would shape Southey's entire life: his courtship of Edith Fricker, his friendship with Samuel Taylor Coleridge, and his deepening commitment to a life of poetry and letters. Southey met Sarah, Edith, and Mary Fricker, the daughters of a widowed milliner, in the fall of 1793. A bond of affection quickly developed between Edith and the lonely young poet, and two years later, on 14 November 1795, they married in secret. Edith Southey never shared her husband's imaginative and intellectual life—Coleridge later remarked that Southey's true wife was his library—but she was a devoted helpmate and mother for more than forty years, until her mind failed and she died in 1837.

What Edith Southey could not provide in the way of intellectual partnership, Coleridge offered in abundance. The two young poets met in June 1794 at Oxford; both were ardent republi-

Southey in his study at Greta Hall, 1804, with Derwent Water visible through the window (drawing by Henry Edridge; by permission of the National Portrait Gallery, London)

cans and Revolutionary sympathizers. Southey had of late been thinking about immigration and social experiment as a way out of personal and political dilemmas. The advent of Coleridge proved catalytic, and the two poets, in concert with some of their respective college friends, concocted the utopian scheme of "Pantisocracy," a Coleridgean coinage signifying "equal power, or rule, of all." Twelve young men and their wives were to immigrate to the New World as a kind of Noachic or Mosaic remnant and there establish in the Susquehanna Valley an agricultural and literary commune based on community property and the reintegration of physical and intellectual labor.

Southey left Oxford that summer. For a year or so the two poets busied themselves planning and trying to raise money for the venture by giving lectures and by publications, including a hackwork play, *The Fall of Robespierre* (1794), for which Coleridge wrote the first act and Southey provided the second and third, and a slim vol-

ume of poetry by Southey and Robert Lovell, a fellow Pantisocrat and husband of Mary Fricker. But the funds did not materialize in sufficient quantity–Elizabeth Tyler cut off her nephew when she learned of his plans and of his engagement to a mere seamstress–and ideological and practical differences soon developed between the more radical but dilatory Coleridge and his thrifty, revisionary friend and temporary roommate. Southey eventually abandoned the project as unfeasible and accepted an invitation to Portugal from his uncle, Herbert Hill, and an offer from his school friend Charles Wynn to finance a study of law with an annuity of £160 to begin in October 1796. Coleridge, who had let himself be persuaded for Pantisocracy's sake to become contracted to the third of the Fricker sisters, the pretty but uncongenial and somewhat frigid Sarah, felt entrapped and betrayed, and the friendship suffered an acrimonious breach. The ironies of the relationship did not end there; Southey would in due course wind up in Coleridge's house, taking care of Coleridge's family.

The most important legacy of Southey's Oxford years was, of course, his turn, in earnest, to a life of letters. Already during his dreary childhood and adolescence he had cheered himself by writing plays, epics, and various kinds of descriptive, reflective, and satirical verse totaling close to 30,000 lines. He now became a poet in earnest. Besides lyrical pieces in the vein of sensibility, including satires on politics and academe, nostalgic meditations and retrospects à la Mark Akenside, odes modeled on Thomas Gray and William Collins, and sonnets in the manner of William Lisle Bowles, Southey wrote his first epic, *Joan of Arc* (1796), a poem of more than six thousand lines on the career of Jeanne d'Arc from her emergence at Vaucouleurs to the relief of Orleans and the coronation of Charles VII at recaptured Rheims. Although in many ways a juvenile work, especially in its original (1796) version, marred by conventional "poetic" and Miltonic diction, the use of supernatural machinery, and sentimental rhetoric and melodrama, *Joan of Arc* is revolutionary in several respects. As a pointed analogue to current events, it champions the cause of France, the traditional national enemy, against the British invader. Moreover, it is essentially pacifist in outlook, the war it describes being a war against war. Above all, its protagonist is a woman, a kind of medieval Mary Wollstonecraft or "Tom Paine in petticoats" as Coleridge called her. The choice of subject is not an ideal one for a pacifist and republican poet, since the action, especially that surrounding Joan's comrade-in-arms, Conrade, is still largely martial and culminates in the coronation of a worthless king (contrast the early lines in praise of "Marten the Regicide," written 1793 / 1794). Just as Southey felt free to use a Catholic visionary to serve as his mouthpiece for his sentimental deism and nature worship, so he turned a feudal action into a vehicle for the denunciation of monarchy, priesthood, and dynastic wars and a celebration of "The Triumph of Woman" (the title of an early ode).

Southey extensively revised the work for its second edition (1798), removing the supernatural "machinery"–angelic interventions, a prophetic inset originally supplied by Coleridge (republished by him as "The Destiny of Nations"), and a visionary descent to the underworld subsequently republished as "The Vision of the Maid of Orleans"–and generally pruning and polishing his language. The cleavage between feudal vehi-

cle and republican tenor, however, was past mending–even in the final version of 1837, when Southey, ironically, dropped most of his earlier republican sentiments and transformed the poem into a parable of national independence. But with all its weaknesses, *Joan of Arc* was a considerable success. It sold well and established Southey both as a poet and, eventually, as the chief target for the polemics of the *Anti-Jacobin* review.

Less problematic in the choice of vehicle were two other works written during Southey's early republican phase, *Wat Tyler*, a play about the English peasant rebellion at the time of Richard II, which was dashed off in a week in 1795 but did not see print until it was published surreptitiously by Southey's political enemies in 1817 as a means of embarrassing the "renegade" laureate with the ghost of his Jacobin past; and the "Botany Bay Eclogues," two monologues and two dialogues whose speakers are transported convicts: prostitute, thief, poacher, soldier, and sailor (written 1794; published 1797). Most of the characters in these productions are wooden and two-dimensional, and the ideological thrust is at times undercut by conventional moral and sentimental clichés. Nevertheless, *Wat Tyler* contains some stretches of impassioned egalitarian rhetoric, and the "Botany Bay Eclogues" radically belie not only the traditional pastoral but also the mock-pastoral mode by showing criminals as the victims of social injustice and oppression.

Southey's abandonment of the Pantisocratic dream, his clandestine marriage, and his prompt departure for Portugal on 8 December 1795 marked in fact the end of both his revolutionary radicalism and his adolescence. While the appalling spectacle of poverty, disease, and ignorance that met him on his travels through Portugal and Spain confirmed the need for revolutionary change in Europe in his mind, it also persuaded him of the relative superiority of conditions in England. The answers he had sought in a political millennium and then in the Pantisocratic exodus he now looked for in domestic happiness with his wife–the home life he had never known as a child. The change of outlook is reflected in the "Hymn to the Penates" he wrote after his return to England. Southey would have opportunities for change in his existence in after years–by entering the diplomatic service, embarking upon an academic career, or leading the life of a journalist. But in each case he chose to stay put and to deal with life within the safe domestic context of his family, his household, and his li-

Editorial cartoon that appeared in 1817, after Southey's political enemies had published his early, republican verse play
Wat Tyler *(written in 1795) to embarrass the conservative poet laureate (engraving by C. Williams)*

brary. The worship of the *dii penates* is the true essence of his creed.

Southey's sojourn on the Iberian Peninsula had other effects upon him as well—effects that were reinforced by his second stay there in 1800: his lifelong detestation of Catholicism—what he saw as its stultifying superstitions, "miracle-mongering," and priestly "hagiomania"—and his concurrent passion for Spanish and Portuguese history, culture, and geography, a passion reflected in poetic, journalistic, and historiographic works and one that made him the leading English Hispanist of his day. The first fruit of these experiences was *Letters Written During a Short Residence in Spain and Portugal* (1797), a volume that proved popular and went through several editions (the record of Southey's second sojourn on the Peninsula, his *Journal of a Residence in Portugal 1800-1801,* was not published until 1960).

The period after Southey's return from Por-

tugal in the summer of 1796 was a time of continued ferment and unrest. While ostensibly reading for the law at Gray's Inn in London as stipulated by Wynn's annuity, Southey heartily disliked the subject and did little actual studying. He also disliked London and was only too glad to leave the city in May 1797 when it appeared that its climate did not agree with Edith Southey. For the next several years the Southeys lived in various places in the south of England, including the village of Westbury, outside Bristol (1798-1799). Although this period brought great personal gains, including a reconciliation with Coleridge and friendships with the young scientist Humphry Davy and the litterateur and amateur Germanist William Taylor of Norwich, Southey was understandably anxious about his future and was plagued by ill health. It was a sudden fear of consumption that prompted him to return to Portugal in 1800–this time with Edith Southey.

Literarily, however, these years were perhaps the most creative and exhilarating of Southey's career. To eke out his income, he began to review, at first for the *Monthly Magazine* with a series of notices on Spanish and Portuguese literature, and then, starting in 1798, for the *Critical Review*, for which he wrote his rather unflattering review of Wordsworth and Coleridge's *Lyrical Ballads* (October 1798). Moreover, the period was for him a time of lyrical efflorescence, helped along by his engagement to write verses for the *Morning Post* at a guinea a week. Between 1797 and 1800 he published two volumes of *Poems*, as well as the two volumes of *The Annual Anthology*, comprising verse that was mostly his own.

Southey's lyrics are of interest more for their formal and thematic variety and innovativeness than for more central qualities of complexity and figurative power. He experimented successfully with the sonnet and the ode–especially the "minor" or monostrophic ode–and, less happily, with the irregular ode and certain classical meters such as the Sapphic strophe. Many of his lyrics are emblematic in nature, including "The Ebb-Tide," "The Oak of the Fathers," "The Holly Tree," and poems on animals, such as "To a Spider," "The Dancing Bear," "The Filbert," and especially "The Pig, a Colloquial Poem"–a vein Southey, an ardent cat lover, had opened early with "The College Cat," written at Oxford. His sonnets, too, tend toward the emblematic ("The Evening Rainbow," "To Winter"). At their best these poems combine simple images with some humor and homely, though sometimes hackneyed, household wisdom. Sententiousness and humor are also marks of Southey's inscriptional verse, a form he was to use again some years later in a somberer vein in a series of inscriptions commemorating important episodes of the Peninsular War against Napoleon.

It is as a writer of ballads and quasidramatic poems that Southey comes most into his own as a lyricist. The latter category comprises several "monodramas" as well as a series of "eclogues." The monodrama is a type Southey derived from German models, though its ultimate antecedents are in late antiquity. Unlike the dramatic monologue proper, it is largely an oratorical set piece, usually a suicide speech, eloquent but without psychological or ironic dimension, and its subjects are for the most part remote in time or place. More spontaneous, less formally

rhetorical, are the related "Songs of the American Indians," but they too appeal mainly to the taste for the remote and exotic. Much closer to home are the "English Eclogues," written at Westbury as pendants to the earlier "Botany Bay" poems. Both the monodramas and the eclogues are of interest as contexts for Wordsworth and Coleridge's *Lyrical Ballads,* many of which are similarly dramatic in technique. Especially the "English Eclogues" reveal striking similarities to the *Lyrical Ballads* in their predominantly local, rustic, and anecdotal subject matter and their cultivation of a simple, colloquial style, more unadorned even than Wordsworth's language–most of the eclogues are actual dialogues between rustic characters. The themes, too, are akin to those of *Lyrical Ballads:* the plight of the old and poor, forsaken and suffering motherhood, the psychology of guilt, and the prominence of superstition in untutored minds.

Southey's major lyrical achievement, however, lies in the area of the ballad, especially the ballad of the supernatural. For the most part, his lyricism is paralyzed by the fatal need to defuse feeling by turning it into ready-made abstractions and tepid sentiments rather than braving the perilous music of charged and ambiguous metaphor. But he could tell a story briskly and impressively, especially with the aid of supernatural effects used to disentangle moral and psychological complexities and to disarm terror by making it more grotesque than sublime. He thus holds a key position in the history of the ballad revival brought on by Bishop Thomas Percy's *Reliques of Ancient English Poetry* (1765) and German *Kunstballaden* such as Gottfried August Bürger's ballad of the specter bridegroom, *Lenore* (which William Taylor's 1797 translation had made famous in England).

Some of Southey's ballads are in fact realistic exercises in ironic point of view, such as "The Complaints of the Poor," the well-known antiwar poem "The Battle of Blenheim," and "The Cross-Roads," on a female victim of male brutality, injustice, and bigotry. Others explore (or exploit) the pathology of madness and guilt ("Mary, the Maid of the Inn," "The Mad Woman," "The Sailor Who Had Served in the Slave-Trade," "Jasper"). More often, however, sin and its consequences are treated in terms of poetic justice being rendered by supernatural agencies ("The Inchcape Rock," "Lord William," "Bishop Bruno," "God's Judgment on a Wicked Bishop") and even of overt diablerie ("Rudiger," "The Old Woman of

Cousins Sara Coleridge and Edith May Southey, daughters of the poets, at Greta Hall, 1820 (portrait by E. Nash; by permission of the National Portrait Gallery, London)

Berkley," "Cornelius Agrippa"). Many of these ballads (and longer "metrical tales") were undertaken (like Coleridge's "Rime of the Ancient Mariner") as potboilers. But they were also a means of exorcizing a deep-seated obsession with the diabolic, which, underneath his rational exterior, haunted Southey all his life, especially in his dreams. We may surely sense a personal reference in the ballad of the "Pious Painter" who spends his life portraying Lucifer and is haunted at night by what he "wrought on by day."

An obsession with death and the diabolic pervades not only Southey's ballads but also his second long poem, *Thalaba the Destroyer* (1801), a romance based on a spurious sequel to the *Arabian Nights* and written in the vein of Gothic Orientalism already made popular by William Beckford's *Vathek* (1786) and Walter Savage Landor's *Gebir* (1798), which Southey reviewed for the *Critical Review* (September 1799). During these years of intense creativity, Southey had at first concentrated

his main efforts on an epic about the legendary Welsh prince Madoc, who supposedly discovered and settled in the New World three centuries before Columbus–a project that had intrigued and occupied the young poet ever since his Westminster days. A first complete version was finished during the Westbury period, but Southey then put it aside as unsatisfactory and turned to *Thalaba*.

That poem sprang in part from another consuming poetic ambition he had conceived early on, namely to illustrate the major mythologies of the world in epic form, as the minor poet Frank Sayers had done on a modest scale with Teutonic myth in his *Dramatic Sketches of the Ancient Northern Mythology* (1790). At various times he planned poems on the Deluge, on Zoroasterism, Hinduism, Teutonic mythology, and Islam. Most of these remained in the planning stage. An epic in hexameters on the rise of Mohammed was commenced in collaboration with Coleridge but then

Robert Southey (portrait by T. Phillips; from Edmund Gosse, English Literature: An Illustrated Record, *1904)*

abandoned. Since Southey had already come to regard epic "machinery" as unacceptable in historical contexts, he chose as the new vehicle for his project on Islam the essentially ahistorical romance, as he did again later for his Hindu project. *Thalaba* and *The Curse of Kehama* (1810) thus are the principal results of this extraordinary instance of the Romantic fascination with mythopoesis, though Southey's epics *Madoc* (1805) and *Roderick* (1814) also contain an abundance of mythological material, represented as priestcraft and popular superstition rather than as objectively existing.

Thalaba is, of course, hardly a reliable picture of the Moslem religion, except in its emphasis on *islam*, "submission" to the will of Allah. For the most part it exploits popular beliefs and legends that Southey collected from his reading in contemporary sources on the Near East. Its story concerns the overthrow of the "Domdaniel," an infernal "seminary" of malignant sorcerers, by a champion of Allah, the young Moslem Thalaba,

thence named the Destroyer. The sorcerers seek to prevent the prophesied doom by annihilating Thalaba's family and, when they discover that the young hero himself has escaped, by seeking to entrap, seduce, and corrupt him in various ways. Of course they fail as each trial becomes a step in Thalaba's progress toward selfless dedication and moral strength. The hero's quest takes him to several oracles, through a variety of tempting earthly paradises, including the famous one of Aloadin, the "Old Man of the Mountain," and through many encounters with horrific sorcerers and sorceresses, to the final harrowing of the Domdaniel. There Thalaba recovers his father's magic sword, successfully defeats the necromantic crew, and brings down their den of iniquity by plunging the sword into the heart of the "Living Image" of Eblis, the Moslem Satan, that supports the vault. He is thereupon received into paradise by the "Houri form" of his beloved Oneiza, whose death on their wedding night had been the severest of his trials–a superdomestic denouement that is typically Southeyan.

The poem labors under a plethora of episodes and magical paraphernalia–a result of Southey's antiquarian preoccupation with mythology and "manners"–and a consequent disequilibrium between vehicle and tenor. Though Thalaba's various trials can be construed as a series of tests involving the temptations of pleasure, power, and self-righteousness, thematic and symbolic progression is obscured by the narrative redundancy, a headlong expansiveness reinforced by the rhymeless irregular, "spasmodic" verse Southey adopted from Sayers. Moreover, the central conflict of the story is too crass, abstract, and gratuitous, lacking in psychological density and now also in political relevance, and its hero, who single-handedly defeats the Principle of Evil itself, too overweening in his very naive perfection, to engross the reader as myth or enlighten him as allegory. Nevertheless, *Thalaba* remains an eminent example of Romantic Orientalism, and it established Southey as the temporary leader of the "Lake School" and exercised a powerful influence on such later writers as the young Percy Bysshe Shelley, who prized it as his favorite poem, and the young Francis Newman.

Southey completed *Thalaba* during his second, longer stay in Portugal (May 1800-June 1801)–a period occupied by extensive researches for a planned "History of Portugal" and equally far-flung donkey rides through the countryside, and one he always fondly remembered for its double excitement of literary discovery and personal happiness. After his return to England, he continued in an unsettled state for some time. Having by now abandoned the idea of a legal career, he obtained a post in London as private secretary to Isaac Corry, the Irish Chancellor of the Exchequer, but disliked the sinecure of the position and resigned six months later, in May 1802. For some years he still entertained the thought of entering the diplomatic service–mainly as a way of returning to Portugal–but he was more and more resolved to earn his living by his pen. Besides continuing to review for the *Critical Review*, he engaged himself in 1802 as a reviewer for the newly founded *Annual Review*, for which he reviewed some 150 works during the next six years. Capitalizing on his linguistic proficiencies, he also published a translation of the Spanish *Amadis of Gaul* (1803), which sold well and was followed by his translations of *Palmerin of England* from the Portuguese in 1807 and the Spanish

Chronicle of the Cid in 1808. Also in 1803 he edited, with Bristol bookseller Joseph Cottle, a three-volume edition of the works of his fellow Bristol poet Thomas Chatterton.

The year 1803 proved decisive in other respects as well. At the beginning of 1802, Southey's mother had died. Several months later the Southeys had moved back to Bristol, and there Edith had given birth to their first child, Margaret, in August. When the baby died of hydrocephalus a year later, however, the devastated parents could not bear to remain in Bristol. For the past year, Coleridge had been pressing his brother-in-law to live with his family at Greta Hall in Keswick, where he had meanwhile moved in order to be near Wordsworth. When the invitation was now renewed, the bereaved parents accepted. They arrived in Keswick in September of 1803–never to leave again. Coleridge soon afterward departed for Malta in search of health and returned from there only to separate at last from his wife and to settle in London–leaving Southey in charge of Greta Hall and all its inhabitants for the rest of his life.

Southey's main poetic project during these years was the massive, two-part epic *Madoc* (1805), his principal bid for epic fame by which he hoped to become the most original epic poet since Milton. The Westbury version, whose exploitation of the sentimental interest in the Incas of Peru had ceased to satisfy Southey, was now refitted with an Aztec context and greatly expanded to accommodate the Welsh scenery and antiquities Southey had gone to Wales to collect in the autumn of 1801, the bulk of this work being done in Keswick and with Coleridge's encouragement. The poem represents a joint tribute to two opposite Romantic tendencies: the medievalism of the Celtic Revival, and the New World utopianism of which Pantisocracy had been Southey's personal variant. It thus enabled the poet to combine his penchant for the exotic with his realization, after the Francophilia of *Joan of Arc*, that an English epic poet should have an English subject. The medieval Welsh bards were widely regarded as both the inheritors of the "true," patriarchal faith and–as in Thomas Gray's *Bard* (1757)–spokesmen for freedom from dynastic and ecclesiastical oppression. Wales could thus represent the once and future England, whose pristine heritage could become the *fons et origo* of a redeemed civilization in the New World. At the same time, that new frontier could furnish not only the "natural" state of Romantic primitivism but, in the Aztec culture, also the most abhorrent example of superstition and priestcraft, beyond the worst that Southey had seen in the Catholic south. The final product is thus not so much Pantisocracy writ large as it is Southey's *Aeneid* and *Lusiad*, his epic of colonization and incipient empire.

The poem elaborates on the legendary discovery and settlement of America by the twelfth-century Welsh prince Madoc. Part 1, "Madoc in Wales," tells of Madoc's return from the New World for the purpose of recruiting additional settlers. At the wedding banquet of his older brother David, the current ruler of North Wales, Madoc depicts the conditions of dynastic and fratricidal struggle that had prompted him to brave the unknown for a fresher world beyond the Western sea and relates his discovery of the New World and of the Mississippi Valley, his alliance with a tribe of peaceful nomads, the Hoamen, against the warlike and priest-ridden Aztecs, the war with and the victory over the Aztecs, and the resulting peace and abolishment of the practice of human sacrifice (the story antedates the Aztec migration to Central America). The remainder of "Madoc in Wales" uses Madoc's recruiting project to take the reader through a Romantic round of Welsh local color–the *gorsedd* (congress) of bards at the "Druid circle," the ancient sanctuary of Bardsey, and so on–and to fill out the political picture of usurpation, ecclesiastical dominance, and imminent restoration under Llewelyn the Great. Madoc is impaled on the horns of the Romantic dilemma of nostalgia for the past and utopian futurism but is able to resolve the dilemma, and the part concludes with a splendid embarkation and a twofold, if ideologically rather contradictory, prospect of republican exodus on the one hand and messianic restoration on the other.

Except for this ambivalent note, Southey might perhaps have done well to end the story in its expanded form here. Given the priority of the colonial theme, however, and his horrified fascination with mythology and with Mexican idolatry in particular, it was inevitable that, as in the *Aeneid*, the "Odyssey part" on wanderings should be followed by an "Iliad part" on war. In "Madoc in Aztlan" Madoc returns to face an incipient revolt, and a relapse into the old bloody religion, among both the Aztecs and the hitherto peaceful Hoamen. Madoc is able to interrupt the Hoamen's ritual and to reconvert them by an act of "deicide." At Aztlan, however, the Aztec priests stage a triumphant comeback for their gruesome rituals and succeed in mobilizing the

warriors for an all-out attack on the Welsh intruders. Madoc himself is captured and compelled to undergo a series of sacrificial single combats, but he escapes and, during the ensuing battle, wins the day by killing the Aztec king and smashing (shades of Thalaba) the idol of the god Mexitli. Driven from their city, the Aztecs nonetheless rally again and launch a second massive attack from the lake, but are again defeated. A volcanic catastrophe at an epochal moment in their calendar finally convinces them that their cause is lost, and the poem ends with the hardiest gathering around the image of Mexitli to begin the historic trek south, while the rest are consigned to Madoc's "easy yoke." The utopian exodus from the Old World thus ironically triggers a further exodus in the New, while the quester for Pantisocracy assumes the "white man's burden" of colonization and conversion.

Like *Joan of Arc, Madoc* is divided between its pacifist theme and its dependence on the martial conventions of the epic–between "goodness" and "greatness," as well as between revolution and restoration–though war now seems more nearly justified by the nature of the opposition. (In 1811-1829 Southey attempted to write a New World epic of postrevolutionary nonviolence, *Oliver Newman:* it significantly remained a fragment.) A parallel dichotomy vitiates Southey's treatment of the Indians. Although much of the detail for "Madoc in Aztlan" is faithfully adapted from accounts of Cortés's conquest of Mexico and although the poem represents in many ways the culmination of previous literary treatments of the American Indian, it does not succeed in transcending the abstract dispute between sentimental primitivism and Hobbist savagism that bedeviled most of the literature prior to James Fenimore Cooper. Without a genuine anthropology of culture, Southey, though fascinated as a poet with all forms of ethnicity, almost always belittles them as aberrations from, and corruptions of, some abstract philosophical (and parochial) norm, one that renders the hero who embodies it rather anemic and colorless (Madoc is essentially a sentimental deist rather than a twelfth-century Catholic), while the antagonists are colorful and "ethnic" in direct proportion to their abnormality. The poet and historian of "manners" is thus hamstrung by the philosopher of morals for whom imaginative gusto is always compromised by its moral ambiguity. The same is true of Southey's treatment of character generally, for example in the removal of all carnal elements from

Southey in 1828 (engraving based on a portrait by Sir Thomas Lawrence)

the personality of Madoc in the final version (he originally was to have married an Indian chieftainess), so that only one or two of the Aztecs emerge with any sort of three-dimensional ambivalence and emotional conflict. Within these limitations, *Madoc* is nonetheless a substantial work, written in a pure, unadorned style and rich in action and colorful scenes and settings that periodically rise to genuine poetic, if rarely tragic, intensity.

Madoc did not turn out to be the epochal work Southey had hoped it would be. Although this poem, like the earlier *Joan of Arc* and *Thalaba*, went through several, sometimes heavily revised, editions, sales of these volumes were meager enough to discourage further poetic ventures of the type. Life at Greta Hall after Coleridge's departure, moreover, was not greatly conducive to a carefree poet's life, despite such gains as the beauty of the Lake District and new friendships

with Wordsworth and Walter Scott. A second daughter, Edith May, was born to the Southeys in 1804, a son, Herbert, in 1806, and there was Coleridge's family, and the widowed Mary Fricker, to take care of as well. Even at thirty-two, Southey began to gray and to feel that he was aging.

His principal literary occupations for the next few years, besides the reviewing and the work on his "History of Portugal," were thus his translations, several editorial projects (including *Specimens of the Later English Poets* and *The Remains of Henry Kirke White* in 1807), and a work of journalism and sociocultural criticism, the remarkable, pseudonymous *Letters from England* (1807), purported to have been written by a Spaniard, Don Manuel Alvarez Espriella, and translated from the Spanish. In this book Southey used his knowledge of the Spanish character and mentality to describe and criticize British culture, manners, politics, and social and economic conditions from a "naive" outsider's point of view in the manner of Voltaire's *Lettres Philosophiques* and Oliver Goldsmith's *Citizen of the World* (1762). The *Letters from England* are a mine of information about England at the beginning of the nineteenth century and during the lull in the Napoleonic War achieved by the Peace of Amiens. Southey still retains much of his liberal and reforming spirit as he excoriates the obsolescence and corruption of Britain's political, penal, and social-service systems, or the plight of the new industrial poor created by the unchecked growth of the "manufacturing system" in towns such as Manchester and Birmingham, and satirizes the mélange of British commercialism and British spleen, especially in the religious domain. The epistolary form of the work makes for lack of system but also for spontaneity and drama, as Southey plays his social indignation off against his anti-Catholicism. The *Letters from England* may be said to have launched Southey's later career as a writer of prose.

The best of his poetry, however, was yet to come. Early in 1808 he met and befriended Walter Savage Landor, who encouraged him to go on with his mythological series and offered to pay any costs of publication. Southey thereupon resumed work on his Hindu project, eventually entitled *The Curse of Kehama*, which he had begun after the completion of *Thalaba* but had then put aside. He largely recast it and finished it by the end of 1809, only to set out upon yet another epic venture, *Roderick*, on the reconquest of Spain from the Moors.

The Curse of Kehama is a romance like *Thalaba*, equally bizarre and extravagant, and even more profuse in its mythological machinery and other exotic curiosities from Southey's vast and out-of-the-way reading. Unlike the earlier poem, however, it embodies in the title figure an archetype of evil in the form of a lust for absolute power that, unlike the gratuitous necromancy of the Domdaniel, is not entirely without relevance in an age of Napoleonic–or Nazi–world conquest. And it pits against this antagonist a hero who brings about the overthrow of the tyrant not by violence or puritanical righteousness but by his very predicament as a pariah, an outcast from both society and nature, conjointly with the tyrant's inevitably overreaching himself–the sort of consistently pacifist denouement that had eluded Southey in his other epics and that Shelley would later perfect in *Prometheus Unbound*

(1820), in part through the inspiration of Southey's poem.

Kehama is an Oriental potentate and chief Brahman who, in return for countless austerities and sacrifices to the god Shiva, has acquired nearly total power and who needs only to conquer the kingdom of death to complete his deification. His Promethean opponent is the peasant Ladurlad, who, when the poem opens, has killed Kehama's son Arvalan to save his daughter from rape and has thereby drawn Kehama's most terrible curse upon his head, one that banishes him not only from society but from all the elements and from every creature comfort, including food and drink, age and death, and, worst of all, sleep. But while the predicament of exile from nature's blessings represents the height of the Romantic agony, it also unexpectedly arms the hero with preternatural powers for his struggle against the adversary–whence the motto of the poem (Grecified from one of Southey's uncle William Tyler's sayings): that curses like chickens "always come home to roost." Thus, while Kehama increasingly consolidates his conquest of earth and heaven, Ladurlad is able to retard this conquest and to protect both his daughter Kailyal and the angelic *glendoveer* Ereenia, who has befriended and fallen in love with Kailyal, from the ghoulish revenant of Arvalan and from Kehama himself. The quest leads again through various paradises, sunken cities, and sacred mountains to a grand denouement in *Padalon*, the Hindu Hades. Here Kehama, having deposed the death god Yamen, demands the *Amreeta* or Water of Immortality but finds that by the justice of the awakened god Shiva he obtains from it only an eternity of torment–the fate he had pronounced upon Ladurlad. While Kehama is thus hoist on his own petard, Kailyal becomes the immortal consort of Ereenia, and Ladurlad regains the blessing of sleep and, like Thalaba, is rewarded by a reunion with his dead wife in a domestic Elysium.

The poem is again vitiated by its melodramatic division of characters into goats of unmixed malignity and lewdness and sheep of pure, Platonic virtue. Yet the figure of Kehama himself is intelligible despite his cosmic megalomania. Conversely, the champion of good, while now without decisive effect on the final outcome of the struggle, by the same token commands admiration by his patience and lack of self-righteousness: the ultimate "Destroyer" is now the god Shiva rather than a mortal hero. Moreover, the poem's poetic caliber is often high:

Southey's addition of rhyme to the free verse of *Thalaba* makes for some enchanting music, the magical and exotic settings, both luminous and somber, often touch the imagination, and the narrative acquires a measure of depth from its ironic reverses and its incorporation of suggestive, if inchoate, symbols of suttee and *amreeta,* juggernaut and lingam. Besides, the poem's influence on Shelley gives it some importance in literary history.

The ideal of nonviolent resistance does not carry over, however, to Southey's last major poem, *Roderick, the Last of the Goths* (1814). Between the completion of *Kehama* and that of *Roderick* four years later, Southey's general orientation underwent the decisive turn to the right, a change that would in due course earn him the stigma of renegade and turncoat from liberals such as Byron, Shelley, and William Hazlitt and the *Edinburgh Review.* The change coincided, roughly, with his appointment, by the prince regent, to the post of poet laureate (in 1813); but it was not caused by that appointment, as his enemies charged or implied. What prompted Southey to relinquish his remaining republican sympathies for the monarchist, establishmentarian, and generally authoritarian stance of his later years was, on the one hand, the callous laissez-faire attitude of the Whigs toward the plight of the laboring poor and, on the other, the threat of anarchy and a *"bellum servile"* Southey saw in the leftist Burdett and Luddite riots and in the assassination, in 1812, of Prime Minister Spencer Perceval. Above all, however, Southey was incensed by the attitude of compromise and outright sympathy of the liberals toward Napoleon, a man whom Southey had come to regard as the devil incarnate. In place of the "war-mongers" whom he had still denounced in the *Letters from England,* he now inveighed against the "peace-mongers," whose willingness to negotiate with the adversary seemed impious treason to him. Southey's anti-Bonapartism reached its peak with the outbreak of the Peninsular War, whose phases he chronicled in the *Edinburgh Annual Register* between 1809 and 1812 and eventually in his three-volume *History of the Peninsular War* (1823, 1827, 1832). *Roderick* must be seen in this context.

The story of Spain's betrayal to the Moors in retaliation for the rape of the daughter of a noble, Count Julian, by Roderick, the last of the Visigothic kings, had been the subject of one of Southey's monodramas as early as 1802. By 1805 Southey had decided to base a final epic on the "Catholic mythology" on this story, now expanded to include the beginning of the *reconquista* under Pelayo, the founder of the new Spanish monarchy. Fired by the popular uprising of the *Dos de Mayo* in Spain in 1808, Southey began the poem, to be called "Pelayo, or Spain Restored," as a paean, like the earlier *Joan of Arc,* to national liberation and independence, with Pelayo as the hero and Roderick as another Arvalan and embodiment of the ancien régime. In line with his subsequent ideological about-face, however, the focus of the poem eventually shifted from Pelayo to Roderick himself, whose legendary survival as a penitent, after his defeat by the Moors in the Battle on the Guadalete (711 A.D.), became now the basis for an exoneration of legitimatist monarchy and of Roderick himself. Southey has the king eventually quit the life of a remorseful anchorite ascribed to him by the monkish chroniclers to rally the Gothic barons against the Moors. Ordained as a priest and traveling incognito under the assumed name Maccabee, Roderick succeeds in freeing his cousin Pelayo from confinement as a hostage at the Moorish court at Cordoba and persuades him to return with him to the mountainous north to organize the *reconquista*–the historical analogue to the *guerrilla* of the Peninsular War. Pelayo is proclaimed king by the Asturian barons, and after several preliminary clashes, the poem climaxes with the legendary ambush and rout of the Moors at Covadonga, popularly regarded as the beginning of the *reconquista.* Roderick, after a series of recognition scenes–with his dog, his mother, the renegade Count Julian, and the violated Florinda (who, it turns out, passionately loved, and was loved by, the unhappy king)–is at last revealed to all by his martial prowess but disappears again after thus having set his country on the road to recovery.

Roderick represents the culmination of Southey's poetic career. The poem was well received–even Byron thought it "the first poem of the time"–and as a result sold well and eventually was translated into both French and Dutch. The story, despite a profusion of characters and intrigues, is well constructed and, as a myth of national foundation and liberation, had an urgent relevance at least for its time. For once, too, in his treatment of Roderick, Florinda, and her father, Count Julian, Southey made allowances for the tragic ambiguities and contradictions of human motives and impulses beyond the usual cartoons of virtue and vice. His firsthand knowledge of Iberian culture and geography also contributes to the poem's attaining an authenticity beyond the bookishness of his other works.

Roderick is, nevertheless, not without flaws. Character, and even setting, is interpreted more than depicted, and many of the subsidiary figures are reduced to the usual fiends and paragons. Although Southey refrains from excessive Catholic baiting in the narrative, he makes up for it in the numerous scholarly footnotes that accompany all his epics and in which epic machinery is, so to speak, converted into scholarly apparatus. Moreover, he compensates in the poem itself by venting his spleen on the Moors, who, as stand-ins for Napoleon's forces, are made into scapegoats for Southey's religious as well as his political bigotry and xenophobia. As a result the poem breathes an appalling spirit of vindictiveness and religious hatred and intolerance that is neither justified by the historical facts nor reconcilable with Southey's own earlier sentiments, though it is abundantly paralleled in the contemporaneous and subsequent laureate poems, especially the anti-Bonapartist odes, such as the *Carmen Triumphale* (1814).

With the publication of *Roderick*, Southey's poetic career is virtually at an end. Most of his laureate verse, even of the fraction that he chose to reprint in his collected poems, is unpalatable fustian, whether diatribe or panegyric, though there are spots of spirited invective. *The Poet's Pilgrimage to Waterloo* (1816) is stylistically accomplished and contains some poignant descriptions and anecdotes of the fateful battlefield, but the elegiac tone is increasingly drowned out by an unctuous and gloating jingoism, and the whole is then capped by a ponderous dream vision, in which revolutionary materialism and postrevolutionary nihilism are evoked to be solemnly exorcised by a homily on divine providence as embodied in British hegemony and a colonial pax Britannica. One must also mention *A Vision of Judgement* (1821)–Southey's absurd endeavor to apotheosize the mad George III and to vindicate his reign sub specie aeternitatis of a Heaven seen as a mere extension of the Tory establishment–not only because of the virulent attack on Byron and the "Satanic School of Poetry" which prefaced it and the brilliant retort it provoked, but also because in its use of hexameters and domestic-celestial machinery it represents an (anticlimactic) coming-full-circle of Southey's poetic career. Except for two late metrical tales (*All for Love; and the Pilgrim to Compostella*, 1829) and the Spenserian *Tale of Paraguay* (1825) about the lives and pious deaths of a

family of Guarani mission Indians in Paraguay, Southey's publications during his later years are in prose.

Although from early on Southey began to earn his living as a reviewer and journalist, his main career as a prose writer may be said to date from 1809, when he was appointed as a regular contributor to the *Quarterly Review*, a publication founded in that year to serve as a conservative countervoice to the liberal *Edinburgh Review*. During the next thirty years, Southey contributed almost ten dozen long review essays to the *Quarterly*, the most important of which he republished as *Essays, Moral and Political* in 1832. In these he became a major, if often immoderate, voice for the Tory establishment and for a humane, in some ways even prescient (though also paternalistic, not to say theocratic) Tory socialism. His religious, political, and socioeconomic philosophy was further elaborated in such polemical publications as *The Book of the Church* (1824), *Vindiciæ Ecclesiæ Anglicanæ* (1826), and *Sir Thomas More: or, Colloquies on the Progress and Prospects of Society* (1829), which acquired a lasting fame from Thomas Babington Macauley's scathing review-essay *(Edinburgh Review,* January 1830).

More than as a polemicist, however, Southey regarded himself as a historian, especially after the waning of his poetic productivity. The great "History of Portugal," begun in 1800, would, he hoped, be the work of the century, rivaling Gibbon's *Decline and Fall of the Roman Empire*, as well as his own epics, as a definitive analysis of old-style, Catholic imperialism and thus be both an inspiration and a warning to the new-style British Empire. Only one brief episode, the masterly *Expedition of Orsua; and the Crimes of Aguirre* (1821), was ever published, and most of what must have been a voluminous manuscript disappeared after Southey's death. However, as an offshoot of the Portuguese project, Southey compiled and published a vast three-volume, more-than-2,300-page *History of Brazil* (1810, 1817, 1819), a pioneering work that is still authoritative today, as its recent retranslation into Portuguese indicates. It reveals Southey as a painstaking scholar who, however, is incapable of selection and synthesis, and sometimes of impartiality–a criticism that also applies to his other historical works, and even to some of his biographies, such as *The Life of Wesley* (1820) and the *Lives of the British Admirals* (1833-1840).

In his last work, *The Doctor, &c.* (1834-1847), a quasi-Shandean, but in fact uniquely

Caroline Ann Bowles, who married Southey in 1839 (from Edward Dowden, ed., The Correspondence of Robert Southey with Caroline Bowles, *1881)*

Southeyan, omnium-gatherum of narrative, veiled autobiography, anecdote, essay, aphorism, and plain buffoonery, Southey elevates his incurable prolixity into a conscious structural principle but does not thereby always avoid tedium either, despite such occasional gems as the charming "Tale of the Three Bears." It is perhaps because *The Life of Nelson* (1813) began as a concise review of the official biography by J. S. Clarke and John M'Arthur that Southey's account of England's greatest naval hero remains today his one undisputed masterpiece. Though uncritical toward Horatio, Viscount Nelson's fanatical jingoism (which he himself shared) and certainly unsympathetic toward Nelson's relationship with Lady Emma Hamilton, Southey nevertheless achieves a portrait of Admiral Nelson that is both heroic and humane, detailed, even technical at times, yet unified and alive, hagiographical, yet down-to-earth–perhaps the ultimate, unex-

pected fruit of his long epic quest.

Southey has had his modest share of scholarly attention, including discussions of some of his works in some larger historical or generic context (for example, Brian Wilkie's *Romantic Poets and Epic Tradition,* 1965) and periodic special pleas in places such as the *Times Literary Supplement.* But only three book-length studies devoted entirely to Southey–those by William Haller, Jean Raymond, and the present writer–have been concerned with the *poet* rather than mainly with the man and moralist and his moment in time. For all his aspirations and Gargantuan productivity, Southey the poet, and even Southey the prosateur, has not achieved a prominent place in the literary canon. In the latest of the periodic *TLS* sallies, Marilyn Butler has argued for Southey's admission to the canon–and for the need to revise that canon generally–by citing the intertextual relations of poems such as *Thalaba* and *Kehama* to the oeuvre of Wordsworth and Coleridge, Byron and Shelley as proof of Southey's importance to the Romantic Movement. Yet it is often precisely the minor, noncanonical writers who initiate, and typify, what the major figures perfect and thereby transcend. Southey's importance is of that encyclopedic kind. Even his "Romanticism" is of the elementary sort that makes him, in Raymond's phrase, essentially a "demi-Romantic."

His place in the history of English prose is more prominent. While less pronounced than the respective styles of Charles Lamb, Thomas De Quincey, or Thomas Carlyle, Southey's prose is essentially modern in its clarity, directness, and vigor. Yet ultimately, his prose, like his poetry, is too often more cumulative than synthetic, extensive rather than profound. He loved best, as he said himself, to read and compile, to rummage and extract, whether in his epics, his histories, or his literary editions, some of which, including those of the works of Cowper and of *Pilgrim's Progress,* have a place in the textual history of these works, but none of which can claim true critical significance. For whatever reason, his unhappy, loveless childhood, or the pains and betrayals of his adult life–of his eight children, for example, he lost four, including his first, and his passionately loved first son, Herbert–he preferred to contend with life from the safe bastion and fetish of his 14,000-volume library rather than at close quarters–an embattled hermit, a crusader in an ivory tower, an admirer of Rousseau's *Confessions* who launched the word *autobiography* and wrote thousands of spirited letters but left no *Prelude,* a lover of the exotic who in forty of his sixty-eight years never budged from the Lake District except for occasional travels abroad, visits, or business trips (such as for the conferral of an honorary doctorate at Oxford in 1820). "My days among the dead are past," he wrote about his books in the best-known and truest of his lyrics.

He was a "demi-Romantic"–or rather Romantic manqué–in other ways as well. He was endlessly fascinated by mythology yet despised it as superstition. He had grave doubts about such cardinal doctrinal points as the Fall, the plenary inspiration of the Bible, and the divine nature of Christ; yet he detested metaphysics and fiercely, even bigotedly, defended both Christianity and the established church as, in his view, the only sufficient guarantees of social and personal harmony. Conversely, while the primmest and most fervent of monogamists, he yet cultivated several intense epistolary friendships with other women: when Edith Southey died in 1837, after three years of mental illness, he married one of them (on 4 June 1839), the minor poet and spinster Caroline Ann Bowles, after twenty years of intimate correspondence. Shortly thereafter, however, his own mind began to fail, worn out from a lifetime of suppressed passion and herculean drudgery of the pen. He died of a stroke on 21 March 1843, and was buried in Crosthwaite Churchyard, Keswick, alongside his first wife and three of his dead children.

Letters:

A Memoir of the Life and Writings of the Late William Taylor, of Norwich . . . (Containing his Correspondence with Robert Southey . . . and Other Eminent Literary Men), 2 volumes, edited by J. W. Robberds (London: Murray, 1843);

Joseph Cottle, *Reminiscences of Samuel Taylor Coleridge and Robert Southey* (London: Houlston & Stoneman, 1848);

The Life and Correspondence of Robert Southey, 6 volumes, edited by Charles Cuthbert Southey (London: Longman, Brown, Green & Longmans, 1849, 1850);

Selections from the Letters of Robert Southey, 4 volumes, edited by John Wood Warter (London: Longman, Brown, Green & Longmans, 1856);

The Correspondence of Robert Southey with Caroline Bowles, edited by Edward Dowden (Dublin: Hodges, Figgis / London: Longman, 1881);

Letters of Robert Southey: A Selection, edited by Maurice H. Fitzgerald (London, New York & Toronto: Oxford University Press, 1912);

New Letters of Robert Southey, 2 volumes, edited by Kenneth Curry (New York & London: Columbia University Press, 1965);

The Letters of Robert Southey to John May, 1797-1838, edited by Charles Ramos (Austin: Jenkins, 1976).

Bibliographies:

Ernest Bernbaum, *Guide through the Romantic Movement,* revised and enlarged edition (New York: Ronald Press, 1949);

Kenneth Curry, "Southey," in *The English Romantic Poets & Essayists: A Review of Research and Criticism,* edited by Carolyn Washburn Houtchens and Lawrence Huston Houtchens (New York: Published for the Modern Language Association by New York University Press, 1966), pp. 155-182;

Curry and Robert Dedmon, "Southey's Contributions to the *Quarterly Review*," *Wordsworth Circle*, 6 (Autumn 1975): 261-272;

Curry, *Robert Southey: A Reference Guide* (Boston: Hall, 1977);

Mary Ellen Priestley, "The Southey Collection in the Fitz Park Museum, Keswick, Cumbria," *Wordsworth Circle*, 11 (Winter 1980): 43-64.

Biographies:

Edward Dowden, *Robert Southey* (London: Macmillan, 1879);

William Haller, *The Early Life of Robert Southey* (New York: Columbia University Press, 1917);

Jack Simmons, *Southey* (London: Collins, 1945);

Malcolm Elwin, *The First Romantics* (New York: Longmans, Green, 1948).

References:

Ernest Bernhardt-Kabisch, *Robert Southey* (Boston: Twayne, 1977);

Marilyn Butler, "Revising the Canon," *Times Literary Supplement*, 4-10 December 1987, pp. 1349, 1359-1360;

Adolfo Cabral, *Southey e Portugal: 1774-1801* (Lisbon: Fernandez, 1959);

Geoffrey Carnall, *Robert Southey* (London & New York: Longmans, Green, 1964);

Carnall, *Robert Southey and His Age: The Development of a Conservative Mind* (Oxford: Clarendon Press, 1960);

Alfred Cobban, *Edmund Burke and the Revolt Against the Eighteenth Century: A Study of the Political and Social Thinking of Burke, Wordsworth, Coleridge, and Southey* (New York: Macmillan, 1929);

Kenneth Curry, *Southey* (London & Boston: Routledge & Kegan Paul, 1975);

Maria O. Da Silva Dias, *O Fardo Do Homem Branco: Southey, historiador do Brazil* (Sao Paulo: Companhia Editora Nacional, 1974);

Richard Hoffpauir, "The Thematic Structure of Southey's Epic Poetry," *Wordsworth Circle*, 6 (Autumn 1975): 240-249; 7 (Spring 1976): 109-116;

Kenneth Hopkins, *The Poets Laureate* (London: Bodley Head, 1954);

Mary Jacobus, "Southey's Debt to *Lyrical Ballads*," *Review of English Studies*, 22 (February 1971): 20-36;

Lionel Madden, ed., *Robert Southey: The Critical Heritage* (Boston: Routledge & Kegan Paul, 1972);

Edward W. Meachen, "From a Historical Religion to a Religion of History: Robert Southey and the Heroic in History," *Clio*, 9 (Winter 1980): 229-252;

Meachen, "History and Transcendence: Robert Southey's Epic Poems," *Studies in English Literature*, 19 (Autumn 1979): 589-608;

Warren U. Ober, "Lake Poet and Laureate: Southey's Significance to His Own Generation," Ph.D. dissertation, Indiana University, 1959;

Ludwig Pfandl, "Southey und Spanien," *Revue Hispanique*, 28 (March 1913): 1-315;

Jean Raymond, *Robert Southey: L'homme et son temps; L'oeuvre; Le role* (Paris: Didier, 1968);

Brian Wilkie, *Romantic Poets and Epic Tradition* (Madison: University of Wisconsin Press, 1965);

Herbert G. Wright, "Three Aspects of Southey," *Review of English Studies*, 9 (January 1933): 37-46.

Papers:

Major public collections of Southey's letters (of which some two thousand remain unpublished) and manuscripts are in the Berg Collection of the New York Public Library, the Bodleian Library, the British Library, the Fitz Park Museum in Keswick, the Huntington Library, the University of Rochester Library, the National Library of Wales, and the Victoria and Albert Museum.

John Thelwall

(27 July 1764 - 17 February 1834)

Stephen Wolfe
Linfield College

SELECTED BOOKS: *Poems on Various Subjects*, 2 volumes (London: Printed for the author & sold by John Denis, 1787);

Ode to Science. Recited at the Anniversary Meeting of the Philomathian Society, June 20, 1791 (London: Printed for the use of the members by Sammells & Ritchie, 1791);

An Essay towards a Definition of Animal Vitality; read at the Theatre, Guy's Hospital, January 26, 1793; in which several of the opinions of the celebrated John Hunter are examined and controverted (London: Printed by T. Rickaby & sold by G. G. J. & J. Robinson, Debrett, and Cox, 1793);

The Peripatetic; or, Sketches of the Heart, of Nature and Society, as Sylvanus Theophrastus, 3 volumes (London: Printed for the author, 1793);

Political Lectures On the Moral Tendency of a System of Spies and Informers (London: Printed for the author & sold at the lecture room and by D. I. Eaton, 1794);

Poems Written in Close Confinement in the Tower and Newgate, under a charge of high treason (London: Printed for the author, 1795);

John Gilpin's Ghost; or, The Warning Voice of King Chanticleer: An Historical Ballad: Written before the Late Trials, and Dedicated to the Treason-Hunters of Oakham (London: Printed for the Author & published by T. Smith, 1795);

The Natural and Constitutional Rights of Britons to Annual Parliaments, Universal Suffrage, and Freedom of Association (London: Printed for the author & sold by J. Symonds, 1795);

Peaceful Discussion and not Tumultuary Violence the Means of Redressing National Grievance (London: Printed for J. Thelwall, 1795);

The Tribune: A Periodical Publication consisting chiefly of the Political Lectures of J. Thelwall, volumes 1-3, nos. 1-50 (London: Printed for the author, 14 March 1795 - 25 April 1796);

Prospectus of a Course of Lectures, to be delivered every Monday, Wednesday, and Friday, during the ensuing Lent. In strict conformity with the restrictions of Mr. Pitt's Convention Act (London, 1796);

The Rights of Nature against the Usurpation of Establishments. A series of Letters addressed to the people of Britain, on the state of public affairs, and the recent Effusions of the Right Honorable Edmund Burke (London: Published by H. D. Symonds & J. March, Norwich, 1796);

Sober Reflections on the Seditious and Inflammatory Letter of the Right Hon. Edmund Burke to a Noble Lord (London: Printed for H. D. Symonds, 1796);

An Appeal to Popular Opinion, against Kidnapping and Murder (Norwich: Printed & sold by J. March, 1796);

Poems chiefly written in Retirement (Hereford: Printed by W. H. Parker, 1801);

The Daughter of Adoration; A Tale of Modern Times, as John Beaufort, LL.D., 4 volumes (London: Printed for R. Phillips, 1801);

Selections, &c. for Mr. Thelwall's Lectures on the Science and Practice of Elocution (York: Printed by A. Bartholoman, 1802);

A Letter to Francis Jeffrey, Esq., on certain calumnies and misrepresentations in the Edinburgh Review (Edinburgh: Printed for the author by J. Turnbull, 1804);

The Trident of Albion; An Epic Effusion; And an Oration on the Influence of Elocution on Martial Enthusiasm (Liverpool: Printed for the author by G. F. Harris, 1805);

A Monody, Occasioned by the Death of the Right Hon. Charles James Fox (London: Printed for the author, 1806);

The Vestibule of Eloquence. Original Articles, Oratorical and Poetical, intended as Exercises in Recitation (London: Printed for the author by J. McCreery, 1810);

Selections for the Illustration of a Course of Instructions on the Rhythms and Utterance of the English Language (London: Printed by J. M'Creery, 1812).

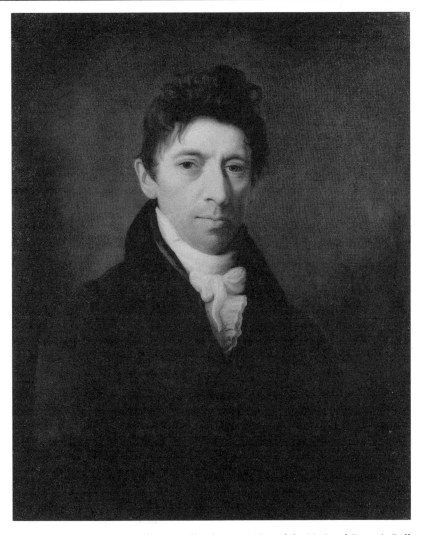

John Thelwall (portrait attributed to William Hazlitt; by permission of the National Portrait Gallery, London)

OTHER: "The Poor Debtor: A Tale," *Politics for the People: or, a Salmagundy for Swine,* 2 volumes (London: Printed for D. I. Eaton, 1794, 1795; facsimile, New York: Greenwood Reprint, 1968), I: 118-121;

The Poetical Recreations of The Champion and his Literary Correspondents; with a selection of essays, literary & critical, which have appeared in the Champion Newspaper, edited by Thelwall (London: Printed at the Champion Press by & for J. Thelwall & sold by Sir R. Phillips, 1822).

John Thelwall is usually seen through the eyes of Samuel Taylor Coleridge or Thomas De Quincey as a figure of demonic Jacobin proportions and of middling poetic talents; however, he can be seen as a writer whose poetry and prose straddles the world of Wordsworth and Coleridge and the world of urban Jacobin political agitation in the 1790s. Thelwall's poetry is seldom studied, but his political writing and lectures have received recent historical and literary-critical attention.

Thelwall was born in London, the son of a silk mercer. When he was nine, he lost his father, Joseph Thelwall. He was brought up by his mother, whose entire energies were devoted to carrying on her husband's business. Thelwall received a rudimentary education at a school in Highgate, but was taken from school at fourteen and put to work behind the counter at his family's business. At sixteen he was apprenticed to a tailor; later he began to study for the clergy, and in 1782 he was articled to John Impey, an attorney of Inner Temple Lane. Thelwall is described

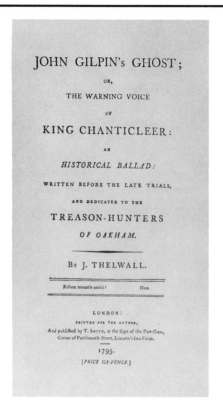

JOHN GILPIN's GHOST;

OR,

THE WARNING VOICE

OF

KING CHANTICLEER:

AN

HISTORICAL BALLAD:

WRITTEN BEFORE THE LATE TRIALS,

AND DEDICATED TO THE

TREASON-HUNTERS

OF *OAKHAM.*

By J. THELWALL.

Risum teneatis amici?   Hor.

LONDON:
PRINTED FOR THE AUTHOR,
And published by T. SMITH, at the Sign of the Pop-Gun,
Corner of Portsmouth-Street, Lincoln's Inn Fields.

1795.

[*PRICE SIX-PENCE.*]

PREFACE.

GOOD wine, says the proverb, requires no bush; and good poetry, it is said by the critics, should require no notes. But when a tavern is opened in a new situation, it may be necessary to hang out a sign; and when poetry is written upon a local subject, it may not be amiss to say a few explanatory words, by way of preface.

This little Ballad will not, however, require much introduction; especially to those who are acquainted with the inquisitorial proceedings of the last two or three years. The occasion of it is simply as follows—An extract from a speech delivered by me at a debating society, having been printed by Eaton, in his Politics for the People, under the title of *King Chanticleer, or the Fate of Tyranny,* that intrepid bookseller was, in consequence, a third time indicted for sedition, and, as the public well knows, was a third time acquitted. Shortly after which, I took an opportunity of sending, by a passenger in the *Stamford* stage, a small packet of books to a brother-in-law who resides in *Oakham,* the county-town of *Rutland,* containing, among other articles, some copies of this ludicrous story, and of the still more ludicrous indictment to which it had given birth. But a conspiracy to intercept my papers had been formed by the *great men* of *Oakham* (particularly Mr. *John Combes,* attorney at law, and agent to Lord *Winchelsea;* the Rev. Mr. *Williams,* who afterwards displayed the critical accuracy of his optics by swearing to my T's and h's, in consequence of having seen me sign my name to the register of my marriage, and Mr. *Apothecary Berry,* who swore he would sell his whole

estate

iv   PREFACE.

estate but he would hang me!) and these books, by some accident or other (being left at *Biggleswade,* the place where the passengers stop to change coaches) fell into *Combes's* hand. The *Oakhamites* were in consequence all in a flame. Nightly meetings were held at " *the Crown,*" which is the principal inn at Oakham; the house of my brother-in-law was broke open, and rifled of papers, books, letters, &c. and *lawyer Combes* was posted to *London* to acquaint the GREAT MAN in DOWNING-STREET with the wonderful discovery.

These particulars gave rise to the following ballad, which was written before the late arrests for High Treason. The copy being in the pocket of an old waistcoat, escaped the general pillage; and has therefore the fortune, good or bad, which I must never expect for any other of the manuscripts written before that time, of coming before the public. It may perhaps excite an innocent laugh at the expence of those who have laboured so ridiculously hard—to make me and my connections, according to the old adage, " laugh on the wrong side of " our mouths."

With respect to the fiction of Gilpin's Ghost, introduced for the sake of machinery, it is perhaps an act of justice due even to an enemy to declare, that it means no reflection upon the birth or family of Combes, about which I neither know nor care any thing whatever. Add to which, that I despise birth and family too much to make any circumstance of that kind an object of satire. I know no difference between legitimate and illegitimate —noble or simple—the republic of letters acknowledges no distinctions but between vice and virtue, wisdom and stupidity. But the conceit about *John Gilpin* having struck my imagination, the fabulous anecdote about *Fetter-Lane* became indispensible, to connect the machinery with the historical parts of the ballad.

Beaufort-Buildings,
28th *Sept.* 1795.

CERRIG-ENION.

Thelwall delin.   *Sutherland sc.*

Why on the moul'dring tomb of other times
Sits the lorn wanderer.

Title page, preface, and illustration by Thelwall for his politically motivated parody of William Cowper's popular comic poem
"The History of John Gilpin" (1785)

Thelwall (right) addressing a meeting in Copenhagen Fields, Islington, on 12 November 1795 (cartoon by James Gillray). The rally was organized by the London Corresponding Society to protest the Treasonable Practices Bill–which broadened the legal definition of treason to include incitement of contempt for King, government, or constitution by speech or writing–and the Seditious Meetings Bill–which severely limited the right to public assembly. Both bills were the Tory government's response to earlier meetings held by Thelwall and his allies, whom Gillray, a Tory, depicted as dangerous radicals inspired by the French Revolution.

as a studious child with a sometimes eccentric character and a highly developed sense of moral and social responsibility. In 1785 he insisted that his indentures be canceled because of his dislike for swearing oaths and because of a growing disenchantment with the legal profession.

In the same year he began to publish poems and articles in literary periodicals and decided to live entirely on his income as a writer. He edited the *Biographical and Imperial Magazine* and became active in meetings of the Society for Free Debate at Coachmakers Hall. His first collection of poems was published by subscription in 1787 and was well received by the *Critical Review* (October 1787), winning him some slight public recognition. The verse in *Poems on Various Subjects* is imitative and rings only slight changes on common eighteenth-century pastoral, Gothic, and Horatian themes.

During 1788-1790 Thelwall came under the influence of the well-known radical Horne Tooke, as he became more active in London borough politics. Tooke was so impressed with Thelwall's skills as a political speaker and writer that he offered to send him to a university and promised to find him a living as a clergyman. In the early 1790s Thelwall joined several radical political organizations in London, including Friends of the People in 1791 and the London Corresponding Society (LCS) in 1792. In his speeches of this period he shares with other members of these groups the use of "reason" to criticize existing political and religious institutions, Painite rhetoric, a self-conscious republicanism, and an insistence upon the political and economic liberties of the "independent" artisan. In 1791 he also studied anatomy and chemistry with freethinking medical men such as Dr. James Hunter, and on 27

July of that year Thelwall married Susan Vellum, whom he called "Stella" in his early poems and with whom he eventually had four children.

By 1792 the Society for Free Debate was silenced by the government, and in November 1793 Thelwall began a series of lectures which the government spy James Walsh attended. From 1793 through 1797 Thelwall was the best-known English Jacobin in London, due to his publications, lectures, and political speeches. His publications during the period begin with three volumes of poetry and prose published pseudonymously in 1793 as *The Peripatetic; or, Sketches of the Heart, of Nature and Society*. This collection of "political-sentimental" travel journals is addressed to an audience who could recognize echoes of Oliver Goldsmith and Thomas Gray, and was familiar with existing debates about the nature of the sublime and the beautiful, enclosure, and the structures of a sentimental education. The volumes are a fictionalized account of a walking tour by Sylvanus Theophrastus and Belmour, each exquisitely tormented by love and "melancholy," and their cynical companion Arisor into the countryside outside London. Each of the characters narrates a verse or prose tale, full of romantic description, tearful emotion, and moral disquisition. Thelwall sets up a dichotomy between the idealized picture of rural life eulogized by Theophrastus and Belmour and Arisor's somber pictures of dullness, rudeness, poverty, and pauperism in the countryside.

This walking tour anticipates William Cobbett's *Rural Rides* (1830, 1833) by focusing on how to read the landscape politically, concentrating on the human cost of "improvement" and the consequences of the gentrification of southern England:

> Whatever be the cause, the poor inhabitant is driven from his cottage, from his little garden, and his bubbling spring, to seek, perhaps, a miserable habitation within the smoky confines of some increasing town; where, among narrow lanes, house crowding upon house, and every floor, every room containing its separate family, . . . he is doomed, in all probability, to behold those infants who, with health and cheerfulness painted on their cheeks, could stretch their little limbs in harmless gambols among the field-flowers with which they loved to decorate their sun-burnt bosoms, now drooping and inactive, confined within a narrow smoky room, and tied, perhaps, (for dread of accident) to a chair; there to languish into decrepitude, leaning the pallid,

wasted cheek upon the shoulder, till friendly death relieves them from the gloomy prospect of helpless manhood.

Thelwall's writing uses the conventions of romance and romantic landscape description to present political and social injustice; however, he is unable to create a language that will demonstrate the power of human action and intervention without a regression to sentimental jargon:

> And though Simplicity and rural Innocence may have little connection with this part of the world, I can never help admiring the neglected neighbourhood, where decent Poverty may find so many comfortable retreats, be hid from gazing scorn, and enjoy a purer gale than the choaked city can afford.

> Far, far away, ye little homely sheds!
> Far from this period be the baneful hour
> When proud Improvement thro' the region
>   spreads,
> Builds o'er each spot, and fells each rustic bower!
> Here still may honest Industry retreat,
> Here Poverty still breathe the untainted gale,
> The rude ear listen to the carol sweet,
> And join the strain the vernal year to hail!

In May 1794 Thelwall was one of the leaders of the London Corresponding Society arrested and imprisoned in the Tower of London and Newgate jail. Habeas corpus was suspended on 23 May and the prisoners were held over the summer until they were formally charged with treason on 25 October. Thomas Hardy, Horne Tooke, and John Thelwall were each brought to trial and acquitted in the next two months. After his acquittal Thelwall had all his speeches and lectures taken down verbatim by a stenographer because of fear of government spies and informers. He published transcripts of these lectures in his weekly periodical, *The Tribune*, from 14 March 1795 to 25 April 1796, when the publication was suppressed. Thelwall was its editor and sole contributor. In addition to his lectures *The Tribune* contains poetry and accounts of his trial and imprisonment. Also in 1795 Thelwall published a collection of sonnets and short poems written when he was a prisoner in the Tower. *Poems Written in Close Confinement* focuses on the poet-patriot who writes "transcripts of the heart, rather than flights of the imagination;–rather intended to rouse the patriotic feeling, than calculated to amuse the admirer of poetical enthusiasm":

> O far the Spartan Fife, to pierce the ear
> Of slumbering Virtue, and again restore

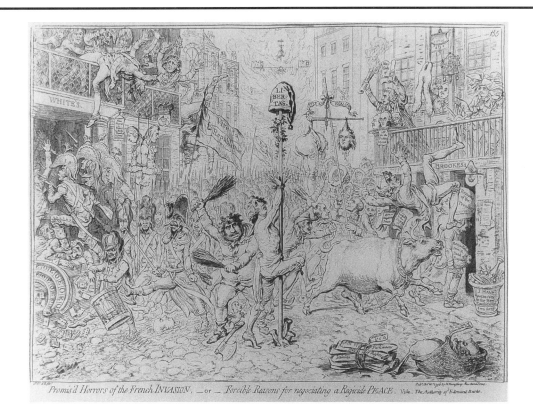

Promis'd Horrors of the French INVASION, —or— Forcible Reasons for negociating a Regicide PEACE. Vide. The Authority of Edmund Burke.

The Tree of Liberty must be planted, immediately!—this is the "Something which must be done and that quickly too!" to save the Country from destruction.—Vide. Sentiments of Whig Club Feb. 22 1797.

Political cartoons by James Gillray published at the height of British fears of a French invasion. Among the advocates of negotiating peace with the "regicide" French government depicted by Gillray in his 20 October 1796 cartoon is Charles James Fox, leader of the Whig opposition in the House of Commons, shown scourging Prime Minister William Pitt; Thelwall goads Francis Russell, Fifth Duke of Bedford (the "Bedfordshire ox"), a leading Fox supporter in the House of Lords, into tossing Edmund Burke, who had broken with the Whigs over the issue of the French Revolution. Gillray's 17 February 1797 cartoon, published as evidence of an imminent French invasion accumulated, presents his Tory view of what should be done with the peace advocates. Fox's head is on the pike; Thelwall's is at far left. The head just to the right of the pike is Richard Brinsley Sheridan's.

Those ancient Manners–simple and severe,
That aw'd encroaching Tyranny!–No more
Should'st thou, degenerate Briton! then deplore
Thy desolated villages–thy plains,
(Where Joy no more, nor rural Plenty reigns)

Thelwall turns from himself to his fellow prisoners in the Tower:

–what are dungeons–what the gloom
Of solitude, to him who thus can turn
From Self to Sentient Nature–to the doom
Of myriads yet in embrio, who shall learn
To bless his virtues, and enjoy secure
The Liberty he toil'd for? Blisful thought!

Thelwall's lectures were often attended by radical literati such as Thomas Holcroft, Elizabeth Inchbald, George Dyer, and perhaps William Wordsworth, during a visit to London, in 1795. Some thought his lectures dangerous, in both style and content. In his *Prospectus of a Course of Lectures* (1796) Thelwall argued that a political orator should leave "the clothing and embellishments" of his speech to the spontaneity of delivery: "for that language will always be most emphatic which the warmth of the moment supplies . . . and those tropes and metaphors will always be most fascinating which springing spontaneously from the collision of passion and fancy, are sketched, perhaps, with *rude*, but with a strong outline, and exhibit, in glowing colors, by the heat and rapidity of their conception."

In *The Rights of Nature* (1796) Thelwall defined himself as an English Jacobin, one who is "attached not to individual men, but to broad and general principles"; whose political goals were annual parliaments, universal suffrage, equal representation among "members unlimited"; and whose economic ideology was of the freedom of the artisan and laborer to set their own conditions and hours of employment and to be free of "the hideous accumulation of capital in a few hands."

In his lectures Thelwall uses William Godwin's *Enquiry concerning Political Justice* (1793) to analyze contemporary government actions and events in France, such as when he compares William Pitt to Robespierre arguing that they both behave like "Jacobins" practicing "retrospective justice." They are both a product of "the old leaven of revenge, corruption and suspicion which was generated by the systematic cruelties of the old despotism." Thelwall also maintains that his ar-

rest in 1794, the suspension of habeas corpus, and the charges and trials of leaders of the LCS, were part of a policy of "terror" copied from the French and designed to remove all opposition to the government. Thelwall's rhetoric in these lectures invokes the "Norman Yoke" and the mythology of the "freeborn Englishman." Unlike Godwin, however, Thelwall gives a positive role to government and encourages political change by attacking particular government abuses and by calling for direct political action through peaceful public demonstrations.

The year 1795 was to prove a turning point in Thelwall's relationship with Godwin, and in the fragile alliance between radical literati and Jacobin artisans of the LCS. There were food riots throughout the country, and large demonstrations in London were addressed by Thelwall and others. The King's coach was attacked on 29 October and immediately Pitt introduced his Anti-Sedition Acts, which curtailed freedom of speech, assembly, and the press. As a consequence of the acts, Thelwall lost his lecture hall and publication and the scanty earnings both provided. Godwin produced an anonymous pamphlet, *Considerations on Lord Grenville's and Mr. Pitt's Bills* (1795), which condemned Pitt's repression but also Thelwall's public calls for continued agitation. Godwin attacked Thelwall as an "impatient and headlong reformer" and his political lecturing as a "hot-bed" of dangerous sedition. Thelwall was angry and disappointed. He immediately sent an indignant letter to Godwin, challenging him to confess his authorship of the pamphlet.

In the preface to the second volume of *The Tribune*, Thelwall addressed Godwin indirectly and tried to answer his charges by contending that a program of effective political reform must involve direct action. Godwin wrote a reply, printed in *The Tribune*, arguing for the gradual enlightenment of mankind and the dangers of demagoguery. Thelwall claimed, however, that Godwin mistook vanity for principle. Rejecting Godwin's educational gradualism and arguing for unlimited agitation Thelwall presented an argument that would resurface in Chartist debates about the use of moral or physical force in the 1840s.

In April of 1796 Coleridge sent a copy of his *Poems on Various Subjects* to Thelwall, and for the next two years these two men sparred in letters about poetry, religion, and politics. Coleridge considered himself a moderating influence

ADVERTISEMENT.

WHEN the author of the majority of the ensuing articles purchased *The Champion* Newspaper, it was his intention to have rendered it, at least, as much a Literary as a Political miscellany. He conceived, that the comparatively unlettered portions of society were already sufficiently excited, by those whose object, or whose taste, it was, to address themselves particularly to those classes; and he persuaded himself that, by rendering his weekly sheet a vehicle, at once, of what he regarded as the legitimate principles of reform, and of critical disquisition upon subjects of polite and elegant Literature, he should carry those principles into circles to which the want of such association had rendered them somewhat repulsive; while, at the same time, by occasioning intellectual refinement to go hand in hand with political enquiry, one great objection to popular politics would, at least, be obviated, as nothing soothes the turbulent emotions of the human mind more than a taste for the elegancies of art and literature.

It wanted not, however, such a motive to have stimulated the author to devote as large a portion of his exertions as circumstances would permit, to subjects of this description; for poetry, in particular, was the first passion of his soul, and critical disquisition had so long been rendered necessary to his professional pursuits, that it had become habitual to the very current of his thoughts. If he understands the structure of his own mind, and the motives by which it is

vi

actuated, he is a votary of the Muses, from elective and natural propensity—a politician, only from a sense of duty.

The peculiar circumstances of the times, however, soon entangled him much more exclusively, in the maze of politics, than was consistent with his original plan or intentions; and his miscellany, by a necessity which he could not controul, has been frequently much less a vehicle than he expected, for the effusions of taste and imagination. Nevertheless, a much larger volume than is now presented, might easily have been selected from its columns; and several of the literary papers, both of the Editor and of his Correspondents, which have been passed over, might, perhaps, have been quite as acceptable to the reader, as those which are here reprinted.

Of the poetry, however, little has been excluded—except a few of the Epigrams, which have been passed over more thro' accident than design, and the omission of which was not observed till it would have been inconvenient to apply the remedy.

There is, at least, this consolation to mitigate his chagrin for the unintentional neglect, that a volume not intended to address itself to political feelings, or to serve any political purpose, is, from those very omissions, so much the more remote from assuming a political character.

JOHN THELWALL.

North Brixton Cottage.
4th Dec. 1821.

INSTRUCTIONS IN ELOCUTION,

AND

THE CURE OF IMPEDIMENTS,

Continue to be given, by Mr. THELWALL, to Select Classes and Private Pupils, at *North Brixton Cottage* (the first embowed Cottage beyond Kennington, on the left hand side of the Brixton Road); and two or three such Pupils, either Ladies or Gentlemen, may be received into his family as heretofore. Mr. T. may also be consulted in all cases of defect or malconformation of the elocutionary organs, either at his own residence or that of the parties afflicted with such imperfections.

TERMS

Of Instruction to Domestic Pupils, with Impediments or Organic Defects.

(The Fees, for Quarterly, Monthly, or shorter Engagements, to be paid at the time of entrance.)

ADULTS.

By the Year......................250 Guineas.
Quarter .... 85 Guineas.
Month.................. 35 Guineas.

PUPILS UNDER SIXTEEN.

By the Year......................200 Guineas.
Quarter .... 75 Guineas.
Month.................. 35 Guineas.

viii

PUPILS UNDER TWELVE.

By the Year....................150 Guineas.
Quarter .... 60 Guineas.
Month.................. 35 Guineas.

COURSES OF LESSONS TO PUPILS WITH IMPEDIMENTS NOT DOMESTICATED.

Twenty-four Lessons.......... 35 Guineas.
Quarterly Course. .... 70 Guineas.

COURSES OF LESSONS TO PUPILS HAVING NO IMPEDIMENT.

Six Lessons.................... 4 Guineas.
Twenty-four Lessons.......... 12 Guineas.
Quarter of a Year............. 30 Guineas.
Single Lessons.................. 1 Guinea each.

Consultations in cases of Impediment, or Organic Defect, where no arrangement is made for Courses of Instruction, 5 Guineas. Ordinary consultations, at the residence of Mr. T., 1 Guinea—at the residence of the Pupil, 2 Guineas.

Advertisement and notice for Thelwall's speech classes in The Poetical Recreations of the Champion *(1822), the volume in which Thelwall collected some of his contributions to the weekly newspaper he published in 1818-1821*

Engraving based on a bust of Thelwall (from the Princeton University Library copy of C. B. Thelwall, The Life of John Thelwall. By His Widow, *1837)*

on Thelwall's fiery temper, counseling a "patience of intellect and action" and the need to move beyond a Godwinian rationalism to a Christian "faith" that was to be found in a balance between intellect and passion. Also in 1796, when it became too dangerous for him to lecture publicly on political events, Thelwall participated in the pamphlet war created by Edmund Burke's speeches and political writing. Coleridge expressed admiration for both Thelwall's replies to Burke and their attempts to demonstrate the relationship between Burke's early aesthetic theories of the sublime and the beautiful and his later theories of society and political behavior.

On 17 July 1797 Thelwall arrived unannounced to visit Coleridge at Nether Stowey, having walked from London. He was seeking a place

to live outside London. He stayed until 27 July and was treated to a dinner party at Alfoxton with the Wordsworths. Having heard rumors of the visit of Thelwall to this "fraternity of French Jacobins" in the district, the Home Office sent the spy James Walsh to investigate. The investigation was later dropped, but it was not the joke Coleridge tried to make it twenty years later when he wrote of Walsh listening to the two poets talking about Spinoza and suspecting that "Spy Nozy" referred to his own alleged red nose.

In 1796, Thelwall began lecturing again in the southern counties and, often to openly hostile audiences and by 1798 he had withdrawn from politics and was farming in Brecon, Wales. For two years he remained silent, but by 1800 he was lecturing on elocution, and in 1801 he published *Poems chiefly written in Retirement.* These poems are a collection of poetry written during 1790-1797 and focus on political themes, the poet's retirement from public life, and the solace provided by family and friends during the treason trials.

> O, let not private wrongs–let not the pride
> Of ill-requited services divide
> Patriot from Patriot, nor in party brawls
> Plunge him, resentful, while the public calls
> For zeal unanimous. . . . Steel my heart
> With all the stoic's firmness; and impart
> A persevering energy, unsway'd
> By Passion or corruption, . . .

By 1804 he had returned to London, where he and his wife began to develop a school of elocution and oratory which concentrated on curing speech impediments. He focused his attention on stammering and stuttering, believing that by having his students recite works of literature he could cure causes of "defective utterance." His school in Lincoln Inn Fields emphasized the mental and moral development of students by using homilies and the best "literary quotation from writers both ancient and modern." His system of treating stuttering through recitation received much favorable publicity and he published papers in the *Medical and Physical Journal* from 1814 to 1818. His papers, lectures, and school provided Thelwall with an interested, if sometimes bemused audience, which included literary figures such as Charles Lamb, William Hazlitt, and Henry Crabb Robinson.

Like many other radicals, Thelwall returned to the political platform in 1818-1819. He often spoke at large public demonstrations in Spa Fields, and he purchased a literary and political journal, *The Champion*, in which he published poems, commentaries on events of political interest, his earlier speeches, and various literary and political reviews. Thelwall tried to direct the journal to the "reflective classes" but without much success. The journal ceased publication in 1821.

In Thelwall's final years he was at work on a "national epic" poem, parts of which he had published as early as 1801. Thelwall returned to teaching elocution, this time in Brixton. In 1822 he edited *The Poetical Recreations of The Champion and his Literary Correspondents; with a selection of essays, literary & critical,* in which he included twelve of

Lamb's poems and some of his own literary and political "effusions." He died at Bath on 17 February 1834. His first wife having died in 1816, Thelwall remarried in 1819 and had a son by his second wife, Cecil Boyle, who wrote a biography of her husband.

Thelwall's place at the center of London Jacobin political and literary activity in the 1790s has been of interest to scholars since the work of E. P. Thompson in the 1960s. Thelwall is seen as an "extraordinary man" whose poetry is imitative and conventional but whose prose writing takes the arguments of Jacobin politics to the borders of revolutionary socialism and provides valuable information about the imagery and ideology of the London Jacobins. His disputes with Godwin and Coleridge have become windows through which we can see some of the literary and political conflicts within English romanticism.

Biographies:

C. B. Thelwall, *The Life of John Thelwall By His Widow,* volume 1 (London: J. Macrone, 1837)–no further volumes published;

Charles Cestre, *John Thelwall: A Pioneer of Democracy and Social Reform in England during the French Revolution.* (London: Swan Sonnenschein / New York: Scribners, 1906).

References:

Nicholas Roe, "Imagining Robespierre," in *Coleridge's Imagination,* edited by Richard Gravil, Lucy Newlyn, and H. Roe (Cambridge: Cambridge University Press, 1985), pp. 161-178;

Roe, "Who Was Spy Nozy?," *Wordsworth Circle,* 15 (Spring 1984): 46-50;

Oliva Smith, *The Politics of Language, 1791-1819* (London: Oxford University Press, 1984), pp. 86-89;

R. Thelwall, "The Phonetic Theory of John Thelwall," in *Towards a History of Phonetics,* edited by R. E. Asher and J. A. Henderson (Edinburgh: Edinburgh University Press, 1981), pp. 186-203;

E. P. Thompson, "Disenchantment of Default? A Lay Sermon," in *Power and Consciousness,* edited by C. C. O'Brien and W. D. Vanech (New York: New York University Press, 1969), pp. 149-181;

Thompson, *The Making of the English Working Class* (London: Gollancz, 1963), pp. 171-182.

William Wordsworth

(7 April 1770 - 23 April 1850)

Judith W. Page
Millsaps College

BOOKS: *An Evening Walk. An Epistle; in verse. Addressed to a young Lady, from the Lakes of the North of England* (London: Printed for J. Johnson, 1793);

Descriptive Sketches. In Verse. Taken during a Pedestrian Tour in the Italian, Grison, Swiss, and Savoyard Alps (London: Printed for J. Johnson, 1793);

Lyrical Ballads, with a few other Poems (Bristol: Printed by Biggs & Cottle for T. N. Longman, London, 1798; London: Printed for J. & A. Arch, 1798; enlarged edition, 2 volumes, London: Printed for T. N. Longman & O. Rees by Biggs & Co., Bristol, 1800; Philadelphia: Printed & sold by James Humphreys, 1802);

Poems, in two Volumes (London: Printed for Longman, Hurst, Rees & Orme, 1807);

Concerning the Convention of Cintra (London: Printed for Longman, Hurst, Rees & Orme 1809);

The Excursion, being a portion of The Recluse, a Poem (London: Printed for Longman, Hurst, Rees, Orme & Brown, 1814; New York: C. & S. Francis, 1849);

Poems By William Wordsworth, Including Lyrical Ballads, and the Miscellaneous Pieces of the Author, 2 volumes (London: Printed for Longman, Hurst, Rees, Orme & Brown, 1815);

The White Doe of Rylstone: or The Fate of the Nortons. A Poem (London: Printed for Longman, Hurst, Rees, Orme & Brown by James Ballantyne, Edinburgh, 1815);

Thanksgiving Ode, January 18, 1816. With Other Short Pieces, Chiefly referring to Recent Public Events (London: Printed by Thomas Davison for Longman, Hurst, Rees, Orme & Brown, 1816);

A Letter to A Friend of Robert Burns (London: Printed for Longman, Hurst, Rees, Orme & Brown, 1816);

Two Addresses to the Freeholders of Westmoreland (Kendal: Printed by Airey & Bellingham, 1818);

Peter Bell, A Tale in Verse (London: Printed by Strahan & Spottiswoode for Longman, Hurst, Rees, Orme & Brown, 1819);

The Waggoner, A Poem. To Which are added, Sonnets (London: Printed by Strahan & Spottiswoode for Longman, Hurst, Rees, Orme & Brown, 1819);

Miscellaneous Poems of William Wordsworth, 4 volumes (London: Printed for Longman, Hurst, Rees, Orme & Brown, 1820);

The River Duddon, A series of Sonnets: Vaudracour and Julia: and Other Poems. To which is annexed, A Topographical Description of the Country of the Lakes, in the North of England (London: Printed for Longman, Hurst, Rees, Orme & Brown, 1820);

A Description of the Scenery of the Lakes in The North of England. Third Edition, (Now first published separately) (London: Printed for Longman, Hurst, Rees, Orme & Brown, 1822; revised and enlarged, 1823); revised and enlarged again as *A Guide through the District of the Lakes in The North of England* (Kendal: Published by Hudson & Nicholson / London: Longman & Co., Moxon, and Whitaker & Co., 1835);

Memorials of a Tour on the Continent, 1820 (London: Printed for Longman, Hurst, Rees, Orme & Brown, 1822);

Ecclesiastical Sketches (London: Printed for Longman, Hurst, Rees, Orme & Brown, 1822);

The Poetical Works of William Wordsworth, 4 volumes (Boston: Published by Cummings & Hilliard, printed by Hilliard & Metcalf, 1824);

The Poetical Works of William Wordsworth (5 volumes, London: Printed for Longman, Rees, Orme, Brown & Green, 1827; revised edition, 4 volumes, London: Printed for Longman, Rees, Orme, Brown, Green & Longman, 1832);

The Poetical Works of William Wordsworth [pirated edition] (Paris: A. & W. Galignani, 1828);

William Wordsworth, April 1798 (portrait by William Shuter; Cornell Wordsworth Collection, by permission of the Cornell University Library)

Selections from the Poems of William Wordsworth, Esq. Chiefly for the Use of Schools and Young Persons, edited by Joseph Hine (London: Moxon, 1831);

Yarrow Revisited, And Other Poems (London: Printed for Longman, Rees, Orme, Brown, Green & Longman and Edward Moxon, 1835; Boston: J. Monroe & Co, 1835; New York: R. Bartlett & S. Raynor, 1835);

The Poetical Works of William Wordsworth (6 volumes, London: Moxon, 1836, 1837; enlarged, 7 volumes, 1842; enlarged again, 8 volumes, 1851);

The Complete Poetical Works of William Wordsworth, edited by Henry Reed (Philadelphia: J. Kay, Jun., and Brother / Boston: J. Munroe, 1837);

The Sonnets of William Wordsworth (London:

Edward Moxon, 1838);

Poems, Chiefly of Early and Late Years; Including The Borderers, A Tragedy (London: Edward Moxon, 1842);

Kendal and Windermere Railway. Two Letters Reprinted from The Morning Post. Revised, with Additions (Kendal: Printed by Branthwaite & Son, 1845; London: Whittaker & Co. and Edward Moxon / Kendal: R. Branthwaite & Son, 1845);

The Poems of William Wordsworth, D.C.L., Poet Laureate (London: Moxon, 1845);

The Poetical Works of William Wordsworth, D.C.L., Poet Laureate, 6 volumes (London: Moxon, 1849, 1850);

The Prelude, Or Growth of a Poet's Mind, An Autobiographical Poem (London: Moxon, 1850; New

Wordsworth's birthplace (top) in Cockermouth, where his father was the legal agent for Sir James Lowther (later Earl of Lonsdale), who owned the house; and Hawkshead Grammar School (bottom), where Wordsworth was a student from May 1779 until summer 1787

York: D. Appleton / Philadelphia: Geo. S. Appleton, 1850);

The Recluse ["Home at Grasmere"] (London & New York: Macmillan, 1888).

Collections: *Poems of Wordsworth,* chosen and edited by Matthew Arnold (London & New York: Macmillan, 1879);

The Poetical Works of William Wordsworth, 5 volumes, edited by Ernest de Selincourt and Helen Darbishire (Oxford: Clarendon Press, 1940-1949; volumes 2 and 3 revised, 1952, 1954);

William Wordsworth: Selected Poems and Prefaces, edited by Jack Stillinger (Boston: Houghton Mifflin, 1965);

The Prose Works of William Wordsworth, 3 volumes, edited by W. J. B. Owen and Jane Worthington Smyser (Oxford: Clarendon Press, 1974);

The Cornell Wordsworth, 14 volumes to date, general editor, Stephen M. Parrish (Ithaca: Cornell University Press, 1975-);

The Prelude 1799, 1805, 1850, edited by Jonathan Wordsworth, M. H. Abrams, and Stephen Gill (New York: Norton, 1979);

William Wordsworth: The Poems, 2 volumes, edited by John O. Hayden (Harmondsworth: Penguin / New Haven: Yale University Press, 1981);

The Poetical Works of Wordsworth, edited by Paul D. Sheats (Boston: Houghton Mifflin, 1982)—revision of the 1904 Cambridge Wordsworth;

William Wordsworth, edited by Stephen Gill, Oxford Author Series (London: Oxford University Press, 1984).

OTHER: Joseph Wilkinson, *Select Views in Cumberland, Westmoreland, and Lancashire,* includes an introduction by Wordsworth (London: Published for Wilkinson by R. Ackermann, 1810).

Although William Wordsworth is now regarded as the central poet of his age, during his lifetime Byron or Scott, and later Tennyson, received more popular acclaim. Even readers in the nineteenth century who argued for Wordsworth's centrality did so on grounds different from those of many twentieth-century critics. For Matthew Arnold, who wanted to bolster Wordsworth's reputation late in the Victorian period, Wordsworth was the great lyrical poet of nature, spontaneity, and affirmation. Readers in this century, such as Geof-

frey Hartman, have found Wordsworth's poetry powerful because of the tensions and contradictions which disturb its sometimes deceptively smooth surfaces. According to this reading of "Wordsworth," the poetry is a site of doubt and conflict, a view recently supported by critics interested in Wordsworth's ideological commitments. The view of Wordsworth as a conflicted and complicated poet whose works document the major events and concerns of his age–the French Revolution and the rise of counterrevolutionary tyranny, the effects of urbanization, mass communication, and war, the desires and limitations of the human mind–appeals particularly to late-twentieth-century readers.

William Wordsworth was born in Cockermouth, Cumberland, into a comfortable middle-class family with roots firmly planted in the Lake Country. His father, John Wordsworth, was legal agent to wealthy landowners, the Lowthers; his mother, Ann Cookson Wordsworth, came to the marriage from a conventionally respectable merchant family in Penrith. Wordsworth was the second child of five: Richard (who became an attorney); William; Dorothy (the poet's lifelong friend and companion); John (a sailor who drowned at sea in 1805); Christopher (who became master of Trinity College, Cambridge). Wordsworth did not leave many descriptions of his parents, but it is assumed that he and his siblings enjoyed a secure early life in Cockermouth, where they lived in a large, attractive house owned by the Lowthers. Although often away from home on business, John Wordsworth took time when home to introduce his children to English poetry and encouraged William to memorize long passages from the works of William Shakespeare, John Milton, and Edmund Spenser, a skill that he would treasure both as an allusive poet and as one who composed his own poetry from memory. William's young imagination was also nurtured by other readings, such as *Don Quixote* and the *Arabian Nights,* works mentioned in *The Prelude,* Wordsworth's long autobiographical poem published posthumously in 1850.

In 1778 Ann Wordsworth died suddenly, and then, over the Christmas holidays of 1783-1784, John Wordsworth followed. In an early version of *The Prelude* (written in 1798-1799), Wordsworth interprets the effect of his father's death on his young consciousness:

The event
With all the sorrow which it brought appeared

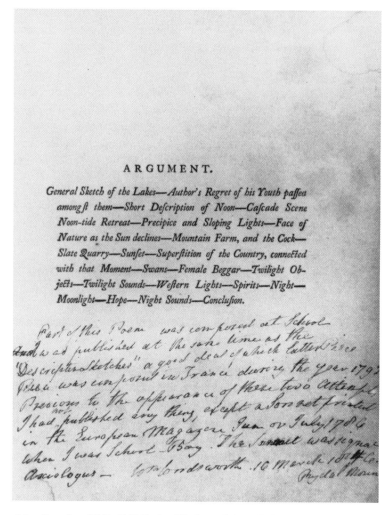

ARGUMENT.

General Sketch of the Lakes—Author's Regret of his Youth paſſed amongſt them—Short Deſcription of Noon—Caſcade Scene Noon-tide Retreat—Precipice and Sloping Lights—Face of Nature as the Sun declines—Mountain Farm, and the Cock— Slate Quarry—Sunſet—Superſtition of the Country, connected with that Moment—Swans—Female Beggar—Twilight Ob- jects—Twilight Sounds—Weſtern Lights—Spirits—Night— Moonlight—Hope—Night Sounds—Concluſion.

Page from the copy of An Evening Walk *(1793) that Wordsworth inscribed to his son William in 1846 (by permission of the Wordsworth Trust)*

A chastisement, and when I called to mind
That day so lately passed when from the crag
I looked in such anxiety of hope,
With trite reflections of mortality
Yet with deepest passion I bowed low
To God, who thus corrected my desires.

John Wordsworth's death had material as well as spiritual consequences for William. At the time of his death, the Lowthers owed their agent well over four thousand pounds, a debt not resolved for almost twenty years, causing much financial difficulty and painful dependency for the Words- worth children. When John Wordsworth died, the household was dispersed, with the boys sent back to school and Dorothy sent to live with rela- tives.

The Wordsworth boys attended Hawkshead Grammar School, known for excellent instruction in mathematics and classics. Rather than live at the school, the Wordsworths boarded with Ann and Hugh Tyson. From Wordsworth's description in *The Prelude*, we know that Ann Tyson inspired love and gratitude in the young poet. She gave him considerable freedom to discover the power of the natural world and to begin to define him- self in relation to that power. Wordsworth was also encouraged at Hawkshead by a young school- master, William Taylor, whose love for poetry– particularly poets of sensibility (Mark Akenside, James Beattie, Robert Blair, Thomas Chatterton, William Collins, John Dyer, Thomas Gray, Char- lotte Smith, James Thomson)–inspired him in his early years. In addition, Wordsworth read Robert Burns's *Poems Chiefly in the Scottish Dialect* (1786), which initiated an admiration of Burns evident in Wordsworth's poetry and in his *A Letter to A*

Friend of Robert Burns (1816).

Wordsworth composed his first verses at Hawkshead in the fall of 1784 on the subject of summer vacation, and in 1785 he wrote verses on the bicentenary of the school. During his last year at Hawkshead, the 1786-1787 academic year, Wordsworth composed most of *The Vale of Esthwaite*, a descriptive poem with Gothic and supernatural elements, of which more than five hundred lines survive. In March of 1787 his first published poem, "Sonnet, On Seeing Miss Helen Maria Williams Weep at a Tale of Distress," appeared in *European Magazine*. Signing his name "Axiologus" (meaning, loosely, "worth of words"), Wordsworth revealed his witty consciousness of his surname and perhaps prefigured his faith in the worth of his own words.

In the fall of 1787 Wordsworth went to St. John's College, Cambridge, as a sizar, a designation applied to students who paid reduced fees. With his strong background in mathematics, Wordsworth was well prepared for the curriculum, but he seems to have decided early in his university career that he would not follow the prescribed path to honors, and he did not distinguish himself at Cambridge. Instead, Wordsworth studied modern languages—particularly Italian with Agostino Isola, under whose direction he developed a lasting admiration for Italian poetry that in turn enriched his reading of Milton and Spenser. *An Evening Walk* (1793), the descriptive poem in heroic couplets that Wordsworth wrote during his Cambridge years, reveals not only his absorption in eighteenth-century descriptive poetry but also his love of and familiarity with Virgil, another lasting interest in his life.

As the end of his course at Cambridge approached, Wordsworth felt increasing pressure from older relatives to excel and to prepare for a career, presumably either in the law or clergy. Rather than commit himself, Wordsworth did what his guardians regarded as mad and dangerous: he left Cambridge from July to October 1790 and went with his Welsh friend Robert Jones on a walking tour of the Alps. The trip was "mad" because Wordsworth could use the time to study and "dangerous" because of the uncertain political climate of revolutionary France. But as Wordsworth confesses in book 6 of *The Prelude* (1805 version), "An open slight / Of college cares and study was the scheme," especially with "France standing on the top of golden hours, / And human nature seeming born again." When he returned to Cambridge in the autumn and

took his B.A. in January 1791, Wordsworth was no closer to pleasing his formidable elders with a plan for his life. After visiting London and Wales, and even returning briefly to Cambridge, Wordsworth returned to France before Christmas in 1791, ostensibly to learn to speak French. During the following year he would learn and experience more than a foreign language.

Although there has been new scholarship on Wordsworth's experiences in France, many questions still remain about the nature and extent of his involvement in the French Revolution. In *The Prelude* Wordsworth claims to have been rather aloof at first, but he sympathized with the Girondins' values and responded to their intellectual connection with the English republican tradition. He became friends with Michel Beaupuy, a highborn Frenchman who supported the revolution. Soon after his arrival in France, Wordsworth became involved with Annette Vallon, a young woman from Blois who would give birth to their child, Anne-Caroline (called Caroline), on 15 December 1792. Wordsworth seems to have been torn by conflicts during this period: while enthusiastic for the revolution, he was repelled by the increasing terror and mob violence, especially as he learned of the September Massacres in Paris in 1792; he was also aware of himself as an Englishman from a Protestant Establishment family involved with Royalist-Catholic Annette. In the midst of these conflicts and nowhere near a resolution, Wordsworth returned to England before the birth of his daughter Caroline, presumably because he was out of money.

The following year was emotionally tumultuous. Wordsworth spent some time in London with his brother Richard, who had followed the more conventional path of establishing a legal career. Then he traveled to the Isle of Wight and back through England on foot from Salisbury to Jones's home in Wales. While wandering across Sarum Plain, Wordsworth began early versions of his Salisbury Plain poems, published in part as the bleak tale "The Female Vagrant" in the *Lyrical Ballads* (1798) and then finally as "Guilt and Sorrow" in 1842; he also memorialized his state of mind and visionary experiences on Salisbury Plain in *The Prelude*. On his way to Bristol from Wales, Wordsworth traveled up the Wye River and visited Tintern Abbey; he later remembered himself in the poem "Tintern Abbey" acting "like a man / Flying from something that he dreads," an apt description of Wordsworth's flight in 1793 from his own inner conflicts. Wordsworth proba-

Racedown Lodge, Dorset, probably as it looked when William and Dorothy Wordsworth lived there in 1795-1797 (painting by S. L. May; by permission of the Wordsworth Trust)

bly made a brief third and dangerous trip to France in October 1793, after England and France were at war. He may have witnessed, as Thomas Carlyle later reported his saying, the execution of the Girondin Antoine Joseph Gorsas. Given the climate in France and the execution of other Girondins, Wordsworth may have left the country in fear of his life. There is no record that he saw Annette or his child.

During 1793 Wordsworth published *An Evening Walk* and the poem he wrote during his year-long stay in France, *Descriptive Sketches*, both appearing under the imprint of the radical bookseller Joseph Johnson. Wordsworth wrote to his Cambridge friend William Mathews (23 May 1794): "It was with great reluctance I huddled up those two little works and sent them into the world in so imperfect a state. But as I had done nothing by which to distinguish myself at the university, I thought these little things might shew

that I could do something." According to Wordsworth, the poems received both "unmerited contempt" and inflated praise; Wordsworth later regretted that he had not submitted them first to readers before allowing them to be published.

Wordsworth also wrote, but cautiously did not publish, "A Letter to the Bishop of Llandaff," an attack on the basic conservative values of the monarchy and the aristocracy associated with Edmund Burke. During this time Wordsworth came under the spell of William Godwin's *An Enquiry Concerning Political Justice* (1793) and its assertion that the "independent intellect" can be divorced from the feelings and affections associated with family and traditional bonds. There is evidence that he helped to plan the radical Godwinian newspaper, *The Philanthropist*, that ran for several months in 1795. Wordsworth had returned to London to earn his way as a journalist, but hopes for a career were complicated by turmoil regarding his personal and political commit-

Silhouette of Dorothy Wordsworth, circa 1806 (by permission of the Wordsworth Trust)

ments in the repressive atmosphere of the 1790s. As he remembers in book 10 of the 1805 *Prelude:*

> I felt
> The ravage of this most unnatural strife
> In my own heart; there lay like a weight,
> An enmity with all the tenderest springs
> Of my enjoyments. I, who with the breeze
> Had played, a green leaf on the blessed tree
> Of my beloved country—nor had wished
> For happier fortune than to wither there—
> Now from my present station was cut off,
> And tossed about in whirlwinds.

Wordsworth was still being tossed about by these winds when in 1795 he inherited nine hundred pounds from Raisley Calvert, a Lake District friend whom he had nursed in his final illness the previous year. In his generosity Calvert hoped that he might free Wordsworth to pursue the only career to which he seemed suited: that of poet. Other friends, the Pinneys, offered Wordsworth their Racedown Lodge in Dorset rent free: here Dorothy and William arrived on 26 September to reestablish their household. It is here that the Wordsworths cultivated their long relationship with Coleridge, whom Wordsworth

had met in Bristol in late summer or early fall of 1795.

Reestablishing close bonds with Dorothy was crucial to William's renewal after his experiences in France and his alienation from his native land. Dorothy is the "beloved woman" addressed in book 10 of *The Prelude* (1805 version), who "Maintained for me a saving intercourse / With my true self," and "preserved me still / A poet." His close relationship with Dorothy, who was to live as a part of William's family for the rest of her life, is the first of several relationships with supportive women who nurtured Wordsworth's career. With Dorothy keeping house and providing moral support and with his developing friendship with Coleridge, Wordsworth began to revive his hopes and ambitions in the spring of 1796.

In this year Wordsworth began composing his first major work, a tragedy in five acts (later titled *The Borderers*), which he would try unsuccessfully to have staged in London. The play was not performed, and it was not published until Wordsworth revised it in 1841 for his *Poems, Chiefly of Early and Late Years* (1842). In this work of 1796-1797 we see both Wordsworth's preoccupation with Godwinism and his growing rejection of it. Although the play does not have dramatic appeal for the stage, in it Wordsworth explores human character and relationships. Whereas in his Salisbury Plain poems he had shown how a person can be led to crime by the injustices of war and poverty, in *The Borderers* he creates the Iago-like character Rivers, who deliberately leads a companion to commit a crime and thus to destroy his own life. The innocent and well-meaning Mortimer abandons the old blind man Herbert to die after being convinced of the old man's evil nature. Without emotional attachment and respect for human affections, Rivers's "independent intellect"—the reason of Godwinian philosophy—proves a destructive and immoral force.

The Borderers, with its dense Shakespearean allusions and echoes, was Wordsworth's only attempt at drama, but it was also his first sustained attempt at blank verse, a metrical form central to his poetic program. And the writing of *The Borderers* led directly into the composition of his first "great" poem, also in blank verse, *The Ruined Cottage,* published in altered form in 1814 as book 1 of *The Excursion.* In this poem Wordsworth not only developed a magnificent blank-verse style, but he also created a narrative structure that would prove important for many later poems: that of having the poet-narrator hear a

*Alfoxden House, near Nether Stowey, where William and Dorothy Wordsworth lived from July 1797 until summer 1798
(illustration by Edmund H. New for William Knight's* Coleridge and Wordsworth in the West Country, *1913)*

story which changes the way he looks at the world and of having the reader and the narrator see objects in the world in a new way. In *The Ruined Cottage* the narrator records the peddler's story of Margaret, a young woman who is deserted by her husband–a victim of the pressures of war and poverty–and slowly loses her home, her children, and her desire to live. The poem begins with the image of "a ruined house, four naked walls / That stared upon each other"–a haunting description which asks the reader and the narrator to discover how and why the house became a ruin. In *The Ruined Cottage* Wordsworth tries to find meaning in human suffering and to establish the grounds for consolation. Both the narrator and the peddler seem to succeed, although Margaret never attained for herself the comfort of their higher knowledge.

To be closer to Coleridge, in July 1797 the Wordsworths moved to Alfoxden House, four miles from the little village of Nether Stowey in

Somerset where the Coleridges lived. They rented Alfoxden House, a mansion with land, including a deer park, for twenty-three pounds. Here Wordsworth continuously revised poems and composed more poetry, including several blank-verse poems that he hoped would one day become part of *The Recluse*, a projected long poem on "Man, Nature, and Society" that Wordsworth would never complete, although he was obsessed for many years by the immense challenge. Recognizing Wordsworth's poetic powers, Coleridge urged him on to this larger task, eventually in lieu of his own attempt to write the great long poem of the age. When Wordsworth published *The Excursion* in 1814, he announced to the world that it was merely part of a much longer and ambitious work yet to be written.

The Wordsworths' unconventional habits (housework on Sunday and walks at all hours of day and night), as well as their association with Coleridge's radical friend John Thelwall, led

Aquatint of Tintern Abbey by William Sawrey Gilpin, from William Gilpin's Observations on the River Wye and Several Parts of South Wales &c. *(1782), a book that William and Dorothy Wordsworth are likely to have taken with them when they visited the abbey in July 1798.*

their neighbors to gossip that they were French spies, or worse. As a result, the Home Office sent a spy to Nether Stowey, who, as the well-known story goes, overheard Wordsworth and Coleridge whispering about "Spy Nozy" (Spinoza), only to learn to his disappointment that they were speaking of the author of an old book. Nothing came of the Spy Nozy incident. In "My First Acquaintance with Poets" (1823) William Hazlitt provides a wonderful retrospective description of Wordsworth at Alfoxden, which demonstrates how he might have aroused curiosity in the locals:

> He answered in some degree to his friend's description of him, but was more gaunt and Don Quixote-like. He was quaintly dressed (according to the *costume* of that unconstrained period) in a brown fustian jacket and striped pantaloons. There was something of a roll, a lounge in his gait, not unlike his own Peter Bell. There was a severe, worn pressure of thought about his temples, a fire in his eye (as if he saw something in objects more than outward appearances), an

intense high narrow forehead, a Roman nose, cheeks furrowed by strong purpose and feeling, and a convulsive inclination to laughter about the mouth, a good deal at variance with the solemn, stately expression of the rest of his face. . . . He sat down and talked very naturally and freely, with a mixture of clear gushing accents in his voice, a deep gutteral intonation, and a strong tincture of the northern *burr,* like the crust on wine.

The Wordsworths remained at Alfoxden until the summer of 1798.

In addition to work on *The Recluse,* during the Alfoxden period Wordsworth wrote the varied poems that would be published anonymously that fall with selections from Coleridge in the *Lyrical Ballads.* These poems–literary renditions of folk ballads, ballad debates, and blank-verse poems–were mostly the products of Wordsworth's happy and productive spring of 1798. Wordsworth and Coleridge planned the volume to earn enough money for a projected trip to Germany, where Coleridge especially wanted to go to learn German and to study German literature and philosophy–not initially to bring about a revolution in English literature. The 1798 volume sold well enough for new editions in January 1801 (with "1800" on the title page), 1802, and 1805, although Wordsworth never regarded the *Lyrical Ballads* as a great popular success. But even Francis Jeffrey, as he was about to launch into an attack of Wordsworth's 1807 book, *Poems, in two Volumes*, sourly admitted in retrospect that "The Lyrical Ballads were unquestionably popular . . . for in spite of their occasional vulgarity, affectation, and silliness, they were undoubtedly characterised by a strong spirit of originality, of pathos, and natural feeling . . ." (*Edinburgh Review*, October 1807). And the *Lyrical Ballads* would earn Wordsworth admirers among the younger writers, including Thomas De Quincey, John Keats, and Percy Bysshe Shelley, who must have been referring to *Lyrical Ballads* when he wrote of "Songs consecrate to truth and liberty" in "To Wordsworth" (1816).

Although the originality of Wordsworth's poems is still being debated, their general artistic superiority to the magazine literature with which they shared some themes–such as celebrations of simplicity and rural life and an interest in the natural world–is beyond dispute. And in a poem such as "Tintern Abbey," the product of Dorothy and William's trip through the Wye Valley in the summer of 1798, Wordsworth produced a nature poem which is not really a nature poem but a profound and anxious meditation on loss and desperately sought consolation. In typical Wordsworthian fashion, the poem focuses not on the present visit of 1798 but on the memory of the 1793 visit and on all that has gone between: the poem celebrates not a visiting but a re-visiting, not vision, but re-vision. Near the end of his meditation, the poet addresses Dorothy, his silent auditor, for confirmation and consolation, a move which has recently sparked feminist critics to consider her part more closely.

Wordsworth added a now-famous preface to the 1800 edition of *Lyrical Ballads* and revised it for the 1802 volume. Although some readers have viewed the preface as unclear or unhelpful in relation to the poems (a tradition perhaps deriving from Coleridge's later repudiation of central ideas in his *Biographia Literaria* [1817]), Wordsworth made significant contributions to poetic theory and clarified his rhetorical strategy. Wordsworth wanted to reach a real audience who could

appreciate the subtleties of his paradoxically artful, complex poems celebrating simple themes and common people–idiot boys, forsaken women, shepherds–and to distinguish these poems from the "trash" in magazines. A frequent charge leveled at Wordsworth from *Lyrical Ballads* to the delayed publication of *Peter Bell* in 1819 was the failure of decorum. In the preface to *Lyrical Ballads* he argues for the seriousness, importance, and permanence of basic human affections and for the use of nonornamental language (later explicitly linked to the King James Bible) to express these affections. Wordsworth outlines his psychological theory of the poetic composition, which reveals his perceptions of the associative processes of the mind. Situating himself in an age of crisis, Wordsworth links his poetic enterprise to the fate of the mind in the modern world:

> For a multitude of causes, unknown to former times, are now acting to blunt the discriminating powers of the mind, and, unfitting it for all voluntary exertion, to reduce it to a state of almost savage torpor. The most effective of these causes are the great national events which are daily taking place, and the increasing accumulation of men in cities, where the uniformity of their occupations produces a craving for extraordinary incident, which the rapid communication of intelligence hourly gratifies. . . . When I think upon this degrading thirst after outrageous stimulation, I am almost ashamed to have spoken of the feeble effort with which I have endeavored to counteract it. . . .

Against this insatiable hunger for incident and titillation, Wordsworth sets the *Lyrical Ballads*.

Perhaps the best representative of Wordsworth's program–for now he had one–is *Michael: A Pastoral Poem*, the last work added to the 1800 edition of the *Lyrical Ballads*. In *Michael*, a stately blank-verse poem, Wordsworth reinterprets the pastoral as a genre depicting a real shepherd living a life based on domestic industry and independent labor. Because of political and economic pressures, Wordsworth saw–and lamented–that the shepherd's simple way of life was dying out. In a letter written shortly after publication, Wordsworth comments to the Whig politician Charles James Fox that he wrote *Michael* and another poem, *The Brothers*, "to shew that men who did not wear fine cloaths can feel deeply." Using a simple, dignified language and verse form, Wordsworth conveys the simplicity and dignity of the shepherd's life and the tragedy of his loss. In a typical Wordsworthian way, the narrator redeems Michael's loss by telling his story, thereby preserving the values of his culture and transmitting those values "to a few natural hearts" who hear—or read–the poem.

The years between the first and second editions of the *Lyrical Ballads* were not uneventful. William and Dorothy accompanied Coleridge to Germany, but they eventually split up, with the Wordsworths settling in the mountain village of Goslar. While Coleridge's intellectual pursuits in Germany were successful, Wordsworth withdrew into himself. He suffered from the nervous headaches that had afflicted him since boyhood and that would be one of several physical manifestations of his anxiety–what Coleridge called his "hyperchondriacal" complaints. In the bitter cold of the German winter (1798-1799), Wordsworth wrote English poetry, explaining in December that "As I had no books I have been obliged to write in self-defence." In this remarkable letter from William and Dorothy to Coleridge, with every inch of paper filled with inserted passages, Dorothy copied her brother's poems for Coleridge, including original versions of the Lucy poems "She dwelt among the untrodden ways" and "Strange fits of passion," the fragmentary "Nutting," and the recollected skating and boat-stealing episodes that would find their way into *The Prelude*. Hence, some of Wordsworth's finest poetry had its origins in this lonely but richly productive winter. Away from England in an alien culture, Wordsworth retrieved his English past and began to ask the questions about the direction of his life that would eventually lead to his central work, *The Prelude*.

The Wordsworths returned to England in May 1799 and traveled directly from Yarmouth to Sockburn-on-Tees, where their old Penrith friends the Hutchinsons were living. Here—much closer to home–they remained for seven months, and here Wordsworth reestablished his ties with his future wife, Mary Hutchinson. Wordsworth composed the second part of what has become known as the "two-part" *Prelude* of 1799: the first part, written mostly in Goslar, had dealt with early childhood; the second part proceeds through adolescence. Although happy to be writing and to be back in England, Wordsworth was plagued by financial troubles, for he had both lent money which had not been returned and borrowed money which he could not yet repay.

With his finances in no better shape and approaching his thirtieth birthday the following spring, in December 1799 Wordsworth moved with Dorothy to Grasmere, where they had rented the cottage at Town End (later known as Dove Cottage) for eight pounds a year, a much more reasonable sum than Alfoxden. William and Dorothy now had their "little Nook of mountain-ground" and quickly established their domestic harmony. Wordsworth worked again on *The Recluse*, celebrating his return to the Lake District and his newly found domestic ideal with what was to be the first book, "Home at Grasmere." In the fall of 1800 he wrote *Michael* and other poems and prepared for the second edition of the *Lyrical Ballads*, which a new publisher, Longman (one with whom Wordsworth was to have a long if not entirely happy relationship), would bring out. Besides keeping house and thereby making Wordsworth's frugal domestic life possible, Dorothy also recorded that life in her Grasmere journals, with concrete details of cooking, cleaning, visiting, walking, and writing.

The year 1801 was not as productive for Wordsworth as the previous few, although the spring (which seemed to be Wordsworth's most productive season) of 1802 brought renewed activity: "The Leech-Gatherer" (later known as "Resolution and Independence"), the beginnings of the Intimations Ode, many lyrics inspired by his reading of sixteenth- and seventeenth-century poetry, revision of the preface to *Lyrical Ballads*, and the Appendix on Poetic Diction. As Wordsworth was struggling with "Resolution and Independence," a poem concerned with the personal and economic fate of poets, he had begun to receive letters from Annette Vallon. By the end of 1801 Wordsworth and Mary Hutchinson had quietly decided to marry, so these letters must have been particularly troublesome. The Peace of Amiens had opened up communications once again between England and France, and Wordsworth decided that he must go to France in order to clear the way for his marriage. With Dorothy accompanying him, William spent the month of August 1802 in Calais with Annette and Caroline. While in Calais, Wordsworth composed a small group of sonnets, which, except for Dorothy's brief journal entry, form the only records of this trip. The sonnets reveal Wordsworth's anxiously intertwined and unresolved thoughts on politics, marriage, and paternity. In contrast to the revolutionary excesses of the 1790s–which gave birth to an illegitimate daughter and an illegitimate ruler in

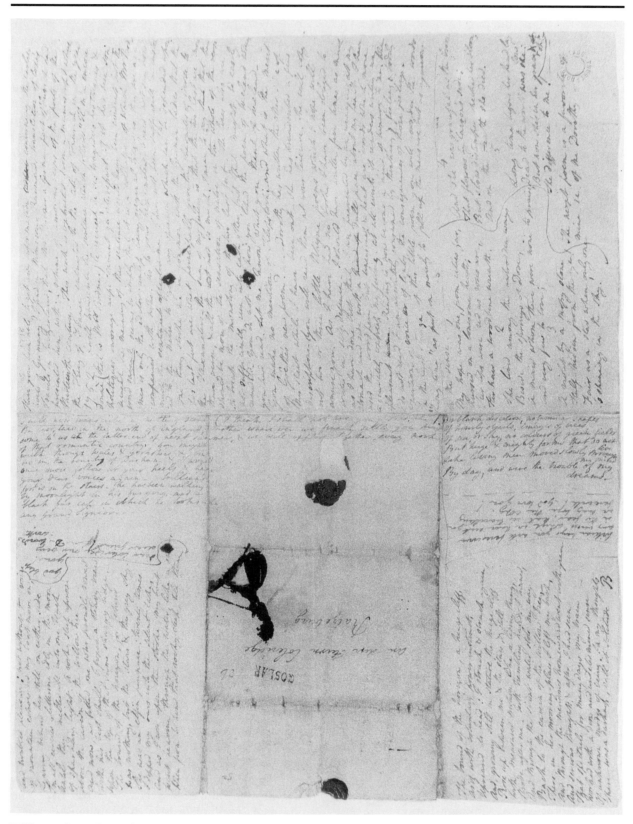

William and Dorothy Wordsworth's December 1798 letter to Coleridge, which includes early versions of "She Dwelt among the Untrod-
den Ways," the skating episode and the moonlight adventure on Ullswater section of the 1799 Prelude, *and "Nutting" (by*
permission of the Wordsworth Trust)

But if the shepherd to his flock should feed...
the herd which each should feed on were it not
Service redundant & ridiculous
And they the tutors of our youth our guides,
And Masters, Wardens of our faculties
And stewards of our labour, watchful men
And skilful in the usury of time
Sages who in their prescience would coerce
All accidents and tracing in their map
The way we ought to tread would chain us down
Like engines, when will they be taught that here
In the unreasoning progress of the world
A wiser spirit is at work for us
A better eye than theirs; most prodigal
of blessings and most studious of our good
Even in what seem our most unfruitful hours.
My playmates! brothers! nursed by the same years
And fellow-children of the self-same hills
Though we have moulded now by various lots
To various characters I do not think
That there is one of us who cannot tell
So manifold the expedients how intense
The unwearied passion with which nature toils
To win us to herself and to impress
Our careless hearts with beauty & with love
There was a boy ye knew him well ye cliffs
And islands of Winander, oftentimes
At evening when the stars had just begun
To move along the edges of the hills
Rising or setting would he stand alone
Beneath the trees or by the glimmering lake

Pages from one of the notebooks Wordsworth used in Goslar during winter 1798-1799 (by permission of the Wordsworth Trust). This fair copy of a draft for "There Was a Boy" was made circa February 1799. The first draft was written during the previous autumn. First published as a separate poem in the 1800 edition of Lyrical Ballads, *"There Was a Boy" was incorporated in* The Prelude *in spring 1804, but appeared by itself again in Wordsworth's 1815* Poems.

And there with fingers interwoven, both hands
Pressed closely palm to palm & to his mouth
Uplifted he as through an instrument
Blew mimic hootings to the silent owls
That they might answer him; & they would shout
Across the watry vale and shout again
Responsive to his call, alternate now
And regular one solitary cry
Came back to him; then quivering peals were heard
And long halloos & screams & echoes loud
Redoubled & redoubled a wild scene
Of mirth & jocund din. And when it chanced
That pauses of deep silence mock'd his skill
Then sometimes in that silence while he hung
Listening, a gentle shock of mild surprize
Has carried far into his heart the voice
Of mountain torrents or the visible scene
Would enter unawares into his mind
With all its solemn imagery its rocks
The woods & that uncertain heaven received
Into the bosom of the steady lake.

Fair are the woods & beauteous is the spot
The vale where he was born: The churchyard hangs
Upon a slope above the village school
And there, along that bank when I have passed
At evening, I believe that near his grave
A full half hour together I have stood
Mute, for he died when he was ten years
old.

Dora Wordsworth's drawing, circa 1826, of her birthplace in Grasmere, the cottage where the Wordsworths lived from December 1799 until May 1808 (based on a circa 1806 drawing by Amos Green; by permission of the Wordsworth Trust). Later called Dove Cottage, it was home to Thomas De Quincey in 1809).

France—Wordsworth looks toward personal and political stability in 1802 through marriage to an Englishwoman of similar background to his own and by reviving Milton's spirit to revitalize the "ancient English dower / Of inward happiness" ("London 1802"). Although he parted on friendly terms with Annette and Caroline and visited them in later years while in France, the poems reveal unresolved personal issues against the fragile background of peace in Calais.

While Wordsworth was no longer the young radical of the early 1790s, recent critics have persuasively argued that there are strong connections between Wordsworth's early radicalism and his later conservatism. Wordsworth did become more conservative, but he never became coldhearted and always maintained his hatred of slavery and tyranny. His response to the Terror in France led to a fear of mob rule and any massive threats to order. But the charges of apostasy, going back to Shelley in 1816, obscure real continuity in Wordsworth's values and locate a dramatic change in Wordsworth well beyond the time when he began to reconsider his moral and ideological commitments in *The Borderers* (written

in 1796-1797, unpublished until 1842).

When William and Mary were married on 2 October 1802, Wordsworth's finances were about to improve. Sir James Lowther, Earl of Lonsdale, had died the previous May, and his heir, Sir William Lowther, agreed to repay the debt to John Wordsworth's estate, which would mean around eight thousand pounds including interest, to be divided among the Wordsworth "children." Although the Wordsworths' finances were never easy, the growing family would live at Dove Cottage with some stability until 1808. Wordsworth's extended family, which included Dorothy, Mary's sister Sara Hutchinson, and often Coleridge and John Wordsworth of the East India Company, was his mainstay during this period, which also saw the birth of John (18 June 1803), Dorothy—whom they called Dora—(16 August 1804), and Thomas (16 June 1806); Catharine (6 September 1808) and William (12 May 1810) were born after the move to Allan Bank. Also at this period the Wordsworths established a lifelong friendship with Sir George and Lady Margaret Beaumont of Coleorton in Leicestershire. Sir George, a lover of poetry, amateur painter, collector of the arts,

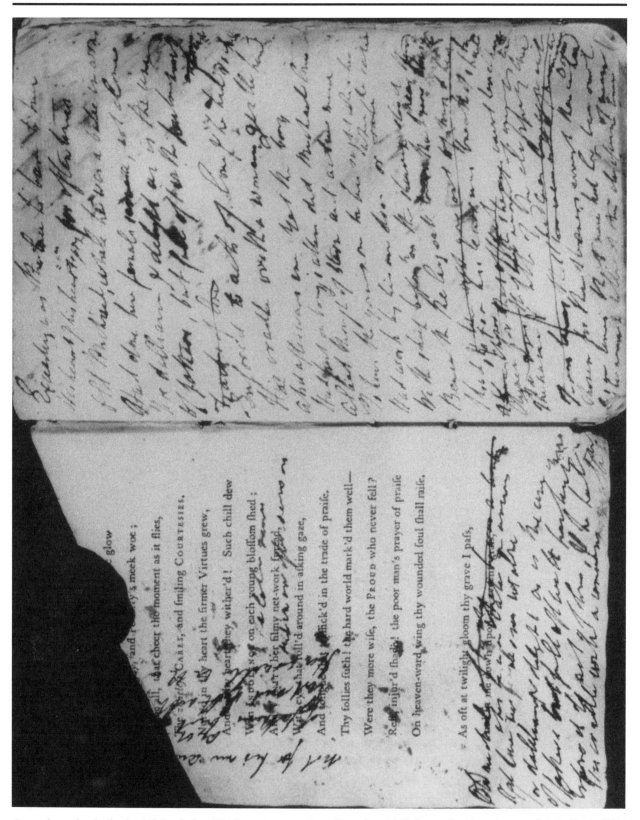

Pages from the drafts for Michael *that Wordsworth wrote circa November 1800 in an interleaved copy of Coleridge's 1796*
Poems on Various Subjects *(by permission of the Wordsworth Trust)*

and a Tory in politics, became Wordsworth's bene-
factor. In 1803 he gave Wordsworth some property at Applethwaite near Keswick, making Wordsworth a freeholder of Cumberland with political
rights. (Later, in 1805, Wordsworth reluctantly accepted Lowther's help in buying property in
Westmorland; he never built on either estate.)

In August 1803 Wordsworth, his sister, and
Coleridge toured Scotland, where the travelers
paid their respects to the memory of Burns and
visited Sir Walter Scott. Although the tour had
such high points, it was not a happy one. Coleridge, who had become increasingly unhappy in
his marriage, especially after he had met and
fallen in love with Sara Hutchinson, and who suffered from bad health and drug dependency,
had decided to go abroad to the Mediterranean.
In his envy of Wordsworth's domestic happiness,
Coleridge complained to Thomas Poole (14 October 1803) that Wordsworth was "more and more
benetted in hyperchondriacal fancies, living
wholly among *devotees*–having every the [*sic*] mi-
nutest Thing, almost his Eating and Drinking,
done for him by his Sister, or his Wife." Although these comments must be filtered through
Coleridge's personal frustrations, they do reveal
the extent to which the Wordsworth women devoted their lives to Wordsworth, providing the domestic harmony that made poetic composition possible. They not only cooked and cleaned and
nursed, but they labored over fair copies of manuscripts and provided the poet with loyal support.
In a lighter tone, but with the same implication,
Henry Crabb Robinson later referred to
Wordsworth's "three wives"–Mary Wordsworth,
Dorothy Wordsworth, and Sara Hutchinson.

But despite tensions on both sides, there
was still love and admiration between the friends–
and Wordsworth still saw Coleridge as an essential inspiration to *The Recluse* project. While Coleridge was trying to regain his health in Malta and
Italy, Wordsworth had hoped that his friend
would send him notes articulating a philosophical
system for *The Recluse*. But the notes never came,
and Coleridge claimed that they had been lost on
his trip back from Italy in 1806. Instead of working on *The Recluse* directly, Wordsworth once
again took up the poem on his own life, which
also became known as the "poem to Coleridge,"
since he decided to address the poem to his
friend, both as a tribute to him and as a way to restore him to hope.

At the beginning of 1804, Wordsworth
began working on *The Prelude* again in earnest,

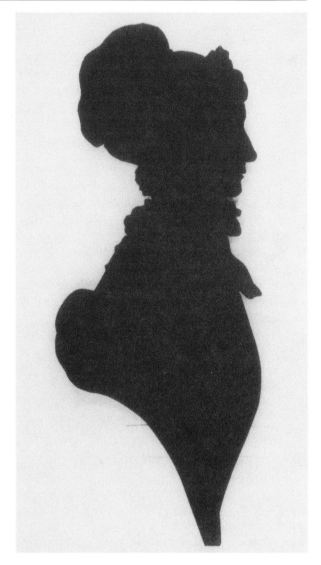

*Silhouette of Mary Hutchinson Wordsworth in early middle
age (by permission of the Wordsworth Trust)*

and by early March he had finished a five-book
version. This version, although it ended with the
visionary experience of climbing Mount Snowdon
in Wales (which Wordsworth had undertaken in
the summer of 1791 with Robert Jones), essentially covers Wordsworth's life through his residence at Cambridge. After completing this version, Wordsworth began to envision an even
longer poem of epic dimensions that would articu-
late how he–as a representative Englishman–had
sustained the disappointments of recent history
caused by the failure of revolution in France and
the growth of tyranny in Europe. In the expanded version, the poet revisits France of the
1790s in his imagination and relives the painful
years of that decade; he shows how his heart and

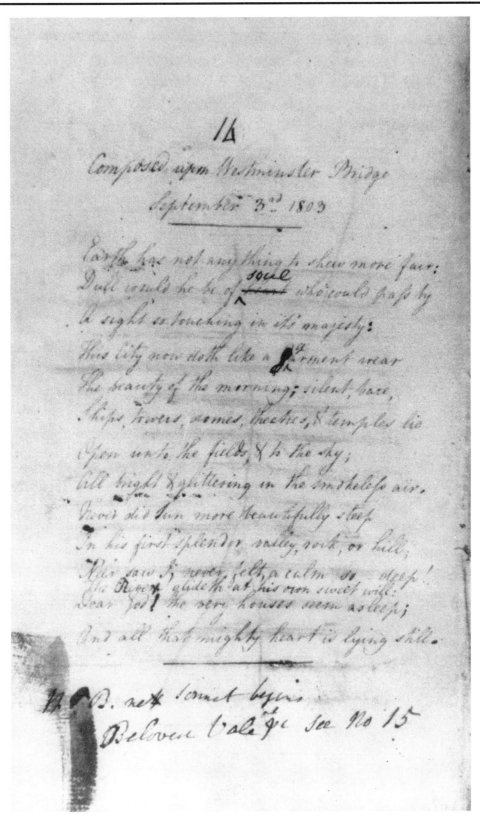

Printer's copy of one of Wordsworth's best-known sonnets transcribed by Sara Hutchinson—and corrected by Wordsworth—some time be-
tween November 1806 and March 1807 for inclusion in his 1807 Poems, in Two Volumes *(Add. Ms. 47864; by permission*
of the British Library). The poem was written on 3 September 1802; the error in the title is Wordsworth's.

Book 8, lines 44-65, from Dorothy Wordsworth's first transcription of the 1805 Prelude, *extensively revised by William Words-worth (by permission of the Wordsworth Trust)*

mind were restored by his links to the natural world and the people who inhabit it.

Although Wordsworth follows a general chronological movement from childhood to maturity, *The Prelude* is not strictly chronological. The actual composition of the poem began in Germany with Wordsworth's memories of childhood experiences, later called "spots of time." But the 1805 poem actually begins with Wordsworth's dedication of himself to poetry, and it ends with the mountaintop epiphany on Mount Snowdon in 1791. In book 1 Wordsworth frames his poem in a Miltonic context, proclaiming that "The earth is all before me," lines which echo the end of *Paradise Lost:* "The world was all before them." But Wordsworth begins his poem in the fallen world and changes the person and number of the pronoun: his quest begins without Eve, without a ready-made community. In the course of book 1, the poet creates the fiction that the poem is in search not only of a hero but of a theme. Wordsworth goes through various possibilities, as indicated by the great writers of the past, perhaps "some British theme, some old / Romantic tale by Milton left unsung." He discovers in the course of this inventory that he is most invigorated by "the story of my life," which will encompass the theme and region of his song.

Wordsworth wrote *The Prelude* as if to suggest that in the act of composition he discovered meanings in past experiences that were not obvious at the time. He typically describes being disturbed or chastened by an event, only to recognize as he writes how that event has unconsciously influenced his life. In order to capture this structure of recollecting and then interpreting a past experience, Wordsworth constantly moves from excited narrative passages to discursive passages, from past to present. A central example of this method occurs in book 6 of the 1805 *Prelude* as Wordsworth describes his walking tour across the Alps in 1790 with Robert Jones. Wordsworth describes himself and Jones as having tremendous expectations of actually crossing the Alps: they are tourists seeking the sublime, adventurers who have "sallied forth" on a quest. As Wordsworth explains, "mighty forms seizing a youthful fancy / Had given charter to irregular hopes." To their astonishment and disappointment, though, the young men actually cross the Alps without realizing that they have done so. From this intensely remembered disappointment, the poet shifts with no transition except a new verse paragraph to this present recognition:

> Imagination!—lifting up itself
> Before the eye and progress of my song
> Like an unfathered vapour, here that power,
> In all the might of its endowments, came
> Athwart me. I was lost as in a cloud,
> Halted without a struggle to break through,
> And now, recovering, to my soul I say
> 'I recognize thy glory'.

Fourteen years later in the process of writing, the poet recognizes how the human mind can compensate for such disappointments.

By May of 1805 Wordsworth had completed the thirteen-book *Prelude*, which he viewed as a tributary to his projected work *The Recluse*, not his major achievement. Wordsworth continued to revise the poem until 1839, when it was beautifully copied as a fourteen-book poem by Dora Wordsworth and her friend Elizabeth Cookson. While critics debate the merits of each version, students now have the advantage of several parallel texts for comparison. Members of Wordsworth's circle provide the only really contemporary response to the 1805 text: after hearing Wordsworth read the poem, Coleridge was moved to record his praise of Wordsworth's "prophetic Lay" in "To William Wordsworth," and family and friends who heard it over the years recognized its greatness. But the public was not to see *The Prelude* until 1850, the same year as the publication of Tennyson's *In Memoriam.*

Shortly after he finished the thirteen-book *Prelude*, Wordsworth wrote to Sir George Beaumont (13 June 1805):

> I have the pleasure to say that I finished my Poem about a fortnight ago. I had looked forward to the day as a most happy one; and I was indeed grateful to God for giving me life to complete the work, such as it is; but it was not a happy day for me—I was dejected on many accounts; when I looked back upon the performance it seemed to have a dead weight about it, the reality so far short of the expectation; it was the first long labour that I had finished, and the doubt whether I should ever live to write the Recluse, and the sense which, I had of this Poem being so far below what I seemed capable of executing, depressed me much. . . .

Wordsworth's sentiments provide a poignant analogue to crossing the Alps: "the reality so far short of the expectation." Far from being the blindly egotistical poet some thought, Wordsworth was vulnerable to doubts and anxieties about his poetic enterprise. *The Recluse* cast a

Wordsworth circa May 1806 (portrait by Henry Edridge; by permission of the Wordsworth Trust)

shadow over the present and made Wordsworth uneasy about the future.

Wordsworth goes on in the same letter to name his most pressing grief: "many heavy thoughts of my poor departed Brother hung upon me; the joy which I should have had in showing him the Manuscript and a thousand other vain fancies and dreams." Wordsworth's much-loved younger brother John, who had planned to retire with his family to Grasmere and join their circle, drowned with many of his crew when his ship, the *Earl of Abergavenny,* was wrecked in a storm near Weymouth Bay on 5 February 1805. The Wordsworths were profoundly grieved. John had been a most sympathetic and affectionate brother, who shared a love of poetry and the natural world. Furthermore, John had wanted to work in order to free William "to do something for the world." Immediately following John's

death, Wordsworth tried to compose tributes to him, but he was so distraught that he could not record the verses that he actually composed because he was too weak to hold a pen and too reluctant to ask another mourner to take dictation. These attempts at composition and composure did, however, have therapeutic effects, and in the spring, as we have seen, Wordsworth returned to *The Prelude*. And in May or June of 1806, thinking of John's death in stormy seas and his own visit to Piel Castle in 1794, Wordsworth wrote his "Elegiac Stanzas Suggested by a Picture of Peele Castle, in a Storm, by Sir George Beaumont." Although the poet remembers from his experience that "Thy [the castle's] Form was sleeping on a glassy sea," he identifies more closely with the painting of the castle braving the angry sea. He sees in the pictured castle an image of his own possible endurance:

Top: the 1806 painting that inspired Wordsworth to write "Elegiac Stanzas Suggested by a Picture of Peele Castle, in a Storm, by Sir George Beaumont," in memory of his brother John Wordsworth, who died in a shipwreck near Weymouth Bay on 5 February 1805 (Private collection; from William Wordsworth and the Age of English Romanticism, 1987). *Bottom: John Constable's* Weymouth Bay *(1816), inspired by Wordsworth's poem (by permission of the Trustees of the Victoria and Albert Museum).*

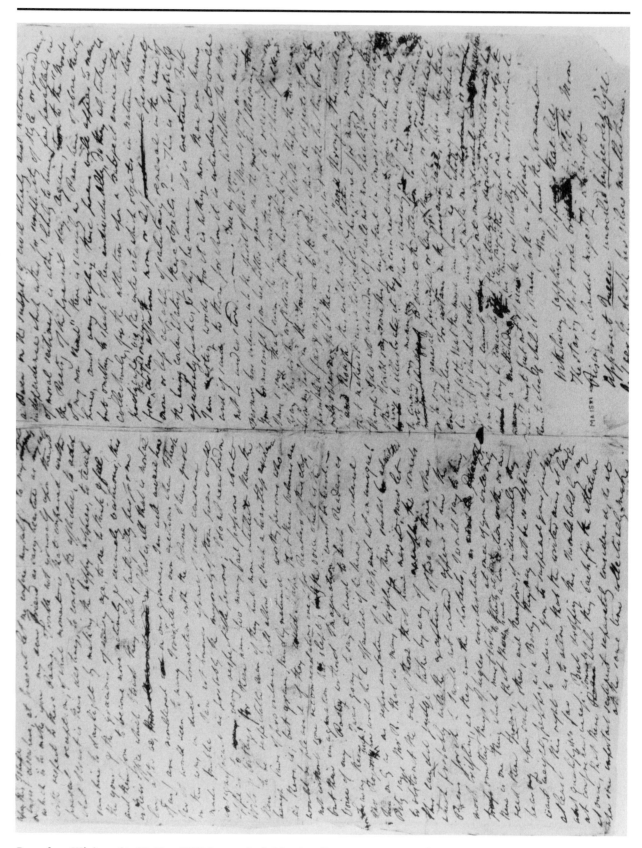

Pages from Wordsworth's 21 May 1807 letter to Lady Margaret Beaumont, expressing his reaction to the unfavorable reception of his recently published collection of poems (MA 1581; by permission of the Pierpont Morgan Library)

And this huge Castle, standing here sublime,
I love to see the look with which it braves,
Cased in the unfeeling armour of old time,
The light'ning, the fierce wind, and trampling
        waves.

John Constable's *Weymouth Bay,* painted with Wordsworth's loss in mind, provides a visual context for Wordsworth's description of the angry sky and sea.

During this period Wordsworth was also constantly worried about Coleridge, and, when he finally saw his friend again in the fall of 1806, he was stunned by his bad health and broken spirit. Coleridge later visited the Wordsworths while they were staying in a farmhouse in Coleorton, but there was to be no repeat of the Alfoxden years. The months at Coleorton (October 1806-June 1807) were not unhappy, though, especially since Hall Farm was so much more spacious for the growing family than Dove Cottage. It is here that Wordsworth read *The Prelude* to Coleridge and the gathered family. For the first time since childhood, the Wordsworths became regular churchgoers, a practice perhaps related to the crisis of John's death. Wordsworth, too, revealed his skill as a landscape gardener, designing a winter garden of evergreens and holly for Lady Beaumont. Wordsworth also traveled a good deal—to London, which he seemed to enjoy more than in his earlier years and in spite of his criticism of urban life—and around the North. A trip in late summer and early fall would lead to the composition in 1807-1808 of *The White Doe of Rylstone* (1815), a poem based on traditional ballads and local legends.

During the spring of 1807 at Coleorton, Wordsworth was preparing copy for his new publication to appear in May as *Poems, in two Volumes.* Included in these volumes were numerous lyrics, many of which had been written in the spring of 1802, forty-six sonnets, poems from the Scottish tour, and other works written over the last five years. The volumes included many poems now regarded as some of Wordsworth's finest lyrics, the Intimations Ode, "Resolution and Independence," "The Solitary Reaper," and "I wandered lonely as a cloud," to name just a few. Despite this artistic wealth, the volumes met with resounding rejections from reviewers. Francis Jeffrey, who might justly be called Wordsworth's nemesis at the *Edinburgh Review,* attacked the volumes without mercy in the October 1807 issue. The leitmotif of his criticism (echoed by other reviewers)

was that Wordsworth as a serious poet wasted his time on mean and uninteresting subjects. Because Wordsworth violated Jeffrey's standard of decorum, his poems seem to be parodies of themselves:

> It is possible enough, we allow, that the sight of a friend's garden-spade, or a sparrow's nest, or a man gathering leeches, might really have suggested to such a mind a train of powerful impressions and interesting reflections; but it is certain, that, to most minds, such associations will always appear forced, strained, and unnatural; and that the composition in which it is attempted to exhibit them, will always have the air of parody, or ludicrous and affected singularity. All the world laughs at Elegiac stanzas to a sucking-pig–a Hymn on Washing-day–Sonnets to one's grandmother–or Pindarics on gooseberry-pye; and yet, we are afraid, it will not be quite easy to convince Mr Wordsworth, that the same ridicule must infallibly attach to most of the pathetic pieces in these volumes.

Jeffrey's comments about such problematic poems as "Alice Fell" and "Beggars" are diminished by his judgment that the Intimations Ode is "the most illegible and unintelligible part of the publication." Jeffrey implies that Wordsworth has feminized the art of poetry with his "namby pamby," his "prettyisms," his "babyish" verse; he approves of "The Character of the Happy Warrior" (written in part as a tribute to Horatio Nelson) because it is "manly." Implicit in Jeffrey's gendered standards is the notion that real poets (men) do not write poems about daisies and daffodils.

Jeffrey's criticism probably helped to ensure much poorer sales for *Poems, in two Volumes* than for the *Lyrical Ballads;* after seven years 230 of the 1,000 copies remained at Longman's. Jeffrey also went far to create the fiction that Wordsworth belonged to a school of poetry, a "brotherhood of poets who have haunted about the lakes of Cumberland." This allegedly conspiratorial fraternity included the likes of Coleridge and Robert Southey, who lived at Greta Hall, Keswick, with the Coleridges. While Wordsworth had known Southey as long as he had known Coleridge, and remained friendly with him all of his life, he did not particularly admire Southey's more-popular poetry. Nevertheless, the legend of the Lake School thrived in reviews for many years and was strengthened by the ideological connection of Wordsworth, Southey, and Coleridge as conservative turncoats. All of this made it perfectly natural for Byron to attack "the Lakers" en masse on political and poetic grounds in the dedication to *Don Juan* (1819-1824).

Following the attacks on his 1807 book, Wordsworth repeatedly expressed to friends his own faith in his work. When Lady Beaumont wrote her consolations, Wordsworth responded: "Trouble not yourself upon their present reception; of what moment is that compared with what I trust is their destiny, to console the afflicted . . . to . . . teach the young and the gracious of every age, to see, to think, to feel, and therefore to become more actively and securely virtuous. . . ." More and more, this group of "gracious" readers became idealized as "the People" as opposed to "the Public." Beyond his sympathetic circle of friends and family, Wordsworth seemed to pin his final hopes on being vindicated by time and not by contemporary readers. In the "1815 Essay, Supplementary to the Preface," published in his *Poems By William Wordsworth* (1815), he bases his overview of literary history on the premise that great writers are not popular in their time. As evidence, Wordsworth points to Samuel Johnson's *Lives of the Poets* (1779-1781) and asks, "where is the bright Elizabethan constellation? . . . where is the ever-to-be-honoured Chaucer? . . . Spenser? . . . Sidney? . . . Shakespeare?" Despite the consolation of implicitly placing himself in this stellar company, Wordsworth still worried over the sale of his books and deeply resented his inability to make enough money from his writing "to buy his shoestrings." (For years he worked to make the copyright laws more responsive to the author's right to earn profits and pass on profits to his heirs.) But the poor reception of his 1807 poems made Wordsworth more reluctant than ever to publish.

Wordsworth's anxiety about publication is evident in the history of *The White Doe of Rylstone*, a poem in seven cantos completed by January 1808. From the beginning, Wordsworth was proud of *The White Doe*, representing it to his sympathetic circle as a spiritual work destined to be misunderstood by the public. Wordsworth felt that the poem would disappoint the expectations of readers looking for the kind of action and adventure found in Byron's popular tales or Scott's metrical romances, particularly *The Lay of the Last Minstrel* (1805). Dorothy Wordsworth wrote to Lady Beaumont on 3 January 1808 that "I certainly misled you when I said that it would be a sort of romance, for it has nothing of that character." Wordsworth exploited neither the early Eliza-

bethan border setting and its Gothicism nor the potential for adventure and suspense inherent in the ballad material about the Norton uprising from Thomas Percy's *Reliques of Ancient English Poetry* (1765). Instead of action or event, the narrative focuses on Emily Norton, whom Wordsworth compares to Edmund Spenser's Una and whose entire family is killed in an uprising against loyalists to Queen Elizabeth. Despite her loss of family and home, Emily finds spiritual consolation in her bond with a mysterious doe, who after Emily's death makes a weekly pilgrimage to Bolton Priory and the Norton gravesite.

Fearing to be misunderstood, Wordsworth went on for seven years before he was willing to publish *The White Doe*. Dorothy wrote to various correspondents, assuring that "we women" urge publication. While separated from William in March of 1808, she even wrote him: "Do, dearest William! do pluck up your Courage–overcome your disgust to publishing–It is but a *little trouble*, and all will be over, and we shall be wealthy, and at our ease for one year, at least." But even this dramatic plea was to no immediate avail. When he did publish the poem in 1815, Wordsworth insisted on an expensive quarto volume (twenty-one shillings) with large type, lots of space on the page, and an engraving of the doe after Sir George Beaumont's painting. Thus, Wordsworth intended his quarto to rival the presentation of Byron's more popular tales, or, as Wordsworth said, to show the world what *he* thought of *The White Doe*.

But *The White Doe* has never received the kind of critical attention Wordsworth thought it deserved and is not now usually included among Wordsworth's greatest accomplishments. While its reception was more mixed than the 1807 *Poems*, reviewers were generally confused about the nature of Emily's consolation and questioned the lack of explicit motivation. In the *Eclectic Review* (January 1816) Josiah Conder disliked the "mystical elements" and added that "The story is . . . so much more like history, than romance, so destitute of plot, and so purely tragical, that it forms a much better subject for a ballad, than for a poem of seven cantos, in which the reader is led to expect more of incident and detail." Jeffrey, too, objected to the "metaphysical sensibility" and "mystical wordiness" while musing that the material might have made an interesting ballad in the hands of Byron or Scott (*Edinburgh Review*, October 1815). But only Jeffrey claimed that "This, we think, has the merit of being the very worst

100   THE WHITE DOE OF RYLSTONE.   CANTO VI.

Such conflict long did he maintain

Within himself, and found no rest ;

Calm liberty he could not gain ;   *Nor liberty nor rest could gain*

And yet the service was unblest.

His own life into danger brought

By this sad burden—even that thought

Exciting   Raised self-suspicion which was strong,

Sway͟i͟n͟g *ed* the brave Man to his wrong :

And how, unless it were the sense

Of all-disposing Providence,

Its will i͟n͟t͟e͟l͟l͟i͟g͟i͟b͟l͟y *unquestionably* shewn,

Finds he the Banner in his hand,

Without a thought to such intent,

Or conscious effort of his own ?

And no obstruction to prevent

His Father's wish and last command !

And, thus beset, he heaved a sigh ;

Remembering his own prophecy

Of utter desolation, made

To Emily in the yew-tree shade ;

How has the Banner clung so fast
To a palsied, and unconscious hand ;
Clung to the hand, to which it passed
Without impediment ? And why,
But that Heaven's purpose might be known,
Doth now no hindrance meet his eye.
No intervention, to withstand
Fulfilment of a Father's prayer
Breathed to a Son forgiven ; and blest
When all resentments were at rest,

Page from Wordsworth's copy of The White Doe of Rylstone *(1815), with his revisions for the 1836 edition of* The Poetical Works of William Wordsworth *(auctioned by American Art Association, Anderson Galleries, Inc., sale number 4154, 14-15 February 1935)*

331

poem we ever saw imprinted in a quarto volume. . . ."

In May of 1808, several months after Wordsworth had finished writing *The White Doe*, the family moved across Grasmere Vale from Town End to Allan Bank, a larger house to accommodate the growing family, but one whose smoking chimneys were to bother the Wordsworths. During this spring and into the fall, Wordsworth composed some poetry intended to be part of *The Recluse*. For the three years he lived at Allan Bank, Wordsworth worked intermittently on what would become *The Excursion* (1814) and wrote a good deal of prose: his *Concerning the Convention of Cintra* (1809), a version of *A Guide to the Lakes*—published as the introduction to *Select Views in Cumberland, Westmoreland, and Lancashire* (1810)—and three *Essays Upon Epitaphs;* the first of the *Essays on Epitaphs* appeared in Coleridge's short-lived publication *The Friend* (22 February 1809), as did "A Reply to Mathetes" (14 December 1809, 4 January 1810). Wordsworth wrote *Concerning the Convention of Cintra* in response to what he saw as the British generals' betrayal of Spanish and Portuguese forces. After the Spaniards and Portuguese had risen against Napoleon's troops, the British negotiated and let the French go. Wordsworth interpreted this action as a betrayal of the cause of liberty, both a betrayal of spirited allies and a betrayal of British values going back to the republicans Wordsworth had celebrated in his sonnets of 1802. Coleridge and Wordsworth's new friend and admirer Thomas De Quincey helped with the long and complicated task of seeing this pamphlet through the press.

In the fall of 1810 came Wordsworth's painful falling out with Coleridge. Coleridge had resolved to go to London, and Wordsworth's old friend Basil Montagu and his wife had offered to take him into their household. Well acquainted both with Montagu's regular habits and with Coleridge's addiction and undisciplined way of life, Wordsworth confidentially warned Montagu that the plan would not work. On the way to London, Montagu carelessly told Coleridge what Wordsworth had said: this indiscretion marked the beginning of a long and painful (and to the outside observer rather ridiculous) string of misunderstandings about exactly what Wordsworth had said. Wordsworth absolutely denied that he had called Coleridge a "rotten drunkard," as Coleridge believed. After many letters and the mediation of such friends as Charles Lamb and Henry Crabb Robinson, Wordsworth and Coleridge halted their dispute in the spring of 1812. Although they remained on friendly terms until Coleridge's death in 1834, they never shared the same intimacy of their earlier years, and Coleridge's interest in and support of Wordsworth's poetry diminished.

Escaping from the discomforts of Allan Bank, the Wordsworths moved to the Grasmere Vicarage in June of 1811. Wordsworth's four-year-old daughter Catharine died in June 1812 after a series of illnesses, and then six-year-old Thomas died in December, following complications from the measles. Wordsworth was a most loving and devoted father, and both he and Mary went through long periods of mourning. Wordsworth expresses his loss of Catharine—and her continuing presence in his mind—in a sonnet published in 1815:

> Surprized by joy—impatient as the Wind
> I turned to share the transport—Oh! with whom
> But Thee, deep buried in the silent tomb,
> That spot which no vicissitude can find.

Following these deaths, Wordsworth became even more solicitous of his surviving children. John was a slow but steady student who would eventually attend Oxford and enter the Church; Willy, a constant worry to his parents, eventually took over Wordsworth's position as Distributor of Stamps in 1842; sadly, Thomas had been the only son who showed real scholarly ability. With his daughter Dora, Wordsworth developed an intensely close relationship; as she grew into womanhood, and especially following Dorothy Wordsworth's decline and Sara Hutchinson's death in 1835, the spirited, talented, and devoted Dora became Wordsworth's companion and amanuensis.

In March of 1813 Sir William Lowther, Earl of Lonsdale, appointed Wordsworth as Distributor of Stamps for Westmorland and part of Cumberland, a position that Wordsworth hoped would eventually help supplement his income by more than four hundred pounds a year. The position required traveling several times a year around the counties to collect revenue, a practice suited to Wordsworth's love of travel, although it was time-consuming. In some circles Wordsworth was never forgiven for accepting this patronage of the Lowthers and the government: he became Browning's lost leader who "left us" for "a handful of silver" (in "The Lost Leader," 1845). Shortly after this, the Wordsworths moved to what would be their final home, the spacious and

*Rydal Mount, Wordsworth's home from 1813 until his death in 1850 (an 1831 watercolor by William Westall;
by permission of the Wordsworth Trust)*

well-situated Rydal Mount, about two miles from Grasmere. Dorothy Wordsworth heralded the family's new comforts: "We are going to have a *Turkey*!!! carpet in the dining-room and a Brussels in William's study." But she went on to assure her friend Catherine Clarkson that at least the Turkey carpet was really economical, if the Brussels was just "smart."

The year after he settled at Rydal Mount, Wordsworth published *The Excursion,* which he dedicated to Lord Lonsdale, and advertised as a portion of his work in progress, *The Recluse. The Excursion,* a long poem in nine books (in two quarto volumes), begins with the much-revised version of *The Ruined Cottage* as its first book. Wordsworth essentially develops four main characters or dramatic voices in the poem: the Wanderer (the Pedlar of *The Ruined Cottage*), the Poet, the Solitary, and the Pastor. The Wanderer introduces the Poet to his friend the Solitary, an unbeliever embittered by the loss of his hopes in the French Revolution and the death of his family.

The trio soon meet up with the Pastor, who joins in the attempt to console the Solitary and reconcile him to himself and to God. In the course of the poem, we overhear many stories pertaining to rural characters and their fates, and discourses on war, colonization, education, and religion as the characters stroll through the countryside. The Solitary remains unconverted.

In his preface Wordsworth explains that "The Recluse will consist chiefly of meditations in the Author's own person," but that in *The Excursion* "something of a dramatic form is adopted." This dramatic or dialogue form allows Wordsworth to present different points of view on various subjects, although, as the astute Hazlitt noted in a three-part review for the *Examiner* (21 and 28 August, 2 October 1814), the main personae also represent parts of Wordsworth's own mind:

> Even the dialogues introduced in the present volume are soliloquies of the same character, taking different views of the subject. The recluse, the pastor, and the pedlar, are three persons in one

poet.... But the evident scope and tendency of Mr. Wordsworth's mind is the reverse of dramatic. It resists all change of character, all variety of scenery, all the bustle, machinery, and pantomime of the stage, or of real life,–whatever might relieve or relax or change the direction of its own activity, jealous of all competition. The power of his mind preys upon itself.

Like *The Borderers*, *The Excursion* might fail as drama, but it tells us a great deal about the conflicts within the poet's own mind. The fact that the Solitary (Hazlitt's "recluse") is not reconciled tells us that Wordsworth had to fight against alienation and melancholy, even though he embraced religion. Perhaps the revelation of this conflict appealed to Keats when he greeted *The Excursion* as one of the three things to rejoice about in the modern world. Keats's "Ode to a Nightingale" pays tribute to the sometimes brilliant poetry of book 4, with its allusions to solemn nightingales and fading anthems.

But *The Excursion* did not meet with universal acclaim. Jeffrey, who gave Wordsworth up as "hopeless," began his review for the *Edinburgh Review* (November 1814) with the infamous quip, "This will never do." Although Jeffrey pointed to the obscurity and "mysticism" of certain passages, his main objection echoed his previous critiques of Wordsworth's lack of decorum: "Did Mr. Wordsworth really imagine, that his favourite doctrines were likely to gain any thing in point of effect or authority by being put in the mouth of a person accustomed to higgle about tape, or brass sleeve-buttons?" Similarly Hazlitt asserted, in the context of his more favorable review for the *Examiner*, that "We go along with him, while he is the subject of his own narrative, but we take leave of him when he makes pedlars and ploughmen his heroes, and the interpreters of his sentiments." In the *Monthly Review* (February 1815) John Herman Merivale perhaps expressed the sentiment of many readers, even today, when he claimed that the poem has "flashes of genius which no weight of pedantry and affectation can entirely suppress or extinguish." It is perhaps this overt didacticism that has most offended modern readers. Interestingly, the major reviewers did not object to the poem on political grounds, although when Shelley launched his attack on Wordsworth the following year, he assumed that *The Excursion* was the product of a reactionary renegade, a position that was later strengthened by the tone of Wordsworth's "Thanksgiving Ode" (1816) celebrating Napoleon's defeat.

The Excursion went into seven editions in Wordsworth's lifetime, but it has never assumed the place in his canon or in posterity that Wordsworth had cherished for it. In stating his preference for Wordsworth's lyric poetry against both *The Excursion* and *The Prelude*, Matthew Arnold helped in his 1879 edition to halt interest in the long poetry. But while *The Prelude* has come to be regarded as the center of Wordsworth's oeuvre, *The Excursion* never made a strong comeback. Nevertheless, as modern scholars want to learn more about Wordsworth's development and his influence on his own contemporaries, *The Excursion* warrants greater attention as the long work that they actually read, discuss, and quote.

In 1815 Wordsworth published, in addition to *The White Doe*, *Poems By William Wordsworth, Including Lyrical Ballads, and the Miscellaneous Pieces of the Author*, two volumes that included poetry written since the 1807 *Poems, in two volumes*. Several of the new poems reveal Wordsworth's passionate rediscovery of the classics: in "Laodamia," for instance, an admired poem in the nineteenth century, Wordsworth has in mind book 6 of the *Aeneid* and Ovid's *Heroides*, as well as other classical sources. Also in these volumes Wordsworth includes an important preface, in which he outlines his method of classifying his poems according to psychological categories or subject matter, as well as his analysis of the two faculties, imagination and fancy.

Although Wordsworth had also planned to publish *Peter Bell* and *The Waggoner* in 1815, he delayed, perhaps because of the poor reception of *The White Doe*. Finally in 1819 Wordsworth brought out *Peter Bell*, written in 1798, and *The Waggoner*, probably written in 1806. *Peter Bell* had the distinction of being satirized before it was published: Keats's friend John Hamilton Reynolds heard the title of the poem and thought it ridiculous enough to write a spoof. Keats implicitly supported this sentiment, writing to his brother in 1819, "Wordsworth is going to publish a poem called Peter Bell–what a perverse fellow it is! Why wilt he talk about Peter Bells?" Keats, who by this time was disillusioned with Wordsworth, seemed to be basing his complaint on Wordsworth's choice of character and subject matter, as Jeffrey and Hazlitt had done for *The Excursion*. Reynolds's satire was but the first of many, which paradoxically made the real *Peter Bell* a much more popular volume than *The Waggoner*, a comic poem admired by and dedicated to Charles Lamb.

Wordsworth in 1818 (portrait by Benjamin Robert Haydon; by permission of the National Portrait Gallery, London). The Wordsworth family, considering this drawing a rather dramatized image of the poet, called it "The Brigand."

Perhaps the most serious attack was Shelley's *Peter Bell the Third,* a work Shelley tried to publish in 1819 but which was not published until 1839–too late to influence the fate of the real *Peter Bell.* Shelley's poem is really not a parody of *Peter Bell* but a critique of Wordsworth's career and the political views that led him to write "odes to the Devil" such as the "Thanksgiving Ode." In Shelley's critique we see disillusionment with Wordsworth based on his political views and recent activities; for in 1818 Wordsworth had campaigned vigorously for the Lowthers in the Parliamentary elections and written *Two Addresses to the Freeholders of Westmoreland* on the occasion. In one of the addresses Wordsworth argues for "mellowed feudality" instead of democracy. In such claims and in his open attack on reform, Shelley saw betrayal and apostasy. Even Keats, who had met Wordsworth through their friend Benjamin Robert Haydon in London in December 1817,

had been disappointed to find Wordsworth away campaigning for the Lowthers when he stopped at Rydal Mount in 1818. Wordsworth, in his turn, defended his actions: he feared the influence of commercial and manufacturing interests and justified support of the Lowthers on the grounds that they would preserve counties like Westmorland and Cumberland and protect them from exploitation by urban areas. Wordsworth would later develop similar arguments in his opposition to the Reform Bill of 1832 and to other liberal measures.

While the younger generation of Romantic poets were becoming disillusioned with Wordsworth on political grounds, Wordsworth was continuing to publish his poetry and beginning to find a new audience. In 1820 the first collected edition of his poems appeared (four volumes excluding *The Excursion*), and then a five-volume collection came out in 1827. In 1828 a pirated edi-

4

Whence but from some celestial urn
These colours wont to meet my eye
Where'er it wander'd in the morn
Of blissful infancy?
This glimpse of glory, why renewed?
Nay rather speak with gratitude;
For, if a vestige of those gleams
Survived, 'twas only in my dreams.
Dread Power! whom Peace and Calmness serve,
No less than Nature's threatening Voice,
If aught unworthy be my choice,
From Thee if I would swerve,
O let thy grace remind me of the Light,
Full early lost, and fruitlessly deplor'd,
Which, at this moment, on my waking sight
Appears to shine, by miracle restor'd!
My soul, though yet confin'd to earth,
Rejoices in a second birth:
— 'tis past — the visionary splendor fades
And night approaches with her shades!

Transcribed by Thos Wordsworth
for Mr Allston, in gratitude for the
pleasure the received from the sight of
his Pictures, in particular, the Jacob's
Dream. Wm Wordsworth

N. B. The Author knows, now far he was indebted
to Mr Allston for parts of the 3d Stanza —
The multiplication of ridges in a mountainous
Country, has Mr Allston has probably observed, are
from two causes, sunny or watery haze or

Page from a fair copy of "Composed during an Evening of peculiar beauty" made by Mary Wordsworth, with a note in William Wordsworth's hand, for Washington Allston, whose Jacob's Dream *was hung at the country house of Sir George O'Brien Wyndham, Earl of Egremont, in 1817, the year this poem was written (Cornell Wordsworth Collection; by permission of Cornell University Library). It was first published, with some textual changes, as "Ode, composed upon an Evening of extraordinary Splendor and Beauty" in* The River Duddon *(1820).*

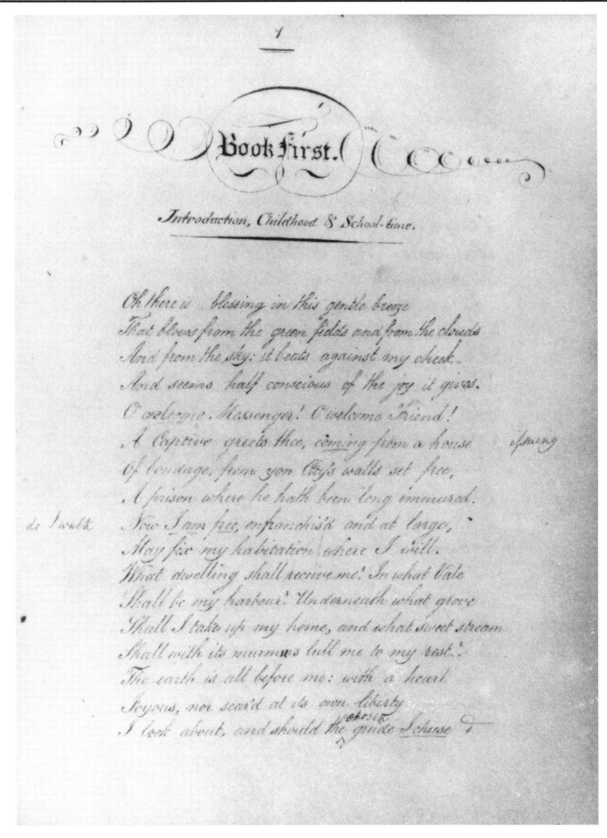

First page of the "Glad Preamble," written as a separate poem in 1799, as it appears at the beginning of The Prelude, *book 1, in the fair copy prepared in 1816-1819 by John Carter, Wordsworth's clerk (by permission of the Wordsworth Trust)*

tion of his complete works came out in Paris. During this period Wordsworth also published (among other works) a well-received collection of sonnets in *The River Duddon, A series of Sonnets: Vaudracour and Julia: and Other Poems* (1820); *Memorials of a Tour on the Continent, 1820* (1822), the fruit of one of his many trips to Europe; and *Ecclesiastical Sketches* (1822), sonnets influenced by his brother Christopher Wordsworth and his work in Church history. The works of this period are varied, although they have one quality in common: they are not part of *The Recluse*. Although Wordsworth continued to refer to this work, his prospects of finishing it diminished. In the sonnet "Nuns fret not" (1807) Wordsworth had praised the boundaries of "the sonnet's scanty plot of ground" for disciplining poetic impulses; he seems never to have found the "plot of ground" to discipline the unwieldy *Recluse* during these years. But he did not give up trying for a long time.

Wordsworth enjoyed growing popularity in the years between the death of Byron in 1824 and the ascension of Tennyson in the 1840s, especially after Scott's death in 1832. At Cambridge in the late 1820s he was admired and promoted by the Apostles, a group including Tennyson, Arthur Henry Hallam, and Richard Monckton Milnes. Debates were held at Cambridge and in London on the relative merits of Byron and Wordsworth. Tennyson himself revered Wordsworth and his poetry. In 1835 while Tennyson was in the Lake District and was rereading poems such as *Michael*, he composed his most Wordsworthian poem, "Dora," about which Wordsworth later reportedly confided, "Mr. Tennyson, I have been endeavoring all of my life to write a pastoral like your 'Dora' and have not succeeded."

By 1835, when Wordsworth's *Yarrow Revisited, And Other Poems*, including poems from the most recent tour of Scotland and other works of the 1820s and 1830s, was published, Wordsworth's reputation was firmly established. In the *Monthly Repository* (1835) he was depicted as a survivor of various attacks and critical battles:

> No poet has ever lived and written down, and that in the most quiet way, a greater host of difficulties than Wordsworth. The common consent which once denied him a place amongst the bards of his age and country, now seems to concede to him the highest rank. He has overcome a world of prejudices, and also some just objections. A new theory of poetry; a practice which

made more startling whatever was most startling in that theory; an offensive defiance of all the common-place, adventitious aids of what is called poetical interest; the political hostility of the two great parties of the state in succession; the heavier charge, with all parties, of apostasy; the repeated, and what appeared the demolishing, attacks of the acutest and most influential criticism of the day; ridicule from all quarters through many years: these are the rocks and brambles over which he has pursued his path up the lofty eminence on whose heights he now peacefully reclines. This is the course of greatness.

There were still critics and readers who would bring various charges against Wordsworth (Browning's "The Lost Leader" was not published until 1845), but in the mid 1830s Wordsworth's poetic achievement could not easily be brushed off. Wordsworth's literary influence later went beyond the genre of poetry: novelists such as Charles Dickens, George Eliot, and Elizabeth Gaskell all revealed their debt to a poet who understood the workings of time and memory and history. Wordsworth also received growing public recognition: honorary degrees from the universities of Durham and Oxford, a Civil List pension in 1842, as well as the poet laureateship in 1843. In his later years Wordsworth received hundreds of curious people at Rydal Mount each year, including, according to Arnold's story, a clergyman who asked whether he had written anything besides the popular *Guide to the Lakes*.

Reading Wordsworth's letters and poetry of the late 1820s and early 1830s, we also see Wordsworth entering the transitional culture of the Victorian age. This is particularly evident in Wordsworth's relationships with women. Although Wordsworth's marriage to Mary Hutchinson was long and happy (and, according to the recently discovered love letters between the two, passionate), he cultivated relationships with other women throughout his life. His later poems and letters reveal a man who greatly admired talented women—writers and poetesses (as they were called)—but always urged that women first fulfill their "womanly virtue" and acquire "Domestic habits" before they thought of anything else. Wordsworth endorsed the developing ideology of womanhood based on notions of female purity and spirituality played out in the domestic sphere. These ideal qualities are evident in a poem Wordsworth published in *The Keepsake* for the 1828 Christmas season, "The Promise" (later "The Triad"), in which he praises the domestic and nur-

Wordsworth in 1832 (portrait by Henry William Pickersgill; by permission of the Master and Fellows of St. John's College, Cambridge)

turing virtues of Edith Southey, Dora Wordsworth, and Sara Coleridge, daughters of the poets.

With his daughter Dora, Wordsworth revealed a possessiveness and dependency not evident in other relationships. Increasingly Wordsworth was bothered by an inflammation of his eyes that he had since his early thirties, and in a poem written in 1816 ("A little onward lend thy guiding hand") he links Dora both to his need for guidance and his need to guide. As she entered her twenties, Dora's health became more fragile, and Wordsworth feared anything that would strain it. But he also depended on Dora's company and her skill as an amanuensis at Rydal Mount. His only conflict with Dora came when she wanted to marry Edward Quillinan, a widower who had been a family friend for many years. Wordsworth agreed to the marriage reluc-

tantly in 1841 when Dora was thirty-seven years old. When Dora died of consumption in 1847, Wordsworth never really emerged from his grief to compose again.

Although Wordsworth remained an inveterate reviser of his poems all his life (and in 1842 finally published *The Borderers* and *Guilt and Sorrow* in *Poems, Chiefly of Early and Late Years*), he did not write much new poetry during his last decade. But he did see several new editions and selections through the press, and he maintained a keen interest in how his poems were presented on the page. During the winter and spring of 1842-1843 Wordsworth dictated notes on his poems to his friend Isabella Fenwick, providing valuable insight into his poetry and his later perception of that poetry.

Letters and memoirs by friends and associates of the Wordsworths paint a picture of the

William and Mary Wordsworth in 1839 (portrait by Margaret Gillies; by permission of the Wordsworth Trust)

poet in his later years as a hearty man, still capable of climbing mountains and of extensive traveling. Wordsworth seems to have maintained a lifelong habit of composing poetry best while walking out of doors, later dictating the products of this activity. To observers such as Henry Taylor, Wordsworth's face seemed to take on the features of the outdoors: "It was a rough grey face, full of rifts and clefts and fissures, out of which . . . you might expect lichens to grow." Like the imposing mountains that he loved, Wordsworth became an image of strength and survival.

To the end, Wordsworth remained a man of conflicting impulses: he loved being settled at Rydal Mount, but he also loved to travel. When he was touring Italy with Crabb Robinson in 1837, he longed for home at the same time that he relished the freedom and discovery recorded in *Memorials of a Tour in Italy, 1837,* published in

Poems, Chiefly of Early and Late Years (1842). Harriet Martineau captures Wordsworth's impulses in her *Autobiography* (1877), when she records that Wordsworth warned her that in order to conserve her resources, she should charge houseguests for meat: "The mixture of odd economies and neighborly generosity was one of the most striking things in the old poet."

The old poet, known affectionately as "the Bard" to Hartley Coleridge, developed his final illness in March 1850. Following his usual habit of walking out of doors in all weather, Wordsworth came down with pleurisy and never regained his strength. He died at Rydal Mount on 23 April 1850, Shakespeare's birthday and sixteen days after his own eightieth birthday. Three months after her husband's death, Mary Wordsworth brought out *The Prelude*, having named the poem appropriately herself. Before his death, Words-

Wordsworth on Helvellyn, *1842 (portrait by Benjamin Robert Haydon; by permission of the National Portrait Gallery, London)*

worth had authorized his nephew Christopher Wordsworth "to prepare for publication any notices of my life that may be deemed necessary to illustrate my writings." The resulting two-volume memoir was longer than the brief notice that Wordsworth imagined, but Christopher Wordsworth thought that this longer work would discourage unauthorized biographies. In preparing his work, Christopher Wordsworth wanted to include mention of the affair with Annette Vallon, but other family members and friends objected. He did say cryptically that his uncle was "encompassed with strong temptations" in France. The memoir thus echoes Wordsworth's treatment of the affair in *The Prelude,* where a fictional story of thwarted lovers (Vaudracour and Julia) is as close as Wordsworth gets to confronting this dimension of his French Revolution. While many of Wordsworth's friends and contemporaries knew of the affair, it was not rediscovered until the beginning of this century.

Reviews of *The Prelude* were generally not bad, although several reviewers criticized the flatness of long discursive passages and were puzzled by the problem of genre, since *The Prelude* was the first English autobiography written in verse and also contained elements of epic, romance, satire, and pastoral. The publication did not substantially change Wordsworth's reputation, which was not as high as that of Tennyson, the new poet laureate. Wordsworth's reputation had sagged enough by 1879 that Arnold felt a need to rehabilitate his poetry. With A. C. Bradley's claim in the *Oxford Lectures on Poetry* (1909) that "Wordsworth is indisputably the most sublime of our poets since Milton" and with the biographical revelations of George McLean Harper (1916) and

Dora Wordsworth, 1839 (portrait by Margaret Gillies; by permission of the Wordsworth Trust)

Emile Legouis (1922), interest in *The Prelude* began to revive.

For the last quarter of a century, critical focus on Wordsworth has been intense. While the New Critics disparaged the Romantics generally, the Romantics–and particularly Wordsworth–have been central to the work of many poststructuralists, who have found his texts particularly rich sites for interpretation. Although most of this work has focused on *The Prelude* and other texts of the great decade (1797-1807), readers with an interest in Wordsworth's historical situation are revaluating the works of Wordsworth's youth and his later years. The Cornell Wordsworth editions, which began to appear in the mid 1970s, have facilitated new research. Although the judgment that Wordsworth's poetry declined after 1807 or 1815 still stands, several recent writers have suggested that we have not yet found a way to read Wordsworth's later poetry for what it

is rather than for what it is not. Perhaps if we think of Wordsworth as a poet who began writing in the eighteenth-century mode, worked through the Romantic period, and then entered the Victorian age, we can better understand the remarkable range of his achievement and of his contribution to English poetry.

Letters:

The Early Letters of William and Dorothy Wordsworth, 1787-1805, 1 volume, edited by Ernest de Selincourt (Oxford: Clarendon Press, 1935); *The Letters of William and Dorothy Wordsworth: The Middle Years,* 2 volumes, edited by de Selincourt (Oxford: Clarendon Press, 1937); *The Letters of William and Dorothy Wordsworth: The Later Years,* edited by de Selincourt (Oxford: Clarendon Press, 1939); revised and enlarged by Chester L. Shaver, Mary Moorman, and Alan G. Hill as *The Letters of Wil-*

Drawing by Leonard Charles Wyon (by permission of the Wordsworth Trust)

liam and Dorothy Wordsworth, 5 volumes (Oxford: Clarendon Press, 1967-1988);

The Love Letters of William and Mary Wordsworth, edited by Beth Darlington (Ithaca: Cornell University Press, 1981);

The Letters of William Wordsworth: A New Selection, edited by Alan G. Hill (New York: Oxford University Press, 1984).

Bibliographies:

Thomas J. Wise, *A Bibliography of the Writings in Prose and Verse of William Wordsworth* (London: Printed for private circulation by Richard Clay & Son, 1916; reprinted, Folkestone & London: Dawsons of Pall Mall, 1971);

Wise, *Two Lake Poets: A Catalogue of Printed Books,*

Manuscripts, and Autograph Letters by William Wordsworth and Samuel Taylor Coleridge (London: Printed for private circulation, 1927; reprinted, London: Dawsons of Pall Mall, 1965);

James V. Logan, *Wordsworthian Criticism: A Guide and Bibliography* (Columbus: Ohio State University, 1947; reprinted, New York: Gordian, 1974);

Elton F. Henley and David H. Stam, *Wordsworthian Criticism 1945-64: An Annotated Bibliography* (New York: New York Public Library, 1965);

Mark L. Reed, *Wordsworth: The Chronology of the Early Years, 1770-1799* (Cambridge: Harvard University Press, 1967); *Wordsworth: The Chronology of the Middle Years, 1800-1815* (Cambridge: Harvard University Press, 1975);

David H. Stam, *Wordsworthian Criticism 1964-73: An Annotated Bibliography* (New York: New York Public Library, 1974);

N. S. Bauer, *William Wordsworth: A Reference Guide to British Criticism, 1793-1899* (London: Hall, 1978);

Karl Kroeber, "William Wordsworth," in *The English Romantic Poets: A Review of Research and Criticism,* fourth edition, edited by Frank Jordan (New York: Modern Language Association, 1985);

Mark Jones and Kroeber, *Wordsworth Scholarship and Criticism, 1973-84, An Annotated Bibliography, with Selected Criticism, 1809-1972* (New York: Garland, 1985);

Jones, "Wordsworth Scholarship and Criticism, 1984-85 Update," *Wordsworth Circle,* 18 (Autumn 1987): 190-208;

Jones, "Wordsworth Scholarship and Criticism, 1986 Update," *Wordsworth Circle,* 19 (Autumn 1988): 220-230.

Biographies:

Christopher Wordsworth, *Memoirs of William Wordsworth,* 2 volumes (London: Moxon, 1851);

Emile Legouis, *The Early Life of William Wordsworth, 1770-1798,* translated by J. W. Matthews (London: Dent, 1897);

George McLean Harper, *William Wordsworth, His Life, Works, and Influence,* 2 volumes (London: Murray, 1916);

Legouis, *William Wordsworth and Annette Vallon* (London & Toronto: Dent, 1922);

Edith Batho, *The Later Wordsworth* (Cambridge: Cambridge University Press, 1933);

Frederika Beatty, *William Wordsworth of Rydal Mount* (London: J. M. Dent, 1939);

Mary Moorman, *William Wordsworth: A Biography,* 2 volumes (Oxford: Clarendon Press, 1957, 1965; New York: Oxford University Press, 1957, 1965);

Ben Ross Schneider, Jr., *Wordsworth's Cambridge Education* (Cambridge: Cambridge University Press, 1957);

T. W. Thompson, *Wordsworth's Hawkshead,* edited by Robert Woof (New York: Oxford University Press, 1970);

Hunter Davies, *William Wordsworth: A Biography* (London: Weidenfeld & Nicolson, 1980; New York: Atheneum, 1980);

Stephen Gill, *William Wordsworth: A Life* (Oxford: Clarendon Press, 1989).

References:

M. H. Abrams, ed., *Wordsworth: A Collection of Critical Essays* (Englewood Cliffs, N.J.: Prentice-Hall, 1972);

F. W. Bateson, *Wordsworth: A Reinterpretation* (London: Longmans, Green, 1956);

Alan J. Bewell, *Wordsworth and the Enlightenment: Nature, Man, and Society in the Experimental Poetry* (New Haven: Yale University Press, 1989);

Don H. Bialostosky, *Making Tales: The Poetics of Wordsworth's Narrative Experiments* (Chicago: University of Chicago Press, 1984);

Frances Blanchard, *Portraits of Wordsworth* (London: Allen, 1959);

James K. Chandler, *Wordsworth's Second Nature: A Study of the Poetry and Politics* (Chicago: University of Chicago Press, 1984);

John Danby, *The Simple Wordsworth: Studies in the Poems 1797-1807* (London: Routledge & Kegan Paul, 1960);

Frances Ferguson, *Wordsworth: Language as Counter-Spirit* (New Haven: Yale University Press, 1977);

David Ferry, *The Limits of Mortality: An Essay on Wordsworth's Major Poems* (Middletown, Conn.: Wesleyan University Press, 1959);

William H. Galperin, *Revision and Authority in Wordsworth: The Interpretation of a Career* (Philadelphia: University of Pennsylvania Press, 1989);

Frederick Garber, *Wordsworth and the Poetry of Encounter* (Urbana: University of Illinois Press, 1971);

Spencer Hall, ed., with Jonathan Ramsey, *Approaches to Teaching Wordsworth's Poetry* (New York: Modern Language Association, 1986);

Geoffrey Hartman, *Wordsworth's Poetry: 1787-1814* (New Haven: Yale University Press, 1964);

Raymond Dexter Havens, *The Mind of A Poet: A Study of Wordsworth's Thought* (Baltimore: Johns Hopkins University Press, 1941):

Mary Jacobus, *Tradition and Experiment in Wordsworth's Lyrical Ballads (1798)* (Oxford: Clarendon Press, 1978);

Lee M. Johnson, *Wordsworth and the Sonnet,* Anglistica, 19 (Copenhagen: Rosenkilde & Bagger, 1973);

Kenneth R. Johnston, *Wordsworth and "The Recluse"* (New Haven: Yale University Press, 1984);

Johnston and Gene W. Ruoff, ed., *The Age of William Wordsworth* (New Brunswick, N.J.: Rutgers University Press, 1987);

John Jones, *The Egotistical Sublime: A Study of Wordsworth's Imagination* (London: Chatto & Windus, 1954);

John Jordan, *Why the Lyrical Ballads? The Background, Writing, and Character of Wordsworth's 1798 Lyrical Ballads* (Berkeley: University of California Press, 1974);

Thèresa M. Kelley, *Wordsworth's Revisionary Aesthetics* (Cambridge: Cambridge University Press, 1988);

Karl Kroeber, *Romantic Landscape Vision: Constable and Wordsworth* (Madison: University of Wisconsin Press, 1975);

Marjorie Levinson, *Wordsworth's Great Period Poems* (Cambridge: Cambridge University Press, 1986);

Herbert Lindenberger, *On Wordsworth's Prelude* (Princeton: Princeton University Press, 1963);

Alan Liu, *Wordsworth: The Sense of History* (Palo Alto, Cal.: Stanford University Press, 1989);

Peter J. Manning, "Wordsworth at St. Bees: Scandals, Sisterhoods, and Wordsworth's Later Poetry," *ELH*, 52 (Spring 1985): 33-58;

David McCracken, *Wordsworth and the Lake District: A Guide to the Poems and Their Places* (New York: Oxford University Press, 1984);

Richard Onorato, *The Character of the Poet: Wordsworth in The Prelude* (Princeton: Princeton University Press, 1971);

W. J. B. Owen, "Cost, Sales, and Profits of Longman's Editions of Wordsworth," *Library*, 12 (June 1957): 93-107;

Judith W. Page, " 'The Weight of Too Much Liberty': Genre and Gender in Wordsworth's Calais Sonnets," *Criticism*, 30 (Spring 1988): 189-203;

Reeve Parker, "Reading Wordsworth's Power: Narrative and Usurpation in *The Borderers*," *ELH*, 54 (Summer 1987): 299-331;

Stephen M. Parrish, *The Art of the Lyrical Ballads* (Cambridge: Harvard University Press, 1973);

Markham Peacock, Jr., ed., *The Critical Opinions of William Wordsworth* (Baltimore: Johns Hop-

kins University Press, 1950);

David Perkins, *Wordsworth and the Poetry of Sincerity* (Cambridge: Harvard University Press, 1964);

Donald H. Reiman, "The Poetry of Familiarity: Wordsworth, Dorothy, and Mary Hutchinson," in *The Evidence of Imagination*, edited by Reiman and others (New York: New York University Press, 1978), pp. 142-177;

Reiman, ed., *The Romantics Reviewed,* part A, volumes 1 and 2 (New York: Garland, 1972);

Nicholas Roe, *Wordsworth and Coleridge: The Radical Years* (Oxford: Oxford University Press, 1988);

Paul D. Sheats, *The Making of Wordsworth's Poetry 1785-1798* (Cambridge: Harvard University Press, 1973);

David Simpson, *Wordsworth's Historical Imagination* (New York: Methuen, 1987);

Gayatri Chakravorty Spivak, "Sex and History in *The Prelude* (1805): Books Nine to Thirteen," *Texas Studies in Literature and Language*, 23 (Fall 1981): 324-360;

Edwin Stein, *Wordsworth's Art of Allusion* (University Park: Pennsylvania State University Press, 1988);

Susan J. Wolfson, *The Questioning Presence: Wordsworth, Keats, and the Interrogative Mode in Romantic Poetry* (Ithaca: Cornell University Press, 1986);

Carl Woodring, *Wordsworth* (Boston: Houghton Mifflin, 1965);

Jonathan Wordsworth, *The Music of Humanity* (London: Oxford University Press, 1969);

Wordsworth, ed., *Bicentenary Wordsworth Studies in Honor of John Alban Finch* (Ithaca: Cornell University Press, 1970).

Papers:

The main depository for manuscripts and papers of Wordsworth and his close circle is the Wordsworth Library, Grasmere. In the United States the libraries at Cornell and Indiana universities have strong Wordsworth collections.

Books for Further Reading

Abrams, M. H. *The Mirror and the Lamp; Romantic Theory and the Critical Tradition.* New York: Oxford University Press, 1953.

Abrams. *Natural Supernaturalism: Tradition and Revolution in Romantic Literature.* New York: Norton, 1971.

Abrams, ed. *English Romantic Poets: Modern Essays in Criticism.* New York: Oxford University Press, 1960; revised, 1975.

Aers, David, Jonathan Cook, and David Punter. *Romanticism and Ideology: Studies in English Writing 1765-1830.* London & Boston: Routledge & Kegan Paul, 1981.

Ball, Patricia M. *The Central Self: A Study in Romantic and Victorian Imagination.* London: Athlone Press, 1968.

Beaty, Frederick L. *Light from Heaven: Love in British Romantic Literature.* De Kalb: Northern Illinois University Press, 1971.

Bloom, Harold. *The Visionary Company: A Reading of English Romantic Poetry*, revised and enlarged edition. Ithaca: Cornell University Press, 1971.

Bloom, ed. *Romanticism and Consciousness: Essays in Criticism.* New York: Norton, 1970.

Bostetter, Edward E. *The Romantic Ventriloquists: Wordsworth, Coleridge, Keats, Shelley, Byron*, revised edition. Seattle: University of Washington Press, 1963.

Bowra, C. M. *The Romantic Imagination.* Cambridge, Mass.: Harvard University Press, 1950.

Brisman, Leslie. *Romantic Origins.* Ithaca, N.Y.: Cornell University Press, 1978.

Butler, Marilyn. *Romantics, Rebels, and Reactionaries: English Literature and its Background 1760-1830.* Oxford & New York: Oxford University Press, 1981.

Clubbe, John, and Ernest J. Lovell, Jr. *English Romanticism: The Grounds of Belief.* De Kalb: Northern Illinois University Press, 1983.

Cooper, Andrew M. *Doubt and Identity in Romantic Poetry.* New Haven: Yale University Press, 1988.

Curran, Stuart. *Poetic Form and British Romanticism.* New York & Oxford: Oxford University Press, 1986.

Enscoe, Gerald E. *Eros and the Romantics: Sexual Love as a Theme in Coleridge, Shelley and Keats.* The Hague: Mouton, 1967.

Ford, Boris, ed. *From Blake to Byron, New Pelican Guide to English Literature*, volume 5. Harmondsworth: Penguin, 1962.

Frye, Northrop. *A Study of English Romanticism.* New York: Random House, 1968.

Frye, ed. *Romanticism Reconsidered: Selected Papers from the English Institute*. New York: Columbia University Press, 1963.

Gleckner, Robert F., and Gerald E. Enscoe. *Romanticism: Points of View*, second edition. Englewood Cliffs, N.J.: Prentice-Hall, 1970.

Harris, R. W. *Romanticism and the Social Order 1780-1830*. London: Blandford, 1969.

Jack, Ian. *English Literature 1815-1832*. Oxford: Clarendon Press, 1963.

Jackson, J. R. de J. *Poetry of the Romantic Period*. London & Boston: Routledge & Kegan Paul, 1980.

Johnston, Kenneth R., and Gene W. Ruoff, eds. *The Age of Wordsworth: Critical Essays on the Romantic Tradition*. New Brunswick & London: Rutgers University Press, 1987.

Jordon, Frank, ed. *The English Romantic Poets: A Review of Research and Criticism*, fourth edition. New York: Modern Language Association, 1985.

Kermode, Frank. *Romantic Image*. London: Routledge & Kegan Paul, 1957.

Klancher, Jon P. *The Making of English Reading Audiences, 1790-1832*. Madison: University of Wisconsin Press, 1987.

Knight, G. Wilson. *The Starlit Dome: Studies in the Poetry of Vision*. London & New York: Oxford University Press, 1941.

Kroeber, Karl. *Romantic Narrative Art*. Madison: University of Wisconsin Press, 1960.

Levinson, Marjorie. *The Romantic Fragment Poem: A Critique of a Form*. Chapel Hill: University of North Carolina Press, 1986.

McFarland, Thomas. *Romanticism and the Forms of Ruin: Wordsworth, Coleridge, and Modalities of Fragmentation*. Princeton: Princeton University Press, 1981.

McGann, Jerome J. *The Romantic Ideology: A Critical Investigation*. Chicago & London: University of Chicago Press, 1983.

Mellor, Anne K. *Romanticism and Feminism*. Bloomington: Indiana University Press, 1988.

Metzger, Lore. *One Foot in Eden: Modes of Pastoral in Romantic Poetry*. Chapel Hill: University of North Carolina Press, 1986.

Prickett, Stephen, ed. *The Romantics*. New York: Holmes & Meier, 1981.

Reed, Arden, ed. *Romanticism and Language*. Ithaca, N.Y.: Cornell University Press, 1984.

Reiman, Donald H. *Intervals of Inspiration: The Skeptical Tradition and the Psychology of Romanticism*. Greenwood, Fla.: Penkevill, 1988.

Reiman. *Romantic Texts and Contexts*. Columbia: University of Missouri Press, 1987.

Renwick, W. L. *English Literature 1789-1815*. Oxford: Clarendon Press, 1963.

Richardson, Alan. *A Mental Theater: Poetic Drama and Consciousness in the Romantic Age*. University Park: Pennsylvania State University Press, 1987.

Rodway, Allen. *The Romantic Conflict*. London: Chatto & Windus, 1963.

Rzepka, Charles R. *The Self as Mind: Vision and Identity in Wordsworth, Coleridge and Keats*. Cambridge, Mass.: Harvard University Press, 1986.

Simpson, David. *Irony and Authority in Romantic Poetry*. London: Macmillan, 1979.

Siskin, Clifford. *The Historicity of Romantic Discourse*. New York: Oxford University Press, 1988.

Swingle, L. J. *The Obstinate Questionings of English Romanticism*. Baton Rouge: Louisiana State University Press, 1987.

Thorburn, David, and Geoffrey Hartman, eds. *Romanticism: Vistas, Instances, Continuities*. Ithaca & London: Cornell University Press, 1973.

Thorlby, Anthony, ed. *The Romantic Movement*. London: Longmans, 1966.

Watson, J. R. *English Poetry of the Romantic Period 1789-1830*. London & New York: Longmans, 1985.

Wilkie, Brian. *Romantic Poets and Epic Tradition*. Madison: University of Wisconsin Press, 1965.

Williams, Raymond. *Culture and Society, 1780-1950*. New York: Columbia University Press, 1958.

Woodring, Carl. *Politics in English Romantic Poetry*. Cambridge, Mass.: Harvard University Press, 1970.

Wordsworth, Jonathan, Michael C. Jaye, and Robert Woof, with the assistance of Peter Funnell. *William Wordsworth and the Age of English Romanticism*. New Brunswick & London: Rutgers University Press / Wordsworth Trust, 1987.

Contributors

David R. Anderson...Texas A&M University

Ernest Bernhardt-Kabisch ....Indiana University

Thomas L. Blanton..Central Washington University

Thomas L. Cooksey..Armstrong State College

Winifred F. Courtney ....Greenwood, South Carolina

A. C. Goodson...Michigan State University

Keith Hanley...University of Lancaster

John R. Holmes ....Franciscan University of Steubenville

Desmond King-Hele..The Royal Society of London

Jonathan N. Lawson ....University of Hartford

Mary Ruth Miller...North Georgia College

Mark Minor ....Westmar College

Judith W. Page..Millsaps College

Nicholas Roe ....University of St. Andrews

Charles Reinhart ....Vincennes University

Alan Richardson ....Boston College

Nicholas Roe ....University of St. Andrews

Marlon B. Ross ....University of Michigan

Patricia L. Skarda...Smith College

N. C. Smith...University of Victoria

Stephen Wolfe..Linfield College

Cumulative Index

Dictionary of Literary Biography, Volumes 1-93
Dictionary of Literary Biography Yearbook, 1980-1988
Dictionary of Literary Biography Documentary Series, Volumes 1-7

Cumulative Index

DLB before number: *Dictionary of Literary Biography,* Volumes 1-93
Y before number: *Dictionary of Literary Biography Yearbook,* 1980-1988
DS before number: *Dictionary of Literary Biography Documentary Series,* Volumes 1-7

A

B

C

D

E

I

Cumulative Index

M

Cumulative Index

P

Q

(Continued from front endsheets)

71: *American Literary Critics and Scholars, 1880-1900,* edited by John W. Rathbun and Monica M. Grecu (1988)

72: *French Novelists, 1930-1960,* edited by Catharine Savage Brosman (1988)

73: *American Magazine Journalists, 1741-1850,* edited by Sam G. Riley (1988)

74: *American Short-Story Writers Before 1880,* edited by Bobby Ellen Kimbel, with the assistance of William E. Grant (1988)

75: *Contemporary German Fiction Writers,* Second Series, edited by Wolfgang D. Elfe and James Hardin (1988)

76: *Afro-American Writers, 1940-1955,* edited by Trudier Harris (1988)

77: *British Mystery Writers, 1920-1939,* edited by Bernard Benstock and Thomas F. Staley (1988)

78: *American Short-Story Writers, 1880-1910,* edited by Bobby Ellen Kimbel, with the assistance of William E. Grant (1988)

79: *American Magazine Journalists, 1850-1900,* edited by Sam G. Riley (1988)

80: *Restoration and Eighteenth-Century Dramatists,* First Series, edited by Paula R. Backscheider (1989)

81: *Austrian Fiction Writers, 1875-1913,* edited by James Hardin and Donald G. Daviau (1989)

82: *Chicano Writers,* First Series, edited by Francisco A. Lomelí and Carl R. Shirley (1989)

83: *French Novelists Since 1960,* edited by Catharine Savage Brosman (1989)

84: *Restoration and Eighteenth-Century Dramatists,* Second Series, edited by Paula R. Backscheider (1989)

85: *Austrian Fiction Writers After 1914,* edited by James Hardin and Donald G. Daviau (1989)

86: *American Short-Story Writers, 1910-1945,* First Series, edited by Bobby Ellen Kimbel (1989)

87: *British Mystery and Thriller Writers Since 1940,* First Series, edited by Bernard Benstock and Thomas F. Staley (1989)

88: *Canadian Writers, 1920-1959,* Second Series, edited by W. H. New (1989)

89: *Restoration and Eighteenth-Century Dramatists,* Third Series, edited by Paula R. Backscheider (1989)

90: *German Writers in the Age of Goethe, 1789-1832,* edited by James Hardin and Christoph E. Schweitzer (1989)

91: *American Magazine Journalists, 1900-1960,* First Series, edited by Sam G. Riley (1990)

92: *Canadian Writers, 1890-1920,* edited by W. H. New (1990)

93: *British Romantic Poets, 1789-1832,* First Series, edited by John R. Greenfield (1990)

Documentary Series

1: *Sherwood Anderson, Willa Cather, John Dos Passos, Theodore Dreiser, F. Scott Fitzgerald, Ernest Hemingway, Sinclair Lewis,* edited by Margaret A. Van Antwerp (1982)

2: *James Gould Cozzens, James T. Farrell, William Faulkner, John O'Hara, John Steinbeck, Thomas Wolfe, Richard Wright,* edited by Margaret A. Van Antwerp (1982)

3: *Saul Bellow, Jack Kerouac, Norman Mailer, Vladimir Nabokov, John Updike, Kurt Vonnegut,* edited by Mary Bruccoli (1983)

4: *Tennessee Williams,* edited by Margaret A. Van Antwerp and Sally Johns (1984)

5: *American Transcendentalists,* edited by Joel Myerson (1988)

6: *Hardboiled Mystery Writers,* edited by Matthew J. Bruccoli and Richard Layman (1989)